Antonia Clare

JJ Wilson

with Damian Williams

speakout

Intermediate
Students' Pack

Pearson Education Limited
Edinburgh Gate
Harlow
Essex CM20 2JE
England
and Associated Companies throughout the world.

www.pearsonelt.com

© Pearson Education Limited 2011
This impression 2012 for Peru only

The right of Antonia Clare and JJ Wilson to be identified as authors of this Work has been asserted by them in accordance with the Copyright, Designs and Patents Act 1988.

First published 2012
Seventh impression 2017
ISBN: 978-1-4479-3798-2
Set in Gill Sans Book 9.75/11.5
Printed in Italy by L.E.G.O.

Acknowledgements

The publishers and authors would like to thank the following people and their institutions for their feedback and comments during the development of the material:

Reporters: Brazil: Stephen Greene, Damian Williams; Germany: Rosemary Richey; Italy: Elizabeth Gregson, Elizabeth Kalton; Spain: Eleanor Keegan; Turkey: Grant Kempton; United Kingdom: Ben Beaumont, Kirsten Colquhoun, Andrew Doig, Fay Drewry, Eileen Flannigan, Sarah Gumbrell, Tad Larner, Fran Linley, Jacqueline McEwan, Zella Phillips, Chris Rogers, Dan Woodard

We are grateful to the following for permission to reproduce copyright material:

Text:
Extract 2.2 adapted from "I want to believe", *BBC Focus*, 01/12/2008, Issue 197, p59 (Blackmore, M.), copyright © BBC Magazines, 2008; Extract 2.2 adapted from "Fraud fugitive in Facebook trap" 14 October 2009 http://news.bbc.co.uk/1/hi/world/americas/8306032.stm, copyright © 2009, The BBC; Extract 3.1 adapted from "Teenagers: Life on Planet Teen" *The Telegraph*, 20/10/2007 (Kavanagh, M.), copyright © Telegraph Media Group Limited; Extract 3.2 from *Longman Active Study Dictionary*, 5th edition, Pearson Longman (2010) p.445, copyright © Pearson Education Ltd; Extract 4.1 adapted from *Think Yourself Rich: Discover Your Millionaire Potential*, published by Vermilion (Sharon Maxwell Magnus 2003), copyright © Sharon Maxwell Magnus, 2003. Reprinted by permission of The Random House Group Ltd, and PFD www.pfd.co.uk on behalf of Sharon Maxwell Magnus; Extract 4.3 after "Wanted: Paradise island 'caretaker'" 12/01/2009, http://news.bbc.co.uk/1/hi/world/asia-pacific/7823812.stm, copyright © 2009, The BBC; Extract 5.1 adapted from Big Ideas Transport Challenge, http://www.open2.net/jamesmay/big_ideas_interactive_html.html, copyright © The Open University; Extract 5.3 adapted from "PC rage hits UK" 29 January 2000, http://news.bbc.co.uk/1/hi/sci/tech/623341.stm, copyright © 2009, The BBC; Extract 6.1 adapted from "Special report on Human Behaviour ", *BBC Focus*, 1/06/2004, Issue 139, p53, copyright © BBC Magazines, 2008; Extract 6.1 from *Longman Active Study Dictionary* 5th edition, Pearson Longman (2010) pp.960,375,826, copyright © Pearson Education Ltd; Extract 7.2 from *Longman Active Study Dictionary* 5th edition, Pearson Longman (2010) p.53, copyright © Pearson Education Ltd; Extract 9.1 adapted from "12 Giant leaps for mankind", *BBC History Magazine*, Vol 10, no 7, 1/07/2009, pp.42-47 (Attar, R.), copyright © BBC Magazines; Extract 10.1 adapted from "I am the Ethical Man" by Rowlatt, J., http://news.bbc.co.uk/1/hi/programmes/newsnight/4736228.stm and http://www.bbc.co.uk/blogs/newsnight/2007/04/we_are_all_ethical_men_and_women_now.html, copyright © 2009, The BBC; Extract 10.2 adapted from "Osaka – the World's greatest food city", *The Guardian*, 13/07/2009 (Booth, M.), copyright © Guardian News & Media Ltd 2009; Extract 10.3 adapted from "10 things you should never do in an airport", http://travel.aol.co.uk/, copyright © AOL.

In some instances we have been unable to trace the owners of copyright material, and we would appreciate any information that would enable us to do so.

Illustration acknowledgements: Jurgen Ziewe p17; Matt Herring pgs38–39, 44–45, 48, 124–125; Dan Hilliard pgs11, 92, 103; Lyndon Hayes pgs26–27, 61, 82–83; Eric Smith pgs14, 38, 62, 80, 145, 149, 151, 153, 156, 165, 166, 167, 168, 169, 170, 173.

Photo acknowledgements: The publisher would like to thank the following for their kind permission to reproduce their photographs:

(Key: b-bottom; c-centre; l-left; r-right; t-top)

Alamy Images: 15, allOver photography 55 (computer), Ancient Art & Architecture Collection Ltd 118 (Chaucer), James R Clarke 19 (girls), culture-images GmbH 65bl, Design Pics Inc. 31 (mother), 62 (A), Garry Gay 43bl (money), Ian Goodrick 62 (E), Nick Gregory 130tc (pass), Dennis Hallinan 111 (drawing), Andrew Holt 130tr, D. Hurst 62 (C), 84bl (rings), Idealink Photography 57 (E), Inspirestock Inc 47 (A), itanistock 95 (B), John James 94tl, Juice Images 76 (C), Iain Masterton 178, MBI 51tl, Photos 12 118 (Chaplin), Chris Rout 105, SCPhotos 99 (home), Jack Sullivan 132tl, Daniel Templeton 51tr, Transtock Inc. 57 (A), Trinity Mirror / Mirrorpix 111 (fashion), Penny Tweedie 84cl, Benjamin Volant 123 (garden), Patrick Ward 50tc; Bananastock: 164 (brother), 164 (brother's daughter), 164 (brother's son), 164 (brother's wife), 164 (me), 164 (son); BBC Photo Library: 36tl, 56r, 119, 124tr; Corbis: Chris Andrews Publications 75 (stress), Bettmann 19 (moon), 23t, 23b, 118 (Einstein), Sara De Boer 88-89 (Cowell), Fred De Noyelle / Godong 127 (A), Tim Graham 21 (C), Catherine Ivill / AMA 88-89 (Beckham), Frans Lanting 108-109 (island), Lorenvu / epa 47 (C), moodboard 29br, NASA 59 (D), Michael Nicholson 118 (Marx), Franck Robichon / EPA 21 (E), Andersen Ross / cultura 52-53 (office), Steve Schapiro 111 (march), Soeren Stache / EPA 43 (models), Buero Monaco / zefa 14; Fotolia.com: Gerald Bernard 61bl, Lane Erickson 157 (factories), 173 (factories), huyang 28-29 (wall), Monkey Business 164 (grandma (left)), 164 (grandpa (left)); Getty Images: 99 (Tribe), AFP 126, 182b, AFP / Don Emmert / Staff 21 (G), Val Doone / Hulton Archive 112 (factories), Asia Images 63, Bruce Ayres 81t, James Baigrie 85br, Barcroft Media 91t, 91b, Hamish Blair / Staff 88-89 (Williams), Lionel Bonaventure / Stringer 128, The Bridgeman Art Library / Giovanni Stradano 120b, Stephen Derr 7bc (interview), GAB Archive / Redferns 88-89c (The Beatles), Martyn Hayhow / Stringer 8 (B), Hulton Archive 118 (Che), Hulton Archive / Trevor Humphries 21 (D), Chris Jackson 21 (B), 108c, Wireimages / Jason Squires 139l, Wirelmage / Juan Naharro Gimenez 136tr, Lambert 155, 171, Ron Levine 47 (B), Lipnitzki / Roger Viollet 182t, Rob Loud / Stringer 135 (Oscar), Dave M. Benett / Contributor 88-89 (Westwood), Martin Mills / Getty Entertainment 139b, Nacivet 117, National Archives / Handout 112tl (rights), Christopher Pillitz 55 (car), Joe Raedle / Staff 21 (H), Martin Philbey / Redferns 116 (C), Tom Stoddart Archive / Contributor 116 (B), Symphonie 90, Roger Viollet 21 (F), Wirelmage 21 (A), 52 (Stacey), 87bl (success), 88-89 (Judi Dench), WireImage / Chelsea Lauren 136bl, Wirelmage / Mark Sullivan 136br, Wireimage / Steve Granitz 136c; Hodder & Stoughton Publishing Group: 'Born On A Blue Day' by Daniel Tammet, reproduced with permission of Hodder & Stoughton Publishers, 2006 87bl (memory man), 177; iStockphoto: Alexskopje 67 (answer), Artmannwitte 74 (football match, inset), Avava 68br, 71, Bluberries 67 (ladder), Steve Debenport 60, Martina Ebel 164 (mother),

Godfried Edelman 68tr, Fatihhoca 69b, Steve Geer 102bl, Laurence Gough 135 (exam), Bill Grove 123 (airport), ilbusca 64-65 (background), Victor Ioramo 85bl, Kemter 164c (ex-husband), Lichtmeister 74 (library), Naphtalina 74 (joystick), David Newton 43br/team, S. Greg Panosian 100-101t, Giorgio Perbellini 140-141 (background), Sergey Peterman 74 (swimming), Tatiana Popova 49, Andrew Rich 48 (astronaut), 48 (astronaut and rocket), Mark Richardson 167 (A), Amanda Rohde 181, Pete Saloutos 135 (sprinter), Chris Schmidt 74 (students), Silvrshootr 167 (B), Alina Solovyova-Vincent 142, James Steidl 35 (record player), Tiridifilm 74 (TV), Track5 68l, Tony Tremblay 74 (business centre), Udo Weber 69t, Brad Wieland 164 (father), Mark Wragg 84 (table top), Steven Wynn 138l, 139br, Yangyin 180; Jupiterimages: 164bl (daughter); Mary Evans Picture Library: 138c, 138r, Edwin Mullan Collection 139r; mytinygarden.com: J. Dykes 59 (B); NASA: data courtesy Marc Imhoff (NASA / GSFC) and Christopher Elvidge (NOAA / NGDC). Image by Craig Mayhew (NASA / GSFC) and Robert Simmon (NASA / GSFC). 40br, 41bl, JPL / ASU 103; Pearson Education Ltd: 164 (aunty), 164 (uncle); Pearson Education Ltd: 72 (inset); Photolibrary.com: A H C. / age fotostock 120-121 (background), 67 (lecture), Banana Stock 12, Walter Bibikow 75c (people), 79 (people), bilderlounge 94tr, A Chederros 62 (B), Corbis 59 (A), Nick Dolding 76 (B), Nick Guttridge 50c (background), Kelly Han 123 (market), Hola Images 106tl, Image 100 76 (A), image100 55 (expert), Ingram Publishing 10, Ingram Publishing RF 106tr, Steven Kazlowski 123 (polar), 132-133, LISSAC LISSAC 99 (cyberspace), John Lund 59 (E), David Madison 77 (E), Roger Marshutz / age fotostock 101br, moodboard RF 95tl, Marvin Newman 111 (statue), Mark Polott 113, Sugar Gold Images 76 (D), Tips Italia 19 (house), 28 (house); Press Association Images: ABACA PRESS / ABACA USA / Empics Entertainment 57 (B), Piovanotto Marco / ABACA 88-89 (Lopez), Martial Trezzini / AP 130tl, Pierre Gleizes / AP 116 (A), Damian Dovarganes 57 (D), Gareth Fuller / PA Archive 87br (challenge), 96bl, 96-97 (background), Fiona Hanson / PA Archive 65cr, Antony Jones 9 (E), Tony Marshall / EMPICS Sport 8 (A), Ian West / PA Archive 50c; Reuters: Ian Waldie 23c; Rex Features: 52 (Gavin), David Fisher 9 (D), David Hartley 8 (C), Rupert Hartley 9 (F), ITV 88-89 (Redgrave), Barbara Lindberg 55 (Top Gear), 64cl, Olycom SPA 88-89 (Branson), 130tc (scan), Marc Sharratt 88-89 (Hendrix), Sipa Press 24, 88-89 (Clinton), 88-89 (Gates), Solent News 57 (C); Science Photo Library Ltd: Mark Garlick 31bl (city), 36-37t, Pasieka 67 (MRI), 112tr (DNA), Maria Platt-Evan 118tl (Da Vinci); Shutterstock.com: Tiplyashin Anatoly 33tl; 'Streetlife' copyright Helen Nagel / 2021 : 99 (neighbours); The Kobal Collection: 136tl; Thinkstock: BananaStock 164 (sister), Brand X Pictures 35 (phone), Toby Burrows 104, Comstock 164 (daughter), Creatas Images 167 (C), Hemera 41br, 52tr, 62 (C battery), 157 (traffic), 157 (water), 164 (cousin), 164 (husband), 173 (traffic), 173 (water), iStockphoto 7bl, 8-9t, 22l, 25, 35 (ink), 35 (tv), 35 (video), 59 (C), 59 (F), 77 (F), 95 (A), 102t, 102b, 127 (B), 129, 157 (aerosol), 157 (deforestation), 164 (father-in-law), 164 (grandma), 164 (grandpa), 173 (aerosol), 173 (deforestation), Jupiterimages 87br (qualified), Photodisc 164 (in-laws), PhotoObjects.net 35 (tape machine), 164 (mother's husband), Stockbyte 75 (news), 95 (C), 102c; TopFoto: 19 (Braveheart), Stapleton Historical Collection / HIP 112 (plane), ullsteinbild 115; Professor Richard Wiseman: 80t

All other images © Pearson Education

Asociación Cultural Peruano Británica
BRITANICO

INDEX:

speakout

PART A

Antonia Clare

JJ Wilson

speakout

Intermediate

Students' Book

CONTENTS

LISTENING/DVD	SPEAKING	WRITING
listen to someone describing their family history	talk about family events; talk about people in your life	write an email of introduction; learn to use formal and informal styles
listen to a set of instructions and do a test	discuss the differences between men and women	
listen to a set of interviews; learn to understand and use two-word responses	talk about type of interviews and interview experiences; role-play an interview	
BBC The Money Programme: Second Life: watch and understand a documentary about life online	discuss and create a new identity	write answers to a questionnaire
listen to a radio programme about important roles in films	talk about life experiences; talk about your life story	
listen to news reports	talk about an important news story/event	write a news report; learn to use time linkers: *as soon as*, *while*, *during*, *until* and *by the time*
listen to people telling anecdotes; learn to keep a story going	tell a true story or a lie	
BBC Hustle: watch and listen to a drama about a burglar and a famous painting	discuss fictional crime dramas; tell a narrative	write a short newspaper article
	discuss attitudes now in comparison to ones you had earlier in life	write messages; learn to use note form
listen to predictions about the future of communication	talk about how things will change in the future	
listen to telephone conversations involving misunderstandings	learn to reformulate and retell a story about a misunderstanding; role-play resolving a misunderstanding	
BBC The Virtual Revolution: watch and understand a documentary about the impact of the internet	talk about communication preferences	write a memo
	discuss the qualities needed for different jobs; complete a survey and discuss the results	
listen to two people describing dream jobs gone wrong	talk about past habits	write a covering letter; learn to organise your ideas
listen to people making decisions in a meeting	learn to manage a discussion; participate in a meeting and create a business plan	
BBC Gavin and Stacey: watch and understand a comedy programme about a man's first day in a new job	describe a day in your life	write about daily routines
	discuss how technology has changed the world; talk about different types of transport and their uses	write an advantages versus disadvantages essay; learn to use discourse markers
listen to people answering difficult general knowledge questions	do a short general knowledge questionnaire; answer questions on your area of expertise	
listen to conversations about technical problems; learn to respond to requests	role-play asking and responding to requests	
BBC Top Gear: watch and understand a programme about a race between a car and two people	present and describe a new machine	write an advertisement for a new machine

| COMMUNICATION BANK page 174 | EXAM BANK page 180 | AUDIO SCRIPTS page 183 |

CONTENTS

CONTENTS

GRAMMAR

1 Read the text and find examples of ...

1 the past simple *he saw*
2 the past continuous *he was dining*
3 the present perfect *have been*
4 the past perfect *had been / had died*
5 a modal verb *might be*
6 a superlative *the best*
7 a relative clause *who was also*
8 a passive *the man was born*

There <u>have been</u> some amazing coincidences throughout history, but this might be the best. In 1900 King Umberto of Italy <u>was dining</u> in a restaurant when he saw that the owner looked exactly like him. The man, who was also called Umberto, was born in Turin on the same day as the king and, like the king, married a woman called Margherita. Amazingly, their weddings had been on the same day. The king invited the restaurant owner to an athletics meeting the next day. As the king sat down, he was told that the other Umberto had died in a mysterious shooting accident. Just as the king heard this news, an anarchist shot him dead.

PRONUNCIATION

2A Find pairs of words that have the same vowel sound.

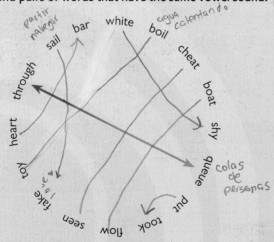

partir
naviegar
sail   bar   white   boil   agua calentando
cheat
boat
through   shy
heart   queue   colas de personas
tol
take   put
seen   flow   took

B ▶ L.1 Listen and check your answers.

C Work in pairs. Think of other words in English that use the same sounds.

VOCABULARY

3A Complete the common phrases below using the correct verb from the box.

~~have~~ ~~take~~ ~~check~~ watch chat ~~go~~ ~~meet~~
~~play~~ do (x2)

1 _have_ a meeting
2 _check_ your email
3 _go_ out with friends
4 _do_ some sport
5 _meet_ a colleague
6 _do_ some work
7 _chat_ on the internet
8 _take_ a break
9 _watch_ a DVD
10 _play_ some music

B Add phrases 1–10 above to the word webs below.

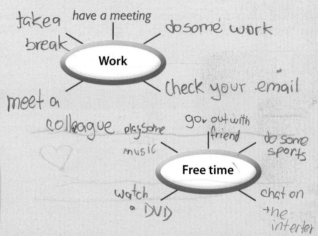

take a break   have a meeting   do some work
Work
meet a colleague   Check your email
play some music   go out with friend   do some sports
Free time
watch a DVD   chat on the internet

C Can you add any more phrases to the word webs? Which of these things do you do on a normal day?

COMMON ERRORS

4A Correct the mistakes.

1 She likes listening ~to~ music.
2 I am ~an~ architect.
3 Are you feeling allright? *all right / alright*
4 When ~I~ can ~I~ visit your house?
5 Let's discuss ~about~ this tomorrow.
6 He don't come here often.
7 We come from ~germany~. *doesn't*
8 Where ~you~ ~did~ you go yesterday?
9 I live in this town all my life. *did*
10 My wife is a really good cook~er~. *I've*

B Which mistakes are connected with ...

a) verb–noun agreement 6
b) spelling 3
c) verb tense 9
d) punctuation/capitalisation 7
e) prepositions 1
f) articles 2
g) vocabulary 10
h) word order 4
i) missing auxiliary verb 8
j) extra words 5

SPEAKING
❯ Talk about family events
❯ Talk about people in your life
❯ Role-play an interview
❯ Create a new identity

LISTENING
❯ Listen to someone describing his family history
❯ Listen to a set of instructions and do a test
❯ Listen to a set of interviews
❯ Watch a BBC documentary about Second Life

READING
❯ Read about a BBC programme that reveals family histories
❯ Read tips on successful interviews

WRITING
❯ Write an email of introduction
❯ Answer a questionnaire

BBC CONTENT
▯ Video podcast: What does *family* mean to you?
◉ DVD: The Money Programme: Second Life

UNIT 1

identity

▶ **Who do you think you are?** p8

▶ **Men and women** p11

▶ **Tell me about yourself** p14

▶ **Second Life** p16

Great Great Grandparent

Take after (be similar physics)

SPEAKING

1A Work in pairs. Take turns to find out as much as you can about your partner. Talk about your family, job/studies, home and likes/dislikes.

B Introduce your partner to the class.

VOCABULARY family

2A Match questions 1–10 with answers a)–j).

1 Do you know a lot about your **family history**?
2 Which do you know best: your mother's or your father's **side of the family**? *H*
3 Where did your **ancestors** come from? *F*
4 Did you ever meet your **great-grandparents**? *J*
5 Do you know most of your **relatives**? *g*
6 Are you **related to** anyone famous? *e*
7 Have you **inherited** any family characteristics? *B*
8 Who in your family do you **take after**? *I*
9 Would you like to know more about your **roots**? *C*
10 Do you live with your **extended family**? *d*

a) Quite a lot. My parents told me a lot of stories about my background.
b) Yes. I'm very shy, like my father and my older brothers.
c) I'd love to, but it's difficult because my parents don't often talk about the past.
d) Yes, I live with my immediate family and my grandparents.
e) No, there are no celebrities in the family!
f) They came from Lagos, in Nigeria.
g) I know about half of them. The others live in New Zealand and I've never met them.
h) My father's. I grew up next door to his sister's family.
i) My mother. We look alike and we have similar characters.
j) No. Unfortunately, they died before I was born.

B Work in groups. Discuss questions 1–10.

▶ page 164 **VOCABULARYBANK**

READING

3A *Who Do You Think You Are?* is a BBC programme that gets celebrities to research their family's roots. What kind of things do you think they discover?

B Read the text to find out.

C Read the text again and answer the questions.

1 Who has a royal ancestor? *Matthew Pinsent*
2 Who has a relative who was a policeman? *Davina Maccall*
3 Who has roots in three continents? *Colin Jackson*
4 Who has a relative who started a second family? *Kim Cattrall*
5 Who has an ancestor who built boats? *Jodie Kidd*
6 Who has a criminal relative? *Nigella Lawson*

1 *Who Do You Think You Are?* is a BBC programme that gets celebrities to research their family's roots. They find out about their ancestors, sometimes travelling across the world to interview relatives. They discover that their family histories include every type of person imaginable: heroes, liars, geniuses, soldiers, inventors and even kings.

2 In one episode, model Jodie Kidd learns that she is the great-granddaughter of newspaper owner Lord Beaverbrook, who was a politician during both world wars. Jodie also discovers that her great-grandfather on her mother's side of the family made a fortune from building ships during World War I and received letters from the King of England and Winston Churchill.

3 And on the subject of kings, Olympic athlete Matthew Pinsent finds that he is related to Edward I, one of the most famous kings in British history. Another Olympic gold medallist, Colin Jackson, takes a DNA test and discovers that he is fifty-five percent sub-Saharan African, thirty-eight percent European and seven percent American Indian. The last result comes as quite a surprise!

A Colin Jackson | **B Matthew Pinsent** | **C Jodie Kidd**

D Underline words or phrases in the text that match meanings 1–5 below.

1 a lot of money (paragraph 2) *fortune* *gold medalist*
2 someone who won a gold medal in sport (paragraph 3)
3 making arrangements so someone is safe (paragraph 4) *security*
4 extremely sad (paragraph 5) *tragic*
5 left someone (or something) in a bad condition (paragraph 5) *abandoned*
6 given a punishment for a crime (paragraph 6) *sentenced*

4 Work in pairs and discuss. Would you like to be on the programme? Why/Why not?

(handwritten note, top left) miserable → unhappy
↓
Sentimiento
Person who feels
unhappy

4 Davina McCall, presenter of *Big Brother*, knows her mother's side of the family is from France. She goes to Paris and finds out that her great-grandfather, Celestin Hennion, was famous throughout France as head of the French police. He once received a medal from King George V to say 'thank you' for organising security for the king's trip to France in 1914.

5 Not everyone on the programme finds good news about their family history. Jerry Springer learns of a tragic story: his parents escaped Nazi Germany three days before the start of World War II but other family members died in the war. And actress Kim Cattrall discovers that her grandfather, from Liverpool, UK, abandoned his family, including three young daughters. He didn't go far. Forty miles down the road in Manchester, he started another family.

6 Finally, Nigella Lawson, a famous chef whose father was a British politician, discovers that one of her relatives was a thief from the Netherlands. After being sentenced to prison, he escaped to England, which is how the Lawsons ended up in London.

| D Davina McCall | E Kim Cattrall | F Nigella Lawson |

LISTENING

5A ▶ 1.1 Listen to an interview with a man describing his family history. Which family members does he talk about?

B Listen again and answer the questions.

1 How many of his great-grandparents and grandparents did he meet? *1*

2 Where did his father's family come from? *Holland*

3 What three types of job did most of his ancestors do? *soldiers, church, sailors → navegadores*

4 How many people are in his 'immediate family'? *3 wife 2 sons*

5 Who does he think tells the best family stories? *He*

(handwritten, top right) My English Lab YAMW-9XXA-3WPX-W4RI

GRAMMAR question forms

6A Read questions 1–6 from the interview. Answer questions a)–e).

1 Do you know a lot about your family history? *yes/no*

2 Did you ever meet your great-grandparents? *yes/no*

3 Where did your ancestors come from?

4 What happened to them?

5 Which members of your family do you feel close to? *e*

6 Who tells the best family stories? *e*

a) Underline the main verb in each question. (The first has been done for you.)

b) Circle the auxiliary verbs. Which auxiliaries refer to the past? Which refer to the present?

c) Which two questions are *yes/no* questions? *1.2*

d) Which two questions end in a preposition: *of, to, by,* etc.? *3.5*

e) Which two questions use *wh-* words to refer to the subject (the person who does the action) and don't use an auxiliary verb? *5.6*

▐▐▶ page 144 **LANGUAGE BANK**

B ▶ 1.2 Listen to the questions above. Are the question words (*wh-* words) in 3–6 said in a higher or a lower voice?

C Listen and shadow the questions (say them at the same time).

PRACTICE

7A Put the words in the correct order to make questions. *do you see your family everyday?*

1 do / every / your / family / you / day / see / ?

2 your / anything / did / teach / grandparents / you / ? *Did your grandparents teach you anything*

3 remembers / who / always / birthday / your / ? *Who remembers always your birthday*

4 read / taught / to / you / who / ? *who taught you to read?*

5 do / do / you / relax / what / to / ? *what do you do to relax?*

6 holiday / do / next / to / you / want / go / on / your / where / ? *where do you want togo on your next holiday?*

7 words / you / what / describe / three / ? *what three words describe you?*

8 happy / what / you / makes / ? *what makes you happy?*

9 knows / best / you / who / ? *who knows you best?*

10 did / speak / first / when / English / you / ? *when did you speak first speaking English*

B Choose three of the questions to ask other students.

SPEAKING

8A Write four dates, four names and four places that are connected with your family.

Dates: *7 May 2008 – My son was born.*

Names:

Places:

B Work in groups. Take turns to explain what you wrote. As you listen, think of questions to ask afterwards.

WRITING emails of introduction

9A When do you need to write a letter or email to introduce yourself? Which of these things have you done or will you do in the future?

- apply for a job/course
- arrange to meet someone for the first time

B Read the emails. Why are the people writing? Which sentences tell us?

To:	CTEBS committee
Subject:	introductions

Dear Colleagues,

As you probably know, next month I will start work as the new director of the Teacher Education Programme. For those of you who don't know me, I would like to take this opportunity to introduce myself. Since 2006, I have worked at the School of Education at Sidis University. My specialisation is in maths and science, and I have been involved in a number of teacher education projects in these fields.

I look forward to working with you.

Yours sincerely,

Nicholas Collett

To:	maxperkin@hotmail.co.uk
Subject:	hi!

Hi Max,

How are you? Zeinab told me it'd be OK to write to you at this email address. My name's Julia. I was at school with Zeinab years ago. I'm coming to Leeds for a week at the end of May. She told me you'd be able to show me some of the sights and help me find my way around. It'd be great if we could meet. Hope to hear from you soon.

All the best,

Julia :)

10 Read the five stages of email writing below. Do the emails in Exercise 9B follow all the stages?

1 **A**im for your **a**udience: think about who you are writing to. Is the email formal or informal?

2 **B**e **b**rief: try not to use too many words. Emails shouldn't go on for pages.

3 **C**ommunicate **c**learly: use simple, clear language and simple sentence structure.

4 **D**o two **d**rafts: write a first version and then rewrite.

5 **E**dit **e**verything: check grammar, vocabulary, spelling and punctuation before sending.

LEARN TO write formal and informal emails

11A Look at the emails in Exercise 9B again. Which one is formal and which is informal? How do you know?

B Answer questions 1–4 with formal (F) or informal (I).

1 Which email uses full forms of verbs (*I am, I would*) instead of contractions (*I'm* and *I'd*)?

2 Which email leaves out words (e.g. *Hope to …* instead of *I hope to …*)?

3 Which email sounds more like spoken English?

4 Which email uses longer, more complex sentences?

C Complete the notes with phrases from the email.

Greeting (formal): [1] _____.
(informal): Hi/Hello.
Opening line (formal): I am writing to …
(Informal): [2] _____
Introduction (formal): I would like to take this [3] _____
(informal): My name's …
Final message (formal): I look forward to …
(informal): [4] _____
Goodbye (formal): [5] _____
(informal): All the best.

12 Read the situations below and write the emails. Think about who you are writing to, the reason for writing and if you need to use a formal or informal style.

Situation 1

Next week you start a new job as Project Manager for a publishing company. Your job is to start new book projects and organise teams to work on the projects. Write to your new colleagues. Introduce yourself.

Situation 2

You are going to Sydney, Australia, for the first time. Your brother's friend, Tom, lives there. You've never met Tom. You want him to show you around the city. Write to Tom. Introduce yourself, and say when you are coming and what you want to do.

SPEAKING

1A Work in groups and discuss. Do you think male and female brains are different? How? What are the stereotypes of men and women in your country?

B Read the BBC blog and discuss the points you agree/disagree with. Can you think of any opinions to add?

GRAMMAR review of verb tenses

2A Match the underlined verbs below with the tenses a)–d).

1 Scientists recently <u>discovered</u> that there are seventy-eight genetic differences. *past simple*

2 Men can't remember what they <u>were wearing</u> yesterday. *past continuos*

3 Women <u>hide</u> things in cupboards. *Present Simple*

4 A baby <u>is crying</u>. *present Continuos*

a) present simple   b) present continuous

c) past simple   d) past continuous

B Complete the rules with the correct tenses a)–d).

> Rules:
> 1 We use *Past simple* for actions, events or situations that are finished.
> 2 We use *Present continuos* for things that are going on at a particular moment in the present.
> 3 We use *Present simple* for habits, routines and things that are always true.
> 4 We use *Past continuos* when someone was in the middle of an action at a particular moment in the past.

C Read about state verbs and underline three examples in the blog opposite.

> Rule: Some verbs are not usually used in the continuous, e.g. *want, like, remember, understand, know*. These are called 'state verbs'.

▶ page 144 **LANGUAGEBANK**

PRACTICE

3A Read the personal profile and put the words in brackets into the correct tense.

> My name is Matsuko Tamazuri. I am twenty-three and I ¹ *am* (be) a student. I study French and Spanish at university in Osaka, where I ² *grew up* (grow up), but at the moment I ³ *am learning* (learn) English in New York. When I first ⁴ *got* (get) here, everything ⁵ *seemed* (seem) different: the food, the clothes and the weather. Now I ⁶ *am enjoying* (enjoy) it and it feels like home! I have a <u>boyfriend</u> called Josh. I ⁷ *met* (meet) him three weeks ago when I ⁸ *was looking* (look) for an internet café! My hobbies ⁹ *are* (be) surfing the net and singing. I ¹⁰ *sing* (sing) every day, usually in the bathroom!

B Work in pairs. Ask questions and write your partner's personal profile. Use the profile above to help.

Scientists recently discovered that there are seventy-eight genetic differences between men and women.

BBC Online News readers suggest what those differences might be.

❝ Women have a multi-tasking gene. Men can never prepare dinner so that everything is ready at the same time. ❞

❝ Men like to have all their stuff (DVDs, CDs) on show to impress their friends. Women hide things in cupboards. ❞

❝ Women have an ability to make men think they are in charge. ❞

❝ Men refuse to pay more than £5 for a haircut because it's not that important. ❞

❝ A baby is crying, a dog is barking, a doorbell is ringing. It doesn't matter: the man of the house is sleeping. Men can sleep through anything. Women can't. ❞

❝ A man can choose and buy a pair of shoes in 90 seconds over the internet. ❞

❝ Women know what to do when someone starts to cry. ❞

❝ Women remember every outfit they've worn for the past twenty years. Men can't remember what they were wearing yesterday without looking on the floor. ❞

❝ Men speak in sentences. Women speak in paragraphs. ❞

LISTENING

4A Read the description of a BBC TV documentary and answer the questions.

1 What is the aim of the documentary?

2 Whose lives does it follow? For how long?

3 What is the purpose of the test?

Child of Our Time

Child of Our Time is a BBC documentary that aims to discover what makes us who we are. The programme follows the lives of twenty-five children and their families for a period of twenty years. During the series, the children and their parents do a number of tests. In this programme, they do a test to discover whether a male brain is different from a female brain and how this affects our character and abilities. ③

B ▶1.3 Take a piece of paper, listen to Parts 1 and 2 and follow the test instructions.

C ▶1.4 Listen to the explanation in Part 3. Turn to page 174 and check your picture. How many parts did your bike have? Could it work? Does it have a person on it? Compare your picture with other students'.

D ▶1.5 Listen to people discussing their pictures of the bicycle. Who says sentences 1–6? A man (M) or a woman (W)?

1 None of us got the chain, did we? W

2 Pedals nor chains, so mine will never work. M

3 None of us drew a person. M

4 I've got a little bird on my handlebars, though. M

5 Yours is the most accurate one. W *exact*

6 And you've got lights on yours. W

5 Discuss the questions.

1 Was the explanation correct for you?

2 Do you agree with the presenter's views about men and women?

> Women think people are important. Men, on the other hand, are more interested in getting the machine right.

VOCABULARY relationships

6A Work in pairs. Look at the words in the box and answer the questions.

> ~~boss and employee~~   classmates   partner   ~~team-mates~~   ~~member~~
> godfather and godmother   mentor and pupil   fiancée and fiancé

1 Which pair works together? *boss and employee*

2 Which pair promises to help guide a child through life? *godfather and*

3 Which pair is going to get married? *fiancée and fiancé*

4 Which pair involves one person learning from the other? *mentor and pupil*

5 Which word describes people who play in the same sports team? *team mates*

6 Which word describes people who go to the same class? *classmates*

7 Which word describes a person who is part of a club? *member*

8 Which word is a general word for 'someone who you do something with'? *partner*

B Work in groups and discuss.

1 Do you associate the roles with men or women or both?

2 Do you think men and women are different in the roles? How?

I think women bosses are often less aggressive than male bosses and they are better at listening.

C ▶1.6 Listen to six sentences. Number the words in Exercise 6A in the order that you hear them.

D Six of the words have two syllables. Find the words and underline the stressed syllable. Say the words aloud, putting the stress on the correct syllable.

speakout TIP

Remember: most two-syllable words in English have the stress on the first syllable. Hold a hand under your chin. Say the word slowly. The jaw (the bottom part of your chin) drops more on the stressed syllable.

SPEAKING

7A Think about your own relationships. Prepare to talk about one man and one woman in your life. Use the questions below to make notes.

• Who are they? *Richard and Giannina*

• What is their role in your life? *Father and Mother*

• How often do you see them? *Mother every day Father every Sunday*

• How have they helped you and how have you helped them? *They take care of me and help me to make some des...*

I'm a member of a football club, and we meet every week. Our coach is fantastic and he has helped our team a lot.

B Tell other students about these relationships.

VOCABULARY PLUS collocations

8A Work in pairs and do the quiz opposite.

B Turn to page 174 and read the text to check your answers.

9A Look at the quiz again. Find and circle five expressions using *take*, *get*, *do* and *go*.

B Write the expressions in italics in the correct places in the word webs below.

1 ~~on a diet~~, ~~home~~, *off something*, ~~for a drink/a walk/a meal~~, ~~grey~~

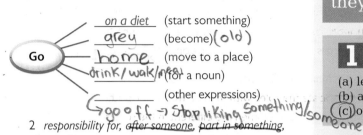

Go
- on a diet (start something)
- grey (become) (old)
- home (move to a place)
- drink/walk/meal (for a noun)
- ___ (other expressions)

Go off → stop liking something/someone.

2 *responsibility for*, ~~after someone~~, ~~part in something~~, ~~a taxi~~

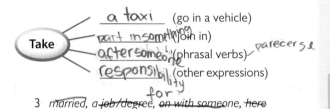

Take
- a taxi (go in a vehicle)
- part in something (join in)
- after someone (phrasal verbs) — parecerse
- responsibility for (other expressions)

3 ~~married~~, ~~a job/degree~~, *on with someone*, ~~here~~

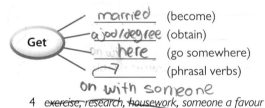

Get
- married (become)
- a job/degree (obtain)
- here (go somewhere)
- on with someone (phrasal verbs)

4 ~~exercise~~, ~~research~~, ~~housework~~, *someone a favour*

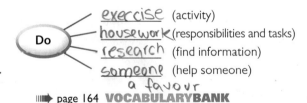

Do
- exercise (activity)
- housework (responsibilities and tasks)
- research (find information)
- someone a favour (help someone)

➠ page 164 **VOCABULARYBANK**

SPEAKING

10A Think about your classmates. Write down the name of someone who:

- never gets angry. Kattia
- does research for his/her job. Rodrigo
- took a test in the last six months. Sofia
- went for a meal last weekend. Luis
- took up a new hobby recently. Jennifer
- always gets here early. Andrea
- went for a walk today. Adriana
- got a new job recently. Jessica

B Work in groups. Ask the other students to check if they agree with your ideas.

What Women Really Think

Stella magazine commissioned YouGov, a research agency, to interview over 1,000 women in the UK about what they really think. How do you think they responded?

1 How many women in the UK would prefer to have a male boss?
- (a) less than 30%
- (b) about 50%
- (c) over 70%

2 How many women have gone on a diet in the past?
- (a) 20%
- (b) between 35% and 45%
- (c) over 50%

3 How many women spend more than seven hours a week doing exercise?
- (a) 4%
- (b) 15%
- (c) 30%

4 What is the biggest challenge for women today?
- (a) staying healthy
- (b) making enough money
- (c) balancing home and work life

5 What do women think is the best age to get married?
- (a) between 21 and 24
- (b) between 25 and 29
- (c) over 30

6 What do 59% of women think fathers should take more responsibility for?
- (a) their children
- (b) doing the housework
- (c) organising holidays

7 According to women, how much housework do they do?
- (a) more than 50%
- (b) over 75%
- (c) nearly all of it

8 How many women aged 45–54 met their husbands through the internet?
- (a) 1%
- (b) 9%
- (c) 16%

► **FUNCTION** | talking about yourself ► **VOCABULARY** | interview advice ► **LEARN TO** | use two-word responses

5 tips to help you do well at interviews

How do you get into the university or the job of your dreams? Even before the interview, you might need to catch someone's attention. The Dean of Admissions at Harvard University says he often receives flowers and chocolates from potential students. One student sent references every day for three months. Eventually, he even sent a letter from his dentist saying how nice his teeth were. He didn't get an interview.

For those of you who do make the interview stage, here are five top tips:

1 Be prepared. Do some research about the university or company so you know what questions to ask.

2 Dress appropriately. You don't have to dress smartly but you should look clean. And don't wear 'bling' (large pieces of jewellery).

3 Arrive on time. Fifteen minutes early is OK.

4 Shake hands firmly and make eye contact. First impressions are important.

5 Speak clearly and try to offer full answers rather than short responses. This shows your enthusiasm.

SPEAKING

1A **What type of interview can you see in the photo? Is it a/an:**

- job interview?
- interview for a place at university?
- newspaper/magazine interview?
- interview for a talk show/other television programme?
- police inquiry?
- placement interview for a language course?

B **Look at the list of interview types above. Answer questions 1–3.**

1 Which types of interview above have you experienced?

2 Which will you experience in the future?

3 Do you think it is possible to show 'the real you' in a short interview? Why/Why not?

VOCABULARY interview advice

2A **Work in pairs. Look at topics 1–3 below and match them to the expressions in the box.**

dress smartly *3*   speak clearly *1*   answer briefly *2*
shake hands firmly *1*   send references *3*
arrive on time *3*   avoid eye contact *2*   do some research *3*
show enthusiasm *1*   be prepared *3*

1 Should do during an interview

2 Shouldn't do during an interview

3 Might do before an interview

B **What else should/shouldn't you do in an interview? Think of as many things as you can in two minutes.**

You should try to ask questions.

FUNCTION talking about yourself

3 **Read the text and answer the questions.**

1 What type of things do people do to get an interview at Harvard University?

2 What should you do before and during an interview?

4A ▶ 1.7 **Listen to three extracts from the audio and answer the questions.**

1 What types of interview are they?

2 Which interviewee doesn't follow the five tips? What does he/she do wrong?

B **Answer questions 1–6. Listen again to check.**
Interview 1

1 What does the student want to practise? *English*

2 What types of classes are in the afternoons? *English idioms Conversation Pronunciation*

Interview 2

3 What did the girl organise on the summer camp? *games children 7-10 years*

4 What 'can be difficult', according to the interviewer? *different ages.*

Interview 3

5 What does the man want to know? *Courses university*

6 Why are online courses more difficult than face-to-face courses, according to the interviewer? *terms of reading and writing*

5A Read the extracts from audio 1.7. Underline the expressions that introduce a question.

Extract I

T: OK. You've got a very good level of English so we'd put you in the advanced class. Is there anything else?

S: <u>Could I ask a question?</u>

Extract 2

I: <u>There are a couple of things I'd like to ask about.</u> Your CV says you have some experience of looking after children?

A: Yes, I was a tutor on a summer camp last year.

I: <u>Can I ask you about that?</u> What type of things did you do?

A: Um, well, I organised games.

Extract 3

I: I think that's about it. <u>Do you have any questions?</u> Any queries?

S: Um, yes, actually <u>I do have a query.</u>

I: Yes, go ahead.

S: It's about online classes at the university.

B Read the extracts below and underline the expressions that are used to introduce an opinion.

Extract I

S: I've studied English for many years and spent time in Britain, but that was a few years ago. <u>So for me the most important</u> <u>thing is to</u> just refresh … and try to remember my English and practise speaking and listening.

Extract 2

I: OK. And you enjoyed it?

A: Yes.

I: What aspect, what part did you enjoy, would you say?

A: <u>I suppose I'd have to say</u> I liked the games best.

I: And any problems?

A: Um, no.

I: What about the different ages? We often find that different ages together can be difficult.

A: It depends. <u>In my opinion,</u> you can usually get the older children to help the younger ones.

Extract 3

S: If I'm accepted, I saw that there are, that it's possible to take some courses online.

I: That's right.

S: So I wouldn't need to attend classes?

I: Not for the online courses. But … well, <u>one thing I'd like to say is that the</u> online courses are, in many ways, more difficult than face-to-face courses.

IIII➤ page 144 **LANGUAGEBANK**

6 Put the words in the correct order to make sentences or questions.

1 query / I / a / have / do *I do have a query*

2 I / a / could / question / ask / ? *could i ask a question?*

3 like / couple / of / are / about / I'd / things / to / a / ask / there
there are a couple of things id like to ask about

4 ask / you / I / can / that / about / ? *can i ask you about that*

5 true / this / opinion / my / isn't / in *in my opinion this isn't true*

6 to / I'd / t / agree / have / say *I have to say I agree*

7 thing / that / like / I'd / one / say / is / to / is / course / the / difficult

8 is / thing / important / most / for / the / me / to / study

→ One thing I'd like to say is that the course is difficult

→ For me the most important thing is to study.

LEARN TO use two-word responses

7A Match expressions 1–5 with expressions a)–e).

1 Of course.
2 That's right.
3 I see.
4 No problem.
5 Go ahead.

a) Please continue.
b) You're correct.
c) You're welcome.
d) Yes, definitely.
e) I understand.

B Which expressions are more formal: 1–5 or a)–e)? Which do you use regularly? Read audio script 1.7 on page 184 to see how the expressions are used.

SPEAKING

8A Work in pairs and role-play the interview. Student A: read the instructions below. Student B: turn to page 174.

You work for a famous business school. Student B wants to do a course at the school. Interview him/her. Use the following prompts and ask about:

- his/her reason for doing the course
- his/her work experience
- his/her expectations of the course
- his/her plans for the future

Prepare the questions. Remember to ask your partner why he/she is a good candidate for the school and, at the end, if he/she has any queries about the business school.

B Change roles and role-play the interview again.

15

DVD PREVIEW

1A What can you do in Second Life? Do you think the statements below are true?

1 In Second Life you can **alter** your appearance. *change*

2 You can become more **attractive** than you actually are. ✓

3 You can **pick** a different skin colour. *choose* *beautiful*

4 You can wear strange **outfits**. *eh clothes* ✓

5 You can **socialise** with people from different countries. ✓ *meet and talk to*

6 You can talk to other **residents** of Second Life. *people who live in one place*

7 You can make money in Second Life's own **currency**. ✓ *+*

B Match the words in bold above with the words/phrases in the box.

~~clothes~~	type of money from one country	
~~change~~	beautiful	~~meet and talk to~~
~~choose~~	~~people who live in one place~~	

C Read the programme information and check your answers to Exercise 1A.

B B C The Money Programme: Second Life

This BBC programme investigates Second Life, a virtual world with its own communities. In Second Life, you reinvent yourself: you choose a different name, change your appearance in any way you want and get a new personality. What is more, Second Life is a world of endless pleasure. You can go shopping, take English classes, meet and chat to people from all over the world, live in a perfect house on a magical island and even make money. There's only one rule in Second Life: there are no rules!

▶ DVD VIEW

2 Watch the DVD and put pictures A–E in the correct order. *D, C, E, A, B*

3A Match pictures A–E with sentences 1–5.

1 Once you've created an account, you can create an avatar. *D*

2 You can be female, male or even something called a 'furry': half-animal, half-human. *C*

3 It turns out there are not a lot of unattractive people in Second Life. *E*

4 But it's more fun flying, and with maps I can find almost anything I want. *A*

5 You can go up to anyone and chat. *B*

B Watch the DVD again to check.

4 Work in groups and discuss.

1 Have you been in Second Life? If not, would you like to spend time there? *No... NO*

2 What might you enjoy about Second Life? What would you not like about it?

3 Why do you think people get addicted to Second Life?

speakout create a new identity

5A ▶1.8 Listen to someone talking about her avatar. Answer the questions.

1 Where did she hear about Second Life? TV
2 What did she change about her appearance? Dark hair
3 What job did she decide to do in Second Life? Business woman
4 What is the 'one thing that hasn't changed'? Personality
5 What type of building does she talk about? SHOPS

B Listen again and tick the key phrases you hear.

Keyphrases

(You can) create a different version of yourself.

I reinvented myself as a …

I created a new image of myself.

I didn't change my appearance that much.

One thing I decided to alter was my …

One thing that hasn't changed is …

My avatar is based on …

C Create your own avatar. Complete your profile using the prompts below:

- name Camila
- age 18
- height 1,67
- weight 50Kg
- hair colour Brown
- eye colour green
- clothes t-shirt jeans trainers
- nationality Peruvian (Spanish)
- languages spoken English Japanesse, Corean&French
- job and/or hobbies Fotagraphy Play the guitar
- favourite places to hang out Beaches and parks
- would like to meet (type of people) funny people
- motto or personal philosophy
- one thing no one knows about you

D Talk to other students. Introduce your new (avatar) self. What do you have in common with other avatars in the class?

writeback answer a questionnaire

6A Read the questionnaire. Choose to be either yourself or your new identity and write answers to the questions. Write 1–2 sentences for each question.

Who are you?

1 What three words best describe you?
2 What is your idea of perfect happiness?
3 What possession is most important to you?
4 What is your greatest achievement?
5 What is your favourite sound, smell and taste?
6 What do you like most about your lifestyle?
7 What do you like least about your lifestyle?
8 What do you always carry with you?
9 Who would be your perfect dinner date? Why?
10 What's your favourite month and why?
11 If you could change one thing about the past, what would it be?
12 If you could learn one new thing, what would it be?

B Share your answers with other students. Decide if the other students' answers are for themselves or their avatar.

FAMILY

1A Complete the sentences with the words in the box.

> history   inherited   after
> extended   ancestors   relative
> great   side   roots   related

1 My parents told me about my family ___history___ .

2 My ancestors probably came from the place where I was born.

3 I once met my ___great___ -grandparents.

4 I take ___after___ my mother, especially my personality.

5 I know someone who inherited a house when their parents died.

6 My family's ___roots___ are in another country.

7 I have a relative living in Australia.

8 I know someone who is related to someone famous!

9 I know my mother's ___side___ of the family much better than my father's.

10 I have a very large extended family: lots of cousins, nephews and nieces.

B Tick the sentences that are true for you. Compare with another student.

QUESTION FORMS

2A Find and correct the mistakes in the questions below. Three of the questions are correct.

1 When you started studying English? *did*

2 Who did helped you to learn English?

3 Do you be enjoy learning languages?

4 Did you to learn anything important from your teachers?

5 What annoys you about your job or your studies? ✓

6 In your job or studies, is there anything you are not happy? *with*

7 When you imagine the perfect career, what do you think of? ✓

8 What keeps you awake at night?

B Work in pairs. Choose four of the questions to ask your partner.

REVIEW OF VERB TENSES

3 Find and correct the mistakes. Five of the underlined verbs are incorrect.

12.10.09

I ¹<u>was walking</u> to work this morning when I ²<u>was seeing</u> Mr Gonzalez, my *saw* old Spanish teacher. He ³<u>was wearing</u> a leather jacket and carrying a guitar. I ⁴<u>ask</u> him how he was. He said, 'Fine. I *asked* ⁵<u>go</u> to my band practice.' I said, 'What *going* band?' He replied, 'I ⁶<u>don't teach</u> any more. It ⁷<u>wasn't</u> really the best job for me. A few years ago I ⁸<u>was starting</u> a *started* band called The Big Easy. We ⁹<u>don't make</u> much money, but I ¹⁰<u>'m liking</u> *like* the lifestyle.' I asked him where he lived and he said, 'I ¹¹<u>'m living</u> in my caravan at the moment. I ¹²<u>travel</u> a lot. I'm a child of the 60s!'

RELATIONSHIPS

4A Put the letters in the correct order to find the names of twelve types of people.

1 tomdogher god mother

2 niface fiancé

3 ilupp pupil

4 nraterp partner

5 ceanife fiancée

6 breemm member

7 stamcasel classmate

8 dethagorf godfather

9 sobs Boss ♡

10 emeyloep employee

11 trenom mentor

12 maatteme team-mate

B Work in pairs. Which of these people do you know or have? Which of these are you?

I have a fiancée. We're getting married next summer.

I'm a member of a gym.

• Mother sister stepfather

• Mexican, canada
  Mom Father Sister Dad

TALKING ABOUT YOURSELF

5A Complete the conversations with the pairs of words in the box.

> query about   like to   to say
> you about   I ask   thing I'd

query about

1 A: I have a the class. Do I have to bring a pen?

   B: No, it's a computer class.

2 A: Could a question? Where *look* does the tennis class meet?

   B: At the tennis courts.

3 A: I'd have I'm not sure you're *to say* qualified. Why should we employ you for the library position?

   B: Because I'm good with children and animals.

4 A: There are a couple of things I'd *like to* ask. Firstly, can you work on Saturdays?

   B: Is that at the weekend?

5 A: One like to say is that you look *thing I'd* good for your age. How old are you?

   B: Thirty.

6 A: Can I ask your latest film, *you about* *Philadelphia*? Where is it set?

   B: In Philadelphia.

B Work in pairs and write a conversation. Use the expressions in Exercises 5 and 7 on page 15 to help.

C Work in groups and take turns to perform your conversations.

BBC VIDEO PODCAST

Watch people talking about their families on ActiveBook or on the website.

Authentic BBC interviews

www.pearsonELT.com/speakout

SPEAKING
- ❯ Talk about life stories
- ❯ Talk about an important news event
- ❯ Tell a true story or a lie
- ❯ Tell a narrative

LISTENING
- ❯ Listen to a radio programme about films
- ❯ Listen to news reports
- ❯ Listen to people telling anecdotes
- ❯ Watch a BBC drama about an art thief

READING
- ❯ Read an article about conspiracy theories
- ❯ Read a news report
- ❯ Read a text about lying

WRITING
- ❯ Write a news report
- ❯ Write a newspaper article

BBC CONTENT
- ▯ Video podcast: When is it OK to tell a lie?
- ◉ DVD: Hustle

UNIT 2

tales

▶ Fact or fiction?   p20

▶ What really happened?   p23

▶ I don't believe it!   p26

▶ Hustle   p28

SPEAKING

1 Work in groups and discuss. Can you think of a film you have seen that has taught you about a person/event in history?

2A Work in pairs and do the quiz. Decide if each question is fact, fiction or partly true. Then check your answers on page 174.

B Discuss. Do you think it is all right for film-makers to change the facts of a story? Why/Why not?

Hollywood versus history

Do you know the difference between what you have learnt from your history books and what you have learnt from watching Hollywood's historically inaccurate movies? Can you tell your facts from fiction?

1 In the film *The Last Samurai*, Tom Cruise plays a US army captain who joins the samurai warriors in Japan in 1876. Was Captain Nathan Algren a real figure from history? *fiction*

2 In *Shakespeare in Love*, William Shakespeare is inspired to write *Romeo and Juliet* by his real-life relationship with a young actress. Did this happen in real life? *fiction*

3 In a scene from *Gladiator*, we see the Roman Emperor Commodus die at the hands of a gladiator. Did he really die like this? *Partly true*

4 In the film *Braveheart*, Mel Gibson plays the character William Wallace, leading an army of men with painted faces, and wearing kilts* as he battles to free Scotland from the English. How much truth is there in the story? *Partly true*

5 In the 1995 adventure, *Apollo 13*, we hear the pilot saying the famous words 'Houston, we have a problem.' But were these his exact words? *Partly true*

* **kilt** – a skirt traditionally worn by Scottish men

VOCABULARY types of story

3A Look at the types of film stories in the box below. Match the types of story with the descriptions a)–i).

> *one person history*
> biopic docudrama disaster romantic comedy
> period drama fantasy/science fiction psychological thriller
> action/adventure mystery/crime

a) Heroes chase and fight. *action/adventure*

b) Characters battle with their minds. *psycholgical thriller*

c) Strange things happen in the future or in imaginary worlds. *fantasy*

d) Things that happen in the life of a real person. *biopic*

e) The good guy (the detective) finds the bad guy (the criminal). *crime*

f) People dressed up in old-fashioned costumes. *period drama*

g) Funny things happen. Two people fall in love. *romantic comedy*

h) Terrible things happen, but people survive. *disaster*

i) A documentary made more interesting with some parts acted. *docudrama*

B Work in pairs and answer the questions.

1 Which types of film do you enjoy watching?

2 Can you name films which match each type of story?

LISTENING

4A ▶ 2.1 Listen to the first part of a radio programme about films and answer the questions.

1 What type of film does the programme talk about? *biopics*

2 Why are these films so popular? *People want to know more from celebritis and teachin a entertaning way*

B Work in pairs and discuss. Look at the photos of actors who have played the roles of famous people in films. How do you think they prepared for the role? Do you think it was difficult?

5 ▶ 2.2 Listen to the second part of the radio programme and answer the questions about the actors and the roles they played.

1 Who met a character they would play in person? *Helen Mirren*

2 Who couldn't meet with the character they played? *Audrey Tautou*

3 Who became good friends with the character? *Will Smith*

4 Who phoned hotels in order to listen to a special accent? *Josh Brolin*

6A Complete the information about the radio programme.

1 Hollywood has always used ___true___ ___stories___ in its films.

2 Hollywood began making films in the ___1920___ s.

3 Some of the best films in recent years have been based on ___true___ ___events___.

4 From these films we've learnt about the ___difficult___ lives of some of the biggest music legends.

5 Many of these actors have won ___oscars___ *won* for their roles.

6 Helen Mirren met the Queen for ___tea___.

7 Josh Brolin phoned up hotels in Texas, to listen to their ___accent___

8 Tatou wanted to look like Coco Chanel, so that we would recognise her ___image___.

B ▶ 2.3 Listen and check your answers.

A Helen Mirren   B Queen Elizabeth II

C Will Smith   D Muhammad Ali

E Audrey Tautou   F Coco Chanel

G Josh Brolin   H George Bush

GRAMMAR present perfect/past simple

7A Read the sentences in Exercise 6A and underline examples of the present perfect and past simple.

B Complete the rules with present perfect or past simple.

Rules:
1 Use the ___P.S___ to talk about experiences or things that happened before now. The time is not specified or important.
2 Use the ___P·P___ to talk about recent events, or an action which started in the past and continues now.
3 Use the ___P·S___ to talk about a specific event in the past (we know when the event happened).
4 Use the ___P·P___ to talk about an action which starts and finishes in the past.

C Look at the sentences in Exercise 6A again and match them with one of the rules above.

➧ page 146 **LANGUAGEBANK**

8A ▶ 2.4 Listen to the pairs of phrases. Notice the difference.
1 I lived / I've lived
2 we met / we've met
3 he decided / he's decided
4 they spent / they've spent

B ▶ 2.5 Listen and write the sentences.

C Listen again and check. Then listen and repeat.

PRACTICE

9 Complete the text with the correct form of the verbs in brackets.

Chris Gardner is a successful businessman and a millionaire. But things ¹_____ always _____ (not be) easy. He ²_____ (not meet) his father until he was twenty-eight years old. This experience made him sure about one thing: he ³_____ always _____ (want) to be a good father to his own children. As a young man, Gardner ⁴_____ (experience) hard times. His wife ⁵_____ (leave) him, he ⁶_____ (lose) his job, and at one stage he and his two-year-old son ⁷_____ (sleep) in train stations and airports. He ⁸_____ (come) a long way since then. His life changed when he ⁹_____ (meet) a man driving a red Ferrari and asked him what job he did. The man was a stockbroker, so Gardner ¹⁰_____ (ask) him out to lunch, and the Ferrari driver introduced Gardner to the world of finance. Since he ¹¹_____ (become) successful, he ¹²_____ (spend) a lot of money helping homeless people, and he ¹³_____ also _____ (write) books about his experiences. His story was told in the film *The Pursuit of Happiness*, starring Will Smith.

SPEAKING

10A Work in pairs. Student A: write *Have you ever …* ? questions using the prompts in the box below. Student B: turn to page 176.

be on TV/in a newspaper   do something embarrassing in public
write a poem/story   go to a country on a different continent
collect something as a hobby   see someone commit a crime

B Take turns to ask and answer questions. Try to find five things that you have done and your partner hasn't done.

SPEAKING

11A Imagine you are going to make a film about your life. Choose five events you would like to include. Write some notes in the film strip below.

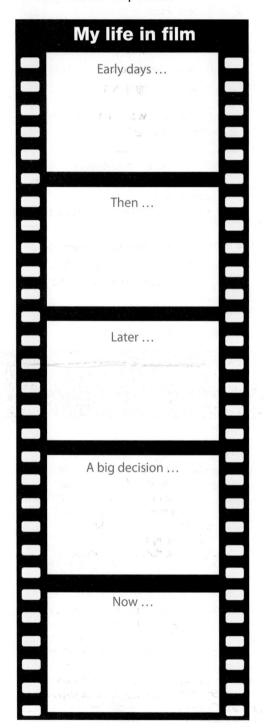

My life in film

Early days …

Then …

Later …

A big decision …

Now …

B Work in pairs. Take turns to talk about the film of your life.

C Think of three questions to ask your partner about the film of their life. Ask and answer the questions.

Why did you choose to … ?

What happened when you … ?

What did you enjoy best about … ?

VOCABULARY **PLUS** prepositions

PAS SIMPLE
Gespecific
time.

Preposition + expressions of time

12 Complete the word webs with expressions in the box.

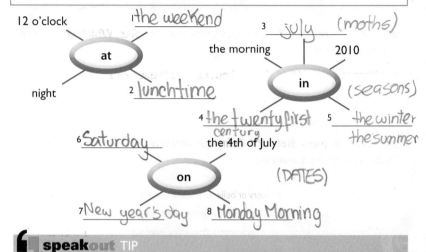

> Saturday   the weekend   Monday morning   New Year's Day   July
> the winter/the summer   the twenty-first century   lunchtime

12 o'clock — ~~the weekend~~

at

night — 2 lunchtime

3 July (moths)

the morning — 2010

in (seasons)

4 the twenty first century — 5 the winter the summer

6 Saturday — the 4th of July

on (DATES)

7 New year's day — 8 Monday Morning

> **speak**out TIP
>
> To help you remember which preposition of time to use, try to memorise this: **on** Monday; **in** winter; **at** that time
> **on** = for specific days, **in** = for time periods, **at** = for specific times

Preposition + noun

13 Complete the sentences with the correct preposition: *on, for* or *by*.

1 It's a book **by** Dan Brown, a film **by** Steven Spielberg, a song **by** Amy Winehouse.
2 I saw it **on** TV. I heard it **on** the radio. I spoke to him **on** the phone. *on foot*
3 We went **for** a walk, **for** a drive, **for** a run, **for** a swim.
4 They travelled **by** boat, **by** plane, **by** coach, **by** train.

Fixed expressions

14 Match the fixed expressions in bold in sentences 1–10 with meanings a)–j).

1 I dropped it **by mistake.**
2 I did the work **on my own.**
3 He's here **on business.**
4 We met **by chance.**
5 It was made **by hand.**
6 We got there **in the end.**
7 She said it **on purpose.**
8 We arrived **on time.**
9 I'll do that **in a moment.**
10 They're **in a hurry.**

a) finally
b) cannot wait
c) by a person, not a machine
d) it was not a mistake
e) alone, not with other people
f) not early, not late
g) in a very short time
h) accidentally
i) not on holiday, but for work
j) it was not planned

15A Look at Exercise 14 again. Write 6–8 questions with phrases with prepositions.

*Do you usually arrive **on time**, or are you sometimes late?*

*Do you prefer to live with someone, or live **on your own**?*

B Work in pairs. Take turns to ask and answer the questions.

▶ page 165 **VOCABULARYBANK**

▶ **GRAMMAR** | narrative tenses   ▶ **VOCABULARY** | the news   ▶ **HOW TO** | talk about important events

SPEAKING

1 Discuss the questions.

1 How do you keep up-to-date with the news?

2 What have been the most important stories in the last five years?

2A ▶ 2.6 Listen to the excerpts from news reports. Which stories can you see in the photos?

B Work in pairs. What do you know about these news stories?

READING

3A Work in pairs. Read the definition and look at the photos below. Then answer the questions.

> **a conspiracy theory:** a theory or belief that there was a secret plan behind a major event

1 What do you think the conspiracy theories were about (the events in the photos)?

2 Which story do you think involved a real conspiracy, according to official reports?

B Read the article to check your answers.

4A Read the article again and answer the questions.

1 Who was killed in a crash?

2 Who was shot?

3 Who was arrested?

4 Who was murdered?

5 Who were the suspects?

6 Who was photographed?

B How are these words and phrases related to the stories?

> shadows   stars   a love story
> alcohol   photographs/photographers
> a man with a gun   a flag
> the FBI (Federal Bureau of Investigation)

C Work in pairs. Answer the questions.

1 What do you think? Do you believe the official reports or the conspiracy theorists?

2 Do you know any other conspiracy theories? What happened?

The World's best-known conspiracy theories
BBC Focus Magazine takes a look

Man on the Moon

There are claims that Neil Armstrong's 'giant leap for mankind' took place in a studio and not on the Moon at all. Many have doubts about the photographs taken by astronauts on the Moon's surface. The conspiracy theorists say that strange shadows were falling in different directions, and surprisingly there are no stars visible. It also seems that the US flag, planted by Buzz Aldrin, was apparently waving in an impossible wind. However, all of these doubts can be explained logically. The lighting conditions on the Moon were complicated, and 'fluttering' on the flag only appeared when the astronauts moved it.

A Royal Affair

Diana, Princess of Wales, was killed on 31st August 1997, after her car crashed as it was driving through the Pont de l'Alma tunnel in Paris. Conspiracy theorists have claimed that Diana's death was not an accident – that she was in fact killed by MI6 (the British Secret Intelligence Service) because of her relationship with Dodi Al-Fayed. However, an inquiry into the accident eventually concluded that Diana's death was simply the result of driver Henri Paul's drunken condition, and the fact that paparazzi photographers were following them. There was also no evidence that Diana was pregnant at the time of the accident, or that she had planned to marry Dodi Al-Fayed.

The Death of a President

Suspects in the assassination of President John F Kennedy included the FBI, the Cuban leader Fidel Castro, and many others. Kennedy was killed in Dallas, Texas, on 22nd November 1963. He was riding through crowds in his car when a gunman shot him once in the head. Lee Harvey Oswald was arrested almost immediately after Kennedy's death, and was himself murdered two days later. A report in 1964 concluded that Oswald had acted alone. But in 1979, the report and the original FBI investigation were criticised. The new report agreed that Oswald had killed Kennedy, but also concluded that the President was killed 'as a result of conspiracy' by people unknown.

GRAMMAR narrative tenses

5A Read the summary. Find and underline examples of the past simple and the past continuous and answer the questions.

> Princess Diana's car crashed as it was driving through the Pont de l'Alma tunnel in Paris. Conspiracy theorists claimed that M16 planned her death because she was having an affair with Mr Al-Fayed.

1 Which tense do we use to talk about the main events in a story? *PS especial time*
2 Which tense do we use to give the background information in a story? *P.C*

B Read the conclusion and answer the questions.

> An inquiry concluded that Diana had not planned to marry Mr Al-Fayed, and that the crash had happened because the driver was drunk.

1 Which of the verbs is in the past simple? *concluded*
2 Which of the verbs is in the past perfect? *had happened*
3 Which tense describes the event that happened first? *Past Simple*

C Underline the correct alternative to complete the rule.

Rule: Use the past perfect to talk about actions which happened *before the past time event we are talking about*/a very long time ago.

➭ page 146 **LANGUAGEBANK**

PRACTICE

6 Read an account of an important news event. Complete the text with phrases a)–h).

11 February 2000: Nelson Mandela's release from prison

I was in the crowd on the parade in Cape Town that day. It was a hot day, and ¹_d_ to see Mandela walk free from the prison. ²_a_ for twenty-seven years. At one point ³_c_ but most people stayed calm. People ⁴_g_ and singing songs. There was a great feeling of solidarity. There was a large tree in the middle of the parade, and ⁵_h_ to get a better view. Suddenly, ⁶_b_ and people fell to the ground. But nobody wanted to leave. Nobody wanted to miss the chance of seeing Mandela for the first time. ⁷_f_ there was a huge cheer. From where I was standing, it was difficult ⁸_e_ but I knew I was there for an important moment in our history.

a) He had been in prison
b) one of the branches broke
c) we heard some shots
d) 50,000 people were waiting
e) to hear what Mandela was saying
f) When he finally arrived
g) were talking to each other
h) many people had climbed onto it

VOCABULARY the news

7A Match the headlines 1–10 with the explanations a)–j).

1 g Prime Minister's wife dies in **crash**
2 a World Trade Center **attacked**
3 j Student demonstration turns **violent**
4 i Workers threaten **strikes**
5 e Massive **earthquake** hits Los Angeles
6 d Most wanted **fugitive** arrested
7 h Floods **destroy** crops
8 b Hostages released after talks with rebels
9 c Music legend **shot** outside his New York apartment
10 f Businesses hit by **collapse** of banks

a) Someone tried to damage or destroy a building.
b) People who were kept as prisoners are allowed to go free.
c) A musician was killed with a gun.
d) Police catch a man who they suspect committed a serious crime.
e) A natural disaster destroys a city.
f) Economic crisis affects businesses.
g) A woman is killed in a car accident.
h) A lot of farmland is under water.
i) Many people might refuse to go to work.
j) People who are protesting begin to fight on the streets.

B Work in pairs. Describe some stories which have been in the news recently using the vocabulary in bold above.

➭ page 165 **VOCABULARYBANK**

SPEAKING

8A Choose one of the news stories in the lesson or another important news story. Make notes to answer the questions below.

1 What was the news story? Where were you when you heard the news?

2 What were you doing? Who were you with?

3 What did you think at first? How did you feel?

4 Did the news change things for you in any way?

B Work with other students. Tell them about your story.

WRITING a news report

9A Read the news report and answer the questions. Underline the parts of the news report which help you to answer.

1 Who is the story about? *Maxi Sopo*

2 What happened?

3 Why did it happen?

4 Where did it happen? *Cancun Mexico*

5 When did it happen? *last month*

6 What is the situation now?
he is in custody in Mexico City

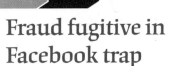

Fraud fugitive in Facebook trap

A man who was on the run from police in the US revealed where he was hiding through a series of Facebook updates.

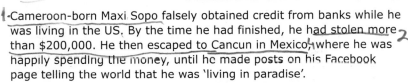

Cameroon-born Maxi Sopo falsely obtained credit from banks while he was living in the US. By the time he had finished, he had stolen more than $200,000. He then escaped to Cancun in Mexico, where he was happily spending the money, until he made posts on his Facebook page telling the world that he was 'living in paradise'.

'He was making posts about how beautiful life is and how he was having a good time with his buddies,' said Assistant US Attorney Michael Scoville. 'He was definitely not living the way we wanted him to be living, given the charges he was facing,' he added.

However, during his time in Cancun, Mr Sopo also befriended a former justice department official on the networking site. This man, who had only met Mr Sopo a few times, was able to discover exactly where Mr Sopo was living. As soon as he had this information, he passed it to the Mexican authorities who arrested Sopo last month.

The twenty-six-year-old is currently in custody in Mexico City.

B Read the news report again. Find examples of the following:

1 quotes used to give someone's opinion

2 a concluding statement which gives us information about the current situation

3 an introductory statement which explains in one sentence what happened

4 more information about the background to the story

LEARN TO use time linkers

10A Look at the news report and find examples of the time linkers in the box.

as soon as   while   during   until
by the time

B Look at the words/phrases in the box above. Which time linker do we use to link an action that:

1 happened previously? *by the time*

2 continues up to that point and then stops?
until

3 happens at the same time as another action? *while*

4 happens at some point in a period of time? *during*

5 happens immediately after something else has happened? *as soon as*

C Complete the sentences with the correct time linker.

1 I came *as soon as* I heard the news.

2 They arrived *while* we were having dinner.

3 Her cat died *during* the night.

4 We waited *until* the lights had gone out.

5 *by the time* the fire engines arrived, the house was destroyed.

11A Work in pairs. Choose a headline and write six questions asking information you would like to know about the story.

> Woman finds suitcase full of money on train

> Huge earthquake destroys city

> Man shot outside his house

B Give your questions to another student.

C Look at the questions and write a short news report (100–150 words). Look at the ideas in Exercise 9B to help you.

speakout TIP

A good news report will give readers all the key information (why? what? how? when? etc.), in a clear and concise way. Does your news report contain the key information?

D Compare your stories with other students. Who has the best story?

VOCABULARY *say/tell*

1A Work in pairs and discuss. How do you know when someone is lying? Do you think their behaviour changes?

B Read the text to check your answers.

How do you know if someone is lying?

From little white lies to lies which can destroy nations, people have lied for as long as they have told the truth. Some people are very good at it. So, how do we know if someone is lying? Here are the things to look out for.

1 The guilty hand: when someone is telling the truth they usually use more body language. They move their hands and their face more. When someone lies, their hands are still.

2 The lying eye: people find it very hard to tell you a lie if they're looking at you straight in the eyes. Normally, they look away just at the moment that they tell the lie.

3 The 'Me': when people tell a story about themselves, they tend to use a lot of 'me' words, like *I*, *me*, and *my*. When they tell a lie, they don't use the 'me' words as much.

2A Match 1–6 with a)–f) to make sentences.

1 I'm terrible at telling (f)   a) 'hello', but she didn't answer.
2 My brother told me (d)   b) a white lie than to upset someone.
3 I think you should say (e)   c) what you mean.
4 Sometimes it's better to tell (b)   d) a funny story yesterday.
5 You should just say (c)   e) sorry.
6 I said (a)   f) jokes. I always forget the punch line!

B Add the phrases with *say* and *tell* from Exercise 2A to the table.

say	tell
'hello'	a story
sorry	jokes
what you mean	a white lie
	what you mean

C Work with other students. Do you agree/disagree with the statements? Why?

1 A lie can travel half way around the world while the truth is putting on its shoes.

2 A good storyteller should mix fiction with truth to make their stories interesting.

3 It's OK to tell lies sometimes.

FUNCTION telling a story

3A Look at the pictures above which tell a story. What do you think is happening in each picture?

B ▶ 2.7 Listen to a woman telling her story. Number the pictures in the correct order.

4A Look at the phrases we can use to help tell the sequence in a story. Add the sequencers from the box to the correct place in the table.

This happened when The next thing I knew
Anyway,   In the end,   Before long,
And then, all of a sudden.

beginning
In the beginning, …
This happened when

describing what happened
Well, Anyway So, And then Before long all of a sudden The next thing I knew

ending
Finally, … In the end

B Listen to the story again, and tick the phrases you hear.

➠ page 146 **LANGUAGEBANK**

5A Work in pairs. Practise telling the story using the sequencers and the pictures to help you. Start like this:
This happened when the woman had an important interview and …

B ▶ 2.8 Do you think the woman was telling a true or false story? Listen to find out.

LEARN TO keep a story going

6A Look at phrases a)–j). Which phrases complete extracts 1–6?

a) What happened then?

b) What did you do?

c) Then what?

d) Oh no!

e) Oh dear.

f) How embarrassing!

g) That's really funny.

h) Really?

i) You're joking!

j) You're kidding!

1 W: So, anyway, erm … I then got on to the tube, um … to go for my interview.

   M: Right, and ___a)___ ?

2 W: I've woken up shouting the word, 'Mum!'.

   M: No! _You're joking!_ (i)

3 W: At the top of my voice, in a packed, quiet tube.

   M: _oh no!_ (d)

4 W: … they're looking at me in a rather strange way.

   M: Right … _then what?_ (c)

5 W: My face had swollen up! … It was bright red, … and covered in blotches, spots …

   M: Oh! _You're kidding_ (J)

6 W: Yes, and the pills that my mother had given me were so out-of-date that they had caused an allergic reaction …

   M: Oh! … ____! _How embarrassing_ (f)

B ▶ 2.9 Listen again and check your answers. Notice how intonation is used to sound interested.

C Listen and repeat the phrases. Try to sound interested. Then repeat but try to sound bored. Can you hear the difference?

speakout TIP

How amazing! When someone tells a story, try to use comments and questions to show that you are interested. Remember to check your intonation. Do you sound interested?

SPEAKING

7A Prepare to tell a story. It can be a true story or a lie. Choose one of the situations below. Talk about when you:

- got stuck in a lift
- missed (or nearly missed) a flight
- slept outside
- spoke to someone famous
- got a tattoo
- appeared on television/in the newspaper
- chased/met a criminal
- were mistaken for someone else
- sung karaoke
- tried a very dangerous sport
- found something unusual
- did something embarrassing on holiday

B Think about the details of your story. Think about the questions below and make some notes or practise telling your story.

- Where were you?
- Why were you there?
- What were you doing?
- What happened?
- How did you feel?

C Work with other students. Take turns to tell your stories and listen and respond. Ask questions to decide if it is a true story or a lie.

A: I once got stuck in a lift.

B: Really?

A: Yes. I was …

D Tell the other students if it is a true story or a lie.

DVD PREVIEW

1 Work in pairs. Discuss the questions.

1 What famous fictional thieves/investigators/detectives do you know about?

2 Which are famous in your country?

3 Have you watched any programmes involving them?

4 Do you watch any crime detective dramas? Which ones? What do you like/dislike about them?

5 What are the features of good detective dramas, e.g. interesting characters?

2 Look at the pictures and read about the programme. What problems do you think Finch had when he stole the painting?

BBC Hustle

*H*ustle is a BBC drama series about a team of criminals who try to obtain and sell things in an illegal or dishonest way. In this programme we meet Finch, a burglar. He's in trouble with Customs, who believe that he has stolen a valuable piece of art. Unfortunately for Finch, when he stole the painting, things didn't go quite according to plan and now he needs the help of a friend.

DVD VIEW

3A Match the words in the two columns to make common crime collocations.

1 guard   a) thief
2 art   b) guard
3 valuable   c) weapon
4 burglar   d) officer
5 customs   e) dog
6 loaded   f) alarm
7 security   g) painting

B Watch the programme. Tick the things above which you see in the clip. Which of the above do you <u>not</u> see?

4A Work in pairs and answer the questions.

1 How does Finch get into the grounds of the mansion? climbing the wall

2 What is the security guard doing? walking around the house

3 What does Finch do when he breaks into the house? look around to find the paiting

4 What sets off the alarm? a monkey

5 How does Finch escape? climbing the wall

6 What happens at the airport?

7 Why do customs officers search Finch? Do they find anything? they think he could have the painting they do don't find

8 What do customs plan to do? follow him

B Watch the DVD again to check.

speakout a narrative

5 Work in groups. Invent details for the story using the questions below to help.

1 What exactly has Finch stolen? *Van gogh*

2 Why did he steal it? *a person offered a lot of money*

3 Is he usually a successful thief? *No, hes bee in Prison*

4 What happens in the airport in Brazil?

5 Where is the painting now? *In a locker in Brazil!*

6 What happens when Finch gets back to the UK?

7 How does Finch plan to get the painting? *for a friend*

8 Does Finch get arrested? Why/Why not? *yes, the*

6A ▶ 2.10 Listen to someone telling the story. How do they answer the questions above?

B Listen again and tick the key phrases you hear. What tense does the speaker use to tell the story? Why is this?

---

keyphrases

In this story, …

The problem is that …

In fact, …

What he doesn't realise/know is that …

However …

Later, …

Because of this, …

In the end, …

C Work in pairs. Take turns to retell the story (or your own version of the story) using the key phrases and the questions in Exercise 5 to help.

writeback a newspaper article

7A Read about a famous art theft. Who stole the painting? Why did he steal it? What happened in the end?

Famous painting stolen

On August 21st, 1911, Leonardo da Vinci's *Mona Lisa*, one of the most famous paintings in the world, was stolen from the wall of the Louvre Museum, in Paris. At first, the police thought one of the guards might have stolen the painting, but seventeen days after the theft, they arrested poet Guillaume Apollinaire. However, he was released when police could find no evidence that he had committed the crime. Two years later, the real thief, Vincenzo Peruggia, was arrested in Italy. Peruggia had worked at the museum, and had stolen the painting because he was angry about how many Italian paintings were on display in France. He had planned to return the painting to the Italian Uffizi gallery, in Florence. The public was so excited at the news of finding the *Mona Lisa* that the painting was displayed throughout Italy before it was returned to France in 1913.

B Write up the story of Finch's art theft as a newspaper article, using the article above and the key phrases to help.

TYPES OF STORY

1A Add the missing letters to complete the types of story.

1 One of my favourite **a**ct**io**n films of all time is *The Terminator*.

2 Jamie Foxx stars in *Ray*, a great b**io**p**i_**c of Ray Charles.

3 *Pretty Woman*, starring Julia Roberts and Richard Gere, is my favourite r**o**m**a**nt**i**c c**o**m**e**d**y**.

4 I'm not a great fan of p**e**r**i**od dr**ama**s, but I thought this production of *Jane Eyre* was brilliant.

5 I loved the psych**o**l**o**g**i**c**a**l thr**i**ll**e**r, *Silence of the Lambs*, but I found it very scary.

6 I still enjoy Agatha Christie's *Murder on the Orient Express*. It's one of the best ever d**e**t**e**ct**i**v**e** films.

7 I can't watch s**ci**enc**e** f**i**ct**io**n films, like *Star Wars* and *Alien*. I can't stand them.

8 I think d**o**c**u**dr**a**m**a**s, films like *Nixon*, are a great way to learn about what really happened during important events.

B Work in pairs. Choose five of the genres and make a 'best ever' list of the films in these genres.

PRESENT PERFECT/PAST SIMPLE

2A Look at the phrases below. Have you done any of these things? Write sentences using *I've ...*, *I haven't ...* and *I have never ...*.

• play in a band/write a song
• ride a horse • visit another country
• run a marathon
• walk in the mountains/go skiing
• organise a big family party
• see a famous band
• swim with dolphins/go scuba diving
• meet someone famous
• go to university/change your job
• start a business
• travel on your own
• write a diary/blog

B Choose one thing you have/ haven't done and tell your partner more about it.

I've played in a band. When I was at university I played in a band called 'The Hooligans'.

THE NEWS

3A Underline the correct option to complete the headlines.

1 Postal *collapse/strike* causes huge delays

2 Police attacked during student *demonstration/crash*

3 *Fugitives/Hostages* released after negotiation with rebel leader

4 Hundreds homeless after *earthquake/collapse* hits

5 *Fugitive/Flood* found hiding in forest

6 Train *strike/crash* kills sixty people

7 House *attacked/crashed* with petrol bomb

8 Young criminal *destroyed/shot* by police

B Work in pairs. Take turns to say a word and respond with a headline.
A: crash
B: Sleeping pilot caused plane to crash.

NARRATIVE TENSES

4A Put the verbs in the correct tense to complete the story.

Sasha [1] **woke** (wake) up late because she [2] **had forgotten** (forget) to set her alarm clock. She [3] **was having** (have) breakfast when the telephone [4] **rang** (ring). It was her boss. He wanted to know why she [5] **hadn't finished** (not finish) the report that he [6] **had ask** (ask) her to do. She quickly [7] **left** (leave) the house to go to work. She [8] **was standing** (stand) on the train when she noticed that lots of people [9] **were looking** (look) at her feet. Then, she [10] **realised** (realise) that she [11] **had forgotten** (forget) to put her shoes on. She [12] **was wearing** (wear) her slippers.

B Can you remember a day when you woke up late? Why? What happened? Tell your partner.

TELLING A STORY

5A Add a word to each speaker's part to correct the conversations.

happened
1 A: This when I was living in Hong Kong.

   B: Oh really? *what* happened?

2 A: I was having a shower when all a sudden I saw a huge spider.

   B: Oh no. What *do* you do?

3 A: Anyway, before I knew ~~it~~ someone called the police.

   B: Really? What next?

4 A: The next I knew, the man was running *thing* towards me and shouting. *happened*

   B: I don't believe it!

5 A: *So* anyway I was going up the ski-lift and I fell off.

   B: *how* embarrassing!

6 A: So, in *the* end, I had to pay all the money back.

   B: *oh* dear.

B Work in pairs. Choose three of the conversations above and expand the stories.

C Work in groups. Take turns to role-play your conversations.

UNIT 3

SPEAKING
> Discuss attitudes now/ earlier in life
> Talk about predictions
> Explain misunderstandings
> Discuss the best ways to communicate

LISTENING
> Listen to people discussing the future of communication
> Listen to a series of misunderstandings
> Watch a BBC documentary about the internet's impact

READING
> Read an article about teenage communication
> Read a story about a misunderstanding

WRITING
> Write a series of messages
> Write a memo

BBC CONTENT
▯ Video podcast: Can new technology help communication?
◉ DVD: The Virtual Revolution

UNIT **3**

contact

SPEAKING

1 Work in groups and discuss.

1 What problems do teenagers and parents of teenagers have? Why?

2 What is the best thing a parent can do for a teenager?

READING

2A Read the article. Does it mention anything you discussed in Exercise 1? What is the main problem it mentions?

B Complete the summary of the article. Use one or two words for each gap.

> The writer is worried about the way she communicates with her ¹_____. She is always asking them questions about their ²_____, but most of the time they ³_____. She thinks that mobile phones and text messages mean that arrangements are always ⁴_____. In the end, she decides to ⁵_____ her own way of making plans. Next time she arranges to meet someone, she's going to be ⁶_____.

C Are the statements 1–5 true (T) or false (F)?

1 Simon usually arrives late.

2 The mother's teenage children always answer her questions.

3 The mother worries about her children when she doesn't know where they are.

4 The teenagers tend to make their plans early.

5 In the end the mother decides to change her behaviour.

D Find words or phrases in the text that match meanings 1–6.

1 changing an opinion or decision (paragraph 1)

2 manage a situation (paragraph 1)

3 too interested in other people's business (paragraph 5)

4 a fear that terrible things might happen (paragraph 5)

5 plans that you make just before they happen (paragraph 7)

6 if you can't change how people behave, then change your behaviour to be like them (paragraph 9)

3 Discuss the questions.

1 Do you think it is important for parents to know about their teenagers' plans?

2 Do you agree that mobile phones have changed the way that people make plans? How?

Life on planet teen

1 My friend Simon is always changing his mind about things. He's never quite sure where he's going to be or whether he'll be busy, and he never arrives when he says he will. This is sad, but I can cope with it. He doesn't live in my house.

2 But I don't like the same situation when it's happening under my own roof. Every day I ask my teenagers questions like an eager reporter. 'Where are you going? When are you coming back? How are you getting home?' And what do I get? If I'm lucky, a small bit of information.

3 'I think it's football after school,' says my fourteen-year-old. 'Unless that was last week.'

4 'I'm going out on Saturday,' says my sixteen-year-old. But most of my questions, however, go unanswered.

5 I don't want to be nosy. I really don't. But I would so love to have a rough idea of where members of the family are going to be. The problem is that I have an over-active imagination. The logic goes: you haven't got football, you didn't say you'd be late, therefore you must be under the wheels of a bus. But while I'm watching the clock in an attempt to stop my panic, my teenagers are changing their arrangements again …

GRAMMAR the future (plans)

4A Read the conversations about plans and complete the rules with the phrases in the box.

the present continuous   *going to* + infinitive   *will* + infinitive   *might* + infinitive

1 A: Are you going to Joel's party?

   B: I <u>might</u> stay at home. I'm very tired.

2 A: Have you spoken to your teacher yet?

   B: No, I'<u>m going to speak</u> to her later.

3 A: What time <u>are you meeting</u> Adam?

   B: At six o'clock.

4 A: Do you want to come with us?

   B: No, thanks. I'<u>ll see</u> you at the stadium.

Rules:

1 Use _____ to talk about plans or arrangements which have already been made.

2 Use _____ to talk about a plan or intention. You have decided that you want to do this, but you may not have made the arrangements.

3 Use _____ when you are not sure what the plan is.

4 Use _____ to talk about the future when you have no specific plan, or you make the decision at the time of speaking.

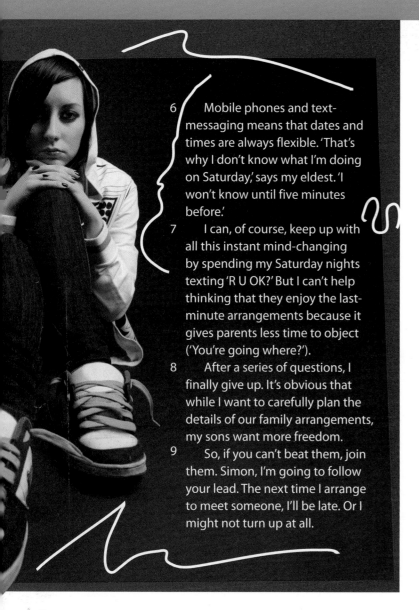

6   Mobile phones and text-messaging means that dates and times are always flexible. 'That's why I don't know what I'm doing on Saturday,' says my eldest. 'I won't know until five minutes before.'

7   I can, of course, keep up with all this instant mind-changing by spending my Saturday nights texting 'R U OK?' But I can't help thinking that they enjoy the last-minute arrangements because it gives parents less time to object ('You're going where?').

8   After a series of questions, I finally give up. It's obvious that while I want to carefully plan the details of our family arrangements, my sons want more freedom.

9   So, if you can't beat them, join them. Simon, I'm going to follow your lead. The next time I arrange to meet someone, I'll be late. Or I might not turn up at all.

B Look at the article above again. Find examples of the structures described below.

1 present continuous for talking about future arrangements
2 *going to* + infinitive for future plans
3 *will* + infinitive for a decision made at the time of speaking
4 *might* + infinitive for a plan which is undecided

▶ page 148 **LANGUAGEBANK**

5A ▶ 3.1 Listen and complete the sentences.
1 What _____ at the weekend?
2 We _____ my brother and his family.
3 Where _____ for them?
4 They _____ a party on Friday.
5 _____ with us tomorrow?
6 I'll ask Marion when she _____.

B Listen again. Notice how they pronounce *going to* in fast speech. Does *going to* have the same pronunciation in sentences and questions? Do we always pronounce *going to* like this? When is it different?

C Listen again and practise saying the sentences fast.
What are you going to do at the weekend?

PRACTICE

6 Underline the correct alternatives to complete the conversation.

Pete: Hey Dax. What ¹*are you two doing/will you two do* on Saturday night?

Dax: I don't know. We ²*might/will* go to the Death City Dread concert. What about you?

Pete: ³*I'll have/I'm going to have* a bit of a party. My parents ⁴*are going/will go* away for the weekend, so I've asked a few people to come over to my place. Kris ⁵*will bring/is bringing* his DJ equipment round, so ⁶*we're having/we'll have* music. And everyone ⁷*is going to bring/might bring* some food and drink. Euan ⁸*will come/is coming* with a few friends. Do you think you can make it?

Dax: It sounds great. ⁹*I'm going to text/I'll text* Leyla to ask her what she thinks. Then ¹⁰*I'm calling/I'll call* you back to let you know. Is that OK?

Pete: That's fine. ¹¹*I'll speak/I'm going to speak* to you later. Bye.

7A Write sentences for situations 1–6 below. Think about whether you have made arrangements already, then decide which tenses to use.

1 something you plan to do at the weekend
Some friends are coming to stay. (I've already arranged this)
I might go out for a pizza on Friday night. (I don't know yet.)

2 something you are going to do after the class
3 something you might buy in the near future
4 something that someone in your family is planning to do
5 a plan or ambition you have, related to your work/studies
6 something that you plan to do for your next holiday

B Work in pairs. Compare your ideas. Ask and answer questions to find out more information.
My sister's moving to Poland.
Really? That sounds exciting. Which city?

VOCABULARY communication

8A Match the words in the box with sentences 1–8.

moan (handwritten)

| ~~gossip~~ compliment moan boast |
| argue ~~warn~~ ~~chat~~ ~~apologise~~ |

1 Have you heard about Vicki? She's got a new boyfriend! ___gossip___

2 I just wanted to say I'm really sorry I missed the match. _apologise_

3 So, how was your day? Did it go well? ___chat___

4 I was the best rugby player in my school, you know. _boast_

5 No, that's not true. I didn't say that you could borrow my mp3 player! _argue_

6 Listen, it's very important that you don't get into cars with people who you don't know. _warn_

7 You look lovely. That top looks really nice on you. _compliment_

8 And when I got home, the house was in a complete mess. They're so lazy. They never help. _moan_

B Decide who is talking in sentences 1–8, parents (P) or teenagers (T).

C ▶ 3.2 Listen and notice the intonation. Then listen and repeat.

➡ page 166 **VOCABULARYBANK**

SPEAKING

9A Think about when you were a teenager. Make a note of things you:

• loved/hated/moaned about
• argued about with your parents/friends
• were warned about by parents/teachers

B Think about your life now. Make a note about people you:

• enjoy chatting to/gossiping with
• tend to argue with
• moan about
• have apologised to

C Work in pairs. Compare your experiences. How have your ideas changed since you were a teenager?

A: I really enjoy gossiping with my girl friends about who we like and who we don't.

B: Do you? Me too! It was the same when we were teenagers!

WRITING messages

10 Work in pairs. Look at messages 1–4 and answer the questions.

1 When do you usually write messages to people?

2 What do you think the relationship is between the writer and the person they are writing to in these messages?

3 Are the messages formal or informal?

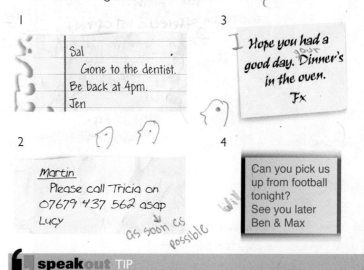

1
Sal
Gone to the dentist.
Be back at 4pm.
Jen

3
I Hope you had a good day. *your* Dinner's in the oven.
Jx

2
Martin
Please call Tricia on 07679 437 562 asap
Lucy
as soon as possible (handwritten)

4
Can you pick us up from football tonight?
See you later
Ben & Max

speakout TIP

Leave it out! When we write notes and messages we don't always write complete sentences. We often miss out small grammatical words to make the message shorter.

LEARN TO use note form

11A Look at the messages 1–4 above. The words in the box have been left out. Which message do they belong to?

| I We'll Your I've Can you I'll |

B Rewrite messages 1–4 below using fewer words.

1
~~Are~~ you feeling hungry? ~~Do you~~ want to meet me ~~for lunch~~ at Pavarotti's 1pm?
R x

3
Pete ~~called to say that~~ he won't be able to come to dinner. Do you think you could call him back on 01954 627 823? Thanks.
Jayne

2
message
We're going to see Elton John in concert. Would you like ~~me to book~~ you a ticket?
Tonya

4
~~I'm really sorry but~~ ~~I~~ can't come to the cinema ~~tonight~~ ~~because I've~~ got too much work ~~to do. I~~ hope you enjoy the film.
Bess

12 Write short messages for the situations below.

1 You're going away for the weekend and would like your flatmate to water the plants.

2 You want to invite a classmate to the cinema.

3 You need to apologise to a work colleague for missing a meeting.

▶ **GRAMMAR** | the future (predictions)   ▶ **VOCABULARY** | future time markers   ▶ **HOW TO** | make predictions

LISTENING

1 Look at the photos and answer the questions.

1 What has replaced the objects in the pictures?

2 In your opinion, are the replacements better than the original things?

2A Work in pairs and discuss.   *translator*

a) In the future how will we communicate with people in other countries?

b) In the future will we still use pen and paper to write?

c) In the future will we watch TV the same way we do now?

B ▶ **3.3 Listen to some people discussing the questions above. Do they mention any of your ideas?**

C Find and correct three factual mistakes in the notes. Listen again to check.

> System for translating foreign languages
> Talk to foreigner on the phone & his/her words = translated into your ear
> Online translation services already exist BUT often make mistakes, e.g. English to Chinese *Japanesse*

> TV programme says handwriting will disappear in 1~~00~~ years
> Will use thumbprints/digital signatures, e.g. scans, instead
> Man says people will still carry pens
> Woman says 'kids' (10–12 yrs old) may stop writing

> They think there'll still be a large TV in the living room
> BUT TV programmes will be 'on demand' – watch what you want
> Man thinks it'll change 'in the long term' – a long time in the future *short*
> Woman agrees

3 Look at the words and phrases in the box. What do you think they mean? Use audio script 3.3 on page 186 to help you.

person translate something   change the system

| an intermediary   (that) will stop barriers   thumbprints |
| retina scans   the most straightforward way (to do something) |
| on demand   a large screen   method of delivery |

VOCABULARY | future time markers

4A Read sentences 1–9 and underline the time markers.   EXAM

1 <u>In the near future</u>, there will be a system for translating foreign languages.

2 They don't think that handwriting will exist <u>in the next ten years</u>.

3 This new system for watching TV could happen <u>in a month or two</u>.

4 Certainly <u>in the long term</u> this will be the future.

5 I think these changes will happen <u>in the short term</u>.

6 <u>In ten years' time</u> children won't be able to write with pen and paper.

7 There will still be TV sets <u>a long time from now</u>.

8 I don't think there will be any big changes <u>next year</u>.

9 Phones that can translate languages will be with us <u>shortly</u>.

B Look at the time markers again. Put them under the correct heading below.

1 **An exact time in the future**

in ten years time – next year

2 **Not an exact time in the future – soon**

in the near future   in a month or two   shortly
in the next ten years   in the short term

3 **Not an exact time in the future – not very soon**

in the long term, a long time from now

C Work in pairs. Ask and answer questions 1–3, using both parts of the question.

1 Will you still live in the same place: a) in the near future? b) in ten years' time?

2 Will you still attend classes: a) six months from now? b) next year?

3 What projects will you work on: a) in the short term? b) in the long term?

GRAMMAR the future (predictions)

5A Read the preview of a programme. What is the programme about?

Visions of the future

In this new BBC three-part series, physicist and futurist Dr Michio Kaku explores the science of today, tomorrow, and beyond. He argues that we are at a turning point in history. In this century, we will move from being passive observers of nature to its active designers. This will give us amazing new possibilities but also great responsibilities.

B Read some of the predictions from the BBC programme. Are they certain (C) or possible (P)?

you are sure

1 Artificial intelligence <u>will</u> revolutionise homes, workplaces and lifestyles. C

2 Robots with human-level intelligence <u>may</u> finally become a reality. P *maybe*

3 The human body <u>could</u> be repaired as easily as a car. *maybe* P

4 We <u>are going to</u> make the … transition from the 'Age of Discovery' to the 'Age of Mastery'. C

5 We <u>are likely to</u> live longer because of developments in genetics and biotechnology. *probably* P

C Look at the underlined words above. Complete the rules with *will*, *could*, *to* or *be*.

Rule:

1 We use ___will___ + infinitive to make predictions about the future. *verb in base form*

2 We use __be__ *going to* + infinitive to make predictions when there is present evidence. *a prediction base on an evidence*

3 We use *may* or __could__ + infinitive to say something is possible but not certain.

4 We use *likely* + infinitive with __to__ to say something will probably happen.

⟹ page 148 **LANGUAGEBANK**

PRACTICE

Diana te quiere :3

6A Circle the correct alternative, a), b) or c), to complete the programme review.

Dr Michio Kaku says that in the near future we ¹__a__ new worlds that look like our own world. To prove it, he flies around in Second Life and tells us that virtual reality is ²__c__ more like real reality.

Kaku then jumps into a remote controlled car, and tells us the car is so intelligent that the words 'traffic jam' and 'traffic accident' ³__c__ from the language.

It isn't just cars that will be intelligent. In a few years' time microchips will be so cheap they ⁴__b__ into every product we buy – our walls, our furniture, even our clothes. And they ⁵__c__ to be so small we ⁶__c__ they exist. The internet, he tells us, will also be everywhere. Kaku says our sunglasses ⁷__a__ our future home entertainment centre.

Kaku then does a virtual dance using 3-D technology (his dance partner is hundreds of miles away) and explains that one day in the near future, 3-D technology ⁸__a__ the telephone and ⁹__c__ air travel.

Then he looks at the popularity of robots. He concludes that, in the long term, some of our closest friends ¹⁰__b__ people.

1 (a) will design (b) will be design (c) will to design
2 (a) become (b) going become (c) going to become
3 (a) going to disappear (b) are going to disappearing (c) are going to disappear
4 (a) are could be built (b) could be built (c) could built
5 (a) likely (b) likely are (c) are likely
6 (a) won't to know (b) not will know (c) won't know
7 (a) may become (b) may of become (c) may to become
8 (a) could replace (b) is could replace (c) could be replace
9 (a) reduce might (b) might to reduce (c) might reduce
10 (a) not might be (b) might not be (c) might be not

B Discuss. Which predictions, if they come true, will be good/bad for the world? Why?

SPEAKING

7A Look at the picture of the future above. Is it realistic? Why?

B Think about the topics in the box. How do you think they will change in the future? Make some notes.

> communication   technology   work habits   cities
> the environment   food

C Work in pairs and discuss your ideas.

Communication: I think we will probably have video conference calls on our mobile phones. There probably won't be …

VOCABULARY *PLUS* idioms

Idiom /ˈɪdiəm/ *[C]*   a group of words that have a different meaning from the usual meaning of the separate words. For example, 'under the weather' is an idiom meaning 'ill'.

8A Read the definition of an idiom and underline the idioms in sentences 1–5.

1 In the future, mobile phones won't only be used for small talk or for taking photos.

2 For people who work against the clock, new ways to communicate will be important.

3 We'll use pen and paper for writing things that are on our mind and for personal notes.

4 Home-made programmes won't be everyone's cup of tea, but that's the future of TV.

5 Music is an issue that's close to my heart because my husband is a musician.

B Look at the underlined idioms and decide if these statements about idioms are true (T) or false (F)?

1 Idioms are usually formal.

2 You cannot usually change the order of words in an idiom.

3 You can sometimes change the verb tense and the subject of an idiom.

4 You can usually guess the meaning from one word in the idiom.

C Work in pairs and compare your answers. Then turn to page 176 to check your answers.

Then turn to page 176 to check your answers.

When you learn new idioms write them in a special place in your vocabulary notebook. To remember idioms better, record them in context and add your own examples. Do this for the idioms in Exercise 8A. Then try them out. Make sure it's the right situation and you remember to use the exact words.

9 Work in pairs. Look at the idioms organised by topic. What do the underlined idioms mean?

> PROBLEMS
> 1 We forgot to pay our taxes. Now we're in hot water.
> 2 I said the wrong thing again. I always put my foot in it.
> TIME
> 3 We're working against the clock. We have two hours to finish the project.
> 4 I'm sure we can win this match but we're running out of time.

10 Look at the idioms organised by key words. Match idioms 1–6 with meanings a)–f).

> BODY PARTS
> 1 Keep an eye on him. b
> 2 Can you give me a hand? c
> FOOD AND DRINK
> 3 It's not my cup of tea. a
> 4 It was a piece of cake. f
> ANIMALS
> 5 You're a dark horse! e
> 6 I want to get out of the rat race. d

a) I don't like it

b) watch

c) help me

d) the competitive world of work

e) you have a lot of secrets

f) easy

11A Find and correct the mistakes. There is a mistake in each sentence.

1 When was the last time you gave someone the hand?

2 Which student do you think is a horse dark?

3 When's the last time you put your feet in it?

4 Which issues are close by your heart?

5 Do you often have to work against the clocks?

6 When were you last in warm water?

B Write an answer to each question. Then compare your answers with other students.

➠ page 166 **VOCABULARYBANK**

SPEAKING

1A Work in pairs. Look at the cartoon and read the story. What do you think happened next?

One year a US TV show called *Late Night with David Letterman* was nominated for an award. To celebrate, the eighty people involved in the show went to a restaurant in Malibu, where they sat at twelve different tables and ate outside. That night someone told the show's producer that Johnny Carson, a famous American talk show host, was in the restaurant.

The producer went over to Carson's table and said, 'It would be so nice if you could say hello to David and meet some of the people. It would mean a lot to them.' So at the end of his dinner, Carson came over and said hello. He sat at the table, talked for a while and then left.
At the end of the evening the producer went to pay the bill.

B Read the end of the story on page 176.

C Work in pairs. Retell the story using the words in the box.

TV show	nominated for an award	celebrate	restaurant
talk show host	say hello	pay the bill	generous	called
didn't know	at the table	ten thousand dollars	

VOCABULARY misunderstandings

2A Complete sentences 1–8 with phrases a)–h).

1 Make sure you go to the King's Street in the centre of town because … *accidentil*
2 We mistakenly left home at 5.30 because d
3 I was expecting to see Pete, my old school friend, but e.
4 I didn't do the homework because h.
5 We thought her birthday was 16th July but c.
6 I ended up at the wrong house because b
7 When I called Mary Lou, she thought I was a stranger because g.
8 I answered the phone but a

a) it was a **wrong number**.
b) I'd got the **wrong address**.
c) we **got the date wrong**.
d) **we thought** it started at six.
e) it was a **different** Peter Smith.
f) there are two streets **with the same name**.
g) she **didn't recognise** my voice.
h) I **didn't realise** it was for today.

B Which expressions in bold do you know? Which have you used?

FUNCTION dealing with misunderstandings

3A ▶ 3.4 Listen to four telephone conversations involving misunderstandings. What type of misunderstandings are they?

B Listen again and answer the questions.

Conversation 1
1 Who did the woman want to speak to? Tom
2 Who did she speak to? Willy's burger … KD

Conversation 2
3 How did David make his hotel reservation? in call
4 What hotel does he want to stay in? sheldon hotel

Conversation 3
5 What time does the show finish? 7:00
6 What time did the show start? 5:00

Conversation 4
7 What does the woman want to rent? car
8 What is the date? 4th July

C Complete expressions 1–7 with the words in the box.

tell	~~that~~	me (x2)	~~saying~~	~~mean~~	~~name~~	~~again~~

1 I didn't catch any of that.
2 You've lost me.
3 Could you repeat the last name?
4 Can you say that again?
5 What exactly do you mean?
6 I don't get what you're saying.
7 Do you mean to tell me..?

D ▶ 3.5 Listen and check. Then listen again and copy the intonation.

▶ page 148 **LANGUAGEBANK**

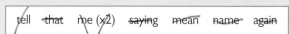

4A There is one word missing in each response. Complete the responses with the missing word.

1 A: Oh no! I can't find the key.

    mean

  B: Do you to say we're going to be locked out all night?

2 A: And after Jimmy left Minnie, he married Millie, who used to be married to Billy.

  B: You've me. Who are all these people?
    lost

3 A: There was a little accident with the spaghetti bolognese and your sofa.

    do

  B: What exactly you mean?

4 A: The boss wants to see you. It's about the money that's missing from the accounts.

  B: I don't what you're saying.
    I get

5 A: Um, er, I think my new phone number is, um, 654 0987 6743.

  B: I catch any of that. What's the number?
    didn't

6 A: My home address is 39 Kings Street, Manchester, Lancashire, M8 2TO.

    say

  B: Can you that again? I didn't hear.

7 A: We're leaving Los Angeles at 11.00p.m., OK? Then we arrive in Sydney at 5.50a.m.

  B: Could you the last part? I didn't hear you.
    repeat

B Work in pairs. What does speaker A say next? Continue the conversations with your own words.

LEARN TO reformulate

5A Read the extracts from the audio 3.4. Underline five examples of how the speaker reformulates what he/she heard.

1 A: We've got no reservations in the name of Cullinan, and we're fully booked tonight.

  B: So you're saying I can't stay here. This is the Sheldon Hotel, yes?

2 C: Didn't you say it starts at 7.00?

  D: No, it starts at 5.00 and finishes at 7.00!

  C: So what you mean is I've missed the whole show.

3 E: Yes, but today's a holiday and all the cars have been booked already.

  F: Do you mean to tell me that there's nothing at all? No cars available?

  E: There's nothing till tomorrow, I'm afraid.

  F: But I definitely booked a car for today, the third of July.

  E: It's the fourth of July today. In other words, your booking was for yesterday.

B ▶ 3.6 Listen to the phrases. Notice how the words are linked together in fast speech.

So‿you're‿saying …

C Listen again and repeat the phrases.

SPEAKING

6A Work in pairs and role-play the situation.

Student A   Student B

> You are a guest at a hotel. Twenty minutes ago you called reception, asking for some soap to be sent to your room. Room service brought you some tomato soup. You want them to take the soup back and bring some soap. Call reception to make your complaint.

> You are a receptionist at a hotel. A guest calls to make a complaint. Start the conversation by saying 'Reception. How can I help you?'

> *Hello. Yes, I'm afraid I have a problem … * Explain the problem.

> Apologise for the misunderstanding and say you will send someone with soap.

> Check details and thank the receptionist for their help.

> Confirm details, apologise again and end the call.

B Change roles and turn to page 178.

C Work in pairs and take turns. Student A: ring reception and make a complaint. Student B: apologise and offer a solution. Use the flow charts to help and role-play the situations.

DVD PREVIEW

1 Discuss. How has the internet changed the world?

2A Did you mention any of the following?

1 It **creates wealth**. (make money)
2 It allows us to **challenge authority**. (question people in power)
3 It allows authorities to **spy** and **censor**.
4 It has created a generation of **web addicts**.
5 It **opens up new realms of knowledge**.
6 It has allowed the **pioneers** and **key players** in technology to become powerful.
7 It has made **e-shopping** possible.

B Work in pairs. Check you understand the meaning of the words/expressions in bold.

3 Read the introduction to the programme. What is it about? Who does the presenter speak to?

BBC The Virtual Revolution

This BBC documentary looks at the revolutionary impact of the internet. Dr Aleks Krotoski tells the story of the internet from its early days through to its most recent successes and innovations. She looks at the good and bad sides of the internet, revealing statistics that show how much we use it and how it has changed the world. The programme also includes comments from some of the best-known internet pioneers.

▶ DVD VIEW

4 Watch the DVD. Put the statistics in the order they are mentioned.

a) 18 million people read blogs. 5
b) People in the UK spend a billion pounds a week on the net. 3
c) A quarter of the planet now uses the web. 1
d) In the UK 35 million people log on to the internet every day. 2
e) 5 million people in the UK use a dating website every month. 4

5A Match the people below to extracts a)–g).

1 Aleks Krotoski, the presenter (x 2) G · g
2 Al Gore d
3 Mark Zuckerberg e
4 Stephen Fry f
5 Bill Gates b
6 Steve Wozniak c

a) In the ten years that I've been studying the web and writing about it as a journalist I've seen it take our world and shake it apart.
b) Well, the web is how mankind communicates nowadays.
c) It's like the internet has become a brain. It's the smartest brain in the world.
d) It is an empowering tool that has more potential than any other that human civilisation has ever developed.
e) The world is just going to keep on getting more and more open and there's going to be more information available about everything.
f) This is astounding technology and we should just take a moment to celebrate the power and the reach that it gives us.
g) The web is a revolution.

B Watch the DVD again to check.

C Discuss in groups.

1 Do you think there are any negative sides of the internet or is it all positive?
2 What do you like best about the internet: (a) it helps us to communicate, (b) it opens up new realms of knowledge, (c) it creates wealth or (d) other?
3 'Well, the web is how mankind communicates nowadays.' (Bill Gates). Do you agree?

speakout communication preferences

6A ▶ 3.7 Listen to a woman talking about how she prefers to communicate (via phone calls, emails, letters, text messages or face-to-face). What does she say about the first four topics below?

- giving good news *face to face – email – phonecall*
- giving bad news *face to face – email*
- arranging social activities *text friends (phone) / phone call*
- sending a 'thank you' message *letter, card*
- catching up with friends
- making a formal complaint
- asking for information, e.g. to get tickets
- giving opinions on issues

B Listen again and tick the key phrases you hear.

keyphrases

It depends (on …)
It's much better to …
I prefer to …
On the other hand,
In those circumstances I'd rather ..
The best way to do this is to send …
It's more convenient.
People really appreciate .
I like it when …

C How do you prefer to communicate? What does it depend on? Make some notes to prepare for the discussion.

D Work in groups and discuss your opinions. Which ways of communicating are the most popular in your class?

writeback a memo

7A Your company has decided to have email-free Fridays. Read the notes below. What are the reasons for doing this?

Rules: no internal emails — last Friday of every month
Short memos allowed
Emails OK for external clients
Reasons: Encourage face-to-face communication
Encourage phone conversations
Reduce time spent on emails
Change routine
Additional info: trial email-free Fridays for 6 months. Then review: questionnaire to all staff. Final decision made next year.

B Your boss has asked you to write a memo explaining the idea to the staff. Read the opening lines and complete the memo using the key phrases to help.

Subject: memo

Dear staff,
Starting next month, we have a new initiative.

COMMUNICATION

1 Work in pairs. Take turns to think of three different situations for each verb in the box.

> moan   argue   chat   gossip
> warn   apologise   boast
> compliment

A: OK. Moan. You moan when it's raining and you have to go on your bike.

B: And you moan when you have too much work to do.

A: Yes, and when the prices of things go up, so everything costs more.

THE FUTURE (PLANS)

2A Complete the paragraphs with phrases from the box.

> 'm going to have   having
> 'm organising   might
> 'm finishing   are going   I'll be
> are coming   will   going to

1 ¹m finishing, work at the end of the month. I've been a teacher here for nearly twenty years, so ² I'll be sad when I leave the school for the last time. But in the future, I ³ m going to have more time to do some of the things I enjoy. My wife and I ⁴ are going travelling. We ⁵ might visit Australia, which I've always wanted to do.

I'm ⁶ going to be forty next month, so I'm ⁷ having a big party. Lots of people ⁸ are coming that I don't see very often, so I'm really looking forward to it. I ⁹ m organising a band, and lots of delicious food and drink, so everyone ¹⁰ will have a good time.

B Write a short paragraph describing a plan you have for the future. Then compare your ideas with a partner.

I'm going to have a meeting with mi friends of my school, We're organasing a marathon of films.

FUTURE TIME MARKERS

3A Match 1–6 with a)–f) to make sentences.

1 I might live in *a foreign country* in the long   d
2 I hope to *be retired* in twenty years'   a
3 I will finish *this course* in a month   f
4 I hope to *write my autobiography* a long time   e
5 I want to buy *a new car* in the near   c
6 I'm going to *go travelling* next   b

a) time.
b) year.
c) future.
d) term.
e) from now.
f) or two.

B Choose four of the sentences above. Change the words in italics so they are true for you.

THE FUTURE (PREDICTIONS)

4A Find and correct the mistakes. Seven of the predictions contain grammatical mistakes.

1 Man not will fly for fifty years. (1901)
2 There isn't going be any German reunification this century. (1984)
3 Democracy will to be dead by 1950. (1936)
4 By 1980 all power (electric, atomic, solar) is likely be almost free. (1956)
5 The Japanese car industry isn't likely to be successful in the US market. (1968)
6 Man will be never reach the Moon. (1957)
7 Television won't very matter in your lifetime or mine. (1936)
8 The internet may to become useful for business but never for the general public. (1989)

B Change the verbs so they mean the opposite and become intelligent predictions. You may need to change some other words.

Man will fly within fifty years.

There is going to be German reunification this century.

DEALING WITH MISUNDERSTANDINGS

5A Put the words in the correct order to make responses in dialogues 1–3.

1 **A:** I've heard that a lot of our employees like you.
B: get / I / saying / you're / what / don't
A: And I'm looking for someone to take over the business when I retire.
B: you / do / what / mean / exactly?

2 **A:** The flight should land at 4.00, but it's going to land at 4.15 or 4.20 because of the delay.
B: didn't / that / I / of / any / catch
A: Instead of landing at 4.00 we're going to land at 4.15 or 4.20 because of the late take off.
B: you / that / can / again / say?

3 **A:** David Johnson and Johnny Thomson are going to meet Tommy Davies tonight.
B: me / lost / you've
A: Johnson, Thomson and Davies are the company directors. They're meeting to discuss the company's future.
B: say / do / mean / to / you / they're meeting without me?

B Work in pairs and practise the conversations. Then change roles and repeat.

BBC VIDEO PODCAST

Watch people talking about how modern technology has affected our everyday communication on ActiveBook or on the website.

Authentic BBC interviews

www.pearsonELT.com/speakout

UNIT 4

SPEAKING
> ❯ Discuss the qualities needed for different jobs
> ❯ Talk about past habits
> ❯ Participate in a meeting
> ❯ Describe a day in your life

LISTENING
> ❯ Listen to people describing dream jobs gone wrong
> ❯ Listen to people making decisions in a meeting
> ❯ Watch a BBC comedy about a man's first day in a new job

READING
> ❯ Read an article about millionaires
> ❯ Read a covering letter
> ❯ Read job advertisements

WRITING
> ❯ Write a covering letter
> ❯ Write about daily routines

BBC CONTENT
> Video podcast: Is your job a 'dream job'?
> DVD: Gavin and Stacey

UNIT 4

jobs

> ▶ Millionaires   P44

> ▶ Dream job   P47

> ▶ That's a good idea   P50

> ▶ Gavin and Stacey   P52

VOCABULARY personal qualities

1A Read about the qualities people need to do their jobs. Which jobs do you think they are talking about?

> Winning is the most important thing for me. I've always been **competitive**, so I love my job. I think I'm **a good leader**. It's important that all the players know what they're doing and it's my job to tell them. The decisions I make are important for the whole team, so I can't be **indecisive**.

coach

> I have classes of 80 to 100 children so I have to be **hard-working**. I do my best, because education is so important for the children. You need to be **a good communicator** in my job, so that you can get the children interested in what they have to learn. Often, we don't have very many resources, so we also need to be creative and be able to **think outside the box**.

teacher

> I'm **a risk taker**, so starting my own business wasn't difficult for me. I've always been very **motivated** and **ambitious**. I start work at 4.30a.m. every day. I don't enjoy sleep. You can't afford to be lazy if you want to make money.

Bussines man/woman

♡ :3

B Match the words and phrases in bold above with the definitions 1–9.

1 work with a lot of effort ___*hard working*___
2 have problems making a decision ___*indeciseve*___
3 think differently or in a new way ___*think outside the box*___
4 want to be more successful than others ___*compettive*___
5 want to be successful or powerful ___*ambitious*___
6 want to achieve something ___*motivated*___
7 person who does things which are dangerous ___*a risk taker*___
8 person who has the qualities to manage a group of people ___*a good lider*___ *RM SUITO*
9 person who can express ideas or feelings clearly to others ___*good comunicator*___

C Which qualities do you think you have? Work in pairs and compare your answers.

▶ page 167 **VOCABULARYBANK**

Camila + Charo ♡

READING

2A Read statements 1–6 about millionaires. Do you think they are true (T) or false (F)?

1 Most millionaires are born rich. *F*
2 Millionaires think that money is more important than love or marriage. *T*
3 They work more than sixty hours a week. *T*
4 They don't like to work when they're on holiday. *F* ✓
5 They do well at school and usually go to university. *F*
6 They like spending money on designer goods. *F*

B Read the article and check your answers.

Have you got what it takes?

1 So you want to be a millionaire, but have you got what it takes? To find out what millionaires are really like and what motivates them, the BBC programme *Mind of a Millionaire* did a survey. Psychologists looked at self-made millionaires to try and understand what qualities are needed to make a million. So, what is really important to a millionaire?

> **You don't have to be born rich to be a millionaire.**

2 The answer, not surprisingly, is money, money and more money. Money is more important than love or marriage. And if you give a millionaire money, they won't spend it, they'll invest it to make more money. But you don't have to be born rich to be a millionaire. Most millionaires come from relatively poor backgrounds. And you don't have to work hard at school either. A lot of successful entrepreneurs were lazy at school and didn't get good results. However, you must have a clear idea of what you want to do (get rich) and you really ought to start early. A lot of millionaires left school early, to start their own businesses.

3   If you want to be a millionaire, not only do you have to work hard, but you should enjoy your work. And you shouldn't take too many holidays. Most millionaires work more than sixty hours a week. Half stay in contact with the office while they're on holiday and 14 percent of them refuse to switch off. Having a good work-life balance is fine for people who only want to be moderately successful, but if you're really ambitious, you have to put in the hours.

4   What are millionaires like as people? The survey found that they are competitive, they like taking risks, and they are aggressive and self-confident. They'll do anything they can to get what they want.

5   Millionaires can break all sorts of rules. The only thing they mustn't do is break the law. Surprisingly, most millionaires are careful spenders. They prefer Gap to Gucci. Many of them choose not to spend money on expensive designer clothes – they would rather find a bargain on the high street. And they don't spend lots of money on expensive meals in restaurants either. They prefer to eat at home. However, they do like to drive Mercedes and go on at least three expensive holidays a year. One last thing: millionaires don't care what other people think of them. So, if you want to be a millionaire, you shouldn't worry about what other people think of you. Just do your own thing.

3   Underline words or phrases in the article that match meanings 1–6.

1   their family didn't have much money (paragraph 2)
2   they never stop thinking about work (paragraph 3)
3   having enough time for work and for the things you enjoy (paragraph 3)
4   work long hours (paragraph 3)
5   find something for a good price (paragraph 5)
6   do what you want without worrying about what other people think (paragraph 5)

4A   Work in pairs. Take turns to say things which millionaires do and don't do. Find as many points as possible.
Millionaires think a lot about money. Most millionaires …

B   Think of millionaires you have heard of. Do you agree with what the article says?

GRAMMAR   *must/have to/should (obligation)*

5   Match the words in bold in sentences 1–6 with the meanings a)–e). One meaning matches with two sentences.

1   You **don't have to** be born rich to be a millionaire. b)
2   If you want to be a millionaire, you **have to** work hard. c)
3   You **must** have a clear idea of what you want to do. c)
4   You **should** enjoy your work. a)
5   You **shouldn't** take too many holidays. e)
6   You **mustn't** worry about what other people think of you. d)

a)   It's a good idea.
b)   It's not necessary. You don't need to be/do this.
c)   It's necessary. You have no choice.
d)   It's important that you don't do this.
e)   It's not a good idea.

page 150 **LANGUAGEBANK**

PRACTICE

6A   Make sentences with the prompts. Use the positive or negative form of the word in brackets.

1   postmen / get up early in the morning (have)
Postmen have to get up early in the morning.
2   window cleaners / be afraid of heights (must) mustn't
3   nurses / be patient and care about other people (should)
4   businessmen often / travel a lot (have)
5   politicians / do their job because they want fame (should)
6   teachers / enjoy working with children (must)
7   doctors / train for several years before they can work (have)
8   teachers / work in the school during the holidays (have)
9   police officers / good communicators (have)

page 167 **VOCABULARYBANK**

B   Think about three different jobs. Make sentences to describe what qualities are/aren't important for these jobs. Compare your ideas with a partner.
Teachers have to be motivated. They should be good communicators, but they don't have to be competitive.

Have you got what it takes to be a millionaire?

Can you work your way to success? Try our survey to find out.

1 When your boss goes on holiday, do you:

a) come in later and leave earlier?

b) work as normal?

c) work harder – you want to impress your boss's boss?

2 You see your dream job advertised. Unfortunately, it asks for five specific skills and you've only got two. Do you:

a) resolve to get at least two more of the skills in the near future, so you can apply next time?

b) apply for the job anyway, focusing on the skills you've got and ignoring the ones you haven't?

c) not apply – what's the point of being rejected again?

3 You have gone to a meeting across town, but your client is keeping you waiting. Do you:

a) get angry – why should you wait for anyone?

b) use the time to phone a friend?

c) use the time to make work-related calls?

4 If you don't like a job, do you:

a) leave – nobody should have to work all the time?

b) leave as soon as you've got a better job, or have the finance to start your own business?

c) do nothing – all jobs are miserable?

5 You are helping a friend out in their clothes shop. The store closes at 6p.m. At 5.55p.m. a woman rushes in saying she is looking for a dress to wear for a party. Do you:

a) tell her you are closing and shut up shop?

b) tell her you've got nothing in her size?

c) tell her you've got some in stock and show her?

SPEAKING

7A Work in pairs. Do the survey above. Then check your score on page 175.

B Discuss. Do you agree with what the survey says about your score? Why/Why not? Do you know anyone who would make a good entrepreneur? Why?

VOCABULARY *PLUS* confusing words

8 Read the vocabulary notes and complete sentences 1 and 2.

> ### job · work
>
> **Work** is what you do to earn money:
> *What kind of **work** does he do?*
>
> A **job** is the particular type of work that you do:
> *Sam's got a **job** as a waiter.*
>
> **Job** can be plural, but **work** cannot.

1 I've finished my degree, so I'm looking for a ___job___.

2 It's not easy to find ___work___ when you're my age.

9A Underline the correct alternative in the sentences below. What is the difference between these words?

1 He suddenly *remembered*/*reminded* that he had to go to the bank.

2 Can you *remember*/*remind* me to call him later?

3 I've *forgotten*/*left* my keys in the car.

4 Did you *hear*/*listen* that noise?

5 Can you say that again? I'm sorry, I wasn't *listening*/*hearing*.

6 Being ill on holiday isn't much *fun*/*funny*.

B Turn to page 175 to check your answers.

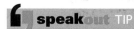 **speakout** TIP

To help you remember confusing words and vocabulary, write them in personalised sentences in your notebook. Write sentences about your life using some of the words from Exercise 9.

10A Complete questions 1–6 with a suitable word from Exercises 8 and 9.

1 What are the best paid ___jobs___ in your country?

2 Is there anything you often ___forget___, like phone numbers, or someone's name?

3 If you ___listen___ carefully, what noises can you hear at the moment?

4 Do you write notes to ___remind___ yourself about important things?

5 How much did you ___earn___ for your first job? What did you buy?

6 What do you like doing for ___fun___? Do you like playing games?

B Work in pairs. Take turns to ask and answer the questions above.

➡ page 167 **VOCABULARYBANK**

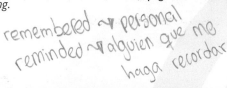

remembered ~ personal
reminded ~ alguien que me
haga recordar

▶ **GRAMMAR** | *used to, would*   ▶ **VOCABULARY** | strong adjectives   ▶ **HOW TO** | talk about past habits

LISTENING

1 Work in pairs. Look at the photos and answer the questions.

1 What are these jobs? Would you like to do them? Why/Why not?

2 What is your idea of a dream job?

2A ▶ 4.1 Listen to people talking about their dream jobs. Match the speaker to the photos opposite.

B What problem does each speaker talk about?

C Listen again and answer questions 1–10. Write Angie (A), Pauline (P) or Monty (M).

1 Who works very long hours? *A*

2 Who got bored of eating restaurant food? *P*

3 Who gave up their dream job? *P*

4 Who travels a lot for their job? *A*

5 Who sometimes works seven days a week? *M*

6 Who thought their job looked exciting? *A*

7 Who is interested in the science of what they do? *M*

8 Who previously worked in a bank? *M*

9 Who has always loved fashion? *A*

10 Who had put on a lot of weight? *P*

VOCABULARY strong adjectives

3 Read audio script 4.1 on page 188 and find the strong adjectives in bold. Match them to the gradable adjectives below.

1 good: wonderful, *amazing* brilliant

2 bad: awful, *terrible*

3 big: enormous

4 small: tiny

5 tired: *exhausted*

6 hot: boiling

7 cold: *freezing*

8 tasty: *delicious*

9 angry: *furious*

10 interesting: *fascinating*

11 pretty: *beautiful*

12 difficult: *impossible*

absolutely freezing

4A Complete conversations 1–6.

1 A: The food here's very tasty.

   B: Yes, it's *delicious*

2 A: It's really hot outside today.

   B: I know. It's absolutely *boiling* .

3 A: Was your girlfriend angry?

   B: Yes, she was really *furious* .

4 A: The view of the lake is really pretty.

   B: Yes, it's *beautiful* isn't it?

5 A: Do you find the job interesting?

   B: I think it's absolutely *fascinating*

6 A: It's difficult to understand what he's saying.

   B: I know. It's *impossible*

B ▶ 4.2 Listen and mark the stress on the strong adjectives. Notice how speaker B emphasises the stressed syllable in their intonation.

C Listen again and shadow speaker B's response.

A Pauline

B Monty

C Angie

GRAMMAR used to, would

5A Read the texts. What did the children dream of doing? Have they achieved their dreams?

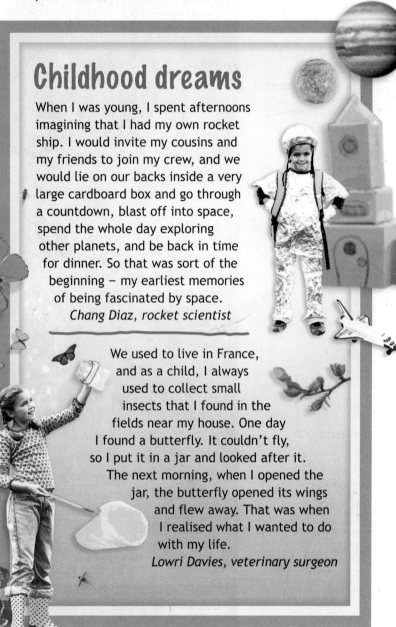

Childhood dreams

When I was young, I spent afternoons imagining that I had my own rocket ship. I would invite my cousins and my friends to join my crew, and we would lie on our backs inside a very large cardboard box and go through a countdown, blast off into space, spend the whole day exploring other planets, and be back in time for dinner. So that was sort of the beginning – my earliest memories of being fascinated by space.
Chang Diaz, rocket scientist

We used to live in France, and as a child, I always used to collect small insects that I found in the fields near my house. One day I found a butterfly. It couldn't fly, so I put it in a jar and looked after it. The next morning, when I opened the jar, the butterfly opened its wings and flew away. That was when I realised what I wanted to do with my life.
Lowri Davies, veterinary surgeon

B Look at the underlined words in sentences a)–d) and match them with rules 1–3.

a) I <u>would invite</u> my cousins and my friends to join my crew.

b) We <u>used to live</u> in France.

c) I always <u>used to collect</u> small insects.

d) One day I <u>found</u> a butterfly.

Rules:

1 Use the past simple, not *used to* or *would,* to talk about specific events in the past. ____d____

2 Use *used to* or *would* to talk about a past habit. You can also use the past simple. ____a____ and ____c____

3 Use *used to* to talk about a past state. You cannot use *would* to talk about a past state. ____b____

▀▀▶ page 150 **LANGUAGE**BANK

PRACTICE

6A Complete the texts. Where possible, use *would*. Where neither *used to* or *would* are possible, use the past simple.

It's every young girl's dream to be an actress when she grows up. I [1] *used to* (love) watching beautiful actresses on television. I was so sure that was what I wanted to do that I [2] *would* (practise) my Oscar speech in front of the mirror in the bathroom. I [3] *would* (use) a shampoo bottle instead of a microphone, and I [4] *would* (thank) all my family and friends, even my three cats, for helping me!

My family [5] ~~would~~ *used to* (live) in Sheffield, just near the football stadium, so as a child, I [6] *would* (go) to football matches most weekends. I remember the first match I went to, my granddad [7] *took* (take) me. I was very young, and I had never seen so many people in one place at one time. It was quite frightening, and I don't think I [8] *watched* (watch) the game very much. But I remember that we won, and the crowd went crazy. After that, every week I [9] *would* (ask) Granddad if he had tickets, and usually he did.

B ▶ 4.3 Listen and repeat. Notice the pronunciation of *used to* /juːstə/. Practise saying the sentences.

1 I used to play football when I was a kid.

2 I used to practise every day.

3 We used to live in London.

4 I didn't use to like classical music.

5 My father used to take me fishing.

6 I used to ski, but now I snowboard.

7 We used to go to the cinema a lot.

C Did you use to do any of the things mentioned above? Tell your partner.

SPEAKING

7 Work in pairs and discuss.

1 What were your childhood dreams? Have you achieved them?

2 Did you have any interests or hobbies in the past which relate to your life (job/studies) now? What were they?

3 How have your ideas, opinions, hobbies, etc., changed? Are there any things that you used to do, which you don't do now? Why did you stop? Would you do these things again?

As a child, I always used to dream about being an artist …

Wanted:
Paradise Island Caretaker

We are looking for someone to work on a tropical island off the Queensland coast. No formal qualifications are needed, but candidates must be willing to swim, snorkel, dive and sail.

- The successful applicant will receive a salary of A$150,000 ($103,000, £70,000) for six months and get to live rent-free in a three-bedroom villa, complete with pool.

- The new recruit will work for just twelve hours a month. Duties include feeding some of the hundreds of species of fish and collecting the island's mail.

- They will also need to prepare a blog, a photo diary and video updates to attract tourists to the area.

WRITING a covering letter

8 Read the advertisement and answer the questions.

1 What kind of person would be good at this job? *a good swimers with* *capacitacion*
2 Would you like to do this job? Why/Why not? *yes,*

9A Read the covering letter. Do you think this person would be good for the job? Why/Why not?

---

¹Dear Richard Smith,

²I'm writing to you regarding your advertisement for a caretaker on Paradise Island which I saw on www.findajob.com. I would like to submit an application for the post. Please find my CV attached.

As an experienced photo journalist who has spent the last five years travelling around the world, I believe that I meet all the requirements you outline in your advertisement.

³• Good communicator with broad IT skills: I've published newspaper and magazine articles, given TV and radio interviews and kept a journal and video weblog on my website with up-to-date photos and stories of my travels.

• Interest in nature and conservation: During a six-month stay in Bermuda, I worked for a dolphin conservation programme, where I had hands-on experience of teaching visitors about these amazing animals and why we need to protect them.

• Proven ability in project management: Before travelling the world, I worked for a small company, organising community projects.

⁴If you require any further information, or would like to arrange an interview, please call me on 077895367289 or email me at alisj@yahoo.com. I look forward to hearing from you at your earliest convenience.

⁵Yours sincerely,

Alison Jessop

B Is the wording of the letter formal or informal? Find examples of expressions which tell you this.

C Underline phrases in the letter which match meanings 1–6.

1 about (paragraph 2)
2 I want to apply for the job (paragraph 2)
3 I think I would be good for the job. (paragraph 2)
4 practical experience of doing the job (paragraph 3)
5 I have shown that I am able to do this. (paragraph 3)
6 as soon as you have the opportunity (paragraph 4)

D Underline any other useful phrases.

LEARN TO organise your ideas

10 Match the parts of the letter 1–5 with notes a)–e).

Preparing a covering letter

a) What qualities are they looking for? Write three to four points that show you have these qualities. Use the same words as they use in the advertisement.
b) Address your letter to an individual. Only use 'Dear Sir/Madam' when you can't find out the recipient's name.
c) Finish with a call to action. What is going to happen next? Are you going to call them or should they call you?
d) Explain why you are contacting them. What is the job? Where have you seen it?
e) Use 'Yours sincerely' if you know their name or 'Yours faithfully' if you don't.

11 Look at the job advertisements on page 179 and write a covering letter for one of the jobs. Use the sample letter and useful phrases to help you.

VOCABULARY business

1A Read the review below. What do you think the programme *The Apprentice* is about?

The Apprentice

'This is a job interview from hell. First prize, you get to work for me. Second prize – doesn't exist.' This is how Lord Alan Sugar greets the contestants who have come to join him for the latest series of *The Apprentice* (broadcast on the BBC).

Fifteen young businessmen and women from around the UK have come to London to compete for a job which could earn them a six-figure salary, working for the UK's most difficult boss. Lord Alan Sugar is a successful businessman who owns a vast business empire, and he's looking for an apprentice to work for him and learn business skills. But Lord Sugar is not easy to please. To get their dream job the contestants need to work as a team, but also show that they have individual talent, because in the end there is only one job.

During the competition, the contestants live together in a luxury house. Each week, Lord Sugar sets the teams a task. They have to work as a team to complete the task and earn as much money as possible. The team which wins gets a luxury treat, paid for by Lord Sugar. The team which loses has to go back to Lord Sugar and explain what happened. And each week one of the contestants gets fired.

B Complete the questions with words from the box.

> ~~fired~~　salary　~~boss~~　compete　businessmen
> interview　team

1　Do you know any successful _businessmen_?
2　When was the last time you and your friends worked as a _team_?
3　Have you ever worked for a difficult _boss_?
4　When did you last go for a job _interview_?
5　Have you ever had to _compete_ for a job?
6　Which jobs earn a six-figure _salary_?
7　What kinds of things does someone have to do to get _fired_ from their job?

C Work in pairs. Would you apply to be on a programme like this? Why/Why not? Take turns to ask and answer the questions above.

FUNCTION reaching agreement

2A ▶ 4.4 Listen to a team having a meeting to decide how to complete the task below. Underline the options they decide on.

Set up a catering company

Your team must start a business that organises and prepares food for customers, either for their businesses, or for events they organise.

Name: Food4events / Italy on the move / <u>Buon Appetito</u>

Company based: in central London / <u>outside central London</u>

Type of catering: company catering / <u>events catering</u>

Speciality Food: British / <u>Mediterranean (Italian)</u> / Indian

B Listen again and tick the option you hear.

1　a) The way I see things, … ✓
　 b) The way I see it, …
2　a) That's a good idea.
　 b) That's a good point. ✓
3　a) I suggest we think about … ✓
　 b) I think we should think about …
4　a) That's fine by me. ✓
　 b) That's OK by me.
5　a) I'm not sure that I agree, actually.
　 b) I'm not sure that … is a good idea. ✓
6　a) How about if we (call it) … ?
　 b) Why don't we (call it) … ? ✓

LEARN TO manage a discussion

ESTABA MOJADO! (handwritten)

5A Complete the underlined phrases for managing a discussion.

1 First of _all_ we need to decide what food we want to sell.

2 Let's _focus_ on the issue of a theme for our food, you know like Indian, or Mediterranean …

3 OK. So, <u>moving on to the next _point_</u>, where do we work from?

4 OK, so _let's_ recap: the company is called Food4events and we sell at parties, events, weddings, etc. We're based outside London. Erm … What else do we need to think about?

5 <u>I think we need to come _back_</u> to the kind of food we want to sell. I really feel that we need to specialise, so perhaps we could be Italian.

6 So, <u>let's _sum_ up</u> what we've decided.

B ▶ 4.6 Listen and check your answers.

6 Find and correct the mistakes. One word in each line is incorrect.

1 A: First of ~~it~~, we need to decide what we want to cook. _all_

  B: That's a good ~~issue~~. How many people are coming to the party? _idea / point_

2 A: OK. So, let's focus ~~with~~ cooking something really simple. _on_

  B: Yes, that is OK ~~of~~ me. _by_

3 A: So, moving ~~up~~ to the next point. Who's going to bring what? _on_

  B: I think we need to come back ~~for~~ what kind of food we want. _to_

4 A: So, let's review. We're cooking pasta and people are bringing salads. _recap_

  B: OK, let's sum ~~for~~ what we've decided so far. _up_

SPEAKING

7A Read the task and write down some ideas.

Set up a company to promote tourism

You are going to set up a tour company to promote tourism in your town/city/country. You need to decide the following:

• the name and location of the company

• what type of tours you will organise (themed tours/language tours/sports tours, etc.) and where they will go

• how you will promote tourism

• how the company will be different from other tour companies

B Work in groups. Read your roles and come up with a plan for the business. You have five minutes.

Student A: It's your job to keep the meeting focused. Try to cover all the points.

Student B: Make sure you make notes about any decisions which are made. You will be the group's spokesperson and will have to sum up at the end of the meeting.

Student C: Try to come up with as many ideas as possible.

C When you are ready, start the discussion like this.

A: Shall we start? First of all, …

D Tell the other groups about your business plan. Which group do you think has the best plan?

---

3 Add the phrases from Exercise 2B to the table below.

Giving opinions
I (really) feel that … *the way i see it* *the way i see thing*

Commenting on other opinions
I (don't) see what you mean. *that's a good idea* Exactly! *That's a good point* *That's fine by me* *I'm not sure that is a good idea*

Suggestions
What about …? *I suggest we think about* I suggest we focus on … *I think we should think about* *how about if we? why don't we?* *(call it)*

▶ page 150 **LANGUAGEBANK**

4A Put the words in the correct order to make sentences and questions.

1 decide / I / on / name / we / think / a / should *I think we should decide on a name*

2 good / a / that's / point *that's a good point*

3 you / see / mean / what / I *I see what you mean*

4 suggest / products / the / on / I / focus / we *I suggest we focus on the products*

5 fine / that's / me / by *that's fine by me.*

6 sure / I'm / that / agree / not / I *I'm not sure that i agree*

7 we / about / don't / it / Why / think / ? *why don't we think about it*

8 business / a / the / about / what / for / name / ? *what about the name for the business*

B ▶ 4.5 Listen to the phrases. Which words are stressed? Listen again and repeat.

DVD PREVIEW

1A Match DVD extracts 1–7 to the correct responses a)–g).

1 Mr Davies, good to see you again. *b)*
2 Did you get your welcome pack? *d)*
3 In the event of a fire, my motto is ... *e)*
4 Ready when you are. *f)*
5 Now here's somebody you've not met yet. *c)*
6 Parcel for you. *a)*

a) It's from my wife.
b) Please, call me Huw. *1*
c) Hi. Nice to meet you.
d) Yeah, I think so.
e) Run for your life?
f) Right, let's show you around.

B What type of situation do you think the DVD clip shows? Read about the programme below to find out.

BBC Gavin and Stacey

Gavin and Stacey is a BBC programme about a young couple. Gavin comes from Essex, near London, and Stacey comes from Cardiff, Wales. After a long-distance relationship conducted online and by telephone, they eventually get married and Gavin moves to Wales. In this episode, Gavin starts a new job. On his first day, his family want him to do well and be happy at work.

2 Work in pairs and answer the questions.

1 What type of things do you think Gavin needs to learn on his first day at work?
2 Who will he need to meet and what advice will they give?

DVD VIEW

3 Watch the DVD. Tick which of the things below happen.

1 He goes to his office. ✓
2 He meets his new boss. ✓
3 He learns how to use the phone in his office. ✓
4 He speaks to a client on the phone. ✓
5 He finds out what to do if there is a fire. ✓
6 He learns how to use the company's website.
7 He meets the website manager. ✓
8 He meets his personal assistant.
9 He is visited by a family member. ✓
10 He receives a package. ✓

4A Answer the questions.

1 Why is Gavin's wife, Stacey, worried? *job*
2 What does Huw, the boss, give Gavin? *plate name*
3 Why does Gavin feel embarrassed in front of Huw? *the family phone calls*
4 What does Owain, the website manager, invite Gavin to do? *rugby*
5 What does Uncle Bryn bring for Gavin? *lunch*
6 Who sends Gavin a message in a box? What does it say? *wife "Good Luck"*

B Watch the DVD again to check.

speakout a day in the life …

5A ▶ **4.7 Listen to someone describing a typical day in her life. Do you think she likes her job?** *Kinder garten Teacher*

B Read the key phrases below. Complete each phrase by adding one word.

> ### keyphrases
> I wake up __at__ (about) 6.30.
> I leave home by 7.20 at the __latest__
> The first __thing__ I do is check my mail.
> I check everything is __ready__ for the children.
> We try to do this at least __once__ a day.
> I make __plans__ for the next day.
> I'm usually home __by__ 5.00.

C Listen again to check. Then tick the key phrases you hear.

D Prepare to tell other students about a normal day in your life. Write notes about:

- hours of work/studying
- tasks you have to do
- people you spend your day with
- problems and challenges
- how you relax
- the best parts of your day

E Tell other students about your typical day. What do you have in common?

writeback your daily routine

6A Read an entry from normallives.com, a website that publishes descriptions of people's daily routines. Is Frank's routine similar to yours? How is it different? *NO,*

I work as a gym instructor in a sports centre. **I get up at** 5.00a.m. every morning and make a cup of coffee. I can't function until I've had my coffee! I drive to work – it takes about fifteen minutes on a good day – **usually getting there at about** 5.40. **The first thing I do is** switch on the lights and the air conditioning if it's summer (heating if it's winter), and then the radio. We have the radio on all day because our clients like listening to the news and the music. The sports centre opens at 6.00a.m.

I work in a team of four, although only two of us are ever in the gym at the same time. The instructors all wear sports clothes. **It's important to be** comfortable because we sometimes need to show new clients how to use the machines. Apart from this, **our other tasks are** quite simple: we check that everyone has their membership card when they come in, and we check that the machines are clean and safe.

I have a one-hour break for lunch, and I usually do two more hours after lunch. **I go home at about** 2.30.

The best part of the job is meeting people. Our clients range from eighteen-year-old body builders to eighty-year-olds who come to exercise and chat. I've never had any problems at the sports centre. It's a really nice job, though it doesn't pay very well. In the evenings **I relax by** reading a book and cooking for myself, and I'm usually in bed by 9.30p.m.

Frank Carduna

B Write about your daily routine using the sentence starters in bold above and the key phrases to help.

PERSONAL QUALITIES

1 Work in pairs. Take turns to define a word and guess the meaning. Student A: describe a word/phrase from the box in your own words, starting with '*I am/ like/enjoy*, etc.'. Don't say the word/phrase. Student B: listen and try to guess the word or phrase.

> hard-working   indecisive
> a risk taker   a good leader RMV
> ambitious   competitive
> think outside the box
> a good communicator

A: *I enjoy working and want to succeed in what I do.*

B: *You're motivated?*

A: *Correct. Your turn to describe a word.*

MUST/HAVE TO/SHOULD (OBLIGATION)

2A Underline the correct alternative to complete the sentences.

1 I *have to/mustn't* call my mother today. It's her birthday.

2 I really *must/mustn't* do more exercise. I'm so unfit.

3 I'm lucky because I *don't have to/shouldn't* get up early in the morning. I'm a student.

4 I think you *should/shouldn't* study harder. Your exam results weren't very good.

5 You *mustn't/should* be afraid of taking risks, or you will never live your dreams.

6 I *shouldn't/don't have to* waste so much time on the computer. I'll never finish my work.

B Complete the sentences so that they are true for you.

1 I have to … this evening. *do homework*

2 I really must do more …

3 I'm lucky because I don't have to *get up early in the morning*

4 I think you should … because …

5 You mustn't worry about … *the exam*

6 I shouldn't waste so much time *relaxing*

i have to to study for my exam

C Compare your ideas in pairs.

STRONG ADJECTIVES

3A Replace the underlined words in the sentences below with strong adjectives in the box.

> ~~brilliant~~   fascinating   ~~awful~~
> ~~exhausted~~   ~~tiny~~   ~~boiling~~
> ~~impossible~~   ~~delicious~~   ~~furious~~

1 I'm <u>very tired</u>. I didn't sleep well. *exhausted*

2 Shall we open a window? It's <u>very hot</u> in here. *boiling*

3 My boss just called. He's <u>very angry</u>. *furious*

4 I find phrasal verbs <u>very difficult</u> to remember. *impossible*

5 The holiday was <u>very good</u>, but the weather was <u>very bad</u>. *brilliant awful*

6 How can you work in this office? It's <u>very small</u>. *tiny*

7 I find astronomy <u>very interesting</u>. *facinating*

8 Did you cook this? It's <u>very tasty</u>. *dilicious*

B Work in pairs and take turns to test each other.

A: *Very big.*

B: *Enormous.*

A: *Correct. Your turn.*

USED TO, WOULD

4A Replace the past simple with *used to* or *would* where possible. Where both are possible, choose *would*.

1 My family lived in Paris, but we moved when I was a teenager. *used to*

2 I spent a lot of time with my grandparents when I was younger. *would*

3 For my first job, I washed dishes in a restaurant.

4 I didn't think money was important. Now I have lots of bills to pay. *use to*

5 We had a lot more free time before we had children. *use to have*

6 My best friend at school lived just across the road from me. *use to*

B Change four of the sentences so that they are true for you.

C Compare with a partner. Find three things that you both used to do as children, that you don't do now.

REACHING AGREEMENT

5A Complete the conversations.

1 **A:** The way I s*ee* things all cars should be banned from city centres.

  B: E*xactly*

2 **A:** I really f*eel* that we need to look at immigration.

  B: That's a good p*oint*.

3 **A:** The w*ay* I see it, the company is making too much money.

  B: I don't see what you m*ean*.

4 **A:** I th*ink* we should ask for more money.

  B: I'm not s*ure* agree, actually.

5 **A:** I s*uggest* we try to meet again next week.

  B: T*hat's* fine by me.

B Work in pairs and practise the conversations.

6 Work in groups. Look at the questions below and discuss. Try to reach agreement on each answer.

1 Should there be a limit to the number of hours people can work in one week?

2 Should there be a minimum wage? What should it be?

3 How long should men/women be allowed to stay off work after they have children?

4 Should everyone be allowed to work from home at least once a week?

5 Should employees be allowed to wear to work whatever clothes they want?

BBC VIDEO PODCAST

Watch people talking about their real jobs and their dream jobs on ActiveBook or on the website.

Authentic BBC interviews

UNIT 5

SPEAKING

› Talk about different forms of transport and their uses

› Present and answer questions on your area of expertise

› Explain/Solve problems

› Describe a new machine

LISTENING

› Listen to people answering difficult questions

› Listen to conversations about technical problems

› Watch a BBC programme about a race between a car and two people

READING

› Read about how technology changed the world

› Read about a book review

WRITING

› Write an advantages/ disadvantages essay

› Write an advertisement

BBC CONTENT

▯ Video podcast: Are you good at solving problems?

◉ DVD: Top Gear

UNIT 5

solutions

speakout DVD

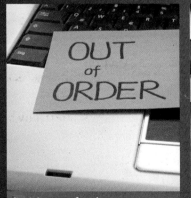

VOCABULARY technology

1A Discuss. How have machines and technology changed the world? Have they made it a better or worse place?

B Work in pairs. Put the words/phrases in the box into the correct word web.

> electricity   nuclear power
> antibiotics   vaccinations
> computer networks   motorbikes
> genetic engineering   washing machine
> vacuum cleaner   space travel
> commercial aeroplanes   solar power
> communications satellites

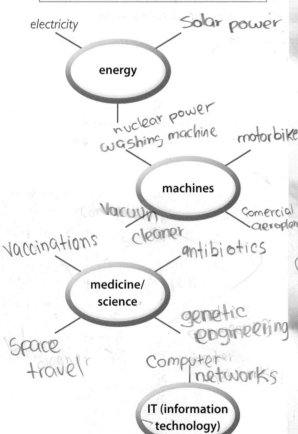

C Look at the words/phrases above and underline the main stress(es). Sometimes there can be more than one per word/phrase.

electri<u>ci</u>ty   <u>nu</u>clear <u>po</u>wer

D ▶ 5.1 Listen and check. Then listen again and repeat.

E Work in pairs. Can you add any more words to each word web?

▶ page 168 **VOCABULARY**BANK

JAMES MAY'S 20th CENTURY

In this BBC series, presenter James May takes a tour of the twentieth century, looking at some of <u>the most surprising</u> and influential technological advances of the past hundred years.

At the beginning of the twentieth century, long-distance travel was only for the military and the very rich. But the invention of <u>commercial aeroplanes</u> and cars changed all that. Travel became <u>easier</u> and more affordable, and the world, as a result, became a little bit smaller. In the programme *Honey, I shrunk the World* James soon discovers that driving a car in those days wasn't as easy as it is today. But shrinking the world wasn't just about travel. For the first time in history, we could bring the world to us via the cinema, then the television, and later the computer.

Each day, 180,000 people move into a city somewhere on the planet. In *Big City, Bright Lights*, James sets out to discover how we've created this high-rise, 24/7 experiment in urban living. He heads for New York – to the top floors of the Woolworth building, once the tallest building in the world. He looks at how, in the last hundred years, our cities have become a lot taller, and how we use <u>electricity</u> to power them.

In the twentieth century the teenager was invented. But how? James May finds out. First, he looks at fashion. The twentieth century introduced fantastic new fabrics in fantastic new colours, made possible by the invention of materials like nylon, which were much cheaper and more colourful than materials we used before. Then, he looks at transport. As a teenager, James always dreamed of having his own <u>motorbike</u>. The motorbike gave teenagers more freedom by allowing them to travel further away from home, and their parents. Finally, he looks at the electric guitar – one of the most important symbols of teenage rock music even today. He talks to Francis Rossi, from the band *Status Quo*, who explains that 'Volume is like speed – you buy a fast car because you want to be faster, you buy a big amplifier because you want to be louder.'

In other programmes, James looks at how advances in medicine have made many people's lives better, and what we have learned from <u>space travel</u>.

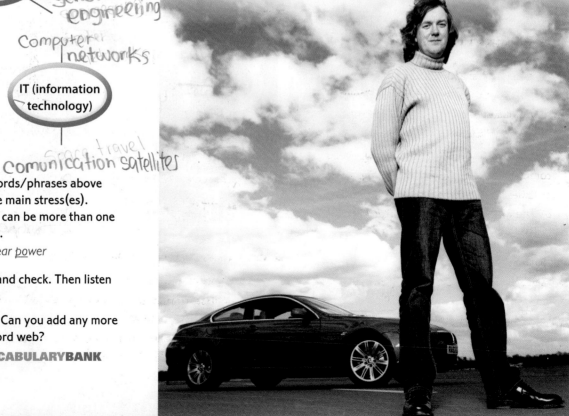

READING

2 Read the article on page 56. Tick the inventions in Exercise 1B which are mentioned. Which other inventions does the article talk about?

3A Read the article again and answer the questions.

1 What kind of people travelled long *military* distances in the early twentieth century? *and rich people*

2 What two things happened in the twentieth century to make the world seem smaller? *commercial aeroplanes and cars*

3 How have cities changed in the last 100 years? Why? *Taller (tall buildings)*

4 What was special about the invention of nylon? *Colourful and cheaper.*

5 Why does James May think that motorbikes are important for teenagers? *for freedom*

6 What invention was an important symbol of teenage rock music? *electric guitar*

B Discuss. What do you think has been the most important piece of technology (medicine/education/home/travel) invented in the last 100 years?

GRAMMAR comparatives and superlatives

4A Read the article again. Find examples of comparatives and superlatives.

B Look at your examples and complete the rules. How do we form the comparatives and superlatives of common adjectives?

Rules:

1 Adjectives with one syllable
comparatives: add *-er/-ier*,
superlatives: add _____.

2 Adjectives with two or more syllables
comparatives: add *more*,
superlatives: add *the most*

C Look at the sentences below and complete the rules with *small* or *big*.

a) Cities have become *a lot/much/far* taller.

b) The world became *a little/a little bit/slightly* smaller.

Rules:

1 Use quantifiers *a lot/much/far* to talk about *big* differences.

2 Use quantifiers *a little/a little bit/slightly* to talk about *short* differences.

➠ page 152 **LANGUAGEBANK**

PRACTICE

5A Complete the statements with the prompts in brackets.

1 The invention of the bicycle made it *a lot easier* (lot/easy) for people to travel from one village to another, to meet new people.

2 The world has become a *much safer* (much/safe) place to live since the invention of antibiotics. People are *by far healthier* (far/healthy) now than 100 years ago. *healthy*

3 The invention of the washing machine has meant that it is *a lot quicker* (lot/quick) for people to wash their clothes. I think it's *the best* (good) invention of the last century.

4 Although we have computers, paper is still the *cheaper* (cheap) and *the most flexible* (flexible) way to record the written word.

5 Electricity is the *most important* (important) invention because without it many of the other things we have would not have been possible.

6 The invention of the telephone and the computer have meant that we are *much busier?* (much/busy) now than we were in the past.

B Work in pairs. Choose an invention from the last 100 years. Write sentences to describe how this invention has changed our lives.

C Read your sentences to other students. Which invention do you think has been the best/worst? Why?

SPEAKING

6A Work in pairs. Look at the photos and read about James May's challenge on page 177. Which of these transport ideas exist at the moment?

A **AEROCAR**

speed: +110 mph
consumes: 13 mpg

B **SPACE PLANE**

speed: 15,000 mph
consumes: 0.12 mpg

C **ROCKET PACK**

speed: 60 mph
consumes: 0.06 mpg

D **ROBOT CAR**

speed: 120 mph
consumes: 45 mpg

E **SOLAR CAR**

speed: 60 mph
consumes: n/a

B Turn back to page 177 and complete the task.

C Work in groups and discuss.

1 Which of these forms of transport do you like/like the idea of? Why?

2 Are there any types of ideas here that you would not try? Why not?

3 Think about all the different types of transport you use. Write a list. Which do you enjoy the most/least? Why?

[handwritten top margin: next to reasons of the / Maintenance / Although]

WRITING advantages/disadvantages essay

7A What do you think are the main advantages and disadvantages of technology in everyday life? Write a list.

B Read the model essay. Does it mention any of your ideas?

The advantages and disadvantages of modern technology

1 It's easy to see the advantages of modern technology in our everyday lives. Technology has given us mobile phones, computers, televisions and many other useful things. However, there are also disadvantages with modern technology.

2 One of the main advantages of modern technology can be seen in medical science. The discoveries of antibiotics and vaccinations have saved millions of lives around the world. In addition to this, modern technology has made industry more efficient.

3 On the other hand, modern technology is responsible for the development of weapons, which have caused a lot of destruction. Another disadvantage of modern technology is that it makes people lazy. Nowadays too many people spend their lives sitting in front of computer screens and this is certainly not a good thing.

4 In my opinion, modern technology is a good thing. In general, the advantages outweigh the disadvantages. However, it's important to remember that technology itself is not the problem. The problem is that people use technology for their own benefit and do not think about the harmful consequences.

C Match paragraphs 1–4 with descriptions a)–d).

a) discussion of disadvantages — *3*
b) conclusion — *4*
c) introduction — *1*
d) discussion of advantages — *2*

D Work in pairs. Complete the guidelines for writing an essay with the words in the box.

personal opinions	examples	notes	beginning	logical order

1 Sort out the facts – make *notes* of all the relevant information you have on the subject.

2 Plan your argument – organise your notes and arrange the ideas in a *logical order*

3 Give your essay an appropriate *beginning* Describe what you are planning to say.

4 Decide how many paragraphs you need for your argument. Each paragraph should discuss one point. Use *examples* to support your arguments.

5 Write a logical conclusion. Though the style of the essay is generally formal and impersonal, this might be the place to include some *personal opinions*

LEARN TO use discourse markers

8A Look at the underlined words and phrases in the essay. Put them in the correct place in the table.

introduce advantages
The most important advantage is …
One of the main advantages
introduce disadvantages *the problem*
The main disadvantage is … *is that*
Another disadvantage
contrasting ideas
Although, … *On the other*
However had
additional reasons
As well as that, …
And another thing, …
In addition to
personal opinion/conclusion
In general, …
As far as I'm concerned, …
In my opinion

B Underline the correct alternatives.

Satellite TV: good or bad?
More and more people are watching satellite television. ¹*The main advantage / As well as that* is that you can choose exactly what you want to watch, and ²*in addition to this / however* you can watch programmes in other languages. ³*However, / Although* this means that whereas people used to talk about programmes with colleagues and friends, now they usually don't watch the same programmes. ⁴*On the other hand / And another thing*, there is too much choice. There are so many programmes to choose from that people can't decide what to watch. ⁵*This means that / As far as I'm concerned*, they watch too much television. ⁶*In my opinion / The problem is that*, satellite television is a good thing, as it gives people more choice. ⁷*However, / In general,* people need to be careful that they choose their programmes carefully.

9 Choose one of the titles below and write an advantages and disadvantages essay. Look at Exercises 7 and 8 to help you.

The advantages and disadvantages of:
- modern technology in everyday life
- owning a car/bicycle
- playing computer games
- using a digital camera
- using email/text messages
- cheap flights

[handwritten bottom notes: need to rest / Travel with persons · Traffic · more expensive · maintenance / go to just relax]

▶ **GRAMMAR** | question tags   ▶ **VOCABULARY** | questions   ▶ **HOW TO** | confirm information

SPEAKING

1A Match photos A–F to the questions below.

1 Is it possible to surf a tidal wave? A
2 Does cheese really give you nightmares? F
3 Why are sumo wrestlers so fat? E
4 Do any wasps make honey? B
5 Is there an easy way to prove the Earth is round? D
6 Why do onions make you cry? C

B Work in pairs. How many questions above can you answer in two minutes?

C Turn to page 176 and check your answers.

VOCABULARY questions

2A Match the pairs of verbs in the box with situations 1–5.

> question/wonder   discuss/debate
> respond/reply   research/investigate
> inquire/look into

1 Someone tells you something. You are not sure you agree. *question/wonder*
2 Someone writes you a letter. respond/reply
3 There is an interesting topic in class. discuss/debate
4 You are writing a thesis for your Master's degree. research/investigate
5 You need to find some information, e.g. about cinema times or to book a table. inquire/look into

B Five of the verbs above are also nouns. Which five?
'Wonder' is a verb and a noun.

C Look at all the verbs again and write their noun forms. N.B. One verb doesn't have a noun form. Use a dictionary to help you.
'Response' is the noun of 'respond'.

D Underline the correct alternative to complete the sentences.

1 The police officer continued his *investigation/ wonder/inquire* into the robbery.
2 Didn't you get my email? You didn't *response/ look into/reply*.
3 We had a very interesting *discuss/debate/ wonder* about the death penalty.
4 I've nearly finished my *research/investigate/reply* into nuclear particles.
5 When I hear about all these social problems, I have to *inquire/question/respond* the education system.
6 You want a job here? No problem. My cousin is the boss. I'll *inquiry/debate/look into* it for you.

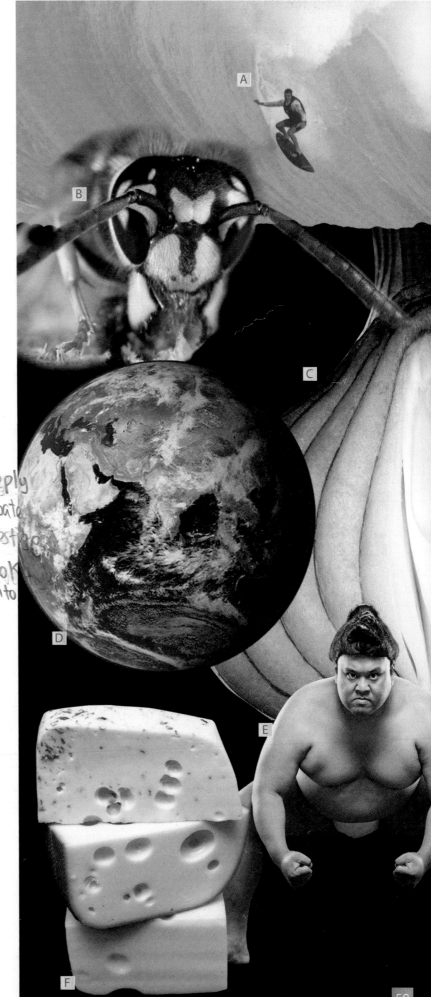

LISTENING

3A Work in groups and discuss.

1 How do you prefer to find information? On the internet, in books or by asking people? What does it depend on?

2 What type of questions do children ask? Think of some examples.

They sometimes ask difficult questions like: 'Why is snow cold?'

B Read a review of a book about questions children ask. How did the author get the idea for the book?

Questions Daddy Can't Answer

It all began with a question asked by Dean, a four-year-old boy: 'Why do ships have round windows?' His father didn't know. And when his sister started behaving badly, Dean asked another question: 'Why can't we just cook her?' On a long drive the boy wondered why the road was so loud. His father replied, 'Because the people who live next to the road have their vacuum cleaners on. The boy's inquiries kept coming: 'Why is the sky blue? Are rainbows hot or cold? What was it like living in the 1940s? What would hurt more – getting run over by a car or getting stung by a jellyfish? Why do police officers like doughnuts?

Eventually, Jamieson decided to write down the questions. He thought it might be fun one day to show them to his son. Then he had a better idea: he'd research the answers. Some people might do their investigations on the internet. Not Mr Jamieson. He contacted experts ranging from astronomers to Buddhist monks to scientists to magicians, and asked lots of questions. He later turned these – and the experts' responses – into a book: *Father Knows Less.*

4A ▶ 5.2 Listen and number the questions below in the order you hear them.

How many hairs are there on the human head?

Why are the windows on ships always round?

Why is there war?

Why did The Beatles break up?

What happens when your plane flies over a volcano?

B Look at the questions again and try to answer them. Compare your ideas with other students.

5A ▶ 5.3 Listen to some people trying to answer the questions in Exercise 4A. Are they the same as your ideas?

B Listen again and complete the notes.

1 Ships' round windows: _____

2 Number of hairs on a human head: _____

3 A plane flies over a volcano: _____

4 The Beatles broke up: _____

5 Reasons for war: different ideologies, a sense of honour, _____

GRAMMAR question tags

6A Complete questions 1–6. Then look at audio script 5.3 on page 189 to check.

1 Round windows are stronger, _____ they?

2 No, it's not that many, _____ it?

3 It depends whose head, _____ it?

4 Nothing happens, _____ it?

5 They got old _____ they?

6 John Lennon went off with Yoko Ono, _____ he?

B Underline the correct alternative to complete the rules.

Rules:

1 Use question tags to confirm information.

2 To form a question tag, repeat the auxiliary verb. For example, use *do* or *does* for *the present/the past.* Use *will* or *won't* for the future.

3 After the auxiliary verb, use a *pronoun/main verb* (e.g. *he, she, it, they*).

4 If the sentence is positive, the question tag is *positive/negative.*

5 If the sentence is negative, the question tag is *positive/negative.*

▶ page 152 **LANGUAGEBANK**

PRACTICE

7 Look at the statements below and complete the question tags.

1 You're Italian, *aren't* you?

2 You aren't a doctor, _____ you?

3 You don't smoke, _____ you?

4 You play a musical instrument, _____ you?

5 You didn't know any of the other students before, _____ you?

6 Our teacher hasn't taught you before, _____ she?

7 You will be here tomorrow, _____ you?

8 This is your pen, _____ it?

9 You went to bed late last night, _____ you?

10 You've travelled a lot, _____ you?

11 You were good at sport when you were a child, _____ you?

12 It wasn't your birthday recently, _____ it?

8A ▶ 5.4 Listen to two questions. Notice how the intonation goes down when the speaker is sure of the answer. Notice how the intonation goes up when the speaker is not sure.

1 You're Italian, aren't you? (the speaker knows the answer)

2 You aren't a doctor, are you? (the speaker is not sure of the answer)

B ▶ 5.5 Listen to the questions in Exercise 7. Which answers is the speaker sure about? Listen and repeat the questions, using the same intonation.

C Work in pairs. Choose six questions to ask your partner. Make sure your intonation is correct in the question tags.

A: You play a guitar, don't you?
B: Yes, I do. I play bass in a band.

SPEAKING

9 Work in groups and follow instructions 1–4 below.

1 Think of one subject each that you know a lot about. Write your topics on a piece of paper.

tennis, Japanese cars, hip hop

2 Exchange papers with another group.

3 Brainstorm questions to ask the other group about their subjects.

Who is the best tennis player in history?
Which Japanese cars are the most popular?

4 Take turns to ask and answer the questions.

VOCABULARY *PLUS* word-building: adjectives

10A Read the text below. How was the ice cream cone invented?

For over a hundred years ice cream was sold mainly in dishes. Then one day, a <u>creative</u> ice-cream seller turned a <u>hopeless</u> situation into a <u>profitable</u> one. In 1904, at a festival, he ran out of spoons and dishes. He bought some wafers from a vendor next to him and put the ice cream into them. The customers loved them and the idea spread quickly. The world has been <u>thankful</u> ever since!

B Underline four adjectives in the text and add them to the word web below. Can you think of other examples of adjectives that fit these patterns?

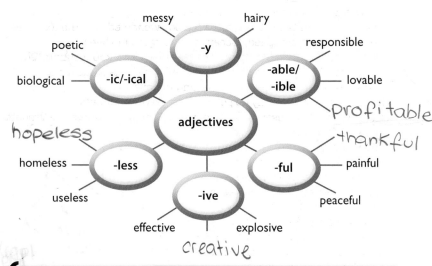

messy   hairy

poetic   **-y**   responsible

biological — **-ic/-ical**   **-able/-ible** — lovable   *profitable*

hopeless   **adjectives**   *thankful*

homeless — **-less**   **-ful** — painful

useless   **-ive**   peaceful

effective   explosive

creative

> ▌ **speakout** TIP
>
> Use L1. L1 is your First Language. Some suffixes in your L1 might have similar meanings to suffixes in English. For example, the Italian *-ivo/a* means the same as the English *-ive*. Can you think of any examples from your language?

11 Complete the text. Add suffixes to the words in brackets.

The city of Detroit, USA was famous for its ¹ _valuable_ (value) car industry. In the early days, the city was ² _responsible_ (response) for the majority of cars in the USA, and Detroit's streets were full of cars. A police officer called William Potts saw that the organisation of the traffic was ³ _hopeless_ (hope) and the traffic was very slow. So, in 1920, he developed an ⁴ _effective_ (effect) system of lights to regulate the flow of cars. He used the same colours as the railway system and put the lights in a tower so that it would be ⁵ _easy_ (ease) for drivers to see them even on ⁶ _rainy_ (rain) days. Potts's system was very ⁷ _successful_ (success). When other countries realised how ⁸ _useful_ (use) it was, the system spread all over the world.

12A Complete the words by adding suffixes.

Find someone who:

1 has a peace_ful_ hobby.
2 is hope_less_ at maths.
3 is a good, care_ful_ driver.

4 is quite mess_y_ at home.
5 thinks he/she is quite creat_ive_.
6 is quite knowledge_able_ about politics.

B Work in groups. Ask and answer questions about the information above.

▶ page 168 **VOCABULARYBANK**

► FUNCTION | polite requests ► **VOCABULARY** | problems and solutions ► **LEARN TO** | respond to requests

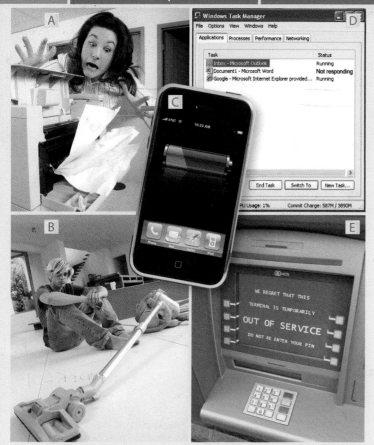

2A Do you have problems with your computer when you work/study? What do you usually do when this happens?

B Read the article. What four things do people do when their computer crashes?

Do you get angry with your computer?

As we rely more on computers in the workplace, people are starting to use violence when their PCs break down, say researchers. When faced with technical problems, most people shout at colleagues, hit the PC or even throw parts of the computers. The most frustrating problem was when people lost their work after their computer crashed or froze. The study found that nearly half of all computer users had become angry at some time. A third of people had physically attacked a computer, 67% experienced frustration and anger, and more than 70% swore at their machines. John Blake (UK) says, 'When my computer crashes, I use swear words such as *Windows*, *Microsoft* or, when I'm really mad, *Bill Gates*!'

VOCABULARY problems and solutions

1A Think of two pieces of technology you have used in the last twenty-four hours. Did you have any problems with them? What problems can you have with them?

B Work in pairs. Look at the photos. What is the problem in each case?

C Look at the phrases in bold. Are they problems (P) or solutions (S)? Which phrases can you use to talk about the problems in pictures A–E above?

1 It's **broken down**. P
2 It **needs recharging**. P
3 It's **out of order**. P
4 It **needs fixing**. P
5 There is no **reception** (for my phone). P
6 **Try switching it off** (and on again). S
7 It **keeps making this strange noise**. P
8 It's **crashed/frozen**. P
9 It **doesn't work** (any more). P
10 We have to **sort it out**. S
11 **Save it onto a memory stick**. S
12 Shall I **print it** for you? S

D Work in pairs and answer the questions.

1 Have any of these problems happened to you or anyone you know recently?
2 How did you feel when it happened?
3 How did you try to solve the problem?

FUNCTION polite requests

3A ▶ 5.6 Listen to four conversations. What is the problem in each case? 1. the machine is no working ATM
2. the laptop crashed.

B Listen again and complete the extracts in the table.

Could you	1 _hold_ the line, please?
	2 _give me_ me a refund?
Could you tell me	who I should 3 _speak_ to?
	what the 4 _problem_ is?
Do you know	what the problem is?
	if there's another 5 _machine_ somewhere?
Would you mind	6 _looking_ at it for me?
	7 _calling_ him for me?

C ▶ 5.7 Listen and repeat the requests.

⟶ page 152 LANGUAGEBANK

3. Vacum cleaner anoying noise funny
4. Machine not working

LEARN TO respond to requests

4A Read some conversation extracts from Exercise 3. Complete the responses with the phrases in the box.

> Yes, I can ~~Yes, I can~~   I'm not sure ~~I'm not sure~~   I'm afraid I can't
> Yes, of course (x2)   ~~Of course not~~   Sure/OK
> ~~Let me have a look~~

1 M: Do you know if there's another machine somewhere? I really need to get some money.

W: Hmm ... _Let me have_. There might be one in the shopping centre. _& look_

2 W: Would you mind looking at it for me?

M: _Of course not_

3 W: Do you know what the problem is?

M: _I'm not. sure_

4 W: Could you tell me what the problem is, sir?

M: _Yes, I can_. It keeps making a funny noise. And it's just not working properly.

5 W: Could you hold the line, please?

M: _Yes_.

6 M: Could you give me a refund?

W: _I'm afraid_ do that. _I can't_

M: Well, could you tell me who I should speak to?

W: _____. You need to speak to the manager.

M: OK. Would you mind calling him for me?

W: _____. I'll just call him.

B Read audio script 5.6 on page 189 to check.

5A Make polite requests with the prompts in brackets.

1 A: I can't concentrate. (Would / mind / turn / music down)?

would you mind turn down the music?

B: Sure. Sorry about that.

2 A: I need to speak to the manager. (Do / know / if / anyone in the office)?

Do you know if there

B: Let me have a look.

3 A: I'm afraid Mr Soul isn't here at the moment.

B: (Do / know / when / _he's_ coming back)?

A: (not / _you_ sure). Do you want me to check?

B: Thank you.

4 A: (Could / tell / how / machine works)? I don't know how to turn it on.

B: (Yes / course).

5 A: I need to take this machine to the repair service. (Would / mind / help / me)?

B: (course / not). Leave it here.

6 A: My computer has frozen (could / tell / who / I / speak / to)?

B: OK. (Let / have / look).

B ▶ 5.8 Listen to check your answers.

C Does the speaker's voice start high or low? Listen again and repeat the requests copying the polite intonation.

SPEAKING

6A Work in pairs. Read your role and think about the phrases you are going to use. Then role-play the situation below.

Student A   **Student B**

> You need to call your sister but you can't get any reception on your phone. Ask Student A if he/she knows where you can get reception.

> Tell Student B that you have reception on your phone. Suggest that he/she tries standing outside.

> You still can't get any reception. Ask Student A if you can borrow his/her phone to send a text message.

> Tell Student B he/she can borrow your phone to make the phone call.

> Thank Student A for his/her help.

B Change roles and role-play the situation below.

Student A   **Student B**

> You can't get onto the internet. Ask Student B if he/she can help.

> Suggest Student A tries turning the modem off and then on again. Ask if that has worked.

> It still doesn't work. Ask Student B if you can try using his/her computer.

> Tell Student A he/she can use your computer.

> Thank Student B for his/her help.

C Choose one or two situations from Exercises 4 and 5. Write a conversation using the flow charts above to help. Then role-play it with a partner.

DVD PREVIEW

1 Work in pairs and answer the questions.

1 Look at the people at the bottom of pages 64–65. What type of sport are they doing?

2 Would you like to try this sport? Why/Why not?

2 Read about the DVD. Who do you think will win the race? Why?

BBC Top Gear

Top Gear is the BBC's international award-winning television series about motor vehicles, mainly cars. More than 350 million viewers worldwide enjoy watching the presenters Jeremy Clarkson, James May and Richard Hammond with their quirky, humorous style. On the show they compare and test-drive cars, and organise all kinds of crazy races. In this programme, James May, possibly the slowest driver in Great Britain, challenges two freerunners to a race in Liverpool city centre. James has to drive six miles towards the Liver building in the city centre in a Peugeot 207. The two teenagers who try to beat him will run and jump over buildings, taking a much more direct route. Who do you think will get there first?

▶ **DVD VIEW**

3 Watch the DVD to see if you were right. Number the events in the correct order.

a) The men jump over James's car. *1*

b) James arrives at the Liver building. *5*

c) James checks his speed. *3*

d) The men jump over people eating at a restaurant. *2*

e) James stops at a red traffic light. *4*

4 Watch the DVD again. What does James May say? Complete the phrases.

1 As we can see, it's a very pretty car, but is it any _____?

2 I'm going to have a race, and it's against the latest French development in urban transport solutions: a couple of young men in silly _____.

3 Parkour: that's a French invention, and it involves that sort of thing. Running around the _____ leaping across buildings and benches.

4 Come on – we're not all _____!

5 I must have averaged ten or twelve miles an hour. I should _____.

6 They are not here. There's no sign of combat trousers man. I've _____!

speakout present a new machine

5A Work in pairs. Answer the questions and complete the tasks.

1 Write a list of jobs you have to do every day.

2 Are there any jobs on this list which you don't enjoy? Could a machine do them for you?

3 Invent a machine which would help you do one of these jobs. Draw a picture of your machine.

B ▶5.9 Listen to someone talking about a new machine. What is the invention? What does it do?

C Listen again and tick the key phrases he uses.

---

key phrases

I'm going to tell you about …

Basically, …

The way it works is this.

It works like this …

First of all, ….

Then/Also, you can …

All you have to do is …

Make sure you …

The best thing about it is that …

D Prepare and practise a short presentation about your new machine. Use your picture and the useful phrases to explain how it works.

E Present your ideas to the class. Which invention do you think is the best?

writeback an advertisement

6A Read the advertisement and answer the questions. What is the musical shower? How does it work?

The musical shower

If you like listening to music when you have a shower, then you might already have a stereo in your bathroom. But imagine how much better it would be if your shower-head also had an mp3 player attached to it.

It will download your favourite tunes, or radio programmes at night. Then in the morning, your shower will automatically play your favourite tunes for you. Try our musical shower.

There's no better way to start the day.

B Write an advertisement (advert) for your invention (120–180 words). Use the advert above and the key phrases to help.

TECHNOLOGY

1A Complete the words in sentences 1–6.

1 I don't agree with nu*clear* po*wer*. I think it's a dangerous way of making el*ectricity*

2 Sp*ace* tr*avel* is a waste of money. Why do we need to send people to the Moon?

3 I couldn't live without my wa*shing* ma*chine*. I hate having dirty clothes.

4 I had to have loads of va*ccinations* when I went to Malawi. I didn't want to get ill.

5 I think ge*netic* engi*neering* is a bit worrying. People might start to only want babies which are beautiful and intelligent.

6 Doctors give people too many an*tibiotics*. So now, some medicines don't work any more.

B Work in pairs. Choose three sentences you disagree with. Tell your partner why.

COMPARATIVES/SUPERLATIVES

2A Look at the information and complete sentences (1–4) using the prompts in brackets.

100 years ago in the US: the average life expectancy was forty-seven years, only 8 percent of homes had a phone, the maximum speed limit in most cities was 10 miles per hour, the average wage was 22 cents per hour, and 90 percent of all doctors had no college education.

1 100 years ago, people didn't live *as long* as they do today. (long)

2 It used to be *far more difficult* to communicate with people on the other side of the world. (far, difficult)

3 It is *far more expensive* for modern businesses to pay their employees. (far, expensive)

4 Nowadays, doctors are *much more educated* than they were in the past. (much, educated)

B Write sentences about how life was different in your country a hundred years ago and compare them with your partner.

QUESTIONS

3A Put the letters in italics in the correct order to find words related to questions.

1 In class last week, we *used discs* …
In class last week, we discussed …

2 I can't answer *nose quits* about … *questions*

3 I try to *pen rods* quickly to . *respond*

4 In the next few months I'm going to *took lion* … (2 words) *look into*

5 I recently *quid rein* about *inquire*

6 I *own red* what happened to … *wonder* *Andrea*

7 I enjoy a good *tea bed* especially about … *debate*

8 It would be interesting to *sit negative* a crime like . *investigate about kidnap*

B Complete the sentences so that they are true for you.

QUESTION TAGS

4A Complete the sentences with the correct question tag.

1 She wrote the first Harry Potter book in a café, *didn't she*?

2 This man, who is U2's singer, does a lot of humanitarian work, *doesn't he*? *Bono*

3 This actor has won an Oscar for *Forrest Gump*, *hasn't he*? *Tom Hanks*

4 He was probably the greatest basketball player in history, *wasn't he*? *Michael Jordan*

5 She lived in Calcutta, where she helped street children, but she wasn't from India, *was she*? *Mother Teresa de Cal*

6 He became Cuba's leader in 1959 and he didn't transfer power to his brother until 2006, *did he*?

7 Her full name is Madonna Louise Ciccone, *isn't it*? *Madonna*

8 Her husband was US President, but she probably won't try again to become President, *will she*?

B Who are these sentences about?

1 J K Rowling

C Work in groups. Play twenty questions. One student thinks of a famous person. The others ask tag questions to find out who it is.
A: You're a man, aren't you?
B: Yes.

POLITE REQUESTS

5A Match requests 1–5 with responses a)–e).

1 Excuse me, could you tell me where I can find the bathroom? *b*

2 Could you call me a taxi? *c*

3 Would you mind helping me with my bags? They're very heavy. *e*

4 Would you mind opening the window? *a*

5 Could you tell me what time the restaurant opens? *d*

a) Sure. It's very hot in here, isn't it?

b) Yes, of course. It's just over there, down the stairs and on the left.

c) Yes, of course. Where do you want to go to?

d) I'm not sure. Let me have a look. Yes, it opens at 11a.m.

e) Of course not. Let me take your suitcase.

B Work in pairs. Take turns to practise the conversations using the prompts below.

Student A:
- where / bathroom?
- call / taxi?
- shop / close?
- get / door?

Student B
- open / window?
- restaurant / open?
- help / shopping?
- tell / platform the train leaves from?

BBC VIDEO PODCAST
Watch people talking about problem-solving on ActiveBook or on the website.

Authentic BBC interviews
www.pearsonELT.com/speakout

66

REVIEW

1

learning

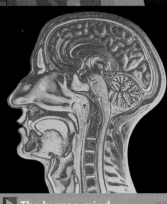

R1.1 FURTHER EDUCATION

▶ **GRAMMAR** | verb tenses; modal verbs; question forms   ▶ **PET SKILLS** | listen for specific information; listen for detail

LISTENING

1 Look at the photos and discuss. What opportunities are there for adult education in your country? If you could study a course at college, what would you like to learn?

2A Work in pairs. Match the sentence halves below to make useful tips for *Cambridge English: Preliminary* (PET) Listening Part 3.

' listening tips PET Part 3

1 Don't try to understand everything *b)*
2 Read the sentences before you listen and think about what kind of information is missing *a*
3 When you listen, check your predictions from before listening *e)*
4 Don't write too many words *c)*
5 Check your answers after listening *d)*

a) is it a number, date, noun, verb or adjective?
b) only listen for the missing information.
c) the answer will usually be one or two words, and never more than three.
d) small spelling mistakes are okay (e.g. *recepcion* for *reception*), but not for common spellings (e.g. *bank*).
e) the second time you listen, focus on the more 'difficult' answers.

B Work in pairs. Look at the exam task below and decide what type of information is missing in each gap. Is it a *date*, *name*, *time*, etc?

3A Read the exam task again and write your predictions for the missing information.

B ▶ R1.1 Listen and check.

Part 3

Questions 14–19

You will hear someone talking on the radio about an adult education centre.

For each question, fill in the missing information in the numbered space.

THE HOME OF LEARNING

Centre started in: (14) ....*1975*....

Other colleges only offered courses in English,
(15) ....*maths*.... and Science.

Courses include: *Local History, Building Relationships, How to Write a Computer* (16) ....*program*....

Location: 61 Camden Road, next to the (17) ....*bookshop library*....

Course times: evenings and (18) ....*weekend*....

Closing date for enrolment: (19) .... March

GRAMMAR   verb tenses

4A Complete the listening extracts with the correct tense: present simple, present continuous, past simple or past continuous.

1 Perhaps you *want/ are wanting* to know how to build perfect relationships with family and friends.
2 No other colleges *provided/ had provided* courses like this before.
3 They only *offered/ offer* more traditional courses ...
4 ... our college *was already offering/ had already offered* a range of interesting courses.
5 This year, we *extend/ are extending* our range of courses to include ...
6 Courses *have/ are having* flexible times, ...

B Look at audio script R1.1 on page 190 and check your answers.

5A Correct the mistakes in the following sentences.

1 I'm really wanting to go on holiday this year.
2 I was sitting where I usually sit in class today.
3 Last night I was staying at home and watching TV.
4 While I came to class today an interesting thing happened to me.
5 I'm really liking where I'm living at the moment.
6 I'm hating doing homework.

B Discuss. Which of the sentences are true for you? Ask questions to find out more information.

Studied /finished /was playing /entered

Part 2

Questions 8–13

You will hear someone enrolling for a course at an adult education centre.

For each question, put a tick (✓) in the correct box.

8 What is the man's job?

  A an author ☐

  B a journalist ✓

  C a web designer ☐

9 What does he say about his job?

  A it's less interesting than it sounds ✓

  B he sometimes works for 'big' newspapers ☐

  C it's glamorous ☐

10 What does he want to get from the course?

  A to learn to cook ☐

  B to improve his writing ☐

  C to make decisions more quickly ✓

11 When does he decide to study?

  A at the weekend ☐

  B on Thursday evening ✓

  C on Saturday afternoon ☐

12 How did he find out about the course?

  A an advertisement in the newspaper ☐

  B from someone he works with ✓

  C his sister ☐

13 What does the receptionist say about the course tutor?

  A he lives in America ☐

  B he has written several books on decision-making ✓

  C He's funny ☐

GRAMMAR modal verbs

6A Choose the correct alternative in the rules below about The Home of Learning.

I You *don't have to*/*mustn't* be an expert in any subject.

2 You *must*/*shouldn't* enrol before 1st March.

3 You *should*/*shouldn't* choose a course you'll find interesting.

4 You *have to*/*don't have to* enrol on the website.

5 You *have to*/*don't have to* study in the evenings.

B Change the sentences so they are true for the place where you study English.

C Work in pairs and compare your answers.

LISTENING

7A Read the exam tips for *Cambridge English: Preliminary* (PET) Listening Part 2. Decide if each one is before listening (B) or during listening (D).

listening tips PET Part 2

I The questions always follow the order of the information you hear, so if you can't answer a question the first time, leave it and move on to the others. *During*

2 You need to choose the option which answers the question exactly, so read the question carefully. *Before*

3 Underline key words in the questions, so that you'll know what to listen for. *Before*

4 Read the instructions carefully – you can get a lot of information here such as who is talking, and what they are talking about. *Before*

5 Listen to find the answer to the question, then choose which option, A, B or C, is closest. *During*

B Read the exam tips again. Then look at the exam task in Exercise 8 and answer questions 1–3.

I Who is talking?

2 What are they talking about? *A Job*

3 Underline the key words in each question.

C Work in pairs and compare your answers.

8 ▶ R1.2 Listen and complete the exam task.

GRAMMAR question forms

9A Correct the mistakes in each of the questions from the listening above.

I I can help you? *yes/no*

2 Which course do you want *to* join?

3 What *do* you do?

4 About what kind of things do you write?

5 Which do you want to get from the course?

6 How *want* you heard about us?

7 Who did us recommend? *Subject*

8 Who *does* teach the course? *Subject*

B Work in pairs and compare your answers. Is each question a *subject question* (S), *object question* (O), *yes/no question* (Y) or question *with* a preposition (P)?

C Look at the questions above again. Then write eight questions of your own to ask another student.

D Work in pairs. Take turns to ask and answer your questions.

how often Do Martin plays fotbal

69

READING

1A Underline the correct alternative to complete the exam tips for *Cambridge English: Preliminary* (PET) Reading Part 2.

❝ reading tips PET Part 2

1 There are eight texts and five people, so three of the texts are *not necessary/necessary*.

2 Make sure you match a different text to each person. The same text *can/cannot* be used twice.

3 Underline the *unimportant/important* parts of each text about each person, so you are clear about what information you are looking for.

4 Read the texts *twice/once*. The first time you read, match the people and the texts.

5 The second time, read the texts *quickly/more carefully* and check your answers – make sure the text matches *some/all* of the information about the person.

B Read the exam tips again. Then look at the exam task below and underline the most important information in each description.

C Work in pairs and compare your answers.

2 Do the exam task.

Part 2

Questions 6–10

The people below all want to choose a course at Goldingham College.
On the opposite page there are descriptions of eight courses.
Decide which course would be suitable for the following people.
For questions **6–10**, mark the correct letter (**A–H**) on your answer sheet.

6   Tom works as a manager and is very **competitive** and a **risk-taker**. He's also **independent** and is looking for a new challenge. *D*

7   Jill owns a local small business, but she's very **ambitious** and wants it to grow. She needs to promote her company cheaply, perhaps using technology.   *C*

8  Flori has two **moody** teenage children who cause her problems at home. She has also recently separated from her husband and moved to a new area where she doesn't know anyone. She isn't a very **good communicator**, but would like to meet people. *A*

9   Frances has recently retired from her job as a journalist, and is looking for a new hobby/interest. She is able to **think outside the box** and is very **motivated**. She loves reading books. *B*

10   John is very **hard-working** and ambitious. He's a **good leader** and is the director of a large company. However, his wife complains that he doesn't spend enough time at home with his children. *H*

A How to Build Great Relationships with Family and Friends
Problems at home? Feel like you should go out and enjoy yourself more? Then this course is for you. Learn how to build and maintain great long-lasting relationships with family and friends.

B Writing Successful Crime Fiction
You could be the next best-selling crime author with this new course. Learn how to build characters and stories into the next big novel. If you've got enough time and motivation on your hands, then we'll show you how to create stories with interest.

C Building your First Website
Learn how to build, design and launch your own website. Whether it's to help build your business, inform people or just for fun – this could be the course for you!

D How to Start a Small Business
Ever dreamed of being your own boss? Do you have that next great business idea? Then join this course and learn everything you need to know about starting your own business – and achieving success.

E How to Write Computer Programmes
If you're interested in how computers work, and you're not afraid of a bit of hard work, then come along and learn about programming. You'll learn the most important programming languages, and at the end of the course you'll write your very own programme!

F Make Better Decisions
If you hate making decisions, from deciding what shoes to wear, to what to spend your money on, it can be difficult to make fast, confident decisions. Sign up for this course and learn how to make decisions confidently and sensibly.

G Car Maintenance
Problems with your car (again)? Fed up with paying mechanics too much to repair it? Join this course and learn how to repair your car yourself. You'll practise basic skills in classes with real cars.

H Balancing Work and Life
This course is for people who have a hard time balancing the conflicting pressures of work and life. We'll show you how to get the most out of your job, while at the same time making sure you spend quality time with your family.

VOCABULARY personal qualities

3A Use the words/phrases in bold from the descriptions of the people in Exercise 2 to complete the sentences below.

1 We call her 'Super-Mavis', because she's so _har-working_. She works forty hours a week, and almost never has a holiday.

2 James is so _moody_____. You never know what you're going to get with him – happy one minute, then angry the next!

3 I work in marketing, and to succeed in this profession you really need to be able to _think outside_ – to consider all possibilities, however strange they might sound at first.

4 To succeed in management you need to be a _good leader_.

5 I like working from home, but you need to be really _motivated_ to make sure you do your work, and not just watch TV all day!

6 To succeed in business you have to really want to be better than everyone else. You need to be a _competitive_ person.

7 Working in a shop means I need to be a _good comunicator_.

8 I wish Richard was more _independent_, he always relies on me to help him.

9 My company is great – they regularly promote people to higher positions, as long as you show you are _ambicios_ and want to move up in the company.

10 I could never do dangerous sports, as I'm not really a _risk_____ _taker_, I like being safe too much!

B Compare answers with a partner. Which of the words/phrases best describe you?

4A Work in pairs. Match the words/phrases in the box to the courses in Exercise 2 where you would expect to see/hear them. There may be more than one answer.

get in touch	arrested	relatives	indecisive	boss
break down	take after	reboot	mother-in-law	
fugitive	gossip	team-mates	mystery	chat
motorbikes	kidnapped	related to		

B Discuss. Which of the courses would you choose to do? Why? What other courses would you like to study?

READING

5A Work in pairs. Which of the exam tips below are good (G) advice, and which are bad (B)?

reading tips PET Part 4

1 You don't need to read the whole text. B

2 You should read the text quickly first to get a general idea of what it's about. G

3 Remember questions 21 and 25 are always about the whole text. G

4 Watch out! The text is about opinions, not just facts. G

5 If you are not sure about a question, sit and think about it until you get the right answer. B

B Look at the exam tips again and change the bad advice to good advice.

6A Work in pairs. Read the text on page 180 and choose the best title.

1 The best course I've ever done.

2 A learning experience.

3 How to cook.

B Turn to page 180 and do the exam task.

VOCABULARY strong adjectives

7A Match the adjectives in bold from the text in Exercise 6 to the strong adjectives below.

1 boiling, _hot_
2 awful, _bad_
3 brilliant, _good_
4 tiny, _small_
5 furious, _angry_
6 freezing, _cold_
7 impossible, _difficult_
8 fascinating, _interesting_
9 delicious, _tasty_
10 beautiful, _pretty_
11 exhausted, _tired_
12 enormous, _big_

B Work in pairs. Which of the adjectives would you use to describe the following?

1 Your classroom
2 Your job/studies
3 English grammar
4 People from your country
5 The last place you went on holiday
6 A film you recently saw
7 our hometown
8 The climate in your country
9 What you had for lunch yesterday
10 How you feel today

DVD PREVIEW

1 Work in groups and discuss.

1 Did you do any sports as a child? Which ones?

2 Have you ever won a sporting competition?

3 Do you think it's a good idea for children to do sports? Why/Why not?

4 Are there any sports that are not good for children?

2 Read about the BBC documentary. How do you think the technique of visualisation can help a gymnast?

**BBC
The Human Mind**

In this documentary, Professor Winston looks at the human mind and how it works. He explores different areas such as how we learn, how our memory works, how we make friends and how we control our emotions. He also looks at how different techniques can help us to learn a new skill. Rebecca Owen is a gymnast and she needs to learn a new move. Can the technique of visualisation help her?

▶ DVD VIEW

3 Watch the DVD. Did visualisation help Rebecca? How?

4A Are the statements true (T) or false (F)?

1 Rebecca has been doing gymnastics since she was five years old.   F

2 She has already won an Olympic gold medal.   F

3 When she learns a new move, she watches other gymnasts do the move first.   T

4 Rebecca never gets nervous or thinks about what could go wrong.   F

5 Visualisation helps Rebecca to rehearse the move in her mind, without moving her muscles.   T

6 The process helps Rebecca to learn the move, and realise her dream of being chosen for the Olympic team.   F

B Watch the DVD again to check your answers. Correct the false statements.

C Discuss the questions.

1 Have you ever tried visualisation?

2 Do you think it could help you? Why/Why not?

speakout a learning experience

5A ▶ R1.3 **Listen to someone describing a recent learning experience and answer the questions.**

1 Why did he decide to learn this skill?
2 What exactly did he learn?
3 Was it difficult?
4 How did he feel in the end?

B Listen again and tick the key phrases you hear.

keyphrases

In the beginning …
This happened when …
The next thing I knew …
Well, …
So, …
Anyway, …
Before long …
In the end …
Finally, …

6A Think of a learning experience you have had. Use the prompts below to make notes.

• What did you learn?
• Why did you decide to learn it?
• What were the most difficult things to learn?
• What did you find easy?
• Would you do it again?

B Work in pairs. Take turns to describe your learning experiences.

writeback emails

7A Read the exam tips and the exam question below. Then decide which of the two emails is better and why.

writing tips PET Part 2

1 Make sure you include all of the information.
2 Keep it brief – don't write more than forty-five words.
3 Check your answers carefully for mistakes.

B Write your own answer to the exam question.

WRITTING

Part 2

Questions 6

You recently took an interesting course at an adult education centre in which you learnt a new skill.

Write a short email to the tutor, Laura. In your email, you should

• Thank the tutor for the course.
• Say what you liked best.
• Ask her what other courses she can suggest for you to take. *100 – 120 WORDS*

Write 35–45 words on your answer sheet.

Email 1

To: laura24@mailbank.com

Dear Laura   HOMEWORK
I am writing to thank you for the very interesting course I recently took with you. I really enjoyed it, and I know that everyone else on the course did too. I really liked your style of teaching, and the whole course was a really useful learning experience for me. I hope I have the opportunity to study with you again in the future. Thank you again.

James   *I look forward to hearing from you sincerely*

Email 2

To: laura24@mailbank.com

Dear Laura
Thank you for the recent course on web design you gave. I really liked your style of teaching and learnt a lot. Could you suggest any other courses I might like?

James

▶ **FUNCTION** | reaching agreement; introducing an opinion   ▶ **PET SKILLS** | interactive communication

REACHING AGREEMENT

1A Work in groups and discuss.

1 What do you like about the place where you study English?

2 What facilities does it have for students?

3 What other facilities would you like it to have?

4 What are the three most important facilities for a school to have?

B ▶ R1.4 Listen to two people doing the exam task below. Which of the questions above do they answer?

Part 2

Examiner: I'm going to describe a situation to you.

A local adult education centre has decided to spend some money on providing some leisure facilities for its students. Talk about which facilities the centre could provide, then decide which is the best idea.

Here are some picture prompts to help you.

C Listen again and tick the key phrases you hear.

keyphrases

I (really) feel that ...

The way I see things, ...

I suggest we think about ...

That's a good idea.

That's a good point.

That's fine/ok by me.

I'm not sure that I agree, actually.

I'm not sure that ... is a good idea.

How about ...?

Why don't we ...?

2A Work in pairs. Match the sentence halves below to make useful tips for the *Cambridge English: Preliminary* (PET) Speaking Part 2.

speaking tips PET Part 2

1 Listen carefully to the instructions for the task — b

2 Don't dominate the discussion d)

3 Speak to your partner a)

4 Listen carefully to what your partner says e

5 Give your opinion c

a) not the examiner.

b) so you know exactly what you need to do.

c) and explain why you think that.

d) you are tested on how well you interact with someone else in this part of the test.

e) so that you can link your answers to what he/she says.

B Listen to the exam task again. Do the speakers follow all of the tips above?

3 Work in pairs. Do the speaking task from Exercise 1B.

INTRODUCING OPINIONS

4A Work in pairs. Which of the exam tips below are good (G) advice, and which are bad (B)?

speaking tips PET Part 4

1 Don't ask your partner for their opinions, just try to say as much as possible. B

2 If you can't think of much to say at first, don't worry because the examiner will help you. G

3 If you can't think of examples from your own experience, G think of someone you know and describe theirs.

4 Ask the examiner for their opinion. B

5 If you agree or disagree with your partner, don't just say 'yes' or 'no', say *why* you agree or disagree. G

B Work in pairs. Change the bad advice above to good advice.

5 Underline the correct alternative to complete the phrases for introducing an opinion.

1 For me, the *more/most* important thing is ...

2 *I'd/I'll* have to say ...

3 *From/In* my opinion, ...

4 One thing I'd like to *say/tell* is ...

5 I *suppose/supposed* ...

6 It seems *to/for* me, that ...

7 I *think/'m thinking* ...

8 We *shouldn't/don't have* forget ...

6 Work in pairs. Do the exam task below.

Part 4

Examiner: Now, I'd like you to talk together about when and where you study, what things you use to help you study and if you prefer to study alone or with other people.

SPEAKING
> ❯ Talk about your emotions
> ❯ Discuss what you would do in different situations
> ❯ Introduce/Respond to news
> ❯ Talk about memorable moments

LISTENING
> ❯ Listen to a radio show about therapies
> ❯ Listen to conversations where people hear news
> ❯ Watch a BBC comedy about a man's terrible day

READING
> ❯ Read about basic emotions
> ❯ Read about a BBC programme *The People Watchers*

WRITING
> ❯ Write a letter of advice
> ❯ Write a website entry

BBC CONTENT
> 🔋 Video podcast: How are you feeling today?
> ◉ DVD: My Worst Week

UNIT 6

emotion

▶ **Feeling stressed?** p76

▶ **The people watchers** p79

▶ **That's great news!** p82

▶ **My worst week** p84

▶ **GRAMMAR** | zero and first conditionals ▶ **VOCABULARY** | -ing/-ed adjectives ▶ **HOW TO** | talk about your emotions

A   C   E   D   B

The Six Basic *Emotions*

According to BBC Focus Magazine, there are six basic emotions which we all experience, recognise in other people, and show in our own facial expressions. They are:

1 FEAR – probably the most basic emotion, fear activates a part in our brain which allows us to escape from danger.

2 ANGER – our ancestors used this emotion to try and deal with a problem rather than run away from it.

3 DISTRESS – loss or tragedy prompt a feeling of sadness. This often results in tears, a lump in the throat and a feeling of heaviness in the chest. See a sad person and you may feel sad, too.

4 JOY – the simplest things can induce this, like a kind word, or a sunny day. This is the most positive emotion and a great motivator as we will actively try to repeat activities which bring us joy.

5 SURPRISE – life is unpredictable, so surprise is a useful emotion. When something surprising happens to us, we raise our eyebrows to open our eyes wider, to allow us to see what is happening.

6 DISGUST – we will naturally feel disgust at certain objects and smells (like the smell of rotten food). We move away from these things (which may carry disease) so this emotion protects us.

SPEAKING

1A Look at photos A–F. What emotions do you think these people are feeling? Why are they feeling them?

B Read the text and match photos A–F with the emotions.

C When was the last time you felt these emotions? Give some examples.

VOCABULARY   -ing/-ed adjectives

2A Work in pairs and complete the questions.

1   What makes you angry or **annoyed**?
2   What sorts of things do you find **relaxing**?
3   Do you enjoy spending time alone, or do you get **bored**?
4   Is there anything you are **frightened** of?
5   What kinds of things make you **worried**?
6   Have you ever been really **embarrassed**?
7   What makes you feel **exhausted**?
8   What sorts of things do you find **confusing**?
9   When was the last time you were **shocked** by something? What was it?
10 Do you find your job/hobbies **satisfying**?

B Look at the quiz again and answer the questions.

1   Which ending is used to talk about feelings: -ed or -ing?
2   Which ending is used to talk about the cause of feelings: -ed or -ing?

C Complete the sentences with the correct form of the adjectives above. Remember to use -ed or -ing endings.

1   It's very __worrying__ watching the news at the moment. I think there's going to be another war.
2   I'm going to bed. I'm __exhausted__ because I've been working late every night this week.
3   My face went bright red when I realised what I'd said. It was really __embarrassing__
4   I can't watch sport on television. It's so _____ that I just go to sleep.
5   I don't understand the grammar. I find the rules very __confusing__
6   I go to yoga every week, because it makes me feel so __relaxed__.

D Choose two sentences above and make them true for you. Compare your ideas with a partner.

▶ page 169 **VOCABULARYBANK**

F

LISTENING

3 ▶ 6.1 Read the definition and listen to the radio programme. Answer the questions.

therapy treatment of a physical or mental illness, often without the use of drugs

1 Which two therapies does the programme talk about? distraction / Laugh terapy

2 The therapies are used in different situations. What situations are mentioned in the programme? Anger, stressed, place ful of cars / people go around people and act nice and funny

4A Are the statements true (T) or false (F)?

1 Eight out of ten people have trouble controlling their anger. F

2 With destruction therapy you use your anger to destroy something in a controlled way. F

3 If you think about a situation when you were angry, the therapy will be more enjoyable. F

4 In Spain, some companies pay for their workers to build hotels. F

5 In Mexico, they use destruction therapy in hospitals. F

6 Laughter therapy can help people to feel less pain. T

7 On average, children laugh 100 times a day, and adults laugh seventeen times. F -17

B Listen again to check. Correct the false statements.

C Discuss the questions.

1 Do you think destruction therapy and laughter therapy are good ideas? Why/Why not?

2 Would you try any of the ideas in the programme?

GRAMMAR zero and first conditionals

5A Look at four sentences from the programme. Which talk about a general situation (GS) and which talk about a specific/future situation (FS)?

a) When people get angry, they don't know what to do with their anger.

b) When we get there, I'll give you a hammer.

c) If I smash the car to pieces, will I feel better?

d) If people laugh about something, they feel better.

B Underline the correct alternative to complete the rules.

Rules:
1 Use the zero conditional (*If/When* + present simple + present simple) to talk about a *general/specific* situation (fact), or something which is always true.

2 Use the first conditional (*If/When* + present simple + *will/might/could*) to talk about a *general/specific* (possible) situation in the future.

▶ page 154 **LANGUAGEBANK**

6A ▶ 6.2 Listen and underline the alternative you hear.

1 If he shouts, *I get/I'll get* angry. O

2 If I see him, *I tell/I'll tell* him. 1ST

3 When they arrive, *we eat/we'll eat*. 1ST

4 When we get there, *I phone/I'll phone* you. 1ST

5 If I finish early, *I go/I'll go* home. O

B Listen again and repeat. Pay attention to the weak form of '*ll* /əl/ in the contraction *I'll* /aɪəl/ or *we'll* /wɪəl/.

PRACTICE

exam

7A Complete the sentences with the correct form of the verbs in brackets. Mark each sentence zero (0) or first (1st) conditional.

1 a) If I go running every day, it __makes__ (make) me feel good. O

   b) I'm feeling down. If I go for a run, I __'ll feel__ (feel) better. 1ST

2 a) When I finish reading this book, I __'ll give__ (give) it to you to read. 1ST

   b) When I __finish__ (finish) reading a book, I usually feel O disappointed.

3 a) I'm meeting my boss later. If I tell him about my new job, he __'ll get__ (get) angry. 1ST

   b) If I __get__ (get) angry, I take a deep breath and count to ten. O

4 a) If I'm tired, I __like__ (like) to eat in front of the television and go to bed early. O

   b) I'm planning to drive through the night. If I get tired, I __stop__ (stop) and sleep. 1ST

B Complete the sentences so that they are true for you. Compare your ideas with a partner.

When I get older ...I'll buy a house.

When my English gets better, I'll travel around the world.

If I'm happy, I usually ...listen to music.

When I get home this evening ...I'll read a book.

If I'm stressed, I usually …

Conditionals ~ { * Zero Conditional: Facts
\> * first conditional: Future prediction

SPEAKING

8A Work in pairs. What do you do in situations 1–5? Write three pieces of advice to give to someone in the same situation.

1 You're nervous about a job interview/exam.

2 You're annoyed with someone in your family.

3 It's the weekend and you're bored.

4 You're stressed about your work/studies.

5 You've got too many things to do.

B Work in groups and compare your ideas. Who has the best ideas?

VOCABULARY *PLUS* multi-word verbs

9A Match the following topics: *Clothes, Computers* and *Love and friendship* with paragraphs 1–3.

1_____: I met my ex-boyfriend when he **chatted me up** in a bar. We **got on** really well. We were together for two years and we were planning to **settle down**, but then I **went off** him!

hablar por interes
llevarse bien
terminar
y por malisar

2_____: You have to **scroll up** and then **click on** the arrow icon. And don't forget to **log off** before you **shut down**.

3_____: I love **dressing up** so when I **tried on** that purple suit, I thought it was perfect for my first day at work! So I arrived and the receptionist told me to **take off** my tie because everyone **dresses down** at the company!

speakout TIP

There are different ways to group multi-words verbs (including phrasal verbs) in your notebook. For example, you can group them by topic (e.g. weather, travel, work), or by preposition (e.g. multi-word verbs with *on, over, by*). Decide how you want to group them and then add the phrases to your notebook.

B Match the multi-word verbs in bold in Exercise 9A with the correct definition in the word webs. You will need to use the infinitive form.

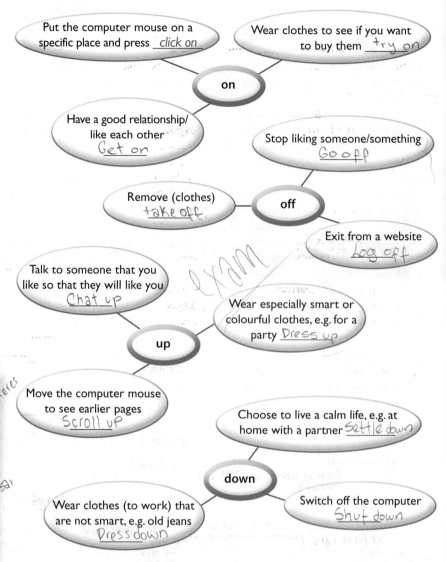

Put the computer mouse on a specific place and press _click on_

Wear clothes to see if you want to buy them _try on_

on

Have a good relationship/like each other _Get on_

Stop liking someone/something _Go off_

Remove (clothes) _take off_

off

Exit from a website _Log off_

Talk to someone that you like so that they will like you _Chat up_

exam

Wear especially smart or colourful clothes, e.g. for a party _Dress up_

up

Move the computer mouse to see earlier pages _Scroll up_

Choose to live a calm life, e.g. at home with a partner _Settle down_

down

Wear clothes (to work) that are not smart, e.g. old jeans _Dress down_

Switch off the computer _Shut down_

10A Look at the dictionary definitions below and answer the questions.

1 Which verb needs an object? _shut down / try on_

2 Which verb does not need an object? _Shut down / get on_

3 Which verb can be followed by another preposition? _get on_

> **try** sth ↔ **on** *phr v* to put on a piece of clothing to find out if it fits or if you like it: *Can I try these jeans on, please?*

> *can't separate*
> **get on** *phr v* 1 *Br E* if people get on, they have a friendly relationship: + **with** *She doesn't get on with my mum very well.*

> **shut down** *phr v* if a company, factory, machine etc shuts down, or if you shut it down, it stops operating: *Hundreds of local post offices have shut down.* | **shut** sth ↔ **down** *Did you shut the computer down?*

Can seperate

B Use the dictionary definitions to help you decide which sentences are possible. Mark the sentences with a tick or a cross.

1 I **tried** the suit **on** / I **tried on** the suit.

2 I **get on** really well with Simon / I **get** Simon **on** really well.

3 You need to **shut down** the computer / You need to **shut** the computer **down**.

C Choose 3–4 verbs from above and write your own example sentences. Use a dictionary to help. Then compare them with a partner's.

▶ page 169 **VOCABULARYBANK**

▶ **GRAMMAR** | second conditional   ▶ **VOCABULARY** | collocations   ▶ **HOW TO** | give advice in hypothetical events

IF you wanted to persuade someone to dress up as a tree in public, what would you do? If you wanted to raise money for charity on the streets, who would you ask to help you? What would you do if you wanted to sell cakes and nobody was buying them? What would you do if you needed to think creatively but didn't have any ideas?

One thing you could do is watch a programme from the BBC series *The People Watchers*. The programme asks the question 'Why do we do what we do?' Through twenty episodes, Professor Richard Wiseman, two psychologists and a neuroscientist do experiments involving members of the public, secretly filming them with a hidden camera. The experiments show why we behave the way we do in everyday situations. If you wanted to know how to get a seat on a crowded train, stop people from jumping queues, get someone to do you a favour, work out if someone is lying, and get a complete stranger to lend you a mobile phone, you could find out by watching.

In one experiment, two of Wiseman's psychologists pretended to be cake-sellers. They stood at a stall on the street and tried to sell cakes for a pound each. No one bought any. So they did what shops do: they held a sale. But it wasn't a real sale. They pretended that one cake cost two pounds, and if you bought a cake, you would get another one free. People started buying! Later they told people that the cakes usually cost two pounds but they were doing a special deal and selling them for just one pound. Again, people bought the cakes. It seems that everyone loves the idea of a bargain even if they aren't really getting one.

Another experiment looked at 'experts' who aren't. Emma, a psychologist, pretended to be a hairdresser. While 'cutting' three people's hair, she talked like a hairdresser, saying all the right things, and dropped a few bits of fake hair. The three volunteers later said they were very happy with their haircuts. In reality, Emma hadn't cut any hair. Richard Wiseman's conclusion? People would do better if they didn't always listen to 'experts'. Instead, they should trust their own eyes.

In another experiment, Jack, a psychologist, had to persuade ordinary people to dress up as a tree. The trick was to 'start small'. First, Jack asked a man to wear a badge; then he asked him to wear a cap; and finally the tree suit. This, Wiseman says, is called 'The foot in the door technique': if you want a big favour from someone, first ask for a small favour!

READING

1A Work in pairs and discuss. What do you think 'people-watching' means? What professions need to be good at people-watching? Why?

B Read the article and check your ideas.

2A Work in pairs and answer the questions.
1 Who is in Professor Wiseman's team?
   2 psicologist and neuroscientis 1
2 What question does the programme answer?
   Why do we do what we do?
3 Why did people suddenly start buying the cakes?
   love the idea of a bargain
4 How much hair did Emma cut?
   nothing
5 What is 'The foot in the door technique'?
   If you want a big favour, first ask of a small favour

B Read the article again. Make notes under headings 1–3.
1 People involved in the programme
2 Situations
3 Conclusions from the experiments

C Work in pairs and take turns to explain the article using your notes.

VOCABULARY verb–noun collocations

3A Match verbs 1–7 with nouns a)–g).

1 hold g)	a) money (for something)
2 raise a)	b) experiments
3 do b)	c) a programme
4 get (f)	d) hair
5 jump (e)	e) a queue ¬ cola de personas
6 cut d)	f) a seat
7 watch c)	g) a sale

B Which do you do:
1 to sell something cheaply? *hold a sale*
2 to avoid standing up in a train/bus/waiting room, etc.? *get a seat*
3 to help a charity? *raise money*
4 to be informed or entertained? *watch a programe*
5 to make someone look more beautiful? *cut hair*
6 to obtain new scientific information? *do expeeriments*
7 to avoid waiting in a long line (for example, to get tickets)?
   jump a queue

GRAMMAR second conditional

4A Read a review of *The People Watchers*. Why does the reviewer like the programme?

Pick of the month

My own favourite series this month? *The People Watchers*. Presented by Professor Richard Wiseman and his rather attractive psychologist friends, the show asks some very interesting questions. <u>If no one saw you, would you take something without paying for it?</u> <u>How close to someone would you stand if you didn't know them?</u> It's all good stuff, but <u>maybe the programme could be even better if we heard from more experts.</u> Unfortunately, for most of the series, we only hear Professor Wiseman's voice. And <u>it would also be nice if we had more statistics.</u> Some of the experiments using hidden cameras show only one or two people in action – not enough to make big conclusions about human nature. But overall, this is good TV: light, easy on the eye, and fun.

B Look at the four underlined sentences above and complete the rules with the words in the box.

| would | could | hypothetical | imaginary | past |

Rules:
1 We use the second conditional to describe a _imaginary_ or _hipothetical_ situation.
2 In the *if* clause, we use the _past_ simple.
3 In the result clause, we use _would_ or 'd.
4 If we are not sure of the result, we can also use _could_.

C Find other examples of the second conditional in the article on page 79.

➡ page 154 **LANGUAGEBANK**

5A ▶ 6.3 Listen and complete the conversations.
1 A: What _would_ _you_ _do_ if your laptop exploded?
   B: If my laptop exploded, I'd call for help!
2 A: What would you do if you lost your house keys?
   B: If I lost my house keys _I'd_ climb through the window!
3 A: How would you feel if your car broke down?
   B: If my car broke down, I _woudn't be_ happy!

B Listen again and answer questions 1–3.
1 How do we pronounce *would* in the question form?
2 How do we pronounce *would* in fast spoken English in positive sentences?
3 How do we pronounce the negative of *would*?

O ~ General truth — more real
1st ~ Specifics predictions
2do Conditional: Imaginary Situations
If Past simple , would

PRACTICE

6 Complete the sentences with the correct form of the verbs in the box.

| ~~write~~ ~~work~~ ~~do~~ ~~can~~ ~~learn~~ ~~fail~~ ~~have~~ ~~not/rain~~ ~~see~~ (x2) ~~go~~ ~~like~~ ~~not/have~~ ~~not/be~~ ~~not/work~~ ~~tell~~ |

1 I would _write_ my autobiography if I _didn't have_ so much work to do.
2 If I _had_ enough time, I _would Learn_ Japanese.
3 If I _can_ go anywhere in the world, I _go_ to the Caribbean.
4 If it _didn't rain_ so much, I _like_ to live in Norway.
5 You _wouldn't be_ very happy if you _fail_ the exam.
6 Who _would you work_ for if you _didn't work_ for our company?
7 What _would you do_ if you _saw_ a UFO?
8 If you _saw_ a friend stealing something, would you _tell_ the police?

7A Complete the sentences about your classmates.
1 If _Nelida_ could go anywhere, he/she _Africa_
2 If _Nelida_ wasn't so busy, he/she _play piano_
3 If _Johano_ was able to speak to the President of his/her country, he/she _organize more the garbage_
4 If _Nelida_ knew how to, he/she _travel with family or friends_
5 _Nelida_ would feel very happy if _buy a house_
6 _____'s life would be easier if …
7 _____ wouldn't like it if …
8 _____ wouldn't care if …

B Ask your classmates if your sentences are true.

SPEAKING

8A Work in pairs and discuss. What would you do if …
1 you saw a very young child smoking in the street?
2 you found a bag of money in the street?
3 you inherited a house on the other side of the world?
4 you discovered that one of your colleagues was taking drugs?
5 you heard someone saying bad things about your friend?
6 one of your relatives asked to live with you?
7 someone asked you to take part in a TV programme?
8 you saw someone stealing bread in the supermarket?

It depends. If they looked like they were hungry, I might not say anything.

B Tell other students your ideas. Which dilemmas were the most difficult?

WRITING a letter of advice

9 Look at the photo and discuss. What do you do when you need advice? Would you ever consider getting professional help, going online or asking a relative/friend/experienced older person? What does it depend on?

10A Read the dilemma. What do you think the person should do?

> My cousin has asked me to lend her some money to start an internet business. **She is intelligent and reliable, and I like her, but she is only twenty years old. Also, I know nothing about internet businesses. Should I lend her the money?**

B Read the responses. Which do you agree with? Why?

YES

You have the money. She has the ideas, the energy and the expertise. If I were you, I wouldn't worry about her age. As a young person, in all likelihood she knows more about the internet than you do. And she isn't asking for your advice, only your money. So, come on - you're a member of her family. What do you have to lose apart from a bit of money? And if you're really worried, maybe tell her you want 50% of the money back within two years. If she's reliable, you'll probably get it.

NO

So your cousin wants money. Perhaps you really trust her, but aged twenty, she probably doesn't have much experience in business. If I were you, I'd ask a lot of questions first. I'd find out how much research she has done, how well she knows the market, and who else is involved. It's possible that she will be successful, but over 90% of new companies disappear within the first year. The other thing is time. In all probability, it'll take her a few years to start making a profit. Can you wait that long to get your money back? And think about this: if it wasn't your cousin asking, would you lend the money?

C Tick the things a letter of advice might include. Compare your ideas with other students.

1 a short summary of the situation
2 a few sentences describing your qualifications
3 some ideas about what the person should do
4 some background information explaining your ideas
5 a question for the reader to think about

D Find the things you ticked in the letters of advice in Exercise 10B.

LEARN TO qualify what you say

11A Look at the words/phrases in the box. Find and underline these in the letters of advice in Exercise 10B. Then answer the questions.

> maybe   probably   perhaps   in all likelihood
> It's possible that   in all probability

1 Which words/phrases mean 'there is a strong possibility'?
2 Which two phrases have the same meaning?

B How do you feel about statements 1–4? Qualify them, using the words and phrases above.

1 As life in the twenty-first century gets more complex, people will have more complex problems.
2 In the future, machines will 'read' our emotions and 'know' if we have a problem.
3 In the future, most young people will prefer to talk to strangers online about their problems rather than have face-to-face conversations with family and friends.
4 I'd never write to a problem page if I needed advice.

Most people ask their family and friends for advice. They don't need to write to problem pages.

*Most people **probably** ask their family and friends for advice. **In all likelihood**, they don't need to write to problem pages.*

12A Read the problem below. Work with other students and think of possible solutions.

> I have a problem. **My twenty-six-year-old brother has always loved football, but now it's becoming an obsession. He goes to watch matches every weekend even though the tickets are expensive and he doesn't have much money. At his house, he sometimes watches three or four matches on TV a day! His only friends are football fans, and his last girlfriend broke up with him because of his obsession. I want to help him, but he's older than me and he thinks it's none of my business what he does in his free time. Please can you give me some advice?**

B Write a letter of advice to the letter writer above.

C Work in groups and take turns to read your letters. If you were in the person's situation, which letter would you like to receive?

▶ **FUNCTION** | giving news ▶ **VOCABULARY** | life events ▶ **LEARN TO** | respond to news

VOCABULARY life events

1A Look at phrases 1–12. Are they good news (G), or bad news (B)?

G 1 pass your exams 7 fail a test B
B 2 have an accident 8 split up with a partner B
G 3 be offered a job 9 win a competition/match G
G 4 get a place at university 10 get promoted G
G 5 get engaged/married 11 get a degree G
B 6 lose your job/money 12 buy a house G

B Work in pairs and answer the question. Have any of the things above happened recently to you, or anyone you know?

2A Work in groups and discuss. What is the best way to give bad news?

B Complete the article with the phrases in the box. Does it mention any of your ideas?

> give a reason tone of voice prepare your listener
> making people too upset bad news good news

Good ways to give bad news

It's easy to give someone good news, but what about when you have some ¹bad news to tell? Are there any good ways to give bad news without ²making ? The following steps might help:
(people too upset)

• Say something positive: Try to start or end the conversation with some ³good news, so that it's not all bad. For example, 'You did very well in the interview, but unfortunately we've given the job to somebody else.'
• ⁴prepare your listener for the news: Use phrases to introduce what you're going to say, like 'Unfortunately, …', 'I'm really sorry, but …' or 'I'm afraid I've got some bad news.' This gives the listener time to prepare for what you're going to say.
• Try to ⁵give a reason People like to know why things go wrong. Try to explain the decision: If someone doesn't get the job, can you explain why? If you have to cancel an arrangement, try to give a reason.
• Use a soft ⁶tone of voice: If you're giving someone bad news, try to use a soft, calm voice to make you sound kind. Say things to show you understand, like, 'I'm really sorry.' or 'I know this must be disappointing.'

C Read the article again. Do you agree with the advice? Why/Why not?

A ·travel C lottery

B D MANAGER

1. not invited/wedding ·hot holiday

FUNCTION giving news

3A ▶ 6.4 Listen to seven conversations. Match the conversations to pictures A–G.

B Look at the pictures again. What is the good news or bad news in each situation?

4A Look at the phrases the speakers use to introduce their news. Listen again and write the conversation number next to each phrase.

good news	I've got some good news (for you). 5
	I'm really pleased to tell you . 5
	You'll never guess what. 3
bad news	Bad news, I'm afraid. 7
	I'm sorry to have to tell you, but . 2
	I'm afraid / Unfortunately, . 712
	I'm afraid I've got some bad news . 4
	There's something I've got to tell you. 5
good or bad news	You know …? Well, …
	I've/We've got something to tell you. 1

B ▶ 6.5 Listen to some of the phrases in the table again. Underline the stressed syllables.

C Listen again. Is the speaker's voice high or low for good news? Is it high or low for bad news? Practise the phrases.

▶ page 154 **LANGUAGEBANK**

5 Put the words in the correct order to make sentences.

1 news / afraid / I'm / bad – / the / we / match / lost
Bad news, I'm afraid we lost the match
2 to / I'm / the / you / tell / got / pleased / you / really / job / that
I'm really pleased to tell you that you got the job
3 going / I'm / to / late / we're / be / afraid
I'm afraid, we're going to be late
4 got / you / there's / tell / I've / to / something
There's something I've got to tell you
5 never / what / you'll / guess
you'll never guess what
6 got / news / I've / for / good / you / some
I got some good news for you
7 was / concert / the / unfortunately, / cancelled
Unfortunately the concert was cancelled
8 lost? / you / the / we / cat / know / we / again / found / him / well,
you know we lost the cat? well we found him

Handwritten annotations on image:
Inpress interview
offer someone else the job
2.
4
↑ bad↑ X
friend's car
(3) he's safe

LEARN TO respond to news

6 How do the speakers respond to the news? Complete the conversations with the words in the box.

> ~~Joking~~ sorry ~~lucky~~ ~~annoying~~ pleased
> ~~Congratulations~~ ~~done~~ shame terrible

1 W: We're getting married.
  M: Wow! That's fantastic. _Congratulations_!

2 W: We've offered the job to someone else.
  M: Oh. That's a _shame_. Thanks, anyway.

3 W1: I've just won some money on the Spanish lottery.
  W2: You're _joking_? … How much did you win?
  W1: 1,000 euros.
  W2: You _lucky_ thing!

4 M1: I've crashed the car.
  M2: Oh no. That's _terrible_.

5 W: They've offered me a place.
  M: That's wonderful news. Well _done_! I'm so _pleased_ for you.

6 W1: Steve's lost his job.
  W2: Oh no. That's awful. I'm really _sorry_ to hear that.

7 M: I've got too much work to do.
  W: Oh no. That's really _annoying_.

speakout TIP

Exaggerate! Sometimes when you speak in a foreign language, your intonation can sound flat. This can mean that you don't sound as polite or enthusiastic as you want to. Try to exaggerate the intonation pattern to sound enthusiastic or concerned. Say the responses in Exercise 7A with an exaggerated intonation.

7A ▶ 6.6 Listen to responses 1–4. Notice the intonation patterns.

1 Congratulations!

2 That's fantastic news!

3 That's a shame.

4 That's awful.

B Practise saying the phrases with the correct intonation.

C ▶ 6.7 Mark the main stress on sentences 1–6. Which ones use a higher voice? Listen and check, then listen and repeat.

1 You lucky thing!

2 That's terrible.

3 Well done.

4 I'm so pleased for you.

5 That's really annoying.

6 That's awful. I'm really sorry to hear that.

SPEAKING

8A Work in pairs and role-play the situation. Student A: you interviewed your partner for a job last week. You have asked him/her back to the office to give them the job. Student B: you were interviewed for a job last week, but since then you have been offered a better job with another company, and you have decided to accept their offer.

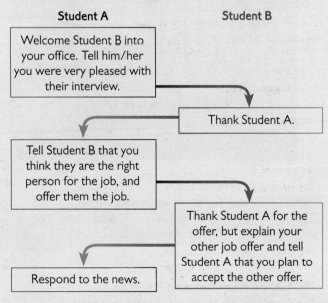

Student A — Student B

Welcome Student B into your office. Tell him/her you were very pleased with their interview.

Thank Student A.

Tell Student B that you think they are the right person for the job, and offer them the job.

Thank Student A for the offer, but explain your other job offer and tell Student A that you plan to accept the other offer.

Respond to the news.

B Work in pairs. First, think of three pieces of good/bad news to tell your partner. Then take turns to give and respond to each other's news using expressions in Exercises 4 and 6.

DVD PREVIEW

1 Read about a BBC comedy. Why is this week supposed to be special for Howard? What's the problem?

BBC My Worst Week

The week before a wedding can be a difficult time, but for publisher Howard Steele, marrying the beautiful Mel, it becomes a complete **nightmare**. Everything that can possibly go wrong does go wrong, even though Howard tries desperately to do the right thing. During the week, Howard accidentally kills his in-laws' dog, puts Mel's granny in hospital, and loses the wedding ring (which has been in the family for many generations) twice. It's not a good start, and what should have been a very special week soon turns into the worst week of his life.

▶ DVD VIEW

2 Watch the DVD then number the events in the correct order.

a) Mel calls Howard in his office. _4_

b) Eve tries to take the ring off using soap in the bathroom. _6_

c) Howard arrives in his office and shows his secretary, Eve, the ring. _2_

d) Mel reminds Howard to collect the ring. _1_

e) The ring gets stuck. _5_

f) Eve bursts into tears, so Howard lets her try the ring on. _3_

3A Who says this: Howard (H), Eve (E) or Mel (M)?

1 'Don't forget the ring.' _M_

2 'It's been in Mel's family for 150 years. They have this rather charming tradition where they (uh) pass it down from generation to generation.' _H_

3 'I always wanted a fairy-tale wedding of my own.' _E_

4 'Try it on. See what it feels like.' _H_

5 'When the vicar asks me to put the ring on my fiancée's finger, it would be very nice if my secretary was not attached.' _H_

6 'No, really – it's stuck.' _E_

7 'I'll get a plumber.' _E_

B Watch the DVD again to check.

4A Complete the sentences about how the characters felt.

1 Mel is worried about _the plans of the wedding_

2 Eve is impressed when she sees _the ring_

3 Eve gets upset about _she doesn't had a wedding_

4 Howard is annoyed when …

5 Eve is anxious about _the ring is stuck_

6 Howard is shocked when _the ring fall on the_

B Compare your ideas with another student.

speakout memorable moments

5A ▶ 6.8 Listen to a man talking about a special weekend. Which of the following statements is <u>not</u> true?

1 His brother organised a surprise weekend away.

2 They went on a boat trip to a lighthouse, and slept there.

3 They went shopping with his brother's money.

4 They went to the theatre and then ate an expensive five-course meal.

B Listen again and tick the key phrases you hear.

keyphrases

One of the most memorable moments/events in my life was …

The happiest moment of my life was when …

It all started one day when …

I was so embarrased/delighted/shocked/terrified when …

I had absolutely no idea.

The funniest thing that ever happened to me was …

(The) next thing/morning …

That weekend/day is one of my happiest memories.

C Choose one of the following questions. Plan your answer using some of the key phrases.

1 What are your strongest memories of your childhood?

2 Have you ever done anything you regret?

3 What's the most embarrassing/funniest/scariest thing that has ever happened to you?

4 What do you remember about the house you lived in as a child?

5 Can you remember a time when you felt very proud?

6 What is your happiest memory?

D Work in groups and tell your stories.

writeback a website entry

6A Read the website entry. What kind of things do people write about on this website? What was special about Ross's car journey?

100 lives: real life, real people, real experiences

Join people from around the world who want to share their stories and experiences. Read true personal stories, chat and get advice from the group

Q: What's your happiest memory?

One of my happiest memories is of a car journey I took with some friends from Canada down to California nearly fifteen years ago. It was a clear night with a full moon, and as we drove we listened to music, and talked. The roads were empty, and there was a wonderful sense of freedom and adventure. We were driving away from our families and everything we knew so well. We drove with the windows open and I can remember the warmth of the wind on my face, and the sound of the music playing out to the open skies. Even now, when I hear any of the songs on that album, it takes me straight back to that journey, and that feeling. I hope it never goes away.

Ross, Calgary

B Choose another question from Exercise 5C and write your story (150–200 words). Use the website entry above and the key phrases to help.

-ING/-ED ADJECTIVES

1A Work in pairs. Use adjectives to describe how you feel in the following situations.

1   you lose your bus/train ticket

2   you get lost at night in a foreign city

3   you wait for a delayed flight

4   you forget someone's name (when you should know it)

B Write situations for the adjectives in the box.

annoying   worried   boring
embarrassing   relaxing
confusing   exhausted
frightening   satisfied

annoying – When you discover your phone has run out of power, it's …

worried – My exams are tomorrow. I'm really …

C Work in pairs. Take turns to read your situations. Don't say the adjectives they describe. Can your partner guess the adjective?

ZERO AND FIRST CONDITIONALS

2A Match 1–7 with a)–g) to make sentences.

1   If you drink too much coffee, b)

2   If you go to bed early, f)

3   If you go to bed late all the time, d)

4   If you listen to loud music when you study, c)

5   You won't get fit if you a)

6   If you don't like your job, g)

7   You'll have problems at work if you e)

a)   drive everywhere in your car.

b)   you won't sleep tonight.

c)   it's difficult to concentrate.

d)   you'll exhaust yourself.

e)   don't finish that report on time.

f)   you'll feel better in the morning.

g)   look for a new one.

B Look at the sentences in Exercise 2A. Can you think of other ways to complete them? Compare your ideas with a partner.

3 Work in pairs and take turns. Student A: write down three things you would like to achieve this year. Show your list to your partner. Student B: look at Student A's list and make *if/when* sentences to give advice.

A: one: find a new job   two: get fit three: improve my English

B: one: find a new job: If you look on the internet, you might find a new job.

VERB–NOUN COLLOCATIONS

4 Rearrange the letters in blue to complete the sentences with *watch/ hold/ raise/ do/ get/ cut.*

1   We should go to the concert early so we can est gates. *get seats*

2   They are going to heal roads to sell their old clothes. *hold a sale*

3   The schoolchildren decided to ease my from for cancer research. *raise money*

4   I'm going home early because I want to grammar two peath on TV. *watch a programme*

5   He gave up his job because he didn't want to opened term six on animals. *do experiments*

6   My cousin is shut car for a living. *cuts hair*

SECOND CONDITIONAL

5 Work in pairs. Student A: use an *if* clause with the phrases in your box. Student B: respond with the correct *would* clause from your box.

A

I/be/rich   there/be/no war
there/be/more hours in the day
I/have/more/energy
nobody/smoke   I/give up/coffee
can/paint/well

B

dance/all night   sleep/better
people/be/healthier
do/a portrait of you
give/money/charity
people/work/more
the world/be/peaceful

A: If I was rich …

B: I'd give some money to charity.

GIVING NEWS

6A Each conversation has two words missing. Write in the missing words. You may have to change the punctuation.

1   A: Bad news, *I'm* afraid.

    B: What's the matter?

    A: The computers aren't working.

    B: Not again! *that's* Annoying.

2   A: You'll never *guess* what.

    B: What?

    A: I got the job.

    B: Congratulations! That's *good* news.

3   A: I've got some good news *for* you.

    B: What is it?

    A: I've been promoted.

    B: Well. That's great news. *done*

4   A: I'm *sorry* to have to tell you, but I'm leaving the company.

    B: What? Why?

    A: The company has got problems, so they're reducing the number of managers.

    B: I'm sorry to *heard* that.

5   A: You *remember* that exam I did last week?

    B: Yes?

    A: Well, I passed.

    B: Congratulations! I'm so *pleased* for you.

B Work in pairs and practise the conversations.

BBC VIDEO PODCAST

Watch people talking about whether they are an optimist or pessimist on ActiveBook or on the website.

Authentic BBC interviews

www.pearsonELT.com/speakout

UNIT 7

UNIT 7

success

▶ The secret of success p88   ▶ The memory men   p91   ▶ Are you qualified?   p94   ▶ Water ski challenge   p96

SPEAKING

1A Work in pairs and read the quotes. What do they tell you about success? Do you agree or disagree?

> 'The difference between failure and success is doing a thing nearly right and doing a thing exactly right.'
> **Edward Simmons**

> 'Success doesn't come to you … you go to it.' **Marva Collins**

> 'The secret of success in life is for a man to be ready for his opportunity when it comes.'
> **Benjamin Disraeli**

B Write the names of three very successful people. Answer the questions.

1 How and why did these people become successful?

2 Do you think they have a special talent, or have they just been lucky?

3 What advice would you give to someone who wants to be as successful as these people?

VOCABULARY success

2A Complete sentences 1–8 with the phrases in the box.

> work hard (at something)   have a natural talent   focus on
> get better at   have the opportunity (to do something)
> believe in yourself   practise (something)   be a high achiever

1 You will never achieve anything, if you don't _work hard_ at it.
2 I don't _have a natural talent_ for languages. I find them difficult to learn.
3 If you _believe in yourself_ and your abilities, then you can achieve anything.
4 It's amazing what children can achieve if they _have the opportunity_ to try different skills.
5 If you want to develop any skill, you have to _practise_ regularly.
6 I'm sure she will _be a high achiever_. She is determined to do well at everything.
7 When I really want something, I try to _focus on_ my goal.
8 If you keep trying, you'll _get better at_ it. Don't give up!

B Find phrases above to match meanings 1–6.

1 be sure about your ideas/abilities _believe in yourself_
2 only think about one objective _focus on_
3 improve _get better at_
4 do something again and again _practise_
5 have the chance to do something _opportunity_
6 be successful in your work or studies _be a high achiever_

C Choose two of the phrases and make sentences which are true for you. Compare your ideas with a partner.

▶ page 170 **VOCABULARYBANK**

LISTENING

3A Read the introduction to an article about success. What do you think the secret of success is?

What is the secret of success?

BBC Focus Magazine investigates

What makes the most successful people on the planet different from the rest of us? If we were more like Albert Einstein or John Lennon, surely we could enjoy the same level of success they did. In truth, however, we pay too much attention to what high achievers are like, and not enough to where they come from and the opportunities they had along the way. In his new book, Malcolm Gladwell reveals that there is one factor – so obvious that it's right under our noses – that all successful people share ...

B ▶ 7.1 Listen to the radio programme to find out.

C Listen again and complete the summary.

In this new book, *The Outliers*, Gladwell argues that Beethoven, The Beatles and Bill Gates all have one thing in ¹ _comun_. They ² _practise_ what they do, and they practised a lot. In fact, Gladwell discovered that in order to be truly ³ _successful_ in anything, it is necessary to practise the ⁴ _skills_ for more than ⁵ _10 tausend_ hours. These people have done that which is why he believes they have been so ⁶ _successful_.

4A Are the statements true (T) or false (F)?

1 If we want to learn from Bill Gates' achievements, we need to look at where he came from and the opportunities he had. _T_

2 If you're going to be world-class at something, you need to have parents who are high achievers. _F_

3 The Beatles played all-night concerts in Hamburg, and this helped them to master their craft. _T_

4 Bill Gates got into computer programming, and through a fortunate series of events, he was able to do lots and lots of programming. _F_

5 Bill Gates had access to a computer at home during the 60s and 70s when computers were 'the size of rooms'. _T_

6 In order to be very successful, you need a very talented teacher, and enough money to pay for your tuition. _F_

B Listen again to check.

SPEAKING

5 Discuss the questions in groups.

1 Do you have a special skill/interest? How many hours do you think you have spent practising it? (10,000 hours is approximately ten hours per week for twenty years.)

2 Do you agree that if you practise something enough, you can become world-class at it, or do you think you need to have a natural talent?

3 What things have you been successful at? Why?

GRAMMAR present perfect simple versus continuous

6A Read sentences a)–e). Underline examples of the present perfect simple and circle examples of the present perfect continuous.

a) Martina's been playing tennis since she was three years old.

b) She's been going to ballet lessons since she was a child.

c) I've known Max for years.

d) How long have you been studying French?

e) He's always enjoyed playing sport.

B Match sentences a)–e) with rules 1–3. Some sentences will match more than one rule.

Rules:

1 Use the present perfect continuous to emphasise that an action has been long and repeated.

2 With state verbs (e.g. *like, love, understand, remember, know,* etc.), we cannot use the present perfect continuous, so we use the present perfect simple.

3 We often use *for, since* and *How long have you ...?* with the present perfect simple and the present perfect continuous.

➡ page 156 **LANGUAGEBANK**

PRACTICE

7A Complete the sentences with the present perfect simple or continuous form of the verbs in brackets.

1 I ____ (write) books for years, but I haven't written a best-seller yet!

2 They ____ (play) music for hours! I can't get to sleep.

3 I ____ always ____ (love) art, but I'm not very good at it.

4 She ____ (not study) a lot because she's been ill.

5 How long ____ you ____ (know) Sheila?

6 I ____ (learn) Mandarin for two years.

7 I ____ (have) my own car since I was twenty.

8 Will Smith? I've never ____ (hear) of him.

B ▶ 7.2 Listen to check. Notice the pronunciation of *have*. Is it strong or weak? Practise saying the sentences.

8A Make questions with the prompts.

1 how long / you / know / best friend?

2 how long / you / do / your hobby?

3 how long / you / study / English?

4 how long / you / live where you live now?

5 how / you / spend / your days off recently?

B Work in pairs. Take turns to ask and answer the questions above. Think of two or more follow-up questions for each question.

A: How long have you known your best friend?

B: For about fifteen years.

A: Where did you meet?

VOCABULARY *PLUS* verb phrases

9A Choose the correct preposition to complete the verb phrases in sentences 1–7.

1 I don't **have a lot in common** *to/with/for* my sister.

2 We don't **have access** *with/at/to* the internet at work.

3 She's **world-class** *in/for/at* playing the violin.

4 He works very hard. He **puts** *in/to/with* a lot of hours.

5 I've got a lot to **think** *with/for/about* at the moment.

6 The film **picks up** *on/to/at* the difficulties people experienced during the war.

7 She **has a talent** *about/for/in* finding a bargain.

B Add the verb phrases to the correct group below.

1 agree		5 depend	
argue	with	rely	on
2 worry		6 look	
complain	about	laugh	at
3 belong		7 succeed	
pay attention	to	believe	in
4 pay			
wait	for		

speak**out** TIP

There are many verbs in English which use prepositions. Keep a record of which prepositions go with which verbs in your notebook. Can you add any more phrases you know to the diagram in Exercise 9B?

C Write three questions using the verb phrases above.

*Do you **argue with** anyone in your family?*

*What kind of things do you **worry about**?*

D Work in pairs. Ask and answer your questions.

➡ page 170 **VOCABULARYBANK**

VOCABULARY ability

1 Work in pairs. Take turns to ask and answer as many questions as you can about the things you are good/bad at.

When did you start playing the drums? How often do you play? Do you …

2A What do the phrases in bold mean?

1 He**'s an expert in** Italian art. He's written several books about it.

2 He**'s gifted at** painting. He had his first exhibition when he was sixteen.

3 She **has** a lot of **ability** as a dancer. I think she could become a professional.

4 She's the most **skilful** footballer I've ever seen. She can play in any position.

5 He **has an aptitude for** maths. He learns new formulas very quickly.

6 He is a really **talented** musician. He can play six instruments.

7 I'm **hopeless at** geography. I failed my exam three times.

8 I'm **useless at** ball sports. I can't play any.

B ▶ 7.3 Look at the words in bold above. Then listen to the sentences from above and answer the questions.

1 Which parts of the words in bold are stressed? Underline the stressed part.

2 Which five words have two syllables? Where do we normally put the stress on two-syllable words?

C Listen again and repeat the sentences. Focus on the stressed parts.

3A Write the name of:

• an expert in your own area of interest.

• someone in the class who is talented.

• a gifted musician.

• something you are useless at.

• something you have an aptitude for.

B Work in groups. Ask each other to explain what they wrote and why.

READING

4A Work in pairs. Look at the photos opposite and on page 177, then discuss. The men in the photos have been called 'The human camera' and 'The human computer'. What special abilities do you think they have?

B Student A: read the text opposite to see if your ideas are mentioned. Student B: turn to page 177.

The human camera

There is no one quite like Stephen Wiltshire. Born in 1974, Stephen was always different. As a child, he couldn't make friends. In fact, he talked to nobody, showed no interest in school subjects and wasn't able to sit still. Stephen was diagnosed as autistic. He didn't learn fully to talk until he was nine years old and he didn't manage to pass his exams, but he found one thing he liked doing: drawing. Art became his way to communicate.

He started by drawing funny pictures of his teachers, but soon began to draw buildings. His eye for detail was perfect. He could see a building just once and remember everything about it. In 1987, aged twelve, he saw a train station in London called St Pancras. Hours later, in front of TV cameras, he managed to draw this complicated building, with the time on the station clock saying 11.20, the exact time when he was there. The drawing showed every detail perfectly.

Since that television programme made him famous in the UK, many great things have happened to Stephen. He has become a well-known artist, published four books of his drawings, taken helicopter rides above the world's great cities – including London, Rome, Hong Kong and New York – and drawn amazing pictures of them, and opened his own art gallery, where he now works, in London.

His drawings are incredibly accurate – he always manages to draw everything in the right place – but also beautiful to look at. In 2006, he was given an MBE by the Queen of England for services to art.

* autistic /ɔːˈtɪstɪk/ *adj* – having a mental condition that makes it hard for someone to understand other people and form relationships

* MBE – Member of the British Empire, an award given by the Queen for outstanding achievements

C Student A: read the text above again and answer the questions.

1 How was his behaviour different from other children's?

2 What special talents does he have?

3 How did the public learn about his special talents?

4 What country/countries has he been to and what did he do there?

5 What has he published?

6 What is his 'job' now?

D Tell your partner about your text. Use questions 1–6 to help.

mf = base form (handwritten)

GRAMMAR present and past ability

5 Read sentences 1–9. Which describe present ability and which describe past ability? Which three sentences are negative?

1 If you tell Daniel your birth date, he <u>can</u> tell you what day of the week you were born on. *present ability*

2 He <u>could</u> see a building just once and remember everything about it. *Past* (handwritten)

3 As a child, he couldn't make friends. *Past / negative* (handwritten)

4 He is able to do extremely difficult mathematical calculations. *present* (handwritten)

5 He was able to calculate 82 × 82 × 82 × 82. *Past* (handwritten)

6 He wasn't able to sit still. *Past / negative* (handwritten)

7 He always manages to draw everything in the right place. *Present* (handwritten)

8 He managed to learn Icelandic in a week. *Past* (handwritten)

9 He didn't manage to pass his exams. *Past / negative* (handwritten)

▶ page 156 **LANGUAGEBANK**

PRACTICE

6 Complete the text with the words in the box.

| ~~can~~ ~~isn't~~ ~~can't~~ ~~managed~~ ~~could~~ ~~to~~ ~~couldn't~~ ~~able~~ |

When four-year-old Derek Paravacini heard the sound of the piano, he ran towards it. Although he was blind, he ¹*managed* to reach the instrument. He pushed the piano player – a small girl – off her stool, and started to play. Adam Ockleford, a piano teacher, said, 'It was … extraordinary. He was hitting the notes with his hands, his feet, his nose, even his elbows.' Paravacini was ²*able* to play the tune he had just heard and at that moment Ockleford realised the boy was a genius.

Paravacini was born blind and autistic and had great learning difficulties. As a child, he ³*couldn't* do many things that ordinary children do. Even today, as an adult, he ⁴*can't* count to ten, and he ⁵*isn't* able to dress or feed himself. But Paravacini has one incredible gift: music. Like Mozart, he ⁶*can* remember every piece of music he hears.

It started when his parents gave him a plastic organ when he was eighteen months old. He couldn't see the notes, but he managed ⁷*to* play tunes on it. By the time he was four, he ⁸*could* play many pieces on the piano. With Ockleford's help, Paravacini developed his technique and played his first major concert at the Barbican Hall in London, aged nine. He has performed all over Europe and the US and in 2006 recorded his first CD.

SPEAKING

7A Look at the activities opposite and read the instructions below.

1 Put one tick next to the things you can do now.

2 Put two ticks next to the things you could do when you were a child.

3 Put three ticks next to the activities you are very good at.

B Work in groups. Compare your abilities. Say how often you do these things, and which ones you enjoy(ed). Describe any special experiences you have had while doing these things.

change the wheel on a car

paint pictures

run for an hour

Toc! Toc!   Qui est là?

tell a joke in a foreign language

catch and cook a fish

write with your 'wrong' hand

remember important dates from history
1066 1901 1666 1837

climb a mountain

play tennis

ride a motorbike

WRITING a summary

8A Read the summary and answer questions 1–3.

Daniel Tammet and Stephen Wiltshire are two gifted young Englishmen who suffer from forms of autism. These men have one thing in common – they are able to remember large amounts of information – but their talents are very different. Wiltshire has an ability to draw complicated images after seeing them only once, while Tammet has an amazing aptitude for remembering numbers. They have both appeared on television programmes, which helped make them famous, and both published books. While Tammet and Wiltshire experienced difficulties during their childhood, their great achievements are now recognised by the public. And best of all: they both seem happy with their lives.

1 Does the summary explain the main idea of the text(s) (who, what, where and why)?

2 Is the summary shorter or longer than the original text(s)?

3 Does the writer of the summary copy sentences from the original text(s) or does he/she use his/her own words?

B Work in pairs. Look at phrases 1–5 from the summary. What details do these phrases leave out? What information is missing?

1 Wiltshire has an ability to draw complicated images.

He drew a train station in London and pictures of other cities, including Rome, Hong Kong and New York.

2 Tammet has an amazing aptitude for remembering numbers.

3 They have both appeared on television programmes.

4 Both published books.

5 (They) experienced difficulties during their childhood.

LEARN TO make notes for a summary

9A Read the notes and find examples of 1–6 below.

THE MEMORY MEN
Tammet & Wiltshire = very gifted. They are able 2 remember
lots of info. Their abilities → them becoming famous
The artist
Wiltshire remembers things he sees
The mathematician
Tammet remembers numbers & does maths problems

1 an abbreviation info .
2 symbols for: a) *and* & b) *resulted in* →
3 a number to represent a word that sounds the same 2
4 a heading The memory men
5 a subheading The artist
6 highlighted information things he sees
                         numbers

B Look at suggestions 1–8. Are they good or bad ideas for taking notes? Change the bad ideas.

1 Use abbreviations and symbols.

2 Use diagrams or drawings.

3 Try to write down every word you hear/copy down every word you read.

4 Write fast. Don't worry about handwriting.

5 Don't worry about spelling. You can check later.

6 Highlight important information.

7 Don't use your own words – you might make mistakes.

8 Use a space or a new heading when there's a change of speaker or topic.

10A ▶ 7.4 Listen to three people talking about memory. Tick the things they talk about in the box.

names faces dates words birthdays
directions to places books you've read places
films jokes information about products
things that happened to you when you were very young

B Read the notes about Peggy. Listen again and use the same headings to write notes about John and Tim.

PEGGY
Job
sales rep 4 publishing company
Memory
needs 2 remember lots
not good at directions → used to get lost all the time.
has to remember names & faces of people she talks to +
information about products

John: Good   Bad
  words   . Dates
           . Birthdays

Tim: Good   Bad
  . Dates   . Jokes
  . Names   . films

C Compare your notes with a partner. What else can you remember about what they say? Use the phrases below to help you.

Sally or Samantha?   makes mistakes
blocking   all other students
after an hour of watching a film

She spent an hour calling a woman Sally when her real name was Samantha.

11A Work in pairs. Ask and answer the questions.

1 Do you have a good memory, generally?

2 Which things in the box in Exercise 10A are you good at remembering?

3 Which would you like to be better at remembering?

4 Do you use any special strategies to remember things?

B Write a summary (100–120 words) of what you learned about your partner.

▶ **FUNCTION** | clarifying opinions   ▶ **VOCABULARY** | qualifications   ▶ **LEARN TO** | refer to what you said earlier

VOCABULARY | qualifications

1A Discuss. Which jobs do you think require the most qualifications?

In my country you have to study for six years to become an architect.

B Read the text. What did Steve Eichel do? Why?

Steve Eichel, a psychologist, was worried about the number of therapists with false diplomas and degrees. He thought it was too easy to get these qualifications. So, one day, he decided to do an experiment. Eichel had a cat called Zoe. Using the name Zoe D Katze (in German, the name means Zoe the Cat), Eichel applied for a number of diplomas and a degree in hypnotherapy for his cat. He completed some forms, paid the money, and invented a CV and a job for Zoe at the Tacayllaermi Friends School (Tacayllaermi backwards spells 'I'm really a cat'). In a few weeks, the cat had two diplomas and a PhD.

2A Work in pairs. What do the words in bold mean? Which words are shown in the photos?

1 What **qualifications** do you have? Apart from school exams, what other exams have you taken or will you take in the future?

2 In your country, when you leave school do you get a **certificate**?

3 Do you have a **driving licence**? What other **licences** can you get?

4 Have you ever done an **online course**?

5 Is **distance learning** popular in your country? Is it more popular than **face-to-face learning**? Which do you prefer?

6 For which professions do you have to **do an apprenticeship**? Does the company usually pay you while you do your training?

7 Do you have a **degree**? From which university?

8 Do you know anyone with an **MA** or a **PhD**? What subject, and in which university, did they do it?

B Discuss the questions in groups.

FUNCTION | clarifying opinions

3A Work in pairs and discuss. Do you think people with a lot of qualifications are usually intelligent?

B ▶ **7.5** Listen to two people discussing intelligence. What do they talk about?

a) intelligent animals
b) intelligent people
c) 'intelligent' technology

C Answer the questions, then listen again to check.

1 Why does the man think the boy from Egypt is intelligent? *a lot of languages | 50*

2 Why does the woman think her two friends are intelligent? What did/do they do? *build his house / parts → new car*

3 Why are qualifications useful, according to the woman? *complete a course / you are able*

4 What does the woman say about 'real life experience, going out and meeting people, talking, travelling'? *amazing education*

4A Complete the phrases in the table.

offering opinions
The [1] ~~reason~~ *reason* I say (he's intelligent) is (that)
For me
In [2] *my* view
I do think
I must say
giving examples
For example,
Let me [3] *give* you (an/another) example.
For [4] *one* thing

B ▶ **7.6** Listen to some three-word phrases from Exercise 4A. Which word is stressed?

C ▶ **7.7** Listen to the full sentences. Copy the stress patterns.

�▶ page 156 **LANGUAGEBANK**

5 Complete the sentences with the words/phrases in the box. Do you agree with the statements?

> ~~must~~   ~~In my~~   Let me give   ~~The reason I~~
> ~~For one~~   ~~For example~~   ~~I do~~   ~~For~~

1 I ___must___ say many creative people are bad students. _For example_ most artists and musicians don't have many academic qualifications.

2 ___For___ me, qualifications aren't that important. _For one_ thing, they don't show a person's character.

3 _In my_ view, face-to-face learning will disappear. _The reason I_ say that is because people want to study from home, so they prefer distance learning.

4 ___I do___ think geniuses usually have personal problems. _Let me give_ you an example: Vincent Van Gogh suffered from depression.

LEARN TO refer to what you said earlier

6 Read the phrases from the audio script and answer questions 1–3.

a) **Like I said,** he doesn't go to school but, for me, he's super-intelligent.

b) **Having said that,** I do think qualifications are useful.

c) Exactly. **That's what I was saying.** Just like the boy from Egypt.

Which phrase shows that you:

1 have already given an opinion that someone else is now giving? _That's what i was saying._

2 have already said something? _Like i said_

3 have said something but now want to give a different opinion? _Having said that_

7 Complete the conversation using the phrases below.

> Like I said,   ~~Having said that,~~   That's what I was saying.

A: I think online courses are great if you can't travel to class. _Having said that_ prefer to have a real teacher.

B: I agree. You learn more with other people in the room.

A: _Like i said_, an online teacher is not the same.

B: I've done some online courses, though. It was really convenient because I could study at home.

A: _that's what_. They're great for people who can't travel.
i was saying

8A Read the job advertisement. What qualifications does it mention?

> **Guides needed for Eco-Tours cruise ships**
>
> **Location:** along the River Nile
> **Salary:** £20,000
> **Duration:** 6 months (includes four 5-week tours)
> **Date posted:** 18th July 09.22
>
> Duties: introduce tourists to the plant and animal life of the Nile, organise day trips for tourists, write a regular blog. Must speak Arabic and English plus one other language. Must have a tour guide licence, a university degree, and basic qualifications in biology and/or land management.

B Work in groups of three. Student A: read about candidate A. Student B: read about candidate B. Student C: read about candidate C. What benefits can they bring to the job? Are there any skills or qualifications they don't have?

> ### Candidate A
> Suresh Perera,
> Sri Lanka, 42
> * was a tour guide in Sri Lanka (2 years), geography teacher in Saudi Arabia (10 years)
> * has a tour guide licence and MA in Geography
> * speaks English, Arabic, Tamil
> * visited Egypt many times, knows the culture and people
> * hobbies: sailing and swimming

> ### Candidate B
> Dr. Ahmed Nasari, Egypt, 54
> * biologist (20 years), experience in 11 countries.
> * PhD in marine biology
> * published three books about marine biology, writes regularly for biology journals
> * speaks Arabic, English, basic German
> * will take the exam for a tour guide licence next month
> * wants to research animal life in the Nile

> ### Candidate C
> Delilah Olufunwa, Nigeria, 28
> * former TV actress and model, then tour guide in Nigeria
> * degree in performing arts
> * excellent physical fitness (qualified scuba diver, strong swimmer)
> * speaks English, Arabic, Spanish, Portuguese, French, is studying Japanese
> * loves animals and nature

C Present your candidate to your group. Who should get the job? Why?

DVD PREVIEW

1 Work in groups. Discuss the questions.

1 Do you enjoy sport? Which ones?

2 Have you ever tried to learn a new sport? How successful were you? Why?

3 Have you ever won a sporting competition or attempted a sporting challenge? How did you feel?

2A Read about the programme below. What is Christine's challenge exactly? Why is she doing it? What are the problems?

BBC The One Show: Water Ski Challenge

Sport Relief is a UK charity which asks celebrities to perform sporting <u>challenges</u> in order to raise money for people in Africa. After visiting Uganda with Sport Relief Christine Bleakley, a presenter on *The One Show* (a BBC magazine show), decided to accept a sporting challenge herself. She agreed to <u>water ski across the English Channel</u> from the UK to France. It was an incredibly <u>tough</u> challenge because Christine had never been on water skis before. After a few months training, she <u>attempted</u> the crossing in the middle of winter. Would her physical and mental <u>determination</u> help her to complete the challenge, or would she <u>give up</u> half way? Could she add this <u>outstanding</u> achievement to her already successful career?

B Match the words/phrases in bold in the text with their definitions 1–6.

1 very difficult

2 tried

3 stop doing something (because it is difficult)

4 something that tests your skill or ability

5 excellent/very impressive

6 desire to continue doing something even when it is difficult

▶ DVD VIEW

3 Watch the DVD. Choose the correct summary.

1 Christine completed the challenge without ever falling off her skis.

2 Christine attempted to cross the Channel but failed.

3 Christine crossed the Channel successfully despite falling a lot during the first half.

4 Christine nearly completed the challenge, but fell at the end and broke her leg.

4A Watch the DVD and number the statements in the order you hear them.

5 a) 'My arms and body hurt so much, but I just don't want to give up.'

4 b) 'She's fallen in ten times in ten miles, and that simply isn't good enough for this challenge. She has got to (dig in now, and) start to focus.'

3 c) 'After several falls into the freezing water, I already feel like I can't take much more.'

6 d) 'I can see France, and nothing is going to stop me.'

7 e) 'The first woman to water ski across the Channel, in the winter, having only got on water skis four months ago. She is remarkable. It's a truly outstanding achievement.'

1 f) 'This challenge is incredibly tough. She is going to be operating in sub-zero temperatures for over 90 minutes.'

2 g) 'I am determined not to fall in, but I soon realise that determination might not be enough.'

B Watch the DVD again and decide who says what. Mark statements with a C (Christine) or a T (trainer).

C Discuss. What do you think of what Christine achieved? Would you do anything like this in order to raise money to help people in Africa? Why/Why not?

speakout an achievement

5A ⏵ 7.8 **Listen to someone talking about a recent challenge/ achievement. Answer the questions.**

1 What was her challenge? ~scuba diving~

2 Was it a good or bad experience? ~difficuld expirience~

3 What did she find easy? ~practical training~

4 What problem(s) did she have? ~cold water / practical~

5 Did she succeed? ~yes~ ~↳ more try → harder- ears block up~

B Listen again and tick the key phrases you hear.

keyphrases

I found it really easy/quite difficult.

It was the … I had trouble with.

I was/We were very nervous.

At first, I couldn't … but then I started to …

One thing I tried …

I tried to/experimented with … but it didn't work/I couldn't …

I got very frustrated/annoyed/tired.

I didn't know how to …

I'm (so) glad/Eventually I managed it.

It was a (really) difficult challenge/good experience …

For me, it was quite an achievement. ~Slies~

C You are going to talk about a recent challenge/achievement. Before you talk, make some notes on the following:

• What was your challenge? (Were you learning a new sport/how to drive, etc?) ~↳ zip line~

• Where were you? ~Arequipa/my family~

• How did you feel? ~exited~

• What was the experience like?/What did the challenge involve?

• Who helped you? ~He persons that are~ ~↳ there are To places that are connected with a line~

• Did you try any special techniques?

• Did you succeed? ~YES ^^ ⌐~

D Work in groups and take turns. Tell each other about your experiences. Who had the funniest/most interesting/most embarrassing experience?

writeback an internet post

6A Read the internet post and answer the questions. What was Jim's challenge? What helped him to learn?

A Beautiful Language, by Jim

I was never very good at languages when I was at school so learning Welsh **was a huge challenge for me. I wanted to learn** Welsh because I was living in Wales and my wife spoke Welsh. **So, I decided** to enrol for a course at the university and go for classes twice a week. I **soon** fell in love with the language – it's so gentle and musical. **I began to realise** how many people living around me loved and treasured their national language. Welsh has beautiful expressions and has often been called the language of poets. **It's not an easy** language **to learn, but it's very satisfying**. I feel like **I've achieved a lot**. **Now**, when I go into my local shop, I try to speak to people in Welsh. I'm sure **I make a lot of mistakes**, but everyone is very kind to me, and they always smile.

B The *My Story* website publishes stories from the public about their experiences and achievements. Write your own story (120–180 words) to submit to the website. Use the words in bold above and the key phrases to help.

SUCCESS

1A Underline the correct alternative to complete the quotes. Which quotes do you think could be important for you? Why?

1 'When you are not *believing/practising*, remember someone else is *believing/practising*, and when you meet him he will win.'

2 'I was seldom able to see *an opportunity/a talent* until it had ceased to be one.'

3 'Focus *on/in* where you want to go, not on what you fear.'

4 'Some people dream of success, while other people wake up and work hard *on/at* it.'

B Work in pairs and discuss.

1 Do you know anyone who is a high achiever? What have they done?

2 What are you focusing on at the moment in your work/studies?

3 How do you think you can get better at speaking English?

PRESENT PERFECT CONTINUOUS

2A Complete the sentences with the present perfect continuous form of the verbs in brackets.

1 I _____ (practise) learning my lines. Rehearsals start next week.

2 I _____ (visit) patients in their homes.

3 I _____ (mark) homework for hours.

4 I _____ (try) some new ideas for a recipe.

5 I _____ (research) a news story.

B Think of a job to go with each sentence above. Write two or three sentences that this person could say at the end of a busy day. Use the present perfect continuous.
I've been reading all day. I've been saying my lines out loud.

C Work in pairs. Take turns to say your sentences. Can your partner guess the job?

ABILITY

3 Complete the text with the words in the box.

| ~~hopeless~~ | gifted | skilful |
| useless | expert | ability | have |

As a child, I was [1] *hopeless* at school. I was [2] _____ at maths, English, science, everything, because I just didn't [3] _____ an aptitude for that kind of study. One day we were playing football and the ball got stuck in a tree. I climbed the tree to get it, and one of my teachers, John Marston, looking out of the staffroom window, noticed that I was a talented climber. He was an [4] _____ in climbing – he'd been in the Alps and up Mount Kilimanjaro – and he invited me to try it one weekend. I really enjoyed it. After a month, he told me I was a very [5] _____ climber for my age. I left school three years later with no qualifications, but I kept climbing regularly until I became very [6] _____ at it. In my early twenties, I became a professional climber. I'll always remember Mr Marston because he showed me I had an [7] _____ which no one else, including me, knew about.

PRESENT AND PAST ABILITY

4A Underline the correct alternative.

1 I *can to/am can/can* type very fast.

2 When I first heard English, I *not able/not could/couldn't* understand anything.

3 Even when I'm stressed, I'm usually *able to/can/able* sleep.

4 I recently had a problem but I *can able to/was able to/managed* solve it.

5 I *'m not able/was able not/wasn't able* to do the job of my dreams (not yet, anyway).

6 Last weekend I *managed to/managed/am managed to* relax completely.

B Tick the sentences that are true for you. Compare your answers with other students.
I can't type very fast, but I don't have to look at the letters when I type.

CLARIFYING OPINIONS

5A Complete the conversations by adding your opinions and giving examples.

1 A: I think that, to be happy, people need to have dreams and ambitions.

   B: For me, _____. Let me give you an example: _____.

2 A: The most important thing to remember is, if you want to be successful in anything, it's hard work, not talent that gets you there.

   B: I do think _____. The reason I say this is _____.

3 A: Being rich or famous is not the same as being successful.

   B: In my view, _____. For example, _____.

4 A: There is too much focus on sporting achievement. Games aren't important.

   B: I must say _____. For one thing, _____.

5 A: If you want to be successful in your job, you need a good education and you need to understand modern technology.

   B: In my opinion, _____. For one thing, _____. For another, _____.

B Work in groups and take turns. Share your opinions with each other and ask follow-up questions.

BBC VIDEO PODCAST
Watch people talking about their greatest achievements on ActiveBook or on the website.

Authentic BBC interviews
www.pearsonELT.com/speakout

SPEAKING
> ❱ Describe your neighbourhood
> ❱ Compare real-world and online activities
> ❱ Discuss social situations
> ❱ Design a community

LISTENING
> ❱ Listen to descriptions of online communities
> ❱ Listen to people describing guest/host experiences
> ❱ Watch a BBC documentary about a remote community

READING
> ❱ Read a text from a BBC website about neighbours
> ❱ Read about how to be a good guest

WRITING
> ❱ Write a website review
> ❱ Write an advertisement

BBC CONTENT
> 🔲 Video podcast: What makes a good neighbour?
> ◉ DVD: Tribe: Anuta

UNIT 8

communities

VOCABULARY getting on

1 Work in pairs and discuss.

1 Do you know your neighbours? How well do you know them?

2 Do you have a good relationship with them? Why?

2A Work in pairs. Match sentences 1–6 with the opposite meanings a)–f).

b) 1 I **get on well with** my neighbour – she's always smiling.

e) 2 It's never a problem if I **ask a favour** of my neighbours.

f) 3 I prefer to **mind my own business** so I don't ask the neighbours personal questions.

d) 4 I sometimes **invite** my neighbour **over** for coffee.

a) 5 My neighbour's dog is **a nuisance** – he's always barking early in the morning.

c) 6 We didn't **get to know** our neighbours for years.

a) My neighbour has pets but they never **disturb** me.

b) My neighbour **gets on my nerves** – he's always complaining.

c) We **made friends with** our neighbours immediately.

d) I like to **keep myself to myself** so my neighbour hasn't been in my house.

e) I'm always **doing favours** for my neighbours.

f) I can be quite **nosy** so I often ask my neighbours about their lives! *⌐gossip*

B Which sentences are true for you? Tell other students.

▥▶ page 171 **VOCABULARY BANK**

READING

3A Circle the option you think is correct to complete statements 1–4.

1 _____ of people in the UK say they know their neighbours.

(a) 27% (b) 50% **(c) 77%**

2 If you live in a flat, you probably know your neighbours _____ if you live in a house.

(a) better than **(b) less than** (c) about the same as

3 _____ year-olds are more likely to know their neighbours than people of other ages.

(a) 18–24 (b) 30–40 **(c) 55–64**

4 The people most likely to know their neighbours are: _____.

(a) women (b) men (c) (neither. There is no difference between them.)

B Read the text to check your answers.

4 Answer the questions.

1 What question did the radio programme try to answer?

2 What is ICM and what did it do? *research group ask people*

3 Which people who wrote to the website say they have a good relationship with their neighbours? *Rx Karen Jilcove Toto*

4 Which person says they had a bad start with a neighbour? *Looby Graham*

How well do you know your neighbours?

The BBC's iPM radio programme asks its listeners for interesting questions. One question that came up:

'I would like to ask a question about neighbours, by which I mean other people who live in your immediate neighbourhood. Many people we have spoken to have said they don't know any of their immediate neighbours.'

What about you? Do you know any of your immediate neighbours, in the sense of something more than exchanging 'Good morning' or 'Good afternoon', for example?

The BBC liked the question and found the answer. A research group called ICM asked people how well they know their neighbours and this is what they discovered.

Surprisingly, 77% of you say you know your neighbours. It also emerged that if you live in a house, regardless of town or rural area, a massive 80% of you know your neighbours. However, the figure drops to 75% if you're in a flat. The survey also revealed that we appear to get friendlier as we get older. In fact, only 64% of 18–24 year-olds know their neighbours, but for people aged 55–64 this number climbs to 88%. Interestingly enough, it turns out that men are a little less likely to say they know their neighbours than women, and the rich say they are closer to their neighbours than the less well-off.

GRAMMAR articles

5 Look at the words underlined in the sentences below. Match sentences a)–f) with the rules below.

a) The BBC liked <u>the question</u> and found the answer.

b) <u>A research group</u> called ICM asked 1,002 people how well they know their neighbours.

c) <u>Men</u> are less likely to say they know their neighbours than women.

d) Here are a few of <u>the best</u>.

e) We moved into our house in <u>Leeds</u> three years ago.

f) I'm <u>a police officer</u>.

Rules:

1 Use *a/an*:
  • the first time something is mentioned (new information). __b__
  • with jobs. __f)__

2 Use *the*:
  • when we know which one we are talking about. __a__
  • with superlatives. __d__

3 Use no article:
  • to talk generally about people or things. __c__
  • with most names of places. __e__

The topic was very popular with lots of BBC listeners and provoked plenty of comments on the BBC's iPM website. Here are a few of the best:

I only really got to know mine when their house caught fire. We're good friends now.
RxKaren

When we moved into our house in Leeds three years ago, the first remark our neighbour made was, 'So you're moving in? I hope you don't have noisy kids.' We reassured him we had no children and tried to make conversation but with no success.
Loobygraham

I live in a small block of 16 flats. We all know each other and we have 8 nationalities living in these flats so we have our own mini United Nations! If I – or any of my neighbours – needed help or advice or assistance of any kind we could all knock on anyone's door and get it.
Jilcove

I'm a police officer. My neighbours are always extremely friendly. They probably think that if they have any problems, I'll rescue them.
Todd

PRACTICE

6 Complete comments below with *a/an*, *the* or – (no article).

My neighbours have ¹ __a__ cat that climbs through my window and terrorises my goldfish. It's so annoying! I'm going to buy ² __a__ dog next week.

My neighbour is ³ __a__ doctor. He keeps himself to himself. Once, my son got sick and I asked ⁴ __the__ doctor to come and have a look and he said, 'My office hours are from 8.00 until 6.00.' Charming!

I have ⁵ __the__ nicest neighbour in the world. I really get along well with her. She often invites me over for dinner, which is great because she's ⁶ __a__ professional chef!

⁷ __–__ People are funny! My neighbours here in ⁸ __–__ Birmingham have an apple tree that hangs over my garden. Once, some apples fell onto my grass, and they came round to collect them!

My neighbour is ⁹ __an__ old lady who lives on her own. My wife and I made friends with her and sometimes do favours for her. ¹⁰ __The__ old lady is always really grateful.

I'm sure that I'm not ¹¹ __the__ quietest person in the world, but my neighbour is so noisy. She's always playing extremely loud music. I can't escape ¹² __the__ noise! What is wrong with people?

▐▌▶ page 158 LANGUAGEBANK

GRAMMAR quantifiers

7A Read sentences 1–6 and underline the words that describe quantity.

1 The topic was very popular with <u>lots of</u> BBC listeners.
2 The topic provoked <u>plenty of</u> comments.
3 Here are <u>a few</u> of the best.
4 We reassured him we had <u>no</u> children.
5 We could <u>all</u> knock on anyone's door.
6 <u>Many</u> people … don't know their immediate neighbours.

B Look at the underlined words above and answer the questions.

1 Which mean *a large number/amount*? Many
2 Which mean *a small number/amount*? a few
3 Which means *none*? no
4 Which two quantifiers can only be used with countable nouns (things we can count)?

▐▌▶ page 158 LANGUAGEBANK

PRACTICE

8A Underline the correct alternatives in the comments below.

1 My neighbour gets on my nerves. She always invites herself over at dinner time so I have to feed her. How *much/many* times have I eaten at her house? *None/No*.

2 My apple tree hangs over my neighbour's garden. There are *a little bit/plenty* of apples for everyone but my neighbours steal them! Once *some/much* of my apples fell on their grass so I went to get them!

3 In fifty years, I've never had *much/many* trouble with my neighbours. But these new ones are a nuisance. They're so nosy – they won't mind their own business. I spend *many of/a lot of* time hiding in the kitchen to avoid them!

4 My neighbour used to leave *a bit of/all of* his windows open. My cat went in there *a few/a little* days a week and played with the goldfish. Then the stupid neighbour bought a dog, and it bit my cat!

5 I'm a doctor. *Several/A bit of* times a year, my neighbours ask, 'Can you give me *a bit of/many* advice?' For free, of course! How do they think I make money? Not by offering free advice!

B Work in groups. Look at the situations above and in Exercise 6 and discuss.

1 Who do you think is the good/bad neighbour in each situation?

2 What makes a good neighbour? What qualities should they have?

VOCABULARY *PLUS* compound nouns

9A Read sentences 1–4. Are they positive (+), negative (-) or both (+/-)?

1 I live next to the <u>main road</u>, so it's a bit noisy. −

2 There's a wonderful bookshop near where I live. +

3 There's a lovely public swimming pool by my house, and it's free for children. +

4 Where I live is good for window shopping but too expensive to buy anything! +/−

B Find and underline a compound noun in each sentence. The first has been done for you.

C Look at the compound nouns and match them with patterns a)–d).

a) noun + noun   c) verb + noun

b) adjective + noun   d) noun + verb

speakout TIP

Compound nouns combine two related words. The first word gives us more information about the second, e.g. *shoe shop, history teacher, paper bag*. What other words make compound nouns with *shop, teacher* and *bag*? Compound nouns can be written as one word, two words or with a hyphen. Use a dictionary to check.

10A Which words complete the compound nouns?

1	*trafic*	jam	6	sports	*centre*
		lights		city	
2	*car*	park	7	high	*street*
		rental		one-way	
3	*shopping*	centre	8	semi-detached	*house*
		mall		terraced	
4	super	*market*	9	housing	*estate*
	outdoor			industrial	
5	primary	*school*	10	*Lotte* duty-free	*shop*
	language			gift	

B ▶ 8.1 Listen to check your answers. Then think about the stress patterns. Which word is usually stressed: the first or the second? Listen again to check.

C Discuss. Think about the place where you are studying now. Which of the compound nouns does it have nearby?

➧ page 171 **VOCABULARYBANK**

SPEAKING

11A Work in pairs. What features do you like/dislike where you live? Use the photos below to help you. Make notes about the following:

• things you like

a beautiful city centre with lots of trees and parks

• things that are nice but not essential

a good local supermarket

• things you hate

graffiti on the buildings

B Think about your neighbourhood. What would make it:

• more beautiful?

• better for your health?

• more interesting?

• safer?

• more of a community?

I'd really like to see a good shopping mall, where people can meet.

My neighbourhood would be healthier if there was less traffic congestion in the mornings.

C Compare your ideas in groups.

VOCABULARY the internet

1A Work in groups. Look at the picture. Which type of website would you use to:

1 find out what is happening in the world? *News site*
2 book a holiday? *Travel site*
3 contact friends? *Social networking*
4 show your holiday pictures? *Photo sharing*
5 meet the partner of your dreams? *Dating site*
6 show your wedding video? *Photo home*
7 find out whether a new film or book is good? *Rating*
8 find out about a big company? *Corporate*
9 share facts about yourself? *Personal home*
10 read and write opinions about anything and everything? *Blog*
11 read or write factual information about a topic? *Wiki*
12 find information quickly? *Search*

B Discuss. Which of these do you use regularly? Which do you use occasionally? Which do you never use?

LISTENING

2A ▶ 8.2 Listen to four people talking about their online communities and answer the questions.

1 What did Speaker 1, Lynn, do a year ago?
2 What does she say about the community?
3 Why does Speaker 2, Rick, say it's 'a twenty-first-century community'?
4 What does he say about 'the best blogs'?
5 What type of place does Speaker 3, Nathan, live in?
6 What does he like about using the internet?
7 What two things does Speaker 4, Abbie, do on her favourite website?
8 How often does she use it?

B Work in pairs. Listen to each speaker again. When the speaker finishes, take it in turns to use the words in the box to explain what the speakers say.

| artists' colony | paintings | business | trust | social networking | cheap |
| loyal readers | engaged | shop online | bloggers | pictures | grows |

3 Discuss the questions.

1 Do you think websites are real communities?
2 What are the benefits of online communities?
3 Are there any dangers or problems in spending a lot of time in online communities?

GRAMMAR relative clauses

4 Read about the origins of a website. Why did the website become successful?

The rise and rise of YouTube

Early in 2005, three friends, Chad Hurley, Steve Chen and Jawed Karim, who were also colleagues, were having problems trying to email a video clip. Within two hours they came up with an idea which would solve the problem and change internet history. They decided to create a video sharing platform and YouTube was born. It's a familiar story for anyone who follows the development of the internet: technology-minded entrepreneurs under thirty, a garage or bedroom, where dreams become reality, little money and a big communicative need. The site was an instant success. The key was a number of features: links to the videos, which made them easy to email; tell-a-friend functions; a feature that allowed YouTube videos to be played on other social networking sites; and another feature that let users comment on the videos. This helped to develop the site's sense of community: YouTube was a place where you posted videos but also chatted about them, complained, smiled (😊) or laughed out loud (LOL). Two years after the launch, Google Inc., bought YouTube for $1.65 billion.

5A Look at the underlined clauses in the sentences below. Which is a defining relative clause and which is a non-defining relative clause?

a) Chad Hurley, Steve Chen and Jawed Karim, <u>who were colleagues</u>, were having problems trying to email a video clip.

b) YouTube was <u>a place where you posted videos</u>.

B Read rules 1 and 2 to check your answers. Then complete rule 3 with *which, who, where* and *that*.

Rules:

1 Defining relative clauses tell us exactly which thing, person or place we are talking about.

2 Non-defining relative clauses add extra information to a sentence. They tell us what a thing, person or place is or does. The sentence is still grammatically possible without the extra information.

3 _where_ is used to talk about places

   who is used to talk about people

   witch is used to talk about things

   that can be used to talk about places, people or things (in defining relative clauses only)

C Read the text in Exercise 4 again. Find and underline eight relative clauses. What type of relative clauses are they: defining (D) or non-defining (ND)?

▸ page 158 **LANGUAGEBANK**

PRACTICE

6A Circle the correct alternatives to complete the text.

For people who liked to send and receive very short messages, Twitter.com was a dream come true. This social networking site, ¹*that/which was/who was* the fastest growing site in 2009, became amazingly popular in a short space of time. So how does it work? You write your message, ²*of which must be/what must be/which must be* no longer than 140 characters, onto your profile via a web, SMS or phone application. Then the message, ³*what is called/this is called/which is called* a 'Tweet', is sent automatically to your subscribers or 'followers'. The people ⁴*use/that use/are who use* Twitter say it's fantastic. Jerry Jones, ⁵*who works for/who works where/which works for* an internet company, describes it as 'a mini-revolution'. He says that when Twitter arrived, it was the moment ⁶*which online/for online/when online* communication changed. No more boring blogs, ⁷*what go/where people go/who people go* on and on about nothing. 'Me and my friends, ⁸*who all use/all use/we use* Twitter, have a saying: Keep your Tweet short and sweet!'

B Discuss the questions.

1 Do you or does anyone you know use Twitter?

2 What social networking websites do you know?

3 Which are the most popular now?

7A ▶ 8.3 Listen for the pauses where there are commas. Tick the sentence you hear.

1 a) The travel site which we developed is really popular.

   b) The travel site, which we developed, is really popular.

2 a) Those children who spend too much time on the net don't communicate well.

   b) Those children, who spend too much time on the net, don't communicate well.

3 a) Video sharing sites which are free are a great resource for students.

   b) Video sharing sites, which are free, are a great resource for students.

4 a) On that dating site where I met my wife there are hundreds of single people.

   b) On that dating site, where I met my wife, there are hundreds of single people.

5 a) Bloggers who write regularly often get their stories from news websites.

   b) Bloggers, who write regularly, often get their stories from news websites.

B Work in pairs. Take turns to choose a sentence from Exercise 7A and read it aloud. Your partner says which sentence you read, a) or b).

SPEAKING

8A Look at the activities in the box below. Do you prefer doing them online or in the real world? What are their advantages/disadvantages?

> shopping   meet new people   find out the news   learn a language
> book flights/hotels   watch films/programmes   speak to friends
> look up information   explore new places

B Work with other students. Discuss your opinions.

I prefer shopping online because I don't have to leave my house, park the car and deal with crowds of people. It's really convenient and easy.

WRITING   a website review

9A Read the website review and answer the questions.
1 What type of website is it? *WIKI*
2 Why does the writer recommend it?
3 Who uses the website? Why?

> Website of the Month for January is **magportal.com**. It's a website which you can use to find magazine articles on lots of different topics. One reason I'd recommend it is the range of subjects, which include health, finance, entertainment, science and technology, sports and even pets and animals.
>
> The best thing about magportal.com is that the design is very simple, which makes it really easy to use. There's a menu of categories and a search engine if you want something specific. Another excellent feature is that you can get articles by typing the date – the most recent ones are shown first – or the name of a specific magazine.
>
> I know several journalists who use magportal.com for research. I suggest that readers try it out; there's something for everyone.

B Number the features of a review in a logical order.
a) Say the purpose of the website. *2*
b) Say who you'd recommend the website to. *4*
c) Introduce the name of the website. *1*
d) Say what special features the website has. *3*

C Find and underline three phrases we use to recommend something.

LEARN TO   use complex sentences

10A Compare the pairs of sentences. Which sounds more fluent: a) or b)?
1 a) It's a website. You can use it to find magazine articles. The articles are on lots of different topics.

   b) It's a website which you can use to find magazine articles on lots of different topics. *fluent*

2 a) I know several journalists. They use magportal.com. They use it for research.

   b) I know several journalists who use magportal.com for research. *fluent*

> **speakout** TIP
>
> Think about using complex sentences. Simple sentences can be effective, but when we use many simple sentences together, it sounds childish: *I swim every day. I love the water. It's good exercise.* We can make sentences more complex by using conjunctions (*and, because, but,* etc.) and relative clauses: *I swim every day **because** I love the feel of the water **and** it's **also** good exercise.* How have the b) sentences in Exercise 10A been made more complex?

B Rewrite sentences 1–4 to make them sound more fluent.
1 The website is well-designed. The good design makes it user-friendly.
2 The site has too much animation. This makes it very slow. It takes a long time to upload.
3 The website's content comes from its users. Users send in their photos.
4 The site feels friendly. It has user profile areas. Here, users can say who they are.

C Work in pairs and compare your answers.

11A What is your 'Website of the Month'? Choose a website and think about the questions below.
1 What type of website is it (photo sharing, social networking, etc.)?
2 Why do you like it?
3 How often do you visit it?
4 Is there a community of users?
5 Who would you recommend it to?

B Write your review (120–150 words). Show it to other students. Which websites sound interesting to you?

VOCABULARY welcoming

1A Match phrases 1–6 to situations a)–f).

1 Make yourself at home. d)

2 Excuse the mess. a)

3 Be my guest. e)

4 Help yourself. f)

5 Have a seat. c)

6 Put your feet up. b)

a) You are apologising for how your home (or office) looks.

b) You know someone is tired and you want them to relax.

c) You are inviting someone to sit down, maybe at work.

d) You want someone to feel relaxed in your house.

e) You give permission for someone to use something that is yours.

f) You are offering someone food.

B ▶ 8.4 Listen to the phrases and notice how words ending in a consonant sound (e.g. /f/) link together with words beginning with a vowel sound (e.g. /æ/ or /ə/) so there is no pause between them. Then listen and repeat.

Make yourself˘at home. yoursel fat home

C ▶ 8.5 Listen to the conversations. Listen again and repeat the final line.

FUNCTION being a good guest

2A Work in pairs. Discuss the questions.

1 When was the last time you were a guest? What was the situation?

2 When was the last time you had a guest? Was he or she a good guest? Why/Why not?

3 What type of things do good and bad guests do?

B Read the text. Did you mention any of these ideas in your discussion?

How to be the world's best guest

Do you want to be a sensitive, popular guest who gets invited back? Read our six top tips for being a good guest.

1 Clothes – if you are in a formal situation, dress smartly: a suit and tie for men, a long skirt and jacket for women.

2 Gifts – if you are going to stay in someone's house, don't arrive empty-handed. Bring a small gift if you are staying for a short period of time, a bigger gift for longer periods. Expensive chocolate works in most situations.

3 Greetings – to shake hands or to kiss? Wait to see what your host does.

4 Food – always accept it when offered, whether it looks horrible or delicious. Try to eat all of it and say it tastes good. Most people are proud of their cooking even if they shouldn't be. Don't hurt their feelings.

5 Names – in formal situations, don't use first names. Always use titles (Doctor, Professor, Chairperson) until the person tells you not to.

6 Leaving – the most important tip for being a good guest is to know when to say goodbye. The secret is to leave while the host is still enjoying your company and wants you to stay longer.

3 Discuss the questions.

1 Which pieces of advice are useful? Are there any that you think are incorrect?

2 Can you add any other advice? Think about personal space, smoking, paying the bill, speaking a foreign host's language or one of your own topics.

4 ▶ 8.6 Listen to six situations. Which speakers did something wrong? Which speakers are asking for advice?

5 Listen again and complete the notes below.

1 She says her family doesn't …

2 He wants to know if he should bring …

3 He should come back in …

4 She forgot to take …

5 In the restaurant you have to …

6 It's Thanksgiving but her family doesn't eat …

6 Look at the phrases in the table and tick the ones you heard in the conversations in Exercise 4. Read audio script 8.6 on page 196 to check.

asking for advice	
question	answer
Is it OK if I (do this)?	Yes, of course./No, you'd better not. It's considered a bit rude.
What should we do (in this situation)?	If I were you, I'd …
Do I need to (bring a dish)?	Yes, you should./No, it's not necessary.
Did I do something wrong?	No, of course not./It's OK. We can sort it out./Don't worry about it.
Is this a bad time? I can come back later.	Can you come back in ten minutes?/Not at all. It's fine.

apologising
Sorry about that. I didn't know.
My apologies. I didn't realise.

➡ page 158 **LANGUAGEBANK**

7A Complete conversations 1–5 by adding two words from the box to each one.

> that were it OK rude should about
> at wrong realise

1 A: Is OK if I take a call during a meeting?
  B: Not really. It's considered a bit. rude

2 A: I just called the boss by his first name, John. Did I do something? wrong?
  B: Not all. That's normal here.

3 A: Sorry about. I didn't know you were waiting.
  B: Don't worry it.

4 A: My apologies. I didn't this was your seat.
  B: No, it's. You can sit there.

5 A: You know I can't eat butter and cheese, right? What I do if they offer me these?
  B: If I you, before your visit I'd tell them you don't eat dairy products.

B Practise the conversations with a partner.

LEARN TO accept apologies

8A ▶ **8.7** Listen to the extracts from the audio script. Number the phrases a)– f) in the order you hear them.

a) It's no problem.
b) Not at all.
c) That's all right. *1*
d) You really don't have to …
e) It's fine.
f) It's nothing.

B Work in pairs, Read situations 1–4 below and take turns to apologise and accept the apology.

1 You agreed to meet your partner for dinner. You are thirty minutes late.

2 You accidentally wake up your partner by singing loudly. You didn't know he/she was asleep.

3 You borrowed your partner's book. You accidentally ripped one of the pages.

4 You are buying something in a shop. You accidentally walk in front of your partner because you didn't realise there was a queue.

SPEAKING

9A Read the situations. Have you experienced either of these? Work in pairs and discuss what you would do/say.

Situation 1

> You are staying with a host family abroad. The family seemed nice at first but now there are some problems and they don't talk to you much. You want to study, but the family is very noisy. They smoke inside even though you asked for a non-smoking house. In the morning, there is never any hot water left for your shower. You decide to talk to the mother of the family.

Situation 2

> A foreign student is staying with you. He keeps saying that the food, the coffee, and the weather in your country are terrible. He seems lonely, never socialises and eats his meals in his room. You want to help him, but he doesn't want to talk. You decide to talk to the director of the school where the student is studying. You want to know what to do.

B Choose one of the situations. Use the flow chart below to plan and role-play your own situation.

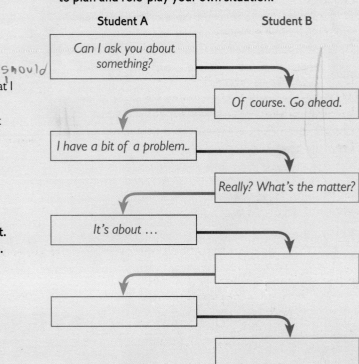

Student A — Student B

Can I ask you about something?

Of course. Go ahead.

I have a bit of a problem..

Really? What's the matter?

It's about …

DVD PREVIEW

1A Work in groups. Look at the photos. Where do you think this is? What do you think life is like for people on an island like this? Do you think their lives are changing in today's modern world?

B Read the programme information. What does Bruce Perry hope to learn from visiting the tribe? *traditions* *how they survive*

BBC Tribe: Anuta

Tribe is a BBC programme in which presenter Bruce Parry goes to some of the world's most isolated places. In this episode, he goes to the Pacific island of Anuta, one of the most remote communities on Earth. There, he learns about their traditions, and discovers how the community survives. There are just twenty-four families on Anuta. Bruce meets them all, and experiences how their customs help to bind the people together.

2 What do you think the words in the box mean? Match them with definitions 1–6.

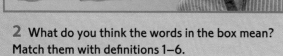

tribe   isolated   remote   customs   survive
bind (people together)

1 form a strong connection between people *bind*
2 continue to live normally even when there are great problems *survive*
3 something that people in a particular society do because it is traditional *customs*
4 a group of people with the same race, language and customs, who live together in the same area *tribe*
5 far away from other places (can also describe a person who is lonely and can't meet other people) *isolated*
6 far away from other places (usually used to describe places) *remote*

▶ DVD VIEW

3 Watch the DVD and number the scenes in the correct order.

a) Bruce meets the children. *2*
b) Bruce meets the community leaders. *4*
c) Bruce catches a fish. *6*
d) Bruce helps to repair a wall in the water. *5*
e) Bruce arrives on the island. *1*
f) Bruce says 'I'm in Paradise'. *3*

4A Circle the correct answer, a) or b).

1 When visitors arrive in Anuta, what must they do?
   (a) Shake everyone's hand.
   (b) Bring gifts to the community leaders.
2 What do the community leaders tell Bruce?
   (a) Their island is like Paradise and he is welcome.
   (b) He can stay in Anuta.
3 What happens during a 'community fish drive'?
   (a) The men catch fish and the women cook.
   (b) Everyone in the community helps to catch fish.
4 What do they do with the fish?
   (a) It is divided amongst all the families.
   (b) The islanders all sit and eat together.

B Watch the DVD again to check.

5 Discuss the questions.

1 Do you think it is good that Bruce visited Anuta? Why/Why not?
2 Would you like to visit this place? Why/Why not?
3 Can the modern world learn anything from places like Anuta?

speakout design a community

6A Read the paragraph from a news report. What is going to happen? Why?

> Mohamed Nasheed, the new President of the Maldives, has a very difficult task: to find a place for the population to live. Most of the two hundred inhabited islands of the Maldives are about three feet above sea level. Scientists have explained that in the future, the Maldives will be under water because of global warming. No one will be able to live there and nothing will remain.

B What would you do if you had to start a new community? Think about the questions below.

1 Where would it be? *warm near france*

2 Who would live there? Would it be a large or small community? *mixture experts small people*

3 What laws would there be? *not hurts somebody else*

4 What type of government would the community have?

5 What special customs would there be? How would these bind the community together?

7A ▶ 8.8 Listen to two people discussing the first three questions above. What do they decide for each question?

B Listen again. Tick the key phrases that you hear.

keyphrases

I'd probably choose ... ✓
I'd go for a place that ...
It'd need to be somewhere ... ✓
They'd need to be able to ... ✓
The most important thing would be ...
Ideally, there would be ... ✓

8 Work in pairs and plan your community. Present your ideas to another pair.

writeback a web advert

9A Read about a project that was the subject of a BBC documentary. What type of community is it?

> *Tribewanted* is a community tourism project on Vorovoro Island, Fiji. The members of *Tribewanted* work with the local people to build a village community. This community combines Fijian traditions with international ideas for environmentally-friendly living. Visitors can stay between one and twelve weeks. While there, visitors work on projects, look after the gardens on the island, feed the pigs and chickens, help with the construction of buildings and write for the *Tribewanted* blog. They can also learn Fijian songs, relax in a hammock, and enjoy the incredible sunsets and sea. It is the adventure of a lifetime.

B You are recruiting people for the *Tribewanted* project. Write a web ad for people to apply. Use the key phrases and the prompts below.

* Amazing opportunity for adventurers!
* We are looking for ...
* We need people who ...   *select*
* We also want people who are able to ...
* Your responsibilities on the island will include ...
* The community is special because ...
* The community will ...
* By the end of your stay you will ...
* Please send ...
* Interviews will be ...   *100 –120*
* Other information ...   *Monday*

1 Title
2 . what is the project

[handwritten: Norma people smoke next to]
[handwritten: Mauricio sometimes]

[handwritten: what kind of things gets on your nerves? how often do you invite people over?]

[handwritten: Are you a nosy person]
[handwritten: Rosio do you mostly keep yourself to yourself? no like to talk]

GETTING ON
[handwritten: Janet no invite]

1A Use words to make phrases connected with 'getting on'. You can use the words more than once in any order.

get — to — well
ask — over — favour
do — on — own
disturb — with — business
make — a — nuisance
mind — your — nerves
invite — yourself to — nosy *[handwritten: yourself]*
keep — friends
know — people
be

B Use the phrases to write four questions to ask other students.

Do you get on well with your dad?

ARTICLES AND QUANTIFIERS

2A Choose the correct option, a), b) or c), to complete the text.

For sixteen weeks, the only thing we saw was ¹_____ sea. One night, fifty miles from ²_____ Solomon Islands, ³_____ storm hit us and ⁴_____ ship swayed like a drunk soldier. ⁵_____ of the sailors were washed into the sea, and ⁶_____ of us were exhausted. The next day we found a hundred fish on the deck, a ⁷_____ of them still alive, mouths open. We ate them with a ⁸_____ bread and salt. A week later, we were attacked by pirates. They didn't kill anyone but they stole ⁹_____ our food. The captain said there was ¹⁰_____ for one week, and we were two weeks away from land.

1 (a) a (b) the (c) –
2 (a) a (b) the (c) –
3 (a) a (b) the (c) –
4 (a) a (b) the (c) –
5 (a) Little (b) Few (c) Some
6 (a) little (b) much (c) all
7 (a) plenty (b) few (c) all
8 (a) little (b) lot (c) few
9 (a) a lot of (b) many (c) lots
10 (a) plenty of (b) too (c) enough

B Work in groups. Write 3–4 sentences to end the story.

THE INTERNET

3A Complete the sentences with the words in the box.

| sites | blog | search | travel |
| video | networking | | |

1 Have you ever booked a holiday using a _____ site? Was it a success?

2 Do you ever use _____ sharing sites, like YouTube.com? Do you have a favourite clip?

3 What _____ engine do you usually use? Do you know others, apart from Google?

4 Do you like social _____ sites? Do you ever get bored with them?

5 Have you ever contributed to a _____? What was the topic and what did you write?

6 What do you think of dating _____? Do you know anyone who uses them?

B Work in pairs. Ask and answer the questions.

RELATIVE CLAUSES

4A Underline the correct alternative.

1 _____ is *which/when/that* four wolves and a lamb vote on what to have for lunch.

2 _____ is a place *that/how/where* animals study humans.

3 _____ is a ship *who/what/that* is big enough for two people in good weather but only one person in bad weather.

4 _____ is the hour *where/which/when* the traffic stops.

5 _____ is a man *whose/where/who* has stopped thinking.

6 _____ is a person *who/whose/which* job is to lend you an umbrella when the sun is shining and take it back when it rains.

B What or who do sentences 1–6 describe? Complete the sentences with the words in the box.

| rush hour | a zoo | a banker |
| friendship | an expert | democracy |

5 *[handwritten: Work in pairs. Look at the list below and take turns to define things. Your partner guesses what/who you defined.]*

• a person in the room
• an object in your bag
• a room in the building
• a famous book or film
• a famous singer
• an object on the table
• a town or city
• a person in the news

He's the singer who ...

BEING A GOOD GUEST

6A Match comments/questions 1–5 with responses a)–e).

1 Did I do something wrong?

2 Sorry about that. I didn't know that was the boss's chair.

3 My apologies. I didn't realise I had to shake everybody's hand.

4 Is this a bad time? I can come back another time.

5 Do I need to bring gifts?

a) No, it's not necessary. We don't expect them in our country.

b) Don't worry about it. She didn't mind at all.

c) No problem. You said hello to everybody, so that's OK.

d) Can you come back tomorrow? I'm busy for the rest of the day.

e) Yes, you did. No one talks during the national anthem, but don't worry – we can sort it out.

B Work in pairs. Cover responses a)–e). Take turns to read the comments/questions in 1–5 and to reply with the correct response/one of your own.

BBC VIDEO PODCAST

Watch people talking about their neighbourhood relationships on ActiveBook or on the website.

Authentic BBC interviews

www.pearsonELT.com/speakout

SPEAKING
> ❯ Talk about important events in history
> ❯ Talk about your own history
> ❯ Compile and do a quiz
> ❯ Describe a role model

LISTENING
> ❯ Listen to descriptions of past decades
> ❯ Listen to people doing a quiz about history
> ❯ Watch a BBC documentary about a great artist

READING
> ❯ Read about important moments in history
> ❯ Read about time travel
> ❯ Read a quiz about history

WRITING
> ❯ Write a short essay
> ❯ Write a wiki entry

BBC CONTENT
> ▯ Video podcast: Do you think life is better now than in the past?
> ◉ DVD: The Divine Michelangelo

UNIT

9

history

▶ Giant leaps   p112

▶ In our time   p115

▶ I have no idea!   p118

▶ Michelangelo   p120

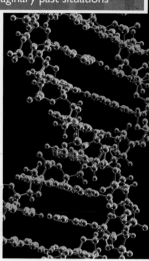

VOCABULARY history

1A Work in pairs and look at the photos. What important developments in history do they show? What do you think are the three most important events in history?

B Read the comments below. Are any of your ideas mentioned?

> A lot of **revolutions** have been important. For example, the Industrial Revolution was a great **turning point** in history.

> The **development** of the internet. The **spread** of the net has been so fast.

> For me, the greatest **advances** in history have been about social justice. There have been some really important **movements**, such as the Civil Rights Movement. These have made the world a better place.

> I'd choose the **invention** of the wheel. It's the **foundation** of most transport and machines.

> Maybe the **discovery** of fire? I think it was the most important thing in human beings' **progress**.

C Put the words in bold above in the definitions below.

1 A moment of great change: _revolution,_
   _____

2 When someone makes or finds something new:
   development, _____ _____

3 Something getting better: _advance,_
   _____

4 When a group of people work to achieve an aim, e.g. human rights: _____

5 The basic idea behind something: _____

6 When something increases and affects more people: _____

D Complete sentences 1–5 in any way you choose. Compare with other students.

1 The biggest turning point in my country's history was …

2 A discovery that changed my life is …

3 My favourite invention is …

4 One thing I hope won't spread is …

5 My country has made progress in …

IIII▶ page 172 **VOCABULARY BANK**

READING

2A Read the introduction to an article from *BBC History Magazine*. What 'alternative moments' do you think the historians will choose?

> *Giant Leaps for Mankind* looks at why we should be celebrating the Moon landing of July 1969 and asks twelve historians to nominate alternative moments in the past that they consider to be giant leaps for mankind.

B Student A: read the texts on the opposite page and make notes with the prompts below. Student B: turn to page 175.

• What?
• Where?
• When?
• Why was it important?

3A Work in pairs. Cover your texts. Look at the notes you made in Exercise 2B. Take turns to tell each other what you read. As you listen, make more notes.

B Work in pairs and answer the questions.

1 Which two books helped the spread of new developments?

2 Which advances help us to study things?

3 Which developments happened mainly because of one person? Which happened because of many people?

C Discuss. Which of the four big moments did you know about? Which do you think are the two most important?

GRAMMAR third conditional

4A Read the sentences below. Do they describe an imaginary situation in the past or an imaginary situation in the present?

1 If he hadn't written *Doctrinale*, education would probably have remained the same.

2 If Galileo hadn't defended his theories, he would have been a free man.

B Look at the sentence patterns and find one other example in your texts.

If + subject	had(n't) + past participle		would(n't) + have + past participle	
If we	had invented	the wheel earlier, life	would have been	easier.
	hadn't discovered	fire, man's progress		slower.

C Read two more sentences from the article. How is the grammatical structure different from the sentences in Exercise 4A?

1 We wouldn't have become the most imaginative of the animals if we had continued eating only plants.

2 Life would have been different if we hadn't invented the steam engine.

➡ page 160 **LANGUAGEBANK**

PRACTICE

5A Complete the sentences with the correct form of the verbs in brackets.

1 Machu Picchu ~~would have remained~~ (remain) unknown if Hiram Bingham ~~hadn't explored~~ (not explore) the Andes in Peru.

2 If the 'I love you' virus ~~had been~~ (be) found earlier, forty-five million computers ~~wouldn't have crashed~~ (not crash).

3 The first experiments in cloning ~~would have been~~ (be) impossible if Gregor Mendel ~~hadn't discovered~~ (not discover) genes.

4 If John Lennon ~~hadn't met~~ (not meet) Paul McCartney, they ~~wouldn't have formed~~ (not form) The Beatles.

5 The invention of the mobile phone ~~wouldn't have been~~ (not be) possible if Alexander Graham Bell ~~hadn't invented~~ (not invent) the telephone.

6 If the Nestor Film Company ~~hadn't opened~~ (not open) a film studio there in 1911, Hollywood ~~wouldn't have remained~~ (remain) a quiet community.

B ▶ 9.1 Listen and check your answers.

C Listen again and repeat. Pay attention to the pronunciation of *had, hadn't, would* and *wouldn't have*. How are they pronounced in fast speech?

6 Make a note of three things that have happened to you in the last year. Write third conditional sentences about how your life would have been different if they hadn't happened to you.

I got a new job. If I hadn't got a new job, I would have been bored in my old job!

SPEAKING

7A Work in pairs. You are going to describe a big moment in history. Choose an important historical event. If you need help, Student A: turn to page 179; Student B: turn to page 176. Think about the questions below.

1 Why was this event important? *When the man go to the moon*

2 What happened before and after the event? *made of /conspocition*

3 Would the world have been different if this event had not happened?

B Describe your big moment to other students. *arrived in*

If the man hadn't ~~been~~ gone to the moon people wouldn't have knowed

Learning to eat meat

Humans are badly designed animals. We are slow, we have weak teeth, and we don't have tails. That's why we need something extra to match other animals. And that's why eating meat – a development that probably started in Africa around 2.5 million years ago – became so important. Meat gives you fats and proteins that you can't get with other food. But more importantly, meat-eating led to hunting, and hunting helped to develop our imaginations. When you hunt, you need to see what isn't there, to see what's behind the next tree or over the next hill. We wouldn't have become the most imaginative – and the most intelligent – of the animals if we had continued eating only plants.

Teaching people to read

Until the end of the twelfth century, Latin was very difficult to learn. Students read and memorised texts for years. Then a Frenchman called Alexander de Villedieu developed a fast method to teach Latin: he used simple rules and wrote them in verse so the students could remember them more easily. Seeing the success of his method, Alexander wrote a grammar book, *Doctrinale*, published in France in 1199. It became a bestseller and spread quickly through Europe, and started a great literacy movement. This new type of learning became the foundation of modern education. If he hadn't written *Doctrinale*, education would probably have remained the same for hundreds of years.

we say we both loved hieghier than we knew we could go~ A

WRITING a short essay

8 Work in pairs. Put the six stages of essay-writing in order.

a) Write a second, final draft. __5__

b) Proofread before you submit your work. Look for errors in grammar, spelling and punctuation. __6__

c) Look carefully at the task/title you are given. What do you need to do: analyse, compare, argue? __1__

d) Check that the sections of the first draft are well-organised. Think about how you can reorganise any unclear parts. __4__

e) Brainstorm ideas. Write down lots of thoughts quickly and don't worry if they are not all good ideas. __2__

f) Write a first draft quickly – it doesn't have to be perfect. __3__

9 Read the short essay below and answer the question. What does the writer think would have happened if China had reached the Americas before the Europeans?

WHAT IF ... Chinese explorers had landed in the Americas first?

Once, China led the world in technology. Centuries before Europe, they had printing and gunpowder. They also had the compass, which meant they could navigate without relying on the position of the Moon. Furthermore, they were brilliant shipbuilders. This ability to build large, strong ships went hand in hand with their other talent: exploration.

In 1405, a Chinaman called Zheng He went on a journey. The idea was to create new trade routes for China. On his first trip, he took 28,000 men in sixty-two ships. Zheng He landed in India and brought home many things that were new to the Chinese: plants, animals, even people.

Zheng He made seven westward journeys. If he had continued to explore, he would probably have reached the Americas before Columbus and the Europeans. However, for political reasons, China stopped exploring. Its leaders believed that China didn't need to trade with these simple, uncivilised people so the country became isolated.

Now, let's imagine Zheng He had reached the Americas first. What would have happened? He would have seen the incredible size of the land and the riches in the ground. He probably would have returned with more men and farmed the land. They would have got rich. The new Chinese colony would have grown and grown, and perhaps they would have later spread to other lands.

Would China have created the next great empire if Chinese explorers had landed in the Americas first? We will never know.

LEARN TO structure paragraphs

10A Read the paragraph below. Then complete statements 1–3 using the labels from the key.

> Chinese ships were extremely advanced compared to ships in other parts of the world. Firstly they were larger; the biggest was 400 feet long and weighed 1,500 tons. They were also better designed; unlike European ships at the time, they had rooms which were 'watertight' – water could not get inside them. What's more, Chinese ships had better equipment: they all had compasses, which meant the sailors would never get lost.

Key:

⬭ =	linking words
▢ =	topic sentence
▨ =	supporting sentence 1
▨ =	supporting sentence 2
▨ =	supporting sentence 3

1 Each paragraph should have a __topic__ __sentence__ that explains the main idea. Often this is the first sentence.

2 Each paragraph needs several __supporting__ __sentence__ to provide examples that illustrate the main idea.

3 The examples should connect well, using __linking__ __words__.

B Label the parts of the first paragraph in the essay in Exercise 9 using the labels above.

11A Read instructions 1–4 for a *What if ...?* essay.

1 Choose an important development in history: an invention, a discovery or an event.

2 Think about the world without this development. How would life be different? How would people's ideas or actions be different? Brainstorm ideas.

3 Plan and write your essay.

4 When you finish, follow the instructions in the Speakout Tip.

speakout TIP

1 Check the 'big' things first: did you answer the question in the title? Are the paragraphs in the right order? Is there anything missing?

2 Check the 'little' things second: grammar, spelling, punctuation, missing words.

B Exchange your essay with another student and check each other's work.

GRAMMAR   active versus passive

1 Write three words or ideas that you associate with teenagers. Compare them with other students.

2A Read the paragraph and choose the best title.

1 Music through the ages

2 How the young found their voice

3 The Death of James Dean

The word 'teenager' was invented in the 1950s. This was the first decade in which teenagers had their own style, their own heroes, their own music and their own way of looking at the world. The 'safe' world of adults was rejected by teenagers, and their heroes were more likely to be actors Marlon Brando on a motorbike (in *The Wild One*, 1954) or James Dean, who was killed in a car crash in 1955, aged twenty-four. The business world immediately saw its opportunity. Magazines, cosmetics and cars were designed to appeal to teenagers, who could usually be found in coffee bars listening to Elvis Presley songs. The truth is that young people want to be different. Many styles in music and fashion have been created since the 1950s: punk music, techno, hip hop. It's safe to say the teenager is here to stay.

B Read the sentences below and answer questions 1–3.

a) The word 'teenager' was invented in the 1950s.

b) Teenagers had their own style.

c) The 'safe' world of adults was rejected by teenagers.

d) The business world immediately saw its opportunity.

e) Many styles in music and fashion have been created since the 1950s.

1 What are the main verbs in each sentence? Find and underline them.

2 Two of the sentences don't say who 'did' the action (because we don't know or it's not important). Which two?

3 Which sentences use active verbs? Which use the passive?

C Look at the sentences again. Complete the rule.

> Rule: We form the passive with: subject + the verb
> ___to be___ (in the present, past or other tense)
> + past participle.

D Find three more examples of the passive in the text.

▶ page 160 **LANGUAGEBANK**

b/d = Active
(→ the subject appear in the sentence "first word")

PRACTICE

3A Rewrite the sentences below using the passive.

1 People all over the world wear jeans.
   Jeans are worn by _____people all over the world_____.

2 Companies are designing mobile phones especially for teenagers.
   Mobile phones _are being designed_

3 The media has always influenced teenagers.
   Teenagers _have always influenced_ _by_ _the media_ .
   been

4 In Sweden they made a great film about a teenage vampire.
   A great film about a teenage vampire _was made in Sweden_

5 In the past, we saw children as mini-adults.
   In the past, children _were seen as mini-adults_

6 In the future, the government will prevent people from smoking until they are twenty-one.
   In the future, people will _be prevented from s_

7 In Mexico they hold a party called *quinceañera* when a girl reaches the age of fifteen.
   In Mexico, a party called quinceañera _were held when_ . _is held_

8 Teenagers will design many of the computer games of the future.
   Many of the computer games of the future _will be desinged_
   by _teenager_ .

B ▶ 9.2 Listen and check your answers.

C Listen again and notice the pronunciation of *are* /ə/, *has been* /həzbɪn/, *was* /wəz/ and *were* /wə/. Then listen and repeat.

a)c)e) = passive → it is not important → verb in the end
who did the action / what happened

VOCABULARY periods of time

4A Put the words and phrases in order from the shortest to the longest periods. Use a dictionary to help you.

> a decade   a millennium   an era   a century   a quarter-century
> a fortnight   an age   the nineteen-seventies/eighties (1970s, 1980s)
> the seventies/eighties (70s/80s)   a generation

B Finish sentences 1–8 with your own words.

1 The best thing about this decade so far has been …

2 The worst thing about this decade so far has been …

3 The thing I remember most about the nineteen-nineties is …

4 One thing I don't know or understand about the nineteen-nineties is …

5 My parents' generation criticises my generation for our …

6 My generation will criticise the next generation for their …

7 One thing that represents my parents' era is …

8 One thing that represents this era is …

C Compare your sentences with other students. Are there any that you agree on?

LISTENING

5A Look at photos A–C. Which decades do you think they are from?

B ▶ 9.3 Listen to three people speaking about different decades. Which decades did they grow up in? Generally, do they feel positive or negative about that decade?

C Listen again and answer the questions.

1 What 'two important aspects' of his life does Speaker 1 mention? Film / Music

2 What 'celebrations' do you think Speaker 1 is talking about?

3 Where is Speaker 2 from? London, England

4 Which musician was 'an icon' for Speaker 2? John Lenon

5 What two things did Speaker 3 think he didn't like during the 80s (he later changed his mind)? fashion music

6 What trend did Madonna start in the mid-eighties? hair short

6A Read the underlined sentences in audio script 9.3 on page 197 and answer the questions.

1 Which decade do you think was good for film and music?

2 What was 'one of the most memorable moments' of the decade in which you grew up?

3 Were things 'developing and getting better' for your generation?

4 What part of your past do you like 'in retrospect'?

B Discuss your answers with other students.

SPEAKING

7A Choose a period when you were a child, a teenager or in your twenties. What did you listen to/do/watch/wear? How did it change as you got older? Make some notes about the following:

- music
- sport
- fashion
- TV and/or films
- technology
- issues in the news

B Work with other students and talk about your personal history. What do you have in common with other students? Tell the class.

VOCABULARY PLUS collocations

8A Read the text and answer the questions.

1 According to the writer, why is time travel difficult for people to believe in?

2 Why is time travel probably boring?

3 Why is it probably not the solution to man's problems?

B Read the text again. Find and underline eight phrases with *come*, *give*, *have* and *make*. The first two have been done for you.

Time travel

All theoretical physicists (have) the same dream. They want to travel in time. Normal people like you and me (have) trouble believing that time travel is possible. The idea is outside our imagination and such thoughts just don't come naturally to us. We can't imagine seeing our parents as little children taking their first steps, or our grandparents' youthful faces as smooth and unlined as glass. We can't imagine watching Stone Age men dragging dead animals to their caves, or watching Alexander the Great conquering half the world, or seeing Mozart at his piano. And the truth is, even if we could travel in time, unless we could also choose an exact moment in an exact place, it would probably be very boring. When we read history books, the past always sounds exciting. But humanity (makes) progress slowly. And Stone Age man didn't own TVs for entertainment.

If time travel is ever possible in the future, time travellers are probably with us now, today. And if they exist, they (have) (come) back from a time in the future and are watching while we (make) a mess of the world. Why don't they (give) us directions on how to save the planet? Why don't they (give) instructions about the environment or how to stop war? Here's a sad thought: maybe they don't know the answers either.

C Look at the underlined phrases and add them to the word webs below.

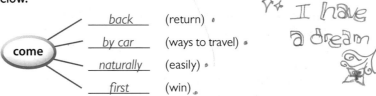

come
- back (return)
- by car (ways to travel)
- naturally (easily)
- first (win)

I have a dream

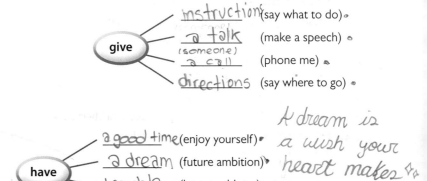

give
- instructions (say what to do)
- a talk (make a speech)
- (someone) a call (phone me)
- directions (say where to go)

A dream is a wish your heart makes

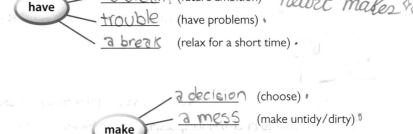

have
- a good time (enjoy yourself)
- a dream (future ambition)
- trouble (have problems)
- a break (relax for a short time)

make
- a decision (choose)
- a mess (make untidy/dirty)
- progress (improve)
- a profit (get more money than you invested)

D Look at the words in the box and add them to the word webs above. Then add any other phrases with *come*, *give*, *have* and *make* you can think of.

> by car   first   a talk   a break   a profit   a good time
> a decision   (someone) a call

➡ page 172 **VOCABULARY BANK**

9A Complete the topic headings 1–10.

1 How to have a good time in your home town

2 How to give instruction to children

3 How not to get fired when you're having trouble with your boss

4 How to make progress when you've been learning English for years

5 How to give directions to the best restaurants in town

6 How to relax and have a complete break from work

7 How to give a talk to an audience of a hundred

8 How to make a profit on your investments

9 How to come first in a competition or game

10 How not to make a mess when you're cooking

B Which of the topics above do you know more about? Choose one or more and prepare to talk about it/them.

C Work with other students. Tell them which you chose and explain how to do it.

SPEAKING

1 Work in pairs and discuss.

1 What are the most famous quiz shows in your country? Do you like them?

2 What type of questions do they ask (history, general knowledge, culture, etc.)?

3 If you had to answer quiz questions on one subject, which subject would you choose?

4 If you had to answer questions on one famous person in history, who would you choose?

I'd choose Walt Disney because I loved his films when I was young and I read his biography.

VOCABULARY describing people

2 Work in pairs. Do the quiz about famous people in history. If you don't know the answers, guess or look at the photos opposite to help.

1 Which highly **original** writer was once kidnapped in France?
(a) Geoffrey Chaucer (b) Isabel Allende
(c) Jane Austen

2 Which **influential** political thinker was famously messy?
(a) Karl Marx (b) Confucius (c) Machiavelli

3 Which **innovative** and **inspirational** actor and film-maker was stopped by the US government from entering the US?
(a) Jodie Foster (b) Charlie Chaplin
(c) Yoko Ono

4 Which **charismatic** scientist spent his free time playing the violin when he wasn't changing the world?
(a) Galileo (b) Albert Einstein
(c) Isaac Newton

5 Which **brave** and **exemplary** freedom fighter went on a road trip across a continent before becoming famous?
(a) Che Guevara (b) Nelson Mandela
(c) Joan of Arc

6 Which amazingly **creative** artist rarely finished the work he started?
(a) Pablo Picasso (b) Edgar Degas
(c) Leonardo da Vinci

3A Work in pairs and look at the quiz again. What do the words in bold mean? Use a dictionary to help you.

B Think of one famous person for each of the adjectives in Exercise 2A. Compare your ideas with other students.

Diego Maradona – He is probably the most influential sportsperson in the history of Argentina.

FUNCTION expressing uncertainty

4A ▶ 9.4 Listen to someone giving the answers to the quiz to her friend. Which answers did the friend know?
1 – 2 – 3 ✗ 4 – 5✗6✗

B Look at the phrases in the box. Match them to the groups of phrases below.

> I don't know   I used to know   I know it isn't …
> I'm not sure but I think …

1 *I don't know* , I have no idea, I haven't a clue

2 *I'm not sure but i think* , I'm not a hundred percent certain but it might be …, I'm fairly sure it's …

3 *i know it isn't* , It's definitely not, I'm sure it isn't

4 *I used to know* , I can't remember, I've forgotten

C Listen again and tick the phrases you hear.

▶ page 160 **LANGUAGEBANK**

(handwritten top margin: mountains different colors / Bolivia lake of Salt)*

5A Complete speaker B's responses in the conversations by adding the pairs of words in the box.

~~have no~~	fairly sure	~~percent certain~~	~~sure it~~
haven't a	~~I've forgotten~~	~~I can't~~	it's definitely

1 **A:** Which sculptor is famous for the statue of David?
  Was it Leonardo da Vinci or Michelangelo?
  have no
  B: I ᵢidea. I don't know anything about art.

2 **A:** What's the name of that American politician who
  made a film about the environment?
  I can't
  B: Oh, um, remember. Was it Rumsfeld? No, um, Bush?

3 **A:** Who was the white South African leader who freed
  Mandela?
  fairly sure
  B: I'm it was Botha, wasn't it?

4 **A:** Who's that Mexican actor who was in *Amores Perros*?
  I've forgotten
  B: Oh, his name but I know who you mean. He's quite
  small and good-looking.

5 **A:** Which company invented the CD-ROM?
  percent certain
  B: I'm not a hundred but it might be Sony.

6 **A:** Do you know who wrote *The Lord of the Rings*?
  Wasn't it William Golding?
  it's definitely
  B: I don't know, but not Golding.

7 **A:** Who won the last football World Cup?
  sure it
  B: I'm wasn't England.

8 **A:** What was the name of that Steven Spielberg film
  about dinosaurs?
  haven't a
  B: I clue. I don't watch Hollywood movies.

B Work in pairs and answer the questions. Then turn to page 176 to check your ideas.

C Work in pairs and practise the conversations.

LEARN TO react to information

6A ▶ 9.5 Read the extracts from audio 9.4 below. Then listen and notice the intonation patterns speaker B uses.

1 **A:** It was Chaucer. I think he worked for the British
  government.
  B: Did he? I didn't know that.

2 **A:** It was Karl Marx.
  B: Oh really?

3 **A:** It was Einstein. He was a very good violinist,
  apparently.
  B: Was he? That's interesting.

4 **A:** Yeah, Guevara was a medical student …
  B: Oh yes, I knew that. I just couldn't remember.

5 **A:** Who went on a road trip with his friend?
  B: Ah, that's right.

6 **A:** It was da Vinci. He invented the parachute.
  B: Oh yeah, I was just about to say that!

B Answer the questions.

1 Which information did speaker B know already? *4/6*
2 Which information was new? *1/2/3*

SPEAKING

7 Work in pairs. Student A: you are going to ask your partner the questions below. First, add two more questions of your own. The answers can be found on page 174. Student B: turn to page 178.

Geography
1 *What's the capital of Australia? Is it Sydney,*
  Melbourne or Canberra?
2 *Which country has the second biggest population?*
  Is it China, India or Russia?
3 *Which one of these countries is not next to the*
  sea: Venezuela, Ecuador or Paraguay?
4
5

DVD PREVIEW

1 Discuss. What do you know about the painting at the bottom of page 121, and the artist who created it?

2 Read the sentences about Michelangelo. What do you think the words in bold mean? Which two pairs of words have opposite meanings?

1 His work is **unique** – no one has ever done anything similar.

2 Some said his work was **divine** because only God could create such beauty.

3 His fame is **eternal**. He will never be forgotten.

4 The sculptures are **extraordinary**. They are incredibly beautiful and realistic.

5 Although he was **mortal**, his work will never die.

6 His art is **awe-inspiring**. We feel small when we look at it. *↳ incredible*

7 His painting on the ceiling of the Sistine Chapel is an incredible **feat**. *→ achivement*

8 In those days, many normal men worked with stone, but he was far from **ordinary**.

9 Even as a child, he had **aspirations** to be a great artist.

10 As a young man in Florence he began his **quest** for fame. *↳ search*

3 Read about the BBC programme, *The Divine Michelangelo*. What is the contrast between Michelangelo's life and his art? *↳ diferencia.*

BBC The Divine Michelangelo

This BBC documentary examines the life and work of Michelangelo Buonarroti, one of the greatest artists in history. It looks at his background as a child in Florence, and how he went on to produce works such as the statue of David, the awe-inspiring ceiling of the Sistine Chapel, and the dome of St Peter's Cathedral, described here as 'the jewel in the crown on the Roman skyline'. The programme also reveals Michelangelo's tempestuous life, his fights with rivals and with his own demons, showing that an imperfect life can produce perfect art.

▶ DVD VIEW

4A Which of these sentences do you think are true?

1 Michelangelo was a sculptor, painter and architect. T

2 He said he was divinely inspired (inspired by God). T

3 He lived and worked three hundred years ago. F

4 His mother died when he was a child. T

5 He was from a rich family. F

6 His father always wanted him to be an artist. F

B Watch the DVD to check.

5A Read the notes. Which words do you think are missing?

Who was Michelangelo?

... a tempestuous genius ... he wanted eternal fame and ¹ _riches_

... an outsider who created works so big and so ² _beautiful_ nobody believed they were produced by a mortal

... NOT an ordinary labourer or honest, ³ _simple_ stonecutter

Background
... had an ⁴ _happy_ childhood
father, Ludovico, was a lowly-paid local official

What did he do?
... persevered and produced works which showed an extraordinary ⁵ _talent_

... created a unique vision of heaven on ⁶ _earth_

B Watch the DVD again and complete the notes.

C Work in groups and discuss. What do you think of Michelangelo's work? Have you ever seen any of his work? How do you think his work has influenced other artists?

Gabriel Marques (Nobel)
1 handred years of solity
Ralistic and magic

speakout influential work

6A ▶ 9.6 Listen to someone talking about someone whose work influenced her. Who does she talk about? How did this person's work change her life?

B Listen again and tick the key phrases you hear.

> **keyphrases**
>
> I fell in love with his novels. ✓
> That book really made its mark on me. ✓
> It had a big impact on me.
> He's one of the best-known writers. ✓
> I'm a big fan of that type of writing. ✓
> The style is brilliant. ✓
> It was very influential.
> He/She/Their work (really) inspired/influenced me … / to (do) …

C Plan to describe someone whose work influenced you. Write brief notes about the following:
• what they did *JK rowling*
• their place in history *20..?*
• what you learned from them *brave*
• how it has influenced the way you do things *confident person*

D Work in groups and take turns to describe your person.

writeback a wiki entry

7A Read the proposal.

> Subject: proposal
>
> Dear student,
> We are compiling a student wiki about world-famous, influential people in the arts and sciences. Please write a short piece (no more than 200 words) including information about where they live(d), when they did their work, their place in history, why they are influential, and who they have influenced. Do not write about political leaders, sports stars or businesspeople. Send your entry to the web address …

B Read an example entry. Does it fit the requirements in the proposal? Is anything missing?

IMPORTANT

Ravi Shankar is probably India's most famous musician. A sitar-player, composer, performer, musical director and teacher, he is best known in the west for his collaborations with George Harrison of *The Beatles*, who studied sitar under him and later produced some of Shankar's records.

Born into a wealthy family in 1920, at the age of ten Shankar went to Paris with his brother's dance group. By thirteen, he was part of the group, working as a dancer and playing different instruments. A few years later he decided to focus full time on the sitar and soon became a master of the instrument. In the 1950s and 60s he toured the world, giving Indian classical music a wider audience. It was during this time that he met and influenced Harrison and other well-known musicians from the UK and the United States.

Shankar wrote film scores and recorded numerous popular albums. He was deeply committed to playing live music, and even performed at Woodstock during the hippie era. In his seventies and eighties he was still performing regularly. He has been very influential because he helped to bring Indian music to the rest of the world.

C Now write your wiki entry about the person whose work influenced you. Use the wiki above and the key phrases to help.

HISTORY

1A Work in teams. Write ten sentences. Each sentence must use a different word from the box. The first team to finish wins!

revolution turning point development movement spread advance invention foundation discovery progress

B Read your sentences to the class.

THIRD CONDITIONAL

2A Complete the sentences with your own words.

1 Dayo left his job because …
2 Lily didn't pay for the meal at the restaurant because …
3 Cristian asked for a replacement phone because …
4 I didn't go on my free holiday to Jamaica because …
5 Kim didn't go to see U2 because …
6 I stopped talking to my mother because …

B Exchange sentences with a partner. Write third conditional sentences for each of the situations your partner completed.

Dayo left his job because he didn't like his boss. If he had liked his boss, he wouldn't have left his job.

PERIODS OF TIME

3A Complete the sentences with words for periods of time.

1 In which d_ _ _ _ _ were you born?
2 What can you remember about the n _ _ _ _ _ _ _-n _ _ _ _ _ _ _?
3 How did you celebrate the new m _ _ _ _ _ _ _ _ _?
4 What's your favourite e_ _ in history?
5 If you could go back in time for a f _ _ _ _ _ _ _ _, where and what c_ _ _ _ _ _ would you choose?
6 What do you think your g _ _ _ _ _ _ _ _ _ are/will be famous for?

B Work in pairs. Take turns to ask and answer the questions.

THE PASSIVE

4A Complete the sentences with the correct passive or active form of the verbs in the box.

~~discover~~ ~~assassinate~~ become ~~build~~ ~~climb~~ ~~declare~~ destroy ~~elect~~ ~~release~~ ~~identify~~

1 The tomb of Tutankhamun _was discovered_ in the Valley of the Kings, Egypt.
2 US and French scientists _identified_ the AIDS virus. 1984
3 A wall _was built_ between East and West Germany. 1961
4 Edmund Hillary and Tenzing Norgay _climbed the_ Mount Everest. 1953
5 The Titanic _was destroyed_ after hitting an iceberg in the North Atlantic. 1912
6 Nelson Mandela _was released_ from prison. 1990
7 Mahatma Gandhi _was assassinated_ by a terrorist. 1948
8 Margaret Thatcher, the UK's first female prime minister, _was elected_. 1979
9 The UK and France _declared the_ war on Germany. 1939
10 Two-year-old Pu Yi _became_ Emperor of China. 1908

B Match the events above with the dates in the box.

~~1922~~	1908	1912	1939
1948	1953	1961	1979
1984	1990		

1922: The tomb of Tutankhamun was discovered.

C Work in groups. Compare your answers and correct each other's work if necessary.

EXPRESSING UNCERTAINTY

5A Put B's words in the correct order to complete the conversations.

1 A: Where's the nearest bank?
   B: no / I / idea / have / sorry,
2 A: Is there anywhere you can smoke in this building?
   B: allowed / it's / definitely / no, / here / not
3 A: What time does this school open in the morning?
   B: at / fairly / opens / sure / I'm / it / 7.00a.m.
4 A: What was your last teacher's name?
   B: remember / can't / I
5 A: Do you know where the nearest restaurant is?
   B: clue / sorry, / haven't / I / a
6 A: What's the school director's name?
   B: it / not / a / might / I'm / percent / but / certain, / be / hundred / Timothy
7 A: How far away is the nearest supermarket?
   B: isn't / it / sure / far / I'm
8 A: What was yesterday's homework?
   B: forgotten / sorry, / I've

B Work in pairs. How many of your partner's questions can you answer?

UNIT 10

UNIT 10

world

▶ **Ethical man** p124

▶ **World food** p127

▶ **When you travel, …** p130

▶ **The great melt** p132

VOCABULARY the environment

1A Work in pairs and discuss. How important is 'green living' to you?

B Look at the sentences below and try to explain the meaning of the words/phrases in bold. Then use a dictionary to check.

1 How much of the food you buy is **pre-prepared** or **processed**? How much is **organic**?

2 How much of the food you eat is produced in the country you live in?

3 How is your home heated? Do you use **energy-saving light bulbs**?

4 Is your house **insulated** and/or **double-glazed**?

5 Do you turn lights/machines off or leave them **on standby**?

6 When you're buying a product, do you consider how to recycle the **packaging**?

7 How often do you buy, sell or give away **secondhand items**?

8 How much of your rubbish is **recycled**?

9 How many hours, on average, do you spend flying a year?

10 How often do you use a car?

C Answer questions 1–10 above.

D Work in pairs and compare your answers.

➠ page 173 **VOCABULARYBANK**

READING

2A Justin Rowlatt, a BBC journalist, decided to try living a greener lifestyle for a year. What changes do you think he made?

B Read the article to find out.

C Work in pairs and answer the questions below.

1 Why did Justin decide to try living ethically for a year?

2 Did he and his family enjoy the experience?

3 What kinds of things did they try to change?

4 What kinds of challenges does Justin say that other journalists have to face?

5 Did Justin and his family manage to reduce their impact on the environment?

6 Did the 'experiment' change the way that they have decided to live?

D Discuss. Do you think the 'Ethical Man' experiment is a good idea? Why/Why not?

1 Hi – I'm Justin Rowlatt and I'm the BBC's 'Ethical Man'. So, what does living ethically mean? Giving up the car, recycling wine bottles, not using plastic bags? I spent a year trying to find out.

2 I want to be clear about one thing right from the start – it wasn't my idea to become the BBC's ethical man. I had just started working for the BBC and on my first day the editor asked me to come into his office.

3 What did I think about the idea of a journalist trying to live as ethical a lifestyle as possible for a year, he wanted to know. He asked me if I liked the idea. What did I think? It was my first day; I said I thought it was a great idea!

4 That's why my family (Bee, my wife, thirty-five, and daughters Eva, five and Zola, four) and I agreed to spend a year doing everything we could to try to reduce our impact on the environment. We changed the light bulbs in our house to energy-saving bulbs. We changed the way we heat and power our home. We stopped flying and we got rid of the car. Instead we walked, used bicycles, or took public transport. We did our supermarket shopping online, ate organic vegetables and I even stopped eating meat (for a month). My heavily pregnant wife, Bee, walked two miles to hospital in the middle of the night, to give birth to our third daughter, Elsa. When we went on holiday to France, instead of choosing a two-hour flight, we went on a nightmarish twelve-hour journey on the train, in a heatwave.

5 You expect to face challenges as a journalist. Many of my colleagues regularly report from war zones. Others have just minutes to prepare before they are expected to give a clear explanation of complex economic data. Some have to work with criminal gangs. But few journalists have faced the sorts of challenges I have during my 'year of living ethically'.

6 It has been a tough year. I put my family through hell and there were many rows and arguments. But the overall result? We managed to reduce our carbon footprint by 37 percent – nearly double the total we had hoped to achieve a year ago.

7 Being forced to go green has shown me that anyone can achieve more than we think. However, I believe most people are too busy to go through all this without being compelled – as I was – to give it a go.

8 Having said that, we don't regret doing it, we aren't planning to get the car back and many of the other changes will remain, too.

3 Read the article again. Underline words/phrases in the text that match meanings 1–6.

1 the amount of damage we do (by our actions) to the air, water and land on Earth (paragraph 4) *impact*

2 threw away or destroyed (paragraph 4) *got rid of*

3 terrible – like a bad dream (paragraph 4) *nightmarish*

4 period of very hot weather (paragraph 4) *headwave*

5 made my family go through a bad experience (paragraph 6) *well put my family through hell*

6 be forced to do something (paragraph 7) *being compelled*

GRAMMAR reported speech

4A Complete the table to show how tenses change in reported speech.

direct speech	reported speech
'We ¹ **aren't** planning to get the car back …' *Present continuos*	He said they **weren't planning** to get the car back … *Past continius*
'Many of the other changes ² **will** remain.' *future will*	He said many of the other changes **would** remain. *Past would inf*
'My heavily pregnant wife, Bee, *Past simple* ³ **walked** two miles to hospital.'	He said he that his wife **had walked** to hospital. *Past perfect*
'I **think** it's a great idea!' *Present simple*	He said he ⁴ **thought** it **was** a great idea! *Past simple*
'It ⁵ **has** been a tough year.' *Prosnt Perfect*	He said it **had been** a tough year. *Past perfect*
'I ⁶ **had** just started working for the BBC.' *Past perfect*	He said he **had** just **started** working for the BBC. *Past perfect*
'Do you **like** the idea?' *Present Simple*	He asked me if I ⁷ **liked** the idea. *Past simple*

B Check your answers using the article in Exercise 2B.

C Look at the table again and underline the correct alternatives to complete the rules.

Rules:

1 When we report speech, we often move the tenses *back (backshift)/ forwards*, e.g. present simple → past simple, present continuous → past continuous, present perfect → past perfect, will → would.

2 If what the person says is still true, we can *keep the tenses the same/change the tense to a future form*, e.g. 'It's the 16th.' → She said it's the 16th.

3 In reported speech, we may also need to change *names and places/ pronouns and time references*, e.g. 'I'll see you <u>tomorrow</u>.' → He said he would see her <u>the next day</u>.

4 In reported questions, the word order is *the same as/different to that* for statements.

▸ page 162 **LANGUAGE**BANK

PRACTICE

* answers*
173 → more vocabulary

5A Complete the sentences by adding one word.

1 I'll see you in my office. [Editor to Justin]
He said he would see Justin in ___*his*___ office.

2 I've got a new job. [Justin to his wife]
He said he ___*had*___ a new job.

3 We're going to try and live a more ethical lifestyle. [Justin to Bee]
They said that ___*they*___ were going to try and live a more ethical lifestyle.

4 I'm going to take a taxi to hospital. [Bee to Justin]
She said she ___*was*___ going to take a taxi to hospital.

5 We're hot. [children to parents]
The children said ___*they*___ were hot.

6 We've achieved a lot. [Justin and Bee]
They said they ___*had*___ achieved a lot.

7 I didn't eat meat for a month. [Justin]
Justin said he ___*hadn't*___ eaten meat for a month.

8 I had expected to face challenges as a journalist. [Justin]
He said he ___*had*___ expected to face challenges as a journalist.

B ▶ 10.1 Listen to check your answers. Listen again and shadow the sentences.

direct
have to/must/can/can't
would/could/might
musn't

reported
had to/had to/could/couldn't
would/could/might
musn't

please don't try

She will be Loved

125

unaware

SPEAKING

6A Work in two groups. Group A: look at the photo, read the fact file below and discuss the questions. Group B: look at the photo and read the fact file on page 178.

The plastic bag problem

Did you know ...?

• The world uses 1 million plastic bags per minute.

• The 'Pacific Ocean Garbage Patch' is an area in the Pacific Ocean filled with waste plastic. The area may be as big as 5 million square km (more than twice the size of the USA). Millions of marine animals die when they eat the plastic, become caught in it, or feed it to their young.

• Plastic bags can now be found in all parts of the world, from the top of Mount Everest, to the bottom of the oceans, and the deserts of Mongolia. Each plastic bag takes more than 1,000 years to disintegrate and never completely disappears.

1 Why does the problem exist?

2 What should be done about it?

3 What laws/schemes would you introduce to deal with the problem?

B Work in pairs with a student from the other group. Tell them about the discussions you had in your group, and any ideas you had.

We talked about the problem of plastic bags. We thought it would be a good idea to make people pay for plastic bags in shops.

VOCABULARY *PLUS* word-building (prefixes)

7A Look at the example sentences 1–10 and underline the prefixes.

un-

1 It's very <u>un</u>usual to have snow in April.

2 The whole situation was completely <u>un</u>real.

re-

3 Most glass bottles and aluminium cans can be <u>re</u>cycled.

4 Don't throw away the bottles. They are <u>re</u>usable.

dis-

5 Roth doesn't like anybody who <u>dis</u>agrees with him.

6 She would never <u>dis</u>obey her parents.

mis-

7 Don't <u>mis</u>understand me. I want to help.

8 I always <u>mis</u>pronounce his name.

over-/under-

9 She hardly eats anything, and she's very <u>under</u>weight.

10 I think I've <u>over</u>cooked the pasta.

B Match the prefixes above with meanings 1–5.

1 not: ___un-___ and ___dis___

2 again: ___re___

3 too much: ___over___

4 too little: ___under___

5 wrong: ___mis___

8 Add prefixes to the words in brackets to complete the sentences.

1 He's lying. His story about how he cycled across Africa was completely ___unbelivable___ (believable).

2 It's easy to ___misjuge?___ (judge) somebody's character by looking at the clothes they wear.

3 Much of the snow in the Arctic has completely ___disappear___ (appeared).

4 These organic potatoes are delicious. Be careful not to ___overcook___ (cook) them.

5 Jessica decided not to accept the job because the company's policies were ___unethica___ (ethical).

6 I think I've done this all wrong. I probably ___misunderstood___ (understood) the instructions.

7 My house is always ___untidy___ (tidy). I don't have enough time to organise my things.

8 She walks to work every day, despite her ___disability___ (ability).

speakout TIP

Use prefixes to guess the meaning of words you don't know. Look at the words in bold below. Can you use the prefix to guess their meaning?

9 Work in pairs and take turns. Ask and answer the questions.

1 Which professions in your country do people often **mistrust**?

2 Who in your country is very famous now, but was **unknown** last year?

3 What kinds of documents do you sometimes need to **renew**?

4 Do you believe scientists have **overestimated** or **underestimated** the problem of climate change?

5 Do you **disapprove** of people who drive their cars everywhere? Why/Why not?

➡ page 173 **VOCABULARYBANK**

▶ **GRAMMAR** | verb patterns   ▶ **VOCABULARY** | reporting verbs   ▶ **HOW TO** | talk about food culture

A   B   C

READING

MOCHI♡

1 Work in pairs and discuss.

1 What countries do you think the food in the pictures comes from?

2 Would you eat these dishes? Why/Why not?

2A Read the text. Why is Osaka the world's greatest food city?

What's the greatest, most exciting food city in the world today?

There used to be one great food city in the world, and that was Paris. At least, that's what most people believed. People now agree that there is incredible food all around the world. Michael Booth, a writer, traveller and food-lover, thinks that the Japanese city of Osaka is the best.

With its busy food halls and small, exclusive restaurants, Osaka is 'bursting' with amazing places to eat. All around the city, you can find delicious fast food dishes which were invented here. Osaka is the city that invented both sushi and instant noodles in the same year (1958), but there are many more local dishes, too.

In Osaka, people love life and they love their food. They even have a saying, '*kuidaore*', which means 'eat until you are bankrupt' because they love to spend money on food. So, what about you? Which city is your culinary favourite?

B Read the text again and answer the questions.

1 What type of food is Osaka famous for?

2 Where can you eat it?

3 How do the people of Osaka describe their food?

LISTENING

3A ▶ 10.2 Listen to two people talking about their favourite food city. According to the speakers, which city, Hiroshima (H) or Madrid (M), has the following:

1 a small, cheap restaurant which serves wonderful seafood? **M**

2 informal restaurants where you order lots of dishes which everyone shares and eats from the middle of the table? **H**

3 something to eat which is like a cross between a pancake and a pizza? **H**

4 people getting together at Sunday lunchtime to have a few bites to eat? **M**

5 a restaurant which specialises in grilled chicken? **H**

B Listen again and complete the extracts below. Then check your answers in audio script 10.2 on page 198.

1 They've got the very famous sushi that everyone thinks about when they think of Japanese food, but they've got so much else to _offer_.

2 Hiroshima is really ~~famous~~ for its *okonomiyaki*.

3 *Tempura* is prawns and _vegetables_ deep fried in a really light, fluffy batter.

4 I lived in Madrid, in Spain, for around _10_ years on and off.

5 The quality of the food is _wonderful_

6 *Tarta de Santiago* is a great pastry _dessert_

7 I once tried pig's ear, which I have to say was possibly the _worst_ thing I've ever tasted.

C Do you know any cities which are good for food? What types of food are they best known for? Which areas have good restaurants? Plan to talk about your favourite food city. Use these phrases from the listening to make some notes.

My favourite food city is …   They've got all sorts of …
XXX is really famous for its …   It's a kind of …
It's really good (for) …   I think my favourite restaurant in … is …
One of my favourite restaurants is a place called …, which specialises in …   It's a cheap/basic/smart/expensive …   You can get …
I'd love to take you to XXX; you'd love it!
I know a really good … that I should take you to.

D Work in groups and take turns to talk about your favourite food city.

127

VOCABULARY reporting verbs

4A Match the verbs with the statements.

1 offer ~~~~ a) I can't eat anything else, thank you.

2 warn ~~~~ b) Would you like a coffee?

3 refuse ~~~~ c) Be careful. It's hot.

B Look at the statements/questions below. Rewrite each statement in reported speech using a verb from the box.

| ~~warned~~ explained ~~refused~~ promised invited suggested ~~offered~~ |

1 'You have to be careful not to eat too much.'

She _warned_ us not to eat too much.

2 'Why don't you come to Palermo and I'll take you to my favourite restaurant?'

He _invited_ us to Palermo, and he _offered_ to take us to his favourite restaurant.

3 'It will definitely be good value for money. I'm 100 percent certain of that.'

She _promised_ that it would be good value for money. ← sentence

4 'I think Lima could be one of the greatest food cities in the world.'

She _suggest_ that Lima could be one of the greatest food cities in the world. ← sentence

5 'The restaurant specialises in grilled chicken.'

He _explained_ that the restaurant specialises in grilled chicken. ← sentence

6 'I don't believe that there is any better food than in Singapore.'

He _refused_ to believe that there was any better food than in Singapore.

GRAMMAR verb patterns

5A Look at the verb patterns in bold in sentences a)–e). Then complete the table below with the sentences.

a) We **explained that** it was our first trip to the area.

b) He **agreed to show** us around Palermo.

c) She **suggested trying** some of the local dishes.

d) They **promised to cook** for us.

e) He **warned us not to eat** the chillies.

verb + infinitive with *to*	verb + *-ing*
She offered to show us around.	They recommended taking the bus
1 b) agreed to show	3 c) suggest trying
2 d) promised to cook	
Verb + object + infinitive with *to*	**Verb + *that***
They invited us to stay.	She decided that she would stay.
4 e) warned us not to eat	5 explained that

suggest agreed promised

B ▶ 10.3 Listen to the sentences above and underline the stressed words.

C Listen again and check your answers. Pay attention to the weak forms of *to* /tə/, *for* /fə/ and *that* /ðət/. Then listen and repeat.

D Some verbs use more than one pattern. Find two examples in Exercise 4B of verbs which can use different patterns.

*Agree: She **agreed to** show us around. They **agreed that** it was a good idea.*

▶ page 162 **LANGUAGEBANK**

promised suggest

PRACTICE

6 Complete the second sentence so that it means the same as the first. Use the correct form of the verbs in bold.

1 'During the festival, street vendors sell nothing but chocolate.' **explain**

She _explained that_ during the festival street vendors only sell chocolate.

2 People should come to the Tomatina festival in Spain. **suggest/visit**

Beatrix _suggested visiting_ Spain during the Tomatina festival. suggest

3 You shouldn't eat anything before the cheese-tasting festivals. There are more than 1,000 cheeses to try. **warn/eat**

He _warned_ us not _to eat_ anything before going to the cheese-tasting festivals.

4 'We'll definitely go to the Mango festival in India in July.' **promise/take**

He _promised to take_ me to the Mango festival.

5 'Would you like me to show you around the Eurochocolate festival?' **offer/show**

The tour guide _offered to show_ us around the Eurochocolate festival.

SPEAKING

7A Read the comments about food below. Do any of the people have similar ideas to you?

'I love good food, but I never cook it myself. I would rather go to a restaurant.'

'Food isn't at all important to me. I just eat when I'm hungry.' >:[

'Food is like a passion for me. I love cooking for lots of people.'

'People who eat in restaurants are lazy. It's such a waste of money.'

B Work in pairs. Tell your partner how you feel about food and cooking. Try to give examples.

C Work with another student. Tell them about your last partner.

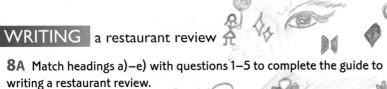

WRITING a restaurant review

8A Match headings a)–e) with questions 1–5 to complete the guide to writing a restaurant review.

a) Information about the price
b) Information about the menu
c) Details of the restaurant
d) Information about the service
e) Information about the atmosphere

1 ___ : Where is it? How can you contact them? How do you get there? What are the opening hours?

2 ___ : What's the décor like? Is it child-friendly? Is it noisy? Is it romantic?

3 __b__ : What kind of food does it serve? Are there any specialities? Do they serve vegetarian food? Are there any particular dishes you recommend?

4 ___ : Are the staff friendly? Do you have to wait a long time?

5 ___ : Is it good value for money? How much does it cost per person? Are there any special offers?

B Read the reviews below. Try to answer the questions above for each restaurant. Which one would you like to visit and why?

> **Are you hungry? You will be at some point. Here's a guide to some of the best restaurants in town.**

4,550 Miles from Mumbai (Indian): Boxhill Way, 0265 958 834

An unusual name for an unusual Indian restaurant, 4,550 Miles from Mumbai offers diners a totally different kind of curry experience. This restaurant has such incredibly stylish and modern décor that it goes against everything you expect from an Indian restaurant, and they even have jazz music playing in the background. Whilst the food is not cheap, it's delicious, so considering the surroundings, it is reasonably priced. They also offer different kinds of Indian treats such as deep fried stuffed green chillies and salmon tikka.

Feast (Vegetarian), Long Row, off Market Square, 0265 955 101

Feast specialises in vegetarian and vegan food and offers mainly light meals and snacks. Although the room is quite small, the atmosphere is cosy, due to the size of the room. And the coffee and homemade cakes which they serve during the day are so good that you'll want to come back. Feast becomes more of a bar in the evening, so look out for different DJs during the week.

Marcelo's (Italian), Lower East Street, 0265 979 994

Marcelo's is a large restaurant that is good at catering for big parties. They serve a wide variety of Italian food, and all pizzas and pasta dishes are reasonably priced. The restaurant itself is decorated in an elegant Mediterranean style and has such an authentic Italian atmosphere, complete with soft Italian music in the background, that you could easily forget which country you're in. They do a two-for-one deal on selected meals throughout the week so be sure to check which nights these are available.

LEARN TO link ideas

9A Look at the examples and answer questions 1–3.

*The food was **so** delicious **that** I didn't mind spending more than usual.*

*It was **such** an enjoyable meal **that** I would recommend this restaurant to anybody.*

*It was so expensive that I wouldn't go back there **unless** I wanted to impress a client.*

***Although** it's a five-star restaurant, the service was appalling.*

***While** the staff are friendly, and the atmosphere is fun, the food isn't anything special.*

1 Which linking words do we use to connect ideas which contrast with each other?

2 Which do we use to talk about the consequences of a situation?

3 Which do we use to suggest a condition?

B Read the reviews in Exercise 8B again. Find and underline the linking words.

C Write sentences to connect the five pairs of ideas below. Use the words in brackets to help.

1 Starbucks has been very successful. Now they want to open new stores in China. (so)

2 The restaurant has had very bad reviews. Nobody wants to go there. (such)

3 The food was very bad. I will only go back there again if they get a new chef. (unless)

4 The food was delicious. The service was poor. (although)

5 The restaurant had a good atmosphere. The food was disappointing. (while)

10 Choose a restaurant in your town/city. Write a short review (80–100 words). Use the guide in Exercise 8A to help you. Use the linking words in Exercise 9B to connect your ideas.

▶ **FUNCTION** | giving advice/warnings ▶ **VOCABULARY** | airports ▶ **LEARN TO** | make generalisations

VOCABULARY airports

1A Discuss the questions.

1 Do you ever travel by plane?

2 Do you enjoy it?

3 What do you like/dislike about air travel?

B Complete the questions/statements you might hear in an airport with the words in the box.

> proceed   aisle   card   passport
> priority   X-ray   hand   gate
> check   boards

1 Can I see your _____?

2 Your _____ number is 42.

3 In a few moments we will be calling all passengers with _____ boarding.

4 Would you like an _____ seat or a window seat?

5 Your flight _____ at 09.30.

6 Please have your boarding _____ ready for inspection.

7 How many bags do you have to _____ in?

8 Do you have any _____ luggage?

9 Please _____ to gate number 30.

10 Put your hand luggage through the _____ machine.

C Put the phrases in the order you might hear them in an airport.

FUNCTION giving advice/warnings

2A Work in pairs. Write a list of three things you must and mustn't do in an airport.

B Read the article. Does it mention your ideas?

C Work in pairs and discuss. Do you agree with the advice? Have you ever experienced any of these problems?

Ten things NOT to do in an airport

1 Pick the wrong terminal – Most airports have more than one terminal, so check which terminal you need before your taxi drops you off and drives away.

2 Annoy the check-in desk – They may be taking a long time, but getting annoyed with them will get you nowhere.

3 Make jokes about bombs or drugs – You might end up in jail instead of enjoying your holiday.

4 Take more than one bag – If it says one bag only for hand luggage, then you can't bring your handbag and shopping bags, too.

5 Go crazy on liquids – 100 ml is the limit. No extra bottles of suncream, shampoo and hair conditioner.

6 Waste people's time – Take off your jewellery, watch and belt before you go through the X-ray machine, so people don't have to wait while you go through the machine again and again.

7 Leave things in the trays – Don't wait until you get to the departure gate before you remember that you left your phone, iPod, keys and passport in the tray.

8 Use the airport internet terminals – They are slow and expensive, and you'll soon wish you hadn't bothered.

9 Shop because you're bored – You got cheap flights and a budget hotel, so why waste money on things you don't need, like giant-sized chocolate bars?

10 Leave the toilet stop until it's time to board – You'll keep the other passengers waiting, and then have to make that embarrassing walk down the aisle when you finally board.

3A ▶10.4 Listen and match conversations 1–4 with situations a)–d).

a) crime in a city

b) the journey to Heathrow airport

c) travelling in the north of the country

d) arriving at the airport

B Listen again. What problems do they talk about in each conversation?

4A Match 1–10 with a)–j) to complete the warnings/advice.

1 Watch out for

2 Make sure

3 Don't … (or else)

4 You'd better

5 If I were you,

6 Be careful

7 Don't forget to

8 Whatever you do,

9 You need to

10 The most important thing is

a) when you take trips into the jungle.

b) you find out how much the journey is supposed to cost.

c) watch out for groups of young children on the streets.

d) the taxi drivers who tend to hang around outside.

e) I'd allow about an hour and a half.

f) don't drink the water.

g) leave plenty of time.

h) get in until you've agreed the price with the driver, or else you could …

i) to remember to hold on to your handbag.

j) take your malaria tablets.

B ▶10.5 Listen and check your answers. Then listen and repeat the phrases. Which words are stressed?

▸ page 162 LANGUAGEBANK

5 Find and correct the mistakes. There is one mistake in each sentence.

1 The most important thing to remember is not going out alone.

2 If I were you I'll bring waterproof clothes.

3 Make sure if you wear a helmet and protective clothing when you ride a bike.

4 Be carefully when you're on the main roads. They're always very busy.

5 Don't forgetting to keep your luggage with you at all times.

6 Whatever you are do, don't buy food from the street sellers. It's terrible.

7 Watch out for people try to sell you fake watches.

8 You'll better leave your valuables in the hotel.

LEARN TO make generalisations

6A Look at how the speakers make generalisations. Cross out the alternative which is **not** possible.

1 Watch out for the taxi drivers who *tend to/are tend to/have a tendency to* hang around outside the airport.

2 You'd better leave plenty of time, because *often/never/usually* there are delays on the tube.

3 Be careful when you take trips into the jungle. *Sometimes/Generally/Always* there are a lot of mosquitoes there, so remember to take mosquito nets and insect cream.

4 *On the whole/It doesn't often happen/It's not very common*, but don't walk around the city obviously carrying money in a big money belt or anything.

5 There isn't really much crime. *On the whole/For the whole/Generally*, it's a pretty safe city.

B ▶10.6 Listen and underline the words/phrases the speakers use.

⁶speakout **TIP**

English speakers often make generalisations because they want to 'soften' a statement. Generalisations sound less direct and less aggressive. Can you use any of the phrases in italics in Exercise 6 to talk about travelling in your country?

7 Look at the sentences below. Then make generalisations using the prompts in brackets.

1 Men use the internet more than women. (tend)

Men tend to use the internet more than women.

2 I go to bed early in the winter. (whole)

3 The beaches are clean and safe. (generally)

4 The trains to the airport are not delayed. (not common)

5 Criminals target tourists. (tendency)

6 English people complain about the weather. (often)

SPEAKING

8A Work in pairs and role-play the situation. Student A: read the instructions below. Student B: turn to page 176.

Student A: you are a tourist. You want to go on a tour in the Australian Outback. Ask the Tourist Information for advice, e.g. Are there any animals to be careful of? What special clothes/equipment do you need?

I'd like some information about going into the Outback. First of all, what animals do I need to be careful of? …

B Change roles and role-play the following situation. Student A: you work in a diving centre. A customer would like to go snorkelling on the reef. Give him/her some advice using the prompts below:

1 most important thing / wear T-shirt / don't get sunburn Suncream / washes off in the sea

2 whatever do / not / touch the coral / break pieces off

3 watch out / stingrays – they can give you nasty sting

4 careful – strong currents – make sure / you can swim to shore/the boat

5 make sure / take underwater camera – take photos

DVD PREVIEW

1 Read about the BBC documentary. Why do you think life gets difficult for the polar bears?

BBC Nature's Great Events: The Great Melt

This BBC nature documentary, narrated by Sir David Attenborough, shows how life changes when the Arctic ice melts in the summer. This is the greatest seasonal change on the planet. During the long winter, the sun never rises, and temperatures plummet to minus 40 degrees. When the ice melts in the summer, the landscape changes completely and life gets difficult for the polar bears.

▶ DVD VIEW

2 Watch the programme and answer the questions.

1 Why is the melting ice a problem for the polar bears?

2 Is the problem worse than it was in the past?

3A Complete the sentences using the words in the box below.

ice flicker rises drown summer sea islands

1 The Northern Lights _____ across the sky.

2 Polar bears are in their element, hunting for seals on the frozen _____.

3 In February, the sun _____ for the first time in four months.

4 At the height of _____, even the permanent ice-caps are touched by the power of the sun.

5 Over 2.5 million square miles of ice have melted away, uncovering thousands of _____, surrounded by open ocean.

6 A mother bear and her adolescent cub rest on a fragment of _____.

7 If future melts are as extreme as this one, bears like these may either starve or _____, lost at sea.

B Watch the programme again to check your answers.

4 Work in groups and discuss.

1 Do you think man can do anything to improve the situation? What?

2 Do you think television programmes like this help to change the situation? How?

BBC

speakout an endangered place

5A ▶ 10.7 You are going to give short presentations about 'Places to see before they disappear'. First, listen to someone else's presentation. Which question below does he not answer?

1 What is the place?
2 Why is it in danger?
3 Why should you go there/see it?
4 How much does it cost to go there?
5 What can be done to change the situation?

B Listen again and tick the key phrases you hear.

> **keyphrases**
>
> One of the most beautiful places … (is under threat)
>
> One of the most endangered places is/has …
>
> One of the biggest problems …
>
> Something that everyone should have the chance to see is …
>
> The problem is that …
>
> Fortunately/Unfortunately, …
>
> Interestingly/Hopefully, …
>
> Many/Much of the … have/has been
>
> We have an opportunity to …
>
> In the past, … but now …
>
> … before it's too late.

6A Work on your own and plan a three-minute presentation. Do some research if necessary, or turn to page 179 for ideas. Use the prompts below and the key phrases to help.

- What is the place?
- Why is it in danger?
- Why should you go there/see it?
- What can be done to change the situation?

B Work in pairs and take turns.

Student A: practise your presentation. Use your notes, but try not to read all the information. Try to look up when you're talking.

Student B: help your partner improve their presentation. Time the presentation. Was it long enough? Give him/her feedback about his/her style and language.

Then change roles, and practise your presentations again.

C Give your presentation to the whole class. Watch the other students' presentations. Which places would you like to visit?

writeback email for action

7A Read the email and answer the questions. Where is Little Green Street? What is the problem?

Writting

name Place + Descriptio

Little Green Street is an old cobbled street just outside the centre of London. It is only 2.5m wide, and the houses here were built more than 225 years ago. The street, with its pretty, painted houses, and cobblestones, survived World War II. But now it is under threat from a developer who plans to build a car park and houses on the land near to it. The houses on Little Green St are protected by law (nobody can get permission to demolish them), but the street itself is not. In order to build his car park the developer plans to send heavy work lorries and machinery up and down this little old street. We are in no doubt that the lorries would destroy the street, and possibly the houses along with it. If you would like to join us in our protest against these plans, please sign your name at the bottom of the email. Thank you.

introduce problem

explain

mention consequence

call for action

B Write an email calling for action to protect one of the places talked about in Exercise 6. Use the email above and the key phrases to help.

133

THE ENVIRONMENT

1A Complete the words/phrases in bold with the missing letters.

1 I only eat **o_____c** food because it's grown without using chemicals.

2 I buy **p__-_r_____d** food because I don't have time for cooking.

3 I don't use **e___g-s___g** light bulbs because they're expensive.

4 My house isn't **in__l___d** very well, so it's always cold in the winter.

5 I try to **r__y___** glass, plastic and paper, but nothing else.

6 I'm careful to turn the computer and TV off at night, and not leave them **o_ s___d__**.

7 I buy a lot of **s____dh___** clothes – I like them and they're cheap.

8 I think **p____ss__** food is great because you can always make a quick meal at home.

B Write two statements that are true for you using the words/phrases in bold. Compare your sentences with a partner.

REPORTED SPEECH

2 Rewrite the reported conversation using direct speech.

> Samantha introduced me (Franco) to Tom who said he was pleased to meet me. I replied that it was a pleasure to meet him, too, and that I hoped Tom was enjoying his stay in Milan. He said he thought Milan was a beautiful city, and he had very much enjoyed his stay there. He said that he had met lots of wonderful people and eaten some delicious food. I asked Tom if he had had the chance to do any sightseeing. Tom told me that unfortunately he hadn't had very much time at all, but that he had enjoyed seeing the cathedral. I asked Tom if he planned to visit Italy again soon. He replied that he would have loved to, but that Italy was a long way from Queensland. I said that was true, and then invited Tom to come and join us for a coffee before he had to leave for the airport. Tom accepted.

Samantha: Franco, this is Tom.
Tom: Pleased to meet you, Franco.
Franco: It's …

3A Work in pairs. Take turns to ask and answer questions 1–5. Make a note of your partner's answers.

1 What are your plans for your next holiday?

2 Where did you grow up? Is it different there now?

3 What do you usually do on a Saturday afternoon?

4 What are you going to do later?

5 What two promises can you make concerning your English studies?

B Work with another student. Tell them what you learned about your partner using reported speech.

REPORTING VERBS

4 Work in pairs and take turns. Student A: choose a word from the box. Don't say the word, but say something in the manner of the word. Student B: listen and guess which word your partner is describing.

| explain | refuse | promise |
| warn | invite | suggest | offer |

A: If you do that again, I'm leaving.
B: warn?
A: That's right.

VERB PATTERNS

5A Circle the correct alternative.

1 He promised *to give/giving* me back the money.

2 I refused *to answer/answering*.

3 She invited us *to stay/for staying*.

4 He's offered *pay/to pay*.

5 In the end, everyone agreed *it to be/that it was* the best thing to do.

6 They explained *wanting/that they wanted* our address.

B Work in pairs and discuss. When was the last time:

• you promised to do something?

• you agreed with someone's idea?

• someone explained something to you?

• you warned someone about something?

• someone offered to do something for you?

GIVING ADVICE/WARNINGS

6A Complete the advice/warnings using the words in brackets to help.

1 _____, don't tell the teacher. (whatever)

2 _____ buy a phrase book. (forget)

3 _____ you get fit before you do it. (make)

4 _____ wear that old shirt, _____ you'll never get the job. (else)

5 If _____, I'd buy her some flowers. (were)

6 _____ you don't oversleep and miss the plane. (careful)

7 You _____ look for a hotel on the internet (better)

8 _____ ask your manager who can approve it. (need)

B Match the advice/warnings above with situations a)–h).

a) I haven't done my homework.

b) I forgot my mother's birthday.

c) I arrive in New York late at night. I don't know where I'm going to stay.

d) My plane leaves at 6a.m., but I don't have an alarm.

e) I'd like to have a holiday but I'm not sure who I have to get permission from.

f) I'm planning to run a marathon, but I haven't done any training.

g) I can't speak the language.

h) I've got a job interview, but I don't have any clean clothes to wear.

C Work in pairs. Take turns to give each other advice using the situations above.

BBC VIDEO PODCAST

Watch people talking about the biggest problems facing the world on ActiveBook or on the website.

Authentic BBC interviews

www.pearsonELT.com/speakout

REVIEW

2

drama

speakout DVD

▶ **GRAMMAR** | present perfect; relative clauses; conditionals   ▶ **FCE skills** | listen for main ideas; listen for detail and opinion

LISTENING

1 Discuss the questions.

1 Who are the most famous actors from your country?

2 Are they famous for anything besides acting?

2A Work in pairs. Match the sentence halves below to make useful tips for *Cambridge English: First* (FCE) Listening Part 3.

❝ listening tips FCE Part 3

1 Read the instructions carefully first C

2 Read sentences A–F e

3 The first time you listen, a

4 The second time you listen, d

5 People speak faster in this part of the test b

a) listen for the main idea and choose which sentence (A–F) is closest.

b) so don't worry if you don't catch every word.

c) What are the people talking about? What do you need to listen for?

d) check the main ideas – does the sentence fit *exactly*?

e) and try to predict main ideas.

B Work in pairs. Look at the exam task below and answer the questions.

1 What are the people talking about?

2 What do you need to listen for?

3 What ideas can you predict from sentences A–F?

3A ▶ R2.1 Do the exam task.

Part 3

Questions 19–23

You will hear five different people talking about a famous actor/actress they admire. For questions **19–23**, choose from the list (A–F) the reason why they admire this actor/actress. Use the letters only once. There is one extra letter which you do not need to use.

A	He/She inspired me to do my present job.	Speaker 1	C	19
B	He/She had a difficult childhood.	Speaker 2	D	20
C	I was impressed by something he/she did recently.	Speaker 3	F	21
D	I'm impressed by how successful he/she has been.	Speaker 4	A	22
E	He/She has used his/her success to help others.	Speaker 5	E	23
F	He/She is typical of a nationality.			

B Listen again. Do you want to change any of your answers?

GRAMMAR present perfect

4A Complete the sentences from the listening in the correct tense: present perfect simple or present perfect continuous.

1 I've always *thought/been thinking* he was a great actor.

2 She's *made/been making* films since the early 1990s.

3 She's *made/been making* many successful films.

4 She's often *been called/been being called* the 'English Rose'.

5 He's *played/been playing* a number of major roles over the years.

6 He's recently *worked/been working* on a film about the Vikings.

7 Since then, she's *visited/been visiting* the places round the world where similar problems exist.

8 Over the years she's *donated/been donating* millions of dollars to charity.

B Look at audio script R2.1 on pages 199–200 and check your answers.

5A Think of a famous actor/actress you admire. Change the sentences in Exercise 4A so they are true for this person.

B Work in pairs. Take turns to show your sentences to your partner and tell them about your chosen actor/actress.

[handwritten: information no important no utilizas that]

GRAMMAR relative clauses

6A Join the sentences below to make relative clauses.

He's a type of actor. He remembers he's still a real person.

He's the type of actor who remembers he's still a real person.

1 One actor is Johnny Depp. I really admire him.

[handwritten: One actor that i really admire is J.D.] *who that*

2 The children at the school watched him perform as Captain Sparrow for fifteen minutes. The school is in south London.

[handwritten: The children at the school, which is in south London, watched him]

3 After *Titanic*, she became the youngest actress to gain two Oscar nominations. *Titanic* made her a huge celebrity.

[handwritten: After titanic, who made her a huge celebrity, she] *which*

4 I can remember watching *Braveheart* and wanting to find out more. *Braveheart* is a film about Sir William Wallace.

[handwritten: I can remember watching Braveheart witch is a film about Sir willian Wallece,]

5 He's a person. He made me decide to be a history teacher.

[handwritten: he's a person that made me decide to be a]

6 It's a location. Parts of *Tomb Raider* were filmed there.

[handwritten: It's a location were Parts]

B Look at audio script R2.1 on pages 199–200 and check your answers.

C Look at your sentences again. Which of the sentences are defining relative clauses, and which are non-defining relative clauses?

7A Correct the mistakes in the following sentences.

1 It's a film which tells the story of a famous crime. *[handwritten: that / wich]*

2 The film, that is set in New York, is full of action.

3 He's the actor what is most famous in my country. *[handwritten: who]*

4 It's the place my favourite film where was made. *[handwritten: were / at the]*

5 I thought the film was very successful was actually quite boring. *[handwritten: witch]*

B Work in pairs. Think of films/actors/places that the sentences could describe.

LISTENING

8A Read the exam tips for *Cambridge English: First* (FCE) Listening Part 4. Decide if each one is before listening (B) or during listening (D).

listening tips FCE Part 4

1 Read the instructions carefully. Predict what information you might hear. *[handwritten: B]*
2 Read through the questions and underline key words. *[handwritten: B]*
3 The first time you listen, choose the correct answer. *[handwritten: D]*
4 The second time you listen, check your answers carefully. *[handwritten: D]*
5 If you're not sure, try to 'eliminate' the two wrong answers. *[handwritten: D]*

B Work in pairs. Look at the exam task in Exercise 9 on page 181 and underline the key words in each question.

C Work in pairs. Compare which words you underlined with your partner. Can you predict any information?

9 ▶ R2.2 Turn to page 181 and do the exam task.

GRAMMAR conditionals

10A Match the sentence halves from the listening in Exercise 9 to make conditional sentences.

[handwritten left margin: 1st, 2st, 0, 2st, 3st, 0, 1st, 0]

1 If you only want to be famous, *[C]*
2 If I were that person, *[e]*
3 When you watch yourself on the screen, *[a]*
4 If you could play any part, *[f]*
5 I wouldn't have fallen over *[b]*
6 If you want to succeed, *[h]*
7 You won't perform well *[g]*
8 If you don't enjoy it, *[d]*

a) you feel real pride in what you've achieved.
b) if I'd looked more carefully.
c) you'll just end up playing minor parts.
d) you'll never be happy as an actor.
e) what would I do in this situation?
f) what would it be?
g) if you take a role you're not really suited to.
h) don't just take the first offer that comes along.

B Look at the audio script R2.2 on page 200 and check your answers.

C Work in pairs. Look at the sentences above again and decide if each sentence is in the zero conditional (0), first conditional (1), second conditional (2) or third conditional (3)?

11A Use the prompts to write eight conditional sentences which are true for you.

[handwritten left margin: 0, 1st, 2nd, 3rd, 0, 2nd, 1st, 2nd]

1 When I get home in the evening, I usually _____ .
2 When I get home tonight, I'll *[handwritten: will do my homework]*
3 If I could be famous for something, I *[handwritten: would like to be a famous writter]*
4 If I had been born in another country, *[handwritten: I would have had other life]*
5 When I feel bored, *[handwritten: I usually play guitar]*
6 If I could meet a famous person, *[handwritten: I would take a picture with him]*
7 I won't *[handwritten: be late, if I get out of my house at time.]*
8 I wouldn't have *[handwritten: passed, If i havent studied]*

B Work in pairs. Compare your sentences.

[handwritten: subject have/has PP]
[handwritten: I've studied for six year]
[handwritten: I've been living here for year]
[handwritten: subject + have/has + verbing]

▶ **VOCABULARY** | history; success; ability   ▶ **FCE SKILLS** | understand text structure; read for specific information

READING

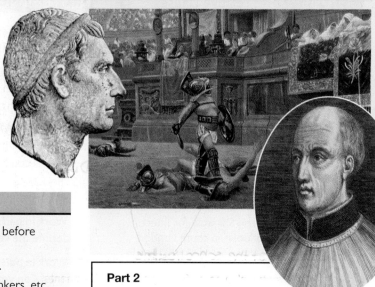

1 Work in pairs. Discuss the questions.

1 What were your ambitions when you were young? Did you want to be famous?

2 Why do you think people want to become famous?

2A Put the exam tips for *Cambridge English: First* (FCE) Reading Part 2 in the correct order.

reading tips FCE Part 2

1 Match the sentences to each gap. Check for links both before and after each gap.

2 Predict what kind of information is missing in each gap.

3 Underline reference words: pronouns, conjunctions, linkers, etc.

4 Read the paragraph again to make sure it makes sense with the sentence added.

5 Read through the main text for general understanding. 1

B Work in pairs. Look at the first part of the exam task on pages 138–139 and answer the questions.

1 What is the text about?

2 What kind of information is missing in each gap?

3 Which words in the paragraphs would you underline?

C Do the exam task.

VOCABULARY history

3A Use the words/phrases in bold from the text in Exercise 2C to complete the sentences below. You may need to change the form of the words/phrases.

1 The Georgian *era* was a time when a lot of people suffered.

2 The 21st Century was *turning point* in politics.

3 My country was *colonised* in the 16th Century, but became independent 200 years later.

4 Slavery ended in the 17th Century. Former slaves were *liberated* and given small plots of land.

5 There are many different political parties, each with very different *leaders*.

6 Fifty years ago there was a period of rapid economic *development*

7 In the 1960s, the civil rights _____ changed the lives of many people. *movement*

8 We have never had a _____. We still have a monarchy. *revolution*

B Look at the sentences again. Change the sentences so that they are true for your country.

C Work in pairs and compare your sentences.

4 Discuss the questions in groups.

1 Do you agree that modern society is obsessed by fame?

2 Why do you think over half of the teenagers in the survey want to be famous?

3 Would you like to be famous? Why/Why not?

Part 2

Questions 9–15

You are going to read an article about the history of fame. Seven sentences have been removed from the article. Choose from sentences **A–H** the one which fits each gap (**9–15**). There is one extra sentence which you do not need to use.

I can still remember discussing future careers at school quite clearly. I wanted to be a pilot, and among my classmates there was, among other jobs, a future doctor, designer and police officer.
[H 9]

A recent study of teenagers in the UK, however, shows that over half of them want to be famous during their lifetimes, and it doesn't matter what for or how.

So why this modern obsession with fame? Is it because of the increasing number of TV talent shows, offering stars and glory to fame-hungry young people? Is this just a modern phenomenon?

[B 10] Some of the earliest 'celebrities' were monarchs: kings, queens, emperors, etc. In 44BC Julius Caesar, famous for his **colonisation** of Gaul and Engand, became the first Roman to have his face put on a coin during his lifetime.

[D 11] His celebrity status actually continued until the 19th Century, when the 'epithet Roscius' was awarded to actors who were considered to be at the very top of their game.

A Even today, the place attracts thousands of visitors who come to see the place where he was murdered.

B Apparently not. In fact, the way we celebrate famous people is by no means just a modern occurrence.

C Dr van Wees added that this could have been 'the next best thing to appearing on TV'.

But celebrity status also came from sporting achievements. According to Dr. Hans van Wees, who lectures in ancient Greek history at University College London, winning athletes in the ancient Olympic games 'were not only widely talked about, but were given the equivalent of red-carpet treatment'.

They were also given free meals for life, and had hymns of praise performed in their honour. **⌐ 12**

Roman gladiators were also celebrities in their time, and their fights attracted thousands of spectators at a time. **G 13**

Religious figures have also gained fame throughout the ages. After he was murdered in Canterbury Cathedral in 1170, Thomas Becket's name spread across Europe, and pilgrims began to arrive at the place he was murdered to show their respect. **A 14**

A real **turning point** was the start of the industrial **revolution** in the 18th Century. Times were changing, with **advances** in science, religion and culture. One of the most significant of these for creating celebrities was the **development** of printing techniques, and by the Victorian **era**, authors such as Charles Dickens made their stories well-known by publishing them in parts, in newspapers and magazines.

Dickens even started his own weekly magazine, 'Master Humphrey's Clock', in which he published his own stories with considerable success. **F 15**

In more recent times, political campaigners have also enjoyed fame, such as Martin Luther King Jr., one of the main **leaders** of the civil rights **movement**, which led to the **liberation** of many oppressed minority groups in the USA.

So it seems that celebrity is no modern thing, though perhaps our obsession with it has reached new heights in modern times. Celebrity status is to be prized, whatever it's for.

D And during the same era, the Roman actor Quintus Roscius Gallus was praised by the Emperor Sulla for his acting skills.

E You couldn't get much more famous at this time.

F This made him internationally famous, even across the Atlantic in the USA.

G News of their battles would **spread** by word of mouth, and boys admired them.

H At this time, though, 'the future' was still a long way away, and inevitably only a few of us realised our childhood dreams.

READING

5A Work in pairs. Which of the exam tips below are good (G) advice, and which are bad (B)?

reading tips FCE Part 3

1 Read each question and underline the key words.

2 Read the text carefully, stopping after each sentence, and look for the question which matches the information.

3 The text will contain the same words as the questions – you only need to look for these.

4 When you find the relevant section, read it carefully to make sure it fits.

5 The questions are in the same order as the information in the text.

B Look at the exam tips again and change the bad advice to good advice.

6A Read the questions in the exam task on page 182 and underline the key words.

B Work in pairs and compare the words you underlined.

C Turn to page 182 and do the exam task.

VOCABULARY success/ability

7A Correct the mistakes in the sentences below.

1 If you want to succeed, it's important to focus at what you want. _on_

2 You need to work hard in grammar if you want to learn English. _at_

3 I have a friend who is an expert of computer programming. _in_

4 I'm hopeless about cooking. I can't even fry an egg! _at_

5 To be good at sport you have to believe of yourself. _in_

6 I would love to have the opportunity for travel around the world. _to_

7 I have a natural talent at music, I think. _for_

8 My sister is a natural highly achiever, she always did really well at school.

9 If you want to get better on English you should watch films in English. _at_

10 If you want to be successful at something, you should practising it for 10,000 hours.

B Look at the sentences again. Then change the sentences so they are true for you.

C Work in pairs and compare your sentences.

DVD PREVIEW

1A Work in pairs and look at the photo opposite. What do you think the relationships between the people are?

B Underline the correct alternative to complete the sentences below.

1 Alan *proposed/got engaged* to Jodie on holiday, she said 'yes' and they *proposed/got engaged*. The wedding is in June.

2 We thought Denise didn't like Ben so we were surprised when he asked her to marry him and she *accepted/turned him down*. We all thought she would *accept/turn him down*.

3 Last week Neil and Carmine *went on a date/were dating* together for the first time and now they are *going on a date/are dating* each other.

4 After their big argument and breakup, Pascal and Marie *got back together/made up with* each other and decided to *get back together/make up*.

5 After they'd been together for two years, Owen and Mariska gradually *drifted apart/went their separate ways*. They realised the relationship wasn't working so they finally *drifted apart/went their separate ways*.

C Work in pairs and discuss. What is the difference between each pair of verbs above?

I propose = ask someone to marry you; get engaged = agree to get married

2 Read the programme information and find out where the series is set, what a *laird* is (in your opinion) and what is about to happen.

BBC
Monarch Of The Glen

Monarch of the Glen is a long-running and popular BBC series about a community in the Highlands of Scotland in the 1920s and 1930s. It centres on the affairs of the Macdonald family, who have been lairds of Glenoble for hundreds of years. In this episode, Iona McLean, a local shepherdess is to marry Malcolm McRae. The current Laird of Glenoble, Paul Bowman-Macdonald, has agreed to accompany Iona to the ceremony and give her away.

▶ DVD VIEW

3A Watch the DVD and choose the correct summary.

1 Iona tells Paul she doesn't love him, and decides to marry Malcolm.

2 Iona tells Malcolm she doesn't love him, and decides to marry Paul. *(ticked)*

3 Malcolm tells Iona he doesn't love her, and that she should marry Paul.

B Watch again and answer the questions. Write I (Iona), P (Paul) or M (Malcolm).

1 Which of the characters is feeling anxious? *Iona*

2 Which of the characters is deeply in love with Iona? *Paul*

3 Which of the characters was once engaged to her? *Malcolm*

4 Which of the characters is angry with Paul? *Malcolm Iona?*

5 Which of the characters doesn't want to marry Iona? *Malcolm*

6 Which of the characters does Iona love? *Paul*

C Watch again and complete the phrases.

1 'Well, at least he ___*turn up*___ this time.'

2 'And it's the hardest thing I *'ve ever done*___

3 'Just ___ out, I suppose. Couldn't quite keep a lid on it.' *slipped*

4 'You *take* that *back* right now!'

5 'It came *from the heart*___

6 'You only *propose* to me this time because, because you felt *guilty* about what happened the last time.'

7 'You don't want to *settle* with me, here, now. Do you?'

8 'Don't you *dare* speak to me! You've just given me away!'

9 'And I' *taking* repossession.'

D Work in pairs and discuss. What do you think happened before the clip? What do you think happens after it?

speakout favourite film moments

5A ▶ R2.3 **Listen to someone describing their favourite moment from a film. Answer questions 1–5.**

1 What was the film? *28 days later*

2 Was the moment he describes at the beginning, middle or end of the film? *beginning*

3 What aspects of the film does he describe? *Danny Boil? amazing shots*

4 What did he like best about it? *My style how they music film this the way was it filmscene*

5 Who does he recommend the film to? *people to like to see something original*

B Listen again and tick the key phrases you hear.

key phrases

• I found it really / quite ...

• I fell in love with (the character) ✓

• It really made its mark on me. ✓

It had a big impact on me.

He's / She's one of the best-known actors / directors / etc.

• I'm a big fan of ... ✓

• The style is brilliant ... ✓

• What I liked best was ... ✓

• I'd definitely recommend this film for people who ... ✓

If you like ____, then you should definitely see this.

6A Think of your favourite film moment. Use the prompts below to make notes.

• What was the film? What type of film is it?

• Which actors starred in it?

• What happened in your favourite moment?

• How did you feel?

• What did you like best about it?

• Who would you recommend it to?

B Work in pairs. Take turns to describe your favourite film moments.

writeback a film review

7A Work in pairs. Read the *Cambridge English: First* (FCE) Writing Part 2 exam task and the exam tips below, then answer the questions in the writing tips box.

writing tips FCE Part 2

1 Read the question carefully and underline what you have to include. *What must you put in your report?*

2 Think about who the target reader is and what style you need to use. *Who is it for? Should it be formal or informal?*

3 Think about the type of language you will use. *What vocabulary can you use? Which key phrases from Exercise 5B could you include?*

4 Think about organisation and which paragraphs you will use. *What will you include in each paragraph?*

5 When you've finished, read your work again and check for any spelling or language errors.

Part 2   *100-120*

Write an answer to question 3. Use 120–180 words in the appropriate style.

---

3 You recently saw this notice on a film website.

> ### Write a review for us!
>
> Have you seen a film recently that made its mark on you? If so, could you write a review for our website? Include information about what type of film it is, where it's set, the main actors and the plot, and say what you liked/disliked about it, and whether you would recommend it.

Write your review.

B Read the sample answer on page 181. Does it contain all the necessary information from the exam task? Which information is included in each paragraph?

8A Use the planner below to plan your review.

• Paragraph 1: Introduction, type of film, where it's set, main actors

• Paragraph 2: The plot/main events

• Paragraph 3: What you liked/didn't like about it

• Paragraph 4: Whether you would recommend it (and who to)

B Do the exam task in Exercise 7A.

EXPRESS UNCERTAINTY

1 Read about Part 2 of the *Cambridge English: First* (FCE) Speaking Test and answer the questions below.

speaking tips FCE Part 2

In Part 2 you are given two photos connected by topic, and have to speak on your own for about one minute. The examiner will ask you to compare the pictures, then answer a question about them. Don't describe the pictures in detail, but do talk about general similarities and differences. Don't interrupt your partner when they are speaking – when they have finished you will be asked another question about their photos, and have twenty seconds to respond. If you aren't sure what you have to do you can ask the examiner to repeat the question. If you don't know a word in one of the pictures, this is okay, but you should describe it using other words you know.

1 How long do you have to speak for when talking about the photos? *1 min*

2 How should you describe the pictures? What else should you do? *similarities differences*

3 Can you talk about your partner's photos? *nop no interrup*

4 What should you do if you don't understand the task? *ask it again*

5 What should you do if you don't know a word that's in the pictures? *discribe with other words*

2A ▶ R2.4 Listen to Ana and Marc doing the exam task below. Who performs better? Why?

> How do you think the people performing are feeling?

> What personal qualities are important to achieve success? *X*

B ▶ R2.5 Listen again to Ana's part and tick the key phrases she uses.

keyphrases

I'm not a hundred per cent ✓ certain, but it might be …

I'm not sure, but I think …

I know/I'm sure it isn't …

It's definitely not … ✓

I used to know …

I can't remember/I've forgotten …

---

3 Work in pairs. Take it in turns to be the examiner and the candidate, and practise the exam task below.

> Why is it important for celebrities to do these activities?

CLARIFY OPINIONS

4A Work in pairs. Match the sentence halves below to make useful exam tips.

speaking tips FCE Part 4

1 Personalise your opinions ✓ *c*

2 The examiner may ask questions to each of you in turn *e*

3 You don't have to agree with your partner, *d*

4 Always have an opinion – *d*

5 Use this as your last opportunity *b*

a) it doesn't matter if it's right or wrong!

b) to show the examiner how well you can speak English!

c) and give real or hypothetical examples to support your ideas.

d) but try not to interrupt them too much. ✓

e) or general questions to both of you.

B Read the quotes from candidates about the *Cambridge English: First* (FCE) Speaking Test Part 4. Who do you think did well (W), and who do you think badly (B)?

1 'The examiner asked me a question which wasn't very interesting, so I changed the subject and talked about my career.' *B*

2 'The examiner didn't say very much. Most of the discussion was just between me and my partner.' *W*

3 'I expressed a few opinions which I think weren't right, but I thought I'd say them anyway.' *W*

4 'I hadn't said much in the other parts of the test, so I didn't say much here. I thought that up to this point I had already failed, anyway.' *B*

5 'I enjoyed this part, as I could just relax and talk about my opinions. Me and my partner had a really good discussion, and were surprised when the examiner told us it was the end of the test!' *W*

---

5 Put the phrases in the box in the right place in the table.

> For me, …   Like I said, …
> I do think …   In my view, …
> The reason I say (that's important) is that …
> For one thing, …
> Having said that, …
> That's what I was saying.
> I must say, (I agree with …)
> For example, …
> Let me give you an/another example.

Giving opinions
For me, …
I do think   *in my view*
I mus say

Giving examples
For one thing   *Let me giv*
For erample

Referring to what you said earlier
The reason i say …
having said tha
that's what i was saying
like i said

6 Work in pairs. Do the exam task.

> ### Part 4
>
> - Why do you think some people want to be famous?
> - What would you like to be remembered for after you die?
> - Some people would prefer to be rich than famous. What do you think?
> - Do you think we pay too much attention to celebrities nowadays?
> - What advice would you give to someone who wants to be successful in their career?

IRREGULAR VERBS

VERB	PAST SIMPLE	PAST PARTICIPLE
be	was	been
beat	beat	beaten
become	became	become
begin	began	begun
bend	bent	bent
bet	bet	bet
bite	bit	bitten
bleed	bled	bled
blow	blew	blown
break	broke	broken
bring	brought	brought
broadcast	broadcast	broadcast
build	built	built
burn	burned/burnt	burned/burnt
burst	burst	burst
buy	bought	bought
catch	caught	caught
choose	chose	chosen
come	came	come
cost	cost	cost
cut	cut	cut
deal	dealt	dealt
dig	dug	dug
do	did	done
draw	drew	drawn
dream	dreamed/dreamt	dreamed/dreamt
drink	drank	drunk
drive	drove	driven
eat	ate	eaten
fall	fell	fallen
feel	felt	felt
feed	fed	fed
fight	fought	fought
find	found	found
fly	flew	flown
forbid	forbade	forbidden
forget	forgot	forgotten
forgive	forgave	forgiven
freeze	froze	frozen
get	got	got
give	gave	given
go	went	been/gone
grow	grew	grown
hang	hung	hung
have	had	had
hear	heard	heard
hide	hid	hidden
hit	hit	hit
hold	held	held
hurt	hurt	hurt
keep	kept	kept
know	knew	known
lay	laid	laid
lead	led	led
leap	leapt	leapt
learn	learned/learnt	learned/learnt

VERB	PAST SIMPLE	PAST PARTICIPLE
leave	left	left
lend	lent	lent
let	let	let
lie	lay	lain
light	lit	lit
lose	lost	lost
make	made	made
mean	meant	meant
meet	met	met
mistake	mistook	mistaken
pay	paid	paid
put	put	put
read /riːd/	read /red/	read /red/
ride	rode	ridden
ring	rang	rung
rise	rose	risen
run	ran	run
say	said	said
see	saw	seen
sell	sold	sold
send	sent	sent
set	set	set
shake	shook	shaken
shine	shone	shone
shoot	shot	shot
show	showed	shown
shrink	shrank	shrunk
shut	shut	shut
sing	sang	sung
sink	sank	sunk
sit	sat	sat
sleep	slept	slept
slide	slid	slid
smell	smelled/smelt	smelled/smelt
speak	spoke	spoken
spell	spelt	spelt
spend	spent	spent
spill	spilled/spilt	spilled/spilt
split	split	split
spread	spread	spread
stand	stood	stood
steal	stole	stolen
stick	stuck	stuck
sting	stung	stung
swim	swam	swum
take	took	taken
teach	taught	taught
tear	tore	torn
tell	told	told
think	thought	thought
throw	threw	thrown
understand	understood	understood
wake	woke	woken
wear	wore	worn
win	won	won
write	wrote	written

LANGUAGE BANK

GRAMMAR

question forms
object questions

Object questions use the word order: question word + auxiliary verb + subject + infinitive.

question word	auxiliary verb	subject	verb
Where	do	you	work?
What	did	she	say?
When	are	they	coming?

yes/no questions

Yes/No questions don't use a question word. The answer to the question is Yes or No.

auxiliary verb	subject	verb
Does	he	smoke?
Did	we	win?
Have	they	arrived?

subject questions

When the *wh-* question word is the subject of the question:
- we don't use an auxiliary verb (*do, did,* etc.).
- we use the same word order as in an affirmative sentence.

question word	verb	object
Who	wants	ice cream?
What	happened?	---
Who	ate	the cheese?

questions with prepositions

When we use a verb + preposition expression (but not multi-word verbs) such as *look for, depend on, write about,* etc., we usually keep the verb and preposition together.

*What did you **talk about**? Who are you **looking for**?*

In very formal English we sometimes move the preposition to the front of the sentence. Compare:

*What does it **depend on**? **On** what does it **depend**?*

review of verb tenses
present simple

+	He **looks** happy.
-	He **doesn't look** happy.
?	**Does** he **look** happy?

Use the present simple to talk about something that is always or generally true, habits, routines, with *be* and other state verbs (see below).

present continuous

+	We**'re staying** here.
-	We **aren't staying** here.
?	**Are** we **staying** here?

Use the present continuous to talk about an activity happening at the time of speaking or a temporary activity happening around now. It may be happening at the moment, but maybe not.

past simple

+	They **worked** hard.
-	They **didn't work** hard.
?	**Did** they **work** hard?

Use the past simple to talk about finished actions, events or situations in the past.

past continuous

+	I **was living** there during the 90s.
-	I **wasn't living** there during the 90s.
?	**Were** you **living** there?

Use the past continuous to talk about an action or situation in progress at a particular time in the past. This action was not finished at that time.

state verbs and dynamic verbs

State verbs are not usually used in the continuous form. The most common state verbs are:

- attitude verbs: *love, hate, like, want, prefer*
- thinking verbs: *believe, know, remember, understand, mean, imagine*
- sense verbs: *see, hear, sound, appear, seem*
- belonging verbs: *own, possess, belong to, have, contain, include*

Some state verbs can be used in the continuous form when they describe actions, e.g. *see, have, think.*

*I**'m seeing** Phil tonight.* (see = meet)

*We**'re having** a party.* (have = organise)

*I**'m thinking** of going to university.* (think = consider)

talking about yourself

introducing a question
Could I ask a question?
There are a couple of things I'd like to ask about.
Can I ask you about that?
I have a query.

introducing an opinion
For me (the most important thing is) …
I'd have to say …
In my opinion, …
One thing I'd like to say is that …

PRACTICE

1 Write questions for the answers in italics.

1 Where _do you live_?
   I live *in Madrid*.

2 Who _won the game_?
   Nick won the game.

3 Does _he eat meat_?
   No, he doesn't eat meat.

4 What _are they doing_?
   They are *sleeping*.

5 What _are you writing_? about
   I'm writing about *my first holiday*.

6 When _did you arrive_?
   We arrived *yesterday*.

7 Who _ate the chocolate_?
   We ate the chocolate.

8 Did _you like the film_?
   Yes, we liked the film.

2 Put the words in brackets in the correct places to make questions.

1 the President? (killed, who)
   who killed the president?

2 were you thinking? (what, about)
   what were you thinking about?

3 to the old theatre? (happened, what)
   what happened to the old theatre?

4 Where your great-grandparents come? (from, did)
   where did your great-gradparents come from?

5 your ancestors from here? (come, did)
   did your ancestors come from here?

6 she here for a long time? (worked, has)
   has she worked here for a long time?

7 is all that noise? (who, making)
   who is making all that noise?

8 house you looking for? (are, which)
   which house are you looking for?

---

1 Underline the correct alternatives.

'Like most translators, I [1]*'m speaking/speak* several languages. At the moment, I [2]*'m attending/attend* a conference. I [3]*was doing/did* some work for an internet company when I [4]*was hearing/heard* about this conference. I [5]*was arriving /arrived* three days ago and I'm going to stay until Monday, when it ends.'

My best friend is called Gina. We [6]*aren't speaking/don't speak* to each other every day, but we're very close. I [7]*was meeting/met* her on my first morning at university. I [8]*was looking/looked* for the library when she came up to me and asked, 'Excuse me, [9]*do you know/are you knowing* where the library is?' We [10]*were finding/found* it together!

2 Put the verbs in brackets into the correct tense.

1 Sit down and watch the game! We _are wining_ (win) 2–1. Ronaldo scored two minutes ago.

2 John wasn't here last summer. He _traveld_ _was travelling_ (travel) around Africa.

3 Fifty years ago, my favourite writer _died_ (die).

4 I didn't do the homework because I _wasn't_ (not listen) when the teacher told us what to do. _listening_

5 DVDs _don't work_ (not work) very well on my laptop, so I use the TV and DVD player.

6 What's that smell? Can you turn off the oven? I think the food _is burning_ (burn).

7 _Did you see_ (see) that film last night? What did you think?

8 Everyone knows that smoking _causes_ (cause) cancer.

---

1 Find and correct the mistakes in the conversation below. There are six mistakes.

1 A: There are a couple of things I'd like ask about. _to_

   B: Go ahead.

   A: Firstly, which of your films do you think is the best?

   B: I'd having to say *Millennium Dreamer*. For me, it's my best film and it was my first comedy. _have to_

   A: Can I ask you around that? You've never done comedy before. Why not? _about_

   B: I don't know. I suppose people think I'm a serious actor.

   A: Could I ask question about your image? Is it accurate? Are you really the strong silent type in real life? _a_

   B: No. One of thing I'd like to say is that these images are invented by the media. By my opinion, good actors are never just one thing. That's why they're actors. _IN_

LANGUAGE BANK

GRAMMAR

2.1 present perfect/past simple

time up to now

+	I**'ve been** to Marrakesh.
-	He **hasn't been** here.
?	**Have** you **tried** it?

Use the present perfect for actions which have happened in your life before now. These are often general experiences. It isn't important exactly when these things happened.

He**'s played** in an Indie band **for a couple of years**. I **haven't travelled** to other countries.

We often use the adverbs *ever* and *never* with the present perfect.

We **'ve never** been to China. Have you **ever** been to the Opera?

recent events

Use the present perfect to talk about events which happened a short time ago. We often use the adverbs *just*, *yet* and *already*.

I've **just** finished his book. It was brilliant.

We've **already** eaten.

Have you done your homework **yet**?

We've seen a lot of Jude **recently**.

present perfect or past simple?

Use the past simple to talk about a specific event which happened at a specific time.

I**'ve been** to Sweden. (At some time in my life up to now. We don't know when.)

We **went** to Stockholm in 2002. (Not *We've been to Stockholm in 2002.* This is a specific occasion and date, so we use the past simple.)

2.2 narrative tenses

past simple

Use the past simple for states and actions in the past. We often specify the time when they happened.

I **left** university **in 1996**. He **didn't know** the way to Sal's house.

past continuous

Use the past continuous to talk about the background information for a story. Use the past simple to talk about the main events.

As I **was walking** through the park, the sun **was shining** and the birds **were singing**. Suddenly, I **heard** a loud noise.

Often the past continuous action is interrupted by another action (in the past simple).

I **was having** a bath when the phone **rang**.

We can use conjunctions like *as* and *while* to talk about two actions which were happening at the same time.

While I was reading the paper, I watched the women buying vegetables in the market.

For more information on state and dynamic verbs section 1.2, page 144.

past perfect

+	I **had finished** my work.
-	They **hadn't had** time.
?	**Had** they **been** there before?

Use the past perfect to make it clear that one action happened before the other.

```
        PAST                                NOW
  I lost my wallet.     I didn't have any money.
_____X_____X_____|
 past perfect        past simple          present
```

I **didn't have** any money because I **had lost** my wallet.

When *before* or *after* is used in the sentence, it's already clear which action comes before the other, so we can use the past simple instead of the past perfect.

She **had lived** in London for five years **before** she moved to New York. She **lived** in London for five years **before** she moved to New York.

We often use the past perfect with 'thinking' verbs like *remember, realise, think, discover, find out*, etc.

When I got to the school, I **realised** I'd left my books at home.

2.3 telling a story

beginning the story	This happened when …
	In the beginning, …
describing what happened	Well, …
	Anyway, …
	So, …
	Before long, …
	And then, all of a sudden …
	The next thing I knew, …
ending the story	In the end, …
	Finally, …

questions to keep a story going	So, what happened?
	What did you do?
	What happened next?
	Really?
responses to show interest	I don't believe it!
	Oh no / Oh dear.
	How embarrassing!
	That's really funny.
	You must be joking.
	Yes, I know.

PRACTICE

1 Tick the correct sentences, a) or b).

1 a) I've been to India last year.
  b) I went to India last year.

2 a) I finished my studies in 2005.
  b) I've finished my studies in 2005.

3 a) Did you have lunch yet?
  b) Have you had lunch yet?

4 a) Did you ever see Metallica play live?
  b) Have you ever seen Metallica play live?

5 a) Is this the first time you've tried judo?
  b) Is this the first time you tried judo?

6 a) It's the most beautiful place I've ever been to.
  b) It's the most beautiful place I ever went to.

2 Use the prompts to make short conversations.

1 A: you / be / here / before? (ever)
  B: no / not

2 A: you / see / the film *The Reader*?
  B: no / not / see (yet)

3 A: he / be / to Budapest?
  B: yes / go / last summer

4 A: you / finish / that book? (yet)
  B: yes / start / the next one (already)

5 A: you / see / Maria?
  B: yes, she / leave / a message for you

6 A: he / decide / what job / want to do? (yet)
  B: no / have / not

1 Underline the correct alternatives to complete the story.

I remember when Marvin Gaye [1]*died/had died*. I [2]*had been/was going* to one of his concerts a few months before. In fact, he [3]*hadn't played/wasn't playing* very well and I was disappointed. I also remember when JFK was shot. I [4]*had lived/was living* with my parents in New York and I [5]*studied/was studying* at the time. I remember the cleaning lady [6]*came/was coming* into the room, and said to me, 'Hey, President Lincoln has been shot.' I [7]*replied/was replying*, 'I know that.' 'No,' she said. 'President Lincoln has been shot!' So I said, 'What do you mean?' And she said, 'Oh no, I mean … President, you know, what's his name, the one now. President Kennedy's been shot.' So then I [8]*was turning/turned* on the radio.

2 Find and correct the mistakes. One sentence is correct.

1 I was leaving the room when I ~~had~~ heard someone shouting.

2 I couldn't open the door because I *had* left my keys at home.

3 We drove through the tunnel when the car broke down. *were driving*

4 As soon as the film started I realised I seen it before. *had*

5 I never been to Egypt before, so I was really excited to see the pyramids. *'d*

6 By the time we arrived at the party, everybody ~~else is~~ leaving. *was*

7 We had waited for nearly an hour before the waiter took our order.

8 I looked through some old photographs when I found this one of you. *was looking*

1 Complete the conversation with the words and phrases in the box.

In the end   ~~don't believe it~~   The next thing I knew
~~So, this happened when~~   ~~So, what happened~~   Well
~~really funny~~   Anyway   ~~You must be joking~~
So

A: Well, [1] *So this happened when* I was working in a photographic store.
B: [2] ___? *So what happened*
A: [3] *Well*, one day, a woman came in and asked if we could fix the problem she had with a photograph. [4] *Anyway* I asked her what the problem was.
B: OK.
A: [5] *the next thing I knew*, she had taken this old photo out of her bag which showed an old man sitting behind a cow, milking it.

[6] *So*, when I asked her what she wanted us to do to the photo, she said, 'Can you move the cow?' 'Move the cow?' I asked. 'Yes,' she replied. 'I want to see what my grandfather looked like. She pointed to the feet sticking out from under the cow.
B: Oh no. [7] *you must be joking*
A: No, seriously. She wanted us to move the cow, so that she could see her grandfather's face.
B: I [8] *don't believe it*! So, what happened next?
A: [9] *In the end*, when I told her we couldn't do it, she got quite angry, and left the shop saying, 'Then I'll have to take it to someone else.'
B: That's [10] ___. *really funny*

LANGUAGE BANK

the future (plans)

be going to

3.1

+	I'm **going to** start university next year.
-	He **isn't going to** get a job this year.
?	Where **are** you **going to** stay?

When using *be going to* use the word order: subject + *am/are/is* + *going to* + infinitive. Use *be going to* to talk about future plans or intentions. When the verb is *go* or *come*, we often use the present continuous.

We're going to (go to) Spain. We're going to Spain.

I'm going to come and see you later. I'm coming to see you later.

present continuous

+	I'm start**ing** my course in September.
-	We're not go**ing** away for very long.
?	What time **are** you leav**ing** in the morning?

The present continuous is formed: subject + *am/are/is (not)* + verb + *-ing*. Use the present continuous to talk about future plans, when arrangements have already been made. We usually specify a future time such as *next week*, *on Friday,* etc., unless it is already clear that we are talking about the future.

We're flying to Greece on Friday. (We've already bought the tickets.)

She's staying in a hotel near the airport. (The hotel is already booked.)

In some cases it doesn't matter if it's the present continuous or *be going to*.

I'm playing football on Saturday. I'm going to play football on Saturday.

will

+	We'll **meet** you at the station.
-	I **won't see** you tomorrow.
?	**Will** you **want** a taxi?

When there is no plan or arrangement (when we make a decision at the time of speaking), we often use *will*.

I'm tired. I think I'll go to bed.

(subject + *will* + infinitive)

For use of *be going to* and *will* for prediction, see section 3.2 below.

might

+	I **might go** out later.
-	We **might not be able** to finish all this work tomorrow.

Use *might* (+ infinitive) to talk about plans, when we are unsure what the plan is.

I might stay at home and watch a DVD. (But I'm not sure. I might go out.)

spoken grammar

We do not usually use *might* + infinitive in the question form. It seems old-fashioned and formal. **Do you think** you might see Evelyn? NOT ~~Might you see Evelyn?~~

the future (predictions)

will

3.2

Use *will* to make predictions.

Smartphones will organise our lives.
She's so talented that I'm sure she'll become famous.

We often use *I think* and *I hope* with *will*.

I think John will become a doctor.
She hopes she will work in the theatre.

be going to

Use *be going to* to make predictions when there is present evidence.

We only have two cars. It's going to be difficult to take eleven people tomorrow.

We use *probably* to make the prediction less certain. *Probably* usually comes after *will*.

The dollar will probably get stronger this year.

Probably comes after *to be* when we use it with *be going to*.

E-readers are probably going to become cheaper.

may and might

Use *may* or *might* to make predictions which are less certain. The negative forms are *may not* and *might not*.

Some of our workers may lose their jobs because of the restructuring.
We might not go away this year because we don't have any money.

could

Use *could* to make predictions which are less certain.

Global warming could destroy large parts of Asia in the next thirty years.

be likely to

Use *be likely to* to make predictions when something is probable. The negative is *be unlikely to* or *not be likely to*.

Regina is likely to be late because she works until seven.

We're unlikely to reach Paris before lunch because of all the traffic.

Are you likely to be hungry later?

Likely/Unlikely are adjectives.

Will we start at 5.00? It's unlikely.

spoken grammar

Might is more common than *may* in spoken English. *May* is a little bit more formal.

dealing with misunderstandings

3.3

saying you didn't hear something	I didn't catch any of that.
saying you don't understand someone's opinion	You've lost me.
	I don't get what you're saying.
asking someone to explain something more clearly	What exactly do you mean?
	Do you mean to say …?
asking someone to repeat something	Can you say that again?
	Could you repeat the last part/name/thing you said?

PRACTICE

1 Complete the conversation. Use the prompts in brackets where necessary.

A: Where ^{1}_____ you going?

B: I'm ^{2}_____ to Paul's house. We'^{3}_____ going to watch the football.

A: OK. Who ^{4}_____? (play)

B: Real Madrid versus Barcelona.

A: I see. And what time are you ^{5}_____ home? (come)

B: I don't know.

A: How ^{6}_____ getting home?

B: I'm not sure. I ^{7}_____ his dad to drive me home, or I ^{8}_____ catch the bus. (ask/might)

3.1

2 Find and correct the mistakes. There is one mistake in each sentence.

1 Will you going out this weekend?

2 I'm sorry I can't come. I playing tennis after work.

3 I don't feel very well. I think I stay at home.

4 What you going to do?

5 We go for a picnic, so I hope it doesn't rain.

6 Is that the phone? Don't worry – I'm going to get it.

7 They might going to a concert.

8 I'm sorry we can't come, but we're to visit my mother this weekend.

---

1 Rewrite the sentences below using the words in brackets.

1 We probably won't win the cup this year. (might)

We _might not win the cup this year_.

2 I may be late. (likely)

I'm _likely to be late_.

3 That company will close in July. (going)

That company _is going to close in July_.

4 He probably won't call after 10.00. (unlikely)

He _is unlikely to call after 10.00_.

5 I'm not going to give up exercise. (won't)

I _won't going to give up exercise_.

6 We might have a problem with the flight. (may)

There _may have a problem wil_.

3.2

7 She'll get angry when she sees this. (going)

She'_s going to get angry when she_.

8 Are you going to visit us? (will)

Will you visit us.

9 I would love it if he comes to the party. (hope)

I hope he comes to the party.

10 It is thought prices will rise if they complete the development. (could)

Prices _could rise if the complete_.

2 Put the pairs of words in the box into the correct place to complete the sentences.

| ~~will be~~ aren't going won't know ~~might not~~ |
| ~~likely to~~ ~~may arrive~~ ~~is going~~ not likely |

1 Jenny be able to meet us tonight because she has to work late.
   might not

2 Several of our workers are lose their jobs this year because of the economic recession.
   likely to

3 In twenty years' time, cars able to fly.
   will be

4 The predicted storm at any moment.
   may arrive

5 The children to stay with me because I'm busy.
   aren't going

6 I my exam results until August.
   won't know

7 It's that we'll arrive before 6.00 because there are train delays.
   not likely

8 Watch out! That painting to fall off the wall!
   is going

---

1 Match 1–7 with a)–g) to make sentences and questions.

1 I didn't catch   a) you're saying.

2 You've lost   b) you mean?

3 I don't get what   c) that again?

4 What exactly do   d) to say …?

5 Could you repeat the   e) any of that.

6 Do you mean   f) last name?

7 Can you say   g) me.

3.3

GRAMMAR

4.1 must, have to, should (obligation)

must, have to

+	I **must** get up at 5 tomorrow.
	They **have to** start work early.
	We **must** start on time.
	She **has to** get there early.
-	You **mustn't** do that!
	We **don't have to** worry.
	They **mustn't** be late.
	He **doesn't have to** bring anything.
?	Do I/we/you **have to** bring …?
	(**Must** you go so early?)*
	Does he/she/it **have to** go?

* Question forms with *must* are not very common, and sound quite formal. We usually use *Do I have to …?* instead.

Use *must* and *have to* to talk about obligations. These things are necessary or important. *Must* is often used for a personal obligation (something we have decided for ourselves that we must do).

*I **must** give up eating chocolate.*

Must is also used in written rules.

*All applicants **must** provide proof of identity.*

Have to is used for external obligation.

*We **have to** wear a uniform.* (It's a company rule.)

Often you can use *must* or *have to* with the same meaning, but in spoken English *have to* is more common.

Don't have to and *mustn't* have different meanings. *Mustn't* means 'it is not allowed'. *Don't/Doesn't have to* means it is not necessary, but you can do it if you want.

*You **mustn't** smoke cigarettes anywhere in the building.* (It is not permitted and it's dangerous.)

*You **don't have to** work after 6.* (It's not necessary.)

Must can only be used to talk about present or future obligation. To talk about a past obligation, use *had to*.

*We **had to** get up early to catch the plane.*

spoken grammar

Have/Has got to means the same as *have/has to* in the context of obligation and is used a lot in spoken English.

*I**'ve got to** get some money from the bank. She**'s got to** get another job.*

should/shouldn't

+	I/You/He/She/	**should** see this film.
-	It/We/They	**shouldn't** smoke in the house.
?	Do you think we **should** …?*	

* *Should we …* is more formal, and not very common.

Use *should* to talk about weak obligations (not as strong as *must* or *have to*). Often it is used for things which you think are a good idea (advice), e.g. *You **should** come to work in smart clothes.* Use *shouldn't* to talk about things which are not a good idea, e.g. *You **shouldn't** go to bed so late. Ought to* has the same meaning as *should*, but is not usually used in the negative or questions, e.g. *You **ought to** call her. = You **should** call her.*

4.2 used to, would

used to

+	I/You/He/She/	**used to** live in France.
-	It/We/They	**didn't use** to see my parents.
?	Did they **use to** visit?	

Use *used to* to talk about past habits/states, which have often changed or are not true now. You can also use the past simple.

*As a child, I **used to** love eating sweets. As a child I **ate** a lot of sweets.*

We can also use *would* to talk about past habits, but not to talk about past states.

*I **would go** to the sweet shop every day.* (habit)

*As a child, I **was** happy. As a child I **used to be** very happy.* (state) NOT *As a child, I would be happy.* (state)

Do not use *used to* to talk about things that happened only once, or for a specific number of times/length of time. Use the past simple for this.

*My family **moved** to America last year.* NOT *My family used to move to America last year.*

*We **went** to Italy twice on holiday.* NOT *We used to go to Italy twice on holiday.*

*I **studied** at university for three years.* NOT *I used to study at university for three years.*

spoken grammar

Never used to is more common in spoken English than *didn't use to*.

*We **never used to** see them, except for during August.*

In spoken English, we often leave out the verb or phrase after *used to*

*Do you smoke? No, I **used to**, but I **don't** any more.*

4.3 reaching agreement

giving opinions	suggestions	commenting on other opinions	
I (really) feel that …	What about …?	That's a good idea.	I (don't) see what you mean.
The way I see things, …	I suggest we focus on …	That's a good point.	I'm not sure that I agree, actually.
The way I see it, …	I think we should think about …	That's fine by me.	
	I suggest we think about …	That's OK by me.	I'm not sure that … is a good idea.
	How about if / Why don't we (call it)…?	Exactly!	

PRACTICE

1 Underline the correct alternative to complete the text.

The worst jobs in the world?

If you like travelling to exotic places, perhaps you [1]*should/shouldn't* try this job. Helge Zieler is a mosquito researcher. In order to study the biting habits of the mosquito which spreads malaria in Brazil, Helge [2]*has to/doesn't have to* sit inside a mosquito net while hundreds of mosquitoes bite him. Every time he sees a mosquito land on his body, he [3]*must/have to* suck it into a tube in his mouth, and then blow it into a container. On a good evening, Helge can catch 500 mosquitoes in three hours. But to do this, he receives 3,000 bites (an average of seventeen bites per minute for 180 minutes). He [4]*mustn't/must* forget his anti-malaria tablets. Once he caught malaria and it took him two years to recover.

You [5]*shouldn't/don't have to* drive too fast on the roads, especially when you're driving in the countryside. Why? Because more than 400 million animals are killed on the roads every year. Joanne Keene knows, because she [6]*has to/shouldn't* remove them. Car drivers [7]*don't have to/must* pick the animals up, so Joanne drives around in a huge truck full of dead cats and raccoons. 'It's a hard job,' she says, 'because we work very long hours. We [8]*mustn't/must* be on call 24 hours a day.'

4.1

2 Match 1–8 with a)–h) to make sentences.

1 It's a good job but we *a)*
2 I love Saturday mornings, because I don't have to *f)*
3 I think you should *h)*
4 The doctor told me that I *b)*
5 You mustn't *c)*
6 You don't have to *g)*
7 Francois is very lucky. His father is very rich, so he *d)*
8 I really must *e)*

a) have to work hard.
b) should do more exercise.
c) come to work dressed in jeans. You have to look smart.
d) doesn't have to work at all.
e) give up smoking. It's not good for my health.
f) get up for work. I can stay in bed until 10a.m.
g) send the forms in until September, but it's a good idea to send them early.
h) think about whether you really want to apply for the job.

---

1 Cross out the alternative which is <u>not</u> possible.

1 I *used to play/played/play* a lot of tennis when I was younger.
2 After school I *would take/used to take/take* the bus home.
3 He *never used to play/would play/played* the guitar, but he doesn't play any more.
4 I *didn't use to enjoy/didn't enjoy/wouldn't enjoy* school, but I worked hard anyway.
5 Tim *used to have/would have/had* long hair.
6 I *studied/used to study/didn't use to study* French for five years.

4.2

2 Make sentences with *used to* or *would* using the words in brackets. Sometimes both may be possible.

1 In Ancient Greece, people *used to* (think) the world was flat, but Aristotle thought it was round.
2 In the olden days, people *didn't used to* (not have) cars, so they rode horses.
3 *did* people really *used to* (enjoy) watching gladiator fights in Ancient Rome?
4 In the sixteenth century, ladies *would / used to* (put) a white powder containing lead on their faces. It was poisonous.
5 Two hundred years ago, they *both* (not use) anaesthetics to perform operations.
6 Before iron was invented, soldiers *both / wouldn't* (fight) using bronze swords, but they weren't very strong and often changed shape in battle.
7 The Romans *both* (make) themselves sick, so that they could eat more during their huge banquets.
8 Why *did* people *used to* (eat) garlic in Ancient Egypt? It was to cure toothache.

---

1 Using the words in italics, rewrite the second sentence so it has the same meaning as the first.

1 Let's begin.
   I think we _____should begin_____.
2 I suggest we look at the emails first.
   Why *don't we* ?
3 I don't understand.
   I *don't see what* you mean.

4 I agree with that idea.
   It's *fine by* me. It's OK by me
5 From my point of view, it works very well.
   The way *I see* things, it works very well.
6 I agree with what you have just said.
   That's *a good* point.

4.3

LANGUAGE BANK

comparatives and superlatives

one-syllable adjectives and two-syllable adjectives ending in -y

adjective	comparative	superlative	notes
cheap fast	cheaper faster	the cheapest the fastest	+-er/the +-est
easy friendly	easier friendlier	the easiest the friendliest	-y changes to -i + -er/the +-est
big	bigger	the biggest	adjective ending in *CVC double final consonant
large	larger	the largest	adjective ending in -e, add -r / the + -st

two-syllable and longer adjectives

adjective	comparative	superlative	notes
important	more/less important than	the most/ least important	+ more/less ... than, or the most/the least ... in the ...

irregular adjectives

adjective	comparative	superlative
good	better	the best
bad	worse	the worst
far	further/farther	the furthest/farthest

ways of comparing

Here are some common expressions used for making comparisons: *It's exactly/about the same as ...,   It's very similar to ...,   It's not as ... as.*

It's **exactly the same as** the one we had last year.
It's **very similar to** somewhere I stayed last year.
He's **not as tall as** I expected.

It's a lot/much/far more + adjective: It's **far more beautiful** than I imagined.

It's a little/a little bit/slightly: It's **slightly smaller** than the last flat I lived in.

using superlatives

Here are some common expressions used with superlatives: *by far the most ..., one of the most ... the second (third/fourth) most ...*

It's **by far the most** delicious meal I've ever eaten.

It's **one of the most** beautiful places in the world.

We often use superlatives with a phrase beginning *in the ...*

She's by far the best student **in the class.**

It's one of the tallest buildings **in the world.**

*CVC – consonant, vowel, consonant

---

question tags

To make question tags, add auxiliary verb + pronoun at the end of the question. For a positive sentence, use a negative tag: *You **play** tennis, **don't you**?* For a negative sentence use a positive tag: *They **weren't** here, **were they**?*

Use contractions in the tag, not the full verb: *He's nice, isn't he?* NOT *He's nice, is not he?* N.B. Use a comma before the question tag and a question mark after it.

	positive verb + negative tag	negative verb + positive tag
present	You're twenty, aren't you?	She doesn't swim, does she?
past	They came back, didn't they?	You didn't see Tim, did you?
present perfect	You've lost it, haven't you?	He hasn't seen us, has he?
future	I'll be back by 10.00, won't I?	We won't lose, will we?

Use question tags to check information that you think is true. Also use question tags to sound less direct (a way to sound polite).

If we are sure of the information, the intonation falls on the question tag.

You're coming tomorrow, aren't you? (expect the answer 'yes'.)

If we are really not sure, the intonation rises on the question tag.

She's from Europe, isn't she? (maybe she isn't)

---

polite requests

request	responses
Could you carry this bag **for me**? **Could you** bring your laptop with you?	Yes, of course. I'm afraid I can't/I'm sorry, I can't.
Could you tell me the way to the hotel? **Could you tell me** what time it is?	Yes, I can. It's ... Let me have a look.
Do you know what time the shops open? **Do you know** how to get there?	I'm not sure.
Would you mind coming a little bit earlier? **Would you mind** booking us a table?	Of course not. OK./Sure.

watch out!

Could you tell me ...? and *Do you know ...?* are not direct questions; the word order is the same as for statements.

Could you tell me what time it is? NOT *Could you tell me what time is it?*

Do you know what time the shops open? NOT *Do you know what time do the shops open?*

Would you mind ... + -ing

Would you mind watering my plants when I go away? NOT *Would you mind to water ...?*

Would you mind ...? is followed by a negative response.

Would you mind helping me? No, of course not. (I'm happy to help you) NOT *Yes, of course* (I would mind helping you = I'm not happy to help you)

PRACTICE

1 Complete the sentences with the comparative or superlative form of the adjectives in brackets.

1 We usually fly to Italy instead of going in the car, because it's ~~quickly~~ (quick) *quickier*

2 They had to travel ~~further~~ *farther* than they wanted to find a hotel. (far)

3 When I was a teenager, I was much _____ than I am now. (not confident) ~~more~~ *less* confident

4 He's one of _____ children in the class. (naughty) *the naughtiest*

5 Exams are much _____ now than they were when I was at school. (easy) *easier*

6 Sweden is ~~bigger~~ than Norway. (big)

7 K2 is the second *highest* mountain in the world. (high)

8 This book is slightly ~~more difficult~~ to understand than his last book. The plot is very complicated. (difficult) *more difficult*

9 He used to be a teacher, but he's decided to become a firefighter. It's a much _____ job. (dangerous) *more dangerous*

10 It's by far _____ film I've ever seen. (good) the ~~better~~ *Best*

2 Rewrite the sentences using the words in bold, so that they have the same meaning.

1 My brother is slightly taller than I am. **bit**
My brother is a little bit Taller than I am.

2 The journey to the coast took ~~much longer~~ than we had expected. **far** *far*
The journey to the coast is farther than we

3 It's easily the most expensive restaurant I've ever been to. **by**
It's by far the most expensive...

4 Your shoes and my shoes are almost the same. **similar**
Your shoes and my shoes are similar.to

5 People here are much healthier now that they have clean water. **lot** *very*
People here are a lot healthier now

---

1 Match 1–8 with a)–h) to make tag questions.

1 Clive was an engineer, (g)   a) have they?
2 You're from Ethiopia, (d)   b) won't he?
3 Shania isn't an actress, (e)   c) has she?
4 They haven't been here before, (a)   d) aren't you?
5 He'll be home soon, (b)   e) is she?
6 You work here, (h)   f) will they?
7 She hasn't met you, (c)   g) wasn't he?
8 They won't finish on time, (f)   h) don't you?

2 Find and correct the mistakes. There is one mistake in each question.

1 You weren't happy, ~~weren't~~ *were* you?
2 It'll probably rain, ~~doesn't~~ *won't* it?
3 She researched her roots, didn't ~~her~~ *she*?
4 They always ask tricky questions, they ~~don't~~ *don't they*?
5 I take after my dad, ~~doesn't he~~ *don't I*?
6 You've met Kevin's fiancée, have ~~not~~ *haven't* you?
7 I put my foot in it yesterday, ~~haven't~~ *didn't* I?
8 My mentor will give me a hand, he ~~won't~~ *won't he?*
9 You had a lot on your mind, ~~doesn't~~ *didn't* you?
10 Phil and Luke are on holiday, ~~are not~~ *aren't* they?

---

1 Find the mistakes and correct them. There is an extra word or two in each line.

1 A: Excuse me, could you ~~is~~ hold the door for me?
  B: Yes, ~~I do~~ of course.

2 A: Do you know when the next train ~~does to~~ leaves?
  B: I'm not ~~OK~~ sure.

3 A: Would you ~~to~~ mind staying behind after the meeting?
  B: ~~It's~~ Sure. That's fine.

4 A: Could ~~is possible~~ you tell me what Tim's phone number is?
  B: Let me have a ~~to~~ look.

5 A: Would you mind ~~to~~ looking after my bag while I go to the bathroom?
  B: No, of course not ~~mind~~.

6 A: Could you tell ~~for~~ me the way to the station?
  B: Yes, ~~so~~ I can.

5.1

5.2

5.3

zero and first conditionals

Zero and first conditionals are sometimes called ' real conditionals' because they talk about situations which are always true, or events which are possible or probable in the future.

zero conditional

if/when +	present simple +	present simple
If/When	You* **heat** water to 100° Centigrade,	it **boils**.

* Here *you* is a general subject meaning 'anyone' or 'people in general'.

Use the zero conditional to talk about a general situation, or something which is always true (a fact).

If plants **don't have** water, they **die**. Ice **melts** if you **heat** it. (*You* here refers to 'anyone', or people generally, not 'you' specifically.)

If/When can come at the beginning or in the middle of the sentence.

6.1 *If* I'm not in the office by 8a.m., my boss gets angry. My boss gets angry **if** I'm not in the office by 8a.m.

If and *when* have the same meaning in zero conditional sentences. In this case *if* means 'when this happens' or 'every time this happens'.

When I'm feeling stressed, I eat chocolate. **If** I'm feeling stressed, I eat chocolate.

first conditional

if/when +	present simple +	will/could/might + verb
If	you **give** me your phone number,	I'**ll call** you when we're ready.
When	you **go** into the kitchen,	you'**ll see** the keys on the table.

Use the first conditional to talk about possible situations in the future and their consequences. If you are sure about the result, use *will/won't*. If you're not sure, use *could/might*.

We can change the order of the sentence, but *if/when* is always followed by the present simple.

If my train **arrives** on time, I'll meet you at ten o'clock. Or I'll meet you at ten o'clock *if* my train **arrives** on time. NOT *if my train will arrive on time*.

In first conditional sentences, *if* and *when* have different meanings. Use *if* when you are not sure if the situation will happen: *If* I pass my exams, *I'll be very happy*. Use *when* for a situation which you know will happen: **When** I pass my exams, **I'll have a party**.

Unless has the meaning of 'if not' or 'except in this situation'.

*I'll go straight to the restaurant, **unless** you call me first.* (I will go straight to the restaurant, if you don't call me first.)

Note the difference between zero and first conditional in the sentences below.

If you sit in the sun, you **get** sunburn. (Zero conditional for a general situation/ fact. 'You' means anyone, or people in general.)

If you sit in the sun, you'**ll get** sunburn. (First conditional for a specific situation. I'm talking to you (personally) about what will happen today.)

second conditional

if +	past simple +	would clause
If	I **lived** to be 100,	I **would** probably **be** very tired.
	he **was** the President,	he'**d make** a lot of changes.
	we **bought** the house,	we'**d need** to sell our car.

6.2 Use the second conditional to talk about an unreal or imaginary situation and its consequences.

In spoken English, *would* is contracted in the positive and negative form.

*I'**d** be there if I had time. If she had enough food, she'**d** feed us all.*

Would is not usually contracted in the question form.

*If you passed your exam, **would** you go to university? **Would** you help me if I paid you?*

Use *If I were you ...* to give advice: *If I were you, I'd change teams.*

Instead of *would*, we can use *could* or *should*: *If you got really fit, you **could** probably play again.*

It is common to use other expressions in the *would* clause: *would be able to*, *would need to* and *would have to*.

*If I lost my job, I'**d need to** find another one!*

*We **would have to** cancel the game if it rained.*

*If you bought a larger quantity, we'**d be able to** offer you a better deal.*

giving news

good news	I've got some good news (for you).
	I'm really pleased to tell you …
	You'll never guess what.
bad news	Bad news, I'm afraid.
	I'm sorry to have to tell you, but …
	I'm afraid/Unfortunately, …
	I'm afraid I've got some bad news …
	There's something I've got to tell you.
good or bad news	You know …? Well, …
	I've/We've got something to tell you.

6.3

responding to good news	Wow! That's fantastic/great news.
	Congratulations!
	You're joking!
	You lucky thing!
	Well done.
	Have you?/Did you?
responding to bad news	That's a shame.
	That's terrible/awful.
	That's really annoying.
	I'm really sorry to hear that.

PRACTICE

1 Complete the sentences with the correct form of the verbs in brackets.

1st 1 If I _pass_ (pass) my exams, my teacher _will be_ (be) very surprised. 1st

Ø 2 When we _visit_ (visit) my mother, she usually _looked after_ (look after) the children. Ø

1st 3 When Gaby _leave_ (leave) her job in the summer, she _'ll worried_ (worry) about what to do next.

1st 4 If I _don't find_ (not find) any cheap tickets, we _won't go_ (not go) to Malta.

6.1 Ø/1st 5 If you _don't water_ (not water) plants, they _will die_ (die).

1st 6 I_'ll be_ (be) surprised if Martha _comes_ (come) to the party. She said she wasn't feeling well.

Ø 7 If you _get_ (get) lost, do you usually _ask_ (ask) someone for directions?

1st 8 They _don't come_ (not come) unless you _will invite_ (invite) them.

Ø 9 If it _is_ (be) a nice day, I _'ll like_ (like) to go for a run in the morning.

Ø 10 I _listen_ (listen) to classical music when I _want_ (want) to relax.

2 Underline the correct alternative.

1 You can't come to the conference ~~unless~~/if/ when you're invited.

2 I'm not talking to you ~~unless~~/if/when you calm down first.

3 They'll arrive as soon as dinner ~~is~~/will be/ won't be ready.

4 They'll cancel the flight if/unless/when the weather is bad.

5 If you eat all of that chocolate mousse, you ~~'ll feel~~/feel/won't feel ill.

6 We'll organise a taxi when we ~~know~~/will know/might know what time the concert starts.

7 When I see a spider, I always ~~scream~~/might scream/will scream.

8 I'll get some money as soon as the bank will open/~~opens~~/might open.

---

1 Complete the sentences with the correct form of the verbs in brackets. Use contractions where possible.

1 If I _sold_ (sell) my house now, it _wouldn't be_ (not/be) worth very much.

2 _Would_ (your parents/come) _came_ if I _organised_ (organise) a party?

3 He _wouldn't be_ (not/be) able to study here if _didn't pass_ (not/pass) that exam.

4 If you _lost_ (lose) your passport, _you'd need_ (need) visit the consulate.

6.2 5 They _'d be_ (be) healthier if _they didn't be_ (not/eat) so much junk food.

6 If you _wrote_ (write) a novel, what _would call_ (call) it?

7 If the students _didn't have_ (not/have) internet access, _would find_ (find) it difficult.

8 We _wouldn't work_ (not/work) there if the boss _didn't give_ (not/give) us a lot of freedom.

9 Where _would she live_ (she/live) if _had_ (have) to move to a different country?

10 If he _could_ (can) study on Tuesdays, _he wouldn't need_ (not/need) to come on Wednesday.

2 Write answers to the questions using the prompts. Use contractions.

1 A: Can we walk to the game?

B: No. (be/late)

If we _walked to the game, we'd be late_.

2 A: Why doesn't the team enter the competition?

B: (it/lose)

If the team _entered the competition, it would lose / it'll lose_

3 A: Can I borrow his car?

B: No. (get/angry)

If you _borrowed his car, he would get angry_

4 A: Why don't we call her now?

B: No. (we/wake her up)

If we _called he now, we'd wake her up_.

5 A: Why can't we start the project again?

B: (waste/money)

If we _started the project again, we'd waste money_

6 A: Can we extend our holiday?

B: No. (miss/school)

If we _extended our holiday, we'd miss school_.

---

1 Complete the conversations.

1 A: You'll never _guess_ what.

B: What?

A: I'm moving to Australia.

B: You're _joking_

6.3 A: No, I'm leaving in March.

B: You _lucky_ thing.

2 A: I've passed my exams!

B: _have_ you? Congratulations!

A: Yes, I got the results this morning.

3 A: There's _something_ I've got to tell you.

B: What is it?

A: I've decided to leave my job at the university.

B: I'm _sorry / afraid_ to hear that. What's the problem?

4 A: I'm _afraid_ we're going to be late.

B: Why? What's happened?

A: The flight's been delayed.

B: Oh, that's a _shame_. That's really _annoying_

LANGUAGE BANK

present perfect simple vs continuous
present perfect continuous

7.1	+	I	've/have	been	reading a book.
		She	's/has		playing the piano.
	-	You	haven't		listening to me.
	?	Have	you		going there for a long time?

Use the present perfect simple or continuous for actions/activities which started in the past and continue until now.

I've studied German for six years. *I've been studying* German for six years.

Often, there is little change in meaning between the two tenses (especially for verbs such as *live, work, teach, study*).

I've lived here for years. *I've been living* here for years.

Use the present perfect continuous to emphasise the length or duration of an activity.

I've been doing yoga for years. (but I'm still not very good at it)

He's been playing football since he was three.

As with other continuous forms, do not use the present perfect continuous with state verbs (e.g. *love, hate, enjoy, know*, etc.). With these verbs, use the present perfect simple.

I've known him for ages. NOT *I've been knowing* him for ages.

We often use *for, since* and *How long have you …?* with the present perfect simple and continuous.

How long have you been waiting *for*? She's been working here *since* 2010.

present and past ability
modal verbs to talk about ability

FALTA POCO
AHSJKLQMÍ

7.2		present	past
	+	I **can** cook.	I **could** run fast.
	-	I **can't** drive.	He **couldn't** do maths.
	?	**Can** you **speak** Spanish?	**Could** you **cook** when you were younger?

We can also use *be able to* to talk about ability.

		present	past
	+	She **'s able to** write well.	Aged three, I **was able to** read.
	-	He **'s not able to** drive.	Aged two, he **wasn't able to** walk.
	?	**Is** he **able to** speak French?	**Were** you **able to** get a job?

...ressions to talk about ability at a particular moment ...can use *be able to* to talk about one particular situation.

We **are able to** offer you a special discount on the fridge today. She didn't answer her phone so I **wasn't able to** speak to her.

Use *manage to* to show that an action is/was difficult.

		present	past
	+	I usually **manage to** finish my work on time.	We **managed to** book a great hotel.
	-	I **don't** always **manage to** speak to my parents every week.	She **didn't manage to** pass the exam.
	?	**Do** you **manage to** see the grandchildren regularly?	**Did** you **manage to** finish washing the dishes?

clarifying opinions

giving opinions	giving examples
The reason I say this **is that** he didn't ask our permission.	**For example,** she forgot her keys yesterday.
For me, there are two options here.	**Let me give you an example:** there was a festival last week.
In my view, we should stop selling the product.	**For one thing,** I don't like caviar.
I do think we should talk to them first.	
I must say I agree with Robert.	

7.3

PRACTICE

1 Complete the sentences with the present perfect simple or continuous form of the verbs in the box. Where both forms are possible, choose the present perfect continuous.

> do sit (not) listen hate (not) watch study teach (not) know read live wait

7.1

1 I'm tired. I _'ve been sitting_ in boring meetings all day.
2 They _have been studying_ for their exams since five o'clock this morning.
3 I'm glad you're here. We _have been waiting_ for you all day.
4 I can't listen to jazz. I _'ve_ always _hated_ it.
5 He _'s been doing_ karate for nearly twenty years.
6 You _haven't been listening_ to me. You haven't heard what I said.
7 She's got a new job. She _has been teaching_ economics at the university since June.
8 How long _have_ you _been living_ in the UK? When did you move here?
9 I _haven't been_ TV. I _have been reading_ my book.
10 We _haven't known_ each other for very long.

2 Underline the correct alternative to complete the sentences.

1 Hi Tariq. I haven't _seen_/been seeing you for ages!
2 I have been knowing/_known_ Justin since we were at school.
3 Yes, we've _met_/been meeting each other before.
4 I _'ve been playing_/did played the guitar for as long as I can remember.
5 My brother _has been travelling_/have been travelled around the world for the last two years.
6 He has always been enjoying/_enjoyed_ travelling.
7 Excuse me. I _'ve been waiting_/have wait for this phone call all morning.
8 I have studying/_have been studying_ Mandarin for more than ten years, and I still find it difficult.

1 Find and correct the mistakes. There are five mistakes in the text.

7.2

Johnny isn't able _to_ make full sentences but he can ~~to~~ say several words such as *Mama* and *Dada*, which he couldn't _is_ a month ago. He able to understand various commands like 'No!' and 'Come here' and he recognises his name. He's becoming more mobile: _able_ yesterday he managed _to_ crawl from the living room to the kitchen. He's also getting better with his hands. He can hold a pen and he sometimes manages to ~~drawing~~ simple pictures.

2 Rewrite the sentences using the words in brackets. Write three words (contractions are one word).

1 She knows how to ride a motorbike.
She can ride a motorbike. (can)
2 I'm not able to play any instruments.
I can't play any instruments. (can't)
3 Seyi and Denia couldn't come last night.
They _weren't able to_ come last night. (able)
4 Were you able to take any photos?
Did you manage to take any photos? (manage)
5 Can you make pizza?
are you able to make pizza? (able)
6 I can usually sleep for eight hours even on a plane.
Usually I _manage to sleep_ for eight hours even on a plane. (manage)
7 Were you a fast runner when you were a child?
could you run fast when you were a child? (could)
8 I haven't finished my homework.
I _haven't managed to_ finish my homework. (managed)

1 Underline the correct alternative.

7.3

1 Jackie has been so nice. _For example,_/For me, she took us to the cinema.
2 You all think that new restaurant is great, but for one thing/_in my view_ the food isn't that good.
3 Ibrahim said the concert was disappointing, and _I must say_/the reason I say I agree.
4 Shakespeare borrowed most of his stories. _Let me give you an example:_/I must say the plot of *King Lear* is taken from a much older story.
5 I like that laptop. For one thing/_I do think_ it's a bit heavy, though.
6 People love the Rolling Stones, _but for me,_/the reason I say this is Led Zeppelin is the greatest rock band.
7 Dogs are the best pets. For another/_The reason I say this is because_ they are so faithful.
8 You should buy that mobile. For one thing, it looks fantastic. _For another,_/For example, it's cheap.

LANGUAGE BANK

articles

8.1

Use **a/an** (indefinite article):

- the first time something is mentioned. *I saw a mouse in the kitchen.*
- before singular nouns. *She's watching a film.*
- with jobs. *I'm a doctor. He's an artist.*

Use **the** (definite article):

- when there is only one of something. *I see the sun.*
- when something has been mentioned before. *The mouse (that I was talking about) was huge!*
- with seas, oceans, rivers and country names that are plural or use extra words like Kingdom, e.g. *the River Danube, the Pacific Ocean, the United Kingdom*
- before the names of some areas, e.g. *the south of France, the coast of Italy*
- with superlatives. *Ali was the greatest boxer.*
- with some defining expressions, e.g. *the first, the only*
- in some phrases with prepositions, e.g. *in the morning, at the end, by the next day*
- with dates in spoken English, e.g. *the fifth of June*

Use **no article** (zero article):

- to talk generally about things or people. *Doctors make more money than nurses.*
- with most names of towns, cities, and countries.
- before plural nouns. *I bought six bottles of water.*
- in some phrases with prepositions, e.g. *on Monday, at work, for lunch, on foot*
- with sports. *I like tennis. He plays football.*

quantifiers

Use **some** and **any** when talking about 'a limited amount/number' (not a large or small amount/number). We often use *some* in positive sentences. In this instance *several* can also be used. *I have some close friends. I have several close friends.*

We also use *some* in questions, especially in requests and offers. *Can you give me some sugar? Do you want some help?*

We often use *any* in negatives and questions. *I don't have any children.* Use **much** and **many** in questions and negatives. *Much* is used with large amounts of an uncountable noun: *How much time do we have? Many* is used with large numbers of a countable noun: *I don't have many friends.*

All means 'everything/everyone'. We can use it with or without *of*. *All the people here are friendly. All of the people here are friendly.*

We use **a lot**, **lots of**, and **plenty of** with large amounts/numbers. We usually use these in positive sentences. *Plenty of* means 'more than enough' (so there won't be a problem). *I spend a lot of time in Paris.*

Too and **too much/many** mean 'more than necessary'. We use *much* with uncountable nouns. We use *many* with countable nouns. *This film is too long. There's too much salt on this meat.*

Enough means 'as much as we need'. We use it in positive and negative sentences and questions. *I don't want this task because I have enough to do. There isn't enough time. Do you have enough sugar?*

None and **no** can mean 'zero'. We use *none of* + noun/pronoun. We use *no* + noun (without article or possessive adjective). *None of the cinemas showed the film. There are no reasons for this.*

A few means 'a small number'. We use it with countable nouns. We usually use it in positive sentences. *She knew a few actors.*

A little and **a bit of** mean 'a small amount'. We use them with uncountable nouns. We usually use them in positive sentences. *I asked for a little water. I need a bit of help.*

relative clauses

8.2

defining relative clauses

Use relative clauses to talk about what a person, place or thing is or does.

Use relative pronouns to join the main clause and the relative clause:

- *who* for people *He's the man **who** sold me the coat.*
- *where* for places *This is the town **where** I was born.*
- *which* for things *That computer **which** you showed me is very cheap.*
- *when* for times *This was the moment **when** Mr Moran knew he was in trouble.*
- *whose* for possessions (it means 'of which or of who') *This is Sarah, **whose** husband you met yesterday.*

We can use *that* instead of *which* or *who*. *Are you the lady **who/that** I spoke to on the phone? Is that the book **which/that** you lent me?*

We can leave out *who*, *which* and *that* when these words are not the subject of the relative clause. Compare: *She's the girl (**who**) I saw yesterday.* (The subject of the relative clause is *I* (not *who*). So we can omit *who*.) with *She's the girl **who** speaks French.* (The subject of the relative clause is *who*. So we cannot omit *who*.)

non-defining relative clauses

Use non-defining relative clauses to add extra non-essential information about a place, person or thing. The sentence is grammatically correct without the non-defining relative clause. Use a comma before the non-defining relative clause. Use a comma or a full-stop after it. We cannot omit the relative pronoun (*who*, *which that*, etc.) *They spoke to Tara, **who** was in a good mood.* We cannot use *that* instead of *which* or *who*. *I saw his latest film, **which** was terrible.*

being a good guest

8.3

asking for advice	
Is it OK if I (do this)?	Yes, of course. / No, you'd better not.
What should I do (in this situation)?	If I were you, I'd …
Do I need to (take off my shoes)?	Yes, you should. / No, it's not necessary.
Did I do something wrong?	It's OK. We can sort it out. / Don't worry about it.
Is this a bad time?	No. Come in. / Can you come back later?

apologising
Sorry about that. I didn't know (you were in a meeting).
My apologies. I didn't realise (you were busy).

PRACTICE

8.1

1 Find and correct the mistakes. There is one mistake with quantifiers or articles in each sentence.

1 Why don't you come and join us? There are plenty ~~the~~ *of* seats.

2 Bobby's girlfriend is ~~engineer~~ *an* engineer.

3 Thousands of people were at the game, so there was *a* lot of noise.

4 Yesterday we saw a doctor ~~about~~ *for* my illness. Fortunately, a doctor said it was nothing serious.

5 Laila was hungry so she ate a ~~bit~~ bread.

6 ~~The~~ women live longer than men.

7 We went to the party but there weren't ~~much~~ *a lot of / the* people there.

8 We looked up and saw an aeroplane in *the* sky.

9 I can't buy it because I only have a few money left.

10 My wife and I have lived in United States for several years.

2 Complete the story with the words in the box.

| a an the (x3) much many few little lot |

¹ *an* old man reaches his 120th birthday. ² *a* journalist comes to interview him. 'What is the secret of your long life?' he asks. 'Well,' says ³ *the* old man, 'I don't have ⁴ *many* problems, I don't drink ⁵ *much* alcohol, I eat a ⁶ *lot* of good food, and I spend a ⁷ *little* time every day relaxing. But do you want to know my real secret? I never disagree with anyone.'

'That's ridiculous!' says ⁸ *the* journalist. 'There must be another secret.'

A ⁹ *few* moments later, ¹⁰ *the* old man says, 'OK, you're right.'

8.2

1 Complete the sentences with who, which, where, when or whose.

1 I met a man _____ house had burned down.

2 This was the moment *when* we knew we would win.

3 I spent several months in Rome, *which* is my favourite city.

4 The village, *where* Teresa grew up poor but happy, was very small.

5 The girl _____ sold you the carpet is from Morocco.

6 That blog, _____ he writes every day, is one of the most popular in the country.

7 Jill married a guy _____ she met on a dating site.

8 I don't want to be with someone _____ whole life is spent surfing the net.

2 Rewrite the sentences using relative clauses. Use the words in italics and the words in the box,

| that who (x2) which (x2) where when whose |

1 What's this programme? Did you want to watch it?

Is this the programme _____ that you wanted to watch _____?

2 Last year I met a translator. She spoke six languages.

Last year I met a translator _____.

3 It was six o'clock on the fifth of August. At that moment, the world changed forever.

It was six o'clock on the fifth of August _____.

4 They gave Jodie an apple. She ate it quickly.

They gave Jodie an apple, _____.

5 You see that apartment? Felipe lived there.

That's the apartment _____.

6 She spent a month in Manchester. She loved it.

She spent a month in Manchester, _____.

7 The boss's office is next to mine. He's always shouting!

The boss, _____.

8 My boyfriend is coming to visit me. He lives in Barcelona.

My boyfriend, _____.

8.3

1 Put the words in the correct order to make conversations.

1 A: do / to / hand / I / everyone's / shake / need / ?

B: no, / necessary / not / it's

2 A: / is / if / it / I / into / take / meeting / coffee / OK / the / ?

B: yes, / course / of

3 A: I / to / realise / didn't / I / send / by / the / information / had / email.

B: It's OK. we / out / it / sort / can

4 A: did / wrong / something / do / I / ?

B: don't / it / about / worry

5 A: what / I / late / do / if / should / am / I / ?

B: if / you / I / were, / I'd / an / train / earlier / catch

6 A: / sorry / that / about. I / you / know / here / were / didn't

B: No problem.

7 A: is / a / bad / time / this / ?

B: fine. / it's / No,

LANGUAGE BANK

GRAMMAR

third conditional

if clause	*would* clause
if + *had* + past participle	*would have* + past participle
If I **had seen** my friend,	I **would have spoken** to her.

9.1

Use the third conditional to talk about hypothetical or imaginary situations in the past. It describes an unreal or impossible situation, e.g. Real situation = I woke up late. Hypothetical situation (third conditional): *If I had heard my alarm clock, I wouldn't have woken late.* (I didn't hear my alarm clock. I woke up late.)

We can start sentences and questions with the *if* or *would* clause.

They **wouldn't have been** late if they had caught the bus.

If they **had caught** the bus, they **wouldn't have been** late.

What would you **have done** if I hadn't called? **If I hadn't called**, what **would you have** done?

Note: When the sentence starts with *if*, we use a comma after the *if* clause.

In written and spoken English, we use contractions with third conditional sentences except in very formal documents.

She'd have told us if **she'd** heard anything. We **wouldn't** have left early if **we'd** known you were coming.

The defendant would not have been caught if he had stayed in his home. (formal)

active vs passive
the passive

	active	passive
present simple	The shop **doesn't accept** credit cards.	Credit cards **aren't accepted** here.
present continuous	Is anyone **using** that computer at the moment?	Is that computer **being used** at the moment?
past simple	Someone **told** us to be here at 8.00.	We **were told** to be here at 8.00.
present perfect	No one **has asked** us about the date.	We **haven't been asked** about the date.
will	Someone **will give** me a car on my next birthday.	I'll **be given** a car on my next birthday.

9.2

Use the active voice to talk about the things people do, e.g. *Sam ate the chicken.*

To make the passive, use subject + *be* + past participle. Use the passive voice:

• to talk about what happens to things or people. *Khaled has been given a prize.*

• when we don't know the doer (the person or thing that does the action). *The film star was murdered.*

• when the identity of the doer of the action is not important. *This cheese is made in Italy.* (It's not important who actually makes it.)

• if the doer of the action is obvious. *The thief was arrested.* (The police are the only people who could arrest the thief.)

If we want to say who does/did the action, we use *by*. *The microwave oven was invented by Percy LeBaron Spencer.*

We sometimes use the passive to emphasise a particular part of the sentence. Compare:

Frank Lloyd Wright designed the Guggenheim Museum of Art in New York. with *The Guggenheim Museum of Art in New York was designed by Frank Lloyd Wright.*

In the second sentence, the emphasis is on Frank Lloyd Wright.

The passive is often used in newspaper reports and other formal writing.

expressing uncertainty

saying you don't know
I have no idea.*
I haven't a clue.*

*These are both informal.

saying you are not sure, but you have an idea
I'm not a hundred percent certain* but it might be …
I'm fairly sure* it's …

*Sure and certain mean the same thing. We can use either of them in these expressions.

9.3

saying you know what it isn't
It's definitely not …
I'm sure it isn't …

saying you used to know
I can't remember.
I've forgotten.

PRACTICE

1 Match 1–8 with a)–h) to make sentences.

9.1

1 If we had arrived earlier,
2 I wouldn't have told her
3 If he hadn't fallen asleep,
4 We would have called you
5 If I'd done all my homework,
6 John would have brought a present
7 If the teacher hadn't helped him,
8 I would have bought that computer

a) he would have failed the exam.
b) if he'd known it was your birthday.
c) he wouldn't have crashed the car.
d) we wouldn't have missed the plane.
e) if it had been on sale.
f) if I'd known it was a secret.
g) I would have passed the course.
h) if we'd had your number.

2 Rewrite the sentences using the third conditional.

1 Maya was late for the meeting. Her car broke down.
   If Maya's car hadn't _____.
2 She felt ill so she didn't come to the concert.
   She would _____.
3 I didn't get the job. I wasn't qualified.
   If I had _____.
4 They didn't buy the house. They didn't have enough money.
   They would _____.
5 We lost the game. Our best player was injured.
   If our best player hadn't _____.
6 You didn't tell me you were coming so I didn't cook a meal.
   I would _____.

1 Underline the correct alternative.

9.2

1 Oh no! My wallet *has being stolen/has been stolen/has stolen*!
2 Were those documents *be sent/send/sent* by email or by post?
3 Not many houses *are been built/are being built/are being build* at the moment.
4 That piano *isn't been played/hasn't be played/hasn't been played* for years.
5 Cars that are parked illegally will *be removed/ being removed/ to be removed*.
6 Are those toys *make/be made/made* by hand?
7 We *weren't employed/not were employed/weren't employ* by the government until 1998.
8 We can't use the photocopier because it's *being repaired/repairing/be repaired* right now.

2 Complete the sentences with the active or passive form of the verbs in brackets. Use the verb tense in italics.

1 The magazine _____ (read) mainly by teenagers. It _____ (publish) every month. *present simple*
2 Most of his programmes _____ (not film) in Europe; he usually _____ (work) in Asia. *present simple*
3 The book _____ (write) by an ex-soldier. It _____ (describe) the war in Vietnam. *past simple*
4 My last company _____ (make) clothes. It _____ (buy) by a multinational company called Zed. *past simple*
5 The buildings _____ (clean) and the walls _____ (paint). *present perfect*
6 I _____ (give) a new office but I _____ (not move) my things in there yet. *present perfect*
7 Today this dish _____ (not cook) in the oven. Instead, we _____ (use) the grill. *present continuous*
8 English _____ (not spoken) everywhere in future. Lots of people _____ (not speak) it. *future (will)*

1 Underline the correct alternative to complete the sentences.

9.3

1 What's my PIN number? *I'm forgetting/I forgotten/I've forgotten*.
2 Can you smoke in the restaurant? *I'm sure isn't/I sure it isn't/I'm sure it isn't* legal.
3 What is this drink? It's *definitely am not/definitely not/definite not* orange juice.
4 How old is he? I'm *surely fair/fair sure/fairly sure* he's twenty.
5 What's Maria's second name? I *haven't the clue/have a clue/haven't a clue*.
6 What's the world's biggest building? I *have no idea/have not idea/am no idea*.
7 Where do the Smiths live? I *not remember/can't to remember/can't remember*.
8 When does the game start? I'm not *a hundred percent certain/certain hundred percent/the hundred percent certain* but it might be at 2.00.

LANGUAGE BANK

GRAMMAR

reported speech

direct speech (actual words)	reported speech
'I always **buy** organic food.'	He said (that) he always **bought** organic food.
'I'm **going** to see my mother **tomorrow**.'	She told me she **was going** to see her mother **the next day**.
'I've **passed my** exams.'	He said he **had passed his** exams.
'We **saw** her at the station.'	They said they **had seen** her at the station.
'I'll meet you **here**.'	He said he **would** meet me **there**.
'I **can't** hear you.'	She said she **couldn't** hear me.
'We **might** be late.'	They said they **might** be late.
'I **must** leave at midday.'	He said he **had to** leave at midday.

10.1

Use reported speech to report what someone said earlier. After a past tense reporting verb, e.g. *said, told,* etc., the original verb often moves one tense back (this is sometimes called 'backshifting').

There may be other changes to pronouns, possessive adjectives, and to references of time or place.

'I'll go.' → *She* said *she would* go.

'It's my car.' → *He* said it was *his* car.

'We'll see you tomorrow.' → *They* said they would see *us the next day*.

'I'll be here.' → *She* said *she would* be there.

Must changes to *had to*, but *mustn't* doesn't change.

'We mustn't be late.' → *They* said *they mustn't* be late. NOT ~~They said they didn't have to be late.~~

Could, would and *might* also don't change in reported speech.

'We **might** see you later.' → *They* said (that) *they might* see us later.

Say and *tell* are the most common reporting verbs. Note the different verb patterns.

He **told me** that he'd be late. She **said** (to me) that she wanted to stay.

Sometimes there is no need to change the tenses (no backshift). This is the case when the reporting verb is in the present tense.

'I'll meet you at the airport.' → He **says** he'**ll meet us** at the airport.

If the information we are reporting is still true in the present, we do not need to change the tenses but if the reporting verb is in the past, we can.

'It's a great film.' → *She said that it's a great film.* (This is still true now.) or *She said that it was a great film.* (Implies she's seen it and thought it was good at the time.)

reported questions

Reported questions have the same tense and word changes as reported statements. To report a *yes/no* question, use *if/whether* after the reporting verb.

'Do you live in Peru?' → *She asked me if I lived in Peru.* or *She asked me whether I lived in Peru.*

To report a *Wh-* question, use the question word.

'Where is the restaurant?' → *She asked me where the restaurant was.*

In reported questions, the word order is the same as for statements. We do not use an auxiliary *do/does/did*.

'Do you like eating sushi?' → *She asked me if I like eating sushi.*

---

verb patterns

Many different structures can follow a verb in English. Some verbs are followed by an -*ing* form, and some are followed by the infinitive.

I can't **stand listening** to opera. He **learned to speak** Mandarin when he moved to China.

verb + infinitive with *to*: agree, ask, tell, expect, learn, manage, help, decide, offer, promise, want, refuse, need

10.2

We **managed to get** to the theatre on time. They **agreed to give** us cheap tickets.

verb + -*ing*: like, love, hate, can't stand, (be) keen on, look forward to, miss, enjoy, fancy, give up, practise

I **miss spending** time with my friends and family. We **look forward to seeing** you.

Reporting verbs use many different verb patterns, so it's

important to learn the patterns. Some verbs can use more than one structure, e.g. *suggest*

He **suggested that** we meet at 6p.m. She **suggested having** lunch in the cafeteria.

verb + infinitive with *to*: offer, promise, refuse, agree

They **offered to give** us a lift to the station. They **promised to phone** when they arrive.

verb + object + infinitive with *to*: invite, warn, tell, ask

They **invited us to stay** for the weekend. He **warned them not to tell** anyone.

verb + -*ing*: suggest, recommend

They **suggested trying** another restaurant. He **recommended eating** at Café Fish.

verb + *that*: explain, warn (someone), promise (someone), suggest

She **explained that** she had to leave the meeting. He **promised that** he would take me out tonight.

---

giving advice/warnings

10.3

advice	warnings
Make sure you … / If I were you, I'd …	Watch out for … / Be careful to/of …
Don't forget to … / You need to …	Don't … (or else …) / You'd better …
The most important thing is to …	Whatever you do, don't …

PRACTICE

1 Complete the reported statements using tense changes (backshift).

1 'We're going to have a baby.'

He said (that) _____ _____ going to have a baby.

2 'I've lived here for more than twenty years.'

She _____ that she had lived _____ for more than twenty years.

3 'We grew these carrots in our garden.'

They told us that they _____ grown the carrots in _____ garden.

4 'I have to go to the dentist tomorrow.'

He said (that) he _____ to go to the dentist the _____ day.

5 'I've lost my passport.'

She said that _____ had lost _____ passport.

6 'I'm feeling a bit stressed.'

She _____ me that she _____ feeling a bit stressed.

7 'We'd never been to the US before.'

They said that _____ _____ never been to the US before.

8 'I can't stay long because I have to go to a meeting.'

She said that she _____ stay long because she _____ to go to a meeting.

2 Using the words in italics, rewrite the sentences as reported speech.

1 'I think that La Tasca's is my favourite restaurant.'

She said that _____.

2 'I'm going to meet Mr Susuki this afternoon.'

He told me _____.

3 'Maja called me yesterday.'

He said that _____.

4 'We'll meet you here tomorrow.'

They told us that _____.

5 'We haven't received your application.'

We told her that _____.

6 'I might see you at the party, Matt.'

She told Matt _____.

7 'I've already sent you an email explaining the situation.'

He said that _____.

8 'I can't type very fast.'

She told her boss that _____.

10.1

---

1 Complete the reported statements below with the verbs in the box and any other necessary words.

| ~~refuse~~ agree promise suggest offer warn invite explain |

1 'I'm afraid I'm not going to pay for this meal.'

He _____refused to pay_____ for the meal.

2 'You need to show your passport to immigration,' she said to him.

She _____ he _____ his passport to immigration.

3 'If you book your tickets in advance, you'll get two for the price of one,' she told us.

She _____ our tickets in advance.

4 'I'll pick you up on the way to the station.'

He _____ pick me up on the way to the station.

5 'Why don't you all come for lunch on Sunday?'

She _____ us _____ for lunch on Sunday.

6 'I'll definitely cook something for dinner.'

He _____ something for dinner.

7 'Be careful to hold on to your bags at the station.'

She _____ on to our bags at the station.

8 'Yes. It's a good idea to have the meeting on Tuesday.'

He _____ the meeting on Tuesday.

2 Find and correct the mistakes. There are mistakes in six of the sentences.

1 The company has agreed that pay for the trip.

2 They recommended going to a different hotel.

3 I suggested to that she look for another job.

4 She suggested to call an ambulance.

5 We offered helping, but there was nothing we could do.

6 The manager refused let us leave the hotel before we met his wife.

7 We promised to sending her a postcard.

8 I explained that there had been a delay.

10.2

---

1 Make sentences giving advice/warnings using the prompts.

1 forget / set / alarm.

2 you / need / buy / ticket / before / get on the train

3 if I / you / call them / before you leave

4 watch out / speed cameras. There / lots on the road.

5 make sure / apply for a visa

6 whatever / do / don't / leave valuable items / the room

7 important / thing / check / flight times

8 forget / take your mobile phone

10.3

VOCABULARY BANK

FAMILY

1 Complete the family tree with the words in the box.

~~in-laws~~   ~~sister-in-law~~   ~~niece~~   ~~nephew~~   grandparents on my mother's side   ~~ex-husband~~   ~~stepfather~~   ~~stepdaughter~~

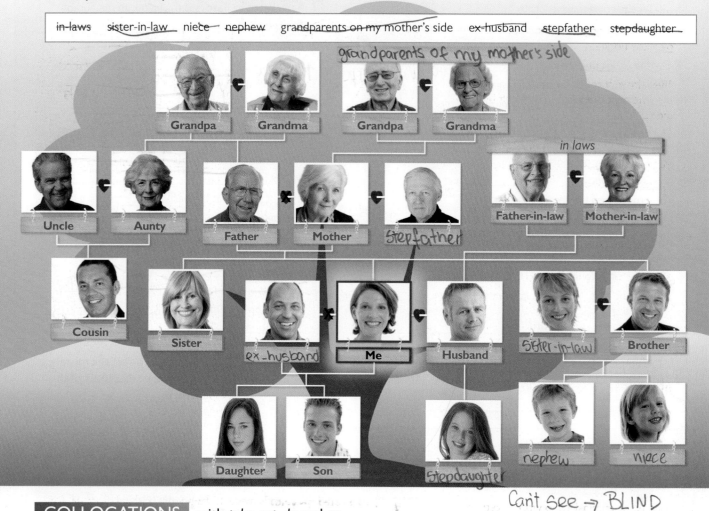

grandparents of my mother's side

Grandpa   Grandma   Grandpa   Grandma

in laws

Uncle   Aunty   Father   Mother   *stepfather*   Father-in-law   Mother-in-law

Cousin   Sister   *ex-husband*   **Me**   Husband   *Sister-in-law*   Brother

Daughter   Son   *Stepdaughter*   *nephew*   *niece*

COLLOCATIONS with *take*, *get*, *do* and *go*

1 Add the words/expressions in italics to the correct places in each word web.

1 ~~your best,~~ *exercise, ~~nothing for you,~~ ~~the cleaning~~*

2 ~~fired,~~ ~~a prize,~~ ~~excited,~~ *food poisoning*

3 ~~a look,~~ *the blame, sugar, ages*

4 ~~on holiday,~~ *crazy, ~~together,~~ badly*

Can't see → BLIND
HEAR → DEAF
SPEAK → MUTE
SMELL → ANOSMIC

Do
- a hobby / *exercise* (action)
- well / *your best* (good effort)
- the washing up / *the cleaning* (something at home)
- you good / *nothing for you* (be affected)

Get
- a good salary / *a prize* (earn)
- a job / *fired* (change your work situation)
- flu/a cold / *food poisoning* (become ill)
- depressed / *excited* (become)

Take
- medicine / *sugar* (swallow)
- ten minutes / *ages* (use time)
- a photo / *a look* (action)
- responsibility / *the blame* (accepting something)

Go
- blind / *crazy!* (become)
- well / *badly* (happen)
- by bus / *on holiday* (travel)
- with / *together* (fit)

PREPOSITIONS of place

1 Match descriptions 1–5 with pictures A–E.

1 They drove <u>along</u> the motorway, and <u>over</u> the bridge.

2 They went <u>around</u> the city.

3 They drove <u>through</u> the main square, <u>past</u> the post office and turned left <u>by</u> the station.

4 The hotel is <u>near</u> the city centre, <u>between</u> the National Museum and the cathedral.

5 The house is <u>next to</u> the supermarket, <u>opposite</u> the cinema.

A

B

C

D

E

NEWS

1 Read the text and match the words/phrases in bold with definitions 1–13 below.

1 continued to *proceeded to*

2 a group of criminals who work together *gang*

3 took someone away because they have done something illegal *arrested*

4 thieves carrying weapons *armed robbers*

5 an attack by criminals on a bank, shop, etc., to steal money or valuable things *raid*

6 (doing something) while threatening to shoot someone *at gunpoint*

7 people whose job it is to protect people or a place, or to make sure that a person does not escape *security guards*

8 leave a place or dangerous situation when someone is trying to catch you *escape*

9 people who saw the crime *Eye witnesses*

10 tried *attempted*

11 warn people that something bad is happening *raise the alarm*

12 made someone do this *forced*

13 a vehicle for the escape *getaway vehicle*

Two **security guards** were kidnapped and held hostage for twelve hours by a **gang** of **armed robbers**, who **attempted** to **raid** a security depot. The robbers held the guards **at gunpoint** and **forced** them to hand over keys and security information. They then **proceeded to** fill a lorry with more than £53 million in notes. Another £150 million was left behind because there was no more room in the **getaway vehicle**. Luckily, one of the guards managed to **raise the alarm**, and the police arrived and **arrested** the gang before they could **escape**. **Eye witnesses** said that they saw at least eight men being arrested.

VOCABULARY BANK

COMMUNICATION

1A Underline the phrases in sentences 1–8 which involve communicating.

1 She tried to <u>get hold of you</u> but your mobile was dead.
2 I'm going to <u>have a chat with</u> Tom about his appearance. ✓
3 The film director <u>got in touch with</u> him through his agent. ✓
4 I don't <u>get what you mean</u>. ✓
5 She <u>goes on and on</u> about her problems – it's so boring! ✓
6 I'm so pleased we've <u>stayed in touch</u> all these years. ✓
7 We <u>said sorry</u> for the mess.
8 They sometimes <u>have arguments about</u> money.

B Match the underlined phrases in Exercise 1A with phrases a)–h) below.

a) talk to *have a chat with*
b) disagree *have arguments about*
c) contact you *get hold of you*
d) apologised *said sorry for*
e) understand *get what you mean*
f) maintained contact *stayed in touch*
g) contacted *got in touch with*
h) talks too much *goes on and on*

IDIOMS

1A Match pictures A–F with the idioms in the box.

> be in two minds let your hair down break the ice travel light
> learn (something) by heart go window shopping

A *break the ice*

B *learn by heart*

C *go window shopping*

D *travel light*

E *let your hair down*

F *be in two minds*

B Complete the sentences with the idioms above.

1 Tomorrow there's a test on this poem. I have to *learn* it *by heart*.
2 I'm *in two minds*. I don't know if I want the black one or the red one.
3 Everyone was nervous, so Jackie told a few jokes to *break the ice*.
4 He always *travels light*. He only takes one suitcase even for long trips.
5 I've got no money at the moment but we can go *window shopping* if you want.
6 You've been working non-stop. Why don't you go out and *let your hair down*?

C What do you think the idioms mean? Use a dictionary to help you.

PERSONAL QUALITIES

1A Complete the sentences with the adjectives in the box.

you can trust in someone ↓   *relax person*

reliable   sensible   ~~easy-going~~
~~aggressive~~   ~~clever/bright~~   honest
~~lazy~~   ~~punctual~~   ~~moody~~   *bipolar*
~~independent~~

1 She is very _independent_. She works well by herself. +

2 You never know what to expect. She's very _moody_, so one minute she's happy, and the next minute, she's shouting at you. −

3 She's very _sensible_. I'm sure she will know what to do if there's a difficult situation. +

4 He's extremely _punctual_. He is never late for appointments. +

5 My new manager is very _easy-going_. She doesn't mind what time we get to work, what we wear. She never looks stressed. +

6 He always tells the truth. He's very _honest_. +

7 She likes to do as little work as possible. She's a bit _lazy_.

8 He's very _clever/bright_. He learns very quickly. +

9 You know that you can trust and depend on him. He's hard-working and very _reliable_. +

10 He nearly attacked one of his employees when he arrived late for the meeting. He's very _aggresive_. −

You're late!

B Look at the adjectives in the box again. Do they describe positive or negative characteristics? Do you have any of these characteristics?

WORKING LIFE

1A Match descriptions 1–3 with jobs A–C.

1 I work as a _B_ for a large corporation. I usually **work nine-to-five**, but sometimes I have to **work late**. My job involves **checking and responding to emails**, **answering phone enquiries** and **organising** my boss's diary.

A Window cleaner

2 I'm an _C_. I tend to **work long hours**. I'm **responsible for** a small team of people. I spend a lot of my time **attending meetings**, and **dealing with problems**. I **advise clients** on their **accounts** and **write updates and reports** for the website.

B Personal assistant

3 I'm a _A_. Lots of people wouldn't like what I do, because it's an **outdoor job**, and it's a **physical job**, but I love it. I **work for myself**, so I can be very **independent**, and I **work flexible hours**, which is good for me. It's a very **sociable job**, too. I talk to people all day long. I couldn't do an **office job**. I would die of boredom!

C Accountant

B Work in pairs. What do the phrases in bold mean?

CONFUSING WORDS

1A Choose the correct option from the words in bold to complete the pairs of sentences.

1 **actually • currently**

a) I expected the first week in my new job to be awful, but _____ it was fine.

b) I am _____ working in London, but before I was working in Paris.

2 **career • course**

a) She's doing a Spanish _____ at the moment, and she's really enjoying it.

b) Ted spent most of his _____ as a teacher.

3 **borrow • lend**

a) Do you think you could _____ me a pen?

b) I had to _____ some money from a friend.

4 **argument • discussion**

a) We had an interesting _____ about the Prime Minister and we all agreed he should resign.

b) I had an _____ with my mother. She's always telling me what to do!

5 **miss • lose**

a) Hurry up, or we'll _____ the bus.

b) Why do I always _____ my car keys?

B Check your answers in a dictionary.

VOCABULARY BANK

TECHNOLOGY

1 Match words/phrases 1–10 with pictures A–J.

1 ~~plug it in~~
2 ~~press the button~~
3 ~~have an injection~~
4 ~~have an operation~~
5 ~~run out of petrol~~
6 ~~break down~~
7 ~~(not) get a connection~~
8 ~~restart/reboot the computer~~
9 ~~do an experiment~~
10 ~~switch it on/off~~

A switch it on/off

B run out of petrol

C press the button

D do an experemen

E have an injection

F plug it in connection

G (not) get connection

H restart/reboot the computer

I have an operation

J break down

WORD-BUILDING nouns (suffixes)

1A Look at the table which shows six different suffixes used to form nouns from verbs and adjectives.

-ation	education relaxation imagination immigration
-ion	pollution instruction depression competition
-ment	entertainment improvement employment agreement
-ing	running smoking laughing eating
-ness	weakness loneliness happiness kindness
-ity	creativity stupidity sensitivity responsibility

B Cover the table and complete sentences 1–10 with the correct form of the verbs/adjectives in brackets.

1 I think a bit of _____ (compete) in schools is a good thing.

2 There has been a great _____ (improve) in his work recently.

3 Dealing with problem clients is not my _____ (responsible).

4 _____ (lonely) is one of the worst aspects of getting old.

5 He suffers from _____ (depress).

6 Try to use your _____ (imagine).

7 I couldn't believe my own _____ (stupid)!

8 There is live _____ (entertain) from 8p.m.

9 I was amazed by his _____ (kind).

10 I didn't hear the last _____ (instruct).

EMOTIONS

1 Complete definitions 1–10 with the correct form of the adjectives in the box.

> exciting/excited   terrifying/terrified
> astonishing/astonished   tiring/tired
> fascinating/fascinated
> disappointing/disappointed
> disgusting/disgusted
> frustrating/frustrated
> depressing/depressed
> interesting/interested

1 you want to know more about it and you give it your attention: *I was* <u>interested</u> *in what he had to say.*

2 being happy, interested and hopeful because something good has happened, or is going to happen: *The kids are getting really* <u>excited</u> *about the trip.*

3 very surprising: *It's* <u>astonishing</u> *that you didn't know about this!*

4 making you feel that you want to sleep or rest: *It was a long,* <u>tiring</u> *journey.*

5 extremely interesting: *Istanbul is a* <u>facinating</u> *city.*

6 unhappy because something you hoped for did not happen: *I was* <u>frustrated</u> / <u>disappointed</u> *that I hadn't won.*

7 making you feel sad: *It's a very* <u>depressing</u> *book. I didn't like it at all.*

8 extremely unpleasant and making you feel sick: *What's that smell? It's* <u>disgusting</u>!

9 feeling annoyed, upset or impatient because you cannot control/change a situation: *He gets* <u>frustrated</u> *when people don't understand what he's saying.*

10 very frightened: *I'm absolutely* <u>terrified</u> *of spiders!*

MULTI-WORD VERBS

1A Match the phrasal verbs in sentences 1–10 with meanings a–j.

verb + off

1 I called him on the phone but we got **cut off**. b

2 They had to **call off** the football match because of the weather. f

3 I have to do this work. I can't **put** it **off** any longer. a

verb + out

4 I'd like to **check out** some other options. d

5 He's wearing a pink jacket so he'll **stand out** from the crowd. g

6 I can't **work out** what to do about the problem. j

verb + after

7 My neighbour is **looking after** my cats when we go away. h

8 He **takes after** his father. They are both very good-looking. c

verb + in

9 Can you print out and then **fill in** the form and send it back to me? i

10 Saskia, please **let** me **in**! e

a) delay doing something
b) the phone suddenly stopped working.
c) look/behave like an older member of the family
d) get more information about something
e) allow someone to come in
f) decide that a planned event won't happen
g) be easy to see/notice
h) take care of something or someone
i) write the necessary information in an official document
j) decide/plan something to solve a problem

B Label pictures A–E with the sentences above.

A allow someone to come in
B write the necessary information in an official document
C I I
D be easy to eee/notice
E
F the phone suddenly stopped working.

VOCABULARY BANK

SUCCESS

1A Match expressions 1–10 with definitions a)–j).

1 be on a shortlist *b)*
2 come first *a)*
3 be nominated *c)*
4 be awarded *d)*
5 win a medal *f)*
6 win an award *e)*
7 be on the winning team *g)*
8 be a runner up *h)*
9 get an 'A' *j)*
10 win a prize *i)*

a) win
b) be named in a list (chosen from a larger group) to be considered for a prize or job
c) be officially suggested as a possible prize winner (or candidate for an important job)
d) be given an official prize/money
e) receive a prize/money because of an achievement
f) receive a valuable piece of metal because of success in a competition (or bravery, e.g. in war)
g) be part of a group that wins a game/competition
h) come in second place in a competition, race, etc.
i) get something because you are successful in a competition, race, etc.
j) get the highest grade for a piece of academic work

B Look at the situations opposite and complete the captions with the words in the box.

> awarded   ~~winning~~   ~~medal~~   award   got   prize
> ~~nominated~~   ~~runner up~~   ~~shortlist~~   came

'I ¹ came first.'
'I was the ² runner-up'
'I won the bronze ³ medal.'

'I won a ⁴ prize for best student! I ⁵ got A's in all my exams!'

'I was ⁶ nominated for Best Actor but I didn't win. The Oscar was ⁷ awarded to Rick Rooney.'

'My book was on a ⁸ shortlist for Book of the Year, but it didn't win. I've never won an ⁹ award.'

'I was on the ¹⁰ winning team!'

VERB PHRASES with prepositions

1A In each sentence the same preposition is missing twice. Complete the sentences with the prepositions in the box.

> to   on   in   ~~for~~   ~~about~~   with

1 I couldn't cope **with** my boss any more so I decided to part **with** the company.
2 The journalist wrote **about** the farm workers, who were protesting **about** their low salary.
3 Always stick **to** what you believe in; this will lead **to** true happiness.
4 She worked **for** a rich family, and her job was to care **for** the sick grandmother.
5 The scientists started working **on** a project, but without any money they couldn't go **on**.
6 Aged ten, she took part **in** a play and this resulted **in** her love of the theatre.

B Match the verb phrases in Exercise 1A with definitions a)–k).
a) create a text *write about*
b) look after *care for*
c) refuse to change your mind *stick to* about
d) be involved in *take part in*
e) be employed by *work for*
f) cause something to happen (two phrases) *lead to / result in*
g) spend time and effort doing something *working on*
h) leave *part with*
i) continue *go on*
j) deal with a difficult problem or situation successfully
k) show publicly that you think something is wrong *protest about*

GETTING ON

1A Match 1–6 with a)–f) to complete the sentences.

My neighbour:

1 is very helpful. For example, b)
2 sometimes borrows my tools a)
3 pops over most days, because d)
4 lends me sugar or milk f)
5 is really unfriendly. She c) *Kookie*
6 is always gossiping e)

a) but he never gives them back!
b) he fixed my car last year.
c) doesn't even say 'good morning'.
d) she likes to chat.
e) about people who live in the street.
f) if I need it.

B Underline the words/phrases in 1–6 which match definitions a)–f).

a) comes to my house (informally) *POPS over*
b) not friendly *unfriendly*
c) uses my possessions ~~borrows~~ *borrows*
d) gives me things (which I will later return) ~~borrows~~ *Lends me*
e) helps a lot *helpful*
f) talking about other people (usually bad things) *gossiping*

COMPOUND NOUNS

1A Put the words next to the correct key word to make compound nouns. Which compound nouns are written as one word? Use a dictionary to check.

~~racket~~ office barrier cream code shop machine player lab tan court cup learner card glasses

1 tennis | *racket*
          | _____

2 coffee | _____
          | _____

3 post | _____
          | _____

4 language | _____
          | _____

5 sun | _____
          | _____

B Put the key words in the correct places. Which compound nouns are written as one word? Use a dictionary to check.

book   machine   phone   room   shoes

1 running | _____
   sports |
   high-heeled|

2 cheque | _____
   picture |
   text |

3 bed | _____
   dining |
   changing |

4 sewing | _____
   washing |
   drinks |

5 mobile | _____
   pay |
   cell |

VOCABULARY BANK

HISTORY

1 Use one word from each row in the table to complete sentences 1–12.

noun	verb	adjective	person
invasion	invade		invader
history		historical/historic	historian
colonisation/colony	colonise		coloniser
democracy	democratise	democratic	democrat
liberation	liberate		liberator
discovery	discover		discoverer
leadership	lead		leader
politics		political	politician
development	develop	developing	developer
invention	invent	inventive	inventor
foundation	found	founding	founder
independence		independent	

1 1066 is the date of the Norman _invasion_ of Britain.
2 Edward Gibbon was a great _____. He wrote *The History of the Decline and Fall of the Roman Empire*.
3 India was a _____ of Great Britain until 1947.
4 South Africa's first _____ elections, in which black people could vote, took place in 1994.
5 In the eighteenth and nineteenth centuries, William Wilberforce led a movement to _____ slaves.
6 Alexander Fleming is known for his _____ of penicillin.
7 Fidel Castro was the _____ of the Cuban revolution of 1959.
8 The Kennedys and the Bush family are known for their involvement in American _____.
9 The World Bank lends money to _____ countries, particularly in Asia and Africa.
10 In 1901 Wilhelm Rontgen won the Nobel Prize in Physics for his _____ of the X-ray.
11 Bill Gates is the _____ of Microsoft.
12 Angola gained its _____ from Portugal in 1975.

COLLOCATIONS with *come, give, have* and *make*

1 Put the words/expressions in italics into the correct places in each word web.

1 *across the mountain, with instructions, to dinner, nearer*

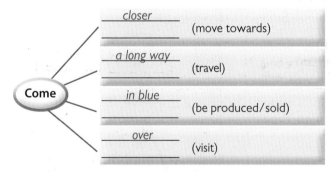

3 *a cold, a chance, ideas, 100 calories*

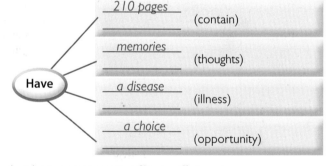

2 *a prize, permission, orders, me a headache*

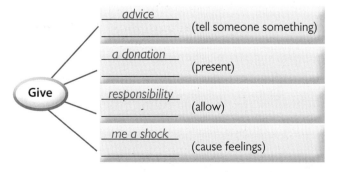

4 *a living, an agreement, a film, an effort*

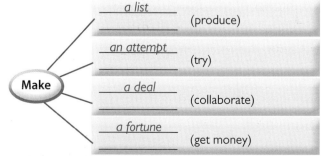

THE ENVIRONMENT

1A Complete the text with words/phrases from the box with the same meaning as the words/phrases in brackets.

> global warming   pollution   aerosol cans   protect   industrial waste
> factory smoke   natural resources   destroys the environment
> harmful   environmentally-friendly   car exhaust fumes
> destruction of the rainforest

Many people are worried about the state of the planet, and the effects of ¹*global warming* (an increase in world temperatures, caused by an increase in carbon dioxide around the Earth). A growing human population is putting pressure on the Earth's ²*natural resources*, (things that exist in nature and can be used by people, for example oil, trees, etc.) like food and water. Also, a lot of human activity is ³*harmful* (causes damage), either because it causes ⁴*pollution* (dirty air, water or land), or because it ⁵*destroys the environment* (damages the air, water and land so badly that it might not recover). Some of the most common causes of damage are:

- ⁶*industrial waste* (chemicals and unwanted materials which factories throw away)
- ⁷*factory smoke* and ⁸*car exhaust fumes*
- ⁹*aerosol cans* (which contain CFCs – a chemical which damages the ozone layer)
- ¹⁰*destruction of the rainforest* which increases the amount of carbon dioxide in the atmosphere.

Environmentalists try to ¹¹*protect* the environment (keep it safe from harm) by encouraging people to change the way they live (recycling more, using ¹²*environmentally-friendly* or 'green' products which do not damage the environment, wasting less, etc.) and persuading governments to take environmental issues more seriously.

B Complete the table with words from the text in Exercise 1A.

noun	verb
¹ destruction	destroy
protection	² protect
³ pollution	pollute
⁴ damage	damage
waste	⁵ waste

WORD-BUILDING (prefixes)

1 Look at the prefixes in the table and complete sentences 1–12 with a suitable form of the words in brackets.

in-	invisible
	inappropriate
	inaccurate
	inadequate
	inability
im-	immature
	impossible
	impolite
	immobile
	immoral
ir-	irresponsible
	irregular
	irrelevant
	irrational
ex-	ex-girlfriend
	ex-Prime Minister
	ex-husband
	ex-boss
	ex-wife

1 The number is not correct. It's _inaccurate_ (accurate)
2 Let me introduce you to my _ex-wife_, Amelia. (wife)
3 I can't do it. It's _impossible_! (possible)
4 It's difficult to travel because the buses and trains are very _irregular_. (regular)
5 You can't leave without saying goodbye. It's _impolite_ (polite)
6 She behaves like a child. She's very _immature_ (mature)
7 You can't come to the office dressed like that. It's _inappropriate_. (appropriate)
8 He left his laptop on the train. He's very _irresponsible_ (responsible)
9 I used to work for him. He's my _ex-boss_. (boss)
10 There is no good reason for it. It's completely _irrational_ (rational)
11 It doesn't do the job. It's _inadequate_ (adequate)
12 She refused to move at all. She was _immobile_ (mobile)

COMMUNICATION BANK

1.2

4C Look at your drawing. Does it include these things?

1 wheels   2 handlebar   3 saddle   4 chain

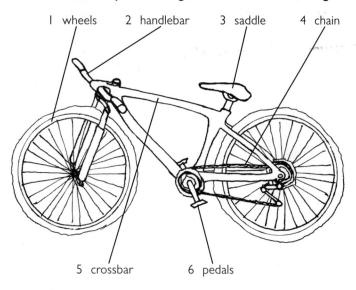

5 crossbar   6 pedals

1.2

8B Read the text and check your answers.

Stella magazine commissioned YouGov, a research agency, to interview over 1,000 women in the UK about what they really think. Here are some of the results.

80% of women say that losing their health is their greatest concern, followed by putting on weight (52%) and losing their jobs (24%). It seems that British women aren't too happy with their bodies: 23% of women are on a diet now and 58% have **gone on a diet** in the past. Only 4% of women **do** more than 7 hours' **exercise** per week, while 21% do no exercise at all.

The biggest challenge for modern women is balancing home and work life (82%), followed by bringing up happy children (56%) and finding time for themselves (52%).

As for their love lives, 9% of women aged 45–54 met their husbands through the internet, and 49% of women believe that the best age to **get married** is between 25 and 29.

And what about the relationships between men and women? 59% think fathers should **take** more **responsibility** for their children. These women are also less than content with their husbands' efforts at home: 51% say they currently **do** over 75% of the **housework**. Despite this, over 70% of women would prefer to have a male boss than a female.

And their heroes? The woman they most admire is ex-Prime Minister Margaret Thatcher (7%), followed by the Queen (5%).

1.3

8A Student B: read your instructions below.

You want to do a course at a famous business school which is well-known for its practical courses. It will give you contacts in the business world. Think about these things:

• the business you want to start
• relevant work experience you have with another company

Student A will interview you for the course. He/She will ask about your:

• reason for doing the course
• work experience
• expectations of the course
• plans for the future

Prepare your answers and think of some questions to ask about the school.

2.1

2A Read and check your answers.

Fact or fiction:

1 Fiction: the film *The Last Samurai* does tell the story of the samurai rebellion, but the character Nathan Algren did not exist.

2 Fiction: in truth, we know very little about William Shakespeare's personal life, or what provided his inspiration.

3 Partly true: whilst *Gladiator* did take a few liberties with history, it's true that the Emperor was killed by a gladiator in the Roman baths.

4 Partly true: the film *Braveheart* does tell the story of how William Wallace fought to free Scotland, but kilts were not worn in Scotland until 300 years later. And there are many other historical inaccuracies.

5 Partly true: the film *Apollo 13* was praised for its accuracy. Much of the dialogue was taken directly from recordings. However, the pilot's exact words were, 'OK, Houston, we've had a problem here'.

9.3

Student A

7 Check Student B's answers to your questions.

1 Canberra; 2 India; 3 Paraguay

9.1

Student B

2B Read the texts below and make notes with the following prompts.

- What?
- Where?
- When?
- Why was it important?

Galileo explores the heavens

When Galileo became the first person to look at the sky through a telescope, it changed our view of the universe. His discoveries about the Sun, Moon and other planets completely disagreed with older theories. He then wrote a book, *Two World Systems*, published in Italy in 1630, which led to his problems with the Roman Catholic Church. At his trial, Galileo was found guilty and it was only in the twentieth century that the Vatican finally agreed with him. If Galileo hadn't defended his theories, he would have been a free man, but we wouldn't have understood the science of our universe.

The steam engine

For most of human history we were not very different from other animals, which also have language, act as a group, and have organisational systems. But the steam engine gave us the ability to do things faster and to do things that other animals couldn't. This development, which took place in Britain in the 18th century, was not one invention, but many. Different people were involved at different stages: Thomas Newcomen, James Watt and George Stephenson. The steam engine allowed us to transform the way we use energy. It changed so many things, including transportation, manufacturing and communication. Life would have been totally different if we hadn't invented it.

4.1

7A Work out your score. Add up the number of points (0, 1 or 2) for each answer. Use your total to find out if you work like a millionaire.

Question 1: a) 0 b) 1 c) 2
Question 2: a) 1 b) 2 c) 0
Question 3: a) 0 b) 1 c) 2
Question 4: a) 1 b) 2 c) 0
Question 5: a) 0 b) 1 c) 2

1+1+2+2+2=8

Key:

Score 8–10 You work like a millionaire!

You are very ambitious and enjoy your work. Keep going. Sooner or later all your hard work will pay off and you can live like a millionaire, too.

Score 6–7 You have millionaire potential!

You understand hard work, and if you make it your top priority, you could be a millionaire, too. Keep focused on your goal.

Score 0–5 You don't work like a millionaire!

The clearest characteristics of self-made millionaires are that they work hard and they enjoy their work. You seem to prefer a work–life balance, where work and money are not your top priorities.

4.1

9B Read the vocabulary notes and check your answers.

remember • remind
If you **remember** something, a fact or event from the past, or something you earlier decided to do, comes back into your mind:
He suddenly remembered he had to go to the bank.
If someone **reminds** you to do something, or something reminds you of something, they make you remember it:
Remind me to call him later today.

forget • leave
If you want to talk about the place where you have left something, use the verb **leave**, not the verb **forget**. Compare:
I've forgotten my book and I've forgotten my keys.
I've left my keys in the car.
Don't say: *I've forgotten my keys in the car.*

listen • hear
If you **hear** something, you know that sound has been made, and can often recognise what it is:
Did you hear that noise?
If you **listen** to something or someone, you pay attention to the words, sounds and music that they are making:
I am sorry, could you repeat the question? I wasn't listening.

fun • funny
Use **fun** to talk about events and activities that are enjoyable, such as games and parties:
Let's go to the beach and have some fun.
Funny is an adjective that describes someone or something that makes you laugh:
Bob's jokes are really funny.

earn • win
Use **earn** to talk about getting money by working:
She earns about $50,000 a year.
Use **win** to say that someone gets a prize in a game or competition.
Brian won first prize in the skating competition.

COMMUNICATION BANK

2.1

10A Student B: make *Have you ever ...?* questions using the prompts.

1 win an award/competition/some money

2 eat something very unusual

3 break a bone in your body

4 lock yourself out of the house

5 ride a horse/donkey/camel/motorbike

6 climb a mountain/run more than 2 km

3.2

8C Check your answers.

1 False. Compare: *I said the wrong thing.* (formal) *I put my foot in it.* (informal) *Not everyone will want them.* (formal) *They are not everyone's cup of tea.*

2 True. *I hate small talk. I just want to talk about the important business.* We can't say: *I hate talk small.*

3 True. *They don't have much time. They're working against the clock.* (present continuous) *Tomorrow we have a lot of things to do. We're going to work against the clock.* (be going to for future plans)

4 True. *What's on your mind?* = *What are you thinking?* or *It's an issue close to my heart.* = *I feel passionate about it.*

3.3

1B Read the end of the story.

The waiter said, 'Mr Carson has already paid your bill.' The producer thought this was incredibly generous. So the next morning he called Carson and said, 'That was so nice of you. How generous you are!' Carson started to laugh and said, 'I didn't know that all those people outside were with you. I thought it was just the people at the table!'

The bill? About ten thousand dollars.

9.1

Student B

7A Look at the notes and describe a big moment in history. Think about the questions on page 113 to help you.

The rise of the computer

1981 – IBM launched the first personal computer. Microsoft wrote the software.

By 1984 IBM was selling three million PCs a year. Apple launched a rival, the Macintosh, which used a mouse and icons.

1985 – Microsoft launched Windows and used some of the same tools.

5.2

1C Check your answers.

1 Nobody has ever done it, but in theory, yes it is possible.

2 Any heavy meal can make you dream more (because you spend more time in REM sleep). But cheese doesn't cause more dreams (good or bad) than any other food.

3 Because the heavier you are, the more difficult it is to push you out of the ring (which is how you win a sumo wrestling match).

4 No. Wasps do drink nectar from flowers but they don't use it to make honey.

5 Yes. If you travel, you'll notice that you can see different constellations of stars. This is because the surface of the Earth is curved.

6 When we cut an onion, it releases a substance called lachrymatory-factor synthase. When a very small amount goes in your eye it irritates the eye. We then produce tears (we cry) to wash the substance away.

9.3

5B Check your answers.

1 Michelangelo; 2 Al Gore; 3 F W de Klerk; 4 Gael García Bernal; 5 Sony and Philips in a joint project; 6 J R R Tolkien; 7 Spain (in 2010); 8 *Jurassic Park*

10.3

8A Student B: read the instructions below.

You work in the Tourist Information centre. A customer would like to visit the Australian Outback. Give him/her some advice, using the prompts below:

1 whatever do / don't approach dingoes – they can bite. Remember / throw away any leftover food.

2 watch out / snakes – some are poisonous. If see one / move slowly away.

3 flies – If I were you / buy fly net to fix onto your hat

4 not forget / wear / hat / suncream / take plenty of water / drink

5 don't wear high heels / new, expensive clothes – land is rough and rocky

B Change roles and role-play the following situation. Student B: you are a tourist. You want to go snorkelling on the reef. Ask the dive instructor for advice, e.g. **Are there any special clothes you should wear? What equipment do you need?**

I'd like some information about going diving. First of all, what clothing do I need to wear?

9.3

Student B

7A Check Student A's answers to your questions.

1 Uruguay; 2 The body of a 5,000-year-old man; 3 1999

5.1

6A Which do you think is the best form of transport, A–E, for each challenge? Why? Compare your ideas with other students.

Hi, I'm James May. I'm a car journalist and BBC presenter. Welcome to my Big Ideas. In this challenge, we're going to explore some of the ways of getting from A to B using a range of transport options.

Mostly we're looking at transport available today but there's a couple that are just around the corner, so we'll pretend we're a few years into the future.

Challenges

1 Challenge: Get to Scotland – easily
I'm in London and need to get to Scotland. I need to get there as quickly as I can. The only problem is I'm too tired to actually drive anything. I want to put my feet up and do the crossword on the way.

Transport: _____

2 Challenge: Get to concert in Hyde Park – without sitting in traffic
OK, for this challenge I've got to get to a classical music concert in Hyde Park (Central London). If I fly, I'll need transport from the airport. Got any good ideas?

Transport: _____

3 Challenge: Go to see elephants in Africa – quickly
Do you ever want to experience the wonders of the world? Me, too. Right now I want to see elephants, maybe even feed a few and I'm not talking about a trip to a zoo here in Great Britain. I want to see them in their natural environment. Get me to Africa. And get me there, and back again, fast.

Transport: _____

4 Challenge: See Moulin Rouge in Paris – efficiently
I fancy an expensive night out, let's go to Paris to see the Moulin Rouge. But, I want to be green, so I want to get there using the most energy-efficient way possible.

Transport: _____

5 Challenge: Get out of here – quickly
Oh dear – I've upset someone. I need to get out of here quickly.

Transport: _____

7.2

4B Student B: read the text below to see if your ideas were mentioned.

The human computer

Daniel Tammet says he was born on a blue day, 31st January 1979. He knows it was blue because Wednesdays are always blue, like the number nine or the sound of people arguing.

As a child, Daniel was diagnosed as autistic. He couldn't make friends. He was too different from the other children. Aged eight, he was able to calculate 82 x 82 x 82 x 82 in his head, but he couldn't tie his own shoe laces, or ride a bicycle.

The thing that makes Daniel special is that he has an incredible ability with numbers. He imagines them as shapes and colours ('289 is an ugly number', he says) and is able to do extremely difficult mathematical calculations. On the TV programme that made him famous in the UK, he managed to recite 22,514 numbers from pi perfectly. If you tell Daniel your birth date, he can tell you what day of the week you were born on, and what day of the week it will be on your 65th birthday.

Daniel counts everything. He eats exactly forty-five grams of porridge for breakfast each morning and he brushes his teeth for exactly two minutes. He doesn't like walking on the beach near his home because there are too many pebbles to count.

Daniel's other great love, besides numbers (which he calls 'his friends'), is learning languages. He speaks ten, and he managed to learn Icelandic in a week for a TV programme in Iceland. He now runs a language teaching business on the internet and in 2007 published a book, *Born on a Blue Day*.

* **porridge** – a type of cereal

* **pebbles** – small stones

* **pi** – a mathematical expression represented by the Greek letter π

C Read the text again and answer the questions.

1 How was his behaviour different from the other children's? he is autistic
2 What special talents does he have? really good at numbers
3 How did the public learn about his special talents? On a TV programe
4 What country/countries has he been to and what did he do there? iceland, learn icelandic
5 What has he published? a book
6 What is his 'job' now? teaching business launguage

D Tell your partner about your text. Use questions 1–6 to help.

appliances ~ refrigeradora, cosas de casa electronicas

10.1

Group B

6A Look at the photo and read the fact file below. Then discuss the questions.

> ## The carbon problem
>
> ### Did you know ...?
>
> • Transport is responsible for 25 percent of the UK's carbon footprint, and that doesn't include flying. In the UK, there are more cars than the number of households. In California, there are more cars than the number of people living there.
>
> • Currently cars are used for 18 percent of trips under a mile and for 62 percent of trips of between one and two miles. 38 percent of car trips are taken by one person alone, and 34 percent are shared by two people.
>
> • Lighting and household appliances like washing machines are responsible for around 35 percent of the carbon pollution from your home, and most of your electricity bills. If every household in the UK put a solar panel on their roof, we would produce more electricity than we need as a nation.

1 Do you think every family needs to have access to a car? Why/Why not?

2 What do you think should be done to reduce the number of miles people drive in cars/fly in aeroplanes?

3 Do you think people should generate their own electricity using wind/solar power, etc., or should governments choose options like nuclear power?

4 What laws/schemes would you introduce to deal with these problems?

9.3

Student B

7 You are going to ask Student A the questions below. First, add two more questions of your own. The answers can be found on page 176.

> *History*
>
> *1 Which football team won the first World Cup in 1930? Was it Brazil, Argentina or Uruguay?*
>
> *2 What was discovered in the Alps mountain range in 1991? Was it the body of a 5,000-year-old man, the body of a hairy elephant, or a World War II aeroplane?*
>
> *3 When did the European Union introduce the euro? Was it 1979, 1989 or 1999?*
>
> *4*
>
> *5*

3.3

6B Change roles and role-play the situation.

Student A	Student B
	You are a guest at a hotel. Your room is too small. Ten minutes ago you called reception to ask if there are any suites available. Then room service arrived with a trolley of sweets (cakes, ice cream, etc.). Call reception to make your complaint.
You are a receptionist at a hotel. A guest calls to make a complaint. Start the conversation by saying 'Reception. How can I help you?'	
	'Hello. Yes, I'm afraid I have a problem …' Explain the problem again and ask if there is a suite available.
Apologise for the misunderstanding. Explain that there are no suites available at the moment, but there will be tomorrow.	
	Check details and thank the receptionist for their help.
Confirm details, apologise again and end the call.	

9.1

Student A

7A Look at the notes and describe a big moment in history. Think about the questions on page 113 to help you.

> **Twenty-first-century natural disasters**
>
> Boxing Day Tsunami, 2004, killed 230,000 in eleven countries. Badly affected India, Thailand, Indonesia and Sri Lanka. Underwater earthquake measured approximately 9.2 on the Richter scale (second largest recorded in history).
>
> Hurricane Katrina, 2005, killed 1,836, affected mainly poor blacks in New Orleans, USA.
>
> Earthquake in L'Aquila, Central Italy, 2009, killed over 300 people.

If the Hurricane Katrina hadn't happened A lot of people

4.2

11 Choose one of the job advertisements below and write your covering letter.

> **Fashion designer wanted:**
> We are looking for a graphic designer with a background in the fashion trade. You should have relevant experience and be up-to-date with fashion trends. Strong hand illustration as well as computer design is essential. Please submit a copy of your CV with relevant samples of work.

> **Teaching assistant, Bahamas**
> Primary school is looking for a teaching assistant to start ASAP. The school is a short walk from the beach. No formal qualifications are necessary; however, a genuine love for the job is required. Please forward CVs or contact me for further information.

> **Travel writer required.**
> Travel writer wanted to join our small team. The successful applicant will travel around the world, staying in luxury hotels, and dining in fine restaurants. He/She will need to send a weekly update, including a short review. No previous experience required, but good communication skills and a love of travel essential.

10.4

6A Choose one of the places below. Then plan a three-minute report. Use the prompts and key phrases on page 133 to help.

The Taj Mahal

The Taj Mahal receives 3–4 million tourists each year, but the crowds and the air pollution are eating away at the white stone facade. Now there are plans to close the Taj Mahal to the public, leaving its famous domes visible only from a distance.

The Forbidden City

It may have been forbidden once but nowadays nearly seven million visitors come to see the ancient emperor's palaces in Beijing, China every year. Now traffic pollution is a real problem which is damaging the palaces. A huge restoration is planned, but should the government stop people visiting?

Mount Kilimanjaro, Tanzania

The famous snows of Kilimanjaro are melting and may soon be gone. A combination of evaporation, too little snowfall, and internal heat from the dormant volcano have reduced the mountain's ice and snow cover by 90 percent from historic levels and it continues to retreat about 1m (3.25 ft.) per year.

The Pyramids of Giza

Unrestricted development around the area, and the way in which the city of Cairo grows closer and closer to the pyramids, threatens both the pyramids and the Great Sphinx. There are now plans to run a multi-lane motorway around the city of Cairo, which could create further problems.

The Grand Canyon, Arizona

Why might it disappear? There are more requests each year to mine near the Grand Canyon. The number of mining claims increased from ten in 2003 to more than 1,100 in 2008, bringing with them the risk of stream and groundwater contamination from cyanide and other chemicals. Should permission for the mining claims be stopped because of the threat?

R1.2

6A Work in pairs. Read the text below and choose the best title.

1 The best course I've ever done.   2 A learning experience.   3 How to cook.

B Do the exam task.

Part 4

Questions 21–25

Read the text and questions below.

For each question, mark the correct letter A, B, C or D on your answer sheet.

_____ (Title)

I've always found it **difficult** to make simple decisions. Most people don't even give a moment's thought to what clothes they put on in the morning, or what to have for breakfast. For me, every step is a **big** decision: Will I be too **hot** or **cold** in these clothes? Which will be a **tasty** way to start the day: toast, cereal or fruit? I'm **tired** before I've even left the house most days.

That's why when I saw a course advertised at my local adult education centre called; 'Make Better Decisions', I decided to sign up. I thought that at last I'd made a **good** decision.

The problems began as soon as I walked in. "When would you like to study, evenings or weekends?" said the enthusiastic receptionist. A **small** decision for most, you might think, but both times are equally good for me – another decision!

On the first day, the course started well enough, and the tutor used **pretty** visual displays while making some **interesting** points, but I didn't really feel involved. I felt like I could have got the same information from reading a book or a magazine article on the subject. After listening to the tutor go on and on for an hour, we had to work alone to complete a test. We were given situations where we had to make a decision, and write our answers. I felt we went into this too quickly, and didn't have an opportunity to prepare or discuss our answers with our classmates. By the end of the session, I felt **angry** with myself for paying for this.

I'm not saying the course is really **bad**, it just wasn't for me. The course was interesting but the centre needs to remember that different people learn in different ways. I didn't learn in their way. I need opportunities to discuss new information and ask questions, and this felt more like a lecture.

---

21 What is the writer trying to do in the text?

A Describe his personality

B Recommend the course he took to other people

C Describe the experience he had

D Warn people not to study at the college

22 What doesn't the writer like about his life?

A He never has time to eat breakfast

B He can't make decisions

C He doesn't study enough

D He feels tired all the time

23 What was the first problem the writer had?

A Choosing when to study

B The course wasn't interesting

C Deciding what to wear for the course

D Choosing which course to study

24 The writer didn't enjoy the course because

A It was boring

B He/She didn't feel involved enough

C It was too difficult to understand

D The tutor wasn't honest

25 Which of the following ways of learning would be best for the writer?

A

| Traditional – You like listening to a teacher and making notes. |

B

| Visual – You like using colourful charts and diagrams to learn new information. |

C

| Kinaesthetic – You like physical activity, learning through sport or games. |

D

| Interpersonal – You like discussing subjects and asking questions to learn. |

R2.1

9 ▶ R2.2 Do the exam task.

Part 4

Questions 24–30

You will hear an interview with Ben Rosenthal, a young actor. For questions **24–30**, choose the best answer (**A, B** or **C**).

24 What does Ben say is the most important aspect of acting?

   A imagining the character in different situations.

   B making people believe in his character.

   C being famous.

25 What does Ben say about being famous?

   A it's a consequence of acting, but not the main reason to do it.

   B it's the main reason for acting.

   C he likes being recognised.

26 In his work, Ben finds it most difficult to

   A get noticed.

   B rely on luck. →trust

   C find good parts.

27 What does Ben enjoy most about acting?

   A everything.

   B knowing that he's done his job well.

   C seeing himself at the cinema.

28 What does Ben say about Macbeth?

   A it's a character with many dimensions.

   B he has played the part.

   C it's a tragic character.

29 What happened when Ben was acting in a comedy?

   A he met other famous actors.

   B he had an accident.

   C his father was angry with him.

30 What advice does Ben give to new actors?

   A take the first offer you receive and have fun.

   B choose the part carefully and enjoy it.

   C you need to work hard to succeed.

R2.3

7B Read the sample answer below. Does it contain all the necessary information from the exam task? Which information is included in each paragraph?

Forgetting Sarah Marshall

I recently watched this film at home on DVD with my husband. It's a romantic comedy, set mainly in Hawaii, and stars Jason Segel, Russell Brand, Kristin Bell and Mila Kunis. I have to say that although I don't usually like this type of film, I really enjoyed it, and it made me laugh all the way through.

The film starts when the main character, Peter Bretter (played by Jason Segel), an unsuccessful musician, suddenly finds himself alone, after his tv star girlfriend, Sarah Marshall (Kristin Bell) arrives home one day and suddenly announces that she's in love with someone else. Peter is devastated and spends his days in bed, crying and feeling miserable, until his step-brother suggests he goes on holiday to Hawaii to forget about her. As he's checking in to his hotel though, he sees Sarah and her new boyfriend, Aldous Snow (a famous British rock star, played by Russell Brand),

also checking in to the same hotel! Peter goes to his room and starts the loud crying again, until Rachel (Mila Kunis), the sympathetic hotel receptionist, comes to see where all the noise is coming from. They start talking, and inevitably become close, but it obviously isn't easy with Sarah and her boyfriend in the same hotel.

The story is a little far-fetched, and some of the scenes clearly wouldn't happen in real life, but you can't help falling in love with Peter, the desperate hero, and the happy ending, though predictable, will make you cry. What I liked most about the film was the interesting characters, and their brilliant performances. You'll laugh, cry, get angry with them all the way through.

I would definitely recommend this film for people who like traditional romance stories, with a few laughs thrown in for good measure.

R2.2

6C Do the exam task.

Part 3

Questions 16–30

You are going to read a magazine article about four successful writers of fiction. For questions 16–30, choose from the people (A–D). The people may be chosen more than once.

A	Clare Reutgére
B	Sam Golding
C	Julie Sparks
D	James Grieve

Which person

compares writing to travelling? **16** ☐

believes you should use experiences you've had? **17** ☐

thinks writing should be something you enjoy? **18** ☐

thinks you shouldn't listen to other people? **19** ☐

talks about planning? **20** ☐

mentions working hard? **21** ☐ **22** ☐

describes an unusual place to get ideas? **23** ☐

was influenced by someone when they were at school? **24** ☐

says it's hard to find people who write simply because they love it? **25** ☐

describes how you'll feel when you finish? **26** ☐

was rejected before achieving success? **27** ☐

describes how to construct people in a story? **28** ☐

suggests recording what you see every day? **29** ☐

describes different places you can work? **30** ☐

Clare Reutgére The most important thing is to believe in yourself. You need to know that you have that novel inside you, ready to share with the world. You can be sure of one thing – you *will* receive rejections, criticism and lots of 'NO!'s, but you have to believe that you can do it. Most famous authors (me included, though I don't think I'm very famous) were rejected many times before finally getting published. Remember that it only takes one person to accept your idea for you to have the opportunity to get your book published. If you have a natural talent for writing, and you work hard at it, it's only a matter of time before the world is introduced to your novel!

Julie Sparks Write about what you know. That's what my English teacher told me at school, and I still firmly believe this. Obviously you need an original idea to make your story different from the next, and this may well involve exploring unfamiliar territory, but unless you focus on what you know well, it won't be convincing. Start small – keep a journal, write a blog, focus on the small aspects of behaviour you see in your everyday life, and build from there. You may be writing a science fiction novel, whose settings share nothing with your day-to-day life, but the characters will need to share aspects of their personality that the reader can relate to. Your main characters could be based on people you know, or a single character might be a 'collection' of parts of different people's personalities, but always stick to what you've had experience of.

So you want to be a best-selling writer?

Read the advice of four authors on how to achieve success. With useful advice on how to get published, they are all experts in their field.

Sam Golding For me, writing is like a journey. It all starts with a single idea, which can come at any time – sitting at my computer, in the supermarket, or even in the shower! You know when it's an idea that will work – *the* idea, because you get that special feeling, and then it becomes exciting. However, this is only the start of the journey, like when you decide where you're going to go on that next big holiday. To see the idea through to completion, though, takes hard work. Then comes the research: Where will the story take place? Who are your main characters? How will they behave? Only when you're sure about every single little detail does the actual writing begin. Sometimes it can feel like walking on a really long road that stretches into the horizon; you can see it all ahead of you, and you're excited about the experiences you're going to have on the way, but you still have a very long way to go. You'll reach that crucial half-way point, when you feel you can't go on, and that you're hopeless at writing, but it's all worth it when you've finished. So work hard at it, because the sense of achievement makes it all worthwhile.

James Grieve Real writers are rare. And by 'real' writers, I mean people who have a passion for writing. I don't mean people who love *being a writer,* or people who love *having written*, but writers who simply love writing. So my biggest piece of advice would have to be to love what you do. If you do, you'll be a high achiever. If you don't, then writing simply isn't for you. Write at home. Write on holiday. Write on the bus. Write on the sofa. Write while you're sitting in a café, watching the people and the world around you. Practise, practise, practise, and you'll get better at it. The most important thing – as with any job – is to enjoy every minute of what you do. If not, then why do it? Take pleasure from having an idea, constructing a story, watching it grow, then writing it down for other people (or just for yourself!) to enjoy. What have you got to lose? That way, if or when success comes, you'll swim in your own glory. Whatever happens, have fun. I know I do!

AUDIO SCRIPTS

UNIT 1 Recording 1

W = Woman M = Man

W: So, do you know a lot about your family history?

M: I do actually. Yes, erm, cos, one thing we have got is a family tree, so, erm, I've put it all on the computer. So, er, I know quite a lot about them.

W: Did you ever meet your great-grandparents, for example?

M: No, I never met them. Erm, in fact, I've only ever met one grandparent.

W: Oh?

M: Yeah, they all died rather young so I only had … I met my granny. Erm, that was from my mother's side. Mellows, they were from Yorkshire.

W: Oh, I was going to say, where did your ancestors come from?

M: Well, yeah, no, erm, my mother's side they all came from Yorkshire, but my father's family, er, originally came from Holland. They came over with, er, with William of Orange in 1689.

W: Ah! That's fascinating!

M: And my ancestor was William of Orange's, erm, closest advisor. And, er, so that was for the glorious revolution.

W: Wow! And what happened to the other ancestors? Do you know anything about your other side?

M: What?

W: What might have happened to …

M: What, my mother's side?

W: … more recently perhaps?

M: Well, all of, most of my ancestors were either soldiers, erm, or in the church, or sailors, and, erm, very dull apparently. My father's side, incredibly dull lot until, er, my father's ah father married ah a woman whose ah surname was Knowle and they're all eccentrics – barking mad – lovely and great fun, so I like to think that I'm descended from that lot, rather more than the boring lot.

W: So on that note, which members of your family do you feel close to, would you say?

M: Well, I've only got, I don't have. Both my parents are dead now so, my immediate family is the answer to that question, my wife and my two sons who are twenty-five and twenty-one years old.

W: And who tells the best family stories?

M: Me!

W: I thought so!

UNIT 1 Recording 3

P = Presenter
Part 1

P: Is your brain male or female? A strange question? Maybe, maybe not. In a moment, you will be asked to draw a picture of a bike. Make sure you have a pen or pencil. Pause now, and play when you're ready.

Part 2

P: OK, you have exactly one minute to draw a picture of a bicycle. Go! Make it as beautiful or normal as you like. Include as much detail as you can. You've got forty-five seconds left.

You've got another fifteen seconds.

You've got five seconds left … four, three, two, one, zero, stop. Right, stop drawing please. Now, you have to write down on your piece of paper, whether you, the artist, are male or female. That's all we need to know for the experiment. Now turn to page a hundred and fifty-eight to see what a real bike looks like. Please pause the recording now.

UNIT 1 Recording 4

P = Presenter
Part 3

P: Now, count up the parts on your drawing. Did you include wheels? A handlebar? A saddle? A chain? A crossbar? Pedals? Did your bike have at least five parts? And could it work? Now for the difference between the men's drawings of a bicycle and the women's: female drawings often include a person riding the bike; men's drawings don't usually include a person. This is a clear indication that women think people are important. Men, on the other hand, are more interested in getting the machine right.

UNIT 1 Recording 5

P = Presenter W1 = 1st woman
M1 = 1st man W2 = 2nd woman
Part 4

P: Here are some comments from men and women who did the test.

W1: Hmmm. Well, I only got four parts right. How many did you get right?

M1: I only got four. How many did you get?

W2: I've got, I've got five, but none of us got the chain, did we, so …

M1: Mine hasn't even got pedals …

W2: No, mine hasn't got pedals …

M1: Pedals nor chains so mine will never work!

W2: But if you've got pedals and no chain it's not going to work anyway …

M1: It'll have to be going downhill …

W2: And also that, um, that means the explanation for men making the bike work doesn't work because you, you …

M1: That's right … of the two women and one man none of us drew …

W2: Have made the bike work.

M1: … yeah, and none of us drew a person … so the explanation about women wanting to put a person on there is hasn't proven correct for you two …

W1: No, not with us … no.

M1: And mine is meant to be all about functionality and it hasn't … ah, I've got a little bird on my handlebars though …

W2: It's a very clear drawing though, yours …

W1: I think mine is more male than yours, maybe? Yes …

M1: I think you're right …

W2: Yours is much more accurate … yours is the most accurate one.

M1: The way you've used the biro to just kind of make the lines more solid … that's quite a masculine …

W1: And you've got lights on yours and you've got, you've got five, five parts.

W2: Yeah.

AUDIO SCRIPTS

UNIT 1 Recording 6

1 I think I'm a good employee as I always do my best at work.
2 At my school we have a system of mentors who help the younger pupils, and I'm one of the mentors.
3 My nice news is that I recently became godmother to my best friend's little girl.
4 I'm the boss of a small company that sells phone cards.
5 I'll introduce you to my fiancé later. We got engaged two weeks ago.
6 I took up judo six months ago and I'm a member of a local club.

UNIT 1 Recording 7

Conversation 1
T = Teacher S = Student

T: And what about your expectations of the course?
S: Well, as I said, I've studied English for many years and spent time in Britain, but that was a few years ago. So for me the most important thing is to just refresh ... and try to remember my English and practise speaking and listening.
T: OK. You've got a very good level of English so we'd put you in the advanced class. Is there anything else?
S: Could I ask a question?
T: Of course.
S: I can take the morning class from 9.00 to 12.00. Is that right?
T: Yes, that's right.
S: And in the afternoon there are options? Optional classes?
T: Yes, these are special classes with a special focus like English idioms, conversation, pronunciation. We have the full list here.
S: I see. Thank you.
T: No problem. OK, well, thank you very much.

Conversation 2
I = Interviewer A = Applicant

I: There are a couple of things I'd like to ask about, Jade. Your CV says you have some experience of looking after children?
A: Yes, I was a tutor on a summer camp last year.
I: Can I ask you about that? What type of things did you do?

A: Um, well, I organised games.
I: Games for?
A: The children.
I: OK. And what age were the children?
A: Um ... seven to ten.
I: OK. And you enjoyed it?
A: Yes.
I: What aspect, what part did you enjoy, would you say?
A: I suppose I'd have to say I liked the games best.
I: And any problems?
A: Um, no.
I: What about the different ages? We often find that different ages together can be difficult.
A: It depends. In my opinion, you can usually get the older children to help the younger ones.

Conversation 3
I = Interviewer S = Student

I: I think that's about it. Do you have any questions? Any queries?
S: Um, yes, actually I do have a query.
I: Yes, go ahead.
S: It's about online classes at the university.
I: Right.
S: If I'm accepted, I saw that there are ... urm, that it's possible to take some courses online.
I: That's right.
S: So I wouldn't need to attend classes?
I: Not for the online courses. But, erm ... well, one thing I'd like to say is that the online courses are, in many ways, more difficult than face-to-face courses. Certainly in terms of reading and writing, they're really quite demanding.

UNIT 1 Recording 8

A = Annabel Winter

A: I heard about Second Life, um, BBC breakfast TV, and um I decided to sort of get on it because I wanted to see what it'd be like to interact in a, a virtual world so, um, and also to see how it was presented onscreen on our computers. So, um, I went on and you can create your own avatar which means to create a, a sort of a different version of yourself, so um, I ... it ... I, I ... created a new

image of myself, um I didn't change my appearance that much. You can choose different parts of, ah the body so you can change your face, I made myself, I made myself with dark hair rather than with blonde. I'm not sure why. Um, one thing I decided to alter was my job. I, um, decided to be a businesswoman rather than, um, an actress ... um, but one thing that hasn't changed is my personality. You get to talk to people online um as your avatar, so obviously my responses are um still as me. Um, but you can also set up, ah ... your own buildings, you can, you can, um, pay for and build your own buildings, so you can be your own businesswoman in your own shop and people can come in and actually buy things from your shop. So it's really interesting to sort of interact as this alternative being, different version, different version of me.

UNIT 2 Recording 1

R = Rosie (A film historian)
P1 = 1st presenter
P2 = 2nd presenter

P1: Hi and welcome to *The Film Show*, where today we're looking at the Hollywood biopic and why it's become so popular. Now, Hollywood has always used true stories in its films. In fact, they began making successful films in the 1920s, and since then there have been thousands of films based on true stories.
P2: That's right, but in recent years, there've been more and more biopics. Directors have turned to the lives of famous people as a source of material. So, why is it that some of the best films in recent years have been based on true events, or inspired by real people?
P1: Today, we're talking to Rosie Truman, an actor and a film historian. Rosie, why do you think Hollywood is doing so many biopics?
R: Well, one reason is that it seems that audiences really enjoy films about people that they already know something about, but they want to know more. So, from these films we've learned something. We've learned about the difficult

lives of some of the biggest music legends, like Ray Charles and Johnny Cash. We've learned about their history and how they grew up. And we've learned about the lives of politicians, like George Bush, or sporting heroes, like Muhammad Ali. It's a way in which Hollywood can actually teach us about history in an entertaining way. And it's interesting.

P2: Yes, I think that's right.

UNIT 2 Recording 2

R = Rosie (A film historian)
P1 = 1st presenter
P2 = 2nd presenter

P2: But what about the actors, Rosie? I mean, many of the actors have won Oscars for their roles in these films. What's it like for them?

R: Well, I think actors just love these roles. I mean, that's another reason why the films work so well. For an actor, this is a great challenge – you know, taking on a role like this. And it's very exciting to be asked to play a character who everyone already knows. Look at Helen Mirren. She won an Oscar for her role playing the Queen, and it's probably one of her greatest successes.

P1: Oh, absolutely! And I mean there have been some fantastic performances.

P2: Yes, that's right …

P1: So, how do they do it? How does an actor prepare for a role like this? Do they get the chance to meet the person that they're going to play? I mean … What happens?

R: Well, yes, obviously, if that person is still alive, then that's a great way for the actor to study the character: how this person moves, how they respond to people. In fact, I know that Helen Mirren met the Queen for tea, you know, very English. And she has talked about how this really helped her to understand her character. And Will Smith, who played Muhammad Ali … well, when they met, they got on really well, and … and they became friends.

P2: But what about playing a difficult character, like George Bush, for example?

R: Yes, it's funny actually, when you're playing a character everyone knows, you have to work really hard

at it. And especially on the voice, to get it exactly right. Josh Brolin played George Bush. And when he was preparing for the character, he talked to himself all day in a Texan accent. He even phoned up hotels in Texas, just so he could learn the accent.

P1: Really? That's funny. What about actors who can't meet the character in person? What do they do?

R: Well, there are lots of other ways to prepare. Audrey Tautou, for example. She played Coco Chanel. So she couldn't meet her in person, but she watched hours and hours of film footage. She watched her in interviews, and she looked at the photographs. In a way, you have a little bit more freedom to do what you want with the character, when people are not so familiar, you know, with how the person behaves, and with their voice. Tautou wanted to look like Coco Chanel when she was on screen, so that we would recognise the image.

P2: That's right. And it was a beautiful film.

R: It was, and you know one of the things …

UNIT 2 Recording 5

1 I lived there for ten years.
2 We've never met before.
3 He won an Oscar.
4 They've spent all the money.
5 You decided to stay.
6 I've learnt a lot.

UNIT 2 Recording 6

P = Presenter N1 = 1st news clip
N2 = 2nd news clip
N3 = 3rd news clip
N4 = 4th news clip

P: Hello. I know what I was doing. Do you?

N1: Buckingham Palace has announced the death of Diana, Princess of Wales. The Princess, who was thirty-six, died late last night in a car crash in central Paris.

N2: It's one small step for man, one giant leap for mankind.

N3: Breaking news in here at five live. There are reports that a plane has crashed into the World Trade Center in New York. That's a plane is reportedly crashed into the World

Trade Center in New York, setting it on fire …

N4: President Kennedy and Governor John Connally of Texas were shot today from an ambush as President Kennedy's motorcade left the centre of Dallas …

UNIT 2 Recording 7

W = Woman M = Man

M: OK, so, tell me all about it …

W: Well, in the beginning, I was at home, and … um … this was just one morning before a very important interview …

M: Uh-huh.

W: And … um … I didn't feel well, so my mother had given me some pills, and um … then I didn't think anything more about it. So, anyway, erm … I then got on to the tube, um … to go for my interview.

M: Right, and what happened then?

W: Well, um … clearly I must have fallen asleep, because I wasn't feeling great by this time. And um, I'm starting to feel sleepy, so I'm thinking I must have fallen asleep. Anyway, erm … I was getting some funny looks, even before I fell asleep, but anyway. I fell asleep, and then I realised, before long, um … I must have been having a dream, I suppose, about my mother. And all of a sudden, I've woken up, but I haven't just woken up, I've woken up shouting the word, 'Mum!'.

M: No! You're joking!

W: At the top of my voice, in a packed, quiet tube.

M: Oh no!

W: Yes, and everybody's staring at me, and that did not help, er, matters. Anyway, I've got off the tube, and I've then arrived at my interview, put all that behind me, I'm not, I'm still not feeling a hundred per cent perfect, but nevertheless arrived at my interview on time, and go in, and think, actually 'This is going rather well. They're not saying an awful lot, and come to think of it, they're looking at me in a rather strange way.'

M: Right … Then what?

W: Well, the next thing I knew, I have left the interview, and said 'thank you very much for seeing

AUDIO SCRIPTS

me, blah-di-blah … and gone to the ladies' room. And there in the mirror, I could see what everyone was looking at, and why they couldn't say anything,

M: What was it?

W: My face had swollen up!

M: Ah! No way!

W: It was bright red, and …

M: No!

W: and covered in blotches, spots …

M: Oh! You're kidding!

W: Yes, and the pills that my mother had given me were so out-of-date that they had caused an allergic reaction …

M: Oh! How embarrassing!

W: I know.

UNIT 2 Recording 8

W = Woman M = Man
W2 = 2nd Woman

M: OK. What do we reckon? True or false?

W2: Erm … I don't know. I think it might be false because … I don't know …

M: Yeah, she was a little bit slow in telling the story …

W2: I don't know if your mum would give you out-of-date pills …

M: Yeah, would a mother give her daughter out-of-date pills?

W2: I think false.

M: It sounded like she was trying to think of what to say next, so … you think false, I think false.

W: Yes, it was false!

UNIT 2 Recording 10

C = Chris Harris

C: OK. Well, in this story, the painting which Finch has stolen is a Van Gogh. Er, he has stolen it for a Russian art dealer, who offered to pay him huge amounts of money for the painting. The problem is that Finch isn't a very good thief. In fact, he's been in prison before. So, when he's in the airport in Rio, he realises that security men are watching him. They're talking on their radios. Also, he sees a newspaper which has headlines about the stolen painting. He decides to put the painting inside a locker in the airport. Er … He keeps the key, and flies back to

the UK hoping that in a few weeks' time, he can go back to Brazil and collect the painting. However, when he leaves the airport in the UK, he realises that he is being followed by customs officers. Oh, also, he meets the art dealer who wants the painting, and the dealer threatens to break his legs if he doesn't get the painting. So, Finch is worried, but he has an idea. He tells a friend of his about the painting, and gives him the key to the locker. He arranges for the friend to fly to Brazil and collect the painting, and to meet him in Argentina, where they can share the money. What he doesn't know is that the friend has seen that there is a reward being offered for the painting. So he decides to call the police and tell them about the plan. Because of this, when Finch arrives at the airport, he is arrested.

UNIT 3 Recording 3

Conversation 1

W1 = 1st woman M1 = 1st man
W2 = 2nd woman M2 = 2nd man

W1: Erm, so there are many, many ways we communicate with people at the moment and, um, in the near future – I wanted to talk about something that, um, is going to be with us which is, um, a system for translating foreign languages. Um, so potentially you could be on the phone talking to someone from another country who's speaking in a different language and it's being, um, translated into your ear so you can communicate that way. What do we th-

M1: Like an intermediary or something?

W1: Um, yes …

M1: Or by technology?

W1: By technology so you can do this on Skype you know where you've got the erm, the camera filming you and you are talking to someone um in another country … How, how do we feel about that?

M1: Well, it might work in the future but it certainly doesn't work at the moment. I mean if you go to a website that's in a foreign language and you can get these, you know, these online translation services …

M2: It, erm …

W2: It's not quite right.

M1: It's very funny.

M2: He gets it wrong.

M1: He gets it completely wrong, especially English to Japanese and back from it.

W1: See, you see will this type of communication affect the way we work, and … and?

W2: Well, businesses, I mean it works very well for businesses because you will be able to communicate with someone from a different company in a different country and maybe … erm, that will stop barriers in that way.

Conversation 2

W = Woman M = Man

W: I heard a TV programme the other day and they said that they don't think that handwriting will exist in the next ten years. What d'you think about that?

M: Oh really? What, what did they suggest would take its place?

W: Er, well, for things like, erm, signatures, you know, for bank cards, or whatever, or signing things, erm, they suggested that we would use thumbprints or er, digital …

M: Kind of retina scans, things like that?

W: Yeah, that's it, yeah.

M: Well, I personally think that handwriting will be with us y'know for a long time. Erm, I think in years to come, people will still carry a pen around in their top pocket rather than anything else, and erm, that will be the quickest, easiest, and most straightforward way to communicate.

W: Well, maybe in the short term but if you think about – I don't know – sort of kids ten, twelve years old, they're using more and more y'know computers at school and things, and they might actually just stop writing, stop the practice of writing.

Conversation 3

W1 = 1st woman M1 = 1st man
W2 = 2nd woman M2 = 2nd man

W1: Well, before I give my opinion I'd like to know what you all think about the future of television.

M1: Well, it won't be on a television set, that's for sure.

W2: No, it'll be on a computer.

M2: Absolutely.

M1: Through broadband on a, on a computer, and it'll be on demand. Y'know, the difference between push and pull technology.

W1: Yes, I absolutely agree that it will be on demand, but I don't think that it will still be … I don't think … I think there'll be a place for computers, for YouTube, all those things, but ultimately it will not replace a very large screen in your living room.

M1: But the large screen in your living room will still be there. It's just the method of delivery and whether or not it's broadcast to you when you don't want it or whether you …

W2: Oh, I absolutely agree.

M1: … pick it up when you do want it.

M2: How soon do you think it'll change then? I mean are we talking long term? Short term?

M1: It won't be in a month … It won't be in a month or two, and it won't be in the short term, but certainly in the long term this will be the future.

W1: I think, I think it will be in the short term, actually. I would say in the next …

W2: Everything is so quickly changing, isn't it?

W1: Yes, absolutely.

M1: You've already got y'know on-demand, with the iPlayer and …

W1: Yes …

M1: and YouTube where y'know if you want to see it you can go and see it when you want to see it.

W1: And that is phenomenally successful.

UNIT 3 Recording 4

Conversation 1
W = Woman M = Man

W: Hi. Me again. I've sent an attachment with all the figures for the last six months. That should be all you need.

M: Sorry – I didn't catch any of that.

W: I've sent the figures in an attachment. Is that Tom?

M: You've lost me. Who is this?

W: This is Ana Lucia. Is that Tom?

M: No, this is Willy's Burger Bar. What number are you trying to get?

W: 845 6795.

M: I think you've got the wrong number.

W: Oh I'm sorry.

Conversation 2
M = Man W = Woman

M: I've got a reservation in the name of David Cullinan.

W: Just one moment. Umm, could you repeat the last name?

M: Cullinan. C-u-l-l-i-n-a-n.

W: Cullinan. I can't find the name. Did you make the reservation over the phone?

M: Yes, just yesterday.

W: Sorry, let me just see if there are any messages here. I won't be a moment. I'm sorry. We've got no reservations in the name of Cullinan, and we're fully booked tonight.

M: So you're saying I can't stay here. This is the Sheldon Hotel, yes?

W: No, this is The Felton. With an 'f'.

M: Really? So I'm in the wrong hotel.

W: The Sheldon is on Queen's Road, just around the corner.

M: Oh no. Sorry, can you say that again – where is it?

W: On Queen's Road, just around the corner.

Conversation 3
G = Girl F = Father

G: You've missed the best bits. You're late.

F: What exactly do you mean? The show starts at 7.00, doesn't it?

G: No, it finishes at 7.00!

F: Didn't you say it starts at 7.00?

G: No, it starts at 5.00 and finishes at 7.00!

F: So what you mean is I've missed the whole show.

G: Yes.

Conversation 4
M = Man W = Woman

M: We've got nothing for you, I'm afraid.

W: I don't get what you're saying. You're a car rental company, right?

M: Yes, but today's a holiday and all the cars have been booked already.

W: Do you mean to tell me that there's nothing at all? No cars available?

M: There's nothing till tomorrow, I'm afraid.

W: But I definitely booked a car for today, the third of July.

M: It's the fourth of July today. In other words, your booking was for yesterday.

W: It can't be. Is it?

M: It's the fourth today, madam.

W: Oh no, I've got the date wrong.

UNIT 3 Recording 6

1 So you're saying I can't stay here.
2 Didn't you say it starts at 7.00?
3 So what you mean is I've missed the whole show.
4 Do you mean to tell me that there's nothing at all?
5 In other words, your booking was for yesterday.

UNIT 3 Recording 7

L = Lisa Brown

L: I use the internet all the time to communicate, but I think for giving good news it's much, much nicer to be there and to do it face-to-face, though obviously it depends on what type of good news it is. Maybe the news is for someone you don't know personally or someone in a different country or city so you can't deliver it face-to-face. If that's the case, an email or a phone call are fine.

I'd say the same thing about giving bad news. If you know the person, it's much better to give it face to face. On the other hand, some bad news can be really difficult to give face to face. It can be embarrassing if someone's going to start crying in front of you or if they're going to get upset. So in those circumstances I'd rather send an email because it's less personal. I don't think I'd ever give bad news by text.

For arranging social activities I usually text my friends or do it over the phone. It's more convenient. People have such bad memories we kind of need to see arrangements written down. Also, we're always changing our plans at the last minute so we really need our phones

AUDIO SCRIPTS

switched on all the time.
For sending a 'thank you' message I think it's really nice to send a letter or, in my case, usually a card. I still send handwritten cards sometimes, and I think people really appreciate them because it shows you made an effort, whereas just sending a text or something isn't much of an effort. And it's not like they're going to keep the message for more than two minutes. But they might keep a card.

UNIT 4 Recording 1

A = Angela P = Pauline M = Monty
A: As a child, I always wanted to be a model. I used to look at all of the **beautiful** women in the magazines, and on television. And I used to think it looked so exciting. To spend all day wearing beautiful clothes, and going to exciting locations for photo shoots. And I've always loved fashion, so the idea that I could go to fashion shows in Paris, New York, etc. was just **amazing** for me. What I didn't realise is that actually being a model is really, really hard work. The hours are very long, especially when you have to travel. Sometimes, we travel for fifteen hours or more, and when we arrive we need to start work straightaway. And the problem is that you need to look good all the time. But often, you're feeling **terrible**.
P: I have a passion for food, so being a restaurant critic seemed like the perfect job for me. I could spend my days sitting in some of the best restaurants, eating **delicious** food, and get paid for it. The only problem, which I didn't realise at the time, is that actually you can get bored of eating restaurant food. I used to eat three-course meals every day, or sometimes twice a day. And I would often cook at home. So I put on loads of weight. I was **furious!** I used to spend hours in the gym, doing exercise to try and work off the food I was eating. But it was **impossible**. So, in the end, I gave it up.
M: I used to work in a bank, so when I lost my job I decided it was time to do something that I would really enjoy. To follow a dream, if you like. I had this wonderfully romantic idea

of owning my own vineyard, making wine, and spending my life in the beautiful Tuscan countryside. But the reality is very different. I had no idea how tiring the job would be. For a start, there're no holidays. For five months of the year, you don't even have weekends. You work seven days a week and you're **exhausted** all the time. And the other problem is the weather. Bad weather can ruin everything. So, in the winter, you have to get up at two o'clock in the morning when it's **freezing** outside, to turn on the frost control. And in September, a bad storm can ruin the grapes in just a few minutes. At least when I worked in an office, I didn't use to worry about the weather. Having said that, I love my life. And the science of making wine is absolutely **fascinating**. I wouldn't change my job for anything.

UNIT 4 Recording 4

W1 = 1st woman M1 = 1st man
M2 = 2nd man W2 = 2nd woman
W1: First of all we need to decide what food we want to sell.
M1: OK, well, the way I see things, the most important thing is to make sure, in the catering industry, what we want to do, is we want to make sure that we make a seventy percent profit on everything we sell, right? So, we need to think about food that doesn't cost very much to produce, …
M2: OK, so no smoked salmon, or …
W2: Exactly. But I think we should decide on a name for the company first, like 'Lotus foods' or 'Saffron', something which sounds exotic.
W1: Hmm. I'm not sure that I agree. **Let's focus** on the issue of a theme for our food, you know like Indian, or Mediterranean first, because that will influence the name.
M2: That's a good point. Also, I suggest we think about how we're going to sell. Because if we're going to events, then the type of food we cook might change, but we could have a name like Food4events.
W1: Good idea.
M1: Sorry, I missed that.
M2: We could call the company

Food4events, and cater for events, weddings and parties. That kind of thing.
W1: I think that's a great idea. Does everyone agree with that?
All: Yes. That's fine. Yup. That's fine by me.
W1: OK. So, **moving on to the next point**, where do we work from?
M1: We need to be somewhere central, like in central London, and then we can travel to events from there.
W2: Sorry, but I'm not sure that central London is a good idea. It's very expensive. I suggest we look outside the city, where it's cheaper to rent office-space.
M2: Yes, I see what you mean. You're right – we don't need to be based in the centre of the city.
W2: Exactly.
W1: OK, so **let's recap**: the company is called Food4events and we sell at parties, events, weddings, etc. We're based outside London. Erm … What else do we need to think about?
M2: How is our company going to be different from others?
W1: Ah … **I think we need to come back to** the kind of food we want to sell. I really feel that we need to specialise, so perhaps we could be Italian.
W2: How about Mediterranean?
M1: Yes, Mediterranean's really popular.
W1: OK – good point. I like the idea of Mediterranean, actually.
M2: OK. Why don't we call it Italy On The Move?
M1: Or Buon Appetito?
W1: I like that. It sounds good. Oh, let's go with Italian, so it's an Italian catering company, and it's called Buon Appetito. That will make us different from the others, and we can have Luca as our head chef! So, let's sum up what we've decided. The company …

UNIT 4 Recording 7

C = Candace Parker
C: I'm a kindergarten teacher with a class of two-year-olds. So, um, my daily routine: well, I wake up about six thirty, take a shower, and have breakfast with my husband. I have

to be at the Child Development Centre by seven thirty so I leave home by twenty past at the latest. Luckily, I don't have far to drive. The first thing I do is check my mail at work to see if there are any messages. Then I go to the classroom and switch on the lights, and I check everything is ready for the children. They usually start coming in about eight. The first hour is play-time, so we're on the floor with the toys. At nine o'clock we get the children seated at the table for their breakfast, which is usually muffins and apple sauce, or bread and cheese, and fruit juice. Then we clean up. If the weather's good we take the children out to the playground. This is probably the best part of the day because everyone's happy to be outside. We try to do this at least once a day. We have lunch at midday and then most of the children have a little nap for about an hour. After that, we do some art work or play music to the children or read to them. Then it's snack time around three thirty: just biscuits and more fruit juice. Then the parents usually arrive at four to take the children home. When all the children have gone, I write down what we did during the day and clean up a little, and then I make plans for the next day. And that's it! I'm usually home by five. Then I relax by reading or watching TV. It's a lovely job.

UNIT 5 Recording 3

W1 = 1st woman M1 = 1st man
W2 = 2nd woman

W1: Why are the windows round on ships?
M1: Round windows are stronger, aren't they?
W2: Are they? I've no idea.
W1: That's right. According to the book, they're less likely to break.
W2: Ah.
M1: There you go.
W1: What about this second one? How many hairs are there on the human head?
W2: Erm … A million?
M1: No, it's not that many, is it?
W2: It depends whose head, doesn't

it?! On my dad's there are about three.
W1: The answer is about 10,000.
M1: Oh, really?
W2: I think that's a bit of a stupid question because it depends, doesn't it?
M1: Well, it was a four-year-old who asked the question.
W2: Oh yeah, that's true.
W1: Next question: What happens when your plane flies over a volcano?
W2: Ummm.
M1: Nothing happens, does it? Well, it depends on whether the volcano is erupting? Or whether it's active.
W2: Yeah.
W1: Well, according to the book, Jamieson asked a pilot. And the pilot said as he was flying over the volcano, his engines shut down, stopped working completely.
W2: Scary. Did he get hot?
W1: Hmm, it doesn't say. But he obviously survived. So there you go. Anyway, what about this one? Why did The Beatles break up?
W2: Dunno. They got old, didn't they?
M1: No, John Lennon went off with Yoko Ono, didn't he?
W1: Well, Jamieson wrote to Yoko Ono and she replied, 'Because they all grew up, wanted to do things their own way, and they did.'
W2: Oh that's interesting.
M1: I'm amazed she replied.
W1: Me, too. OK, last one. After watching a violent video game, the little boy asked why is there war?
W2: Great question.
M1: That's a really good question.
W2: Hmm, because men like fighting?
M1: Political reasons. One country wants the land or the oil or the gold.
W1: Well, Jamieson asked lots of experts. Most of them didn't or couldn't answer. Then he asked an American army colonel, who said there are four big reasons: different ideologies, a sense of honour, economic reasons, and fear.
M1: Uh-huh.
W2: Good question for a four-year-old.
M1: And a good answer.

UNIT 5 Recording 6

Conversation 1
M = Man W = Woman
M: Arggh. Oh no.
W: What's the matter?
M: Oh. This cash machine's not working. **Do you know if** there's another machine somewhere? I really need to get some money.
W: Hmm … I'm not sure. There might be one in the shopping centre.
M: Thanks.

Conversation 2
W = Woman M = Man
W: Argh!
M: What's the matter?
W: My laptop's just crashed, again. That's the third time it's happened. **Would you mind looking at it for me?**
M: Sure.
W: Thanks. It's so annoying. I keep losing my documents. **Do you know what the problem is?**
M: Let me have a look. There's a lot of stuff on here. Why don't you save the documents onto a memory stick?
W: That's a good idea.
M: And then do you want me to try …

Conversation 3
W = Woman M = Man
W: Customer Services. Good Morning.
M: Um, yes. I've got a problem with my vacuum cleaner.
W: **Could you tell me what the problem is,** sir?
M: Yes, I can. It keeps making a funny noise. And it's just not working properly.
W: You say it keeps making a funny noise …
M: Yes, that's right.
W: OK. Let's see if I can find someone who can help you. **Could you hold the line, please?**
M: Yes, of course.

Conversation 4
M = Man W = Woman
M: Oh. I don't believe it! Excuse me, this machine's not working. It's just taken my money. **Could you give me a refund?**

AUDIO SCRIPTS

W: I'm afraid I can't do that.
M: Why not?
W: Well, I'm not allowed to give refunds.
M: But I've just lost my money. And I still need a ticket.
W: I can sell you a ticket, but I can't give you a refund.
M: Well, **could you tell me who I should speak to?**
W: Yes, of course. You need to speak to the manager.
M: OK. **Would you mind calling him for me?**
W: Of course not. I'll just call him.

UNIT 5 Recording 8

Conversation 1
A: I can't concentrate. Would you mind turning the music down?
B: Sure. Sorry about that.

Conversation 2
A: I need to speak to the manager. Do you know if there's anyone in the office?
B: Let me have a look.

Conversation 3
A: I'm afraid Mr Soul isn't here at the moment.
B: Do you know when he's coming back?
A: I'm not sure. Do you want me to check?
B: Thank you.

Conversation 4
A: Could you tell me how this machine works? I don't know how to turn it on.
B: Yes, of course.

Conversation 5
A: I need to take this machine to the repair service. Would you mind helping me?
B: Of course not. Leave it here.

Conversation 6
A: My computer has frozen. Could you tell me who I should speak to?
B: OK. Let me have a look.

UNIT 5 Recording 9

J = James Carn

J: I'm going to tell you about Robo-Chef. Basically, Robo-Chef can prepare and cook all your favourite recipes. It works like this. First of all, it washes and prepares all the vegetables, then it prepares your dish, and cooks it for you on your cooker. Robo-Chef comes complete with hundreds of menus already programmed. But you can also programme Robo-Chef with your own recipes, or, if you want to try something new, you can download new recipes whenever you like. All you have to do is choose the dish you want, decide how many people you want Robo-Chef to cook for, and what time you want the meal to be ready. So, let's say you would like a vegetable lasagne for six people, ready by eight o'clock. Then, just make sure you have all the ingredients in the kitchen, press the button, and that's it. You can go out to work, and when you come home in the evening, your delicious supper will be ready. What could be easier? Robo-Chef is the chef of the future.

REVIEW 1 Recording 1

E = Examiner
R = Radio personality

E: You will hear someone talking on the radio about an adult education centre. For each question, fill in the missing information in the numbered space. You now have twenty seconds to look at Part 3.
Now we are ready to start. Listen carefully. You will hear the recording twice.
R: Have you ever wanted to learn how to repair your own car, or understand exactly how your computer works? Perhaps you want to know how to build perfect relationships with your family and friends? Well, here at The Home of Learning we have just the right course for you!
We have lots of experience in providing interesting courses which will help you develop your skills. When we started in 1975, no other colleges had provided courses like this before. They only offered more traditional courses, such as English, Maths and Science. By the early 1980s, our college was already offering a wide range of interesting courses, with the focus on learning for enjoyment.

This year, we are extending our range of courses to include even more interesting subjects. For example, you can learn how to write a computer programme, build great relationships with your family and friends, or learn about our local history.

You don't have to be an expert in any subject to join us. Simply give us a call on 0207 453 2781, visit our website at www.thehomeoflearning. co.uk, or even come in and say hello at 61 Camden Road, next to the book shop. Courses have flexible times, in the evenings or at the weekends, and we'll find the right course and time for you. However, don't think about it too long, as the closing date for enrolment is the 1st of March. So don't delay, join us today!
E: Now listen again.

[Main recording is repeated]
E: That is the end of part 3.

REVIEW 1 Recording 2

E = Examiner R = Receptionist
C = Customer

E: You will hear someone enrolling for a course at an adult education centre. For each question, put a tick in the correct box. You now have forty-five seconds to look at the questions for Part 2.

Now we are ready to start. Listen carefully. You will hear the recording twice.
R: Good morning. Can I help you?
C: Hi there, yes, I'd like to enrol for one of your courses, please.
R: Certainly. Which course do you want to join?
C: 'Make Better Decisions'.
R: OK, we've got space available on that course – I just need to ask you a few questions first, if that's ok.
C: Sure, go ahead.
R: OK, first things first, what do you do?
C: Well, at the moment I'm working as a reporter for a local newspaper, er, but I sometimes do some freelance writing work, erm … copy for advertisements, reviews, texts for websites, that sort of thing.
R: Right, ok, sounds interesting. And,

what kind of things do you write about?

C: Er … All sorts, really. Er, for the local newspaper, it's mainly – well, it's not as glamorous as it sounds, really, er – mainly stuff about council meetings, lost cats, and so on … er, but I'm hoping to find work for one of the big national newspapers soon.

R: Right, thanks for that. And what do you want to get from the course?

C: Ah-ha! That's the thing. Er … Let me explain. You see my problem is that I'm terrible at making decisions, no really! I just, sort of, get into a terrible panic sort of thing and end up choosing the wrong thing. Even silly things, like what to have for lunch!

R: [laughs]

C: But you see it's also affecting my work – having to decide what to include or not include in an article or something, and it means a simple article can take me much longer than it should.

R: I see. Well, you've certainly come to the right place! Right, on to the details. Do you want to study evenings or weekends? We have classes for this course on Thursday evenings and Saturday mornings.

C: Hhmm, let me see, both are good, but I might be tired in the evening … but I also like to sleep late on Saturdays, er, so the afternoon would be better … Only Saturday mornings, you say?

R: That's right.

C: … um … well … [groans] … you see what I mean about making decisions?

R: Well, the content on Thursdays is repeated on Saturdays, so why don't I put you down for Thursday evening, then if you can't make it, just come on Saturday instead?

C: Ah, of course! Excellent idea. Put me down for Thursdays, then.

R: Great. And can I just ask – how did you hear about us?

C: Er, sorry?

R: I mean, was it a recommendation, an advertisement, –

C: Oh, I see. A, a recommendation.

R: And who recommended us?

C: It was a colleague at the

newspaper. Erm … She works in the advertising department and saw your advert, then told me about it.

R: Excellent, thanks. Do you have any questions?

C: Yes, just one. Erm … Who teaches the course?

R: Well, that's the best part. The tutor is American, but he lives here in England. He's written quite a few books about decision making, and he's lots of fun to study with!

C: Ah, sounds great.

R: OK, so now on to payment …

E: Now listen again.

[Main recording is repeated]

E: That is the end of Part 2.

REVIEW 1 Recording 3

P = Paul

P: So, this happened recently, when I was round a friend's house. Every now and then, well, about once a month, my friends – David and Sally, sort of, erm, cook a meal and invite people over. It's always something nice, like last time it was duck in an orange sauce, sort of gourmet sort of thing. Well anyway, the food's always really nice, and my wife, on the way home, started saying that I should cook something some time, and invite friends over. Well, I was kind of shocked because I don't, – I really can't cook. So I joked and laughed about it, and sort of forgot about the whole thing.

The next day, though, I started thinking about it and thinking about how I'd really like to try and cook something. The next thing I knew, I was looking up all kinds of recipes on the internet, and making lists of ingredients to take to the supermarket. And then, all of a sudden, I found myself standing in my kitchen with hands full of shopping bags.

I'd decided to cook something simple, as it was my first real attempt – chicken curry. I had the recipe which I'd printed from the internet, all the right ingredients, and David and Sally were coming over later that evening, excited at the thought that I was cooking, for a change.

Although I was really nervous and expected to make a mess (my wife had the number of a local restaurant which does deliveries ready), it was actually surprisingly easy. I followed the instructions in the recipe to the letter, and long before our guests arrived I had a lovely chicken curry cooking away in the oven.

Our friends were genuinely impressed (I could tell they weren't just being polite), and we then agreed that every other month I would cook for them. In the end, I felt really proud of myself and realised that all the time I'd been saying 'I can't cook', I'd just been afraid of learning something new.

REVIEW 1 Recording 4

A = Alicia J = Joel I = Interlocutor

A: OK, I feel that it's important to do exercise, so I think the swimming pool is a good idea. What do you think, Joel?

J: I'm not sure that the swimming pool is a good idea, because it will be very expensive, and I don't think students will go to the centre to do exercise. How about the TV? Because … because … the way I see things people will want to relax.

A: Erm, that's a good point, but what about when people are hungry? Why don't we choose the snack bar? People can buy something to eat in the break.

J: That's fine by me. Let's choose that one then.

A: OK.

I: Thank you.

UNIT 6 Recording 1

R = Radio presenter C = Clip
P = Professor M = Man

R: Welcome to Start the Day!

C: Hello – can I help you?
Your call is important to us.
Hello – can I help you?
Your call is important to us. Sorry, all our operators are busy at the moment. Please hold.

M: They put you in a queue for ages, listening to this terrible music. When you finally speak to someone, you're so angry, you just want to shout …

AUDIO SCRIPTS

R: Anger. We all know the feeling. A report out last year shows that people are getting angrier. One in ten people say that they have trouble controlling their temper. Traffic jams, airports, call centres, computer crashes – they can all leave us feeling angry, and anger is difficult to control. Or is it? Professor Miller from The Metropolitan University is here to tell us about two very different therapies to help deal with stress. First of all, destruction therapy. What's that about?

P: Well, basically, the idea is that a lot of people, when they get angry, they don't know what to do with their anger – they don't deal with it very well. They just keep it inside. But, if you don't deal with your anger, sooner or later it will explode. So with destruction therapy, you use your anger to destroy something, but in a controlled way, and the idea is that if you do that, it helps you to feel better.

R: OK, I get angry a lot. Can destruction therapy help me?

P: Perhaps. We can try it. What we do is we take you to a place full of old cars. When we get there, I'll give you a hammer, and you can use it to smash a car to pieces.

R: Really? Is it that simple? If I smash the car to pieces, will I feel better?

P: Yes, a little. But that's only the beginning. Then, I'll ask you to think about a situation in the past when you felt really angry. And when you think about that anger situation, you'll hit the car much harder. And the therapy will be much more satisfying. When we finish the session, you'll feel much better.

R: That's amazing, and businesses are using this kind of therapy in Spain, is that right?

P: Yes, there are some old hotels in Spain. You can pay to go and destroy the hotel. So, some companies who feel that their workers are stressed, or they need to build a team, send their workers to destroy the hotel. And it's a good way for them to get rid of that stress. It works.

R: That's incredible. But there's another idea I wanted to ask you about. People say that laughter is the best medicine. And nowadays, laughter therapy is used in hospitals to help people with pain.

P: That's right.

R: So, how does that work?

P: Well, if people laugh about something, they feel better. On average, children laugh up to 400 times a day, but when we grow up, we only laugh about seventeen times a day. And it's not enough, because when you laugh, your body produces chemicals – and these chemicals make you feel happier. And they also make you feel less pain. So, in Mexico, for example, they use laughter therapy in hospitals. A group of people go around the hospital, visiting the patients, and basically, they make them laugh, by telling them jokes, or doing something funny.

R: And does it really work? Do people feel better afterwards?

P: Absolutely! They feel better, and they don't need medicine.

R: That's brilliant. So, in Mexico, laughter really is the best medicine?

P: Yes, it looks like it. That's right …

UNIT 6   Recording 4

Conversation 1
W = Woman   M = Man

W: We've got something to tell you.
M: What's that?
W: We're getting married.
M: Wow! That's fantastic. Congratulations!
W: There's one thing I've got to tell you though.
M: Really? What's that?
W: I'm afraid you're not invited.
M: Oh. That's a shame.
W: It's going to be a very small wedding.
M: I see.

Conversation 2
W = Woman   M = Man

W: Hello. You came in for a job interview last week.
M: Yes, that's right.

W: Firstly, I'd like to say that we were very impressed with your interview.
M: Oh. Thank you.
W: However, I'm sorry to have to tell you, but we've offered the job to someone else.
M: Oh. That's a shame. Thanks, anyway.
W: I'm afraid the other candidate had more experience.
M: I understand.
W: But, we'd like to keep your details, in case another job comes up in the future.
M: OK.

Conversation 3
W1 = 1st woman
W2 = 2nd woman

W1: You'll never guess what.
W2: What?
W1: I've just won some money on the Spanish lottery.
W2: Oh, you're joking?!
W1: No, really.
W2: That's amazing! How much did you win?
W1: One thousand euros.
W2: Oh, you lucky thing! How fantastic! How are you going to spend it?
W1: Actually, I've got so many bills to pay, I'll spend it on that.
W2: Well, it's good news anyway.

Conversation 4
M1 = 1st man   M2 = 2nd man

M1: I'm afraid I've got some bad news.
M2: What is it?
M1: I've crashed the car.
M2: Oh no. That's terrible. Are you OK?
M1: Yes, I'm fine.
M2: That's lucky.
M1: But, I'm afraid the car isn't.
M2: Oh, that doesn't matter. You can get the car fixed.
M1: Unfortunately, it was your car.
M2: My car? You mean you crashed my car? How did that happen?
M1: Well, you see I …

Conversation 5
W = Woman   M = Man

W: I've got some good news for you.

M: What is it?
W: You know I was waiting to hear from the university?
M: Yes.
W: Well, I'm really pleased to tell you they've offered me a place.
M: That's wonderful news. Well done! I'm so pleased for you.
W: There's only one problem.
M: What's that?
W: It means I'm leaving home.
M: Yes, of course. But it's fantastic news.

Conversation 6
W = Woman M = Man
W: Guess what!
M: What?
W: I got the promotion.
M: That's fantastic!
W: Yes, but there's something I've got to tell you.
M: What's the matter?
W: I'm sorry, but we'll have to cancel the holiday.
M: What do you mean?
W: Unfortunately, I can't go on holiday. I've got too much work to do.
M: Oh no. That's really annoying. I was looking forward to it.
W: I know. I'm really sorry.

Conversation 7
W1 = 1st woman W2 = 2nd woman
W1: Bad news, I'm afraid.
W2: What is it?
W1: Steve's lost his job.
W2: Oh no. That's awful. I'm really sorry to hear that.
W1: Do you want to hear the good news though?
W2: Yes.
W1: The company is paying him £30,000.
W2: Really?
W1: He's going to travel around the world.
W2: That's amazing.

UNIT 6 Recording 8

S = Stig Vatland
S: One of the most, er, memorable moments, or not moments rather events, in my life … er … was a couple of years ago. Erm … It all started one day when I was at work and my brother phoned me out of the blue and said, um, 'What are you doing the weekend of Sept 23rd?' or whatever it was. And I said, 'I don't know.' He said, 'Well, book a flight to Norway.' My brother lives in Norway, and I live in England so I said, 'Why?', he said, 'Oh I'll let you know when you get there – it's a surprise.' So weeks went on, and I tried to work out what this could be, but I had absolutely no idea. So the weekend in question came about … went to the airport, got on my flight, and ah I was met there by somebody I'd never met before. He just came up and said, 'Are you Stig?'. I said, 'Yes.' And he said, 'OK. Come with me.' So I went with him to the car. We drove for a little while, and I tried to kind of get it out of him where we were going, but he wouldn't tell me anything. He pulled up outside a hotel, and there was my brother, and my half brother, and my two half sisters there waiting for me. I was thinking 'What on earth is going on?' And my brother just said, 'I realise we don't spend enough time together, so I've gathered you all here and I've planned a weekend for you.' We're like 'Oh, cool! So, what are we doing?' 'I'm not telling you.' 'OK fine.' Next thing we got on a boat and, er, he took us out to a lighthouse. And the first night we spent, er, eating Norwegian prawns drinking beer, and we slept in a lighthouse. Next morning we got up, drove off in his car, we said, 'Where are we going?' He said, 'I'm not telling you.' He took us to a local shopping centre and said, er, 'I realise I've done OK in life. I've done better than you guys. Here have a load of money. I want you all to go shopping and buy stuff that you wouldn't normally buy with this money.' He said, 'The one condition is you're not allowed to buy a gift for me or my family.' So off we went in different directions, spent all his money, and, er, bought some very nice things, met back again. In the evening, he took us out to a blues concert, then he took us for a five-course meal. And, er, we stayed that night in a very nice hotel. The next morning we had breakfast, I got back on a plane and went back to England. Yeah, that weekend is one of my happiest memories.

UNIT 7 Recording 1

P = Presenter I = Ian
P: Hello and welcome back to the *Focus* podcast. I'm Jenny Osmond, the editor of *Focus*, the monthly science and technology magazine from the BBC.
He's the hugely influential author of *Blink* and the *Tipping Point*. His work is quoted by academics, presidents and your mates down the pub. And now Malcolm Gladwell has turned that deft mind of his to a new subject: the science of success. In his new book, *The Outliers*, Gladwell argues that if we want to be successful, we should think less about what successful people are like, and more about where they have come from and the opportunities they have had along the way. Now, Ian's read the book and he joins me. Now … his new book is looking at success …
I: Yes, and what he says is, erm, that if we think about somebody like Bill Gates, hugely successful person, and we want to learn from, from his achievements, then what do we look at? We look at what that man is like, you know, what drives him, what does he do on a day-to-day basis, how can we be more like him? Erm … But what Gladwell argues in the new book is, is that we should pay less attention to that side of stuff, and look at where Bill Gates came from. So, how did he get to where he got to, the opportunities he had along the way. Erm … And what he says is that Bill Gates has one thing in common with another group of very successful people, The Beatles.
P: So, what's that?
I: Well, they both practised what they do, and they practised a lot.
P: Right, so how much is a lot?
I: A lot is 10,000 hours. That's like the magic number if you're going to become world-class at anything in the world, you need to put 10,000 hours' practice in.
P: Oh, OK.

AUDIO SCRIPTS

I: So, The Beatles, they, they were doing gigs, you know, like all-night gigs in Hamburg, in these little clubs, and just the number of hours that they put in on the stage, erm, allowed them to master their craft. And the same with Bill Gates. He, er, as he was growing up, got into computer programming, and through a very fortunate series of events, he was able to programme, and programme, and programme, erm, and again …

P: Because he had access to computers at a time when these things were developing.

I: Absolutely! … Exactly! The timing is so, so important. He happened to go to a university, erm, where he had access to er, a computer programming unit. I mean, this was back in the 60s and 70s when computers were the size of rooms and stuff. Erm, and so what Gladwell does throughout the book is pick up on these little things that we really need to go back and look at again if we are to really understand why successful people are as successful as they are.

P: I think the 10,000 hours magic number is really interesting because, as you know, I used to play tennis professionally, and I hit a load of tennis balls when I was younger. And I'm sure, I must have done 10,000 hours' worth, you know, I must have done four hours a day, and stuff. And I remember speaking to Martina Hingis' mum about why she thought her kid was so good, and such a prodigy, and she basically said, 'My daughter has been hitting tennis balls since the age of three and she has hit X number of tennis balls for X number of hours and it's, you know, I'm sure she's … So once you're over that magic number of 10,000 … yeah.

I: The same goes for people like Beethoven, erm … It's incredible how …

P: But at the end of the day you have to have talent.

I: You've got to have raw talent, you've got to have belief in what you can do, and you have to have the will to put those hours in … but you also need the opportunity.

T = Tim   J = John   P = Peggy

T: So what about your memory, Peggy? How good is it?

P: It's OK, which is lucky 'cos I need to remember lots of things.

J: Like what?

P: Well, I'm a sales rep for a publishing company so I'm usually out visiting schools, trying to sell books.

J: So you need to remember … what exactly?

P: Oh, lots of things. The worst thing when I started was just trying to remember how to get to these schools in my car. I used to get lost all the time. I'm not very good at directions. Then once you're there you have to remember the names and faces of the people you're talking to. I once spent a whole hour calling this woman Sally when her name was Samantha.

T: And she didn't tell you?

P: For some reason she didn't tell me. And then there's all the product information.

J: Product information? What, the books?

P: Yes. We sell about five hundred different books and I have to know the difference between all of them. I mean, it gets easier, thank goodness, but I still make mistakes occasionally. What about you, John? You're an actor, right?

J: Yeah. The main thing I have to remember is my lines. Fortunately, I've got a good memory for words, and I don't find it that hard to memorise them. So, I mean, yeah. The other thing you have to remember when you're in the theatre is the blocking.

T: What's that?

J: Blocking? It's where you stand or move to, y'know? Like, when you say your words you might have to walk quickly across the stage. Or move in front of someone. It's all planned and er, you have to remember it.

T: Oh, I see.

J: But it's funny: for, for other things I have a terrible memory. I'm totally useless. I always forget birthdays and dates. I'm always late for things. It's just … yeah … luckily, I'm OK with my lines.

P: What about you, Tim?

T: I'm probably the same as all other students. At least all other history students. I have to memorise dates and also names. But it's not that difficult because you read about them so much you can't really forget them. But for other things I have a really bad memory. I can never remember jokes or films. Sometimes I'm watching a film and after an hour I realise I've seen it already. I'm completely hopeless like that.

J: Oh, me too …

M = Man W = Woman

M: It's interesting: one of the most intelligent people I know is a ten-year-old boy from Egypt. He doesn't go to school and he works on a street in Cairo, in one of the touristy areas. And he sells things like small statues of the pyramids, things like that, to tourists. Now, the reason I say he's intelligent is that he can sell you something in about fifteen languages. I once spent an afternoon watching him, and it was incredible. Most of the time he uses English, but he guesses where you're from by looking at you, and then he starts speaking. He can speak just a little bit of French, Spanish, Japanese, Italian, German, etcetera. It's amazing. He knows just enough in all these languages to say hello and sell you something.

W: How did he learn the languages?

M: I asked him that and he said he learned them by talking to tourists.

W: That is quite amazing.

M: So anyway, that's my example. Like I said, he doesn't go to school but, for me, he's super-intelligent. What about you?

W: I can think of loads of people who don't have any qualifications but are able to do really difficult things. I've got a friend, for example, who built his own house. He just taught himself how to do it, bought a piece of land, bought the materials and the equipment and just did it. No qualifications, no certificates, no university degree. In my view, that's a real practical kind of intelligence.

M: I couldn't do that.

W: Let me give you another example. I've got another friend who takes parts of old cars and makes new cars from them. He does it at the weekend as a way to relax. And the new car actually works!

M: I couldn't do that either.

W: I wouldn't know where to start. And this is someone who left school at fifteen to do an apprenticeship. But, you know, having said that, I do think qualifications are useful in some ways. I mean, for one thing, they show that you are able to complete a course, that you're motivated and committed enough.

M: Yeah, I think that's true.

W: But I must say real life experience, travelling, going out and meeting people, talking … I think these give you an amazing education, too.

M: Exactly. That's what I was saying. Just like the boy from Egypt.

UNIT 7 Recording 7

1 In my view, that's a real practical kind of intelligence.

2 I do think qualifications are useful in some ways.

3 But I must say real life experience, travelling and meeting people give you an amazing education, too.

4 For one thing, they show you are able to complete a course.

UNIT 7 Recording 8

T = Tracy Hackston

T: A couple of years ago, er, I learned how to scuba dive which was, um, really exciting, really good experience and when you're learning half of the, the training is in the classroom and half is er, a practical in a swimming pool. So the classroom stuff was fine erm, I found it really quite easy. I was learning with my mum and she was really worried about doing the kind of more academic stuff and passing the exam but I found that part OK. It was the practical stuff that I had trouble with and she was really lucky, she was erm, really good. But you go and you learn all the technical stuff, you know

how to go under the water, how to clear your mask if you get water in it, that kind of thing. And then you have to do two dives outside in a, in a kind of reservoir or a quarry or, you know, something like that. But obviously because I'm in the UK it was really, really cold and we woke up on the morning of our dive and there was ice on the water so when we got there we were very nervous and didn't want to get into the water. But once I was in it was so freezing that I tried to go under the water but the more I tried the harder it got and then I got very frustrated and started to cry and then all my ears got blocked up and I couldn't get under. But eventually I managed it and erm, went down, passed my test, did all of the skills that you need to do. Despite the fact that I was so terrible at it I managed to pass and now, erm, now I'm passed I can go anywhere I want so I'll make sure it will be somewhere very hot. So, erm, to sum up, all, altogether it was a really difficult, really difficult challenge, I'm so glad I managed it. Erm … For me, it was quite an achievement and, and I'm proud of myself for having done it.

UNIT 8 Recording 2

L = Lynn

L: In real life my husband and I are both artists, visual artists. We paint landscapes and portraits. Well, we've been using the website for about two years now. And about a year ago we started an artists' colony on the internet, and it's been great. There are people like us, who work in the arts but also other people. And we show our paintings, and it's brought some business for us. It's a very creative kind of community, and we love it. We really do.

R = Rick

R: There is definitely a community of bloggers. It's a very twenty-first century community, which means no one knows one another personally. Bloggers might tell you their thoughts but, er, you don't know them as people. The guy who wrote this, who says he's a fifty-year-

old American university professor, might be a sixteen-year-old girl from Bombay – we just don't know. But the best blogs have a following, who are very loyal readers. These are people who log on every day. And they get really engaged in the content. Well, that, to me, is a community.

N = Nathan

N: The place where we live is very small. There's only one shop, which sells all sorts of things like food, newspapers, and everything really. There's a small school, a pub, and then not much else. Actually, our social life is based on the pub, where we have our town meetings. Anyway, when we need to buy other things we shop online. It's cheap and it saves us an hour's drive in the car. And yeah, I've bought all sorts of things there: furniture, clothes … stuff you just can't get where we live.

A = Abbie

A: The website which I use the most is a social networking site. It's like Facebook or MySpace. I put up pictures of me and my family and I write messages – but to be honest, I use it mostly to keep in touch with friends. And the thing that I like is you go onto your friend's homepage to see what they've been doing … and er, you, you can see pictures of all their friends. And then you see pictures of your friend's friends, and it grows and grows so you meet new people. Erm, I think it's great. I check it at least once every day.

UNIT 8 Recording 5

Conversation 1

A: I'm really hungry. Can I have some of this?

B: Help yourself.

Conversation 2

A: Come on in.

B: Thanks.

A: Have a seat.

Conversation 3

A: Hi.

B: What a day! I'm so tired!

A: I'll make you some coffee. Put your feet up.

AUDIO SCRIPTS

Conversation 4
A: Can I just quickly use your phone?
B: Be my guest.

Conversation 5
A: Welcome!
B: Thank you. What a nice room.
A: Make yourself at home.

Conversation 1
W = Woman M = Man
W: Hi Dave. Sorry. Do you mind?
M: Sorry?
W: We don't smoke in the house.
M: Oh, sorry about that. I didn't know.
W: That's all right. It's no problem.

Conversation 2
M1 = 1st man M2 = 2nd man
M1: So they've invited me to dinner at their home.
M2: Wonderful. And they're also from Morocco?
M1: The same as you. From Morocco.
M2: That'll be great.
M1: So, do I need to bring a dish? Like, bring some food?
M2: No, it's not necessary. You can bring a small gift if you want but you don't need to bring food.

Conversation 3
M = Man W = Woman
M: Hello?
W: Hello?
M: Hi, I'm Richard Davies. From Exeter? I'm here to visit your offices.
W: Ah hello.
M: I'm a bit early. Is this a bad time?
W: Umm.
M: I can come back later.
W: I wasn't expecting you so early. Can you come back in ten minutes? I just need to finish some work here, then I'll be able to show you around.
M: Of course. Sorry about that.
W: Not at all. It's fine.

Conversation 4
W1 = 1st woman
W2 = 2nd woman
W1: So, I walked into your parents' house but I forgot to take my shoes off. Did I do something wrong?
W2: Oh, I see.

W1: My shoes weren't dirty or anything but I still felt really bad.
W2: It's OK – I'll tell my parents you forgot. Don't worry about it.
W1: I don't know. Should I call them up to apologise?
W2: No, it's nothing. You really don't have to apologise.

Conversation 5
W = Waiter C = Customer
W: Excuse me sir, would you mind putting this on?
C: What?
W: Put on your jacket. In this restaurant you have to wear a jacket.
C: My apologies. I didn't realise.

Conversation 6
W = Woman M = Man
W: So this American family are going to stay with us for Thanksgiving.
M: For what?
W: For Thanksgiving. You know, people from the United States celebrate it.
M: So what's the problem?
W: Americans always eat turkey on Thanksgiving, don't they? But we're vegetarians – we never eat meat. So, well, what should we do?
M: Um … if I were you, I'd tell them the problem, and maybe they can cook a turkey while you and your family just eat something else.

Extract 1
W = Woman M = Man
W: We don't smoke in the house.
M: Oh, sorry about that. I didn't know.
W: That's all right. It's no problem.

Extract 2
W = Woman M = Man
W: I wasn't expecting you so early. Can you come back in ten minutes? I just need to finish some work here, then I'll be able to show you around.
M: Of course. Sorry about that.
W: Not at all. It's fine.

Extract 3
W1 = 1st woman
W2 = 2nd woman
W2: It's OK – I'll tell my parents you forgot. Don't worry about it.

W1: I don't know. Should I call them up to apologise?
W2: No, it's nothing. You really don't have to apologise.

B = Ben Jacques S = Sharon Hills
B: So Sharon, erm, imagine you had to start a brand new community. Er …
S: Yes?
B: I know it's a difficult question, but ideally where would it be?
S: Erm, I'd probably choose somewhere quite warm, so yeah, so you didn't have any issues of flooding, or you know, too much snow to deal with something like that. And then I'd choose another place most people would probably choose, not an island … erm ….
B: Where … where exactly?
S: But, I think, hmmmm … somewhere in France, I don't know why.
B: Oh somewhere in France? OK and, and who would be there: the French only or a mixture of people?
S: No, I … well, it would need to be a mix of people and they'd need to be able to help one another.
B: In what way?
S: Well, erm … I'd like to take one person who's an expert in one field, another person who's an expert in another field, so you have – you know – arty people, erm, manually skilled people, erm … good orators, good writers.
B: Ah, so a whole range of skills …
S: Exactly!
B: … all going into the melting pot.
S: Yes, but, I wouldn't have too many people to start with, although if it's too small a group then I suppose you risk, erm, falling out. But I think if you keep that group fairly small to begin with then you can draw up your own special laws, you know, to govern yourselves.
B: Would it need laws do you think … this, this utopian society?
S: Mmmm … well, ideally there'd be no laws but because people are human I think you would probably have to come up with some ground rules yes.

B: What would be the most important one?

S: Oh! Erm, I think, erm … not to physically hurt somebody else I suppose.

B: Right, so pretty much like we have at the minute …

S: Yes, I suppose …

UNIT 9 Recording 2

1 Jeans are worn by people all over the world.

2 Mobile phones are being designed especially for teenagers.

3 Teenagers have always been influenced by the media.

4 A great film about a teenage vampire was made in Sweden.

5 In the past, children were seen as mini-adults.

6 In the future, people will be prevented from smoking until they are twenty-one.

7 In Mexico, a party called quinceañera is held when a girl reaches the age of fifteen.

8 Many of the computer games of the future will be designed by teenagers.

UNIT 9 Recording 3

1 Yeah, I grew up in the 90s. Erm, for me film and music are two important ah important aspects of my life, and it was a fantastic decade for both of those. In terms of films, there were some ah excellent ones that came out, erm, my favourites being *Forrest Gump*, *Pulp Fiction*, and *The Shawshank Redemption*. In terms of the music … probably the most famous bands of the time was Oasis and Blur. Ah, one of the most memorable moments of the 90s was Euro 96 … obviously the football tournament. I was lucky enough to go to the opening ceremony myself. Obviously, as we was entering the end of the millennium the celebrations towards the end of the nineties were huge as were the actual celebrations on the night. Tony Blair was elected, erm, so he was the first sort of Labour government for, for a long time. Um and also Mother Teresa died, sort of Mother Teresa was, erm, the famous charitable missionary.

2 Ah, the 70s, well they were wonderful I think if, if I'm asked were they was it a good decade or a bad decade, personally I have to think it was a good decade to grow up in. I think it's very lucky I think of it as a very lucky experience when generally the world that I lived in, which was London and England, which was the post-war period and therefore an era of a certain amount of erm, restriction was all ending and things were freeing up and that happened just at the time that I was leaving home and finding my own independence. It all seemed as though it happened at the same time. Erm, technology was er, changing and improving, um, everything seemed to be developing and getting better in many ways. The fashion was getting rid of short hair and regimented kind of looks, erm, individuality was very much the order of the day. Great people were emerging in the arts. John Lennon, for example, was an icon for me I think as a creative artist with a message as well in his work. Great artists in film, Scorsese, *Taxi Driver*, Spielberg, *Duel* these were emerging artists of tremendous skill and artistry but they were just starting out then when I was.

3 I was a teenager in the 80s and I remember thinking that um I didn't like a lot of the fashion and the music from back then but now it's obvious in retrospect that I did quite like it. I love looking back on like a nostalgia trip at the way we used to dress and how much hair gel I used and how much hair spray the girls used, and er, now in the 2000s there's sort of a trip back into that time you know, girls are wearing big earrings again and geometric patterns of their clothes. Erm, the music in the 80s became quite computerised sounding, quite electronic and er, disco faded away, although we did still have soul although people like Luther Vandross and Billy Ocean, erm, making soul music. Er, New Romantic was another style that came out in the early 80s where the men started wearing lots of make-up and had big shoulders and small waists and erm, there was Madonna was a big trendsetter for girls and er,

at one point she cut her hair really short in the mid 80s and almost like a boy's, and then all the girls started cutting their hair short, too. Erm, I wasn't very fashionable myself, I used to spend most of my money on records not clothes. Erm, there were some good films around in the 80s too things like *Back to the Future* with Michael J Fox, *Desperately Seeking Susan* with Madonna, *ET*, *Police Academy* … Um, I'm gonna be forty this year and I reckon my birthday party is going to be a big nostalgia trip back to the 80s.

UNIT 9 Recording 4

W = Woman M = Man

W: What about this first one? Who was once kidnapped in France?

M: I have no idea. Maybe Isabelle Allende?

W: It was Chaucer. I think he worked for the British government.

M: Did he? I didn't know that.

W: OK, what about the next one? Who was messy?

M: Umm … probably Machiavelli.

W: It was Karl Marx.

M: Oh really?

W: And the third one: who was stopped by the US government from entering the States?

M: I'm not a hundred percent certain but it might be Chaplin. I read somewhere that he had some political views that they didn't like in the States. I'm fairly sure it's Chaplin. Is that right?

W: You're right. It was Chaplin.

M: Yeah, I read something about that.

W: OK, number four. Who played the violin?

M: I haven't a clue. I'll guess it was Galileo.

W: It was Einstein. He was a very good violinist, apparently.

M: Was he? That's interesting.

W: Number five.

M: It's definitely not Mandela. Ermm … Joan of Arc?

W: Didn't you see that film about Che Guevara and his friend travelling across South America on their motorbikes?

M: I don't think I did, actually.

AUDIO SCRIPTS

W: Yeah, Guevara was a medical student …

M: Oh yes, I knew that. I just couldn't remember.

W: Who went on a road trip with his friend?

M: Ah, that's right.

W: And the last one?

M: Umm, well I'm sure it isn't Picasso. Oh, it's da Vinci. He invented lots of stuff but never actually produced any of it, like … um … oh I can't remember, but I know he was an inventor as well as an artist.

W: Correct. It was da Vinci. He invented the parachute.

M: Oh yeah, I was just about to say that!

UNIT 9   Recording 6

L = Lili Lowe

L: OK, well, someone whose work really influenced me is Gabriel García Márquez. I like his short stories, but I fell in love with his novels, particularly *One Hundred Years of Solitude*. That book really made its mark on me. Anyway, erm, well, Marquez is a Colombian writer. I think he was born in 1928. He's a Nobel Prize winner – he won the Nobel Prize in Literature – and his books have been translated into dozens of languages. Erm … He's one of the best-known writers in the style of what's called magic realism. This means he writes kind of realistically but there's magic, I mean magical things happen in his books, like ghosts appear and kind of crazy things happen. I'm a big fan of that type of writing. Anyway, his novels are kind of funny but it's black humour or satire. He invents all these amazing, unforgettable characters, like um, corrupt officials and devoted lovers, vicious policemen and stupid revolutionaries, and through it all you're laughing at the characters but you also see their world is falling apart. I haven't read his work in Spanish, only English, erm, but the style is brilliant. His dialogue is fast and funny and he writes amazing descriptions of places and people. And, um, well, it was finding Márquez's work as a teenager that really made me become a reader.

UNIT 10   Recording 2

1 My favourite food city is ah Hiroshima, in Japan … Umhmm … Ah they've got all sorts of food. They've of course got the really famous sushi that everyone thinks about when they think of Japanese food, but they've got so much else to offer. Ah, Hiroshima's really famous for its okonomiyaki which is like a cross between a pancake and a pizza … and it's kind of egg and like a flour mixture with cabbage and noodles and meat and sometimes cheese. It's really good. One of my favourite restaurants is a place called, ah, Daikichi, which specialises in grilled chicken you can get grilled chicken with cheese, grilled chicken with plum sauce, ah and a really good soup with rice and ginger in it. I'd love to take you to Daikichi, you'd love it. They do good beer, too. Erm, but also you can get tempura in Hiroshima, which is like prawns and vegetables deep fried in a really light, fluffy batter … it's really good. And then, ah, you have also the informal restaurants that are called Izakaya where you go with a group of friends and you order lots of dishes and everyone shares and eats from the middle of the table so it's a great way to try lots of different kinds of food. Actually I know a really good Izakaya that I should take you to.

2 Well, my favourite food city would be Madrid. I lived in Madrid, in Spain for around ten years on and off and the quality of the food is, is wonderful – it's sensational. Spanish people always say that, ah, Spanish food is the best in the world and I always argued while I lived there, that, er, I felt there was a lot more variety of food in the UK, but when I moved back to the UK I really started to miss the richness, the quality of food in Spain. I think my favourite restaurant in Spain was a tiny little, um, Galician which is a part in the north west of Spain, seafood restaurant in a small little bar, it was a very, it wasn't posh or expensive, it was cheap and basic but just served the most wonderful seafood followed by lots of white wine and er, a great Tarta de Santiago, a great pastry dessert, afterwards. Another great thing, obviously about Spanish food which you'll've heard of is 'tapas' where everyone gets together on a Sunday lunchtime before lunch to have a few bites to eat and, and a few beers together and it's a lovely social atmosphere and it's nice to go out and try a variety of different food. I tried once, ah, pig's ear, which I have to say was possibly the worst thing I've ever tasted [laughs], but generally the quality was sensational.

UNIT 10   Recording 4

Conversation 1

W = Woman   M = Man

W: Is there anything I should know for when I arrive at the airport?

M: Yes, watch out for the taxi drivers who tend to hang around outside the airport. Most of them aren't licensed, so you shouldn't really use them.

W: OK.

M: If you do use one, make sure you find out how much the journey is supposed to cost. Don't get in until you've agreed the price with the driver, or else you could find that you have to pay three or four times the amount you should pay for the journey.

W: Oh right. That's good to know.

Conversation 2

M = Man   W = Woman

M: Hi – I'm going to Heathrow tomorrow, and my plane leaves at 3p.m. Latest check in time is 1.40. What time do you think I should leave central London?

W: For Heathrow? Well, you'd better leave plenty of time, because often there are delays on the tube. Are you going on the tube or the train?

M: The tube, I think.

W: The tube? If I were you, I'd allow about an hour and a half. So, if you want to be at the airport at 1.30., then you'd better leave at about twelve o'clock.

M: OK. That's great. Thanks.

Conversation 3

M1 = 1st man M2 = 2nd man

M1: Be careful when you take trips into the jungle in the north. Generally, there are a lot of mosquitoes there, so remember to take mosquito nets, and insect cream. It's a good idea to wear long trousers, and shirts with sleeves in the evening. And don't forget to take your malaria tablets.

M2: Oh yes, I must remember those.

M1: And whatever you do, don't drink the water, or you'll get a bad stomach.

M2: Oh, I didn't know that.

M1: Yes, always be sure to boil the water first, or drink bottled water. You have to be careful when you eat raw food, too, like fruit, if it's been washed in water.

M2: OK.

Conversation 4

W1 = 1st woman

W2 = 2nd woman

W1: We're going there on holiday, and I've heard that there's a lot of street crime. Is that true?

W2: Not really no. I mean, it's like any big city. You need to watch out for groups of young children on the streets. They try to distract you, and then sometimes take your bag.

W1: Oh. Right.

W2: It's not very common, but don't walk around the city obviously carrying money in a big money belt or anything.

W1: Of course.

W2: The most important thing is to remember to hold on to your handbag, and things like that, but no, there isn't really much crime. On the whole, it's a pretty safe city.

W1: That's useful, thanks.

UNIT 10 Recording 5

1 Watch out for the taxi drivers who tend to hang around outside the airport.

2 Make sure you find out how much the journey is supposed to cost.

3 Don't get in until you've agreed the price with the driver, or else …

4 You'd better leave plenty of time.

5 If I were you, I'd allow about an hour and a half.

6 Be careful when you take trips into the jungle.

7 Don't forget to take your malaria tablets.

8 Whatever you do, don't drink the water.

9 You need to watch out for groups of young children on the streets.

10 The most important thing is to remember to hold on to your handbag.

UNIT 10 Recording 7

R = Rob Hustin

R: One place that I think everyone should have the chance to see is Venice. But the problem is that this beautiful and charming city is slowly sinking. Ever since the fourteenth century engineers have tried to work out a way to stop the floods in Venice, but so far nobody has managed. Sometimes there are as many as forty floods per year between March and September, and Venice is actually sinking at a rate of two and a half inches every decade. It's very possible that your grandchildren, and their grandchildren will never have the chance to see this fragile city. Everyone should have the chance to enjoy the city, to walk across its famous bridges, through its ancient squares. There are no cars in Venice, and many people think it helps this to be one of the most romantic cities in the world. So, can it be saved?

Well, they are trying. Barriers are being put in to try and stop the water getting too high. This is viewed as a temporary measure, although they should last a hundred years, so the problem is finding a permanent solution. If you want my advice, go there while you still can, and then together we can put pressure on the government to spend the money it needs to find a permanent way to keep this beautiful and historic city for future generations. We have an opportunity now to save this city, and we must, before it's too late.

REVIEW 2 Recording 1

E = Examiner   W1 = 1st woman

M1 = 1st man   W2 = 2nd woman

M2 = 2nd man   W3 = 3rd woman

E: You will hear five different people talking about a famous actor or actress they admire. For questions 19 to 23, choose from the list, A to F, the reason why they admire this actor or actress. Use the letters only once. There is one extra letter which you do not need to use. You now have thirty seconds to look at Part 3. Now we are ready to start. Listen carefully. You will hear the recording twice.

W1: Well, one actor who I really admire is Johnny Depp. I mean, I've always thought he was a great actor, as he's so … um, you know, versatile in the different types of characters he plays, but it's him as a person which I have respect for. He's the type of actor who remembers that he's still a real person. The other week I read that while he was filming in London, he just turned up at this school, because one of the pupils had written him a letter. The children at the school, which is in South London, watched him perform as Captain Jack Sparrow for fifteen minutes. I mean it's not like, you know, charity work or anything but it made this little girl's dream come true.

M1: The actress that I most admire is Kate Winslet. Her career is really impressive, I think. I mean, she's been making films since the early 1990s, and she's still going strong! She's achieved so much in her career, and she's made so many successful films. After *Titanic*, which made her a huge celebrity, she became the youngest ever actress to gain two Oscar nominations, and she finally won an Oscar for Best Actress in 2008, for her role in *The Reader*. I just hope she continues!

W2: My favourite actress is Helena Bonham Carter. For me, she's just the typical English actress. In fact, she's often been called the 'English Rose', and has acted in typical parts, such as the Harry Potter films, and *Alice in Wonderland*. Her parents

AUDIO SCRIPTS

both had serious health problems when she was young, which can't have been easy for her, but since then she's worked hard to become successful. I think she captures what it is to be typically English – whatever that is – and her acting skills are very impressive.

M2:Favourite actor? Hhmm, that's a tough one, but I think I'd have to say Mel Gibson. He's played a number of major roles over the years, and of course he's a really convincing actor, but the thing I like most about him is that he really brings history to life, especially in films such as *Hamlet* and *Braveheart*. I can remember watching *Braveheart*, which is a film about Sir William Wallace, and wanting to go and find out more. I've also heard a rumour that he's recently been working on a film about the Vikings, too. He's the person who made me decide to become a history teacher!

W3:I really admire Angelina Jolie, who is a famous actor, for all the humanitarian work she's done. In 2000, she was filming in Cambodia. Erm … Cambodia's, the um, the location where parts of *Tomb Raider* were filmed, and erm, while they, uh, while they were there, the crew found that they were restricted in their movements because of landmines. She also met people whose lives had been affected by land mines there, and was so, um, so impressed by their strength and courage that she became Goodwill Ambassador for the United Nations High Commission for Refugees. Since then, she's been visiting the places round the world where similar problems exist, and balancing a busy acting career and bringing up a family. I think a lot of celebrities do charity work just to raise their status or whatever, but I think she genuinely cares. Over the years she's donated millions of dollars to charity, too.

E: Now listen again.
[*Main recording is repeated*]
E: That is the end of part 3.

E = Examiner   I = Interviewer
B = Ben

E: You will hear an interview with Ben Rosenthal, a young actor. For questions 24 to 30, choose the best answer, A, B or C. You now have one minute to look at Part 4.
Now we are ready to start. Listen carefully. You will hear the recording twice.

I: This week, we talk to aspiring young actor Ben Rosenthal, on what it's like to be an up and coming actor in today's world. So, Ben, do you see yourself as becoming the next Robert de Niro?

B: Ha ha, that would be nice. No seriously, I think that if you only want to be famous, you'll just end up playing minor parts all your life. For me, it's much more important to capture the character I'm playing and make it believable. When I accept a part, I always take it seriously, and I hope people watching can see that. I always try to start by thinking; 'If I were that person, what would I do in this situation?'

I: But surely you'd like to be famous?

B: That would be nice, but for me it's a side effect of good acting, not the main purpose.

I: What are some of the biggest challenges you face in acting?

B: I think the hardest thing is finding good work, especially at the beginning. I was lucky, I think, as I was spotted when I was performing in a small theatre group, and then had the opportunity to take a small part in a TV series. If I hadn't been noticed, I wouldn't have gone much further in my career, I don't think.

I: I see. And what do you enjoy most about acting?

B: I love everything about it, to be honest! But the best thing is when you know you've given the best possible performance you can. Then, when you watch yourself on the screen, say at the cinema or something, you feel real pride in what you've achieved.

I: Hmmm … If you could play any part, what would it be?

B: Ah-ha, well there's no doubt about it, it would have to be Macbeth, in the play by William Shakespeare. I don't know how familiar you are with the story, but if you watch a good performance, you'll see that this role has everything: nobility, guilt, tragedy, and more. Er … At home with his wife, the character takes on another dimension, his weakness in the face of his wife's persuasion.

I: Have you ever had any embarrassing moments?

B: Ha ha, yes, too many to mention! Erm … There was one particularly embarrassing time, however, when I was playing the part of an angry father in a comedy. I got so into the part that as I was walking across the set, I didn't notice that some of the furniture had been moved, and went crashing into a chair! I wouldn't have fallen over if I'd looked more carefully! It was really embarrassing as there were some really big actors in this programme, and they all saw it happen!

I: Oh! Oh no, that must have been embarrassing. Well, finally, what advice would you give to any new actors out there?

B: Well the first thing I'd say is that if you want to succeed, don't just take the first offer that comes along. Er, think about the role carefully, and whether you're right for it and if it's right for you. You, you won't perform well if you take a role you're not really suited to, and people won't believe in your character. The second thing is that you should have fun. Acting is hard work, contrary to what most people think. For example, it can take a whole day just to film one short scene. So if you don't enjoy it, you'll never be happy as an actor, and that will show.

I: Well thanks very much for your time, Ben, and we hope to see you in your upcoming film …

E: You'll now hear Part 4 again.
[*Main recording is repeated*]
E: That is the end of Part 4.

REVIEW 2 Recording 3

S = Sarah

S: One of my favourite scenes from a film is the opening scene in *28 Days Later*. It starts when the main character, played by Cillian Murphy, wakes up in hospital after a road accident. As he gets up, he realises he's alone in the hospital, and that the building has clearly been deserted.

As he leaves the hospital, and walks round the streets of London, you can see some amazing shots of a quiet and empty London. The background music slowly builds up as he walks through the streets, building up to a loud crescendo when he realises that the whole country has been evacuated. I found it really moving as he slowly starts to realise he's alone. What I liked best about it was the way it was filmed. The style is brilliant, and you're left asking yourself how they could have possibly filmed these scenes.

We later learn that this was because of the spread of a deadly virus, which turns people into zombies. I later fell in love with the character as he meets up with the other 'survivors' and they make their way to a military base in the north of England.

The film was directed by Danny Boyle, and it really made its mark on me. He's one of the best-known directors of these kinds of films. I'm a big fan of him, because he always adds something new and original to the films he directs. I'd definitely recommend this film for people who like to see something original.

REVIEW 2 Recording 4

I = Interlocutor   A = Ana
M = Marc

I: In this part of the test, I'm going to give each of you two photographs. I'd like you to talk about your photographs on your own for about a minute, and also to answer a short question about your partner's photographs.

Ana, it's your turn first. Here are your photographs. They show people performing in different situations.

I'd like you to compare the photographs, and say how you think the people performing are feeling. All right?

A: Okay, yes, so. In the first picture there are some children performing a, um, show at school, while in the second it's a man performing in the street. I can't remember the name of this but he's standing very still and quiet. In both pictures the people look happy, but in the first picture the children look happier. I'm not a hundred per cent certain, it might be that in the first picture the children have finished performing, so they feel relieved, whereas in the second picture the man is concentrating hard, even though he's smiling. Erm … What else? Yes, in the second picture it's definitely not in a theatre, but the first picture is. I think in both pictures the people are feeling good because they are enjoying what they are doing, and the spect – er – people watching them are enjoying it too.

I: Thank you. Marc, which of these performances would you like to watch?

M: The second.

I: Thank you. Now, Marc, here are your photographs. They show people receiving different awards. I'd like you to compare the photographs, and say what personal qualities are important to achieve success. All right?

M: Erm … In the first picture I can see a woman, she looks like a famous actress. She's wearing very, er, [pause] erm … Yes. She looks very happy because she is getting a prize. She's laughing and she looks very, very happy. Very happy. In the second picture I can see a man, he's a driver, and he's first. He's wearing a, erm, driving clothes and drinking champagne. I think he's very happy also. Erm … the second one is a sports prize and the first is an acting prize. That's it.

I: Thank you. Ana, have you ever won an award?

A: Unfortunately, no. I hope that one day in the future I will, though, it must be very satisfying.

I: Thank you.

PART B

Pearson Education Ltd
Edinburgh Gate
Harlow
Essex CM20 2JE
England
and Associated Companies throughout the world.

www.pearsonelt.com

© Pearson Education Limited 2011
This impression 2012 for Peru only

First published 2012
Seventh impression 2017

Set in Gill Sans 9.75/11.5

Printed in Italy by L.E.G.O.

Illustrations by 195 Eric (kja-artists.com): pp9, 13, 20, 23, 34, 46; 087 Sean (kja-artists.com): pp8, 11, 14, 18, 28, 36, 37, 38, 41, 47, 49, 55, 56

Acknowledgements

Text
We are grateful to the following for permission to reproduce copyright material:
Extract on page 46 adapted from 'CouchSurfers - The Community that won't lie down', www.couchsurfing.org <outbind://35/www.couchsurfing.org> , ³CouchSurfing² and ³CouchSurfer² are registered and unregistered service marks of CouchSurfing International, Inc. - a Non-Profit Organization www.couchsurfing.org <outbind://35/www.couchsurfing.org>
In some instances we have been unable to trace the owners of copyright material, and we would appreciate any information that would enable us to do so.

Photo
The publisher would like to thank the following for their kind permission to reproduce their photographs:
(Key: b-bottom; c-centre; l-left; r-right; t-top)
Alamy Images: Cultura 4, Danita Delimont 20tr, David Gee 4 13, Image Source 7, moodboard 20cl(c), Radius Images 20cr(d); Corbis: Bettmann 16, 26; Earth Hour: 53; Getty Images: Graham Chadwick / ALLSPORT 52l, Rick Graves 19, TORSTEN BLACKWOOD / AFP 21b; Press Association Images: ABACA Press France 52r, Brian Cassey, File 21t; Reuters: Casper Christoffersen / Scanpix 52c; Rex Features: DAVID HARTLEY 40tl, SHAROK HATAMI 40c; Studio 8: Studio 8 35 (Brigitte); The Kobal Collection: 40r; Thinkstock: Ableimages 35 (Olly), Comstock Images 20tl (a), Digital Vision 42, Hemera 20br(f), 57c, iStockphoto 43, 54, 57t, Jack Hollingsworth / Stockbyte 20bl (e), Jupiterimages 23, 35 (Lulu), Nick Daly 35 (Henrik)

All other images © Pearson Education

Every effort has been made to trace the copyright holders and we apologise in advance for any unintentional omissions. We would be pleased to insert the appropriate acknowledgement in any subsequent edition of this publication.

Picture Research by: Kay Altwegg

speakout

Intermediate
Workbook with key

Antonia Clare
JJ Wilson

CONTENTS

CONTENTS

VOCABULARY family

1A Rearrange the letters in italics to complete the sentences.

1 We see our *flexed dynamite* every week. <u>extended family</u>

2 My *transparent dagger* left India in 1920. _____

3 I researched my *fair oily myths* online. _____

4 Vincent is *a tree told* a famous actor. _____

5 It's always nice when *evil tears* come to stay. _____

6 I wish I knew more about my *cat sensor*. _____

7 When Ella's parents died, she *tied her in* an old house. _____

8 He doesn't know anyone on his mother's *emailed fifth soy*. _____

9 I asked Grandma about my French *torso*. _____

10 My son *fake treats* me; we have the same nose. _____

B Underline the correct alternatives.

I am probably more multicultural than most people. I have African, Polish and British [1]*inherits / <u>roots</u> / side*, and I was born in Germany. My [2]*relative / inherited / extended* family is all over the world, with several of them in New Zealand and Australia. I know quite a lot about my [3]*family story / family history / relative history* because my parents told me about it when I was a child. My [4]*great / greater / grand* grandparents on my father's [5]*sides / end / side* of the family were from Poland, while my mother's [6]*relatives / sides / related* are from Nigeria. I don't know much about my [7]*take after / family extended / ancestors* before the 1900s, except that I am [8]*relative / related to / inherited* the chief of a tribe in Nigeria.

GRAMMAR question forms

2A Circle the question with the correct form.

1 a) What you keeps awake at night?
   b) What keeps you awake at night?

2 a) Who you wanted to be when you were a child?
   b) Who did you want to be when you were a child?

3 a) Who taught you a valuable lesson, and what was it?
   b) Who did teach you a valuable lesson, and what was it?

4 a) You ever wish you lived in a different time?
   b) Do you ever wish you lived in a different time?

5 a) What type of music you do listen to?
   b) What type of music do you listen to?

6 a) As a child, did you like school?
   b) As a child, did you to like school?

7 a) When did you first think of yourself as an adult?
   b) When you first thought of yourself as an adult?

8 a) What one thing do you always worry?
   b) What one thing do you always worry about?

B Match questions 1–8 in Exercise 2A with answers a)–h).

a) Tom Cruise or Johnny Depp.   2
b) Yes. I loved every minute of it!
c) My weight. I'm permanently on a diet.
d) The sound of my husband snoring.
e) When I bought my first car.
f) No. I like the twenty-first century just fine.
g) My brother taught me to stand up for myself.
h) All types: jazz, rap, classical, rock.

3 Circle the correct options to complete the text.

It's the honey monster

Kids say the funniest things! As a children's quiz master, I've heard some wonderful answers over the years. In one quiz I asked, 'What is the name of the insect [1]_____ makes honey?' One child answered, 'The honey monster'.

The best sources of funny answers are usually geography questions. I once asked, '[2]_____ country is famous for pizza and pasta?' One little boy shouted out, 'Hungary!' I imagine he was thinking 'hungry'. Another question: '[3]_____ Latin American country do you find *tamales*, *sombrero* hats and *burritos*?' Without hesitating, a child shouted, 'Germany'!

Kids' history isn't always perfect either. When I asked, '[4]_____ leader, whose last name began with 'G', helped India gain independence?', the answer, according to one child, wasn't Gandhi, but Geronimo! Another time, I asked almost a joke question: '[5]_____ the 2008 Olympic Games held in Beijing?' '2010!' shouted an eight-year-old.

Science questions get some nice answers, too. I once asked, '[6]Where _____ a rocket fly to?' The answer? Mysteriously, a six-year-old replied, 'A rocket goes in your pocket!'

1 a) who	b) what	c) which
2 a) Which	b) Whose	c) Where
3 a) In which	b) What	c) At which
4 a) Who	b) Which is	c) Which
5 a) When did	b) When were	c) What year
6 a) is	b) do	c) does

4A ▶ 1.1 Listen and write the questions you hear.

1 _____

2 _____

3 _____

4 _____

5 _____

6 _____

B Listen again and repeat, paying attention to the intonation.

LISTENING

5A ▶ 1.2 Listen to three people answering the questions below. Write their answers.

Which family member influenced you the most? How?

	Who?	How?
Clyde	_____	_____
Luciana	_____	_____
Austin	_____	_____

B Listen again and answer the questions.

1 What expression did Clyde's mother always use?

_____

2 Where did Clyde travel to when he was young?

_____

3 How long did Luciana live with her grandparents?

_____

4 What was her grandfather's 'major thing'?

_____

5 What story did Austin's Uncle Charlie tell?

_____

6 What did Austin's mother say about Uncle Charlie?

_____

C Read the extracts from the recording. What do you think the words and phrases in bold mean? Match them with meanings a)–f).

1 So **in that respect** I think my mother really influenced me.

2 He was very **tough**.

3 He could be very **gentle**.

4 He always **saw the bright side of life**.

5 He was built like a tank. I mean **massive**.

6 He fought a crocodile **with his bare hands**.

a) strong and determined

b) extremely big

c) without using a weapon or tool

d) in this way

e) was optimistic

f) kind and careful not to hurt anyone

WRITING emails of introduction: formal and informal

6A Read the purposes of two emails. Which email needs to be formal?

1 Introduce myself to a member of my host family in Spain before I visit.

2 Introduce myself as the new chairperson of the Teachers' Association.

B Read the emails and underline the correct alternatives.

> To: psanchez@yoohoo.es
>
> Subject: hi!
>
> From: danielagjones@hitmail.com
>
> [1]*Hi Pilar / Dear Madam Pilar*,
>
> [2]*I am writing to greet you. / How are you?* As you know, I'm going to stay with you this summer. I [3]*have decided to / thought I'd* send an email to introduce myself. My name's Daniela, but my friends call me Danny, and I hope you will, too.
>
> I'm eighteen years old and at university here in Manchester, studying Business and Economics. I've got lots of hobbies. I love horse riding, swimming, listening to music, and I also play the flute. My favourite hobby, though, is dancing. I [4]*am particularly keen on / really like* samba and salsa.
>
> I [5]*can't wait to stay / look forward to staying* with you in Spain, though my Spanish isn't very good! [6]*Hope / I do hope* to hear from you soon.
>
> Danny

> To: membership@taas.com
>
> Subject: Introductions
>
> From: hatquistj@ltsu.edu
>
> [7]*Dear members / Hello everybody*,
>
> [8]*I'm writing to say hi / I am writing to introduce myself.* As many of you know, I will begin in the role of chairperson of the Teachers' Association of Amlen State at the end of this month. [9]*I would like to take this opportunity / I really want* to outline my major plans for the Association over the coming year.
>
> I am a maths and physics teacher. I have been in the profession for over forty years in a variety of roles: teacher, administrative assistant, head teacher, and school inspector.
>
> My first priority is to increase membership. In the last six years we have seen a decrease of almost 30% in our numbers. I have various proposals for achieving this, which [10]*I'll tell you about / I will explain* during our first meeting next month.
>
> [11]*I look forward to working with you all / See you all soon.*
>
> [12]*All the best / Yours sincerely*,
>
> Jacqueline Hatquist

C Read the instructions and write an email (120–150 words).

You are going on an adventure trip for students of English. You will join ten other students from all over the world on a one-month tour of India. The tour will include cultural visits and two hours of English lessons every day. Write an email of introduction to the other students.

GRAMMAR review of verb tenses

1 Complete the conversations with the correct form of the verbs in brackets.

1 A: I need a holiday, but flights _____ (be) always expensive at this time of year.

B: That's true, but I _____ (find) a cheap flight to Mexico on the net yesterday.

2 A: Grace _____ (win) the lottery last week!

B: That's right. She _____ (sleep) when her brother called to tell her.

3 A: I _____ (not like) football.

B: Why _____ you _____ (not tell) me earlier? The tickets cost £70 each!

4 A: _____ you _____ (hear) about the accident last week?

B: Yes, the boys _____ (drive) along Court Street when a motorbike hit the car.

5 A: _____ you _____ (need) somewhere to stay? I have a spare room.

B: No, it's OK. I _____ (stay) with my sister.

6 A: I _____ (read) a novel called *The Road* at the moment.

B: Oh yes. I found it so boring that I _____ (not finish) it.

7 A: I like an early start, so I _____ (get up) at six every morning.

B: Me too. I always _____ (leave) the house by seven.

8 A: John! Are you ready? We _____ (wait) for you!

B: OK, here I am! Sorry about that. I _____ (look) for my hat! I couldn't find it anywhere.

2 Match beginnings a) and b) with endings i) and ii).

1 a) Do you use the computer? *ii*

b) Are you using the computer? *i*

i) I need it for a few minutes.

ii) Or is everything done by phone?

2 a) She tries to work

b) She's trying to work

i) , so please be quiet.

ii) on her book for two hours every day.

3 a) It doesn't snow

b) It isn't snowing,

i) much in New Mexico.

ii) so we can go out now.

4 a) What are you doing

b) What do you do

i) for a living?

ii) now? Do you want to go for a coffee?

5 a) He was playing squash

b) He played squash

i) for the team last year.

ii) when he broke his ankle.

VOCABULARY relationships

3A Put the words in the box into categories 1–4.

employee   fiancée   fiancé   classmate   pupil   boss team-mate   godfather   godmother   member

1 Person you work with:

_____

2 Person who studies:

_____

3 Person you are close to (almost family):

_____

4 Person you do a hobby with:

_____

B Complete the sentences with the words in Exercise 3A.

1 This is Marianna, my _____. We're getting married next year.

2 Dave is my _____. We're both in Year 12 at Cokethorpe High School.

3 She asked her _____ for some time off work, but he said no.

4 I'm a _____ of a swimming club. We meet twice a week at the sports centre.

5 Luisa got 100% in her exam. She's the best _____ in my class.

6 He's an _____ of GEO Foods. He's been there for six years.

7 When I was born, my father asked John, his best friend, to be my _____.

8 Leticia is my _____. We play in the same basketball team.

4A Underline the stressed syllable in the words in italics.

1 He was an *employee* here.

2 I had a wonderful *mentor*.

3 All *pupils* wear a uniform.

4 We were *team-mates* for years.

5 Have you met my *fiancée*?

6 Talk to your *partner*.

7 She's my *godmother*.

8 That club is for *members* only.

B ▶1.3 Listen and check. Then listen and shadow the sentences (say them at the same time).

chatzone1.com

Men and Women – What They Say About Each Other

(1) The battle of the sexes has probably been going on since the first caveman left his dirty dishes on the floor of the cave. A subject of endless discussion, it has inspired a million jokes and articles and almost as many books.

(2) However, a recent study tells us that men and women really do think differently. Our brains are built in a different way. The results of the study suggest that men have better spatial perception (driving, ball sports), while women's brains equip them better for remembering words and speaking fluently.

(3) The scientists examined only a small part of the brain, and they say that further research needs to be done. Here at *chatzone1* we have done some less scientific research. We asked people, 'What are the differences between the sexes?' Here are their answers.

What women say about men

(4) Men remember useless information, like how fast an aeroplane can go, even if they'll never fly one. (Heather)

If you ask a man a question, he'll always have an answer, even if it's the wrong one. (Aisha)

Men do things first, and think about the risks later. (Candy)

Men cannot watch sport on TV and talk to women at the same time. (Mai)

What men say about men

(5) Men know that common house spiders aren't as dangerous as rattlesnakes. (Daniel)

Men can drive without looking at themselves in the mirror every ten seconds. (Ron)

Men can watch a whole film without interrupting to ask, 'Who is he?' 'What's her job?' 'Does he like her?' (Alfred)

When men want something, they ask for it instead of making a comment distantly related to the subject and hoping their partner will guess what the real subject is. (Guy)

What men say about women

(6) Women couldn't invent weapons that kill, only weapons that make you feel really guilty until you say sorry. (Kent)

While men speak in sentences, women speak in paragraphs. (Sergio)

Women are happy to own twenty CDs, while men need 200. (Steve)

Women order salad, then eat the man's chips. (Kazeem)

What women say about women

(7) Women have natural instincts about what is dangerous for babies. (Linda)

Women notice when something is dirty or needs replacing. (Carol)

Only women can understand other women. (Xun)

Women have a calendar in their brains: we remember birthdays and anniversaries easily. (Avril)

READING

5A Do you think statements 1–4 are about men or women? Who said them: men or women?

1 They do things first, and think about the risks later.

2 They remember useless information.

3 They notice when something is dirty or needs replacing.

4 They always remember birthdays and anniversaries.

B Read the text and check.

C Write the name of the person who makes similar statements to the ones below.

1 Men hate to say, 'I don't know'. _Aisha_

2 Men cannot 'multi-task'; they can only concentrate on one thing at a time. _____

3 Men are very direct when they need something. _____

4 Women are more fluent than men when they speak. _____

5 Women are more maternal; they understand what is good for young children. _____

6 Women have better memories for dates than men. _____

D Find words in the text to match definitions 1–5.

1 the ability to see the position, size or shape of things (paragraph 2) _____

2 give you the tools or abilities that you need (paragraph 2) _____

3 more or to a greater degree (paragraph 3) _____

4 not closely (paragraph 5) _____

5 natural abilities or feelings that make people and animals know something (paragraph 7) _____

VOCABULARY PLUS collocations with *take/get/do/go*

6 Complete the phrases with *take*, *get*, *do* or *go*. Use each verb three times.

1 _get_ a job
2 _____ off coffee
3 _____ part in a quiz
4 _____ some research
5 _____ my homework
6 _____ on with people
7 _____ grey
8 _____ her a favour
9 _____ responsibility
10 _____ angry
11 _____ up the guitar
12 _____ for a walk

VOCABULARY interview advice

1 Match 1–8 with a)–h) to make advice.

1 Don't avoid eye

2 The most important thing is to be

3 Make sure you show

4 You must arrive on

5 Shake hands

6 Make sure you dress

7 Don't always answer

8 Before the interview, do

a) some research about the company.

b) briefly. Try to give a full response.

c) smartly. Maybe wear a suit.

d) contact. Look at them during the interview.

e) enthusiasm. Smile and ask questions.

f) firmly with your interviewers.

g) prepared. Think about what they will ask you.

h) time. Don't be late!

FUNCTION talking about yourself

2A Add the vowels to complete the conversations.

Conversation 1

A: C__ __ld I __sk a q__ __st__ __n?

B: Sure. Go ahead.

A: Will this type of project become common?

B: In my __p__n__ __n, architecture will become more environmentally friendly.

Conversation 2

A: Th__r__ __r__ a c__ __pl__ __ __ th__ngs I'd l__k__ t__ __sk __b__ __ __.

B: OK.

A: How do you see your future in our company?

B: F__r me, th__ m__st __mp__rt__nt th__ng is to keep developing and learning the job.

Conversation 3

A: I h__v__ a q__ __ry.

B: Yes? Go ahead.

A: A lot of people criticised you because of the cuts in funding for education. Did you ever think about resigning from the government?

B: One th__ng I'd l__k__ t__ s__y is th__t compared to other governments, we invested a lot of money in education.

Conversation 4

A: Earlier, you mentioned your latest film. C__n I __sk you __b__ __t th__t?

B: Yes, of course.

A: Was it difficult not being the star?

B: I'd h__v__ t__ s__y 'yes'. In my last four films I always had the biggest part.

B Match pictures A–D with conversations 1–4 in Exercise 2A.

LEARN TO use two-word responses

3 Circle the correct option to complete the conversations.

1 A: Is it OK if I check my emails?

   B: _____. That's fine.

   a) Go ahead b) That's right c) I understand

2 A: Are you interested in free medical insurance?

   B: _____. How do I sign up?

   a) You're correct b) Yes, definitely c) No problem

3 A: My dog is ill, so I can't come to work today.

   B: _____. Will you be in tomorrow?

   a) You're correct b) Please continue c) I see

4 A: Hi, Nazir. I'm going to be about fifteen minutes late.

   B: _____. There's no hurry.

   a) Yes, definitely b) That's right c) No problem

5 A: I can't travel in June – my wife's expecting a baby.

   B: _____. We'll make sure there's no travel until at least August.

   a) I understand b) Go ahead c) You're welcome

6 A: Do you live at 106 West Smith Road?

   B: Yes. _____.

   a) That's right b) No problem c) You're welcome

7 A: So the answer is probably 15,997.

   B: _____. But how did you reach the answer?

   a) You're correct b) No problem c) Go ahead

8 A: Thank you so much for letting me use your motorbike.

   B: _____. Did you have fun?

   a) Yes, definitely b) I see c) You're welcome

9 A: Excuse the interruption. I'm just showing Mr Liu the classrooms. _____.

   B: Oh, OK. So, students, turn to page 33.

   a) I see b) You're welcome c) Please continue

10 A: Are you able to work next weekend?

   B: _____. We need to finish the project, don't we?

   a) Go ahead b) Of course c) I understand

VOCABULARY types of story

1A Complete the words to describe types of story.

1 *Terminator* is one of the best ever __ct__ __n films.

2 *Walk the Line* is a b__ __p__c of the musician Johnny Cash.

3 *Avatar* won an award for best f__nt__sy film.

4 I enjoy all film genres, particularly historical or p__r__ __d dr__m__.

5 *New in Town* is a r__m__nt__c c__m__dy about an ambitious woman from Miami who moves to a small town in Minnesota, in America's mid-west.

6 *The Wizard of Oz* is a classic children's __dv__nt__r__ story.

7 *2012*, one of the biggest Hollywood d__s__st__r films ever made, shows the end of the world as we know it. The special effects are truly spectacular.

8 Cr__m__ films range from Hitchcock's thr__ll__r *Vertigo* to the dark c__m__dy *Pulp Fiction*.

9 *He Who Must Live* is a d__c__dr__m__ about the life of Fidel Castro.

B Which words in Exercise 1A could be used to describe these films?

1 *Nowhere Boy* talks about John Lennon while he was at school and art college in 1950s Liverpool.

2 *Supervolcano* is based on what would happen if the volcano in Yellowstone National Park erupted.

3 In *My Best Friend's Wedding*, best friends Julianne Potter and Michael O'Neil promise to marry each other if they are still single at the age of twenty-eight.

4 *Daybreakers*: It is the year 2019, and a plague has transformed much of the world's population into vampires.

5 *Die Hard* stars Bruce Willis as a policeman battling against terrorists.

6 *Murder on the Orient Express*: When his train is stopped by deep snow, detective Hercule Poirot is called on to solve a murder when the body of one of the passengers is discovered.

GRAMMAR present perfect/past simple

2 Underline the correct alternatives.

1 A: I *'ve never been / didn't go* to Hollywood.
  B: Haven't you? I *went / 've been* there last year.

2 A: How many films *have you acted / did you act* in so far?
  B: I *'ve acted / acted* in seventeen films up to now.

3 A: He's only twenty-two years old, but he *travelled / has travelled* all around the world.
  B: Really? Which countries *did he visit / has he visited*?

4 A: She *has won / won* four Oscars for her performances.
  B: That's right. She *has won / won* an award for Best Actress last month.

5 A: They *have lived / lived* in California for twenty years.
  B: When *did they move / have they moved* to Texas?

6 A: *Have you been / Were you* here for a long time?
  B: Yes. I *arrived / have arrived* over an hour ago.

7 A: We *'ve been married / were married* for forty years now.
  B: Do you remember the first day we *'ve met / met*?

8 A: *Did you enjoy / Have you enjoyed* the film?
  B: I *didn't have / haven't had* time to watch it yet.

3 Rewrite the second sentence so that it means the same as the first. Use the correct form of the words in capitals.

1 I met Ella ten years ago. KNOW
  I *'ve known* Ella for ten years.

2 She went to Mumbai four weeks ago. BE
  She _____ in Mumbai for four weeks.

3 They started the business in 2009. WORK
  They _____ together since 2009.

4 We moved into the house six months ago. LIVE
  We _____ this house for six months.

5 The last time I saw Robbie was two weeks ago. SEE
  I _____ for two weeks.

6 This is my third visit to London. BE
  I _____ three times.

4A ▶ 2.1 Listen and complete the conversations.

1 A: Have you been here before?
  B: Yes, _____ Naples a few times.

2 A: Have you had time to see the museum yet?
  B: No, _____ time.

3 A: Did you find your hotel OK?
  B: Yes, _____ the hotel without any problems.

4 A: Have you got your guidebook?
  B: Oh no. I _____ it in my room.

5 A: Have you had any lunch?
  B: Yes, _____ eaten.

6 A: Have you enjoyed your stay?
  B: Yes, _____ a wonderful time.

B Listen again and shadow the answers.

VOCABULARY PLUS prepositions

5 Underline the correct preposition to complete the sentences.

1 I'll see you *at / on / in* lunchtime.

2 We often cook outside *at / in / on* the summer.

3 I start work at 8.30a.m. *at / on / in* Monday.

4 I try not to go out alone *at / on / in* night.

5 I just heard it *at / on / in* the radio.

6 *At / On / In* the end, we decided to take a taxi.

7 I'm sorry. I took your coat *at / by / in* mistake.

8 Please be quick. We're *at / by / in* a hurry.

9 Wait there. I'll be with you *at / on / in* a moment.

10 We found the museum completely *at / by / in* chance.

11 I'm afraid Mr Reeves is away *at / on / in* business. Can I help?

12 Nobody wanted to come with me, so I went *at / on / in* my own.

READING

6A What do you know about James Dean? Are the statements true (T) or false (F)?

1 James Dean became famous for his role in the film *Rebel Without a Cause*.

2 He died in a car accident when he was just twenty-one years old.

3 He was speeding in his car at the time of the accident.

4 When he was younger, he nearly died in a motorcycle accident.

5 His favourite drink was whisky.

B Read the article on the right and check your answers. Correct the false statements.

C Circle the correct option to answer the questions.

1 Why do people come to Hollywood?

  a) Because it's dangerous.

  b) To follow their dreams.

  c) To meet other actors.

2 Why was James Dean nicknamed 'America's Rebel'?

  a) He played a teenager in the film *Rebel Without a Cause*.

  b) He was friends with another actor, Ronald Reagan.

  c) Teenagers respected his rebellious attitude.

3 What did he do before he arrived in Hollywood?

  a) He performed dangerous stunts on television.

  b) He raced motorbikes.

  c) He worked in a restaurant.

4 Why did Dean argue with his father?

  a) His father caught him drinking whisky.

  b) He crashed his father's car.

  c) His father didn't want him to be an actor.

FOREVER YOUNG: THE HOLLYWOOD HERO WHO DIED YOUNG

'Dream as if you'll live forever; live as if you'll die tomorrow.'

1 The dream is the same for everyone; actors, dancers, singers, filmmakers. They go to Hollywood looking for money, success, fame and power. And many come to Hollywood as young people, barely out of their teens. But Hollywood can be a dangerous place, and some of Hollywood's heroes even lose their lives because of it. But although they die young, they are heroes forever, immortalised in film history.

2 One such hero was James Dean. Dean once said 'Dream as if you'll live forever; live as if you'll die tomorrow'. Arriving in Hollywood as a young man, James Dean quickly became a star. In the film *Rebel Without a Cause*, Dean showed teenage angst at its best, and he captured the world with his casual style and rebellious attitude. It was an attitude that he held both on-screen and off, and teenagers everywhere found a hero they could both respect and admire. Soon, he was more popular than even his own screen idol, Marlon Brando, and he was nicknamed 'America's Rebel' by Ronald Reagan.

3 Always the rebel, Dean was afraid of nothing. Before becoming famous, he worked as a stuntman for a TV show. Dean loved his car, a silver Porsche 550 Spyder, and it was in this car that on September 30, 1955, Dean crashed and died from his injuries. He was just twenty-four years old. Even though his career in Hollywood was short, he only made three films, he made a lasting impression on everybody who watched him, and even on future generations. James Dean will be forever young.

4 There are many myths about James Dean, but only some of them are true. James Dean loved speed. When he was younger, he had a motorcycle accident and lost his two front teeth. People assumed that Dean was speeding at the time of his car crash – he had been stopped by police for speeding just two hours earlier. But experts now believe that Dean was travelling at 55 mph, and that the accident was just unlucky. As a young man, Dean was a rebel at home. He was thrown out of his father's house when they argued about Dean wanting an acting career, rather than a career in Law. And finally, on-screen James Dean is shown getting into a fight after drinking whisky, but off-screen his favourite drink was coffee.

D Find words or phrases in the text to match definitions 1–5.

1 still very young/in their early twenties (paragraph 1) _____

2 made famous for a long time (paragraph 1) _____

3 opinions or behaviour which are against authority (paragraph 2) _____

4 an opinion or feeling about someone/something that you have for a long time (paragraph 3) _____

5 thought something was true (paragraph 4) _____

LISTENING

1A Read the introduction to a radio programme. Are the statements true (T) or false (F)?

1 A 'flashbulb memory' is a memory of an important event.

2 You do not usually remember small details with a flashbulb memory.

FLASHBULB MEMORIES
– WHERE WERE YOU THEN?

Do you remember where you were when an important event occurred? Can you remember who you were with? Then you may have what is called a 'flashbulb memory'. In 1977, two psychologists, Roger Brown and James Kulick, used the term 'flashbulb memories' to talk about people's recollections of the John F. Kennedy assassination. They suggested that, like a camera's flashbulb, when a truly shocking event happens, the brain 'takes a picture' of the moment when you learn about the event. This enables us to remember, sometimes in great detail, events of an emotional significance to us. Tune in to Radio 6 *Real Lives* and listen to some of the stories.

B ▶ 2.2 Listen to the stories. Match pictures A–D with speakers 1–4.

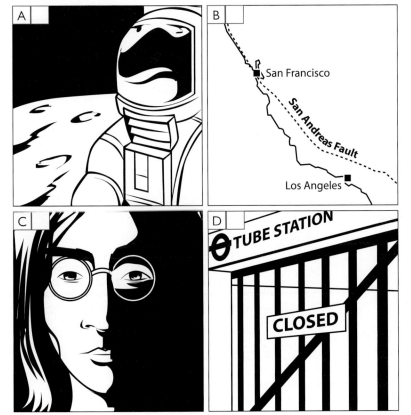

A

B San Francisco
   San Andreas Fault
   Los Angeles

C

D TUBE STATION
   CLOSED

C Listen again and answer the questions.

1 Who was angry about not getting to a meeting on time? _____

2 Who watched the news on a black and white television? _____

3 Who got up to make everyone coffee? _____

4 Who were trying to talk on their mobile phones? _____

5 Who thought that maybe what they remembered was just a dream? _____

6 Who wanted peace for everyone? _____

GRAMMAR narrative tenses

2 Circle the correct option to complete the sentences.

1 Simon was feeling exhausted because
   a) the baby wasn't sleeping all night.
   b) the baby hadn't slept all night.

2 We were driving to the hospital to visit Sam when
   a) they called to say she had gone home.
   b) they were calling to say that she was going home.

3 By the time we got to the beach
   a) the rain had stopped.
   b) the rain stopped.

4 Juan was feeling excited because
   a) he wasn't seeing his parents for ten years.
   b) he hadn't seen his parents for ten years.

5 She was singing an old folk song
   a) which I hadn't heard for years.
   b) which I didn't hear for years.

6 Everyone was dancing because
   a) Porto had just won the match.
   b) Porto were just winning the match.

3 Complete the conversations with the correct form of the verbs in brackets.

Conversation 1

A: What ¹_____ (happen) to you on Saturday night? We ²_____ (wait) for ages, but you ³_____ (not come).

B: I'm really sorry. I ⁴_____ (drive) back from Aga's house when my car ⁵_____ (break) down.

A: Why didn't you call?

B: My phone ⁶_____ (run out) of battery.

Conversation 2

A: ⁷_____ you _____ (enjoy) your dinner last night?

B: No. Actually, I ⁸_____ (hate) it.

A: Why? What happened?

B: Well, we ⁹_____ (book) a table, but I ¹⁰_____ (not realise) it was right by the door. People ¹¹_____ (come) in and out all evening and it was freezing. Then, when the waiter ¹²_____ (pour) my wine, he ¹³_____ (spill) it down my dress. And also, we ¹⁴_____ (order) fish, which they ¹⁵_____ (say) was fresh. But when it ¹⁶_____ (arrive) it ¹⁷_____ (taste) terrible!

VOCABULARY the news

4A Complete the headlines with the words in the box.

> crash   demonstration   attacked
> strikes   earthquake   fugitive   floods
> hostages   shot   collapse

1

Plane _____ in the Mediterranean

2 Thousands killed and more homeless in huge _____ in Haiti

3 Pirates take families as _____

4 HEAVY _____ DESTROY HOUSES AS RIVER WATER RISES

5 _____ arrested at airport

6 Thousands attend anti-war _____

7 JOURNALIST _____ AND KILLED BY GUNMAN

8 PRIME MINISTER _____ WITH EGGS AND ROTTEN FRUIT DURING CONFERENCE

9 Global economic crisis as banks and insurance companies _____

10 Train workers' _____ cause delays

B Circle the correct option to complete the sentences.

1 We need to check our flights. The airport workers are planning _____.

a) strikes   b) demonstrations

2 Fire officers had to clear the area in case the buildings _____.

a) attacked   b) collapsed

3 Police were congratulated when the _____ was finally arrested.

a) hostage   b) fugitive

4 If the rain continues, more _____ are expected.

a) floods   b) earthquakes

5 More than 100 people were rescued when the train _____.

a) crashed   b) shot

WRITING a news report; time linkers

5A Put the sentences/paragraphs in the correct order to complete three news reports, A–C. Each report should have three parts:

1 an introductory statement to say what happened

2 background information

3 a concluding statement (or an opinion in quotes).

REPORT A

a _____ The pupils mark their fingerprints [1]*while / as soon as* they enter the church. They will be monitored over three years.

b _____ [2]*During / Until* that time, if they attend 200 masses, they will be excused from taking one exam.

c _____ A Polish priest has installed an electronic reader in his church in Warsaw for school children to leave their fingerprints when they attend mass.

REPORT B

a _____ But Kiyotaka Yamana, a Tokyo resident who started the 'Love Message Yelling Event' after his marriage failed, said that didn't mean they were unromantic. 'The dominant image of Japanese men is of overworked businessmen, but I wanted to tell people around the world that Japanese men are actually very romantic,' Yamana told reporters.

b _____ [3]*While / During* they are on stage, yelling 'I love you' or 'Let me be with you', they are filmed, and the event is broadcast on national television. [4]*Until / By the time* recently, Japanese men have usually chosen not to talk very openly about love.

c _____ Love is really in the air in Tokyo at the 'Love Message Yelling Event'. [5]*While / During* the event, dozens of people stand on a stage in Hibiya Park in central Tokyo and shout out love messages to their partners.

REPORT C

a _____ However, [6]*by the time / until* they reached the ruins, the area had been cut off by floods and mudslides, and they had to wait [7]*as soon as / until* army helicopters could come and airlift them to safety.

b _____ The travellers had finished the difficult 45-km (28-mile) trek along Peru's Inca trail to see the famous Machu Picchu ruins.

c _____ Over a thousand tourists had to be evacuated from Machu Picchu last week.

B For each report, answer the questions.

1 What happened?

2 Where was it exactly?

3 Why did it happen?

C Underline the correct time linkers to complete the reports.

D Write a short news report (80–120 words) describing a recent news event in your country.

VOCABULARY say/tell

1 Complete the sentences with the correct form of *say* or *tell*.

1 President Obama _____ a joke, and everybody laughed.

2 The manager called to _____ she was sorry about what had happened.

3 I still can't believe that he _____ me such a big lie. I'm furious with him.

4 Someone once _____ me a story about that.

5 Listen. Why don't you just _____ what you mean?

6 As Jodie walked past the table, the young man looked up and _____ 'hello'.

FUNCTION telling a story

2 Underline the correct options to complete the story.

STUCK IN THE SNOW

¹*This happened when / All of a sudden* I was snowboarding with a few friends in Italy. ²*Before long / Well*, most of the group were really good skiers, ³*so / in the end* one day we went to the top of this difficult run. ⁴*In the beginning / Anyway*, the field was full of fresh snow, and in the middle a tree had fallen down, and was covered in snow. It made a perfect jump, so soon everyone was queuing up to perform tricks. ⁵*Well / Before long* it was my turn. Well, I went as fast as possible, and jumped up ready to do a back flip. But I forgot to bend my knees. ⁶*So / The next thing I knew*, I was pointing down, like an arrow. I went head first into the snow, right up to my waist. My legs were sticking up in the air, and I couldn't move. ⁷*In the end / Before long*, they had to dig me out. ⁸*Anyway / All of a sudden* we've all laughed about it ever since.

LEARN TO keep a story going

3 Complete the conversation with the words in the box.

> what   Really   no   then   amazing
> happened   Oh   kidding

A: You'll never guess what happened to Mukul.

B: No. What happened?

A: Well, you know he's working as a taxi driver to help pay for his medical studies.

B: Yes, I know.

A: Anyway, he took a family who were on holiday from Italy in his taxi. And one of his passengers was a seventy-two-year-old grandmother.

B: Yes, so what ¹_____?

A: Well, she left her handbag, with more than $21,000 of the family's travelling money, some very valuable jewellery, and some of their passports, in the back of his taxi.

B: Oh ²_____. You're ³_____. So, ⁴_____ did he do?

A: Well, he looked in the bag to see who it belonged to.

B: Yes, …

A: And he found an address that was fifty miles away. So, he drove all the way there.

B: And what happened ⁵_____?

A: Well, there was no one in …

B: ⁶_____ dear.

A: So he left a note and his telephone number. And when the family called him, he went back and returned the bag.

B: ⁷_____?

A: Yes. As you can imagine, the family were overjoyed, and they offered him a reward.

B: How much?

A: I don't know. He didn't take it. He said he couldn't accept it. He was just happy that he'd done the right thing.

B: I don't believe it. That's really ⁸_____.

3.1 CONTACT

LISTENING

1A ▶ **3.1 Listen to three people talking about their future plans. Who talks about:**

a) their university studies? _____

b) a holiday? _____

c) their weekend? _____

Ruth

Kieron

Amber

B Listen again and circle the correct option.

1 Where is the hostel where Ruth is planning to stay?

  a) near the mountains

  b) near one of the biggest lakes

  c) not far from the sea

2 How far is she planning to walk each day?

  a) 10–20 km   b) 20–30 km   c) 30–40 km

3 What does she plan to do in the evenings?

  a) go out to a restaurant and meet other walkers

  b) write about the walks they have done

  c) have something to eat and go to bed

4 What is Kieron going to study at university?

  a) Sports   b) Law   c) History

5 Where is he going to live? Why?

  a) In a house with friends because it's fun.

  b) In university accommodation because it's cheaper.

  c) With his parents because they live near the university.

6 What clubs does he hope to join?

  a) a wine-tasting club   b) an adventure club

  c) a sports/rugby club

7 Where is Amber going for her honeymoon?

  a) the Red Sea   b) the Nile   c) the Pyramids

8 What does Amber enjoy about travelling?

  a) speaking to people in a different language

  b) learning about a new culture

  c) new experiences, meeting new people, going to new places

9 What does she plan to do while she is on holiday?

  a) a scuba-diving course   b) sightseeing

  c) swimming and sunbathing

C Match the underlined phrases in sentences 1–5 with meanings a)–e).

1 We meet up <u>every now and again</u> for walking holidays.

2 It's not everyone's idea of fun, I know, but <u>I can't wait</u>.

3 <u>To start with</u>, I'm going to stay in the university.

4 I'll have to <u>see how it goes</u>.

5 We're staying in a <u>luxury</u> hotel.

a) in the beginning

b) see what happens

c) very comfortable and expensive

d) I'm looking forward to it very much / I'm very excited

e) occasionally

GRAMMAR   the future (plans)

2 Circle the correct options to complete the conversation.

A: ¹_____ anywhere this weekend?

B: Yes, we ²_____ up to Edinburgh to see some of the sights.

A: That's nice. Where ³_____ to stay?

B: I don't know yet. I ⁴_____ a look online later.

A: I've got some friends in Edinburgh. They ⁵_____ have some space. I ⁶_____ you their number.

B: Thanks. That's great. What about you? ⁷_____ anything exciting?

A: No, I think I ⁸_____ the weekend watching DVDs.

1 a) Do you go   b) Are you going

2 a) 're going   b) 'll go

3 a) are you going   b) might you

4 a) have   b) 'm going to have

5 a) might   b) are going to

6 a) 'll give   b) 'm going to give

7 a) Do you do   b) Are you doing

8 a) 'll spend   b) 'm spending

3 Complete the email. Use the present continuous, *will/might* or *be going to*. There may be more than one possibility.

Hi Ros – ¹_____ (you/do) anything at the weekend? Do you want to come out with us? Danny and I ²_____ (go/out) on Saturday night. It would be great if you could come. We ³_____ (try) one of the restaurants in Trastevere – it's really nice round there.

One thing we've planned is we ⁴_____ (meet) up with a few people from the course for a drink first, in Piazza Santa Maria. Do you know it? We ⁵_____ (be) outside Café Marzo from about 6.30, if you want to join us. I'm not sure how late we ⁶_____ (be). If anyone still has enough energy at the end of the evening, a DJ friend of mine ⁷_____ (play) at the Gioia Music Restaurant, so we ⁸_____ (go) there and dance a bit afterwards. We'll see how things go. I ⁹_____ (call) you tomorrow to see what your plans are.

Speak soon,

Silvia

4A ▶ 3.2 **Listen to the sentences. Which words are stressed? Circle the option you hear.**

1 a) They're <u>going</u> to <u>play</u> <u>squash</u>.
   b) <u>They</u>'re going to play <u>squash</u>.

2 a) I'm <u>going</u> to buy a <u>new</u> <u>phone</u>.
   b) I'm going to <u>buy</u> a new <u>phone</u>.

3 a) She's <u>going</u> to <u>spend</u> a week in <u>Greece</u>.
   b) She's going to spend a <u>week</u> in <u>Greece</u>.

4 a) He isn't <u>going</u> to eat <u>anything</u>.
   b) He <u>isn't</u> going to <u>eat</u> anything.

5 a) Are you <u>going</u> to <u>walk</u> to the <u>station</u>?
   b) Are <u>you</u> going to <u>walk</u> to the station?

6 a) <u>He's</u> going to change his <u>job</u>.
   b) He's going to <u>change</u> his <u>job</u>.

B **Listen again and repeat. Focus on the pronunciation of** *going to* **in fast speech.**

VOCABULARY communication

5 **Use the clues to complete the crossword.**

Across

3 Talk in a friendly and informal way

5 Talk too proudly about something that you have, or that you have done

6 Say something nice to someone in order to praise them, for example about their appearance or about how well they have done something

8 Tell someone that something dangerous or bad may happen, so they can avoid it or prevent it

Down

1 Talk or write about other people's behaviour or private lives

2 Say that you are sorry about something you have done or said

4 Shout and say angry things to someone because you disagree

7 Complain about something in an annoying way

WRITING messages; using note form

6A **Match messages 1–6 with situations a)–f).**

1 Gone to lunch. Back soon.

2 Mr Jackson called. No message. Will call again later.

3 Dentist appointment cancelled. Need to rebook.

4 At the cinema. Dinner in the oven. See you later.

5 Messages — Going swimming after school – want to come?

6 Sorry, didn't tidy bedroom – was late for school.

a) a brother leaving a message for his sister

b) a mother leaving a message for her son

c) a secretary leaving a message for his/her boss

d) a colleague leaving a message for other colleagues

e) a son leaving a message for his mother

f) a person leaving a message for self as a reminder

B **Which words have been deliberately left out of the messages? Rewrite the messages in full.**

1 _____

2 _____

3 _____

4 _____

5 _____

6 _____

C **Write notes for these situations.**

1 To your boss: Tell him that Mr Ali telephoned, and that you have arranged for them to meet at Mr Ali's office tomorrow morning at 9a.m.

2 To your brother: Invite him out to the cinema this evening.

3 To your colleague: Say that you have gone home and will be back in the office tomorrow.

READING

1 **Read the text and choose the best heading.**

a Five Ways to Find ET*   b Man and ET: A Communication Breakdown?   c Music in Space

*ET means extraterrestrial – a non-human, intelligent lifeform that may exist on other planets.

In 1977, Man sent a shuttle (a type of spaceship) called *Voyager 2* into space. The idea was to communicate with extraterrestrial life. In the space shuttle there was a recording specially made to introduce humanity to any aliens who found the shuttle. The recording contained the word *hello* in many languages, the sounds of a baby crying and a couple kissing, a message of peace from the Secretary General of the United Nations, and music from all over the world: Mexican mariachis, panpipes from Peru, a Japanese shakuhachi piece, even a song by Chuck Berry. One TV programme imagined that aliens found *Voyager 2*, listened to the music and sent a message back to humanity: 'Send more Chuck Berry!' 1 _____

For as long as Man has looked at the sky, we have wondered if there is intelligent life in space. In 1984, the SETI (Search for Extraterrestrial Intelligence) Institute was founded. One of its main tasks is sending signals into space in the hope that an intelligent alien life form will make contact. In other words, SETI is doing what *Voyager 2* did, but with 150 full-time scientists, educators and other staff working from sunny California on Planet Earth.

SETI has spent millions of dollars, and used up decades of people's working lives. And still nothing. So the big question: Why are we still waiting for a response? 2 _____

- There is no other intelligent lifeform out there. We are alone in the universe.
- There is intelligent life out there, but it communicates differently. While we use radio waves, maybe the aliens use something we don't know about.
- There is intelligent life out there, but it doesn't want to communicate with us. And who can blame it? Just look at Man's history and how we treat newly-discovered civilisations. When we are not giving them our diseases, we enslave them, steal their land and get them addicted to junk food and bad TV. And now we want to say 'hello' to another species? 3 _____
- We have not searched for long enough or far enough. Man has only been looking for ET for three or four decades. That is a tiny amount of time compared to the age of the universe. 4 _____
- We have succeeded in communicating with extraterrestrials, but government organisations are hiding this information from the public. This is the conspiracy theorists' dream; somewhere in an underground bunker (usually thought to be in Roswell, New Mexico, USA), there are crashed UFOs and the bodies of dead aliens being examined by secret government agencies. But no one has any evidence of an alien. 5 _____

2 **Read the text again and answer the questions.**

1 What was the purpose of *Voyager 2*?

_____

2 Which word was chosen for the recording, and spoken in different languages?

_____

3 How does SETI try to communicate with extraterrestrials?

_____

4 Who works for SETI?

_____

5 How long have we been looking for extraterrestrials?

_____

6 What do conspiracy theorists think?

_____

3 **These sentences have been taken out of the text in Exercise 1. Where should they go? Write the letter in the correct gap 1–5.**

a Even in our own communities, we kill animals, murder each other, and ruin the environment.

b And no one has found the secret bunker either.

c Space is also rather big, and we haven't searched very much of it.

d There are a number of possible answers.

e It may be a good joke, but in reality, after over thirty years we are still waiting for a response.

4 **Find words or phrases in the text to match definitions 1–4.**

1 form of energy that moves through the air, allowing us to send and receive messages (lines 26–28) _____

2 to make someone a slave (lines 29–34) _____

3 a group of animals or plants of the same kind (lines 29–34) _____

4 a strongly built room under the ground (lines 39–46) _____

VOCABULARY future time markers

5A Complete the predictions with the words in the box.

| term | next | future | in | time | short | from | ~~shortly~~ |

1 I'm going to find out my exam results _shortly_ . Then I hope to go to university.

2 In the near _____ I'm going to travel around Europe. I just need to save a bit more money.

3 The economy is weak now, but it will improve in the long _____ .

4 In the _____ term we expect our sales profits to increase by about 3 percent.

5 I'm planning to get married to my boyfriend _____ a year or two. Then we'll start a family.

6 I have no idea where I'll be a long time _____ now, but it won't be in a big city.

7 In ten years' _____ I hope to be a doctor working with children somewhere in Africa.

8 I'm starting a new job _____ month. If all goes well, I'll keep working for the company until I retire.

B Which predictions are about things that will happen soon? Which are about things that will happen more than three years in the future?

GRAMMAR the future (predictions)

6 Rewrite the second sentence so that it has the same meaning as the first sentence. Use the words in capitals.

1 There's a possibility that I will study in Spain.   MAY
   I may study in Spain .

2 Where do you plan to stay?   WILL
   Where _____ ?

3 Will you speak to Ted tomorrow?   GOING
   Are _____ ?

4 Janine probably won't pass her exam.   UNLIKELY
   Janine _____ .

5 The weather forecast predicts a storm.   GOING
   There's _____ .

6 He has a chance of becoming the champion.   COULD
   He _____ .

7 Scientists will probably find a cure for cancer one day.   LIKELY
   Scientists _____ .

8 I don't think we'll be able to attend the meeting.   MAY
   We _____ .

9 There isn't time for us to go shopping.   WON'T
   We _____ .

10 There's an opportunity to meet next week.   COULD
   We _____ .

7 Complete the text with one word in each gap. Contractions are one word.

THE FUTURE OF LANGUAGE LEARNING

In the future we [1]_____ going to see more and more people using technology to learn languages. There will [2]_____ software that gets computers to read texts aloud and translate them. And we [3]_____ only talk on the computer; we will also talk with the computer in any language we choose.

We will also begin to understand the importance of the five senses in language education, and researchers and publishers are likely [4]_____ look at children's toys for inspiration. Music is going [5]_____ play an increasing role in language learning. Short texts and phrases will be set to music and this will help students to remember the words, just as _The A, B, C Song_ helps children learn the alphabet.

Textbooks may [6]_____ unrecognisable when compared to today's books. They will come with microchips that produce smells and sounds. So if we are learning the word _bread_, when we touch that part of the page it will smell of bread. If we are learning the word _cry_, when we touch the word it [7]_____ make a crying sound.

At first, these books [8]_____ likely to be expensive, but market economics will drive prices down. So get ready for fun and games while you learn another language – these changes could happen sooner than you think!

VOCABULARY PLUS idioms

8 Underline the correct alternatives.

1 'I'm no good at [1]_big / small_ talk. I always put my [2]_foot / hand_ in it, and it's really not my cup of [3]_tea / coffee_.'

2 'I joined the [4]_mouse / rat_ race last year when I became a project manager. I have to keep my [5]_ear / eye_ on three or four projects at the same time. We're always [6]_working / running_ against the clock, and quite often we [7]_work / run_ out of time.'

3 'I thought an online course would be a [8]_piece / bit_ of cake, but I soon found myself in [9]_cold / hot_ water. It was really difficult. I told one of the other students what was on my [10]_mind / brain_. He was an A student, and he gave me a [11]_foot / hand_ with one of the assignments and I passed the course.'

FUNCTION dealing with misunderstandings

1 ▶ 3.3 Cover Exercise 2. Listen and match pictures A–D with conversations 1–4.

2 Listen again and complete the conversations.

Conversation 1

A: The living room is too green and the floor's all wrong.

B: Sorry?

A: The living room. Green. And I hate the floor.

B: You've ¹_____ me.

A: I'm talking about Mum's new house. I don't like the colour of the walls in the living room.

B: Oh!

Conversation 2

A: Hello? I'm trying to find my lost luggage.

B: Ah, OK.

A: My bags went missing in Montevideo in Uruguay, after a flight from Curitiba, Brazil.

B: ²_____ you say that ³_____ ? Montevideo?

A: I flew from Curitiba to Montevideo and my bags went missing.

B: Have you reported it already?

A: Yes, the name is Anders Kleeburg.

B: Hang on. Could you ⁴_____ the last name? Anders … ?

A: Kleeburg. K-l-e-e-b-u-r-g.

Conversation 3

A: OK, so cricket. So this is the bowler, OK? He runs up and bowls at the batsman.

B: ⁵_____ exactly do you ⁶_____ ? What's a bowler?

A: A bowler is the person with the ball in his hand, OK? And he tries to get the batsman out. Get him off the field.

B: Do you mean to ⁷_____ he tries to kill the batsman with the ball?

A: No!

Conversation 4

A: Did you read this?! About popcorn. In 1948, two American scientists found some popcorn in a cave in New Mexico and dated it. It was over five thousand years old.

B: I didn't ⁸_____ any of that. Are you talking about popcorn?

A: Yeah, it's an ancient food. Popcorn is thousands of years old.

B: I don't ⁹_____ what you're ¹⁰_____ . You mean the popcorn we ate in the cinema yesterday is thousands of years old!

A: No! Popcorn in general. People have eaten it for thousands of years.

LEARN TO reformulate

3 Put B's words in the correct order to complete the conversations.

Conversation 1

A: I'm afraid you have to wear a tie in this nightclub.

B: we / can't / saying / in / you're / so / come

_____

Conversation 2

A: The show starts at nine o'clock.

B: you / at / it / starts / didn't / ten / o'clock / say?

_____

Conversation 3

A: The pass mark for this exam is seventy percent.

B: what / failed / mean / so / we / you / is

_____

Conversation 4

A: This type of car is twice as expensive as the other one.

B: me / do / costs / to / that / tell / you / it / mean / €50,000?

_____

Conversation 5

A: No other team can catch us.

B: the / words, / we / in / are / other / champions

_____

VOCABULARY personal qualities

1A Complete the words about personal qualities.

1 He won the election because he is a g_____
c_____. People enjoy listening to him talk.

2 Susan's h_____-w_____ nature helped her
through university, when she had to study a lot.

3 Sami's very l_____. He doesn't work hard at
school, and he doesn't help at home, either.

4 Tim started at the bottom of the company, but he was
a_____. He knew that one day he would be the
manager of the whole organisation.

5 Lucy's a very g_____ l_____. She listens to
people, and then decides what's best for everyone to do.

6 He hates to lose a race. He's very c_____.

7 I find it difficult to make decisions. I'm a bit i_____.

8 You need to be more creative and think o_____
t_____ b_____.

9 They are a group of very m_____ students. They
are keen to work hard.

10 Being a racing driver, Anton has to be a r_____
t_____. He isn't afraid of danger.

B Find words or phrases in Exercise 1A which have the opposite meaning to 1–8.

1 makes decisions easily *indecisive*

2 not interested in competing with others _____

3 lazy _____

4 needs someone else to make them work _____

5 doesn't communicate well _____

6 not good at organising a team of people _____

7 doesn't like dangerous situations _____

8 not interested in becoming successful _____

GRAMMAR *must, have to, should* (obligation)

2 Match sentences 1–10 with sentences a)–j). Then underline the correct alternative.

1 We *don't have to / shouldn't* wear a uniform at work.

2 You *shouldn't / have to* stay up all night studying.

3 I think you *should / mustn't* talk to your boss.

4 You *don't have to / mustn't* drink and drive.

5 I think he *mustn't / should* start his own company.

6 Nurses *have to / should* work long hours.

7 You *don't have to / mustn't* cheat during the exam.

8 I *must / don't have to* leave at 4 o'clock.

9 You *should / don't have to* apologise for his behaviour.

10 We *should / must* remember to book the tickets today.

a) He's very ambitious.

b) You need to find out why he shouted at you.

c) It wasn't your fault.

d) You'll be thrown out of the college.

e) We can wear whatever we want.

f) It'll be too late if we wait until tomorrow.

g) It's against the law.

h) Otherwise I'll miss my train.

i) You'll be too tired tomorrow.

j) It's no good if you want a nine-to-five job.

3 Correct one mistake in each sentence.

1 You must ~~to~~ tell him as soon as possible.

2 I've finished this exercise. What I should do now?

3 The clients don't has to come to the office. We can meet
them at the restaurant.

4 I shouldn't to tell you this, but the boss is leaving on
Monday.

5 Do we have wear a uniform?

6 Everybody must leaving the building by 6p.m.

7 She have to be at work by 7.30a.m.

8 I think you should to check what time the film starts.

9 You don't must use a mobile phone in the classroom.

10 We have wait until the IT man comes to fix the system.

LISTENING

4A Look at the pictures. What qualities do you think are important for these jobs?

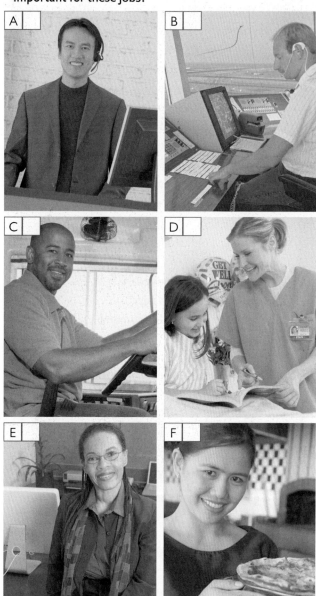

A ☐ B ☐ C ☐ D ☐ E ☐ F ☐

B ▶ 4.1 Listen to six people talking about their jobs. Match pictures A–F above with speakers 1–6.

C Listen again. Who says these things? Write the number of the speaker next to each statement.

1 You have to be organised, and have a good memory, too.
2 And you need to pay attention to detail.
3 You shouldn't get stressed too easily.
4 You have to care about the people you're looking after.
5 You always have to be on time.
6 And you have to be able to work well under pressure.
7 You must be very accurate and observant. /
8 You have to be able to stay calm.

VOCABULARY PLUS confusing words

5A Complete the conversations with the words in the box.

| job work remember remind forget leave hear |
| listen fun funny won earn |

1 A: Oh no, _____ to that. It's raining and I don't have an umbrella.
   B: Why not? Did you _____ it at home?
   A: Yes, I did.
   B: Here. Use mine.

2 A: Can you _____ me to post that letter on the way home?
   B: Sure. Just _____ to bring it with you.

3 A: Did you have a good night last night?
   B: Yes, it was really _____. We danced until two in the morning, but today I feel terrible.

4 A: I got the _____, by the way.
   B: Congratulations! That's brilliant news.
   A: Yes, I'm so excited. Finally, I'm going to _____ a proper salary.
   B: That's great. Well done.

5 A: I've got to go to _____ now. I'll see you later.
   B: Yes, don't _____ we're meeting Chaz at 7.30.
   A: Don't worry. I'll be there.

6 A: Did you _____ the joke about the scarecrow?
   B: No.
   A: He _____ an award for being outstanding in his field.
   B: That's not even _____.

B Complete the sentences with words from Exercise 5A.

1 Can you _____ me to call my brother later? It's his birthday.
2 Did you _____ about that couple who _____ millions of pounds on the Euro lottery?
3 I don't get paid enough. I need to get a new _____.
4 We're having a meeting tomorrow morning. Don't _____!
5 I really enjoy my _____. I find it interesting, and the people I work with are good _____.
6 He's so _____. He always makes me laugh.

DREAM JOB TURNS INTO NIGHTMARE

1 It was advertised as the best job in the world. And it certainly looked good. You would be paid ($189,000 for six months) to surf, sail, and swim. The job came with a beachside mansion, with its own swimming pool, and fantastic views of the ocean. All you had to do was look after tiny Hamilton Island, situated off the coast of Queensland. Duties included feeding the fish, and writing a blog of your experiences to help encourage tourism in the area. There were more than 34,000 applicants for the job from all over the world, so Ben Southall was delighted when he beat them all, and won the contract.

2 But, as it turned out, it wasn't quite the dream job that some people might have expected. Firstly, it was incredibly busy. Ben found himself working seven days a week, and up to nineteen hours a day. He had a busy schedule of events to attend, with promotional events, press conferences, training courses and administrative duties. 'It has been very busy, busier than most people would have imagined, and certainly busier than I had imagined,' Mr Southall told reporters when he finished his contract.

3 In fact, during his six months, Ben visited ninety 'exotic locations', made forty-seven video diaries, and gave more than 250 media interviews — including a chat with popular US TV host Oprah Winfrey. He also posted more than 75,000 words in sixty separate blogs, uploaded more than 2,000 photos, and 'tweeted' more than 730 times.

4 That didn't leave much time for surfing, sailing or simply relaxing and enjoying the sea views. And when he did get the chance to try out his water sports, things didn't always go well. On one trip, Ben was stung by a deadly jellyfish. The Irukandji jellyfish are transparent and very small, so they are very difficult to see in the water.

5 'I was enjoying a post-Christmas jetski session with some friends at a quiet beach on Hamilton Island and as I climbed off the back of the ski and onto the beach, felt a small bee-like sting on my forearm,' Mr Southall wrote on his blog. Within thirty minutes, Ben was feeling the venom. He was hot and sweaty, with headaches and pains in his chest, and high blood pressure. Ben had to be rushed to a doctor who diagnosed the symptoms and gave him some medication. Luckily, Ben was fine, but it was an unwelcome end to his stay in paradise. On the blog he wrote, 'This was not what I'd wanted at all — I'm supposed to be relaxing in my last few days on Hamilton Island.' Ben was lucky to survive.

6 However, he still insists that he enjoyed himself immensely. In fact, Tourism Queensland is offering him a new contract, and he will also write a book about his experiences.

READING

1A Ben Southall got a 'dream job': looking after Hamilton Island, off the coast of Queensland, Australia. This article describes how the job turned into a nightmare. Which of these problems do you think it will mention?

> loneliness   free time   feeling bored   other
> money   illness   problems with animals

B Read the article to see if you were right. Then answer the questions.

1 What three things help to make the job 'the best job in the world'?

2 Why was the job not as 'ideal' as it seemed at first?

3 What happened to Ben towards the end of his contract?

4 What is he going to do now?

2 Tick the things which Ben did as part of his job.

1 gave speeches

2 made video diaries

3 managed a big team of people

4 gave interviews

5 attended press conferences

6 learned a new language

7 met politicians

8 wrote a novel

9 wrote a blog about his experiences

10 learned to surf and sail

3 Find words or phrases in the text to match definitions 1–8.

1 a large house by the sea (paragraph 1) _____

2 a plan that includes a lot of things to be done in a short time (paragraph 2) _____

3 meetings at which someone answers questions asked by people from newspapers, television, etc. (paragraph 2) _____

4 activities involved in managing the work of a company or organisation (paragraph 2) _____

5 posted a comment using the website Twitter (paragraph 3) _____

6 have an opportunity (paragraph 4) _____

7 taken very quickly (paragraph 5) _____

8 very, very much (paragraph 6) _____

VOCABULARY strong adjectives

4 Complete the sentences with the correct word.

1 a) I thought the show was *brilliant / boiling*.

b) Is the heating on? It's *brilliant / boiling* in here.

2 a) Have you heard the news? Isn't it *terrible / furious*?

b) All the trains were delayed. I was *terrible / furious*.

3 a) I'd invite you round, but my apartment is *delicious / tiny*.

b) Have you tried these salads? They're *delicious / tiny*.

4 a) I can't do it – it's *exhausted / impossible*!

b) I'm going home. I'm *exhausted / impossible*.

5 a) It's a *fascinating / huge* book about naval history.

b) $50,000! That's a *fascinating / huge* amount of money!

GRAMMAR used to, would

5 Complete the paragraphs. Use one word for each gap.

I used ¹_____ work for a big company. I ²_____ to work long hours and I ³_____ dream of living in a more exotic location, sitting on a beach with my laptop. Now I run my own website business. I don't earn as much money as I ⁴_____ to earn, but I'm much happier.

I ⁵_____ to work as a computer programmer. Most of the time, I ⁶_____ enjoy it. But I didn't ⁷_____ to like being in an office all day. So, I decided to get a job working outdoors. Now, I train people in forestry skills, so I'm outside most of the time. And my lifestyle is much healthier than it ⁸_____ to be.

6A Rewrite the sentences with *used to*.

1 Did you spend your holidays by the sea?

_____

2 We didn't have a dog when I was a child.

_____

3 Daniel was one of the naughtiest boys in the class, but he's much better now.

_____

4 I loved reading in the evening, but now I'm too tired.

_____

5 I remember how I sat in my grandfather's studio and watched him paint.

_____

6 I was quite fat. Then, I went on a diet and lost ten kilos.

_____

7 Children always played around on the streets in the old days, but there's nobody here now.

_____

8 They lived in a big house, but they had to move.

_____

B Tick the sentences in Exercise 6A where you could replace *used to* with *would*.

7A Look at the underlined words. Are they pronounced with a /s/ or /z/ sound?

1 I <u>used</u> to be very sporty.

2 Can I <u>use</u> your phone?

3 He never <u>used</u> to worry about it.

4 I <u>used</u> to live in the USA when I was 18.

5 This stuff is <u>used</u> to kill insects.

6 I don't <u>use</u> the car much any more.

7 We <u>used</u> to love going there on holiday.

8 I didn't <u>use</u> to live in Europe.

B ▶ 4.2 Listen and check. Then listen and repeat. Focus on the pronunciation of /juːstə/.

WRITING a letter; organising your ideas

8A Put the parts of the covering letter in the correct order.

____ Thank you for your consideration. If you require any further information, please do not hesitate to contact me. I can be reached at vinniej22@dmail.com or 07788 922 123. I look forward to hearing from you ¹<u>soon</u>.

_1_ Dear Ms Nelson,

____ I believe that my communication skills, customer service abilities, and positive work ethic would make me an asset to the shop.

____ I am currently studying English at Exeter University and I am looking for summer work to help me finance my studies. ²<u>I think I would be good at this job.</u> Firstly, I am both hard-working and organised, and I have excellent communication skills. Secondly, I have ³<u>shown that I am good at</u> customer service. In my previous job, on the reception desk at Queen's Hospital, I had ⁴<u>practical</u> experience of providing quality customer service, and working with all types of people.

____ Yours sincerely,

____ I am writing to you ⁵<u>about</u> the summer position at SunnySam's Electronics, advertised on www.summerjobs4students.com. ⁶<u>I want to apply</u> for the post. I attach my CV, application form and all the information required in the advertisement.

____ Vinnie Jessop

B Replace the underlined sections 1–6 in the letter with the phrases in the box. Write the correct number.

hands-on ____   at your earliest convenience ____
regarding ____   proven ability at ____
I would like to submit an application ____
I believe I meet all the requirements of the post ____

C Write a covering letter (120–180 words) for a summer job working as a restaurant/shop manager.

VOCABULARY business

1A Circle the correct options to complete the text.

Hi Lucy,

I'm just writing to tell you about my new job. Remember when I had to ¹_____ for ²_____ last month? Well, I got the job. I'm so pleased about it, because in my last job I worked for a really difficult ³_____, but things here are much better. The people in the office are really good fun, and we work well as a ⁴_____. My new boss is a ⁵_____ businessman, who ⁶_____ a six-figure ⁷_____! But he's very generous with his money, and takes us out to lunch every week. The only problem now is that I still arrive late for work all the time. I hope I don't get ⁸_____.

Let me know how you're getting on at work. Speak soon.

Becca

I	a) be	b) go	c) make
2	a) an interview	b) a job	c) a work
3	a) colleague	b) job	c) boss
4	a) team	b) salary	c) businessman
5	a) difficult	b) successful	c) six-figure
6	a) works	b) is	c) earns
7	a) job	b) salary	c) money
8	a) interview	b) boss	c) fired

IT MIGHT BE BETTER IF WE WORK AS A TEAM

B Use the phrases in Exercise 1A to complete the sentences.

I He's not easy to work for. He's a very _____
_____.

2 They were surprised to find out that the tramp was actually a _____ _____.

3 I like the people in the office. We _____ well as a _____.

4 They're looking for a new manager, so I'm going to _____ for an _____ next week.

5 We don't _____ a _____- _____ salary, but we really enjoy the job.

6 Unless you change your attitude, you will soon _____ _____.

FUNCTION reaching agreement

2 Complete the conversation with the phrases in the box.

not sure that I agree   suggest we think about
see what you mean   see things   that's a good idea
How about if we   That's fine

A: The way I ¹_____, the first thing we need to do is update the website.

B: Yes, ²_____. But we haven't decided what information to put there.

A: I know. I ³_____ what should be on the site, and then decide who's going to work on it.

B: ⁴_____ by me.

C: I'm ⁵_____, actually. I think we need to look at the finances first. We don't know how much money we can spend on the website yet.

B: I ⁶_____, but I'm not sure what to do. ⁷_____ decide what we would like first, and then look at how much it will cost?

A: Fine. That sounds good to me.

LEARN TO manage a discussion

3 Complete the sentences with the words in the box.

on (x2)   all   recap   to   up

I Let's focus _____ the main problems, and talk about the rest if we have time.

2 OK, but first of _____, we need to look at the notes from the last meeting.

3 Moving _____ to the next point. What are we going to do about salaries?

4 So, let's _____ on the main ideas we've discussed, and then we'll stop for lunch.

5 I think we need to come back _____ the decision to relocate.

6 Let's sum _____ what we've talked about.

VOCABULARY technology

1A Underline the correct alternative.

1 He's six months old. He's been to the doctor to get his *genetic engineering / vaccinations*.

2 We are running out of coal, so the government is looking at new ways of making *electricity / computer networks*.

3 The government is planning to build new *nuclear power / genetic engineering* stations, but many people are worried that they are too dangerous.

4 The company has just invested thousands of dollars in its new *computer network / antibiotics* to improve communication between employees.

5 It sounds like you've got a chest infection. I think you need some *solar power / antibiotics*.

6 NASA has decided to restart its *communications satellites / space travel* programme and try to send people to Mars.

7 They rode their *commercial aeroplanes / motorbikes* right up through to the United States and Canada. The trip took several weeks.

B Match words in italics from Exercise 1A with definitions 1–8.

1 The science of changing the genes of a living thing _____

2 The energy created when you split or join two atoms _____

3 Drugs used to kill bacteria and cure infections _____

4 Power carried by wires and used to make lights and machines work _____

5 Exploration of the area beyond Earth where the stars and planets are _____

6 Machines that are sent into space and travel around the Earth, sending radio and television signals _____

7 Energy from the sun _____

8 An injection given to someone to protect them from a disease _____

2A Put the words in the correct column according to the pronunciation of the underlined letter a.

space antibiotics nuclear travel machine communications satellites vacuum commercial aeroplanes solar vaccinations

/eɪ/ make	/æ/ apple	/ə/ polar
space	antibiotics	

B ▶ 5.1 Listen and check. Then listen and repeat.

LISTENING

3A ▶ 5.2 Listen to Mia, Tom and Owen answering the following questions. Write Mia (M), Tom (T) or Owen (O) next to the question they answer.

1 How has your country changed in the last thirty years? __

2 Is the world getting better or worse? __

3 How has your life changed in the last thirty years? __

B Circle the correct option to complete the sentences.

1 Mia thinks that thirty years ago _____.
   a) life was simpler
   b) the pace of life was faster
   c) people were happier

2 Mia thinks that email puts pressure on people because _____.
   a) people's computers crash
   b) emails sometimes don't arrive
   c) we are expected to give an instant response

3 Tom says that Beijing has grown because people _____.
   a) don't have as much money as before
   b) came from around the world to get rich
   c) came from all over China to make money

4 Tom says that life in the countryside _____.
   a) has changed enormously because of the new technology
   b) will never change because they do not have access to technology
   c) has not changed that much, but people have more technology

5 Owen says that living conditions around the world _____.
   a) are improving, even though many people are still living in terrible poverty
   b) are terrible and are going in the wrong direction
   c) are not improving, and more and more people are living in poverty

6 Owen thinks that there are _____.
   a) fewer wars than before, but weapons are getting more dangerous
   b) more wars than before, and weapons are getting more dangerous
   c) the same number of wars as before, and weapons are getting safer

C Listen again and check.

GRAMMAR comparatives/superlatives

4 Complete the conversation with the correct form of the adjectives in brackets.

A: I love my new digital camera. It was [1]_____ (expensive) my last one, but the pictures are much [2]_____ (good) quality, and it's [3]_____ (easy) to use.

B: But it's much [4]_____ (big). Isn't it [5]_____ (heavy) to carry around with you?

A: Actually, it was one of [6]_____ (light) models in the shop. Although you can get [7]_____ (small) and [8]_____ (cheap) cameras, they're not as good as this one.

5 Underline the correct alternatives.

WHAT'S YOUR FAVOURITE GADGET IN THE KITCHEN?

My favourite gadget in the kitchen is the dishwasher. It's [1]*much / a lot more* faster than me at washing up. The problem is that I'm getting [2]*a slightly / a little bit* lazier.
Yuri

The toaster. Morning is [3]*by far / slightly* the best time of the day for me. I enjoy a relaxing breakfast. And toast is [4]*a lot / more* tastier than bread. I love it.
Katia

I don't cook very much, because I'm too busy. I have a microwave, which I find makes it [5]*more / a bit* easier. Now, I eat [6]*slightly / a little far* better than I did before.
Nguyen

WRITING an essay; using discourse markers

6A Look at the task below and the notes a student has made. Tick the advantages and cross the disadvantages.

Discuss the advantages and disadvantages of studying English online, as opposed to in a classroom.

1 flexibility – can study where and when you want, don't have to travel to a school

2 lack of interaction with your teacher or students

3 more choice – can choose to skip parts of the course, focus on other parts

4 IT problems – need to be confident with how the technology works, have good connections to the internet, etc.

5 discipline and time management – have to stay motivated

6 materials are technologically advanced – use a variety of multimedia materials

B Look at the two plans, A and B, for the essay. Which is better? Why?

Plan A

Many people now study English online. There are lots of good materials on the internet for doing this. As the technology increases, more and more people will try online learning.

But there are some problems, too. Online learning is boring because you are on your own. It's difficult to be motivated.

My opinion – I have tried online materials, and they are very good. But going to a class is a better way to improve your English.

Plan B

Introduction:
increase in technology means many people are now choosing to study English online, not in classrooms.

Advantages:
- increased flexibility
- increased choice of materials

Disadvantages:
- lack of interaction with teacher and students
- difficulty with motivation and discipline
- IT problems

Conclusion:
- Online courses offer students more choice and flexibility, but are more impersonal.
- Language is about communication, so face-to-face interaction with people in a classroom is a better way to learn.
- Online courses might be a good way to supplement your learning.

C Look at the essay one student wrote. They forgot to use any discourse markers to link their ideas. Rewrite the essay, including discourse markers from the box where you see an asterisk (*).

One of the main advantages is that	However, (x2)
Another disadvantage is	In my opinion,
The problem is that	And another thing,

With the increase in technology, many people are now choosing to study English online, rather than in the classroom. It's easy to see that there are many advantages to online courses. * There are also disadvantages.

* When you study online, you have increased flexibility to study when you want to, and where you want to. You have an increased choice of the materials you want to study, because you can choose them yourself.

* When you study online, there is a lack of interaction with your teacher and students. * You might find it difficult to stay motivated, and be disciplined with your studies. * You might experience computer problems, which make your study difficult.

* Online courses offer students more choice and flexibility. * They are more impersonal. As language is about communication, face-to-face interaction with people in a classroom is a better way to learn.

VOCABULARY questions

1 Cross out the alternative which is **not** possible in each sentence.

1 The class had a really good *debate / discussion / ~~reply~~* about the environment.

2 In this study I will *investigate / wonder / discuss* the government's economic policy.

3 You should try to *respond to / enquire / reply to* emails as quickly as possible.

4 I *questioned / looked into / enquired about* renting a car, but it was too expensive.

5 A good *enquiry / question / wonder* always leads to more questions.

6 I've always *wondered about / questioned / responded* this man's motivation.

7 The *look into / research / investigation* was a waste of time; we found no solutions.

8 His newspaper column *debates / enquires / discusses* the issues of the day.

2 Add the missing letters to complete the text.

WHO GOES FIRST?

Everyone involved in medical ¹re_search_ is eventually faced with a difficult ²qu_____: who will be my guinea pig? Who will be the first person to try this new medicine before we know if it works?

If we ³l_____ i_____ the history of drug testing, we find that many researchers not only ⁴de_____ this issue, but that a few have a surprising ⁵re_____: they use themselves as guinea pigs.

When scientist Jonas Salk was ⁶in_____ a new polio vaccine in the 1950s, he tried the drug on himself, his wife and children. It worked. Someone later ⁷en_____ about who held the patent (the right to sell the medicine). Salk's ⁸re_____ showed his character: he ⁹wo_____ why anyone wanted to make money from something that the world needed.

GRAMMAR question tags

3 Underline the correct alternative.

1 You're from France, *aren't you / weren't you*?

2 She broke a world record, *hasn't she / didn't she*?

3 They haven't seen us, *have they / haven't they*?

4 Don won't tell anybody, *does he / will he*?

5 That house looks nice, *isn't it / doesn't it*?

6 We didn't see that film, *did we / saw we*?

7 It hasn't rained for months, *has it / have it*?

8 You will come tomorrow, *won't you / will you*?

9 The shop doesn't open at 6a.m., *will it / does it*?

10 You stopped smoking last year, *didn't you / you didn't*?

4 Read the situations and write questions. Use the correct question tags.

1 You think your friend is in love.
You *really like Mary, don't you*____? (really like / Mary)

2 You leave the cinema laughing together.
That film _____? (be / funny)

3 Your friend's younger brother is going to borrow your car.
He _____? (not crash / the car)

4 You leave the football stadium after a boring match.
It _____? (not / be / very good / game)

5 You say goodbye to your friend at the airport.
You will _____? (write / to me)

6 You want to check that your friend got home safely last night.
You _____? (not miss / the last bus)

7 A tourist thinks you speak French.
You _____? (speak / French)

8 You have lost your watch.
You _____? (not see / my watch)

5A Read the conversations. Which responses are genuine questions (where Speaker B really doesn't know the answer)?

1 A: Have you met Yinka's parents?
B: Only once. They're doctors, aren't they?

2 A: There isn't a cloud in the sky.
B: I know. It's a beautiful day, isn't it?

3 A: Are you looking for the scissors?
B: You haven't seen them, have you?

4 A: Have you read Jhumpa Lahiri's new book?
B: Yeah, she's a great writer, isn't she?

5 A: I've got my final exam tomorrow.
B: You'll pass, won't you?

6 A: I think this is the wrong address.
B: Yes, we've made a mistake, haven't we?

B ▶ 5.3 Listen and check. Then listen again and repeat the responses. Use the same intonation in the question tags.

READING

6A Read the introduction to the article. Which questions can you answer? Which can only be answered by experts?

I never knew that!

What is worse for you: boredom or stress? Why is sea air good for you? If you throw water into the air during the Russian winter, will it come back down as ice? What three foods should you take to a desert island?

People love trivia*. In 2005, a book called *Does Anything Eat Wasps?* was a surprise hit. It was a collection of questions and answers from readers of a magazine called *New Scientist*. We at *Lynx Mag* decided to come up with our own questions and then we asked a panel of experts for answers.

*trivia: unimportant facts

B Read the rest of the text to find the answers.

1 Q: You are going to stay on a desert island for several months and you can only choose three foods to take with you. Which do you choose, and why?
Broccoli, walnuts and orange juice. Broccoli has a chemical which helps detoxify your liver. It's also a superfood. Walnuts have protein and plenty of healthy fats. Orange juice is a source of clean water, and the orange contains Vitamin C. *Dr Leah Morecombe*

2 Q: What's worse for you: boredom or stress?
Boredom. Stress can have benefits. Weight lifting is a type of stress. So are other sports and pressures at work. All of these are good for you in small doses. Boredom means you have no purpose in life, and no dose of boredom is good for you. *Dr Samran Naipaul*

3 Q: Why is sea air good for you?
It isn't particularly. It got a reputation for being good for you in Victorian times because there was so much unhealthy smog in big cities. *Dr Robina Whitman*

4 Q: Why do flies like rotting food?
Flies like rotting food because soft environments provide perfect conditions for breeding. When a fly's eggs hatch, the larvae live in and eat the rotting food until they grow into adult flies. *Dr Kelvin Marsh*

5 Q: If you throw water into the air during the Russian winter, will it come back down as ice?
It depends where you are in Russia, and what the temperature is at the time. But, potentially, yes. At a temperature of -30°C, small amounts of water will turn into ice almost immediately. *Immanuel Kanevsky*

C Complete the questions for the answers.

1 Q: _____ helps detoxify your liver?
  A: Broccoli.

2 Q: What does the writer say _____?
  A: It can be good for you, while boredom can't.

3 Q: Who thought sea air was _____?
  A: The Victorians.

4 Q: What creatures live in and _____?
  A: Fly larvae.

5 Q: At -30°C, when will a small _____?
  A: Almost immediately.

D Find words in the text that match meanings 1–5.

1 remove dangerous chemicals or poison from something (paragraph 1) *detoxify*

2 measured amounts of something that you experience at one time (paragraph 2) _____

3 unhealthy air that is full of smoke and pollution (paragraph 3) _____

4 going bad; becoming soft and useless (paragraph 4) _____

5 when an egg breaks and a baby bird, fish or insect comes out (paragraph 4) _____

VOCABULARY PLUS word building: adjectives

7 Complete the text with the correct form of the words in brackets.

THE PNEUMATIC TYRE: HOW DID IT START?

John Dunlop, a Scottish vet, was [1]_____ (response) for one of the world's great inventions.

Dunlop's young son kept falling off his tricycle because the bumpy streets were [2]_____ (hope) for cycling. Dunlop thought of a [3]_____ (create) solution: filling the rubber tyres with air. This, he realised, would be an [4]_____ (ease) way to make the tricycle more stable.

He was right: it turned out to be a very [5]_____ (effect) solution. Lots of cyclists copied the idea and the air tyre became very [6]_____ (success). French car makers realised it was a [7]_____ (value) idea, and produced air-filled car tyres. The tyres also became very [8]_____ (profit); Dunlop Tyres is still a huge company today.

VOCABULARY problems and solutions

1 Complete the sentences with the words in the box.

memory switching crashed sort work print down order recharging fixing

1 I'm on the motorway, and my car's broken _____.

2 My phone isn't working. The batteries need _____.

3 We can't use the machines here because they're out of _____.

4 Can you call the maintenance department and tell them that the photocopier needs _____?

5 If it still doesn't work, try _____ it off and on again.

6 I don't believe it! My laptop's just _____ again!

7 Have you got another pen? This one doesn't _____ any more.

8 Don't worry about that now. I'll _____ it out later.

9 OK. First, you'd better save the documents onto a _____ stick.

10 I've got a copy on my computer. Do you want me to _____ you a copy?

FUNCTION polite requests

2A ▶ 5.4 **Listen to eight conversations. What does the person want each time? Match pictures A–H with conversations 1–8.**

B ▶ 5.4 Listen again. Complete the conversations with one word in each gap.

1 A: Excuse me, _____ you tell me the way to the swimming pool, please?

   B: Yes, of _____ I can. You keep going this way, until you get to the traffic lights. Then, …

2 A: Hello. Do you _____ what time the bank opens?

   B: I'm not _____. I'll just ask someone.

3 A: Do you want us to bring anything?

   B: That would be great. Could _____ bring some salad, and maybe something for dessert?

   A: Yes, _____ course. Anything else?

   B: No, that'll be fine.

4 A: Could you _____ me with my bags?

   B: I'm _____, I can't. I've got my hands full.

5 A: Would you mind _____ the door for me?

   B: Of course _____. There you are.

   A: Thank you. That's very kind.

6 A: Could you _____ me what time the show starts?

   B: _____ me have a look. The afternoon show starts at 3p.m.

   A: Thanks very much.

7 A: Would you _____ coming to get me from the station?

   B: OK. _____. Wait outside and I'll be there in ten minutes.

8 A: Do you know _____ there's a post office near here?

   B: Yes, _____ is – there's one just along this road.

LEARN TO respond to requests

3 Put the words in the correct order to make responses.

1 A: Would you mind saying that again?

   B: of / not / no, / course

   _____

2 A: Do you know how to get there?

   B: sure. / not / I'm / look. / me / have / a / let

   _____

3 A: Could you phone Tilly for me?

   B: course / yes, / of

   _____

4 A: Could you finish doing this for me?

   B: can't / I / afraid / I'm

   _____

5 A: Could you take these folders for me?

   B: I / yes, / can

   _____

LISTENING

1 Read the exam task below and answer the questions.

1 Who is being interviewed?

2 What did he recently win?

3 How many questions are there?

2A ▶ R1.1 Do the exam task.

Part 2

Questions 8–13

You will hear a radio interview with a head teacher of a school who has just won a prize for his work improving the school.

For each question, put a tick (✓) in the correct box.

---

8 What type of school is it?

A a college ☐

B a primary school ☐

C a language school ☐

9 Who does he say was responsible for the school's success?

A himself ☐

B the teachers and pupils ☐

C the teachers, parents and pupils ☐

10 What does he say about the breakfast club and the 'How You Want' project?

A they were an important starting point ☐

B the children loved them ☐

C they were difficult to introduce ☐

11 What does he say about the topics the children chose?

A only the boys like football ☐

B some of them were inappropriate ☐

C all the children wanted to talk about TV ☐

12 Who organised the events outside school?

A the parents ☐

B the children ☐

C the teachers ☐

13 What does the head teacher hope for the future?

A that the children play more sport ☐

B that the government give them more money ☐

C that their success will continue ☐

B Listen again and check your answers.

3 Read the extracts from the recording. What do you think the words and phrases in bold mean? Match them with meanings a)–e).

1 So how did you manage to **turn things around**?

2 She sounds like a very **smart** person!

3 ... being **forced to** learn things which they weren't interested in.

4 We also spent time **finding out** what topics they were interested in.

5 ... which helped **raise money** for the school to spend on new technology.

a) made to do something which you don't want to do

b) collect cash for a good cause

c) completely transform a situation, usually for the better

d) intelligent, clever

e) discovering

GRAMMAR question forms

4A Put the words in the correct order to make questions.

1 to / you / listen / Do / audiobooks / ever

_____ ?

2 you / When / English / learning / did / start

_____ ?

3 country / What / famous / your / for / is

_____ ?

4 you / to / Who / a / bike / taught / ride

_____ ?

5 like / a / As / vegetables / did / child / you

_____ ?

6 last / the / Where / Cup / was / World

_____ ?

7 problem / to / speak / Who / a / you / if / usually / do / have / you

_____ ?

8 your / like / Do / job / you

_____ ?

B Match questions 1–8 in Exercise 4A with answers a)–h).

a) At primary school, when I was seven.

b) My sister. She's a really good listener.

c) Sometimes, usually when I'm driving.

d) Mostly, but I hated broccoli!

e) I love it. I get to meet interesting new people every day.

f) Pizza and pasta. Delicious!

g) Oh, I'm not sure. I think it was in South Africa.

h) My grandfather – he was very patient with me, even when I always fell off!

GRAMMAR verb tenses

5 Complete the sentences with the correct form of the verb in brackets.

1 This is Phil. He _____ (be) a teacher.

2 What _____ you _____ (do) when I called last night? I thought you were at home.

3 I _____ (stay) with my parents at the moment until I can find a flat.

4 I _____ (not know) you like *The White Cliffs*. Me too – they're my favourite band!

5 Please don't call too early on Sunday. I _____ (not get up) before 10a.m. at the weekend.

6 Rrrrr! I _____ (sleep) really well until you _____ me _____ (wake up)!

7 Don't go in that room – they _____ (record) a live radio programme at the moment.

8 I feel really tired today. I usually _____ (go) to bed at 11p.m. but last night I _____ (can not get) to sleep until 1a.m.

6 Circle the correct option to complete the sentences.

1 Susan can be really moody at times,
   a) you never know if she's going to laugh or cry.
   b) you're never knowing if she's going to laugh or cry.

2 The party was really boring,
   a) so we were going home early.
   b) so we went home early.

3 When I called Jim
   a) he had a meeting, so he couldn't speak.
   b) he was having a meeting, so he couldn't speak.

4 I watched a great documentary about the Romans last night,
   a) it was all about how they built cities.
   b) it was all about how they build cities.

5 I plan to move to Japan next year,
   a) so at the moment I study Japanese.
   b) so at the moment I'm studying Japanese.

6 What a disaster! The teacher was waiting for us in room 2
   a) while we were waiting for her in room 8!
   b) while we're waiting for her in room 8!

GRAMMAR modal verbs

7 Rewrite the second sentence so that it means the same as the first. Use the correct form of the words in capitals.

1 It's not a good idea to interrupt the teacher while she's explaining something important. SHOULD
   You _____ the teacher when she's explaining something important.

2 It's necessary to do your homework if you want to pass the exam. MUST
   You _____ your homework if you want to pass the exam.

3 It's not necessary for you to eat in the school canteen, you can go somewhere else if you want. HAVE TO
   You _____ in the school canteen, you can go somewhere else if you want.

4 Priscilla's boss is really strict. It's necessary for her to arrive on time every day or he makes her stay late in the evening. HAVE TO
   Priscilla's boss is really strict. She _____ on time every day or he makes her stay late in the evening.

5 It would be a good idea for you to say sorry to Claudia. I think you really hurt her feelings. SHOULD
   You _____ sorry to Claudia. I think you really hurt her feelings.

6 You can't speak during the exam. MUST
   You _____ during the exam.

8A ▶ R1.2 **Listen and complete the conversations.**

1 A: Children, go and clean your rooms!
   B: Aw, do we _____?

2 A: Can we leave early today?
   B: No, you _____ until you've finished your work.

3 A: I'm really worried about the exam.
   B: Well, I've told you before, you _____ more.

4 A: Can I wear jeans to the party?
   B: Yes that's fine, you _____ formal clothes.

5 A: Is it an important game?
   B: Oh yes, they _____ it if they want to get promoted.

6 A: Don't you just hate her clothes?
   B: You _____ things like that, it's not nice.

B **Listen again and shadow the answers.**

READING

1 Look at the exam task below and answer the questions.

1 What are the people described in the first part of the task all doing at the moment?

2 What have they been offered?

3 What is each person studying?

2 Do the exam task.

Part 2

Questions 6–10

The people below are all university students who have been offered a two-week work experience placement. They want to choose the right placement for them.

Opposite there are descriptions of eight work experience placements.

Decide which placement would be suitable for the following people.

For questions **6–10**, mark the correct letter **(A–H)** on your answer sheet.

---

6 Stacey is studying art. She loves shopping for clothes and going to parties. She's a very creative person.

7  Mike is studying mathematics. He enjoys solving logic problems, and he spends all his free time playing computer games.

8  Claire is studying English literature. She loves writing her own stories and is very good at communicating with people. She gets bored quickly, and doesn't like working in a 'safe' job.

9  Steve is studying economics. He's very motivated and independent – he often works on his own. Outside class, however, he's very popular and has lots of friends.

10  Tasmin is studying biology. She's a good leader when working with other people, and is good at getting the best ideas out of other people.

A Journalist for a local newspaper
On this placement you'll work closely with a local journalist, investigating interesting stories and interviewing people. You'll write a full article of your own, which will be included in our newspaper.

B Computer programmer
If you have an analytical mind and like thinking of new solutions to problems, then this placement is for you. You'll learn basic computer codes for the most popular software, and how to adapt them for different needs.

C Physics researcher
Do you love discovering new things about the world around us? If you want to learn the principles of scientific research, and how to carry out experiments, then this placement is for you.

D Legal intern
In this position you'll work closely with one of our top lawyers. At the end of the placement you'll write your own case report and practise presenting it to a team of critical lawyers. You'll need to be able to take risks and have good communication skills.

E Mechanical engineer
This placement is ideal for someone who likes to get 'hands on' and look at the practical side of how machines work. During your time with us, you'll learn how to see an idea through from start to finish.

F Independent financial advisor
If you are good at understanding financial systems and/or mathematics, and want an opportunity to apply these skills in a practical way, then this placement is right for you. You'll need the ability to work alone and be good at dealing with people.

G Fashion designer
Can you tell what looks good? Can you say what's currently 'hot'? If you've always dreamed of creating your own clothes and seeing other people wear them, then you should choose this placement.

H Ecology advisor
This placement is ideal for people who care about the environment and have a good basic scientific knowledge of ecosystems. You'll need to be good at managing people and selecting and rejecting ideas before offering valuable advice to the government.

3 Find words or phrases in the work-experience descriptions to match definitions 1–6.

1 finding out information about something (Journalist for a local newspaper) i _____

2 change or modify (Computer programmer)
a _____

3 a set of arguments used in a legal process (Legal intern)
c _____

4 use physical contact to work with something (Mechanical engineer) h _____ o _____

5 in fashion at the moment (Fashion designer)
h _____

6 choosing good ideas and not choosing bad ideas (Ecology advisor) s _____ and r _____ ideas.

VOCABULARY personal qualities

4 Underline the correct alternatives to complete the sentences.

1 Should I go by bus or train? Oh, I wish I wasn't so *indecisive / ambitious*!

2 Shaun's so *competitive / lazy*. I asked him to finish this report a week ago and he hasn't even started it yet.

3 Winning isn't everything, you know. You don't always have to be so *lazy / competitive*.

4 In my job I need to be able to *be a good leader / think outside the box*. The problems we have need creative solutions.

5 I don't think I could start my own business. Security is important to me as I'm not a very good *communicator / risk taker*.

6 Paula's always been *competitive / ambitious*. I remember when she was ten years old and she wanted to be a lawyer!

5A Underline the stressed syllables in the words/ phrases.

1 hard-working

2 ambitious

3 a good communicator

4 competitive

5 indecisive

6 motivated

B ▶ R1.3 **Listen and check. Practise saying the words.**

VOCABULARY strong adjectives

6 Use the clues to complete the crossword.

Across

2 very good

5 very interesting

6 very cold

8 very tired

11 very angry

12 very hot

Down

1 very pretty

3 very difficult

4 very small

7 very big

9 very bad

10 very tasty

WRITING

1A **Read the email below. Why is Aldo writing to his friend?**

To:

Deer Stefano

How you are? Yesterday we have a really good English class. We all wrote short articles for a class newspaper, and at the end of the lesson the teacher was posting them on the internet! Are you still studying english?

Aldo

B **Correct the five mistakes in the email.**

2 **Write your own answer to the exam question.**

Part 2

Question 6

You recently had a really good English class on the course you're studying.

Write a short email to your friend Stefano, telling him about the class. In your email, you should

• Ask how he is.

• Say why you enjoyed the class.

• Ask him if he is still studying English.

Write **35–45 words** on your answer sheet.

VOCABULARY *-ing/-ed* adjectives

1A Underline the correct alternative.

1 In three days we cycled 250 km. It was really *exhausted / exhausting*.

2 Everyone is very *worried / worrying* about losing their jobs.

3 I got stuck talking to a really *bored / boring* man.

4 I was *annoyed / annoying* because the class was cancelled again.

5 The car was travelling at a *frightened / frightening* speed.

6 I felt *embarrassed / embarrassing* about how untidy the house was.

7 He was totally *confused / confusing* by the tax form.

8 I'm going to have a nice, *relaxed / relaxing* bath.

9 I'm not really *satisfied / satisfying* with the way he cut my hair.

10 We were *shocked / shocking* when we saw the bill.

B Find adjectives in Exercise 1A to match definitions 1–8.

1 not interesting _____

2 angry or irritated _____

3 very tiring _____

4 content, pleased _____

5 unclear or difficult to understand _____

6 uncomfortable and worried _____

7 upsetting and surprising _____

8 calming, helping you to rest _____

READING

2A You are going to read an article about why people get angry, and what happens. Before you read, number the events in the box according to categories 1–3 below.

1 Reasons   2 Consequences   3 Solutions

> You start to shout. *2*
> You're irritated with someone. *1*
> You throw things around. __
> You do physical exercise. *3*
> You're frustrated about something. __
> You feel tense. __
> You try meditation. __
> People criticise you. __
> You distance yourself from the situation. __

B Read the article and check.

Stressed out?
Take control.

We all know how it feels to get angry. Sometimes anger is mild, when you're just irritated with someone. But at other times anger can be more extreme, with explosive rages. You start to shout and throw things around. You lose control. Your blood pressure increases, your heart races, and you can't think about anything else. But what exactly *is* anger?

Anger is a normal response to a situation where you feel you are being attacked, treated unfairly, let down by others, hurt or rejected. Anger can help you to defend yourself, deal with the problem, and let others know how you feel. But anger can also cause problems. If you always lose control, people might start to avoid you. Friends and colleagues may be afraid of your temper, and leave you alone. Getting angry might make you feel better; giving you energy and making you feel like you're in control. But it might also leave you feeling hurt, and misunderstood. Also, getting angry doesn't usually solve the problem.

So, what can you do about your anger?

1 **Work out what makes you angry** – You need to understand what situations make you angry. Is it when people make comments about your work, or criticise you? Is it that you get angry when you're frustrated, and can't do the things you want? Do you get angry when you're tired? Understanding what makes you angry can help you to deal with the problem.

2 **Understand the signals** – Learn to identify the signs that you're getting angry. Do you start to shout and feel tense? Do you pace about the room? You need to recognise your own signs before you can change your behaviour.

3 **Take control of your mind and body** – Try taking a step back and distancing yourself from the situation, both physically and emotionally. Check your breathing, and take some deep breaths to slow you down, and calm your heartbeat. Ask yourself, 'Am I overreacting?', 'Am I listening to what people are saying?' Can you find a way to be assertive, rather than aggressive? Try to speak calmly, rather than shout. Try the 'Is it worth it?' test. Ask yourself, 'Will it really matter in one month, one year?' Do some physical exercise, like going for a run or a swim. Or try some meditation, listen to music, or do whatever helps to calm you down.

3 Complete the statements with information from the article.

1 When you get angry, your blood pressure _____ and your heart speeds up.

2 Being angry about something can help others to _____ how you feel.

3 Getting angry is not usually a good way to _____ problems.

4 It's a good idea to understand what _____ make you angry.

5 If you recognise the signs that you are getting angry, then you can start to _____ your behaviour.

6 When you are angry, you should try to _____ yourself from the situation.

7 Deep _____ will help to calm your heart beat.

8 Try to speak _____ rather than shout.

GRAMMAR zero and first conditionals

4A Complete the sentences with the correct form of the verb in brackets.

1 When Marianne _____ (find) a job, she _____ (leave) home.

2 Thomas _____ (get) a promotion if he _____ (work) harder.

3 If people _____ (exercise) regularly, they tend to _____ (live) longer.

4 If we _____ (leave) early enough, we _____ (miss) the traffic.

5 We _____ (start) the meeting as soon as everybody _____ (be) here.

6 If the music _____ (be) loud, people always _____ (dance).

7 When the weather _____ (be) good, we usually _____ (eat) outside.

8 If you _____ (use) sun cream, you _____ (not get) burned when we go sailing.

B For each sentence in Exercise 4A, decide if the situation is general (what normally happens – zero conditional), or specific (a possible situation in the future – first conditional).

1 _specific – first conditional_____
2 _____
3 _____
4 _____
5 _____
6 _____
7 _____
8 _____

5 Tick two correct sentences. Correct the wrong sentences.

1 If I find the book, I ʷⁱˡˡ send it to you.

2 If you will go to England, you will improve your English.

3 I'll tell him you called when I will see him.

4 If you give the plant too much water, it will die.

5 If they arrive early, will you to ask them to wait?

6 If you will come to the party tonight, will you bring a friend?

7 When I go to Krakow, I usually will see my aunt.

8 I always call my sister when there's a problem.

9 She will get angry if you will say that!

10 I go to the doctor tomorrow if I feel worse.

VOCABULARY PLUS multi-word verbs

6A Circle the correct option to complete the sentences.

1 Don't forget to _____ when you've finished.
a) click on　　b) take off　　c) log off

2 She's my best friend. We _____ really well.
a) get off　　b) get over　　c) get on

3 I used to love Indie music, but then I _____ it.
a) went off　　b) got on　　c) logged off

4 I _____ lots of different outfits, but I didn't like any of them.
a) tried off　　b) dressed up　　c) tried on

5 Can you _____? I can't read what it says at the bottom of the screen.
a) scroll on　　b) scroll over　　c) scroll down

6 You have to _____ your shoes when you go inside.
a) log off　　b) take off　　c) dress down

7 He's nearly forty. It's about time he _____.
a) settled down　　b) went off　　c) got on

8 I don't like going into bars on my own. I'm worried someone will try to _____.
a) get on with me　　b) chat me up　　c) settle down with me

B Complete the multi-word verbs with a suitable particle.

1 I'd love to settle _____ and have children.

2 Unfortunately, I don't get _____ with his mother very well.

3 A very good-looking young man started to chat me _____ in the nightclub.

4 I think he went _____ me when he met my family!

5 Why don't you try _____ this shirt? I think it will really suit you.

6 Scroll _____ to the top of the page to find our contact details.

7 Do you mind if I take _____ my jacket? It's boiling in here.

8 Sorry, I didn't realise you needed the computer. I've just logged _____.

VOCABULARY verb-noun collocations

1 Complete the sentences with a verb from Box A and a noun from Box B.

A

| watch jump hold get raise do cut |

B

| sale queue money hair experiments programme seat |

1 The scientists in our lab _____ a lot of _____ to find cures for common illnesses.
2 Did you _____ that _____ about UFOs on TV last night?
3 If you don't get to the show early, you won't _____ a _____.
4 The shop manager decided to _____ a _____ of last year's products.
5 Excuse me, you can't _____ the _____. Lots of people are waiting.
6 I asked my sister to _____ my _____ because I couldn't afford the hairdresser.
7 We're trying to _____ _____ for Save the Animals. Our target is €10,000.

GRAMMAR second conditional

2 Rewrite the sentences using the second conditional.

1 Joe goes to bed at 2a.m. He feels tired all the time.
  If Joe _didn't go to bed at 2a.m. he wouldn't feel tired all the time._
2 She doesn't play for the team – she isn't fast enough.
  If she _____.
3 We can't drive to your house because we don't have a car.
  We _____.
4 They won't pass the exam because they don't study.
  They _____.
5 I have a supportive family. My life is so easy.
  My life _____.
6 I'd love to buy that house, but I don't have the money.
  If I _____.
7 I'm so lazy. I don't write to my friends.
  I _____ lazy.
8 You don't water your plants regularly. They look so dry!
  If you _____.
9 Tom and Dave never help in the house. Their mother doesn't ask them.
  They _____.
10 I work on Saturdays. I can't come to the barbecue.
  If I _____.

3 Put the verbs in brackets into the correct form. Use *would* or the past simple.

Henrik Lulu

Olly Brigitte

If you could choose any three things, what three things ¹_would make_ (make) your life better? We asked this question to the public.

Henrik, 25, from Sweden, said, 'If I really ²_____ (have) a chance to change three things, they ³_____ (be) the environment, poverty and peace. My priority? I ⁴_____ (introduce) new laws to save the planet.'

Lulu, 30, from Edinburgh, had different ideas. She said, 'My life couldn't be better, but if I ⁵_____ (have to) change something, I ⁶_____ (change) the colour of my curtains – they're a horrible grey!'

Olly, 16, from London, said, 'OK, if I ⁷_____ (be) able to change three things, first thing: I ⁸_____ (be) Prime Minister. Second thing: I ⁹_____ (make) rich people pay more tax. Third thing: I ¹⁰_____ (not let) people smoke cigarettes because they give you cancer.'

Brigitte, 19, from Germany, immediately said, 'More money! If I ¹¹_____ (be) richer, I ¹²_____ (not have) to work in this stupid shop! I could spend my days painting, which is my real dream!'

4A ▶ 6.1 Listen and write the sentences you hear. Write contractions as one word.

1 _____
  (9 words)
2 _____?
  (8 words)
3 _____
  (10 words)
4 _____
  (10 words)
5 _____?
  (9 words)
6 _____
  (8 words)

B Listen and repeat the sentences. Pay attention to the rhythm and the contractions.

LISTENING

5A ▶ 6.2 Listen to the introduction to a radio programme. What is the topic?

B Look at the picture. Which people do you think are 'potential victims'? Why?

C ▶ 6.3 Listen to the rest of the programme and check.

D Listen again and complete the notes.

> **POTENTIAL VICTIM?**
>
> 1 Woman with dog: <u>No</u>, because dogs are <u>unpredictable</u>.
>
> 2 Woman on mobile phone: _____, because she isn't _____.
>
> 3 Tourists looking at map: _____, because they are concentrating on the map, not _____.
>
> 4 Man leaving cashpoint: _____, because he didn't put the money _____.
>
> 5 Woman in mini-skirt: _____, because of her positive _____.
>
> 6 Big man in coat: _____, because he's looking at his feet and he doesn't know _____.
>
> 7 Couple leaving taxi: _____, because rule number one of the street is: if you have anything valuable, _____.

WRITING a letter of advice; qualifying what you say

6A Read the problem and choose the best summary.

a) Kathy doesn't want her friend to apply for a job because it is Kathy's 'dream job'.

b) Kathy's friend is angry because they both want to apply for the same job.

c) Kathy wants the same job as her friend, but she is worried their friendship will end if she gets it.

> Last week my colleague and best friend Mariela saw a job advertised in the paper. She told me it's her 'dream job' and she intends to apply for it. Unfortunately, it's also my dream job and I really want to apply. I have more experience than Mariela and would probably have a better chance of getting the job. But if I got it, it would ruin our friendship. Should I apply? And if I do, should I tell Mariela?
>
> *Kathy*

B Put the paragraphs in the correct order to make a letter of advice.

Paragraph 1: _____

Paragraph 2: _____

Paragraph 3: _____

Paragraph 4: _____

A How would you feel if you didn't apply, she did, she got the job, and you spent the rest of your career in the same job, bored and unhappy? Or how would you feel if, because of her getting this new job (which you *didn't* apply for), she lost daily contact with you, and your friendship broke up anyway? Wouldn't that be much worse than both of you applying and supporting each other?

B I know that close friendships can be ruined because one person becomes more successful than another. It happens all the time, and not only in Hollywood or on Wall Street. But this is no reason for you not to chase your dreams. Finally, here are a few questions for you.

C If she knows this, then that's the end of your problem. All you have to do is be honest with her and tell her that you want to apply. Then see what she says. If she is really angry, <u>perhaps</u> she isn't such a good friend. If I were you, I would also support *her* application as much as you can. Maybe offer to read through her CV and her application letter. If she gets an interview, give her a 'good luck' card and buy her a new pair of earrings to wear on the day. It's possible that neither of you will get the job, but tell her you'll be happy if either of you gets it.

D OK, so you work together and are best friends, too. This means that Mariela probably knows how you feel about your job and, in all likelihood, also knows your plans for your career. In all probability, she realises that this job is your dream job, too.

C Read paragraphs C and D again and underline six words/phrases for qualifying what you say. The first has been done for you.

D Read the problem. Write a letter of advice (180–200 words).

> In one month, an old friend of mine is getting married. He told me the date nearly a year ago. Unfortunately, I forgot this date and I have now booked a holiday with my new girlfriend on exactly the same day. I can't change the dates of the holiday because my girlfriend can only have this one week off. Her boss says she can't change the date. I really don't know what to do. Help!
>
> *Stefan*

VOCABULARY life events

1A Complete the sentences with the words in the box.

split lost pass won bought accident degree
offered place promoted engaged failed

1 Did you _____ all your exams?
2 Sam had an _____ at work and had to go to hospital.
3 My boyfriend gets on so well with my boss, that he even _____ him a job!
4 Are you going to apply for a _____ at university?
5 Liz and Tony have been _____ for years, but they still aren't married.
6 Tom _____ his job at the factory.
7 I _____ my driving test six times!
8 My parents _____ up when I was three.
9 She _____ an international dance competition.
10 Helen got _____ to manager.
11 He's got a _____ in physics.
12 Last year they _____ a house on the beach in Brazil.

B Match 1–6 with a)–f) to make phrases.

1 pass   a) an accident
2 get   b) your job
3 win   c) with a partner
4 have   d) a competition
5 lose   e) promoted
6 split up   f) exams

FUNCTION giving news

2A ▶ 6.4 Listen and match conversations 1–8 with situations A–H.

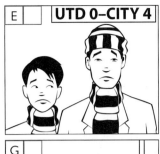

B Cross out one unnecessary word in each sentence. Then listen again and check.

1 Bad news, as I'm afraid.
2 I'm sorry for to have to tell you, but we lost the match.
3 I've got some good unfortunately news for you.
4 I'm afraid of I've got some bad news.
5 There's something who I've got to tell you.
6 You'll never guess what is happened.
7 It's unfortunately, we were burgled last night.
8 I've got something for to tell you.

LEARN TO respond to news

3 Complete the words in the responses.

1 A: I've just passed my motorbike test!
   B: C_____! That's f_____ news.
2 A: Maciej's had an accident.
   B: That's t_____! I'm really s_____ to hear that.
3 A: I've just won the race!
   B: W_____ d_____. That's g_____ n_____.
4 A: He was attacked outside his house.
   B: That's a_____! Do they know who did it?
5 A: Amazing! I've just found €100 in an old coat pocket.
   B: H_____ you? You l_____ thing!
6 A: Unfortunately, he didn't get a place at university.
   B: That's a sh_____. I'm sorry to hear that.
7 A: I just bumped into Samantha on my way here.
   B: You're j_____! What's she doing here?

VOCABULARY success

1 Rewrite the second sentence so that it means the same as the first. Use the words in capitals and one other word.

1 She was born with an ability to play the piano. NATURAL

She has a _natural talent_____ for playing the piano.

2 He needs to concentrate on what he is doing. FOCUS

He needs to _____ what he is doing.

3 She put a lot of effort into her maths project. HARD

She worked _____ her maths project.

4 I want to improve my Russian, so I do it a lot every day. GET

I want to _____ at Russian, so I practise it every day.

5 He's someone who is very successful. ACHIEVER

He's a _____.

6 It's important to think that you have the ability to do what you want. BELIEVE

It's important to _____ yourself.

READING

2A Write down three tips you would give to someone starting their own business.

B Read the text. Does it mention your ideas?

MAKING IT HAPPEN

Women around the world setting up their own businesses may face similar kinds of barriers, despite the different contexts in which they live and work. But in spite of the problems they face, many have success stories to tell. We asked successful entrepreneurs for their tips for success.

BRIDGING TWO CULTURES

When Jiao Lee moved to Ireland from China, she saw the opportunity to start a business which could help to build bridges between the two countries she loved. She started China Tours as a small travel business, setting up tours between the two countries. It was hard at first. She had to learn all about setting up a business in a foreign country, and she struggled with language barriers. But it was all worth it. China Tours now employs more than forty people, and has offices in Ireland and China. Jiao says, 'It has been such an exciting ride setting up China Tours, and I've enjoyed every minute. I wouldn't want to work for anyone else now.'

Success Tip – Always keep an eye open for an opportunity. And don't be put off when things seem hard in the beginning. Stick with your ideas, and soon you will find success.

SWEET SUCCESS

When Carmen Spataro set up Sweet Dreams, a mobile cupcake business in her home city of Washington, she used social media to help spread the word about her new business. Travelling around the city in her pink van, selling her freshly-baked cupcakes, Carmen sends her followers updates on Facebook and Twitter, telling them where and when they can find the van. The idea has been a fantastic success, with customers sending each other messages about the new, delicious range of cakes on offer. 'I'm in cupcake heaven,' tweets one of her happy customers. 'I wasn't very confident with the technology at first,' says Carmen. 'But I learned quickly, and now I love it. Using social media has helped to add to the sense of fun which we wanted to establish.'

Success Tip – Keep up-to-date with technology, and use it to promote your business.

HATS OFF

Melissa Faith had no idea that her designs for children's hats would lead her to success in business. She started by making a few hats to sell at a market. The hats were so popular that they sold out almost immediately. 'It was amazing. People were coming back for more, and I couldn't keep up with the demand,' she explains. Melissa set up a website to sell the hats online. Loopy Kids HatZone was an instant success, and Melissa now exports hats all over the world. 'One of the problems I've had,' says Melissa, 'is that I'm dyslexic, so it's hard for me to keep up with all the paperwork and emailing.' However, she thinks that her dyslexia also helps her to be more creative, and to have a fresh approach to problem-solving.

Success Tip – Be prepared for the unexpected. Some of the best things happen when you don't plan for them.

3 Read the text again and mark the statements true (T), false (F) or don't know (DK).

1 Jiao Lee had previous experience in the travel industry.

2 She found that language was a problem in the beginning.

3 Carmen was confident with new technology.

4 She sells her cakes around the city from a mobile van.

5 Melissa had always planned to start a company selling hats.

6 She finds it difficult to be creative at work.

4 Match words and phrases 1–6 from the text in Exercise 2 with definitions a)–f).

1 barriers

2 struggled with

3 (be) put off

4 spread the word

5 keep up with

6 a fresh approach to (something)

a) tell a lot of people about something

b) found it hard to do

c) make you not want to do something

d) a new way of looking at something

e) things that prevent you from doing something

f) do something as quickly as you need to

GRAMMAR present perfect simple versus continuous

5 Complete the conversations with the present perfect simple or continuous form of the verbs in brackets. If both are possible, use the continuous form.

1 A: Your hair looks nice.

 B: Thank you. I _____ (go) to a new hairdresser. It's much cheaper.

2 A: Do you know what time the package is being delivered? I _____ (wait) all morning.

 B: I'll just check for you.

3 A: You look exhausted.

 B: I know. I _____ (not sleep) well recently.

4 A: Are you OK?

 B: Not really. The baby _____ (cry) all day. I don't know what to do.

5 A: Have you two met before?

 B: Yes, we _____ (know) each other since university.

6 A: You look well. Have you been away?

 B: Yes, we _____ (ski) in the Alps.

7 A: How long _____ they _____ (live) in Australia?

 B: For about five years. They moved there to be closer to his family.

8 A: _____ you _____ (watch) that new detective series?

 B: Yes, it's brilliant. I _____ really _____ (enjoy) it.

6 Complete the email with the present perfect simple or continuous form of the verbs in the box. If both are possible, use the continuous form.

| not decide   find   not have   think   happen   look |
| work (x2)   study   stay |

Hi Nina,

How are you? Sorry I didn't write earlier, but so much ¹_____ in the last few weeks, I just ²_____ any spare time.

Luke and Shauna ³_____ with us. They were over from America, where Luke ⁴_____ on his new film. It was great to see them and catch up on their news. Apparently, they ⁵_____ about moving back to Asia, but they ⁶_____ for sure yet.

Things over here are good. We ⁷_____ for somewhere new to live. Our landlord wants us to leave, which is a shame. But we might ⁸_____ somewhere near the centre. It's a beautiful flat overlooking the river. And it's only five minutes' walk from the restaurant where I ⁹_____ at weekends. So, that would be fine. Jimmy ¹⁰_____ hard for his exams – they're next month, so keep your fingers crossed.

I'll write again soon. Take care of yourself.

Much love,

Kelly

VOCABULARY PLUS verb phrases with prepositions

7A Match verb phrases 1–8 with a preposition from the box.

| on   about   for   to   in |

1 depend _____

2 succeed _____

3 pay attention _____

4 rely _____

5 pick up _____

6 have a talent _____

7 think _____

8 have access _____

B Complete the sentences with a suitable phrase from Exercise 7A.

1 You don't have to decide straight away. Why don't you _____ it for a while?

2 This is important. Try to _____ what the man is saying.

3 Both solutions could be right. It _____ your point of view.

4 I'd like to _____ something you said earlier.

5 You obviously _____ music. You play very well for a beginner.

6 We _____ thousands of books in the university library.

7 I'm not sure if they'll _____ winning the election, but it's a good campaign.

8 I can't _____ you to be there on time, because you're usually late.

VOCABULARY ability

1A Circle the correct options to complete the text.

Princess Diana   John Lennon

Schoolteachers may be experts ¹_____ their subjects, but they aren't always right about their students. Some of the most brilliant people in British history were ²_____ at school and got terrible reports. In his school report, John Lennon was described as '³_____ – certainly on the road to failure'. Winston Churchill, future Prime Minister and probably Britain's most ⁴_____ politician, clearly had a lot ⁵_____ as a student, but his behaviour was so bad that his teacher wrote, 'I really don't know what to do.' Stephen Fry's teacher didn't realise Fry had an ⁶_____ English. A fine actor, comedian and writer, Fry was bottom of his class. Robert Graves, a ⁷_____ schoolboy writer who became one of Britain's greatest poets, left school with this message from his headmaster, 'Well, goodbye, Graves and remember that your best friend is the wastepaper basket.' One of Diana, Princess of Wales's teachers was correct in that Diana wasn't a ⁸_____ student, but the teacher also wrote, interestingly, that she 'must try to be less emotional … with others.'

1 a) at	b) for	c) in
2 a) useless	b) useful	c) gifted
3 a) skilful	b) hopeless	c) an expert
4 a) useless	b) hopeless	c) skilful
5 a) of ability	b) of skilful	c) of talented
6 a) expert in	b) aptitude for	c) aptitude to
7 a) gifted	b) expert	c) talent in
8 a) gifted at	b) expert	c) talented

B Look at the words and phrases in the box and answer the questions.

> expert   gifted   have a lot of ability   have an aptitude for
> hopeless   skilful   talented   useless

1 Which two are negative? _____

2 Which two are adjectives that mean you are naturally very good at something? _____

3 Which is an adjective that means you are good at something (you practised it)? _____

4 Which is a noun that describes someone who knows a lot about something? _____

5 Which two phrases mean you are naturally good at something? _____

GRAMMAR present and past ability

2 Complete the text with the words in the box.

> manage   managed   to   was   wasn't   remember
> couldn't   could

THE REAL RAIN MAN

RAIN MAN

In 1989, actor Dustin Hoffman won an Oscar for his role in *Rain Man*. While accepting it, he said, 'My special thanks to Kim Peek for making *Rain Man* a reality.' But who was Kim Peek? Peek was a man with a mental disability, who ¹_____ do many simple things such as dressing himself, but could remember enormous amounts of information. Peek didn't ²_____ to walk until he was four, but from the age of 16–20 months, he was able to ³_____ large amounts of information. As a teenager, he memorised whole books.

In later life, he ⁴_____ able to read a book in one hour and he remembered approximately 98.7 percent of everything he read. He ⁵_____ recite the content of around 12,000 books about history, geography, sports, and many other subjects. He was also able ⁶_____ remember thousands of different pieces of music, though he ⁷_____ able to play them all because of his physical disability.

Kim travelled with his father all over the US and Canada, speaking about how he ⁸_____ to live a full life even though he was disabled. He died in 2009.

3 Cross out the alternative which is not possible.

1 We *didn't manage to / couldn't / didn't manage* speak to John this morning.

2 I *can / am able to / do able to* speak five languages.

3 Ugo *managed to / could / was able to* finish the report yesterday.

4 Twenty years ago, I *was able to / can / could* run ten kilometres.

5 Few of us *can / are manage to / are able to* work without technology these days.

6 Women *didn't able to / weren't able to / couldn't* vote in Switzerland until 1971.

7 I *can't / 'm not able to / 'm not manage to* come to class tomorrow.

8 When we finished the work, we *were able to / could to / could* have a break.

9 *Are you able to / Do you can / Can you* use a computer?

10 *Did you manage / Were you able / Could you* to do your homework?

4A Read the pairs of sentences aloud. Tick the pairs that have the same number of syllables.

1. a) He's very gifted.
   b) She's really skilful.
2. a) He has an aptitude.
   b) I'm hopeless at this.
3. a) He thinks he's useless.
   b) She has a talent.
4. a) They say he's an expert.
   b) She has great ability.

B ▶ 7.1 Listen and shadow the sentences. Concentrate on the rhythm.

LISTENING

5A Pictures A–F show moments in the life of a genius. What do you think is happening in each picture?

A
seven months

B
NEW YORK TIMES
eighteen months

C
six years

D
nine years

E
DAILY NEWS
Fall of a genius

F
WILLIAM SIDIS
1898–1944

B ▶ 7.2 Listen to William Sidis's story and check your answers.

C Listen again and answer the questions.

1. Where were his parents from originally, and where did they move to?
2. What was William's first word?
3. How old was William when he could speak Russian, French, German and Hebrew?
4. What did he do at Harvard University when he was nine?
5. What did he do two years later?
6. Who 'followed him around'?
7. What two things did his sister say about his ability to learn languages?
8. For most of his adult life, what was Sidis 'running away' from?

WRITING a summary; making notes

6A Read the notes for a summary of the story in Exercise 5. Then read audio script 7.2 on page 86 and answer the questions.

1. Find two mistakes in the notes.
2. Find two examples of places where the writer copied exact words.

THE LIFE OF WILLIAM SIDIS

__Background__
- Lived in New York
- Father: psychologist at Harvard (Russian roots)

__Childhood__
- Born 1898
- 6 months: could speak. First word = 'moon'.
- 18 months: read newspaper
- 3 years: could type
- As a child, spoke Russian, French, German & Hebrew
- As a child, gave Maths lecture at Harvard Uni
- 11 yrs: attended Harvard Uni

__Adulthood__
- Wanted a quiet life
- Journalists followed him around and wrote articles about this young genius
- Didn't like fame
- 1944: died

__Myths__
- His sister = close 2 him & spoke about him after he died
- Knew all world's languages
- Took 1 week to learn a language
- IQ of 250–300

__Conclusion__
- Not all childhood geniuses will produce great things as adults
- Need to leave people alone to live their lives

B Which of the following are included in the notes? Tick the ones you find.

1. an abbreviation
2. a symbol for 'and'
3. a number to represent a word that sounds the same
4. a heading
5. a subheading
6. highlighted information

C Write a summary of the story (120–150 words) using the notes in Exercise 6A.

William Sidis is sometimes called 'the most intelligent man ever', but he isn't famous and his life was not full of great achievements. He was born ...

VOCABULARY qualifications

1 **What are the people in 1–10 talking about? Choose from the words in the box.**

> qualifications   a certificate   a driving licence
> an online course   face-to-face learning
> distance learning   an apprenticeship   a degree
> an MA   a PhD

1 I got my first degree in 1990 and always wanted to study the subject more deeply so I finally began one last year. _____

2 I much prefer it because I like to be with other students in the same room. That's how I learn best. _____

3 My brother did one in a fashion company. They were nice to him and they showed him the basics of the business. _____

4 I don't really have any because I left school when I was fourteen, but I worked hard and was a success. _____

5 Mine is framed and hanging on my wall! It's evidence that I took the one-month course, and it was necessary for me to get a job. _____

6 When I finish school I'd like to go to university to study history, so I hope I'll have one by the time I'm twenty-one or twenty-two. _____

7 You really need it to be a university professor. It's the hardest academic qualification and it involves original research, but it's necessary. _____

8 I did one once. It was interesting because you write lots of messages to the other students but you never meet them. I passed. _____

9 It's the way education has been going for a long time. It means people from isolated parts of the world can study at a good university even if they can't travel there. _____

10 It took me five attempts to get mine! The first time I tried, I crashed and the instructor just said, 'OK, come back next week!' _____

FUNCTION clarifying opinions

2A ▶ 7.3 **Listen to conversations 1–3. What is happening in each one? Circle the correct option to complete the sentences.**

Conversation 1

Parents are discussing a child's _____.

a) behaviour

b) TV-watching habits

c) school grades

Conversation 2

Colleagues are discussing _____.

a) another colleague's work

b) their qualifications

c) the best person for a job

Conversation 3

A presenter is asking a question about _____.

a) directing a play in a school theatre

b) the government's view of education

c) lack of money for the arts in schools

B **Listen again. Which sentence do you hear, a or b?**

Conversation 1

1 a) In my view, it's getting out of control.
   b) For my view, it's getting out of control.

2 a) By example, she watched TV for six hours yesterday.
   b) For example, she watched TV for six hours yesterday.

3 a) I'm saying that's a lot.
   b) I must say that's a lot.

4 a) That's not what I'm saying. She's always in front of a screen.
   b) That's what I was saying. She's always in front of a screen.

Conversation 2

5 a) For me, Elizabeth is the best.
   b) To me, Elizabeth is the best.

6 a) For once, she has the right qualifications.
   b) For one thing, she has the right qualifications.

7 a) She would, but now I've said that, she already has a good job.
   b) She would, but having said that, she already has a good job.

Conversation 3

8 a) Yes, the reason I say this is that funding has been cut for arts subjects.
   b) Yes, it's reasonable to say that funding has been cut for arts subjects.

9 a) Let me give you an example. A school I visited last month wanted to do a play in the little school theatre.
   b) Let's look at the example. A school I visited last month wanted to do a play in the little school theatre.

10 a) I am thinking we could solve a lot of the problems if the government recognised the arts.
   b) I do think we could solve a lot of the problems if the government recognised the arts.

VOCABULARY getting on

1 Put the pairs of words in the box into the correct places in sentences 1–10 below.

> ~~on my~~ ~~us over~~ ~~on well~~ disturb me
> ~~friends with~~ a nuisance ~~ask a~~
> ~~my own~~ to know to myself

on well
1 Joachim gets with his mother, but he's always arguing with his father.

2 Can I favour? Would you mind opening the window for me? *ask a*

3 Whenever they're arguing, I prefer to mind business. I don't get involved. *my own*

4 Hayley has invited for dinner at her house. Can we go? *us over*

5 Those neighbours are – they're always playing loud music and making a mess. *a nuisance*

6 She got her neighbours immediately. They were really friendly and chatty. *to know*

7 Please don't! I'm trying to do some work. *disturb me*

8 One thing that gets nerves is when the neighbours have noisy parties! *on my*

9 Xun hasn't made her neighbours yet, but she only moved in last week. *friends with*

10 I keep myself. I hate chatting about nothing – it's a waste of time. *to myself*

GRAMMAR articles and quantifiers

2 Add *a*, *an* or *the* where necessary.

1 Do you want *a* drink?

2 Have you received letter I sent you?

3 Dogs are wonderful pets.

4 Do you have pen I can borrow?

5 She went to Paris on Wednesday.

6 Is there airport in the city?

7 I'm going to Germany in morning.

8 We live by Pacific Ocean.

9 My brother is actor.

10 Nurses aren't paid enough.

11 He doesn't have children.

12 Did you see film I told you about?

13 I live in United States.

14 She's nicest woman I know.

15 Do you like apples?

3 Make sentences with one word or phrase from each section.

1 ~~We went there for a~~	a) of us love this	i) of friends in this community.
2 There are plenty	b) of good restaurants in the town,	ii) in Poland when I was younger.
3 I don't know	c) many cars in most	iii) I like the architecture.
4 All	d) ~~few days in~~	iv) ~~June last year.~~
5 If you have enough	e) lots	v) place because it's so friendly.
6 There are too	f) much about this city, but	vi) especially if you like French food.
7 I've got	g) time, go	vii) to the museum – it's great.
8 I spent a bit	h) of time	viii) big cities – I hate traffic!

1 *We went there for a few days in June last year.*

2 _____

3 _____

4 _____

5 _____

6 _____

7 _____

8 _____

4 Read the text. Which lines are correct? Which have an extra word?

In the past, a small English village called ~~the~~ Lanreath, in Cornwall,	1 *the*
had three pubs, two shops, and a post office. Now it doesn't have	2 ✓
but any of these. The post office, the last shop and the last pub	3 _____
were all of recently closed down. Now the council wants	4 _____
to close the primary school. The school has had excellent	5 _____
results and is very popular with children and parents. The	6 _____
problem is that the school doesn't have enough students, and	7 _____
the council says it costs too much to money to keep it open for	8 _____
only a small few children. The villagers decided to fight the	9 _____
council's ruling. The whole village packed up, including sheep and	10 _____
cows, and travelled a five hours to London. They went to a	11 _____
park and created a miniature Lanreath. They showed the more	12 _____
best of village life, playing traditional games, doing a traditional	13 _____
dance, and holding a cake sale. Some of all the teachers also taught	14 _____
a lesson for Lanreath Primary School pupils.	15 _____
The BBC made a TV programme about the story: *Power To The*	16 _____
People: The Invasion of Islington, presented by a Tim Samuels.	17 _____

LISTENING

5A ▶ **8.1 Listen to interviews with Elise and Marc about neighbours and answer the questions for each person.**

1 Who are their neighbours?

Elise: _____

Marc: _____

2 Why do they like the situation with their neighbours?

Elise: _____

Marc: _____

3 How often do they see their neighbours?

Elise: _____

Marc: _____

4 How long have the people lived there?

Elise: _____

Marc: _____

B Complete the summaries with one word in each space. Then listen again and check.

Elise says she has the ¹_____ neighbours. She sees them a lot because she works in the ²_____ business. Her extended family consists of ³_____ people. They eat together every ⁴_____. She thinks this situation is ⁵_____ in many countries. She has never asked her ⁶_____ if he likes living so close to her family.

Marc's nearest neighbours are two cows that live ⁷_____ miles away! Marc and his wife used to live in ⁸_____, but they didn't like the crowds, the noise and using public ⁹_____. They bought a ¹⁰_____ ten years ago. Marc and his wife work ¹¹_____. Marc says the interviewer is the ¹²_____ person they've seen this year!

C Circle the best alternative way of saying these extracts from the interviews.

1 if I need a babysitter for my kids …

a) if I need someone to look after my children …

b) if my children need to sit still …

2 You never get fed up with the family?

a) You never eat with the family?

b) You never get tired of the family?

3 We always wanted to live side by side.

a) We always wanted to live in the same town.

b) We always wanted to live next to each other.

4 We really are completely isolated.

a) We really like to be close to nature.

b) There are no other people near us.

5 It's not a functioning farm.

a) The farm doesn't make much money.

b) The place isn't actually used as a farm.

6 We're a bit antisocial.

a) We don't like mixing with other people.

b) We don't like working for big companies.

VOCABULARY PLUS compound nouns

6A Match the words in box A with the words in box B to make compound nouns.

A

~~traffic~~ high housing sports industrial car super language shopping one-way terraced outdoor gift primary

B

houses ~~lights~~ shop school (×2) centre (×2) street (×2) park market (×2) estate (×2)

1 _traffic lights_____   8 _____

2 _____   9 _____

3 _____   10 _____

4 _____   11 _____

5 _____   12 _____

6 _____   13 _____

7 _____   14 _____

B ▶ **8.2 Listen and check. Then listen and repeat. Concentrate on the stress patterns.**

7 Complete the sentences with a compound noun from Exercise 6A.

1 My best friend lives in a house on a big new _____ in Bristol.

2 I'm studying English for six weeks in a _____ in Bath.

3 My son will be old enough to go to _____ next year.

4 You can't drive your car down there – it's a _____!

5 I use the gym in the _____.

6 We live in a row of small _____ in Barton Road.

7 Drive along the High Street and turn left at the _____.

8 We left the car in the _____ while we went shopping.

9 I buy my food in the _____ because it's more convenient than going to lots of small shops.

10 There's a _____ in the art gallery where you can buy postcards of some of the paintings.

11 Our town has an _____ every Thursday behind the bus station – I buy all my vegetables there.

12 Ben's new company has an office on an _____ just outside Coventry.

13 There's an internet café in the _____, between the cinema and the book shop.

14 My daughter and her friends spend most Saturdays in the _____, although I don't think they buy much!

VOCABULARY the internet

1 Read the situations and write the type of website or web page a)–l) the speakers need.

1 'I want to write my day-to-day thoughts and publish them on the internet.' _Blog_

2 'I need my own website that tells people who I am and what I do.' _____

3 'I just need to find some information very quickly.' _____

4 'I'm looking for love.' _____

5 'I want to put my photos on the net so my friends and family can see them.' _____

6 'I need some information about a big company that I might work for.' _____

7 'I want to find out what's going on in the world.' _____

8 'I want to make new friends and find out what my old friends are doing.' _____

9 'I want to find out the best places to go for a holiday.' _____

10 'I'd like to read short reviews of films, restaurants, etc., to see which are the best.' _____

11 'I'd like to see this film clip that my friend uploaded onto the net.' _____

12 'I want to write an online encyclopedia that everyone can contribute to.' _____

a) blog
b) photo sharing site
c) ratings site
d) video sharing site
e) social networking site
f) search engine
g) wiki
h) travel site
i) news site
j) personal homepage
k) dating site
l) corporate website

GRAMMAR relative clauses

2 Match each pair of sentences with the correct explanation, a) or b).

1 The children, who love films, went to the cinema. _b_

2 The children who love films went to the cinema. _a_

   a) Only some of the children went to the cinema.

   b) All of the children went to the cinema.

3 Her brother, who is a musician, lives in New York.

4 Her brother who is a musician lives in New York.

   a) She has one brother. He lives in New York.

   b) She has more than one brother. One of them lives in New York.

5 My house, which is by the beach, has a great view.

6 My house which is by the beach has a great view.

   a) I have more than one house.

   b) I have only one house.

7 They went to the only school in the village, which had good teachers.

8 They went to the only school in the village which had good teachers.

   a) There was more than one school in the village, but only one had good teachers.

   b) There was only one school in the village.

3 Complete the quotations of definitions with the words in the box.

> thing that   who behaves   clothing that   which has
> person who   place where   name that   a place

1 'A jumper is an item of _____ _____ is worn by a child when his or her mother is cold.'

2 'A dictionary is the only _____ _____ success comes before work.'

3 'A coward is a _____ _____, when faced with danger, thinks with his feet.'

4 'Experience is the _____ _____ men give to their mistakes.'

5 'A cigarette is a bit of tobacco in paper _____ _____ fire at one end and an idiot at the other.'

6 'An advertisement is a _____ _____ persuades you to spend money you don't have on things you don't need.'

7 'A babysitter is a teenager _____ _____ like an adult so adults can behave like teenagers.'

8 'A bank is _____ _____ where you keep the government's money in your name.'

4 ▶ 8.3 Listen for the pauses where there are commas. Tick the sentence you hear.

1 a) The website which we built is too slow.

   b) The website, which we built, is too slow.

2 a) Those people who are always working don't enjoy life.

   b) Those people, who are always working, don't enjoy life.

3 a) The ratings site which I check every day is growing fast.

   b) The ratings site, which I check every day, is growing fast.

4 a) Those students who do online courses love studying.

   b) Those students, who do online courses, love studying.

5 a) Near my flat where you're staying there's a supermarket.

   b) Near my flat, where you're staying, there's a supermarket.

COUCHSURFERS – THE COMMUNITY THAT WON'T LIE DOWN

1 One April, Casey Fenton bought a cheap ticket from the United States to Iceland. He planned to stay for a long weekend. There was just one problem: he had nowhere to sleep. He didn't want to stay in a hotel, so he emailed 1,500
5 students in Reykjavik, Iceland's capital, asking if he could sleep on someone's couch. Amazingly, he had dozens of replies. After a wonderful weekend with his new friends, he realised that there was a fantastic opportunity for cultural exchange through 'CouchSurfing'. He decided to start a website to make
10 CouchSurfing possible.

2 www.CouchSurfing.org was launched in 2003. Its mission statement said that the idea was to 'create inspiring experiences', with a focus on cross-cultural sharing. Since then, tens of thousands of people have stayed on strangers' couches
15 in 230 countries, had the chance to see places through the eyes of a local person, and made wonderful friendships.

3 So how does it work? If you want to be a host, you write your profile on the website, saying where you live, your age, job and hobbies. If you want somewhere to stay, you type the
20 name of the city. A list of people appears. You look at their profiles and photos and choose a person. Then you contact them to see if they are free. In many cases, they meet you for a coffee first before allowing you into their home. Then, if you seem normal and friendly, they let you stay on their couch.

25 **4** The idea of CouchSurfing seems dangerous. Would you really want to stay with a stranger? The website has several ways to protect its users. Before choosing a person to stay with, you can read what other CouchSurfers say about them. There is also a system of 'vouching'. This means that other people
30 promise that your host has a good character. It is impossible to make CouchSurfing completely safe, but there have been no horror stories so far.

5 And the benefits? Here's what the CouchSurfers say on the website. 'It offers me a window to see the beautiful planet in
35 the best way.' (Liu, China); 'What a great way to travel and meet people!' (Cecilia, Paraguay); 'CouchSurfing changed my life. Meeting people all around the world, discovering
40 their way of life, their culture, getting new friends, … everything becomes possible with CouchSurfing.'
45 (Kim, Malaysia)

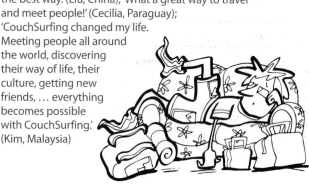

READING

5A Look at the picture and the title of the text. What do you think a *CouchSurfer* is?

B Read the text and answer the questions.
1 What problem did Casey Fenton have concerning his trip to Iceland? _____
2 Who did Fenton write to, and what happened next?
_____
3 What does the website say CouchSurfing focuses on?
_____
4 What are the four stages for finding someone to stay with?
_____
5 How does the website try to make CouchSurfing safe?
_____

C Match words 1–5 from the text with definitions a)–e).
1 a dozen (paragraph 1)
2 to launch (paragraph 2)
3 a mission statement (paragraph 2)
4 inspiring (paragraph 2)
5 a profile (paragraph 3)

a) so good or successful that it makes people want to do something
b) a text that explains the purpose of an organisation
c) to start something big or important or make a new product available
d) a short description that gives the main details of what someone is like
e) twelve

WRITING a website review; using complex sentences

6A Complete gaps 1–4 in paragraphs A–D with the words in the box.

like	feature	best	would

A ☐ Another ¹_____ I like is the book reviews. Regular users of the website often write these. Even though the writers aren't professionals, some of the reviews are excellent, and they give you a good idea of what's in the book.

B ☐ One website I really ²_____ is amazon.com. It is a website for buying books. One reason I'd recommend it is because you can buy used books. This means you can get really good books for half the price they cost in the shops.

C ☐ Finally, I ³_____ recommend this website to anybody who is interested in books. Even if you don't buy anything, it is fun to surf the site, and a great source of information about books of all types.

D ☐ The ⁴_____ thing about Amazon, though, is the fact that it is so easy to use, and you can trust it. I have ordered dozens of books through Amazon, and the books have always arrived quickly and in good condition.

B Put the paragraphs of the website review in the correct order.

C Write a website review (120–150 words).

that's ___ posibilities   *it's <u>fine</u>*
it's not <u>necessary</u>

VOCABULARY welcoming

1A Make phrases for welcoming with the words in the boxes. Then complete the conversations.

> at mess make the yourself help home excuse yourself

1 A: Can I try one of these cakes?
   B: Yes, _help yourself_ .
2 A: Come in. _excuse the mess_ .
   B: It looks very tidy to me. You should see my place!
3 A: Welcome! _make yourself at home_
   B: Thanks. What a nice room.

> my seat up guest put a be your have feet

4 A: May I use your phone, please?
   B: _Be my guest_ .
5 A: Good morning. I'm here to see Mr Drucker.
   B: I'll tell him you're here. _have a seat_ .
6 A: You must be exhausted. _put your feet up_
   B: Thank you. Yes, it was a really tiring day.

B Match pictures A–F with the conversations in Exercise 1A.

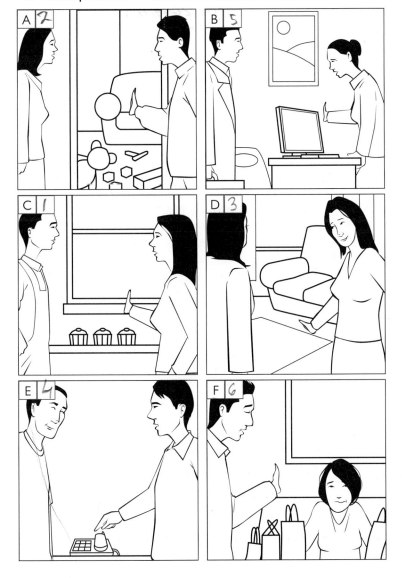

A 2 B 5
C 1 D 3
E 4 F 6

FUNCTION being a good guest

2 Tick the correct sentences.

1 a) Is it OK if I arrive half an hour late?
   b) Is it OK if I am arrive half an hour late?
2 a) What we should do if we get lost?
   b) What should we do if we get lost?
3 a) Do I need to bring a present?
   b) Do I need bring a present?
4 a) Was I did something wrong?
   b) Did I do something wrong?
5 a) Is this a bad time? I come back later.
   b) Is this a bad time? I can come back later.
6 a) If I'm you, I'd apologise.
   b) If I were you, I'd apologise.
7 a) Sorry about that. I didn't know.
   b) Sorry for that. I didn't know.
8 a) My apologise. I didn't realise.
   b) My apologies. I didn't realise.
9 a) No, it's not the necessary.
   b) No, it's not necessary.
10 a) Don't worry. It's fine.
   b) You don't worry. It's fine.

LEARN TO accept apologies

3 Underline the correct alternative.

1 A: I'm really sorry. I broke this cup.
   B: *It's no problem.* / *It's not the problem.*
2 A: Sorry, I didn't phone you before coming. I can see you're busy.
   B: *Not at all.* / *Not all.* I'll be finished in just a minute.
3 A: My apologies. I didn't realise you were working.
   B: *That's too right.* / *That's all right.* I'm not doing anything important.
4 A: Sorry, did I do something wrong? I didn't know I had to shake everyone's hand.
   B: *It's very fine.* / *It's fine.* I don't think anyone noticed.
5 A: I forgot to send you the notes from the last meeting. Sorry about that.
   B: *Nothing.* / *It's nothing.* Don't worry about it.
6 A: I'm sorry. I didn't bring anything for the children.
   B: *You really don't have to.* / *You really haven't to.* They're just happy to see you.
7 A: I'm sorry. I didn't realise I had to print the tickets out.
   B: Don't worry. *We can sort it out.* / *We can sort out it.*

47

VOCABULARY history

1A Find nouns in the word square that match meanings 1–10.

1 A complete change either in the way people think, or in a country's political system.

2 The time when an important change begins to happen. (two words)

3 An event that changes a situation, or the process of growing or changing.

4 When something increases and affects more people.

5 Any change, discovery or invention that makes the world better.

6 A group of people that works to achieve an aim.

7 A machine, tool, system, etc., made for the first time.

8 The basic idea or principle behind something.

9 Something that someone learns about when it was not known before.

10 Change that improves something.

T	U	R	N	I	N	G	P	O	I	N	T
D	A	E	B	P	R	O	G	R	E	S	S
E	C	V	D	E	R	I	O	M	E	I	P
V	F	O	U	N	D	A	T	I	O	N	T
E	E	L	U	F	C	S	S	G	J	V	E
L	S	U	A	V	U	A	P	L	I	E	D
O	W	T	V	A	P	D	R	A	G	N	E
P	D	I	S	C	O	V	E	R	Y	T	X
M	E	O	R	E	K	A	A	E	I	I	H
E	D	N	I	U	F	N	D	O	E	O	O
N	C	I	N	T	I	C	F	R	S	N	E
T	M	O	V	E	M	E	N	T	C	L	F

B Underline the correct alternative.

1 History books say Alexander Fleming was responsible for the *foundation / discovery* of penicillin.

2 The internet has helped the *turning point / spread* of their ideas.

3 After finishing the research, we'll begin work on the *development / advance* of the product.

4 James is making a lot of *progress / discovery* in all his school subjects.

5 There have been amazing *advances / spreads* in technology in the last few years.

6 She was a member of the early feminist *progress / movement*.

7 Only a *foundation / revolution* will destroy this government.

8 I think the wheel is the greatest *invention / movement* in history.

GRAMMAR third conditional

2 Circle the correct option to complete the sentences.

1 They would have said something if we _____ the rules.

   a) were broken   b) would have broken   c) had broken

2 If _____ you, I would have said 'hello'.

   a) I would see   b) I have seen   c) I'd seen

3 He _____ if the ambulance hadn't come.

   a) would died   b) would have died   c) would have been died

4 If I'd known a ticket cost €100, I _____.

   a) wouldn't have come   b) would have came
   c) not would have come

5 She would have arrived at the airport on the wrong day if I _____ her.

   a) haven't phoned   b) hadn't phoned   c) wouldn't phone

6 If the government hadn't lent the company a million pounds, it _____.

   a) had closed   b) would close   c) would have closed

7 They would have had a picnic if it _____.

   a) hadn't rained   b) had rained not   c) had been rained

8 If he hadn't had such a great coach, John wouldn't _____ a great squash player.

   a) have become   b) to become   c) had become

3 Write a sentence with *if* for situations 1–8.

1 Early travellers invented boats. Cross-continental travel became possible.

   If early travellers hadn't invented boats, cross-continental travel wouldn't have become possible.

2 Archduke Ferdinand was assassinated. World War I started.

   _____

3 People from Sumer needed permanent records. They invented writing. _____

4 World War II happened. The United Nations was formed in 1945.

   _____

5 William the Conqueror invaded England in 1066. The English language changed. _____

6 Charles Darwin travelled to South America. He developed the theory of evolution. _____

7 Sailors on the *Titanic* didn't see the iceberg and 1,595 people died.

   _____

8 Captain James Cook sailed to Australia. It became a British colony.

   _____

4A ▶ 9.1 Listen and add two missing contractions to each sentence.

1 If I'd known you were coming, I would've waited.

2 If I waited, I been late.

3 If I been late, I missed the show.

4 If I missed the show, I wasted my money.

5 If I wasted my money, I been angry.

B Listen again and repeat the sentences. Pay attention to the pronunciation of *had* and *would have*.

LISTENING

5A ▶ 9.2 Look at 1–5 below and think about the question: Where and when were these things first used? Listen and complete the answers.

Invention	Where?	When?
1 toothpaste	_Egypt_	_1,600_ years ago
2 biological weapons	_____	_____ years ago
3 football	_____	_____ years ago
4 central heating	_____	_____ years ago
5 umbrella	_____	_____ years ago

B What is the connection between the inventions in Exercise 5A and pictures A–E below? Listen again and check.

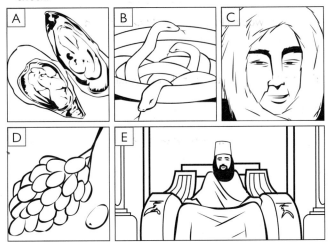

C Read these extracts from the listening in Exercise 5A and find words to match definitions a)–e) below.

1 Was it the same as modern toothpaste? Definitely not. Ancient Greek toothpaste used ingredients like crushed bones and oyster shells.

2 Some generals would even throw dead bodies at the enemy or into the enemy's river.

3 In the 18th century, one way American Indians were killed was through using infected blankets given to them by the Europeans who were colonising America.

4 A rich banker installed it in his house so that he could grow grapes in England's cold weather!

5 Interestingly, it seems that only kings or very important people had umbrellas in these sculptures. So they were a symbol of high social class.

a) the people that your country is fighting against in a war
_____

b) something that represents a special quality or situation
_____

c) placed somewhere and connected ready to be used
_____

d) containing dangerous bacteria which spread disease
_____

e) pressed very hard so it is broken into extremely small pieces _____

WRITING a short essay; structuring paragraphs

6A Read the introduction to a short essay and choose the best title.

a) Sumerian Culture

b) The History of Writing

c) Business throughout History

In 3200 BC, Sumerians invented writing. For these people, who were located in the area we now call Iraq, there was nothing poetic about it. They didn't write to fire the imagination or to tell beautiful stories. Instead, they wrote because it was a way to keep business records. While previous generations had relied on their memory for the details of deals and the things they owned, the new generation decided to make permanent records. As a result, early 'writing' looks like a very simple type of drawing.

B Read the introduction again and:

1 Circle the topic sentence.

2 Underline a linking word (one has already been underlined).

3 Underline one linking expression (three words).

C Read the notes and finish the essay (120–150 words).

> **Symbols** ------------------------------------
>
> At first = pictures of animals, body parts, trees, birds, everyday tools
> Then later symbols = for ideas
> Then later symbols = for sounds
> Could be read left to right or right to left – picture of a head (human or animal) at beginning of line showed readers the direction to read in
>
> **Writing** ------------------------------------
>
> On walls of temples and on papyrus (early paper)
> 99% of people = illiterate – only religious leaders/ scholars read
> Start of writing = start of 'history' – ideas and other info passed down through time

GRAMMAR active versus passive

1A Read the text and correct five mistakes with passives.

WHERE I GREW UP

I grew up in a big old house with a big old family. The house had four floors, one floor for each generation.

The bottom floor was where my maternal grandparents lived. They were give the bottom floor so that they didn't have to climb any steps – that's the story I was told, anyway. But in reality, I think it's because my grandmother escaped the house at 4.00a.m. every morning to go for walks and we didn't want to been woken up.

Mum and Dad's room was on the second floor, and us children were be put on the third floor, out of the way.

At the very top of the steps there was an attic where my great-grandfather was hidden away, out of sight. He was as mad as a box of frogs. He used to play operas on an ancient gramophone and sing Puccini at the top of his voice. When he died, I was given that gramophone and all his records. Amazingly, forty years later, it still works.

The house has be rebuilt many times since those days and the garden, where we used to climb trees and run wild, has been covered with concrete. I read recently that the house will to be sold again. It won't be bought by me, though. My memories are enough.

B Read the text again and underline five correct examples of the passive.

2A Rewrite sentences 1–8 using passives. Do not say who did the action.

1 People give the Institute almost a million euros a year.
   The Institute is given almost a million euros a year.

2 One day they will discover a cure for cancer.
   _____

3 Someone stole the files last year.
   _____

4 They took these famous photos at the end of the war.
   _____

5 Nobody has told the President about the plan.
   _____

6 The searchers have found the missing people.
   _____

7 They cancelled all flights going out of Paris.
   _____

8 Someone cleans the paintings once a year.
   _____

B ▶ 9.3 Listen and check. What happens to the pronunciation of the auxiliary verbs *are*, *were*, *has*(n't) *been* and *have been*? Listen again and repeat.

VOCABULARY periods of time

3 Replace the underlined phrases with the phrases in the box.

| the generation   over a quarter-century   millennium |
| just over a century ago   era   half a century |
| over seven decades   just over a fortnight |

1 The 18th century was a great period of time for music. *era*

2 Nelson Mandela spent twenty-seven years in prison. *over a quarter century*

3 In 1909, Geronimo, the Native American leader, died. *just over a century ago*

4 We are in the first stage of a new thousand-year cycle. *millennium*

5 Louis XIV ruled France for seventy-two years. *over seven decades*

6 A world full of technology is normal for those people born in the 1990s. *the generation*

7 Jack Kerouac wrote *On the Road*, a classic novel about 1960s freedom, in about eighteen days. *just over fortnight*

8 Fidel Castro led Cuba for nearly fifty years. *half a century*

VOCABULARY PLUS collocations with *come*, *give*, *have* and *make*

4A Complete phrases 1–16 with *come*, *give*, *have* or *make*. Use each verb four times.

1 _____ a good time   9 _____ directions
2 _____ progress   10 _____ trouble
3 _____ a talk   11 _____ back
4 _____ naturally   12 _____ a mess
5 _____ a break   13 _____ me a call
6 _____ a dream   14 _____ a profit
7 _____ first   15 _____ by car
8 _____ instructions   16 _____ a decision

B Complete 1–5 using two collocations with the same verb. Make sure you use the correct tense.

1 I'm _____ _____ with this report. It's really difficult to write. I think I'll _____ a _____ and finish it later.

2 In 1998, the company _____ a _____ to close its European offices. After two years, it _____ a _____ of over $1,000,000.

3 Can you _____ me a _____ when you get this message? I need you to _____ me _____ to your house. I'm completely lost!

4 Drawing didn't _____ _____ to me. It took me years to become good at it, but last year I _____ _____ in an art competition.

5 The boss is going to _____ a _____ to the employees next week. He wants to _____ _____ on how to use the new software.

READING

5A Look at the table. What information do you think goes in gaps 1–6? Read the text below and check your ideas.

Four Generations			
Name:	Born:	Origin of name:	Known for:
The Lost Generation	1_____	Gertrude Stein, a writer, named them.	Millions died in World War I (1914–1918)
Baby Boomers	2_____	The 'baby boom' (high birth rates) after World War II	Being successful (in USA)
Generation X	1960s and 1970s	3_____	4_____
Millennials (Generation Y)	5_____	A book: *Millennials Rising: The Next Great Generation*	6_____

Generations and Generalisations

'Young people these days! They contradict their parents, chatter in the company of guests, eat their food too quickly, and are rude to their teachers!' Who said this? Was it a tired, stressed twenty-first century parent? No. These words were said by
5 Socrates in Athens two and a half thousand years ago. It seems that every generation complains about the next generation. But now there's another element: in the twentieth century we began naming each generation.

First came The Lost Generation (born around 1880–1895). This
10 was the generation which fought in World War I (1914–1918), in which over fifteen million people were killed. American writer Gertrude Stein is famous for naming it The Lost Generation, but actually it was her French car mechanic (she lived in Paris) who first used the expression. He complained
15 that the young mechanics who worked for him were useless at their jobs, and he described them as *une génération perdue* – a lost generation! Stein borrowed the expression.

After the Second World War, there was the Boomer Generation, or the Baby Boomers. This was the generation born between
20 1945 and about 1960, a period when birth rates increased throughout the world. In the USA, the Baby Boomers are seen as the great, successful generation which made their country rich.

The next generation was called Generation X. The name was
25 popularised by Canadian writer Douglas Coupland in his 1991 novel, *Generation X: Tales for an Accelerated Culture*. People from Generation X – born in the 1960s and 1970s – rebelled against their parents' values. They didn't want to work for the same company their whole life, and they spent their time
30 listening to 'grunge' music or playing video games.

The next generation has two names: Generation Y and the Millennials. Generation Y was first described in detail in 2000, when Neil Howe and William Strauss wrote *Millennials Rising: The Next Great Generation*. Generation Y – people
35 who were born in the 1980s and 1990s – is known for its love of technology: iPods, mobile phones, digital cameras, digital everything. They are amazing networkers, constantly online, and great multi-taskers. They can read (web pages), listen (to music on their iPods) and write (Instant Messages) all at the
40 same time.

But are these generational names correct? Can we really describe a whole generation as having similar habits and qualities? How similar are the lives of teenagers in New York to the lives of teenagers in rural China or Peru? In 2010, only
45 a quarter of the world's population used the internet. Only a small percentage of those had iPods. So can we say this generation loves technology?

Are we really talking about generations or generalisations?

B Complete the questions.

1 Q: What did _____?

  A: 'Young people these days! They contradict their parents, chatter in the company of guests, eat their food too quickly, and are rude to their teachers!'

2 Q: When did we _____?

  A: In the twentieth century.

3 Q: How many _____?

  A: Over fifteen million.

4 Q: What happened _____?

  A: Birth rates increased throughout the world.

5 Q: Who _____?

  A: Neil Howe and William Strauss.

6 Q: How many _____?

  A: Twenty-five percent of the world's population.

C Match words 1–6 with definitions a)–f).

1 contradict (line 1)

2 chatter (line 1)

3 birth rate (line 20)

4 popularise (line 25)

5 networkers (line 37)

6 multi-taskers (line 38)

a) make something known and liked by many people

b) people who spend a lot of time communicating and sharing information with others

c) the number of children born in a particular year/place

d) talk quickly in a friendly way about unimportant things

e) disagree, saying that the opposite is true

f) people who can do lots of things at the same time

HISTORY NOW MAGAZINE — ASKS 'WHO DO YOU ADMIRE?'

'I admire the explorer Ranulph Fiennes. He walked to both the South and North Poles, crossed Antarctica on foot, and climbed Mount Everest when he was sixty-five. He lost fingers and toes and still kept exploring. You have to be ¹b__ _v__ to do that. He's very ²ch__ __ __ m__ __ __ too: he was on a shortlist to play James Bond, but Roger Moore got the part instead! Fiennes's life has been ³ex__ __ __ __ __ y; one of his greatest achievements is that he has raised over 5 million pounds for charity.'

(Mark, climber)

'I admire Wangari Maathai. She's a Kenyan activist who founded The Green Belt Movement, an organisation that protects the environment. She has also been very ⁴i__f__ __ __ __ __ __ l in the women's rights movement. She was the first African woman to win the Nobel Peace Prize, which, for women all over the world, is absolutely ⁵i__ __p__ __ __ __ __ __ n__ __. It shows that women in poor countries can make a difference.'

(Umunyana, teacher)

'I love Ang Lee's films. I think he's the most ⁶cr__ __ __ __ __ __ director working today. I've watched *Crouching Tiger, Hidden Dragon* seven times. I love the shots of landscapes and people flying through the air. It just seems so ⁷o__ __ __ __ __ __ l compared to most Hollywood films. His films are always really ⁸i__ __ __ __ __ __ __ v__ too – like *Brokeback Mountain*. Who could imagine a story about gay cowboys becoming a classic?'

(Hae Jin, film student)

VOCABULARY   describing people

1 Read the text and complete words 1–8.

FUNCTION   expressing uncertainty

2 Circle the correct option to complete the conversations.

1 **A:** When were the first Olympic Games?
   B: a) I have no idea.
      b) I haven't got an idea.

2 **A:** Do you know who invented the machine gun?
   B: a) I haven't the clue.
      b) I haven't a clue.

3 **A:** What's the world's biggest country?
   B: a) I'm not a hundred percent certain, and it might be Russia.
      b) I'm not a hundred percent certain, but it might be Russia.

4 **A:** Do you know when the first emails were sent?
   B: a) I'm fairly sure it was in the 1970s.
      b) I'm fair sure it was in the 1970s.

5 **A:** Who's the current President of South Africa?
   B: a) It's definitely but not Thabo Mbeki.
      b) It's definitely not Thabo Mbeki.

6 **A:** Which country has reached the World Cup final the most times?
   B: a) I don't know, but I'm sure it isn't England.
      b) I don't know, but I've sure it isn't England.

7 **A:** What year did Yuri Gagarin fly into space?
   B: a) I don't can remember.
      b) I can't remember.

8 **A:** What's the name of that French woman who lived to 122?
   B: a) I've forgotten.
      b) I'm forgotten.

LEARN TO   react to information

3A Complete the conversations.

1 **A:** Marisa had her baby yesterday.
   B: _____ she? What wonderful news!

2 **A:** I'm doing an online project about Second Life.
   B: Oh really? _____'s interesting.

3 **A:** His cousin was an Olympic boxer.
   B: _____ he? Wow!

4 **A:** My sister doesn't eat meat.
   B: _____ she? OK, I'll cook fish.

5 **A:** The King of Italy? There isn't one! Italy is a republic.
   B: I was just about to _____ that.

6 **A:** I love Lady Gaga!
   B: _____ you? I think she's crazy.

7 **A:** The inventor of the internet? It was Tim Berners-Lee.
   B: Oh yes, I knew that. I just couldn't _____.

8 **A:** My parents have never been here.
   B: _____ they? When are they going to visit?

9 **A:** Jake was the number one student in the country.
   B: Really? I _____ know that.

10 **A:** John's got the car. We'll have to travel by bus.
   B: _____ we? Oh, that's annoying.

B ▶ **9.4 Listen and check. Then listen again and shadow B's part. Try to copy the intonation.**

10.1 WORLD

VOCABULARY the environment

1A Put the letters in the box in the correct order to make words and phrases. Then match them with definitions 1–10.

> scoredspe   no tabysdn   gicanpagk
> negery-vangis   naricog   ecdosn-danh
> lebodu gezald   celedrcy   rep-peerdarp
> dnsuiltea

1 not switched off, but ready to be used when needed ___on standby___

2 windows or doors with two layers of glass ___double glazed___

3 food with substances added to it in order to preserve it, improve its colour, etc. ~~pre prepared~~ ___processed___

4 covered with a material that stops electricity, sound, heat, etc. from getting out ___packaging___ ___insulated___

5 grown without chemicals ___organic___

6 food which has already been washed, prepared, cooked, etc. so that it is ready to eat ___pre prepared___

7 the bags, boxes, etc. that a product is sold in ___packaging___

8 using less electricity than normal ___energi saving___

9 glass or paper, etc. which has been processed so that it can be used again ___recycled___

10 not new; has been owned by someone else ___second hand___

B Complete the sentences with words from Exercise 1A.

1 We don't use chemicals. All our fruit and vegetables are ___organic___.

2 I don't buy new clothes – I buy everything from ___second hand___ shops.

3 All the windows are ___double glazed___ so we can't hear the noise outside.

4 If we changed to ___energi saving___ light bulbs, our electricity bills would be cheaper.

5 I don't have time to cook in the evenings, so I buy a ___pre prepared___ meal on the way home.

6 Everything in the café is fresh and natural. We don't use any ___processed___ food.

7 All the paper and plastic from the office is ___recycled___ in these bins.

8 Don't leave the TV on ___stand by___. Turn it off when you go to bed.

9 I don't buy fruit in the supermarket because they use too much ___packaging___ which can't be recycled.

10 The house is much warmer now that we have ___insulated___ the roof.

LISTENING

2A Read the text about Earth Hour. Can you complete it?

EARTH HOUR: HOW SMALL ACTIONS CAN HAVE A BIG IMPACT

Earth Hour is a global event where people around the world switch off the
1_____ in their houses, offices, and at other important landmarks, like the 2_____ in Paris, and the 3_____ in Egypt. It started in 2007 in 4_____, Australia, as a protest against climate 5_____, and has grown into a world-wide event. But not everyone thinks it is a good idea – people have 6_____ opinions about what an event like Earth Hour can achieve.

B ▶ 10.1 Listen to a radio phone-in programme about Earth Hour and see if you were right.

3A Are the statements true (T) or false (F)? Correct the false statements.

1 In 2007, twenty-two million people across Sydney switched off their lights for Earth Hour.

2 In 2010, thousands of cities in 128 countries took part in the event.

3 Organisers say that they want to show what people can do to save energy.

4 Everybody agrees that the event is a good way to help people understand the problem.

5 Amy and her children had dinner by candlelight.

6 Jay-Jay thinks that the event helps people to change their everyday behaviour.

B Complete the phrases in bold so that they mean the same as the phrase in brackets.

1 One city decided to **take a _____ against** climate change. (protest against)

2 Earth Hour quickly **went _____.** (spread across the world)

3 In 2010, thousands of cities in 128 countries **took _____.** (participated)

4 The Eiffel Tower in Paris, the Egyptian Pyramids, New York's Empire State Building and Sydney Harbour Bridge were all _____ **into darkness.** (made to go dark quickly)

5 Organisers want to **draw _____ to** the problem of climate change. (make people notice)

6 Is it a good way to _____ **awareness** about the problems the world is facing? (increase the number of people who know about something)

7 I think it's a **complete _____ of time.** (not a good way to use time)

GRAMMAR reported speech

4 Complete the reported sentences.

1 'I don't understand why you're always late.'
She said that she ~~don't~~ understand why I was always late.

2 'We're meeting outside the gym at 6.15,' Bill told the others.
Bill said that they _were_ meeting outside the gym at 6.15.

3 'I've eaten plenty already, thank you.'
He said that he _had_ eaten plenty already.

4 'My job finished last week,' she told Jim.
She told Jim that _her_ job had finished the week before.

5 'I'll see you tomorrow,' said Adam.
Adam said that he would see us the _next_ day.

6 'It's my favourite programme.'
Luis told his mother that it was _his_ favourite programme.

7 'We'll meet you at the airport.'
They told her that they _would_ meet her at the airport.

8 'Are you enjoying the trip?' the tour leader asked.
The tour leader asked them if _they_ were enjoying the trip.

5A Ali (A) is talking to a travel agent (T) about booking a holiday. Put their conversation in the correct order.

A: _5_ No, I haven't, but it's a good idea.

A: _1_ I want to go to Spain, because I've never been there before.

A: _7_ OK.

A: _3_ I'm thinking of going by plane.

A: _11_ That sounds great!

A: _9_ No, I haven't. Could you show me what accommodation is available?

T: _4_ Have you thought about taking the train instead?

T: _2_ How are you planning to travel?

T: _10_ There's an eco-farm near Valencia where you can stay for free, if you help the farmer pick his olives.

T: _6_ It's cheaper than flying. I'll show you some of the train routes.

T: _8_ Have you decided where you want to stay?

B Complete the sentences reporting the conversation in Exercise 5A. Write one word in each gap. Contractions are one word.

1 Ali said that _she_ _wanted_ to go to Spain because _she'd_ _never_ _been_ _there_ before.

2 The travel agent _____ _____ how she _____ _____ to travel.

3 She said that _____ _____ _____ of going by plane.

4 He asked her if _____ _____ about taking the train instead.

5 Ali said that _____ _____, but that _____ _____ a good idea.

6 The travel agent said that it was cheaper than flying, and that he _____ _____ _____ some of the train routes.

7 He asked her if she _____ _____ where _____ _____ to stay.

8 She said that _____ _____. She asked him to show her what accommodation was available.

9 He said that there was an eco-farm near Valencia where she _____ _____ for free, if she _____ the farmer pick his olives.

10 Ali said that _____ _____.

VOCABULARY PLUS word-building (prefixes)

6 Add prefixes *un-*, *dis-*, *under-*, *mis-* or *re-* to the words in bold to complete the sentences.

1 I _mis_**understood** his directions and got completely lost.

2 Discipline is very important to us. We don't like the children to _dis_**obey** the teacher.

3 Shall I throw these boxes away, or can we _re_**use** them for something else?

4 It's a very _un_**usual** situation. Nothing like this has happened before.

5 I _mis_**estimated** how long the journey would take. It took an hour longer than I expected.

6 The old man walked around the corner, and _dis_**appeared**. We never saw him again.

7 I don't know how you find anything in this office. It's so _un_**tidy**!

8 I have to _re_**new** my driving licence because it has expired.

9 They use children in their factories, which I find completely _un_**ethical**.

10 I'm afraid I have to _dis_**agree**. I don't think that's right at all.

VOCABULARY reporting verbs

1 Circle the correct option to complete the reported statements.

1 'Can I give you a hand?'

He _____ to help.

a) invited b) refused c) offered

2 'I'm afraid the first train leaves at 6.30a.m.'

She _____ that the first train leaves at 6.30a.m.

a) offered b) explained c) suggested

3 'I don't believe you!'

He _____ to believe me.

a) refused b) promised c) offered

4 'Come in and have something to eat.'

She _____ us in for something to eat.

a) offered b) warned c) invited

5 'Don't go there. It's dangerous.'

He _____ us not to go there.

a) warned b) suggested c) invited

6 'I'll buy you a diamond ring.'

He _____ to buy me a diamond ring.

a) explained b) promised c) suggested

7 'Why don't we go for a walk?'

He _____ going for a walk.

a) warned b) offered c) suggested

READING

2 Read the article and match pictures A–E with paragraphs 1–5.

A TASTE OF YOUR LIFE

1 In the BBC chat show series *A Taste of My Life*, TV chef Nigel Slater talks to celebrities about their strongest food memories, and particular dishes which have shaped their lives. Comic actor Sanjeev Bhaskar **reminisces** about the contrast between bland 'meat and two veg' school dinners and the Indian food he was served at home. Fellow chef Nigella Lawson tells her life story through food. Do you have a memory of a favourite dish, associated with a special event? Can you remember who cooked it? We asked for your best food memories.

2 It has to be **boiled** eggs with 'soldiers'. My mum used to give this to us as kids. The egg should be soft-boiled so the **yolk** is still **runny**, and the toast is spread with melted butter, and cut into thin strips (tall and straight, like soldiers), which you can hold and dip into the top of the egg. Now I give it to my kids and they love it. It's healthy, and I hope it will give them the same happy memories.
Claire, UK

3 My grandmother's homemade pasta. She used to make pasta on the kitchen table every day. I can remember her laying out the pasta in the morning when I got up for breakfast. Nowadays, people have pasta machines, but she would roll out the pasta by hand, and when we came home from school, there was always a plate of fresh **tagliatelle** waiting for us. The dry pasta you buy in the shops just doesn't taste the same. *Mariella, Italy*

4 Tortilla. Whenever I feel like I'm missing my home country, I cook a tortilla. It's a kind of omelette made with potato and onion, and you can find it in all the tapas bars in Spain. But, of course, the one I make at home is the best. I have so many happy memories of eating tortilla. They go all through my life, from when I was a child, a student at university, eating with friends. Tortilla is everywhere. I couldn't live without it.
Jorge, Spain

5 When I go back to Penang (Malaysia), I go straight to a hawker (street/café seller) and order a bowl of Penang Hokkien Mee (Prawn Noodle Soup). It's one dish I always **miss**. There is something about the combination of the prawns and the chilli in the soup, with the noodles. I just love it. You can make it at home too, but it tastes better when you eat it out on the street. There's an atmosphere, with the heat, and the noise of the traffic and people shouting. It's more than just a dish – it's an experience. And I always look forward to it. Penang's food is part of my life. In fact, I don't think you can find the same taste anywhere else.
Irene, US

3 Read the article again and answer the questions.

1 Who has happy memories of the dish from different stages of their life?
_____

2 Who likes to eat this dish when they return to a special place?
_____

3 Who wants to feed her children a dish which her mother fed her as a child? _____

4 Who describes how the dish should be prepared? _____

5 Who remembers eating this dish when they came home from school as a child? _____

6 Who thinks the dish tastes better when you eat in on the street?
_____

4 Underline the correct alternative for these words and phrases from the article.

1 reminisces: talk or think about *pleasant / terrible* events in your past

2 boiled: cooked in *oil / water*

3 yolk: the *yellow middle / shell* of an egg

4 runny: *hard / soft; liquid*

5 tagliatelle: a type of *pasta / soup*

6 miss: feel *sad because you haven't got / happy because you have got* something you like

GRAMMAR verb patterns

5 Complete the email with verb patterns which include the verbs in brackets. You may need to add personal pronouns (e.g. *us, me*).

Hi Francesca,

How are things? We've just had a great weekend. Ali and Greg are over from New Zealand, so we ¹*decided to meet* (decide/meet) up. They wanted to see London, so I ²_____ (suggest/spend) a couple of days there. Louise ³_____ (invite/stay) at her place, which made things easier. She also ⁴_____ (offer/take) some time off work, so she could show us around the sights. She ⁵_____ (explain/be) easier to travel around with someone who knows where everything is. We were planning to get an organised bus tour, but Louise ⁶_____ (recommend/travel) by ourselves on the buses and Underground. It was a great way to see the city. There were so many things we all wanted to see, but we ⁷_____ (agree/choose) one or two things each. I was really keen to go on the London Eye, but Louise ⁸_____ (warn/not go) up because the weather was bad. We saw lots of other things though, like Big Ben and the Tate Modern. I ⁹_____ (promise/write) and tell you all about it. Next time, you must come, too!

Hope you're well. Take care.

Matt

6A Complete the second sentence so that it has the same meaning as the first. Use the words in capitals. Use between two and five words.

1 'I'm not coming with you,' said Gina. REFUSE

Gina _____ with us.

2 'I'll definitely call you later,' he said. PROMISE

He _____ me later.

3 'Let's go out for a meal,' they said. DECIDE

They _____ out for a meal.

4 'OK. We won't go on holiday this year,' they said. AGREE

They _____ on holiday this year.

5 'It's a very expensive restaurant,' she told us. WARN

She _____ the restaurant was very expensive.

6 'James, why don't you come to the theatre with us on Friday?' they asked. INVITE

They _____ to the theatre with them on Friday.

7 'The children grow vegetables in the garden.' EXPLAIN

The teacher _____ grow vegetables in the garden.

8 'You should buy your fruit at the market.' RECOMMEND

He _____ our fruit at the market.

B ▶10.2 Listen and check. Then listen and repeat. What happens to the words *to, for, at* and *that* in the sentences? Are they stressed or unstressed?

WRITING a review; linking ideas

7A Read the review. Does the writer recommend the restaurant? Why/Why not?

TIFFANY'S PINE WOODS, 0465 244 963

A colleague of mine recommended Tiffany's. Perhaps I should just say that I won't be following his recommendations any more. As I walked in, the first things I noticed were the large flat-screen TVs all over the restaurant, each one showing a different football game. ¹_____. My first reaction was to walk straight out, but there were quite a lot of people there, and we were hungry, so we decided to stay and see what the food was like.

First of all, we ordered drinks. When they arrived, the waitress had forgotten the water, none of the drinks had ice, and ²_____. We didn't see the waitress again for about another twenty minutes. When she finally reappeared, we tried to order some food. I was amazed when she didn't even write down our order. ³_____. I'm sorry, but a good waiter/waitress will always write down what you want.

The starters arrived, but they were very small. ⁴_____. I ate it, but it was nothing special. If you're looking for somewhere nice to eat, then I wouldn't choose Tiffany's, ⁵_____.

B Complete phrases a)–e) with the words in the box. Then match them with gaps 1–5 in the review.

unless such so while although that

a) ... one of the glasses was _____ dirty that we sent it back.

b) _____ the main courses were a little better, my fish was fried, and not grilled as I had asked for.

c) ... _____ you just want to enjoy the football.

d) She thought she had _____ a good memory _____ she would remember everything.

e) _____ the décor was bright and fun-looking, the atmosphere was uninviting, and the chairs weren't comfortable at all.

8A Read the review again and tick the information it gives. Which information is <u>not</u> given?

1 information about the price

2 information about the menu and type of food served

3 details of the restaurant (name, location, phone number, etc.)

4 information about the service

5 information about the atmosphere

B Write a review of a restaurant that someone has recommended to you (180–220 words). Try to include all the information in Exercise 8A.

VOCABULARY airports

1 Add vowels to complete the words in the texts.

'I was travelling from Italy to Stockholm for work. In a hurry, I picked up my ¹p__ssp__rt and ticket, and left for the airport without checking them. When I went to ²ch__ck __n my bags, instead of asking me if I wanted an ³__ __sl__ or a window seat, and giving me my ⁴b__ __rd__ng c__rd, the lady behind the desk told me I was at the wrong airport! How was I to know that there were two airports in Milan? I was in the wrong one.'

'I couldn't believe what was happening, when I tried to fly to Houston with my son last month. We had just been through the ⁵X-r__y m__ch__n__ when we were stopped by security guards and told we were not allowed to ⁶b__ __rd the plane. The reason? My son's name, Matthew Gardner, was on a list of wanted criminals. The unbelievable thing is that my son is two years old. Apparently he was 'wanted' in connection with a shooting!'

'While waiting for a connecting flight at Hong Kong airport, I decided to do some shopping. I had a ⁷pr__ __r__ty b__ __rd__ng card, but I forgot to keep my eye on the departure boards. One minute before my flight was due to leave, I realised to my horror that the message on the departure board read 'Flight XYZ to London – Please ⁸pr__c__ __d t__ g__t__ n__mb__r 143. Final call.' I grabbed my ⁹h__nd l__gg__g__ and ran to the gate like a marathon runner. When I boarded the plane, everyone was staring at me. As if that wasn't bad enough, when I finally found my seat, I realised I'd left my shopping bags, with my new $250 camera in it, in the duty-free shop!'

FUNCTION giving advice/warnings

2 Circle the correct option to complete the warnings/advice.

1 Watch _____ for crocodiles. The river is full of them.
   a) up   b) out
   c) at

2 Don't walk around outside without a sunhat, _____ sunstroke.
   a) or to get   b) or you will getting
   c) or else you'll get

3 Make _____ plenty of water with you. You'll be thirsty by the time you get to the top.
   a) sure you take   b) sure of taking
   c) be sure to

4 _____ leave your bags here, and we'll bring them up for you.
   a) You will better   b) You'd better
   c) You're better

5 If I were you, _____ the airport to see if the flight has been delayed.
   a) I'm calling   b) I'll call
   c) I'd call

6 Be _____ your hand luggage and make sure there are no sharp objects.
   a) careful to check   b) careful and checking
   c) careless and check

7 _____ book a taxi to pick you up from the airport.
   a) Don't forget   b) Don't forget to
   c) Do you forget

8 _____, don't forget your phrasebook. You'll need it if you can't speak the language.
   a) Whatever you do   b) What you do
   c) Ever what you do

LEARN TO make generalisations

3 Match 1–6 with a)–f) to make generalisations.

1 Italians have a tendency
2 Generally, people eat
3 English people often
4 In Turkey, it's common to find
5 On the whole, grandparents in China
6 In Latin cultures, the family tends to

a) later in Spain.
b) be very important.
c) to drink coffee, not tea.
d) different styles of cooking in different parts of the country.
e) are very involved in bringing up their grandchildren.
f) complain about the weather.

LISTENING

1 Read the exam task below and underline the key words in each of the statements A–F.

2A ▶ R2.1 Do the exam task.

Part 3

Questions 19–23

You will hear five different people talking about their favourite films. For questions **19–23**, choose from the list (**A–F**) what each speaker says about the film. Use the letters only once. There is one extra letter which you do not need to use.

A	I feel emotional every time I watch it.	Speaker 1	19
B	I think modern films rely too much on special effects and violence.	Speaker 2	20
C	I like watching old films.	Speaker 3	21
D	The film had an effect on me which lasted for several weeks.	Speaker 4	22
E	I noticed new things about the film when I watched it again later in life.	Speaker 5	23
F	I became a fan of the film after a surprise visit to the cinema.		

B Listen again to check your answers.

3 Read the extracts from the recording. What do you think the words and phrases in bold mean? Match them with meanings a)–e).

1 It's a **charming** story …
2 It really **made an impression on** me.
3 I know it's a bit **cheesy**, but …
4 Hhmm, that's a **tough** one …
5 … and good that it didn't **take itself** so **seriously**.

a) silly and not easy to believe
b) difficult
c) pleasing and attractive
d) think that it was more important than it was
e) made me think about it

GRAMMAR present perfect

4 Complete the sentences with the present perfect simple or continuous form of the verbs in brackets. If both are possible, use the continuous form.

1 You look exhausted. How long _____have_____ you _been working_ (work) on those reports?

2 My brother's excellent at football. He _has been playing_ (play) since he was two years old.

3 Where have you been? We've been _waiting_ (wait) for hours!

4 I'm sorry but I _'ve never loved_ (never love) you.

5 They _'ve won_ (win) six games so far this season.

6 I can tell when you're lying. I _'ve known_ (know) you since you were a child.

7 Jamie and Linda _have been_ (be) together for years, I don't think they'll ever split up. _been being_ ✗

8 I _'ve been living_ (live) with my brother for the last 3 weeks, while I'm trying to find a place of my own.

5 Complete the text with the present perfect simple or continuous form of the verbs in the box.

---

not appear   watch   be   work (x2)   hear   release
try   separate   interview

---

homework

Paulo's film gossip blog

Well, it [1] _____ a busy month here in Hollywood! All the major studios [2] _____ new films, but XYZ studios [3] _____ particularly hard to finish filming their biggest film of the year: *The White Heart*. Julia Rothschild, who [4] _____ in any major roles since 2008, plays the main role and it's set to be a major success. I [5] _____ a few members of the cast, and they all say they're really happy with what they've produced.

Celebrity news – it looks like Hollywood couple Dan Sears and Candy Sureheart [6] _____ . Candy announced at a recent press conference, 'We [7] _____ really hard to make our relationship work, but Dan [8] _____ hard in Europe on a new film and it's made things really difficult for us'. I'm sure lots of fans who [9] _____ the situation will be disappointed.

That's all for this week, but I'd love to hear your comments. [10] _____ any interesting gossip about upcoming films or celebrities?

GRAMMAR relative clauses

6A Look at the exam task below. Who is being interviewed?

B Look at the questions in the exam task. Which two topics below will they not talk about?

1 Tamara's acting career.
2 A funny experience she had.
3 What the job of a film director involves.
4 How she became a film director.
5 The most difficult part of her job.
6 Her future plans.

7 ▶ R2.3 Do the exam task.

Part 4

Questions 24–30
You'll hear an interview with Tamara Goodliffe, a film director. For questions **24–30**, choose the best answer (**A**, **B** or **C**).

---

24 According to Tamara, the job of a director is
   A to make sure the actors feel comfortable.
   B to put all the parts together and make it believable.
   C difficult.

25 What does she say is the most difficult part of her job?
   A deciding whether to keep her original idea.
   B thinking of new ideas.
   C talking to actors who are difficult to work with.

26 Tamara says the best thing about her job is
   A the hard work she puts in to the job.
   B seeing other people work hard.
   C seeing the finished product.

27 When she was an actor, Tamara says she
   A was difficult to work with.
   B was really good at acting.
   C always did exactly what she was told to do.

28 How did she become a director?
   A she went for an interview.
   B a film company asked her to try directing.
   C she made a short film with her friends and sent it to a film company.

29 What point does she make about her films?
   A she doesn't think they are depressing.
   B they show real people and real situations.
   C people don't need to connect with the characters.

30 What advice does she give to new directors?
   A never move away from your original idea.
   B be open to new ideas as they appear.
   C always be nice to the actors.

8A Put the words in the correct order to make relative clauses.

1 book / the / you / That's / that / about / I / told
   _____ .

2 funny / The / was / who / Oscar / the / very / actor / won
   _____ .

3 the / of / Nice, / is / The / set / France / is / story / south / in / in / which
   _____ .

4 play / saw / That's / week / we / the / last
   _____ .

5 very / was / the / Richard, / She / news / explained / to / upset / who
   _____ .

6 we / Is / last / visited / year / this / place / the
   _____ ?

B ▶ R2.2 Listen and check. Then listen and repeat.

C Look at the sentences in Exercise 8A again. Which are defining relative clauses (D), and which are non-defining relative clauses (ND)?

GRAMMAR conditionals

9A Match sentences 1–8 with endings a)–h).

1 You shouldn't have said that to her. If I *were / am* you, I'd
2 She won't take the job *unless / if*
3 It's my own fault. If I *studied / 'd studied* a bit more, I'd
4 Our teacher always *feels / felt* disappointed if we
5 If they *will win / win* the next game, they'll
6 If I'd known you were coming, I *would / would have*
7 I love that actor. If I *met / meet* him, I'd have to
8 What *would / will* you do if you lost

a) have passed the exam.
b) be through to the final!
c) say sorry.
d) your job?
e) ask for his autograph.
f) don't do our homework.
g) waited for you.
h) they offer her more money.

B Look at the sentences above again. Underline the correct alternatives.

READING

1 Read the exam task. Are the sentences true (T) or false (F):

1 The article is about the history of reality TV.

2 Eight sentences have been removed from the article.

3 You should choose the sentence which best fits each gap.

4 There are two extra sentences which don't come from the article.

2 Underline the words/phrases in sentences A–H which refer to other parts of the text.

A *Many see these programmes as the origin of the popular reality programme Big Brother.*

3 Do the exam task.

Part 2

Questions 9–15

You are going to read an article about the history of reality TV. Seven sentences have been removed from the article. Choose from sentences **A–H** the one which fits each gap (**9–15**). There is one extra sentence which you do not need to use.

The last 10–20 years have seen an explosion in TV talent shows, home improvement shows and similar programmes, and you might think that reality TV is a modern thing. ☐ **9**

Most people agree that the first real reality show on TV was *Candid Camera*, which was first shown on US TV in 1948. This was based on an earlier radio programme (*Candid Microphone*), in which the presenter played jokes on members of the public and recorded their reactions. ☐ **10**

Reality TV programmes have always been with us since this time, such as *The Family*, which followed a normal family in the UK in the mid-1970s, as well as several TV-dating shows.

☐ **11** The 1988 Writers Guild of America strike meant that there was a need for new ideas for TV, and so, in 1989, Fox started broadcasting *COPS*, a fly-on-the-wall documentary which followed police officers as they arrested criminals. Though it started in the USA, it also followed the actions of police officers in Hong Kong, London and even the former Soviet Union.

In 1991, the Dutch TV series *Nummer 28* brought together seven students who didn't know each other and filmed them in a house, with a summary programme at the end of each week. MTV produced a similar series in 1992, called *The Real World*. ☐ **12**

This is perhaps the world's most famous reality TV programme, which also started in Holland and has produced different national versions all over the world.

Another very popular reality TV programme in the 21st century was called *Pop Idol*, in which hopeful singers or 'idols' performed to three judges, and the public were allowed to vote in later stages by telephone and text message. This was the start of a new format in reality TV: the talent show. ☐ **13** It became one of the UK's biggest exports of TV formats, with different versions made in over thirty countries.

It was the success of this and other reality TV programmes which has meant that the UK is now the world leader in reality formats, exporting new ideas to the rest of the world. ☐ **14** Programmes such as *Got Talent*, *Masterchef*, and *Wife Swap* all began in the UK.

Nowadays there are a great number of different types of reality TV, such as types of documentary, talent shows, professional shows such as *The Apprentice*, home improvement shows and even those that cover the supernatural and paranormal. ☐ **15** Recent reality shows such as *Made in Chelsea* show real people saying what they want to, but the storyline is planned.

One thing remains clear though – whether you love it or hate it, reality TV is here to stay.

A Many see these programmes as the origin of the popular reality programme *Big Brother*.

B However, reality TV actually goes back much further than that.

C Hollywood might dominate the film and TV drama industry, but the UK exports more of these types of programmes.

D Many people were interested in what the job involved.

E But it wasn't until the late 1980s that reality TV became really popular.

F However, perhaps now we are seeing a return to traditional TV making.

G The programme was so popular that it continued right up until the early 21st century.

H Although these kinds of shows had already existed, allowing the public to vote made it very popular.

VOCABULARY history

4 Put the letters in brackets in the correct order to complete the dictionary entries.

1 Discoveries or inventions that make the world better.
_____ (scanvead)

2 A period of time in history that is known for something.
_____ (rea)

3 When a country's political system or a way of thinking changes. _____ (nilotreuvo)

4 When something affects more people or a wider area.
_____ (drapes)

5 A group of people who have the same aim.
_____ (teemnovm)

6 A time of important change. _____
_____ (nitrung tipon)

7 When one country establishes political control over another country. _____ (sianolconito)

8 A growth or change which improves a situation.
_____ (pleedtonvem)

9 A person who directs or controls a country or group.
_____ (dreela)

10 When a group of people become free from someone's control. _____ (tribeliona)

VOCABULARY success/ability

5 Use a word from box A and a word from box B to complete the sentences.

A

believe focus gifted expert hard talent better hopeless

B

on at (x4) in (x2) for

1 Before they introduced the new law, the government consulted an _____ _____ education.

2 Sorry the food tastes so horrible, I'm _____
_____ cooking. Shall we order a takeaway?

3 When you go for the job interview, make sure you
_____ _____ your strengths.

4 If she wants to qualify for the Olympics, she'll need to work _____ _____ improving her time.

5 Mozart was especially _____ _____
music. He gave his first concert when he was only six.

6 If you really want to win, you need to _____
_____ yourself.

7 If you don't practise, you won't get _____
_____ painting.

8 He has a natural _____ _____ playing football. He was born with the ability.

WRITING

1A Choose the correct alternative to complete the book review.

> ### *The City and The City* by China Miélville
>
> A friend of mine recently recommended this book, and I have to say that in future I'll be following his recommendations. I don't usually write reviews but I [1]*thought/found* this book really enjoyable and I just had to tell the world.
>
> I'm a [2]*such/big* fan of 'dystopia' stories (such as George Orwell's *1984*), and so this book was just right for me. It's partly a crime story, but also describes in great detail a city divided into two parts and ruled by two very strict authorities. The residents of each city aren't allowed even to see or recognise each other, and so have to practise 'unseeing'.
>
> The style [3]*is/was* brilliant, and the way the author describes the cities and the everyday lives of people who live there really paints a picture in your mind as you read it. What I [4]*liked/thought* best though was the main character. I [5]*'m/fell* in love with Inspector Tyador from the very beginning, and his approach to solving the crime.
>
> I'd definitely [6]*recommend/review* this book for people who like something different in a story.

B Read the book review again. What two things does the writer like about the book?

2A Read the exam task below. What four things do you need to include in the review?

> ### Part 2
>
> Write an answer to question **3**. Use **120–180** words in the appropriate style.
>
> ___
>
> **3 You recently saw this notice on a website which sells books.**
>
> Share your reading experiences!
>
> Here at booksonline.com we're always looking for ways to help you choose the right book. If you recently read a book which you really liked or disliked, help others by writing a short review. Include your opinion of the book, information about the story and characters, and two things you liked/disliked about it.
>
> **Write your review.**

B Do the exam task.

VOCABULARY family

1 Complete the sentences.

1 I recently discovered that I'm _____ to a famous football player of the 1950s.

2 There are several soldiers on my father's _____ of the family.

3 I take _____ my mother; we look very similar.

4 My _____ family consists of four grandparents, six uncles and aunts and fifteen cousins.

5 I always spend Christmas with _____ – usually my uncle, but sometimes my sister.

6 When her father died, she _____ over €10 million.

7 My great-_____ were married for twenty years before they had my grandfather!

8 We moved to Krakow fifty years ago, but my family's _____ are in Warsaw.

GRAMMAR question forms

2A Complete the interview questions. Use the same verbs as the answers.

A: Who [1]_____ ?

B: I work for a small publishing company called Calinet.

A: What type of things [2]_____ ?

B: I do a lot of things – do some editing, contact authors.

A: What problems [3]_____ ?

B: I deal with problems concerning the manuscripts: mistakes, wrong length, wrong style.

A: When [4]_____ working there?

B: I started working there in 2007.

A: [5]_____ the job?

B: Yes, I do enjoy it. It's great.

A: So why [6]_____ for this job?

B: I applied because it's a great company.

B ▶ RC1.1 Listen and repeat the questions with the correct intonation.

GRAMMAR review of verb tenses

3 Put the verbs in brackets into the correct tense to complete the introduction to a speech.

Hello, everybody! My name is Shane Towers. I [1]_____ (be) a teacher, but at the moment I [2]_____ (take) a year off to finish my Master's Degree. I [3]_____ (not start) working with children until 2005, but now I [4]_____ (love) it. Well, today I'm going to talk about Theatre of the Oppressed. I first [5]_____ (see) the name when I [6]_____ (look) through some articles for my degree. I [7]_____ (read) an article about drama in education and suddenly the name [8]_____ (jump) out at me: 'Theatre of the Oppressed'. In my country, the theatre [9]_____ (not be) usually for or about the oppressed; it's for rich or middle-class people. I [10]_____ (want) to find out more …

VOCABULARY relationships

4A Match the sentences with the people in the box.

classmate	boss	team-mate	partner	mentor
employee	pupil	fiancée		

1 'Please finish this report for me by tomorrow morning.' _____

2 'Ian, can I borrow your pen? I forgot to write my name on my homework.' _____

3 'Come on! Together we can win this game!' _____

4 'Let's look at this together; I can give you some ideas.' _____

5 'We still need to send out the wedding invitations.' _____

6 'I have a meeting in the office with my manager at 6.00.' _____

7 'Sorry, sir. I thought we had to hand in our homework tomorrow.' _____

8 'We'll split the costs 50/50, OK?' _____

B Mark the stress on the words in the box.

VOCABULARY PLUS collocations with take/get/do/go

5 Replace banana with take, get, do or go. Use the present simple or the past simple.

1 I *banana* a lot of research before I *banana* my degree. *did, got*

2 A year ago she *banana* up a new hobby: acting. Then she *banana* part in her first play. _____

3 Last night we *banana* some work on the proposal and then we *banana* for a meal. _____

4 Can you *banana* me a favour? Can you help me to *banana* this test? _____

5 You *banana* after your father. I hope you don't *banana* grey when you're twenty-five, too! _____

6 Eventually I *banana* off Jane because she always *banana* angry for no reason. _____

VOCABULARY interview advice

6 Circle the correct option to answer the questions.

1 How should you dress before an interview?

a) messily   b) brilliantly   c) smartly

2 How should you shake hands with someone?

a) nicely   b) firmly   c) heavily

3 When should you arrive for an appointment?

a) on time   b) quickly   c) late

4 What shouldn't you avoid in an interview?

a) foot contact   b) head contact   c) eye contact

5 What should you do before an interview?

a) some research   b) a job   c) the washing

6 What should you show in an interview?

a) your CV   b) your photos   c) enthusiasm

FUNCTION talking about yourself

7 Read the conversation between Ian and his boss, John. Which lines are correct? Which have an extra word?

I: John, could I to ask a question?	1	_to_
J: Of course. What would you like to know?	2	✓
I: There are but a couple of things.	3	_____
J: Yes, go ahead.	4	_____
I: I am have a query about the website.	5	_____
J: Yes. You know it isn't finished yet?	6	_____
I: Can I to ask you when it will be finished?	7	_____
J: It's for me, the most important thing is to get it right.	8	_____
I: I understand, but when will it be ready?	9	_____
J: I'd have really to say, websites have been a big problem for this company.	10	_____
I: In the my opinion, they've been the biggest problem. But when will it be ready?	11	_____
J: One thing I'd like for to say is that we are working hard on the website.	12	_____
I: So you don't have a date?	13	_____
J: Er ... no. Sorry.	14	_____

LEARN TO use two-word responses

8 Put the words in the boxes into pairs to make two-word responses. Then complete the conversations with the correct responses.

of problem welcome course no you're

1 A: Thank you so much.
   B: _____ .

2 A: Sorry about that.
   B: _____ .

3 A: Can I leave early, please?
   B: _____ .

ahead correct see I go you're

4 A: I think the answer is 'Paris'.
   B: _____ .

5 A: Can I tell you what happened?
   B: _____ .

6 A: I couldn't come because I was ill.
   B: _____ .

I right that's please understand continue

7 A: Is your name John Brown?
   B: _____ .

8 A: Sorry I didn't finish it.
   B: _____ .

9 A: So, I was telling you about …
   B: _____ .

VOCABULARY types of story; the news

9 Complete the descriptions of films with the words in the box.

fantasy fugitive strike biopic science period earthquake collapse thriller action crash attack shot comedy

1 This _____ describes the life of César Chávez, the leader who organised a workers' _____ so that people could work under fair conditions.

2 This psychological _____ tells the story of a _____ who hides from the police while trying to prove that he is innocent.

3 This is a very funny romantic _____ that tells the story of two people who fall in love when their cars _____ on a small road.

4 This _____ fiction film describes what happens when aliens _____ Planet Earth, attempting to destroy everything.

5 This children's _____ begins when a hole opens up in the ground after an _____, and a giant, friendly creature comes out to rescue everybody.

6 This _____ drama looks at the _____ of the British Empire and what happened to those who returned to Britain from the colonies.

7 This _____ film, which begins with the President getting _____, involves two minutes of acting and ninety minutes of guns and bombs.

GRAMMAR present perfect/past simple

10 Read the phrases in italics and correct the ones that are wrong.

1 The Berlin Wall *has fallen* in 1989.

2 *Have you been* to any of the Caribbean islands?

3 I started work at 6a.m. but I still *haven't finished*.

4 What time *have you gone* to bed last night?

5 It's so dry here. It *hasn't rained* for weeks.

6 Did you hear about Casey? He's *broken* his leg!

7 Van Gogh *hasn't sold* many paintings during his lifetime.

8 You're a good guitar player. *Have you played* for long?

11 ▶ RC1.2 Listen and tick the sentence you hear.

1 a) I stopped.   b) I've stopped.
2 a) We made it.   b) We've made it.
3 a) He helped me.   b) He's helped me.
4 a) They killed it.   b) They've killed it.
5 a) You worked hard.   b) You've worked hard.
6 a) I thanked her.   b) I've thanked her.

VOCABULARY PLUS prepositions

12 Complete the diary entry with the correct prepositions.

I went ¹_____ a run in the morning while listening to some music ²_____ Eminem. I hate running ³_____ the winter, especially ⁴_____ Monday morning. It's too cold! Unfortunately, Kim is away ⁵_____ business and only gets back late ⁶_____ night, so I had to run ⁷_____ my own. It was hard work running six miles, but I did it ⁸_____ the end. Had breakfast ⁹_____ a hurry and managed to get to work ¹⁰_____ time. Problems with the bus so I went ¹¹_____ train, which was quicker. ¹²_____ chance, I heard ¹³_____ the radio that the new film ¹⁴_____ Roger Graves, an old friend of mine, was coming out ¹⁵_____ June. It's about a man who runs every morning and hates it!

GRAMMAR narrative tenses

13 Complete the sentences with the past simple, past perfect or past continuous form (positive or negative) of the verbs in the box. Use each verb once.

turn on	finish	eat	open	do	leave	stay	listen
wear	go						

1 She went to Hotel Buena Vista, but I _____ in Hotel Primavera!

2 As Bilal closed the door, he realised he _____ the keys in the car.

3 Yannick _____ to music when someone knocked on the door.

4 When I got to work, I saw that I _____ one black shoe and one brown shoe!

5 When we arrived, it was cold because Dad _____ the heating.

6 Bella started the course last year, but she _____ it.

7 Goa was new to us because we _____ there before.

8 It was too hot, so I _____ the window.

9 The police want to know what you _____ between 6.30a.m. and 7.00a.m. yesterday.

10 The food tasted horrible, so we _____ it.

VOCABULARY say/tell

14A Complete the phrases with *say* or *tell*.

1 _____ jokes

2 _____ 'hello'

3 _____ a white lie

4 _____ sorry

5 _____ stories

6 _____ what you mean

B Complete the sentences with the correct form of phrases from Exercise 14A.

1 When I was young, my father always _____ before we fell asleep.

2 Most comedians _____. But his face alone makes you laugh!

3 I explained that I didn't mean to break the window! I _____!

4 She isn't very friendly, is she? She never _____ when I see her in the street.

5 He didn't want to make her cry, so instead of telling the truth, he _____.

6 Instead of talking for hours around the issue, why don't you just _____!

FUNCTION telling a story

15 Underline the correct alternatives.

A: ¹*Happened this / This happened* when I was on holiday in Portugal last year. There were three of us renting this old, scary house in the countryside. It was miles from anywhere.

B: So what ²*happened / did happen*?

A: We'd had a really nice evening. My friend is a good cook and she'd made this lovely meal, so we were feeling very content and full. ³*In anyway / Anyway*, that night, just after we'd all gone to bed, we heard this kind of scratching sound at the door. ⁴*To / In* the beginning, we just thought it was the wind and we went to sleep and forgot about it. But then the following night, the same thing: scratch, scratch at the door.

B: ⁵*But no / Oh no*!

A: ⁶*Well / Very well*, we were all in separate rooms but ⁷*after / before* long we were all sitting together in the living room, really scared. ⁸*So / So on* we talked and talked, trying to work out what to do.

B: And what ⁹*did you do / you did*?

A: ¹⁰*Final / Finally* we decided to get a knife or another weapon and go outside together to see what it was. ¹¹*The next thing / The near thing* I knew, I was at the front of three frightened girls, carrying the kitchen knife and about to unlock the front door.

B: ¹²*Dear / Oh dear*!

A: It went really quiet again. And then, all of ¹³*the sudden / a sudden*, there was the scratching sound.

B: So what ¹⁴*happened then / then happened*?

A: I opened the door and a cat jumped back and ran off into the night. All that panic and ¹⁵*for / in* the end it was just a cat!

B: That's really ¹⁶*funny / fun*!

A: Well yes, we all laughed afterwards, but it was very scary at the time!

TEST

Circle the correct option to complete the sentences.

1 Sarah is _____ a famous nineteenth-century politician.
   a) related to   b) relative   c) related

2 Where _____ last summer?
   a) have you go   b) do you go   c) did you go

3 What music _____?
   a) do you listen   b) you listen to
   c) do you listen to

4 Who _____ you with this homework?
   a) helped   b) did help   c) was helped

5 _____ she like pasta?
   a) Is   b) Does   c) Do

6 I'm _____ a novel.
   a) writing   b) be writing
   c) already written

7 What _____ between 4.00p.m. and 4.30p.m.?
   a) did you do   b) were you doing
   c) you were doing

8 We are _____ of a tennis club.
   a) team-mates   b) partners   c) members

9 They _____ in a concert.
   a) did   b) took place   c) took part

10 Can you _____?
   a) make me a favour   b) do me a favour
   c) do me favour

11 You _____ your father, especially in your character.
   a) take after   b) take over   c) take to

12 I _____ research before I started the project.
   a) did a   b) took some   c) did some

13 I _____ about this topic.
   a) could question   b) ask a question
   c) have a query

14 Why don't you _____ and tell your story?
   a) go ahead   b) be ahead   c) go forward

15 _____ me, the most important thing is to be honest.
   a) By   b) For   c) According

16 I love films about the future, especially _____.
   a) fiction science   b) science fiction
   c) period drama

17 We _____ to Italy yet.
   a) didn't go   b) not have been
   c) haven't been

18 _____ Paul last night?
   a) Were you see   b) Did you see
   c) Have you seen

19 What _____ to your hair?
   a) have you done   b) you have done
   c) you did

20 I didn't want to work _____ my own.
   a) in   b) on   c) by

21 She fired the gun _____ mistake.
   a) by   b) on   c) at

22 He realised he _____ Janine before.
   a) met   b) was meeting   c) had met

23 The alarm went off while we _____.
   a) sleep   b) were sleeping
   c) had slept

24 I was nervous because I _____ a speech before.
   a) wasn't giving   b) didn't give   c) hadn't given

25 When I _____ her, she didn't know who I was.
   a) had met   b) was meeting   c) met

26 The kidnappers wanted a million dollars for each _____.
   a) hostage   b) fugitive   c) flood

27 That boy is always _____ lies.
   a) speaking   b) saying   c) telling

28 If you did something wrong, you should _____ sorry.
   a) ask   b) say   c) tell

29 All _____, the rain came down.
   a) in the end   b) very sudden   c) of a sudden

30 That's impossible – you _____ joking!
   a) must to be   b) must be   c) must

TEST RESULT **/30**

GRAMMAR the future (plans)

1 Circle the correct option to complete the sentences.

1 I'm _____ out with Aleks on Friday night.
   a) going
   b) go
   c) might go

2 _____ married in May.
   a) Are we going get
   b) We're going to getting
   c) We're going to get

3 This film is boring. I think _____ to bed.
   a) I'm to going
   b) I'll go
   c) I might going

4 _____ going to do anything special at the weekend?
   a) You are
   b) Are you
   c) Do you

5 Great idea! _____ have a party to celebrate.
   a) We'll
   b) We going to
   c) We're having to

6 Who _____ invite?
   a) will you
   b) will you going to
   c) you might

7 Peter _____ fifty on Saturday!
   a) is being
   b) is going to be
   c) might be

8 _____ a Thai curry. I'm expecting about twenty people.
   a) I'm going to cook
   b) I will to cook
   c) I'm cooking

VOCABULARY communication; future time markers

2 Complete the sentences with the correct word.

1 a) She likes to *chat / apologise* to friends on the phone.
   b) I really think you should *chat / apologise* for what you have done.

2 a) He's always *warning / moaning* about things: the weather, the economy, the government.
   b) You can't say that I didn't *warn / moan* you. I told you he would be angry.

3 a) When you're stressed, you are more likely to *gossip / argue* about silly things, like who does the washing-up.
   b) They like to go out in the evening and *gossip / argue* about other friends, and what they're doing.

4 a) He *boasted / complimented* me on the dress I was wearing.
   b) She likes to *boast / compliment* about how much money she earns and how she is the best at her job.

5 a) We'll be leaving *shortly / near*.
   b) I can't see him leaving his job in the *shortly / near* future.

6 a) We'd like to buy our own house in a *term / year* or two.
   b) In the long *term / year*, I think she made the right decision.

7 a) I'd like to start my own business at some point in the future, but that will be a *short / long* time from now.
   b) In the *short / long* term, over the next few weeks, we want to see business improve.

8 a) In ten *next / years'* time, I hope to be a surgeon.
   b) *Next / Years'* month, we will celebrate twenty years of marriage.

GRAMMAR the future (predictions)

3 Underline the correct alternative to complete the text.

THE FUTURE OF FREE MUSIC

So, with everybody downloading music on the internet for free, what is the future of the music industry? We asked some music experts for their opinions.

Matthew G – head of Indit Records, UK

'Basically, I think things [1]*aren't likely to / are going to* change very much. People [2]*may / might not* like it, but governments [3]*may / aren't going to* introduce more laws to punish people who steal music by downloading it for free. And this [4]*is going to / isn't going to* force people to move to music download sites where you pay for your music. It's already happening, and I think in the future this process [5]*won't to / is likely to* continue.'

Ian M – music reporter

'I think the future [6]*will / is likely* look very different. People [7]*couldn't / won't* pay for every track which they listen to any more. I think they [8]*are going / may* use a subscription site, so they pay a monthly fee and then can download as much music as they want to listen to, legally. I think we [9]*are going to / may not* see more and more record companies begin to use services like this. There [10]*could / couldn't* also be social networking sites, where people pay to join and then they can listen to each other's music.'

VOCABULARY PLUS idioms

4 Write the second sentence so that it means the same as the first. Use idioms which include the words in capitals.

1 It's so easy.   CAKE

It's _____.

2 He was in trouble.   WATER

He was _____.

3 I said something really inappropriate.   FOOT

I put _____.

4 It's an issue which is very important to me.   HEART

It's an issue which is _____.

5 He left his job in the city to go and become a coffee farmer.   RAT

He decided to leave _____ and become a coffee farmer.

6 Could you help me sort out these papers?   HAND

Could you _____ sorting out these papers?

7 I think about her all the time.   MIND

She's always _____.

8 I don't really like R&B music.   TEA

R&B music isn't _____.

9 I like to follow what's happening in politics.   EYE

I like to _____ what's happening in politics.

10 I'm afraid we have no more time.   RUN

I'm afraid we've _____.

FUNCTION dealing with misunderstandings; reformulate

5 Complete the conversations with the words in the box.

| saying | mean | catch | get | other | repeat | what | say | exactly | lost |

1 A: The picture dates back to the sixteenth century when it was …

B: I didn't _____ any of that.

2 A: So, you take the third turning on the right, go straight on for 200 metres, turn left, take the first right again, and it's straight in front of you.

B: I'm sorry. You've _____ me.

3 A: If you don't have a pink stripe on your ticket, then I'm afraid staff are not allowed to let you in.

B: Apologies, but I'm afraid I don't _____ what you're saying.

4 A: We had a very minor incident involving your new car.

B: What _____ do you mean?

5 A: We are sorry to report that all trains have been cancelled.

B: Do you _____ to say we can't travel today?

6 A: I've come to collect a parcel for Mr Wainwright.

B: Can you _____ that again?

7 A: There's one stop-over, for twenty-four hours, in Bahrain.

B: Could you _____ the last thing you said?

8 A: This desk is now closed.

B: So, you're _____ that we need to move to another desk?

9 A: I'm afraid you need to vacate the premises.

B: So _____ you mean is we need to go?

10 A: We anticipate inconveniences along the route.

B: In _____ words, we're going to be late.

VOCABULARY review

6 Complete the words in the sentences.

1 He always wants to win. He's very co_____.

2 Part of being a good le_____ is being able to listen to people.

3 It's one of the most am_____ films I've ever seen. It's very moving.

4 I have to go to bed as soon as possible. I'm absolutely ex_____.

5 To be a successful entrepreneur, you need to be a ri_____ ta_____.

6 It's minus ten degrees outside. It's fr_____!

7 It's a fa_____ story, really interesting. It's about a man who …

8 I love my job, but I should be earning a much bigger sa_____.

9 He was always telling the bo_____ what to do, and in the end, he got fi_____.

10 I'm very nervous, because I've got to go for this job in_____ tomorrow.

11 I can't believe how angry he was. He was absolutely fu_____.

12 I'm sure she'll do well in her new job. She's very ha_____-wo_____.

7A Put the words in the box into the correct place in the table according to the stress pattern.

| ~~amazing~~ ~~salary~~ tasty competitive successful leader interview furious delicious boiling difficult freezing exhausted impossible |

oOo	Ooo
amazing	*salary*
Oo	oOoo

B ▶ RC2.1 Listen and check.

GRAMMAR *must, have to, should* (obligation)

8 Complete the sentences with the correct form of *must, have to* or *should*. Use the information in brackets to help you.

1 Milo _____ write three ten-thousand-word essays for his course. (It's necessary)

2 We _____ tidy up the house. Jenna will be home soon. (It's a good idea)

3 You _____ park here. You'll get a fine. (obligation not to do this)

4 You _____ pay for children. They can come in for free. (It isn't necessary)

5 The sign says you _____ keep your dog on a lead. (It's necessary)

6 You _____ smoke anywhere in the building. It isn't allowed. (obligation not to do this)

7 You _____ wear a helmet when you ride your motorbike. It's the law. (It's necessary)

8 Do children _____ go to school on Saturdays? (Is it necessary?)

9 You _____ wear jeans to a job interview. (It isn't a good idea)

10 You _____ pay for the coffee. It's free. (It isn't necessary)

VOCABULARY PLUS confusing words

9 Complete the sentences with the words in the box.

listen   funny   remember   won   hear
fun   forgotten   left

1 I'm sorry. I can't _____ your name. Is it Sarah or Sue?

2 I think I've _____ how this machine works. Please show me again.

3 It's in my bag, which I've _____ in the car.

4 You never _____ to what I'm saying.

5 Sorry, the music's too loud. I can't _____ you.

6 I don't believe it. They've _____ the match.

7 I always laugh at his stories. He's so _____.

8 Why don't you come with us to the restaurant? It should be _____!

GRAMMAR *used to, would*

10A Complete the text with *used to* or *would* and the verbs in brackets. Where both *used to* and *would* are possible, use *would*.

FIVE YEARS AGO

Greg and Emily Bishop [1]_____ (live) on a small island in the Caribbean. They had a wonderful life. Greg [2]_____ (work) as a teacher in a local school, and Emily [3]_____ (study) for an online course at a university. They [4]_____ (have) a house on the beach, and after school, the children [5]_____ (play) on the beach with their friends. At the weekends, they all [6]_____ (enjoy) surfing, sitting on the beach, and eating delicious tropical fruit, like mangoes and pineapples. But when Greg's father became ill, the family decided to move back to the UK.

B Read about Greg and Emily's life now. Then complete sentences 1–6 with *used to* or *would*.

NOW

Greg runs his own taxi company, and Emily has a job working in a sports centre. The children don't enjoy school as much, and say they have to wear too many clothes all the time to keep warm. At the weekends, they all stay inside and watch football on television, and eat fish and chips.

1 Greg _____ (not have) his own business.

2 Emily _____ (not work) in a sports centre.

3 The children _____ (enjoy) school more in the Caribbean.

4 The children _____ (not wear) so many clothes to keep warm.

5 The family _____ (not stay) inside at weekends.

6 They _____ (eat) tropical fruit, not fish and chips.

FUNCTION reaching agreement

11A Complete the phrases in the conversation with the words in the box.

don't   sure   suggest   need   about   What   things   that   me
point   agree   should

A: OK. As you all know, we had record sales last year, and we'd like to organise a celebration for all the staff. Any ideas for what we could do?

B: Well, I feel [1]_____ we should have a party here in the office.

A: That's OK by [2]_____.

C: I'm not sure that I [3]_____, actually. I think we [4]_____ think about going somewhere else. The way I see [5]_____, we spend every day in the office. Why [6]_____ we do something different to celebrate?

D: That's a good [7]_____. How [8]_____ if we go on a trip somewhere?

B: Yes. Or we could do a course together. There's a place where you can go and make chocolates, or bake bread or something like that.

D: I'm not [9]_____ that's a good idea. I [10]_____ we focus on things we all enjoy doing, like sport. [11]_____ about spending a day playing golf?

C: Golf! I don't think so.

A: OK. I think we [12]_____ to focus on whether we have a party of some kind, or go on a trip somewhere.

B Which phrases are used to give opinions? Which are responses to a suggestion or idea?

TEST

Circle the correct option to complete the sentences.

1 Hi, Jake. What _____ this evening?

   a) you doing   b) are you doing c) will you doing

2 I'm not sure. I think I _____ stay at home and study.

   a) will to   b) might   c) going to

3 We _____ Italy for our holidays. We love it there.

   a) are going to   b) will go   c) might going

4 We _____ about everything from politics to the weather. It's ridiculous.

   a) compliment   b) boast   c) argue

5 When Roberta comes round, we drink coffee and _____.

   a) apologise   b) chat   c) warn

6 He's changing his job in a month or _____.

   a) term   b) year   c) two

7 I think it will be better for everyone in the long _____.

   a) year   b) term   c) time

8 Look at the sunshine! You _____ have a great time at the beach.

   a) 're going to   b) 're likely to   c) may

9 We _____ never see him again.

   a) aren't likely to b) may   c) won't

10 Yes, we're working against the _____ to finish in time.

   a) pressure   b) life   c) clock

11 Come on. Spill the _____. What did she say?

   a) peas   b) beans   c) tea

12 We don't know much about him. He's a dark _____.

   a) horse   b) dog   c) fish

13 She's been promoted and she's the top _____ now.

   a) fish   b) horse   c) dog

14 I'm sorry. I didn't _____ you were busy.

   a) recognise   b) remind   c) realise

15 I'm afraid I didn't _____ that. Can you say it again?

   a) catch   b) take   c) do

16 André is very _____. He wants to sell his designs all over the world.

   a) lazy   b) ambitious   c) indecisive

17 Françoise is a good _____. People really listen to what she has to say.

   a) risk taker   b) listener   c) communicator

18 The doctor said I _____ take these pills.

   a) has to   b) have to   c) haven't to

19 Help yourself to anything you want. You _____ ask.

   a) don't have to b) have to   c) must

20 It's a wonderful _____. I enjoy it a lot.

   a) work   b) study   c) job

21 I can't believe how big your kitchen is. It's _____.

   a) tiny   b) big   c) enormous

22 The interview was _____. I'll never get the job.

   a) brilliant   b) awful   c) exhausting

23 When I told my boss, he was _____.

   a) furious   b) terrible   c) impossible

24 As children, we _____ play at the bottom of the garden.

   a) used   b) use to   c) would

25 My mother _____ live in the mountains.

   a) used to   b) use to   c) would

26 If we work as a _____, we'll get the job done faster.

   a) boss   b) businessman c) team

27 More than a hundred people had to _____ for a single job.

   a) compete   b) decide   c) get fired

28 The way I see _____, we need to start again.

   a) point   b) things   c) idea

29 That's OK _____ me.

   a) on   b) at   c) by

30 I think we need to sum _____ what we've learned.

   a) up   b) on   c) at

TEST RESULT /30

69

VOCABULARY technology

1 Add vowels to complete the words.

1 I don't believe it. The __l__ctr__c__ty has gone off again.
2 He had to have a v__cc__n__t__ __n against measles.
3 I think sp__c__ tr__v__l is a complete waste of money.
4 I worry about g__n__t__c __ng__n__ __r__ng. I don't think we know enough about it.
5 We've put two huge s__l__r p__n__ls on the roof.
6 They're putting in a new c__mp__t__r n__tw__rk to improve communication.
7 N__cl__ __r p__w__r is dangerous because people make mistakes.
8 The region has much more tourism now that c__mm__rc__ __l __ __r__pl__n__s can fly here.

GRAMMAR comparatives/superlatives

2 Rewrite the second sentence so that it means the same as the first. Use the prompts in brackets.

1 (slightly / warm)
The sea isn't as cold as it was yesterday.
The sea _____ than yesterday.

2 (far / expensive)
These black trainers are much cheaper than those white ones.
Those white trainers _____ these black ones.

3 (delicious)
I have never eaten a meal as good as that one.
That was _____ I've ever eaten.

4 (lot / easy)
I expected the exam to be more difficult.
The exam _____ I had expected.

5 (simple)
All the other solutions to the problem are more complicated.
It's _____ solution to the problem.

6 (much / happy)
I felt terrible yesterday, but today I feel much better.
I'm _____ today than I was yesterday.

7 (bit / short)
My brother is slightly taller than me.
I'm _____ my brother.

8 (bad)
Grandad thinks the world was a better place when he was young.
Grandad thinks the world is _____ it was when he was young.

VOCABULARY questions

3 Underline the correct alternative.

1 I'd like to *discuss / inquire* this with my boss.
2 He didn't *answer / respond* to my email.
3 We need to *look / question* into the problem.
4 I'm *wondering / responding* if he'll take the job if we offer it to him.
5 I need to do some *research / debate* before buying a new computer.
6 The police are going to *wonder / investigate* the burglary.
7 We're getting a lot of *inquiries / question* about the new service.
8 It was a very interesting *debate / discuss* about immigration.

GRAMMAR question tags

4 Complete the questions with question tags.

1 We can walk there, _____?
2 They've already left, _____?
3 We'll see you later, _____?
4 You don't like jazz, _____?
5 The film was great, _____?
6 You spoke to Mr Johnston earlier, _____?
7 You won't need the car, _____?
8 You haven't lost your keys again, _____?

VOCABULARY PLUS word building: adjectives

5 Complete the words with the correct suffix.

1 His shoulder is very pain_____. He says it hurts a lot when he tries to move it.
2 Unfortunately, the number of home_____ people living on the streets has increased.
3 I'm afraid I'm not respons_____ for what happened. It wasn't my fault.
4 He's one of Japan's most creat_____ film directors. His work is very original and exciting.
5 The situation seemed hope_____. What we were trying to do was impossible.
6 It's a very effect_____ way to teach reading – we've had excellent results.
7 Don't worry about the car, I'm just thank_____ that nobody was hurt.
8 She was always a mess_____ child. She just loved getting dirty!

VOCABULARY problems and solutions

6 Put the words in the correct order to make sentences.

1 car's / down / the / broken

_____

2 phone / recharging / my / needs

_____

3 out / it's / order / of

_____

4 printer / fixing / the / needs

_____

5 it / switching / off / try / and / again / on

_____

6 this / it / strange / making / noise / keeps

_____

7 more / work / doesn't / any / it

_____

8 out / have / it / we / sort / to

_____

FUNCTION polite requests; responding to requests

7 Underline the correct alternatives.
1 A: Could you *tell / to tell* me where I can find the manager?
  B: Yes, *of course / afraid*.
2 A: Do you know *if there's / if is there* a supermarket near here?
  B: I'm not *afraid / sure*.
3 A: Would you mind *checking / to check* the system for me?
  B: Of *course / sure* not.
4 A: Could you *see / to see* if anyone has arrived yet?
  B: Let me have a *look / course*.

VOCABULARY -ing/-ed adjectives

8 Complete the sentences with the correct form of the adjective in brackets.
1 Are you _____ with me just because I'm a bit late? (annoy)
2 There's a _____ atmosphere in the school. (relax)
3 It's all very _____. I can't understand the results of this survey. (confuse)
4 She's _____ with doing the same thing every day. (bore)
5 I realised I'd made a terrible mistake. It was so _____! (embarrass)
6 I was still _____ from the race. (exhaust)
7 You look _____. What's wrong? (worry)
8 It was a very _____ experience. (frighten)

GRAMMAR conditionals

9A Underline the correct alternative.
1 If I have time later, *I call / I'll call* you.
2 If I *don't / wouldn't* sleep well enough, I feel terrible the next day.
3 If there *is / would be* anything else you need, just tell me.
4 Those plants *die / will die* unless you water them soon.
5 If we had more room, *I'll / I'd* invite them to stay.
6 It wouldn't be as bad if we *didn't / don't* have so many exams this year.
7 If I didn't have a car, I *will / would* cycle everywhere.
8 If we *won't / don't* leave now, we'll be late.
9 It's more expensive if you *live / lived* in a bigger house.
10 If we *get / will get* hungry, we'll buy some sandwiches.
11 She *would / will* get angry if we asked her.
12 Life would be easier if we *will have / had* more money.

B Circle the correct option to complete the sentences.
1 If it rains tonight, _____.
  a) I take an umbrella
  b) I'll stay at home and watch a DVD
  c) I don't go out
2 If Justine passes her exams, _____.
  a) her mother is delighted
  b) she has worked hard
  c) she'll go to university
3 If you eat too much junk food, _____.
  a) it's not good for your health
  b) you would be too fat
  c) you'll like pizza a lot
4 If I had a garden, _____.
  a) I'd grow my own vegetables
  b) I sit in the sun all day long
  c) I'll grow lots of beautiful flowers
5 When I'm bored _____.
  a) I'd watch the TV
  b) always I cook something to eat
  c) I usually read a book
6 _____ at the cinema if you want.
  a) I'm meeting you
  b) I'll meet you
  c) I'd meet you
7 _____, I'll meet you later.
  a) If I get all my work finished on time
  b) If I'll finish work on time
  c) When I am finishing my work
8 He would look much better _____.
  a) when he'll buy some new clothes
  b) if he would sleep more
  c) if he cut his hair

VOCABULARY PLUS multi-word verbs

10 Complete the sentences with *on, off, up* or *down*.

1 I couldn't believe it when my brother's friend tried to chat me _____ .

2 It was an informal family barbecue, so she dressed _____ in old jeans and a T-shirt.

3 You just need to click _____ the icon to open the file.

4 Can I try these jeans _____ , please?

5 When you've finished on the computer, can you log _____ ?

6 She enjoys spending time with her dad, but she doesn't get _____ with her mum very well.

7 I was so embarrassed when he took _____ his shoes in the theatre!

8 I want to settle _____ and have children one day.

9 I used to drink a lot of coffee, but recently I've gone _____ it.

10 If you scroll _____ , you'll find a link right at the bottom of the page.

VOCABULARY verb-noun collocations

11 Circle the correct option to complete the sentences.

1 They're _____ a plant sale in the village hall on Saturday.
   a) being   b) holding   c) doing

2 She's running a marathon to _____ money for cancer research.
   a) have   b) raise   c) do

3 They're _____ an experiment in bilingual education at my daughter's school.
   a) being   b) doing   c) having

4 If you get to the cinema early, can you _____ us some seats?
   a) have   b) put   c) get

5 Did you _____ that programme last night on killer whales?
   a) watch   b) seeing   c) look

6 How annoying. That man has just _____ the queue.
   a) held   b) walked   c) jumped

7 I think it's time I got my hair _____ . It's far too long.
   a) wash   b) cut   c) dry

VOCABULARY life events

12 Match 1–8 with a)–h) to make sentences.

1 She didn't stop at a red light

2 The relationship wasn't working

3 I got a place at university

4 He did very well in the interview

5 They want to live together

6 She was brilliant at the job

7 He had an accident on holiday

8 He lost his job at the factory

a) so I'm going to study psychology.

b) so she got promoted.

c) so she failed her driving test.

d) so he's looking for work.

e) so they split up.

f) so he had to fly home.

g) so they offered him the job.

h) so they've bought a house.

FUNCTION giving and responding to news

13 Find and correct ten mistakes in the conversations.

Conversation 1

A: I'm sorry to have to telling you, but the train has been cancelled.

B: That annoying.

Conversation 2

A: I've got a good news for you.

B: What is it?

A: I've finished my painting.

B: Congratulation!

Conversation 3

A: There's something I've got to tell to you.

B: What?

A: I'm leaving San Francisco.

B: Oh. I'm sorry for hear that.

Conversation 4

A: You'll never guess to what.

B: What?

A: I got my promotion!

B: That's so fantastic news!

Conversation 5

A: Unfortunate, I didn't get the job.

B: That's real shame.

TEST

Circle the correct option to complete the sentences.

1 Could you go and get the _____? I need to clean the floor.

a) communications satellite   b) washing machine
c) vacuum cleaner

2 Nowadays you can have a _____ to protect you from influenza.

a) antibiotic   b) vaccination
c) genetic engineering

3 Houses in the area have become much _____ recently.

a) more affordable b) more cheaper
c) expensiver

4 People are able to work far _____ hours than before.

a) most flexible   b) more flexible
c) the more flexible

5 The saxophone is _____ to learn than some other instruments.

a) slightly the hard b) slightly easy
c) slightly harder

6 That's a very good _____.

a) wonder   b) inquire   c) question

7 I'm doing _____ into how computers affect children.

a) a research   b) some research
c) some investigate

8 You don't want to come with us, _____?

a) would you   b) did you   c) do you

9 You've brought the camera with you, _____?

a) did you   b) haven't you c) didn't you

10 She _____ one of the best players in the world, isn't she?

a) 's   b) will be   c) was

11 I couldn't do anything to make things better. I felt _____.

a) effective   b) painful   c) useless

12 He's a very _____ puppy.

a) lovable   b) creative   c) biological

13 My computer's _____. Can you help me?

a) needs fixing   b) doesn't work
c) crashed

14 Could you tell me _____?

a) what is the problem   b) what the problem is
c) what the problem

15 Sure. Let me _____.

a) look for   b) have a look   c) look at

16 I've had a really _____ week.

a) exhausted   b) tired   c) exhausting

17 I get really _____ when he doesn't reply to my texts.

a) annoyed   b) annoying   c) boring

18 I'll give you the present when _____ you.

a) I will see   b) I would see c) I see

19 If we can arrange everything, _____ to France for a holiday.

a) we'll go   b) we go   c) we would go

20 _____ very tired when I have to travel a lot.

a) I'll get   b) I get   c) I would get

21 It's a formal evening, so we must _____ in something nice.

a) dress down   b) dress for   c) dress up

22 We're very different characters, but we _____ well.

a) get off   b) get on   c) get on with

23 She's selling the paintings to _____ for charity.

a) buy money   b) earn money
c) raise money

24 I'll get there early and get us some _____.

a) seats   b) entrance   c) chair

25 If he _____ the drums late at night, I would sleep much better.

a) doesn't play   b) didn't play   c) would play

26 Life _____ easier if we didn't have to work so hard.

a) would be   b) is   c) was

27 I wouldn't mind if he _____ back again!

a) always comes   b) never comes c) never came

28 She was _____ a job at their head office in Washington.

a) offered to   b) offered   c) promoted

29 I'm really pleased _____ you that you've won first prize.

a) tell   b) to tell   c) telling

30 A: Their house burned down in a fire.

B: Oh no. That's _____.

a) a shame   b) annoying   c) awful

TEST RESULT   /30

REVIEW AND CHECK 4: UNITS 7–8

VOCABULARY success

1 Tick two correct sentences. Correct the wrong sentences.

1 Our company focuses at quality software.
2 She's getting better at maths.
3 It's important that we work hardly at this.
4 The key is to believe of yourself.
5 He is certainly a high achiever.
6 We'll improve if we are practise every day.

GRAMMAR present perfect simple versus continuous

2 Underline the correct alternative.

1 How long have you *known / been knowing* David?
2 She's angry – she's *waited / been waiting* for an hour!
3 This morning I've *read / been reading* a book called *Infinite Jest* – it's over a thousand pages long!
4 How many people have you *invited / been inviting* for this party?
5 My hands are dirty, I've *worked / been working* on the car.
6 For the last six years I've *learned / been learning* Arabic, but it's really difficult.
7 They don't want to rent *The Godfather* because they've *seen / been seeing* it already.
8 Hello. I don't think we've *met / been meeting* before.

VOCABULARY PLUS verb phrases with prepositions

3 Complete the text with the correct prepositions.

TOP**BLOGGERS**

The best bloggers pay attention ¹_____ what's going on in the world. They listen ²_____ influential people, pick up ³_____ the stories in the air and put ⁴_____ hours reading websites and doing their research. They don't just wait ⁵_____ the big stories; they find them in the corners where other people aren't looking. Of course, they rely ⁶_____ traditional media such as newspapers. All bloggers depend ⁷_____ other sources for their content, but they think ⁸_____ the issues and, rather than just agreeing ⁹_____ the journalists, they look ¹⁰_____ alternative opinions. Often the best bloggers belong ¹¹_____ groups or societies that have access ¹²_____ interesting people, so the bloggers can hear different opinions. The most important qualities for someone to succeed ¹³_____ the 'blogosphere' are to have a talent ¹⁴_____ writing and to believe ¹⁵_____ yourself. In this sense, they have a lot in common ¹⁶_____ traditional journalists, but bloggers don't have to worry ¹⁷_____ newspaper deadlines. The negative side? Bloggers usually don't get paid ¹⁸_____ their work.

VOCABULARY ability

4 Put the words in the correct order to make answers to the questions.

1 A: Why do you think they asked him to write the textbook?
B: subject / because / expert / he's / his / an / in
_____

2 A: Why do you think he'll pass the exam?
B: of / he / maths / because / lot / ability / has / in / a
_____

3 A: Why do you think she'll become an Olympic gymnast?
B: sport / she's / the / at / gifted / because
_____

4 A: Why do you think they'll do well in Hollywood?
B: talent / have / writing / because / a / scripts / for / they
_____

5 A: Why do you think he'll become a professional golfer?
B: aptitude / the / has / an / because / game / for / he
_____

6 A: Why do you think you'll fail the test?
B: science / at / absolutely / because / hopeless / I'm
_____

GRAMMAR present and past ability

5 Rewrite the second sentence so that it means the same as the first. Use the words in capitals. Write three words. Contractions are one word.

1 We don't know how to play cards.   CAN'T
_____ cards.
2 She is a wonderful singer.   CAN
_____ really well.
3 Can you bring some drinks to the party?   ABLE
_____ to bring some drinks to the party?
4 We didn't have time to visit Las Vegas.   MANAGE
We _____ visit Las Vegas.
5 I failed the test.   ABLE
I _____ pass the test.
6 I can usually clean the house in about two hours. MANAGE
I usually _____ the house in about two hours.
7 What languages were you able to speak when you were a child?   COULD
What languages _____ when you were a child?
8 They succeeded in breaking the record.   MANAGED
They _____ the record.

VOCABULARY qualifications

6 Complete the text with the words in the box.

> Master's apprenticeship licence distance
> qualifications online degree learning

YOUTH WORK

When I left school, I had no ¹_____ except my driving ²_____. I needed that because I spent most of my time in stolen cars. When I was eighteen, a friend of my father's told me I could do an ³_____ in his printing company, but because I couldn't read or write, I refused. Instead, I got involved in serious crime. Aged nineteen, I was sent to prison. This was my first taste of real education. Although there was no formal face-to-face ⁴_____, one of the inmates taught me to read and write. Later, he told me about ⁵_____ learning. We were allowed access to computers for a few hours a week, so I started an ⁶_____ course. After three years, I got a ⁷_____ in psychology. It was the best day of my life. When I left prison, I went on to do a ⁸_____, and I became a youth worker, advising young people how to avoid a life of crime.

FUNCTION clarifying opinions

7A Underline the correct alternatives.

A: In my ¹views / view, sport is wonderful. The ²reasoning / reason I say this is that it makes people work in teams. ³For / To me, it's really important.

B: I ⁴can / must say I agree with you. ⁵And / For one thing, it keeps you healthy. For ⁶another / other, it's good for your character. ⁷For / In example, you learn teamwork.

A: That's ⁸it / what I was saying: you learn to work together And like I ⁹told / said, it's also good for your health.

B: That's right. I ¹⁰will / do think children should play more sport in school.

A: And they can join clubs, too. Let me ¹¹do / give you an example: my kids are in an after-school athletics club.

B: That's great. Having ¹²said / spoken that, those clubs can be very expensive.

B Which of the expressions 1–12 in Exercise 7A are for giving opinions (O)? Which are for giving examples (E)? Which are for referring to what you said earlier (R)?

1 _____	7 _____
2 _____	8 _____
3 _____	9 _____
4 _____	10 _____
5 _____	11 _____
6 _____	12 _____

VOCABULARY getting on

8 Put the letters in brackets in the correct order to make a word. Then rewrite the sentences using that word and **two** other words.

1 That music is really annoying. (revesn)
   That music really gets _on my nerves_____.

2 I don't like mixing with other people. (mlseyf)
   I prefer to keep _____.

3 She's always helping me. (frvouas)
   She's always _____.

4 Why don't you stop interfering in my life? (binesssu)
   Why don't you mind _____?

5 They asked us to have dinner with them. (orev)
   They invited us _____.

6 I have a great relationship with my dad. (lwle)
   My dad and I _____.

GRAMMAR articles and quantifiers

9 Are the two underlined parts of the sentences correct? Change the ones that are wrong.

1 I went to school in a small town in ✓/ the ╱United States.

2 My cousin, who is from the West Indies, is an architect.

3 Golf players don't usually make much money, but best ones are millionaires.

4 We saw a rat. The next day our cat killed rat.

5 I didn't enjoy a party – there were too much people.

6 Do you know any good hairdressers? I need the haircut.

7 Plenty of people would happily pay to travel to Moon.

8 I need an MA, but it takes too many time and I don't have enough money.

9 To finish the dish, add a little salt and lot of pepper.

10 Some of us are planning to go to the Barcelona this weekend.

VOCABULARY PLUS compound nouns

10 Cross out the word which does not belong.

1 jam / traffic / lights / ~~person~~

2 car / park / house / rental

3 calling / gift / duty-free / shop

4 industrial / school / housing / estate

5 apartment / primary / language / school

6 one-way / high / news / street

7 shopping / mall / shops / centre

8 semi-detached / flat / terraced / houses

VOCABULARY the internet

11 Tick six correct sentences. Correct the wrong sentences.

1 ~~Blogs~~ *Wikis* are mini-encyclopedias containing useful information.
2 We use search engines to find information quickly.
3 Dating sites contain information about companies and businesses.
4 Wikis tell us which products, films, places, etc. are the best.
5 Photo sharing sites let us upload our pictures so our friends can see them.
6 Ratings sites tell us about individuals – their family, friends and hobbies, etc.
7 News sites tell us what's happening in the world.
8 Social networking sites let us stay in contact with old friends, and make new ones.
9 Travel sites allow us to research places and sometimes book holidays.
10 We use personal homepages to find a partner.
11 Video sharing sites allow people to put film clips on the web.
12 Corporate websites are a type of online journal.

GRAMMAR relative clauses

12 Join the sentences using *which, where* or *who*.

1 I spoke to a doctor. He was very nice.
The doctor _____.
2 We visited a museum. It had a wonderful exhibition.
The museum _____.
3 She was born on an island. It's now under water.
The island _____.
4 My girlfriend is in the fashion industry. She lives in Paris.
My girlfriend, _____.
5 I grew up in a house. It's now a theatre.
The house _____.
6 Tom is my best friend. He works with my father.
Tom, _____.
7 The sale in Macy's lasted for ten days. It's now finished.
The sale in Macy's, _____.
8 They went to a restaurant. It served crocodile.
The restaurant _____.

VOCABULARY welcoming

13 Complete the sentences with a suitable verb.

1 Welcome to the company. Please _____ a seat.
2 You want to use the phone? _____ my guest.
3 Come in. _____ the mess. I've been very busy.
4 Let me take your coat. _____ yourself at home.
5 You look tired. Why don't you _____ your feet up?
6 Hungry? Please _____ yourself.

FUNCTION being a good guest

14 Read the conversations. Cross out eleven extra words.

Conversation 1
Pete: Hi, Don. Is it OK if I ~~to~~ bring a friend to your party?
Don: Yes, of course. No problem.
Pete: Oh, and one other thing. Do I need for to bring anything?
Don: No, it's not the necessary. We have everything we need.

Conversation 2
Joe: I put my feet on the table. Did I do something wrong?
Kat: Oh. It's considered be a bit rude.
Joe: Really? Sorry about that. I didn't know.
Kat: It's OK – we can sort it but out.

Conversation 3
Andre: Is this for a bad time? I can come back later.
Bella: Can you to come back in ten minutes?
Andre: Yes, of course. My apologies. I didn't can realise you were in a meeting.
Bella: It's fine. Don't to worry about it.

Conversation 4
Nick: We caught Roger stealing again. What should we to do?
Tam: If I were you, I'd give him a final warning. You haven't told anyone else?
Nick: No, of course not. OK, I'll do that. Should I tell my boss?
Tam: No, you'd better be not.

LEARN TO accept apologies

15 Add the words in the box to the correct place in B's replies in the conversations.

| all right it's (×2) no at ~~to~~ |

1 A: Sorry I didn't bring a dish. I just didn't have time.
   B: You really don't have ⟋ apologise. We weren't
              to
       expecting anything!

2 A: I'm sorry – I forgot to bring my notes.
   B: It's problem. I can photocopy mine.

3 A: Sorry, did I bump you?
   B: That's. It didn't hurt.

4 A: Sorry, am I late?
   B: Not all. We usually don't start till 3.15.

5 A: Sorry, did I step on your toe?
   B: No, nothing. I didn't even feel it.

6 A: I'm so sorry about missing lunch.
   B: Honestly, fine. Don't worry about it.

TEST

Circle the correct option to complete the sentences.

1 We're going to focus _____ quality.

   a) to   b) on   c) by

2 For the last two hours _____ in the garden, so I'm tired.

   a) I'm working   b) I work

   c) I've been working

3 Jun and I _____ each other for ten years.

   a) have been knowing   b) have known

   c) are knowing

4 I think I like the new flat, but I _____ there long.

   a) haven't been living   b) am not living

   c) don't live

5 Bad news – his dog _____.

   a) is died   b) has been dying   c) has died

6 We really depend _____ our sponsors.

   a) of   b) to   c) on

7 You have _____ for tennis.

   a) an expert   b) an attitude   c) an aptitude

8 I'm hopeless _____ languages.

   a) in   b) on   c) at

9 Will you _____ finish your work on time?

   a) can   b) be able   c) manage to

10 I'm afraid I _____ to help you.

   a) am unable   b) can't   c) manage

11 When he was three, he _____ already talk.

   a) managed   b) was able   c) could

12 I'm _____ an apprenticeship in an internet company.

   a) doing   b) making   c) working

13 She's just got her driving _____.

   a) exam   b) licence   c) certificate

14 In my _____, Tokyo's the world's greatest city.

   a) view   b) opinions   c) thinking

15 Let me _____ you an example of what I mean.

   a) make   b) take   c) give

16 Those people should _____ their own business.

   a) take   b) mind   c) think

17 He's training to become _____.

   a) pilot   b) the pilot   c) a pilot

18 _____ usually start to walk at about twelve months.

   a) Children   b) A child   c) The children

19 There were _____ people at the party.

   a) plenty of   b) a few of   c) lots

20 I ate _____ ice cream, and now I feel sick.

   a) too   b) too much   c) too many

21 We grew up on a _____ estate.

   a) housing   b) house   c) living

22 I often use search _____ to find out information.

   a) machines   b) engines   c) sites

23 I use a video _____ site.

   a) internet   b) loading   c) sharing

24 The road _____ we wanted to take was closed.

   a) that   b) where   c) what

25 Tillie, _____ is already at university.

   a) that's only sixteen,   b) who's only sixteen

   c) who's only sixteen,

26 The town _____ is full of trees.

   a) where I live   b) which I live   c) where, I live

27 Russia, _____ has changed a lot.

   a) which we visited in 1989,

   b) which we visited in 1989

   c) what we visited in 1989,

28 Come in and _____ yourself at home.

   a) be   b) take   c) make

29 My _____. I didn't know you were busy.

   a) disgrace   b) sorry   c) apologies

30 If this is a bad _____, I can come back later.

   a) time   b) hour   c) timing

TEST RESULT   /30

VOCABULARY history

1 Complete the words in these sentences.

1 The government was removed during the rev_____.

2 The change to farming communities was history's greatest tur_____ p_____.

3 Rich countries should help poor countries in their economic dev_____.

4 Because people lived close together, the disease quickly spr_____.

5 In the fight to cure cancer, the result of this research is a great adv_____.

6 She was one of the most important people in the women's mov_____.

7 The personal computer was the twentieth century's best inv_____.

8 The invention of the wheel provided the fou_____ for most machines.

9 The 3,000-year-old body found in the mountains was a great dis_____.

10 In the debate about climate change, we haven't made much pro_____.

GRAMMAR third conditional

2 Complete the sentences with the third conditional form of the verbs in brackets.

1 If Xiulin _____ (not help) us, we _____ (not finish) the project on time.

2 They _____ (go) for a picnic if it _____ (not rain).

3 If I _____ (study), I _____ (not fail) the test.

4 My wife _____ (tell) me if she _____ (have) a problem.

5 If Thierry _____ (not score) that goal, we _____ (not won).

6 What _____ (you/do) if you _____ (miss) the plane?

GRAMMAR active versus passive

3 Rewrite the sentences using the passive.

1 We sell chairs and tables here.
Chairs and tables _____.

2 They don't produce coffee in England.
Coffee _____.

3 They are building a new school.
A new school _____.

4 Someone assassinated the President.
The President _____.

5 Samuel Beckett didn't write *Ulysses*.
Ulysses _____.

6 No one has told us anything about the exam.
We _____.

VOCABULARY periods of time

4 Underline the correct alternative.

1 There was a big party to celebrate the new *millennium / fortnight / seventies*.

2 I stayed for *the eighties / a generation / a decade*, arriving in 1989 and leaving in 1999.

3 In the first part of July, we spent *an era / a fortnight / the century* in Greece, on holiday.

4 She worked in the same school for nearly *an age / the nineties / a quarter-century*.

5 War was a way of life for my grandfather's *generation / decade / age*.

6 I grew up in *a century / an era / the nineties*.

VOCABULARY PLUS collocations with *come, give, have* and *make*

5 Cross out the word which is not possible.

1 The team came *first / by car / well*.

2 I listened while Sam gave *directions / a discussion / instructions*.

3 William made *project / progress / a mess* in his art class.

4 I had a *dream / homework / good time* last night.

5 My ability to speak French came *naturally / forward / back to me*.

6 She's going to give *a talk / me a call / problem* today.

7 The company has to make a *profit / money / decision*.

8 She sometimes has *progress / trouble / a break* while doing her homework.

VOCABULARY describing people

6 Put the letters in bold in the correct order to complete the sentences.

1 I like **tearceiv** _____ people who have their own ideas.

2 She wasn't very **igolirna** _____; her ideas were nothing new.

3 Like most great leaders, he's very **arccisahtmi** _____.

4 Her life, spent helping others, was **xaeeyplrm** _____.

5 She had some **nnvvatiioe** _____ ideas about design.

6 Like many soldiers, he was extremely **reabv** _____.

7 My boss is **spiirotilnnaa** _____ – everyone follows him.

8 Jackson is the most **neflliunati** _____ player in the team.

FUNCTION expressing uncertainty

7 Make sentences with a word or phrase from each section.

1 I've	a) sure	i) clue.
2 I haven't	b) forgotten	ii) isn't Elizabeth.
3 I'm fairly	c) a	iii) it's Jane.
4 It's	d) it	iv) not Sarah.
5 I'm sure	e) no	v) her name.
6 I have	f) definitely	vi) idea.

1 *I've forgotten her name.*
2 _____
3 _____
4 _____
5 _____
6 _____

LEARN TO react to information

8 Underline the correct alternative.
1 A: This film is very similar to his last one.
   B: I was *about just / just about* to say that.
2 A: Jeanette Winterson is the one who wrote *The Passion*.
   B: *Does / Is* she? I didn't know that.
3 A: It took over a hundred years to complete the building.
   B: Did it? That's *interesting / too interesting*.
4 A: *Whole Lotta Love* was written by Led Zeppelin.
   B: I knew that. I just *don't / couldn't* remember.

VOCABULARY the environment

9 Complete the sentences with the words in the box.

> packaging   double glazed   recycled   energy-saving
> pre-prepared   on standby   ~~processed~~   insulated
> organic   second-hand

1 We try not to eat too much *processed* food, and we grow our own _____ food.
2 We are very conscious of the environment: we use _____ light bulbs and the house is _____.
3 We don't waste energy. Our windows are _____ and we make sure our computers are _____ or switched off.
4 We rarely buy _____ food. The _____ is such a waste of plastic.
5 All of our clothes are _____, and most of our furniture is _____.

GRAMMAR reported speech

10 Complete the conversations. B always remembers that A said the opposite earlier.
1 A: That book is very good.
   B: Oh? I thought you said *that book wasn't very good.*
2 A: I know the answer.
   B: Oh? I thought you said _____.
3 A: I haven't been to Germany.
   B: Oh? I thought you said _____.
4 A: I can't swim.
   B: Oh? I thought you said _____.
5 A: I'm going to university.
   B: Oh? I thought you said _____.
6 A: I won't be there on Monday.
   B: Oh? I thought you said _____.
7 A: I'll be able to help.
   B: Oh? I thought you said _____.
8 A: I spoke to Kevin.
   B: Oh? I thought you said _____.

11 Find and correct five mistakes in the reported questions below.
1 He asked me when started the game.
2 He asked me if I do play any instruments.
3 She asked me where my husband was.
4 She asked me if I worked at home.
5 He asked me why was I crying.
6 She asked me if slept my baby all night.
7 She asked me if they did speak English.

VOCABULARY PLUS prefixes

12 Add prefixes to two words in each sentence.
1 Ah, I_{mis}understood the instructions; I thought it was_{un}usual to cook pasta for forty minutes!
2 He judged the cooking time and left the food in the oven too long; now it's cooked.
3 The results of his diet are believable; he used to be weight, but now he looks fit.
4 The kitchen was tidy so I told her to put things in order, but she obeyed me and went out.
5 We use plastic plates instead of throwing them away, and we cycle food packaging.
6 I approved of Dr Kim's behaviour because it's ethical to give bad advice to patients.
7 Don't estimate the time it takes to new a passport; mine took over two months.
8 He was living here, then he suddenly appeared; at the moment his location is known.

VOCABULARY reporting verbs

13 Underline one incorrect verb in each sentence. Which sentence does it belong to?

1 David <u>promised</u> us to his birthday party. *Sentence 6*

2 The tour guide refused us about poisonous spiders.

3 The doorman suggested to let me into the club because I was wearing jeans.

4 I explained to take her for dinner, to say 'thank you'.

5 The teacher invited the grammar clearly so everyone understood.

6 My dad warned to buy me an ice cream if I behaved well.

7 Minty offered going to Greece for our holiday.

GRAMMAR verb patterns

14 Underline the correct alternatives.

World Food restaurant (15 DELANEY ST, SANTA CLARA, 22187)

A friend suggested ¹*for me / that I / me to* go to World Food, and explained ²*me / that / if* I would love the cool, relaxed atmosphere and the outstanding menu. He warned ³*me to / that I / me* expect a big bill at the end, but promised ⁴*me / to / which* that it was worth it.

I arrived at 7.25 for a 7.30 reservation and the receptionist told me ⁵*waiting / wait / to wait* in the bar. I waited for thirty-five minutes before a waiter, with no apology, offered ⁶*for take / taking / to take* me to my table.

The decor was horrible – grey paintings that looked like something your dog might bring home – and I was seated under a speaker playing loud music. I asked the waiter ⁷*give / for give / to give* me a better seat. At first he refused ⁸*to move / moving / move* me, saying the restaurant was full, but finally he agreed ⁹*for / that he / to* give me a window seat.

After the terrible service, I feared the worst, but the food was excellent. My friend had recommended ¹⁰*to try / by trying / trying* the salmon in teriyaki sauce. It was a great choice, as was the apple pie I had for dessert. All World Food needs is a new attitude; the cooking is outstanding.

VOCABULARY airports

15 Match 1–8 with a)–h) to make sentences you hear at an airport.

1 May I see
2 Please proceed
3 Is this hand
4 Would you like to check
5 15D is an aisle
6 Your flight will
7 Can I see your boarding
8 We don't have a gate

a) to gate number 62.
b) seat, sir.
c) card, please?
d) your passport, please?
e) luggage, madam?
f) number yet.
g) in this bag?
h) board at 2.45.

FUNCTION giving advice/warnings

16 Put the words in italics in the correct order to complete the sentences.

Q I'm exploring the Amazon for a few weeks. Can you give me some advice?

A OK, ¹*thing is the important to most* _____ be prepared. Read about the Amazon first. Regarding clothes, ²*sure bring you make* _____ a raincoat as it's very wet. Obviously, it's really wild so ³*snakes watch for out* _____. The truth is ⁴*common not very it's* _____ for people to die from snakebites in the Amazon, but it does happen.

Q I'm climbing Mount Kilimanjaro. Any tips?

A Kilimanjaro is a tough climb, so ⁵*I you, if start I'd were* _____ preparing physically four months before the trip. Also, ⁶*bring to need you* _____ a really good pair of hiking boots. Finally, climbers ⁷*bring tendency a to have* _____ too much stuff. ⁸*you pack don't do, Whatever* _____ too much. You'll have to carry it all up the mountain.

Q I'm travelling around India. Can you give me some advice?

A Firstly, you'll see some amazing sights, so ⁹*bring forget don't to* _____ a camera. Secondly, ¹⁰*whole the on* _____ Indian food is wonderful, but ¹¹*eat careful be to* _____ only food that has been prepared properly in a kitchen. Also, ¹²*some take better you'd* _____ water-purifying pills because the water can be contaminated.

TEST

Circle the correct option to complete the sentences.

1 The _____ of penicillin was an accident.

  a) discovery   b) discoverer   c) discover

2 Because of the internet, ideas _____ quickly.

  a) revolution   b) invent   c) spread

3 He wouldn't have survived if he _____ his medicine.

  a) took   b) hadn't taken c) hasn't taken

4 If you had seen her, what _____?

  a) did you say   b) would you said
  c) would you have said

5 If I _____ that it was so hard, I would have asked for help.

  a) would have known b) knew   c) had known

6 She would _____ famous if she'd been born in another generation.

  a) have be   b) have been   c) had been

7 All articles _____ by our board of editors.

  a) are discussed   b) discussed
  c) be discussed

8 Why _____ about this problem?

  a) wasn't I told   b) was I told not
  c) I wasn't told

9 The money will _____ tomorrow.

  a) collect   b) to be collected
  c) be collected

10 The 1980s was my favourite _____.

  a) century   b) millennium c) decade

11 We are making _____ all the time.

  a) movement   b) progress   c) advance

12 Lu _____ us directions to her house.

  a) did   b) gave   c) had

13 She was a very _____ musician.

  a) influencing   b) inspiration c) influential

14 I have _____ what to do.

  a) a clue   b) no idea   c) ideas

15 I'm a hundred percent _____ of the answer.

  a) knowing   b) certainly   c) certain

16 We never eat _____ food.

  a) processed   b) process   c) reused

17 She said she _____ to talk to her boss.

  a) was going   b) going   c) would

18 You told me you _____ Bill for years.

  a) haven't to see   b) don't see   c) hadn't seen

19 He asked me when _____ in the country.

  a) I arrive   b) I'd arrived c) I am arrive

20 She asked if we _____ how to get to Bristol.

  a) are knowing   b) did know   c) knew

21 I _____ the question.

  a) disunderstood   b) not understand
  c) misunderstood

22 I _____ to pay the bill, but she refused.

  a) offered   b) explained   c) invited

23 She _____ them that the water was dangerous.

  a) refused   b) warned   c) suggested

24 The man refused _____ me the gun.

  a) giving   b) for give   c) to give

25 The guide recommended _____ the museum.

  a) visiting   b) to visit   c) visit

26 My mother suggests _____ early as it gets crowded.

  a) that we are go   b) that we go c) us to go

27 I warned you _____ that.

  a) not doing   b) not to do   c) to not do

28 I took it on the plane as hand _____.

  a) luggage   b) cases   c) bags

29 If I _____ pack some spare shoes.

  a) were you, you should
  b) were you, I'd
  c) am you, I'd

30 Please make _____ you sign your name.

  a) definite   b) sure   c) certainly

TEST RESULT   /30

AUDIO SCRIPTS

Recording 1

1 What's your middle name?
2 Who gave you that?
3 Where's the best restaurant?
4 Why did they arrive late?
5 What did you have for lunch?
6 When does your train leave?

UNIT 1 **Recording 2**

Clyde

When I was growing up, my mother had this expression that she used all the time. She used to say, 'Keep your eyes open'. Very simple, I know, but she always said it. Like ... 'keep your eyes open' all the time. And so, well, we travelled quite a lot in those days, especially around Europe, and she always told us ... or encouraged us ... to look at different cultures and see the things around us. So in that respect, I think my mother really influenced me because now I appreciate other cultures and I do try to see the things around me.

Luciana

Biggest influence? Well, my grandfather was definitely the biggest influence on me. I lived with my grandparents for about five years when I was a child, which is quite common in my country. And my grandfather was really strict. He was very tough. He was an immigrant who came from Italy with nothing, absolutely nothing, and he really believed in hard work. And everyone was frightened of him because he shouted a lot. But because I was his grand-daughter, I saw a different side of him. He could be very gentle, and quite a loving man. But his major thing was honesty. You had to tell the truth. He didn't mind if you made a mistake or did something wrong, but if you lied to him ... oh, he would get very, very angry. He made me an honest person and a hard-working person.

Austin

I had an uncle – he's dead now – my Uncle Charlie. He was my mother's brother. And the thing about Charlie was that he was always happy. He always saw the bright side of life, which is something I've tried to do. He was a real character. He was built like a tank. I mean massive. I think he was some kind of boxing champion. And I remember him coming to our house at Christmas – this is when I was a kid – and laughing all the time. He had this big deep laugh. And he had a story that he always told us. He told it to us every Christmas, about a time in Australia when he fought a crocodile with his bare hands, basically killed this crocodile. And we believed every word of it. Many years later after he'd died, I asked my mother about this story and she looked at me funny and said, 'Your Uncle Charlie never went to Australia. He never left London in his whole life.'

UNIT 1 **Recording 3**

1 He was an employee here.
2 I had a wonderful mentor.
3 All pupils wear a uniform.
4 We were team-mates for years.
5 Have you met my fiancée?
6 Talk to your partner.
7 She's my godmother.
8 That club is for members only.

UNIT 2 **Recording 1**

1
A: Have you been here before?
B: Yes, we've visited Naples a few times.

2
A: Have you had time to see the museum yet?
B: No, we haven't had time.

3
A: Did you find your hotel OK?
B: Yes, we found the hotel without any problems.

4
A: Have you got your guidebook?
B: Oh no. I've left it in my room.

5
A: Have you had any lunch?
B: Yes, we've already eaten.

6
A: Have you enjoyed your stay?
B: Yes, we've had a wonderful time.

UNIT 2 **Recording 2**

1
Christine

A lot of friends were staying in my apartment. We'd had a party the night before, and in the morning, one friend, Danny, got up to make everyone some coffee. While he was making the coffee, he heard the news on the radio. He came back into the room, and told us that John Lennon had died. Someone had shot John Lennon. We were all really shocked. It was a very strange feeling. We couldn't believe it. We had all grown up with the music of John Lennon and The Beatles. We had played his music the night before. And now, suddenly, he was dead. There was a huge feeling of loss. He was such a peaceful man, who had wanted peace for everyone. It was a terrible way for him to die.

2
Rob

I was travelling to a meeting on the Tube that morning, and there were delays everywhere. They closed the Underground station. At first, I was really angry, and worried about not getting to my meeting on time. But gradually, we started to realise that something terrible had happened. People outside the station were trying to talk on their mobile phones, but the networks were all down, because of the panic. Some people started to get news, and soon we discovered there had been bombs all over London. It was a strange and terrible feeling. There were crowds of people outside shops, watching the news on the televisions.

3

Gino

I was sitting in the kitchen of my house in Italy with my family, and I was only a child. Everyone was watching television. I remember the black and white pictures. I watched as this man landed on the Moon. And I can remember thinking how amazing it must be to be an astronaut, and what an exciting job it was. Until then, I had wanted to be a train driver, but for a few years afterwards, I definitely wanted to be an astronaut.

4

Marianne

I was staying in Los Angeles with some friends, and I was only about eighteen years old. In the night I suddenly woke up, and the whole house was shaking. I had never felt an earthquake before, but I knew that was what was happening. It was very frightening. But after a few seconds it stopped, everything went quiet, and I went back to sleep. When I woke up in the morning, I thought perhaps it had all been a dream. But when I went downstairs, and turned on the radio, I heard the news. The quake was in San Francisco, and it had done a lot of damage. So, I was lucky really. But I will never forget that feeling.

UNIT 3 Recording 1

Ruth

I'm really excited about this weekend actually, because I'm ... I'm going walking with some friends in the Lake District. There's a whole group of us and we meet up every now and again for walking holidays. I love walking because it makes you feel so good, so we always have a good time. We're staying in a hostel, near one of the biggest lakes. There are some lovely walks from there and we've stayed in the hostel before. We're planning to do two big walks, one each day. They're about twenty- or thirty-kilometre walks, so it'll be quite hard, I think. We'll be really tired in the evenings, so we won't do much then, just have something to eat in the hostel, and then go to bed. It's not everyone's idea of fun, I know, but I can't wait.

Kieron

I'm starting at Dundee University in September. I'm going to study Law, so I'm really excited about it. I think it's going to be a good course, and I'm hoping to meet lots of new friends and have a good time, too. To start with, I'm going to stay in the university accommodation on campus, until I get to know the city better, and then I might move out and rent a flat with some other students. I'll have to see how it goes. Living on campus is cheaper, so I might stay there for the whole year. I'm planning to join a few clubs, probably the sports club, because I love sports. I enjoy playing rugby so I'll see if I can join the rugby club or something like that.

Amber

We're going to the Red Sea for our honeymoon, which is wonderful. I've never been to Egypt before, and I'm sure I'm going to love it. I love new experiences, meeting new people, and going to new places, and I think Egypt is going to feel really different. The language, the food, the way people behave, everything. We're staying in a luxury hotel right on the beach, and we're going to do a scuba-diving course while we're there. I've always wanted to try scuba-diving. It's going to be fantastic.

UNIT 3 Recording 2

1 They're going to play squash.
2 I'm going to buy a new phone.
3 She's going to spend a week in Greece.
4 He isn't going to eat anything.
5 Are you going to walk to the station?
6 He's going to change his job.

UNIT 3 Recording 3

1

Conversation 1

A: The living room is too green and the floor's all wrong.
B: Sorry?
A: The living room. Green. And I hate the floor.
B: You've lost me.

A: I'm talking about Mum's new house. I don't like the colour of the walls in the living room.
B: Oh!

Conversation 2

A: Hello? I'm trying to find my lost luggage.
B: Ah, OK.
A: My bags went missing in Montevideo in Uruguay, after a flight from Curitiba, Brazil.
B: Can you say that again? Montevideo?
A: I flew from Curitiba to Montevideo and my bags went missing.
B: Have you reported it already?
A: Yes, the name is Anders Kleeburg.
B: Hang on. Could you repeat the last name? Anders ...?
A: Kleeburg. K-l-e-e-b-u-r-g.

Conversation 3

A: OK, so cricket. So this is the bowler, OK? He runs up and bowls at the batsman.
B: What exactly do you mean? What's a bowler?
A: A bowler is the person with the ball in his hand, OK? And he tries to get the batsman out. Get him off the field.
B: Do you mean to say he tries to kill the batsman with the ball?
A: No!

Conversation 4

A: Did you read this?! About popcorn. In 1948, two American scientists found some popcorn in a cave in New Mexico and dated it. It was over five thousand years old.
B: I didn't catch any of that. Are you talking about popcorn?
A: Yeah, it's an ancient food. Popcorn is thousands of years old.
B: I don't get what you're saying. You mean the popcorn we ate in the cinema yesterday is thousands of years old!
A: No! Popcorn in general. People have eaten it for thousands of years.

UNIT 4 Recording 1

1

I work in a busy airport in France. I am responsible for a small group of people. In my job you need to know what you are doing. You must be very accurate, and observant. And you have to be able to work well under pressure and be a good decision maker.

2

I work in a pizza restaurant. In my job you need to have a friendly, relaxed manner. It's important to be friendly to customers, and patient. You have to be organised, and have a good memory, too.

3

In my job you have to be a really good communicator. You need to be able to listen carefully to customers, and find out what the problem is. And then you have to be able to think outside the box sometimes to see if you can find a solution to the problem, which will keep everybody happy. You have to be able to stay calm, even if the customer starts getting angry.

4

I work in a lawyer's office. You have to have good organisational skills, I think, and you shouldn't get stressed too easily. You have to be quite hard-working as well. And you need to pay attention to detail.

5

I work in a children's hospital. I think the most important quality for my job is that you must be a caring person. You have to care about the people you're looking after. And you have to get on with children. That's very important.

6

You need to be very patient in my job, especially when there's a lot of traffic. And you have to be a good timekeeper as well. You always have to be on time.

UNIT 4 Recording 2

1 I used to be very sporty.
2 Can I use your phone?
3 He never used to worry about it.

4 I used to live in the USA when I was 18.
5 This stuff is used to kill insects.
6 I don't use the car much any more.
7 We used to love going there on holiday.
8 I didn't use to live in Europe.

UNIT 5 Recording 1

/eɪ/ make

space
communications
aeroplanes
vaccinations

/æ/ apple

antibiotics
travel
satellites
vacuum

/ə/ polar

nuclear
machine
commercial
solar

UNIT 5 Recording 2

Mia

Well, it's changed a lot, goodness, enormously. I mean thirty years ago, I was still at school. I was ten years old. Life was a lot simpler then. All I had to think about was doing my homework, and enjoying my free time with friends. I think life was simpler for everybody then. We didn't have all this technology, and I think the pace of life was slower. At work, when someone sent a letter, it could take a week or two even before they would get a reply. Nowadays, people email, and they expect an instant response. On the same day, or within an hour or two. That puts a lot of pressure on people. We say that technology has saved us time, but it just speeds things up, and we are expected to do so much more. It's non-stop. We have mobile phones and BlackBerries, iPhones. So we don't just turn off and relax.

Tom

That's an interesting question. It's changed a lot. I live in Beijing. So there has been a huge advancement of technology, and huge growth. There are more people, with more money. There has been an economic explosion here, so the city has grown. All the offices and high-rise buildings, lots of those weren't here thirty years ago. And it's very multicultural nowadays. People from all over the world live in Beijing. People came from everywhere to see if they could get rich, and many of them did get rich. They made millions. I think in a lot of places out in the countryside, things haven't changed that much. Life is quite similar to how it was before, for farmers, and their families. I suppose they have more technology now. They have mobile phones, and televisions, and the internet, so they know a lot more about the wider world, and what is going on. Thirty years ago, they just had a radio, and it was difficult to find out information. That's much easier now.

Owen

Oh, well, both probably. The world is getting better in many ways. I think if we look at living standards across the world, obviously there are still millions of people living in terrible poverty, but I think the situation is getting better. People have better access to food and medicines, and education. So, these are all things which are improving. Medicine is improving, so people live longer, and we can fight infectious diseases. People's lives have improved because of technology, so life is easier now than it was before. A lot of manual work is done by machines. But in some ways, the world is getting worse. War, for example, is a bigger problem all the time. There are more and more wars, which is surprising. And weapons are becoming even more dangerous. I think the environment is definitely suffering, so we are polluting more than we used to because of all the industrialisation. And I think also, socially, things are getting worse. Because people are less social now, than before. They spend more time on their own, with computers and computer games, and less time talking to others, working together, and I think that is a great shame, and a problem for the future, too.

UNIT 5 Recording 3

1
A: Have you met Yinka's parents?
B: Only once. They're doctors, aren't they?

2
A: There isn't a cloud in the sky.
B: I know. It's a beautiful day, isn't it?

3
A: Are you looking for the scissors?
B: You haven't seen them, have you?

4
A: Have you read Jhumpa Lahiri's new book?
B: Yeah, she's a great writer, isn't she?

5
A: I've got my final exam tomorrow.
B: You'll pass, won't you?

6
A: I think this is the wrong address.
B: Yes, we've made a mistake, haven't we?

UNIT 5 Recording 4

1
A: Excuse me, could you tell me the way to the swimming pool, please?
B: Yes, of course I can. You keep going this way, until you get to the traffic lights. Then, …

2
A: Hello. Do you know what time the bank opens?
B: I'm not sure. I'll just ask someone.

3
A: Do you want us to bring anything?
B: That would be great. Could you bring some salad, and maybe something for dessert?
A: Yes, of course. Anything else?
B: No, that'll be fine.

4
A: Could you help me with my bags?
B: I'm sorry, I can't. I've got my hands full.

5
A: Would you mind opening the door for me?
B: Of course not. There you are.
A: Thank you. That's very kind.

6
A: Could you tell me what time the show starts?
B: Let me have a look. The afternoon show starts at 3p.m.
A: Thanks very much.

7
A: Would you mind coming to get me from the station?
B: OK. Sure. Wait outside and I'll be there in ten minutes.

8
A: Do you know if there's a post office near here?
B: Yes, there is – there's one just along this road.

REVIEW 1 Recording 1

E = Examiner I = Interviewer
H = Mr. Hubbard

Examiner: You will hear a radio interview with a head teacher of a school who has just won a prize for his work improving the school. For each question, put a tick in the correct box.

**You now have 45 seconds to look at the questions for Part 2.
Now we are ready to start. Listen carefully. You will hear the recording twice.**

I: Here with me in the studio today is Mr. Roy Hubbard, who has recently won an award for the ambitious work he's done at Cedars School in North London, where he has been head teacher for the last six years. Welcome, Mr. Hubbard.

H: Hello.

I: Could you start by telling us a bit about the school?

H: I'd love to. It's a primary school, and we have pupils from 5 to 11 years old. When I first started at the school six years ago, it was a failing school, and we had one of the lowest average test scores in the country. Parents didn't want to send their children there, and the local council was considering closing the school. Today I'm happy to say that things have improved a lot and we're now one of the top five schools in North London.

I: Wow, so how did you manage to turn things around?

H: Well, let me start by saying that although it was me who won the local government award this year, to quote Isaac Newton, I was 'standing on the shoulders of giants' somewhat.

I: How do you mean?

H: Well, the real reason things improved at Cedars was down to the endless hard work of the teachers, parents and children themselves who I've been lucky enough to work with.

I: Right, important to mention.

H: Yes, well, one of the first things we did when I arrived was start a breakfast club. The idea was that if we could get the children in before lessons started and provide them with a hot, nutritious meal before they started classes, then this would help them concentrate better during the school day and therefore learn better, too.

I: I see. My mother always used to say that breakfast is the most important meal of the day.

H: She sounds like a very smart person! A lot of the children come from poor families, and they don't always have enough money to provide this at home. The next thing we did was start what we called the 'How You Want Project'. What this involved was – quite simply – asking the pupils what they *wanted* to do. A lot of them had already had quite bad experiences of school, being forced to learn things which they weren't interested in.

I: But surely the children just said they wanted to play computer games, watch TV, and so on?

H: Haha, yes, but obviously we asked them to choose from a selection of activities. We also spent time finding out what topics they were interested in, and used these as ways of presenting the information we needed to teach.

I: So what did they come up with?

H: A variety of things – you'd be surprised! Some quite unexpected topics came up such as a soap opera clearly meant for adults, and others which aren't appropriate to mention on the radio! But to take an example we used, a lot of the pupils like football – both boys and girls – and football is a subject which you can use to introduce a whole range of other areas on the school curriculum. You've got maths and geometry looking at the different angles a footballer uses to score a goal, history – a lot of teams have interesting histories which are tied up with the local (and sometimes national) culture, language, biology, etc.

I: That's fascinating. I wish my school had been like that! So were those two projects enough to turn the school around?

H: Oh no, though they were a very important starting point. I have to say that the teachers were brilliant at organising and writing the new syllabus, but the parents of the children also put in a lot of work. They organised lots of events outside school time, such as a local sale, competitions and a fun run, which helped raise money for the school to spend on new technology. This meant that each class had a set of tablet computers they could use with the children to teach them modern skills that they'll need when they leave school.

I: That sounds amazing. And do you have any future plans for the school?

H: Oh yes. Because of our recent success, the local government has agreed to give us a sum of money, with which we plan to build a new sports centre. The children are very excited about it, as you can imagine. I just hope we can continue the success we've had in the future.

I: Well, I'm sorry but I have to stop you there, as we've run out of time. Congratulations on winning your award and to all the parents, teachers and children who helped make it possible, and the very best of luck for the future.

H: Thank you, that's very kind.

Examiner: That is the end of Part 2.

REVIEW 1 Recording 2

1 A: Children, go and clean your rooms!

B: Aw, do we have to?

2 A: Can we leave early today?

B: No, you mustn't go until you've finished your work.

3 A: I'm really worried about the exam.

B: Well, I've told you before, you should study more.

4 A: Can I wear jeans to the party?

B: Yes that's fine, you don't have to wear formal clothes.

5 A: Is it an important game?

B: Oh yes, they must win it if they want to get promoted.

6 A: Don't you just hate her clothes?

B: You shouldn't say things like that, it's not nice.

REVIEW 1 Recording 3

1 hard-working
2 ambitious
3 a good communicator
4 competitive
5 indecisive
6 motivated

UNIT 6 Recording 1

1 If I had more time, I'd learn to ski.
2 If you didn't work, what would you do?
3 If they had to move, they wouldn't live with me.
4 She'd go out at night if her parents let her.
5 Where would you go if you had the chance?
6 I wouldn't sleep if I drank that coffee.

UNIT 6 Recording 2

In the eyes of street criminals, everybody communicates something. Some people communicate strength and power; others communicate 'I am a victim'. Researchers Jean A Hampton and Robert Ealey asked convicted criminals to watch a secret video of a street scene and then say which people look like possible victims of a crime. They did it easily. The potential victims, surprisingly, were not always small women;

sometimes they were big men. For this interview, Robert Ealey looked at this picture of a street scene and explained which people were potential victims.

UNIT 6 Recording 3

I = Interviewer   E = Robert Ealey

I: So which of these people would a criminal go for?

E: Not the ones you think.

I: Can you explain?

E: Yeah, so for example, you've got an old woman, see?

I: Yes.

E: So you're a criminal, OK? You might think, OK, this old woman is small and weak. She's not going to fight me or give me any trouble. But who's she with?

I: She's with a dog.

E: That's right. And the thing about dogs is they are unpredictable. And the last thing you want if you're a criminal is unpredictability. You have about five seconds maximum to commit the crime and you don't want any surprises. OK? So you leave the old woman.

I: Right. Is that really the length of time for a street crime?

E: Five seconds? That's the maximum. Most street crimes take maybe two seconds, then it's over.

I: Wow.

E: OK, so let's take someone else. There's a woman talking into a mobile phone, OK?

I: Yes, I see her.

E: Easy victim or not?

I: Well, if she's talking on a mobile phone, she could tell her friend what's happening, right?

E: And then what?

I: Um, the friend calls the police?

E: And do you think the police are going to get there in five seconds?

I: Well, no.

E: No, this woman on the phone is a potential victim. The phone doesn't matter. The reason she's a potential victim is that she isn't paying attention to what's happening around her. She isn't looking at other people. She's distracted.

I: I see.

E: The same with the tourists looking at the map, OK?

I: Right.

E: They're concentrating on the map, not the people around them. This also tells the criminal that these people are lost and don't know what they're doing.

I: But there are two of them, right, so maybe a criminal would hesitate?

E: Maybe, but don't forget, it takes half a second to steal something and run. OK, what about the man at the cashpoint?

I: The guy taking cash out of the bank?

E: What's he doing wrong?

I: Well, if that was me, the cash would be in my wallet before I turned round.

E: That's right. He's basically saying, 'look at me, I've just taken out lots of money and I'm too stupid to put it in my wallet quickly'. He's a criminal's dream. What about the woman in a mini-skirt?

I: Well, she's attractive and … I don't know. She's not exactly big and strong either. Maybe a victim?

E: But look at her body language. She's confident, she knows where she's going, she's looking straight ahead, and she's probably moving fast. No criminal would go for her.

I: That's interesting. So body language is pretty important.

E: It's extremely important. Look at the man in the coat. Big man, probably strong, but what's his body telling us?

I: He's not focusing.

E: Yes, that's right. He's looking at his feet. He doesn't know who's around him. Any criminal will think, 'nice coat, probably a fat wallet in there, full of money, and he's not concentrating'. The key for a street criminal is surprise. It doesn't matter who the victim is; if you can surprise them, they have no chance.

I: The couple leaving the taxi?

E: Rule number one of the street: if you have anything valuable, don't show it. This man's wearing an expensive watch which everyone can see. The other thing is people leaving cars are always in a weak position. They aren't standing up properly, and they aren't aware of who else is on the street.

UNIT 6 Recording 4

Conversation 1

A: Bad news, I'm afraid.

B: What's the matter?

A: I'm afraid it needs a new engine.

Conversation 2

A: What's the problem?

B: I'm sorry to have to tell you, but we lost the match.

Conversation 3

A: I've got some good news for you.

B: What's that?

A: We've won a holiday for two in Turkey!

Conversation 4

A: I'm afraid I've got some bad news.

B: What's happened?

A: The flight's been cancelled.

Conversation 5

A: There's something I've got to tell you.

B: What's that?

A: I failed my exam.

Conversation 6

A: You'll never guess what happened.

B: What?

A: I was promoted!

Conversation 7

A: Unfortunately, we were burgled last night.

B: Oh no. That's terrible.

Conversation 8

A: I've got something to tell you.

B: What is it?

A: We're getting married.

UNIT 7 Recording 1

1

He's very gifted.

She's really skilful.

2

He has an aptitude.

I'm hopeless at this.

3

He thinks he's useless.

She has a talent.

4

They say he's an expert.

She has great ability.

UNIT 7 Recording 2

A: Sidis was the greatest genius in history.

B: William Sidis? A genius.

C: Probably the greatest mind of the twentieth century.

D: They say his IQ was between two hundred and fifty and three hundred. That's off the scale.

E: A genius.

F: William Sidis? Great brain, difficult life.

G: Sidis? Genius.

Was William Sidis the most intelligent man who ever lived? If so, why isn't he famous? Why isn't his name known like the names of Einstein, Leonardo, and Charles Darwin? What can his life teach us?

William James Sidis was born on April 1st in 1898. That's right: April the first, April Fool's Day. His parents were Boris and Sarah Sidis, Russian-Jewish immigrants who had settled in New York. They were both passionately interested in education. Boris was a psychologist who taught at Harvard University and Sarah used to read Greek myths to her son as bedtime stories.

It soon became clear that their son was something special. Aged six months, William said his first word: 'door'. At seven months, he pointed at the moon and said 'Moon'. At eighteen months, William could read *The New York Times*. And aged three, he reached up to a typewriter and wrote a letter to a shop called Macy's, asking them to send him some toys! At six, he could speak Russian, French, German and Hebrew.

All of this took place at home, but soon he made newspaper headlines. He passed the entrance exam to one of the United States' best universities at the age of eight. Then, aged nine, he gave a lecture on mathematics at Harvard University. Attended by maths professors and graduate students, this lecture put Sidis on the map. He began attending Harvard

University two years later, at the age of eleven.

Now that he was in the public eye, things began to go wrong for William Sidis. The media was fascinated by him. Journalists followed him around and wrote articles about this young genius. Not surprisingly, Sidis began to feel like an animal in a zoo, with everyone watching him.

He wasn't interested in becoming famous, nor in becoming an academic. He just wanted to live a quiet, private life. He tried. He went from job to job, publishing only one book of any academic interest. But everywhere he went, whatever he did, people eventually learned who he was, and the press kept writing about him. In 1944, he died aged 46, almost forgotten.

Since his death, many stories have been told about Sidis. Some said that his genius burned out like an old light bulb. His sister said Sidis knew all the languages of the world and that he could learn a language in a day. None of this was true. Even his IQ – which was supposed to be between 250 and 300 – was just a guess. No intelligence test has been invented to go to that level of genius.

So what can we learn from his life? Firstly, not all childhood geniuses will produce great things as adults. They may think great thoughts or do incredible calculations, but many of them just do normal jobs and find happiness in that way. Secondly, Sidis spent much of his time and energy running away from fame. Unless they want to be Hollywood stars, people need to be left in peace. That's how most geniuses do great work.

UNIT 7 Recording 3

Conversation 1

A: We really need to stop this. In my view, it's getting out of control. For example, she watched TV for six hours yesterday. Six hours!

B: I must say that's a lot.

A: It *is* a lot. She needs to get out more.

B: And when she's not in front of the TV, she's on the internet.

A: That's what I was saying. She's always in front of a screen.

Conversation 2

A: For me, Elizabeth is the best. She would be really good in this job.

B: Why do you think so?

A: For one thing, she has the right qualifications. For another, she obviously really wants the job.

B: Yeah, that's very clear. I think the other woman ...

A: Hayla.

B: Hayla. She would do a good job, too.

A: She would, but having said that, she already has a good job. You can see that Elizabeth is really hungry for this position.

Conversation 3

A= Presenter   B = Mr Dyson

A: Mr Dyson, in your presentation you said that the arts in many schools weren't getting enough attention. Can you explain?

B: Yes, the reason I say this is that funding has been cut for arts subjects. There just isn't enough money. Let me give you an example. A school I visited last month wanted to do a play in the little school theatre, but there was no money for costumes, for music. So in the end there was no school play, and the theatre was closed for the whole summer term.

A: And this is a money issue?

B: I do think we could solve a lot of the problems if the government recognised the arts as it recognises maths or science or reading, yes. Like I said, money isn't everything, but it's part of the problem.

UNIT 8 Recording 1

Elise

E = Elise   I = Interviewer

E: I live next door to my parents, who are on one side, and my brother's family, who are on the other side.

I: Right.

E: It's really, really useful. They're the perfect neighbours.

I: In what sense?

E: Well, I like the situation because we help each other. For example,

if I need a babysitter for my kids, it's no problem.

I: And you see each other a lot?

E: We work together in the family business so we see each other every day. And I guess the whole extended family, which is eleven of us including the children, we eat together maybe once or twice a week, always on Sundays and sometimes during the week. So, yes, we do see each other a lot.

I: You never get fed up with the family?

E: No, I think this situation is quite normal in a lot of countries, maybe like Italy. It certainly is for our family. We've always lived in the same town. I've lived here all my life, and we always wanted to live side by side. I hope our children continue the business and live here, too.

I: And what about your husband? Does he like being so close to your family?

E: Um, I've never asked him actually! Yeah, course he does! I think.

Marc

M = Marc   I = Interviewer

M: We don't have any neighbours. Our nearest neighbours are a couple of cows that live in a field about ten miles away.

I: Are they good neighbours?

M: Fantastic! Very quiet! No, we really are completely isolated.

I: So how come? I mean, was this your dream?

M: Well, it wasn't at first. We were living in Paris, which is a great city, but it's kind of big and we got tired of crowds of people, and all the noise and using public transport. So about ten years ago, we bought an old farmhouse in the middle of nowhere. It's not a functioning farm, but it has an internet connection and me and my wife both work online. And we just love the peace and quiet.

I: So the cows aren't yours?

M: No, they belong to a farmer about ten miles away!

I: And isn't it a bit lonely out here?

M: We love it. We never see our neighbours, apart from the cows, which is just fantastic for us as we're a bit antisocial. Actually, you're the first person we've seen this year!

I: Oh, sorry to interrupt your peace!

M: Not a problem. Just don't stay too long!

UNIT 8 Recording 2

1 traffic lights
2 high street
3 housing estate
4 sports centre
5 industrial estate
6 car park
7 supermarket
8 language school
9 shopping centre
10 one-way street
11 terraced houses
12 outdoor market
13 gift shop
14 primary school

UNIT 8 Recording 3

1 The website which we built is too slow.
2 Those people who are always working don't enjoy life.
3 The ratings site, which I check every day, is growing fast.
4 Those students who do online courses love studying.
5 Near my flat, where you're staying, there's a supermarket.

UNIT 9 Recording 1

1 If I'd known you were coming, I would've waited.
2 If I'd waited, I would've been late.
3 If I'd been late, I would've missed the show.
4 If I'd missed the show, I would've wasted my money.
5 If I'd wasted my money, I would've been angry.

UNIT 9 Recording 2

Hello, and welcome to 'Fascinating Facts!' Today we're going to take a look at some those 'modern' inventions which turn out to be … well, not quite so modern at all!

Let's start with toothpaste. So you think, 'hmm, toothpaste – when was that invented?' A hundred years ago? Maybe two hundred? But we find that actually, toothpaste has been around for sixteen hundred years. People from Egypt used it, and then the Ancient Greeks and Romans used it. Was it the same as modern toothpaste? Definitely not. Ancient Greek toothpaste used ingredients like crushed bones and oyster shells.

OK, another invention for you: biological weapons. Again, you think, 'biological weapons – must be a twentieth-century invention'. Wrong again. Biological weapons have been used for over three thousand years. Probably beginning in Ancient Greece, it was common for one side to poison their enemy's water supply during a war. Some generals would even throw dead bodies at the enemy or into the enemy's river. One leader called Hannibal even put poisonous snakes into pots and threw them onto an enemy's ship. In the eighteenth century, one way American Indians were killed was through using infected blankets given to them by the Europeans who were colonising America.

Next topic: football. Just how old is the game? The answer is, we don't really know. But we do know that forms of it were played in China over two thousand years ago. And it also seems that the game developed by chance in different parts of the world. Wherever European explorers went, they discovered that native people already played some kind of football: Aborigines in Australia, the Inuit in Greenland, Japan and the Americas. So I suppose it really is the people's game.

Right. Central heating. It's been a wonderful thing for us in cold countries and helps us get through the winters. But most of us don't realise it's a very old invention. Once again, the Ancient Greeks were the first in Europe, over two thousand years ago, although there was a similar system in Korea. Both of these civilisations had pipes and controlled fires under the floors to keep the buildings warm. In England, one of the first examples of central heating was in the 1830s. A rich banker installed it in his house so that he could grow grapes in England's cold weather!

The final invention we're going to look at today is the good old umbrella. If we look at a number of ancient sculptures from Egypt and Persia, which is now called Iran, it's clear that the umbrella has been around for a long, long time, certainly more than two thousand years. Interestingly, it seems that only kings or very important people had umbrellas in these sculptures. So they were a symbol of high social class. But what were they for? In Europe we tend to think of umbrellas as things to protect us from the rain. But historically, they protected people from the sun. And later, they became a fashion item.

UNIT 9 Recording 3

1 The Institute is given almost a million euros a year.
2 One day a cure for cancer will be discovered.
3 The files were stolen last year.
4 These famous photos were taken at the end of the war.
5 The President hasn't been told about the plan.
6 The missing people have been found.
7 All flights going out of Paris were cancelled.
8 The paintings are cleaned once a year.

UNIT 9 Recording 4

1
A: Marisa had her baby yesterday.
B: Did she? What wonderful news!

2
A: I'm doing an online project about Second Life.
B: Oh really? That's interesting.

3
A: His cousin was an Olympic boxer.
B: Was he? Wow!

4
A: My sister doesn't eat meat.
B: Doesn't she? OK, I'll cook fish.

5

A: The King of Italy? There isn't one! Italy is a republic.

B: I was just about to say that.

6

A: I love Lady Gaga!

B: Do you? I think she's crazy.

7

A: The inventor of the internet? It was Tim Berners-Lee.

B: Oh yes, I knew that. I just couldn't remember.

8

A: My parents have never been here.

B: Haven't they? When are they going to visit?

9

A: Jake was the number one student in the country.

B: Really? I didn't know that.

10

A: John's got the car. We'll have to travel by bus.

B: Will we? Oh, that's annoying.

UNIT 10 Recording 1

P = Presenter   A = Amy   J = Jay-Jay

P: In 2007, one city decided to take a stand against climate change. Two point two million people across Sydney switched off their lights for an event that would become known across the world as Earth Hour. Earth Hour quickly went global, spreading across the world, and in 2010, thousands of cities in 128 countries took part. Global landmarks like the Eiffel Tower in Paris, the Egyptian Pyramids, New York's Empire State Building, and Sydney Harbour Bridge all plunged into darkness, as millions of people around the world switched their lights off to protest against climate change.

Organisers say that they want to demonstrate what people can do to reduce their carbon footprint and save energy, and thus draw attention to the problem of climate change. However, critics describe the event as meaningless. In today's programme, we're asking what you think. Can Earth Hour really make a difference? Is it a good way to raise awareness about the problems the world is facing? Have you taken part in the switch-off? First on the line, we have Amy. Amy, can you tell us what you think?

A: I think Earth Hour is a great idea. It's a really simple way for people to show that they care about the environment, and want something to change.

P: So, did you do anything for Earth Hour last year, Amy?

A: Yes, I did. I was at home with my two children, who are eight and thirteen years old, and we switched the lights off at home, and had our dinner by candlelight.

P: And how did you find that? What did the children think?

A: It was brilliant. The children loved it, and we enjoyed a really quiet hour, with no television, or music. We talked, actually. And we'll be doing it again this year, definitely.

P: Thank you, Amy. Thanks for calling. Now, we've got Jay-Jay on the line. Jay-Jay, what do you think of Earth Hour?

J: I think it's a complete waste of time. I can't believe it.

P: Wow. And why is that, Jay-Jay? What's the problem?

J: I don't understand how anybody can think that turning off your lights for one hour is really going to make any difference. It's just a way for people to do something which makes them feel better. They turn their lights off for an hour, and then they think they have done something about climate change. And then they can carry on as they were before. What we need is for people to really change how they behave, every day, not just for an hour. They need to use less electricity, not drive around in their cars everywhere. We need governments to make big changes, and turning your lights off ... well, it's just silly.

P: But don't you think, Jay-Jay, that it is a symbol, a gesture that helps to get people around the world thinking about the problems?

J: Yes, you're right. But the main problem is not to get people thinking about it, but to get people to actually change the way that they live, and that's not easy.

P: You're right about that. I suppose …

UNIT 10 Recording 2

1 Gina refused to come with us.
2 He promised to call me later.
3 They decided to go out for a meal.
4 They agreed not to go on holiday this year.
5 She warned us that the restaurant was very expensive.
6 They invited James to go to the theatre with them on Friday.
7 The teacher explained that the children grow vegetables in the garden.
8 He recommended buying our fruit at the market.

REVIEW 2 Recording 1

Examiner: You will hear five different people talking about their favourite films. For questions 19–23, choose from the list A–F what each speaker says about the film. Use the letters only once. There is one extra letter which you do not need to use.

You now have 30 seconds to look at Part 3.

Now we are ready to start. Listen carefully. You will hear the recording twice.

Examiner: Speaker 1.

S1: I'm not sure if it's the best film I've ever seen, but certainly the best film I've seen recently was *Hugo*. It's a charming story about a little boy who lives in a train station in Paris and spends his life trying to recreate a model that his father started working on before he died. The reason I think it was so good is that it has all the things necessary for a good film. The story, the actors and the special effects were brilliant. It really made an impression on me. In fact, I was still talking about it with my friends weeks later!

Examiner: Speaker 2.

S2: I know it's a bit cheesy, but my favourite film of all time has to be *Titanic*. I know the actual story isn't true, but the background events are, and that makes it even more real for me. I love a good romance story, and knowing that this kind of thing did actually happen on that night made me feel the emotions that the people at that time must have felt. I've watched it lots of times now, but it still makes me cry every time I watch it.

Examiner: Speaker 3.

S3: I just love all the *Harry Potter* films, all of them. I had to admit I came to these quite late, after everyone had been telling me all about them. Then one day my boyfriend came home with some cinema tickets. He didn't tell me what we were going to see, just said it was a surprise. Well, it was the first film, and since then I've been a massive fan – I've even read all the books, too!

Examiner: Speaker 4.

S4: Favourite film? Hhmm, that's a tough one, but I think I'd have to say *12 Angry Men*. I know it's a very old film now, and there are no special effects or anything like that, but for me it is what good films are all about. I think modern films show too much violence and explosions and things like that. It's like a lot of directors have forgotten how to tell a good story, which this film does. It also has an important message for all of us in that you shouldn't just believe what everyone else says, but believe in what you think yourself.

Examiner: Speaker 5.

S5: One of my favourite films is *Back to the Future*. I remember watching it when I was a young girl, and falling in love with Michael J. Fox. The main reason I liked it then though was because it was such an unbelievable story, but the characters almost made it believable. I watched it again recently as an adult, and I realised

that the reason for this is because it's actually a comedy. I think it was brilliant for the time and good that it didn't take itself so seriously, as some films like that do. I also now realise that it had a bit of everything – romance, action, suspense, science fiction, and so on. I think that's why it's still such a good film today.

Examiner: Now listen again.

That is the end of part 3.

REVIEW 2 Recording 2

1 That's the book that I told you about.

2 The actor who won the Oscar was very funny.

3 The story is set in Nice, which is in the south of France.

4 That's the play we saw last week.

5 She explained the news to Richard, who was very upset.

6 Is this the place we visited last year?

REVIEW 2 Recording 3

P = Presenter

TG = Tamara Goodliffe

Examiner: You'll hear an interview with Tamara Goodliffe, a film director. For questions 24–30, choose the best answer, A, B or C.

You now have 1 minute to look at Part 4.

P: In the studio with me today is Tamara Goodliffe, who was recently voted the best female British film director in a survey carried out by *FilmReel* magazine. Congratulations Tamara, you must be very proud.

TG: Thank you, and yes, I do feel proud, but perhaps not because of anything I've done.

P: Why's that?

TG: Well, as a director, it's – quite simply – my job to direct. The people who put the hard work into the films are the writers, the actors, the musicians. A good film is basically a combination of all those parts, and it's my job just to put it all together so that people can believe what they see.

P: Ah, I think you're being too modest. Surely it can't be that easy?

TG: Well, yes, sometimes it can get quite difficult. I think the hardest thing is when you have an idea of what a particular scene should look like, but as it comes together it starts to look different. You then have to decide: should I try to make it look more like my original idea, or develop this new way of showing what happens?

P: Interesting. But what's the best thing about being a film director?

TG: Without a doubt, it has to be when it all comes together. Seeing the film for the first time after the final edit, and knowing all the hard work that went into each part. That's the best thing.

P: And what about your beginnings? How did you become a film director?

TG: Well, like a lot of directors, I started out as an actor. I had parts in a few films, but they were only small parts and to be honest I didn't really enjoy acting.

P: No, why was that?

TG: Well, if I'm honest, I don't think I was very easy to work with. I always had very specific ideas about how a particular character should be shown, and directors often disagreed with me. Looking back, I think I was really annoying!

P: Hehe. Oh dear.

TG: Yes, so anyway, a good friend of mine came to me with an idea for a short film. He had already got together the actors, the script and the location, and asked if I'd like to direct it. I'd never done any directing before, but I thought 'why not?' and we filmed the whole thing in a week with my friend's video camera.

P: Wow, that sounds quite adventurous. What happened next?

TG: I sent it to a friend of mine who worked at CGM studios, he passed it on to his director, and they loved it. That was actually the start of what later became *Friends with Wings*, the first feature-length film I directed.

P: That's amazing. Now Tamara, it's often said that your films, while trying to show 'real life', are often depressing. What would you say to that?

TG: Ah yes, this is something I often hear. But I think when you're dealing with the kinds of situations that my films are often about – real people's lives with real people's problems – it will often come out that way. The reality is that a lot of people's lives are a bit depressing! However, I do feel it's important to show real situations, so that people can connect with the films on a personal level. It really helps bring the story to life.

P: Well, you don't need to convince me, I'm a big fan of your films!

TG: Thank you.

P: And finally Tamara, do you have any advice for any new directors?

TG: Oh yes. I'd have to say that for me the most important thing is to have a vision of how you want the film to look, but don't let that restrict you. If, when filming, things start to take another shape, allow that to grow. The end result will be a more realistic piece of work.

P: Thanks very much Tamara. It was a pleasure to meet you.

TG: Thank you.

Examiner: Now you'll hear part 4 again.

RC1 Recording 1

1 Who do you work for?
2 What type of things do you do?
3 What problems do you deal with?
4 When did you start working there?
5 Do you enjoy the job?
6 So why did you apply for this job?

RC1 Recording 2

1 I've stopped.
2 We made it.
3 He helped me.
4 They've killed it.
5 You've worked hard.
6 I thanked her.

RC 2 Recording 1

amazing
successful
delicious
exhausted
salary
interview
furious
difficult
tasty
leader
boiling
freezing
competitive
impossible

ANSWER KEY

UNIT 1

1.1

1A
2 great-grandparents
3 family history
4 related to
5 relatives
6 ancestors
7 inherited
8 side of the family
9 roots
10 takes after

B
1 roots
2 extended
3 family history
4 great
5 side
6 relatives
7 ancestors
8 related to

2A
2 b 3 a 4 b 5 b 6 a 7 a 8 b

B
b 6 c 8 d 1 e 7 f 4 g 3 h 5

3
1 c 2 a 3 a 4 c 5 b 6 c

4A
1 What's your middle name?
2 Who gave you that?
3 Where's the best restaurant?
4 Why did they arrive late?
5 What did you have for lunch?
6 When does your train leave?

5A
Clyde
Who? His mother
How? She encouraged him to 'keep his eyes open' – to look at different cultures and see things around him.

Luciana
Who? Her grandfather
How? He made her an honest and hard-working person.

Austin
Who? Uncle Charlie
How? He was always happy. He always saw the bright side of life.

B
1 Keep your eyes open.
2 He travelled around Europe.
3 For about five years.
4 honesty
5 In Australia he fought and killed a crocodile with his bare hands.
6 He never went to Australia and never left London.

C
1 d 2 a 3 f 4 e 5 b 6 c

6A
Email 2 needs to be formal.

B
1 Hi Pilar
2 How are you?
3 thought I'd
4 really like
5 can't wait to stay
6 Hope
7 Dear members
8 I am writing to introduce myself
9 I would like to take this opportunity
10 I will explain
11 I look forward to working with you all
12 Yours sincerely

1.2

1
1 are, found
2 won, was sleeping
3 don't like, didn't … tell
4 Did … hear, were driving
5 Do … need, 'm staying
6 'm reading, didn't finish
7 get up, leave
8 're waiting, was looking

2
2 a ii, b i
3 a i, b ii
4 a ii, b i
5 a ii, b i

3A
1 employee, boss
2 classmate, pupil
3 fiancée, fiancé, godfather, godmother
4 team-mate, member

B
1 fiancée 2 classmate 3 boss
4 member 5 pupil 6 employee
7 godfather 8 team-mate

4A
1 employee 2 mentor 3 pupils
4 team-mates 5 fiancée 6 partner
7 godmother 8 members

5A
1 men – said by women
2 men – said by women
3 women – said by women
4 women – said by women

C
2 Mai 3 Guy 4 Sergio 5 Linda 6 Avril

D
1 spatial perception 2 equip 3 further
4 distantly 5 instincts

6
2 go 3 take 4 do 5 do 6 get 7 go
8 do 9 take 10 get 11 take 12 go

1.3

1
1 d 2 g 3 e 4 h 5 f 6 c 7 b 8 a

2A
Conversation 1
Could I ask a question?
In my opinion
Conversation 2
There are a couple of things I'd like to ask about.
For me, the most important thing
Conversation 3
I have a query.
One thing I'd like to say is that
Conversation 4
Can I ask you about that?
I'd have to say 'yes'.

B
A 4 B 1 C 2 D 3

3
1 a 2 b 3 c 4 c 5 a 6 a 7 a 8 c
9 c 10 b

UNIT 2

2.1

1A
1 action
2 biopic
3 fantasy
4 period drama

5 romantic comedy
6 adventure
7 disaster
8 crime, thriller, comedy
9 docudrama

B

1 biopic
2 disaster
3 romantic comedy
4 fantasy
5 action / thriller
6 crime

2

1 've never been, went
2 have you acted, 've acted
3 has travelled, has he visited
4 has won, won
5 lived, did they move
6 Have you been, arrived
7 've been married, met
8 Did you enjoy, haven't had

3

2 's / has been
3 've / have worked
4 've / have lived in
5 haven't seen Robbie
6 've / have been to London

4A

1 we've visited
2 we haven't had
3 we found
4 've left
5 we've already
6 we've had

5

1 at 2 in 3 on 4 at 5 on 6 In 7 by 8 in
9 in 10 by 11 on 12 on

6A/B

1 T
2 F (He was twenty-four years old.)
3 F (He wasn't speeding at the time of the accident.)
4 F (He had a motorcycle accident and lost two teeth.)
5 F (His favourite drink was coffee.)

C

1 b 2 c 3 a 4 c

D

1 barely out of their teens
2 immortalised
3 rebellious attitude
4 a lasting impression
5 assumed

2.2

1A

1 T 2 F

B

A 3 B 4 C 1 D 2

C

1 Rob
2 Gino
3 Danny, a friend
4 people outside the station
5 Marianne
6 John Lennon

2

1 b 2 a 3 a 4 b 5 a 6 a

3

1 happened
2 waited
3 didn't come
4 was driving
5 broke
6 had run out
7 Did … enjoy
8 hated
9 had booked
10 hadn't realised / didn't realise
11 were coming
12 was pouring
13 spilled
14 ordered
15 had said / said
16 arrived
17 tasted

4A

1 crash 2 earthquake 3 hostages
4 floods 5 fugitive 6 demonstration
7 shot 8 attacked 9 collapse 10 strikes

B

1 a 2 b 3 b 4 a 5 a

5A

Report A

a 2 b 3 c 1

Report B

a 3 b 2 c 1

Report C

a 3 b 2 c 1

B

Report A

1 A priest installed an electronic fingerprint reader in his church.
2 Warsaw, Poland
3 He wants to monitor whether the children attend mass or not.

Report B

1 There was a 'Love Message Yelling Event'.
2 Hibiya Park in central Tokyo, Japan
3 Kiyotaka Yamana started the event after his own marriage failed, to encourage people to be more romantic.

Report C

1 More than 1,000 tourists had to be evacuated from Machu Picchu in helicopters.
2 Machu Picchu, Peru
3 The ruins had been cut off by floods and mudslides.

C

1 as soon as 2 During 3 While 4 Until
5 During 6 by the time 7 until

2.3

1

1 told 2 say 3 told 4 told 5 say 6 said

2

1 This happened when
2 Well
3 so
4 Anyway
5 Before long
6 The next thing I knew
7 In the end
8 Anyway

3

1 happened 2 no 3 kidding 4 what
5 then 6 Oh 7 Really 8 amazing

UNIT 3

3.1

1A

a Kieron b Amber c Ruth

B

1 b 2 b 3 c 4 b 5 b 6 c 7 a 8 c 9 a

C

1 e 2 d 3 a 4 b 5 c

2

1 b 2 a 3 a 4 b 5 a 6 a 7 b 8 a

3

1 Are you doing
2 are going out
3 might try / are going to try
4 're / are meeting / 're / are going to meet
5 'll / will be
6 're / are going to be
7 is playing
8 might go

9   'll / will call

4A
1 a 2 b 3 b 4 b 5 a 6 b

5
Across
3 chat 5 boast 6 compliment 8 warn

Down
1 gossip 2 apologise 4 argue 7 moan

6A
1 d 2 c 3 f 4 b 5 a 6 e

B
1   I've gone to lunch. I'll be back soon.
2   Mr Jackson called (earlier). He didn't leave a message. (He said that) He will call again later.
3   My dentist appointment has been cancelled. I need to rebook.
4   I'm at the cinema. Your dinner is in the oven. I'll see you later.
5   I'm going (to go) swimming after school – do you want to come (with me)?
6   I'm sorry, I didn't tidy my bedroom – I was late for school.

3.2
1
b

2
1   To communicate with extraterrestrial life.
2   hello
3   SETI sends signals into space.
4   150 full-time scientists, educators and other staff.
5   For three or four decades.
6   They think that secret government agencies are examining crashed UFOs and the bodies of dead aliens.

3
1 e 2 d 3 a 4 c 5 b

4
1 radio waves 2 enslave 3 species 4 bunker

5A
2 future 3 term 4 short 5 in 6 from 7 time 8 next

B
1, 2, 4, 5 and 8 are about things that will happen soon.

3, 6 and 7 are about things that will happen more than three years in the future.

6
2   will you stay
3   you going to speak to Ted tomorrow

4   is unlikely to pass her exam
5   going to be a storm
6   could become the champion
7   are likely to find a cure for cancer one day
8   may not be able to attend the meeting
9   won't have time to go shopping
10   could meet next week

7
1 are 2 be 3 won't 4 to 5 to
6 be / become 7 will 8 are

8
2 foot 3 tea 4 rat 5 eye 6 working
7 run 8 piece 9 hot 10 mind 11 hand

3.3
1
A 4 B 3 C 1 D 2

2
1 lost 2 Can 3 again 4 repeat 5 What
6 mean 7 say 8 catch 9 get 10 saying

3
1   So you're saying we can't come in.
2   Didn't you say it starts at ten o'clock?
3   So what you mean is we failed.
4   Do you mean to tell me that it costs €50,000?
5   In other words, we are the champions.

UNIT 4

4.1
1A
1   good communicator
2   hard-working
3   lazy
4   ambitious
5   good leader
6   competitive
7   indecisive
8   outside the box
9   motivated
10   risk taker

B
2   competitive
3   hard-working
4   motivated
5   good communicator
6   good leader
7   risk taker
8   ambitious

2
1   e   don't have to
2   i   shouldn't
3   b   should

4   g   mustn't
5   a   should
6   j   have to
7   d   mustn't
8   h   must
9   c   don't have to
10   f   must

3
2   I've finished this exercise. What I should should I do now?
3   The clients don't has have to come to the office. We can meet them at the restaurant.
4   I shouldn't to tell you this, but the boss is leaving on Monday.
5   Do we have to wear a uniform?
6   Everybody must leaving leave the building by 6p.m.
7   She have has to be at work by 7.30a.m.
8   I think you should to check what time the film starts.
9   You don't must mustn't use a mobile phone in the classroom.
10   We have to wait until the IT man comes to fix the system.

4B
A 3 B 1 C 6 D 5 E 4 F 2

C
1   2
2   4
3   4
4   5
5   6
6   1
7   1
8   3

5A
1   listen, leave
2   remind, remember
3   fun
4   job, earn
5   work, forget
6   hear, won, funny

B
1   remind
2   hear, won
3   job
4   forget
5   work, fun
6   funny

4.2
1B
1   good salary, beachside mansion, fantastic views of the ocean
2   Because Ben was too busy, and there wasn't much time to relax.

3 He was stung by a deadly jellyfish.

4 He is planning to write a book about his experiences, and he might accept a new contract with Tourism Queensland.

2

2, 4, 5 and 9

3

1 a beachside mansion
2 a busy schedule
3 press conferences
4 administrative duties
5 tweeted
6 get the chance
7 rushed
8 immensely

4

1 a brilliant   b boiling
2 a terrible   b furious
3 a tiny   b delicious
4 a impossible   b exhausted
5 a fascinating   b huge

5

1 to 2 used 3 would 4 used 5 used
6 would 7 use 8 used

6A

1 Did you use to spend your holidays by the sea?
2 We didn't use to have a dog when I was a child.
3 Daniel used to be one of the naughtiest boys in the class, but he's much better now.
4 I used to love reading in the evening, but now I'm too tired.
5 I remember how I used to sit in my grandfather's studio and watch him paint.
6 I used to be quite fat. Then, I went on a diet and lost ten kilos.
7 Children always used to play around on the streets in the old days, but there's nobody here now.
8 They used to live in a big house but they had to move.

B

Sentences 1, 5, 7

7A

1 /s/ 2 /z/ 3 /s/ 4 /s/ 5 /z/
6 /z/ 7 /s/ 8 /s/

8A

1 Dear Ms Nelson
2 I am writing to you about …
3 I am currently studying English …
4 I believe that my communication skills …

5 Thank you for your consideration. If you require …
6 Yours sincerely
7 Vinnie Jessop

B

1 at your earliest convenience
2 I believe I meet all the requirements of the post
3 proven ability at
4 hands-on
5 regarding
6 I would like to submit an application

4.3

1A

1 b 2 a 3 c 4 a 5 b 6 c 7 b 8 c

B

1 difficult boss
2 successful businessman
3 work, team
4 go, interview
5 earn, six-figure
6 get fired

2

1 see things
2 that's a good idea
3 suggest we think about
4 That's fine
5 not sure that I agree
6 see what you mean
7 How about if we

3

1 on 2 all 3 on 4 recap 5 to 6 up

UNIT 5

5.1

1A

1 vaccinations
2 electricity
3 nuclear power
4 computer network
5 antibiotics
6 space travel
7 motorbikes

B

1 genetic engineering
2 nuclear power
3 antibiotics
4 electricity
5 space travel
6 communications satellites
7 solar power
8 vaccination

2A

/eɪ/ **make:** space, communications, aeroplanes, vaccinations

/æ/ **apple:** antibiotics, travel, satellites, vacuum

/ə/ **polar:** nuclear, machine, commercial, solar

3A

1 T 2 O 3 M

B

1 a 2 c 3 b 4 c 5 a 6 b

4

1 more expensive than
2 better
3 easier
4 bigger
5 heavier
6 the lightest
7 smaller
8 cheaper

5

1 much
2 a little bit
3 by far
4 a lot
5 a bit
6 slightly

6A

1 ✔ 2 ✗ 3 ✔ 4 ✗ 5 ✗ 6 ✔

B

Plan B is better because it is more clearly organised into advantages and disadvantages. The paragraphs are planned and there is an introduction and a conclusion.

C

However, there are also disadvantages.

One of the main advantages is that when you study online, you …

The problem is that when you study online, there is … students. **Another disadvantage is** you might find it difficult … your studies. **And another thing,** you might experience …

In my opinion, online courses offer students more choice and flexibility. **However,** they are …

5.2

1

Not possible:

2 wonder
3 enquire
4 questioned
5 wonder
6 responded

7 look into

8 enquires

2

2 question

3 look into

4 debate

5 response

6 investigating

7 enquired

8 reply

9 wondered

3

1 aren't you

2 didn't she

3 have they

4 will he

5 doesn't it

6 did we

7 has it

8 won't you

9 does it

10 didn't you

4

2 was funny, wasn't it

3 won't crash the car, will he

4 wasn't a very good game, was it

5 write to me, won't you

6 didn't miss the last bus, did you

7 speak French, don't you

8 haven't seen my watch, have you

5A

1, 3, and 5 are genuine questions.

6C

1 Which food

2 about stress

3 good for you

4 eat rotting food

5 amount of water turn into ice

D

2 dose 3 smog 4 rotting 5 hatch

7

1 responsible 2 hopeless 3 creative
4 easy 5 effective 6 successful 7 valuable
8 profitable

5.3

1

1 down 2 recharging 3 order 4 fixing
5 switching 6 crashed 7 work 8 sort
9 memory 10 print

2A

A 3 He wants to know if they have to bring anything.

B 4 She wants someone to hold something for her.

C 7 She wants someone to pick her up at the station.

D 2 He wants to know what time the bank opens.

E 1 She wants to know the way to the swimming pool.

F 8 She wants to know if there is a post office near there.

G 6 He wants to know what time the (afternoon) show starts.

H 5 She wants someone to open the door for her.

B

1 could, course

2 know, sure

3 you, of

4 help, sorry

5 opening, not

6 tell, Let

7 mind, Sure

8 if, there

3

1 No, of course not.

2 I'm not sure. Let me have a look.

3 Yes, of course.

4 I'm afraid I can't.

5 Yes, I can.

1

1 a head teacher 2 a prize for improving
a school 3 six

2

8 B 9 C 10 A 11 B 12 A 13 C

3

1 c 2 d 3 a 4 e 5 b

4A

1 Do you ever listen to audiobooks?

2 When did you start learning English?

3 What is your country famous for?

4 Who taught you to ride a bike?

5 As a child, did you like vegetables?

6 Where was the last World Cup?

7 Who do you usually speak to if you have a problem?

8 Do you like your job?

B

a 2 b 7 c 1 d 5 e 8 f 3 g 6 h 4

5

1 is/'s

2 were (you) doing

3 am/'m staying

4 didn't know

5 don't get up

6 was sleeping, woke (me) up

7 are/'re recording

8 go, couldn't get

6

1 a 2 b 3 b 4 a 5 b 6 a

7

1 shouldn't interrupt 2 must do
3 don't have to eat 4 has to arrive
5 should say 6 mustn't speak

8A

1 have to 2 mustn't go
3 should study 4 don't have to wear
5 must win 6 shouldn't say

1

1 studying at university

2 a two-week work experience placement

3 Stacey – art, Mike – mathematics, Claire – English literature, Steve – economics, Tasmin – biology

2

6 G 7 B 8 D 9 F 10 H

3

1 investigating 2 adapt 3 case
4 hands on 5 hot 6 selecting, rejecting

4

1 indecisive 2 lazy 3 competitive
4 think outside the box 5 risk taker
6 ambitious

5

1 hard-<u>wor</u>king

2 am<u>bi</u>tious

3 a good comm<u>u</u>nicator

4 comp<u>e</u>titive

5 inde<u>ci</u>sive

6 <u>mo</u>tivated

6

Across

2 brilliant

5 fascinating

6 freezing

8 exhausted

11 furious

12 boiling

Down

1 beautiful

3 impossible

4 tiny

7 enormous

9 awful

10 delicious

R1.3

1A

to tell him about a really good English class he had yesterday

B

Dear Stefano

How **are you**? Yesterday we **had** a really good English class. We all wrote short articles for a class newspaper, and at the end of the lesson the teacher **posted** them on the internet! Are you still studying **English**?

Aldo

UNIT 6

6.1

1A

1 exhausting 2 worried 3 boring
4 annoyed 5 frightening 6 embarrassed
7 confused 8 relaxing 9 satisfied
10 shocked

B

1 boring 2 annoyed 3 exhausting
4 satisfied 5 confusing 6 embarrassed
7 shocking 8 relaxing

2A/B

Reasons: You're irritated with someone, You're frustrated about something, People criticise you.

Consequences: You start to shout, You throw things around, You feel tense.

Solutions: You do physical exercise, You try meditation, You distance yourself from the situation.

3

1 increases
2 understand
3 solve
4 situations / things
5 change
6 distance
7 breathing / breaths
8 calmly

4A

1 finds, will / 'll leave
2 will get, works
3 exercise, live
4 leave, will / 'll miss
5 will / 'll start, is
6 is, dance
7 is, eat
8 use, won't get

B

2 specific – first conditional
3 general – zero conditional
4 specific – first conditional
5 specific – first conditional
6 general– zero conditional
7 general– zero conditional
8 specific – first conditional

5

2 If **you go** to England, …
3 I'll tell him you called when **I see** him.
4 ✔
5 If they arrive early, **will you ask** them to wait?
6 If **you come** to the party tonight, will you bring a friend?
7 When I go to Krakow, **I usually see** my aunt.
8 ✔
9 She will get angry if **you say** that!
10 **I'll / will go** to the doctor tomorrow if I feel worse.

6A

1 c 2 c 3 a 4 c 5 c 6 b 7 a 8 b

B

1 down 2 on 3 up 4 off 5 on 6 up
7 off 8 off

6.2

1

1 do, experiments
2 watch, programme
3 get, seat
4 hold, sale
5 jump, queue
6 cut, hair
7 raise money

2

2 If she was fast enough, she would / could play for the team.
3 We could drive to your house if we had a car.
4 They would pass the exam if they studied.
5 My life wouldn't be so easy if I didn't have a supportive family.
6 If I had the money, I would buy that house.
7 I would write to my friends if I wasn't so lazy.
8 If you watered your plants regularly, they wouldn't look so dry!
9 They would help in the house if their mother asked them.
10 If I didn't work on Saturdays, I could come to the barbecue.

3

2 had
3 would be
4 would introduce
5 had to
6 would change
7 was
8 would be
9 would make
10 wouldn't let
11 was
12 wouldn't have

4A

1 If I had more time, I'd learn to ski.
2 If you didn't work, what would you do?
3 If they had to move, they wouldn't live with me.
4 She'd go out at night if her parents let her.
5 Where would you go if you had the chance?
6 I wouldn't sleep if I drank that coffee.

5A

The topic is which kinds of people are likely to be victims of crime.

B

2, 3, 4, 6 and 7 are potential victims.

D

2 Yes, (because she isn't) paying attention to what's happening around her. She isn't looking at other people.
3 Yes, (because they are concentrating on the map, not) the people around them.
4 Yes, (because he didn't put the money) in his wallet quickly.
5 No, (because of her positive) body language. She's confident, she knows where she's going, she's looking straight ahead, and she's probably moving fast.
6 Yes, (because he's looking at his feet and he doesn't know) who's around him.
7 Yes, (because rule number one of the street is: if you have anything valuable,) don't show it.

6A

Summary c

B

1 D 2 C 3 B 4 A

C

Maybe, It's possible that, probably, in all likelihood, In all probability

6.3

1A

1 pass 2 accident 3 offered 4 place
5 engaged 6 lost 7 failed 8 split 9 won
10 promoted 11 degree 12 bought

B

2 e 3 d 4 a 5 b 6 c

2A

A 4 B 3 C 1 D 8 E 2 F 7 G 6 H 5

B

1 Bad news, ~~as~~ I'm afraid.
2 I'm sorry ~~for~~ to have to tell you, but
  we lost the match.
3 I've got some good ~~unfortunately~~
  news for you.
4 I'm afraid ~~of~~ I've got some bad news.
5 There's something ~~who~~ I've got to tell
  you.
6 You'll never guess what ~~is~~ happened.
7 ~~It's~~ unfortunately, we were burgled
  last night.
8 I've got something ~~for~~ to tell you.

3

1 Congratulations, fantastic
2 terrible, sorry
3 Well done, great news
4 awful
5 Have, lucky
6 shame
7 joking

UNIT 7

7.1

1

2 focus on
3 hard at
4 get better
5 high achiever
6 believe in

3

1 DK 2 T 3 F 4 T 5 F 6 F

4

1 e 2 b 3 c 4 a 5 f 6 d

5

1 've / have been going
2 've / have been waiting
3 haven't been sleeping
4 's / has been crying
5 've / have known
6 've / have been skiing
7 have … been living
8 Have … been watching, have …
  enjoyed / been enjoying

6

1 has been happening
2 haven't had
3 have been staying
4 has been working
5 've / have been thinking
6 haven't decided
7 've / have been looking
8 have found
9 've / have been working
10 's / has been studying

7A

1 depend on
2 succeed in
3 pay attention to
4 rely on
5 pick up on
6 have a talent for
7 think about
8 have access to

B

1 think about
2 pay attention to
3 depends on
4 pick up on
5 have a talent for
6 have access to
7 succeed in
8 rely on

7.2

1A

1 c 2 a 3 b 4 c 5 a 6 b 7 a 8 c

B

1 hopeless, useless
2 gifted, talented
3 skilful
4 expert
5 have a lot of ability, have an aptitude for

2

1 couldn't 2 manage 3 remember
4 was 5 could 6 to 7 wasn't 8 managed

3

Not possible:
1 didn't manage
2 do able to
3 could
4 can
5 are manage to
6 didn't able to
7 'm not manage to
8 could to
9 Do you can
10 Could you

4A

1 ✔
2 a 6 syllables, b 5 syllables
3 ✔
4 a 6 syllables, b 7 syllables

5B

A When Sidis was seven months old, he
  pointed at the moon and said 'moon'.
B At eighteen months, he could read *The
  New York Times*.
C At six, he could speak Russian, French,
  German and Hebrew.
D Aged nine, he gave a lecture on
  mathematics at Harvard University.
E Journalists followed him around and
  wrote articles about him but he didn't
  achieve much as an adult.
F He died in 1944, aged 46.

C

1 His parents were from Russia. They
  moved to New York.
2 William's first word was 'door'.
3 William was six when he could speak
  Russian, French, German and Hebrew.
4 When he was nine, he gave a lecture
  on mathematics at Harvard University.
5 Two years later, he began attending
  Harvard University.
6 Journalists 'followed him around'.
7 His sister said he knew all the
  languages of the world and that he
  could learn a language in a day.
8 For most of his adult life, Sidis was
  'running away' from fame.

6A

1 **Mistakes:** His first word was *door*, not
  moon

  He took one day to learn a language,
  not one week.
2 **Exact words:** Journalists followed him
  around and wrote articles about this
  young genius

  Not all childhood geniuses will
  produce great things as adults

B

1 Uni (university), yrs (years)
2 &
3 close 2 him
4 THE LIFE OF WILLIAM SIDIS
5 Background
6 leave people alone

7.3

1

1 an MA
2 face-to-face learning
3 an apprenticeship
4 qualifications

5 a certificate

6 a degree

7 a PhD

8 an online course

9 distance learning

10 a driving licence

2A

1 b 2 c 3 c

B

1 a 2 b 3 b 4 b 5 a 6 b 7 b 8 a
9 a 10 b

UNIT 8

8.1

1

2 Can I **ask a** favour?

3 Whenever they're arguing, I prefer to mind **my own** business.

4 Hayley has invited **us over** for dinner at her house.

5 Those neighbours are **a nuisance** – they're always …

6 She got **to know** her neighbours immediately.

7 Please don't **disturb me**.

8 One thing that gets **on my** nerves is when …

9 Xun hasn't made **friends with** her neighbours yet …

10 I keep myself **to myself**.

2

2 Have you received **the** letter I sent you?

3 ✔

4 Do you have **a** pen I can borrow?

5 ✔

6 Is there **an** airport in the city?

7 I'm going to Germany in **the** morning.

8 We live by **the** Pacific Ocean.

9 My brother is **an** actor.

10 ✔

11 ✔

12 Did you see **the** film I told you about?

13 I live in **the** United States.

14 She's **the** nicest woman I know.

15 ✔

3

2 b vi There are plenty of good restaurants in the town, especially if you like French food.

3 f iii I don't know much about this city, but I like the architecture.

4 a v All of us love this place because it's so friendly.

5 g vii If you have enough time, go to the museum – it's great.

6 c viii There are too many cars in most big cities – I hate traffic!

7 e i I've got lots of friends in this community.

8 h ii I spent a bit of time in Poland when I was younger.

4

3 but 4 of 5 ✔ 6 ✔ 7 ✔ 8 to (money)
9 small 10 ✔ 11 a (five hours) 12 more
13 ✔ 14 all 15 ✔ 16 ✔ 17 a

5A

1 Elise's neighbours are her parents and her brother's family. Marc's neighbours are 'a couple of cows' / a farmer.

2 Elise likes this situation because they 'help each other'. Marc likes the situation because they 'just love the peace and quiet'.

3 Elise sees her neighbours every day. They work together and they all eat together once or twice a week. Marc never sees his neighbours, apart from the cows.

4 Elise has lived there all her life. Marc has lived there for ten years.

B

1 perfect 2 family 3 eleven 4 Sunday
5 normal 6 husband 7 ten 8 Paris
9 transport 10 farmhouse 11 online
12 first

C

1 a 2 b 3 b 4 b 5 b 6 a

6A

2 high street

3 housing estate

4 sports centre

5 industrial estate

6 car park

7 supermarket

8 language school

9 shopping centre

10 one-way street

11 terraced houses

12 outdoor market

13 gift shop

14 primary school

7

1 housing estate

2 language school

3 primary school

4 one-way street

5 sports centre

6 terraced houses

7 traffic lights

8 car park

9 supermarket

10 gift shop

11 outdoor market

12 industrial estate

13 high street

14 shopping centre

8.2

1

2 j 3 f 4 k 5 b 6 l 7 i 8 e 9 h 10 c
11 d 12 g

2

3 a 4 b 5 b 6 a 7 b 8 a

3

1 clothing that

2 place where

3 person who

4 name that

5 which has

6 thing that

7 who behaves

8 a place

4

1 a 2 a 3 b 4 a 5 b

5A

A CouchSurfer is a traveller who arranges to stay on a stranger's couch.

B

1 He had nowhere to sleep.

2 He wrote to 1,500 students in Reykjavik, and he had dozens of replies inviting him to stay.

3 The website says CouchSurfing focuses on cross-cultural sharing.

4 1 You type the name of the city. 2 You look at the profiles of people there and choose someone. 3 You contact them to see if they are free. 4 They may ask you to meet for a coffee first before inviting you to their home.

5 You can read what other CouchSurfers say about this person, and there is also a system of 'vouching', in which other people promise that your host has a good character.

C

1 e 2 c 3 b 4 a 5 d

6A

1 feature 2 like 3 would 4 best

B

1 B 2 A 3 D 4 C

8.3

1A

1 Help yourself

2 Excuse the mess

3 Make yourself at home

4 Be my guest

5 Have a seat

6 Put your feet up

B

A 2 B 5 C 1 D 3 E 4 F 6

2

1 a 2 b 3 a 4 b 5 b 6 b 7 a 8 b 9 b
10 a

3

1 It's no problem.

2 Not at all.

3 That's all right.

4 It's fine.

5 It's nothing.

6 You really don't have to.

7 We can sort it out.

UNIT 9

9.1

1A

1	revolution	6	movement
2	turning point	7	invention
3	development	8	foundation
4	spread	9	discovery
5	advance	10	progress

T	U	R	N	I	N	G	P	O	I	N	T
D	A	E	B	P	R	O	G	R	E	S	S
E	C	V	D	E	R	I	O	M	E	I	P
V	F	O	U	N	D	A	T	I	O	N	T
E	E	L	U	F	C	S	S	G	J	V	E
L	S	U	A	V	U	A	P	L	I	E	D
O	W	T	V	A	P	D	R	A	G	N	E
P	D	I	S	C	O	V	E	R	Y	T	X
M	E	O	R	E	K	A	A	E	I	I	H
E	D	N	I	U	F	N	D	O	E	O	O
N	C	I	N	T	I	C	F	R	S	N	E
T	M	O	V	E	M	E	N	T	C	L	F

B

1 discovery

2 spread

3 development

4 progress

5 advances

6 movement

7 revolution

8 invention

2

1 c 2 c 3 b 4 a 5 b 6 c 7 a 8 a

3

2 If Archduke Ferdinand hadn't been assassinated, World War I wouldn't have started.

3 If people from Sumer hadn't needed permanent records, they wouldn't have invented writing.

4 If World War II hadn't happened, the

United Nations wouldn't have (been) formed in 1945.

5 If William the Conqueror hadn't invaded England in 1066, the English language wouldn't have changed.

6 If Charles Darwin hadn't travelled to South America, he wouldn't have developed the theory of evolution.

7 If sailors on the *Titanic* had seen the iceberg, 1,595 people wouldn't have died.

8 If Captain James Cook hadn't sailed to Australia, it wouldn't have become a British colony.

4A

1 If I'd known you were coming, I would've waited.

2 If I'd waited, I would've been late.

3 If I'd been late, I would've missed the show.

4 If I'd missed the show I would've wasted my money.

5 If I'd wasted my money, I would've been angry.

5A

2 Ancient Greece, over 3,000

3 China, over 2,000

4 Ancient Greece / Korea, over 2,000

5 Egypt / Persia (Iran), more than 2,000

B

A Ancient Greek toothpaste used oyster shells.

B Hannibal used snakes as a biological weapon.

C The Inuit played a type of football.

D A rich English banker installed central heating in his house so he could grow grapes.

E In ancient sculptures from Egypt and Persia, only kings or very important people had umbrellas.

C

a enemy b symbol c installed
d infected e crushed

6A

b The History of Writing

B

1 In 3200 BC, Sumerians invented writing.

2 While

3 As a result

9.2

1A/B

I grew up in a big old house with a big old family. The house had four floors, one floor for each generation. The bottom floor was where my maternal grandparents lived. **They were given** the

bottom floor so that they didn't have to climb any steps – that's the story I <u>was told</u> anyway. But in reality, I think it's because my grandmother escaped the house at 4a.m. every morning to go for walks and we didn't want **to be woken up**. Mum and Dad's room was on the second floor, and us children **were put** on the third floor, out of the way. At the very top of the steps there was an attic where my great-grandfather <u>was hidden</u> away, out of sight. He was as mad as a box of frogs. He used to play operas on an ancient gramophone and sing Puccini at the top of his voice. When he died, I <u>was given</u> that gramophone and all his records. Amazingly, forty years later, it still works. The house **has been rebuilt** many times since those days and the garden, where we used to climb trees and run wild, <u>has been covered</u> with concrete. I read recently that the house **will be sold** again. It <u>won't be bought</u> by me, though. My memories are enough.

2A

2 One day a cure for cancer will be discovered.

3 The files were stolen last year.

4 These famous photos were taken at the end of the war.

5 The President hasn't been told about the plan.

6 The missing people have been found.

7 All flights going out of Paris were cancelled.

8 The paintings are cleaned once a year.

B

The auxiliary verbs *are*, *were*, *has(n't) been* and *have been* are contracted (said in a shortened version).

3

2 over a quarter-century

3 just over a century ago

4 millennium

5 over seven decades

6 the generation

7 just over a fortnight

8 half a century

4A

1 have a good time

2 make progress

3 give a talk

4 come naturally

5 have a break

6 have a dream

7 come first

8 give instructions

9 give directions

10 have trouble

11 come back

12 make a mess

13 give me a call

14 make a profit

15 come by car

16 make a decision

B

1 having trouble, have a break

2 made a decision, made a profit

3 give me a call, give me directions

4 come naturally, came first

5 give a talk, give instructions

5A

1 around 1880–1895

2 1945 to about 1960

3 A novel: *Generation X: Tales for an Accelerated Culture*

4 Rebelling against their parents' values, not wanting to work for the same company their whole life, listening to 'grunge' music, playing video games

5 between 1980s and 1990s

6 Love of technology, amazing networkers, constantly online, great multi-taskers

B

1 Socrates say (about the younger generation)

2 begin naming each generation

3 people were killed in World War I

4 after the Second World War (from 1945–1960)

5 wrote *Millennials Rising: The Next Great Generation* / first described Generation Y in detail

6 people used the internet in 2010

C

1 e 2 d 3 c 4 a 5 b 6 f

9.3

1

1 brave 2 charismatic 3 exemplary 4 influential 5 inspirational 6 creative 7 original 8 innovative

2

1 a 2 b 3 b 4 a 5 b 6 a 7 b 8 a

3A

1 Did 2 That 3 Was 4 Doesn't 5 say 6 Do 7 remember 8 Haven't 9 didn't 10 Will

UNIT 10

10.1

1A

1 on standby

2 double glazed

3 processed

4 insulated

5 organic

6 pre-prepared

7 packaging

8 energy-saving

9 recycled

10 second-hand

B

1 organic

2 second-hand

3 double glazed

4 energy-saving

5 pre-prepared

6 processed

7 recycled

8 standby

9 packaging

10 insulated

2A

1 lights 2 Eiffel Tower 3 Pyramids 4 Sydney 5 change 6 different

3A

1 F (2.2 million people)

2 T

3 T

4 F (Some people think the event is meaningless.)

5 T

6 F (He doesn't think the event helps people to change their behaviour.)

B

1 stand 2 global 3 part 4 plunged 5 attention 6 raise 7 waste

4

1 didn't 2 were 3 had 4 her 5 next 6 his 7 would 8 they

5A

A: I want to go to Spain, because I've never been there before.

T: How are you planning to travel?

A: I'm thinking of going by plane.

T: Have you thought about taking the train instead?

A: No, I haven't, but it's a good idea.

T: It's cheaper than flying. I'll show you some of the train routes.

A: OK.

T: Have you decided where you want to stay?

A: No, I haven't. Could you show me what accommodation is available?

T: There's an eco-farm near Valencia where you can stay for free, if you help the farmer pick his olives.

A: That sounds great!

B

2 asked her, was planning

3 she was thinking

4 she'd thought

5 she hadn't, it was

6 would show her

7 had decided, she wanted

8 she hadn't

9 could stay, helped

10 sounded great

6

1 misunderstood

2 disobey

3 reuse

4 unusual

5 underestimated

6 disappeared

7 untidy

8 renew

9 unethical

10 disagree

10.2

1

1 c 2 b 3 a 4 c 5 a 6 b 7 c

2

A 4 B 5 C 2 D 1 E 3

3

1 Jorge 2 Irene 3 Claire 4 Claire 5 Mariella 6 Irene

4

1 pleasant

2 water

3 yellow middle

4 soft; liquid

5 pasta

6 sad because you haven't got

5

2 suggested spending

3 invited us to stay

4 offered to take

5 explained that it would be / explained that it was

6 recommended that we travel / recommended travelling

7 agreed to choose

8 warned us not to go

9 promise to write

6A

1 refused to come

2 promised to call

3 decided to go

4 agreed not to go

5 warned us that

6 invited James to go

7 explained that the children

8 recommended buying

B

unstressed

7A

The writer doesn't recommend the restaurant because they thought the atmosphere was uninviting, the service was poor and the food was not great, either.

B

a so 2

b Although 4

c unless 5

d such, that 3

e While 1

8A

1 no information given

2 no information given

3 ✔

4 ✔

5 ✔

10.3

1

1 passport

2 check in

3 aisle

4 boarding card

5 X-ray machine

6 board

7 priority boarding

8 proceed to gate number

9 hand luggage

2

1 b 2 c 3 a 4 b 5 c 6 a 7 b 8 a

3

1 c 2 a 3 f 4 d 5 e 6 b

1

A I feel <u>emotional</u> <u>every time</u> I watch it.

B I think <u>modern films</u> rely <u>too much</u> on <u>special effects</u> and <u>violence</u>.

C I <u>like</u> watching <u>old</u> films.

D The film <u>had an effect</u> on <u>me</u> which lasted for <u>several weeks</u>.

E I noticed <u>new things</u> about the film when I watched it <u>again</u> <u>later</u> in life.

F I <u>became a fan</u> of the film after a <u>surprise visit</u> to the <u>cinema</u>.

2

19 D 20 A 21 F 22 B 23 E

Extra statement: C

3

1 c 2 e 3 a 4 b 5 d

4

1 have (you) been working

2 has/'s been playing

3 have/'ve been waiting

4 have/'ve never loved

5 have/'ve won

6 have/'ve known

7 have been

8 have/'ve been living

5

1 has/'s been

2 have released

3 have been working

4 hasn't appeared

5 have/'ve been interviewing

6 have separated

7 have/'ve been trying

8 has/'s been working

9 have been watching

10 Have you heard

6A

a film director

B

They won't talk about 2 and 6.

7

24 B 25 A 26 C 27 A 28 C 29 B 30 B

8A

1 That's the book that I told you about.

2 The actor who won the Oscar was very funny.

3 The story is set in Nice, which is in the south of France.

4 That's the play we saw last week.

5 She explained the news to Richard, who was very upset.

6 Is this the place we visited last year?

C

1 D 2 D 3 ND 4 D 5 ND 6 D

9A

1 c 2 h 3 a 4 f 5 b 6 g 7 e 8 d

B

1 were 2 unless 3 'd studied 4 feels 5 win 6 would have 7 met 8 would

1

1 T

2 F (seven sentences have been removed)

3 T

4 F (there is only one extra sentence)

2

B However, reality TV actually goes back much further than <u>that</u>.

C Hollywood might dominate the film and TV drama industry, but the UK exports more of these <u>types of programmes</u>.

D Many people were interested in <u>what the job involved</u>.

E But <u>it wasn't until the late 1980s</u> that reality TV became really popular.

F However, perhaps now we are seeing <u>a return to traditional TV making</u>.

G <u>The programme</u> was so popular that it continued right up until the early 21st century.

H Although <u>these kinds of shows</u> had already existed, allowing the public to vote made it very popular.

3

9 B 10 G 11 E 12 A 13 H 14 C 15 F

Extra sentence: D

4

1 advances

2 era

3 revolution

4 spread

5 movement

6 turning point

7 colonisation

8 development

9 leader

10 liberation

5

1 expert in

2 hopeless at

3 focus on

4 hard at

5 gifted at

6 believe in

7 better at

8 talent for

1A

1 found

2 big

3 is

4 liked

5 fell

6 recommend

B

the style of writing and the main character

2A

your opinion, information about the story and characters, two things you liked/disliked about it

REVIEW AND CHECK 1

1

1 related 2 side 3 after 4 extended
5 relatives 6 inherited 7 grandparents
8 roots

2A

1 do you work for
2 do you do
3 do you deal with
4 did you start
5 Do you enjoy
6 did you apply

3

1 'm   6 was looking
2 'm taking   7 was reading
3 didn't start   8 jumped
4 love   9 isn't
5 saw   10 wanted

4A/B

1 boss
2 classmate
3 team-mate
4 mentor
5 fiancée
6 employee
7 pupil
8 partner

5

2 took, took
3 did, went
4 do, take
5 take, go
6 went, got

6

1 c 2 b 3 a 4 c 5 a 6 c

7

3 but 4 ✔ 5 am 6 ✔ 7 to 8 It's 9 ✔
10 really 11 the (my opinion) 12 for
13 ✔ 14 ✔

8

1 You're welcome.
2 No problem.
3 Of course.
4 You're correct.
5 Go ahead.
6 I see.

7 That's right.
8 I understand.
9 Please continue.

9

1 biopic, strike
2 thriller, fugitive
3 comedy, crash
4 science, attack
5 fantasy, earthquake
6 period, collapse
7 action, shot

10

1 fell
4 Did you go
7 didn't sell

11

1 b 2 a 3 a 4 b 5 b 6 a

12

1 for 2 by 3 in 4 on 5 on 6 at 7 on
8 in 9 in 10 on 11 by 12 By 13 on
14 by 15 in

13

1 stayed
2 had left
3 was listening
4 was wearing
5 hadn't turned on
6 didn't finish
7 hadn't been
8 opened
9 were doing
10 didn't eat

14A

1 tell 2 say 3 tell 4 say 5 tell 6 say

B

1 told stories
2 tell jokes
3 said sorry
4 says 'hello'
5 told a white lie
6 say what you mean

15

1 This happened
2 happened
3 Anyway
4 In
5 Oh no
6 Well
7 before
8 So
9 did you do
10 Finally
11 The next thing

12 Oh dear
13 a sudden
14 happened then
15 in
16 funny

TEST

1 a 2 c 3 c 4 a 5 b 6 a 7 b 8 c 9 c
10 b 11 a 12 c 13 c 14 a 15 b 16 b
17 c 18 b 19 a 20 b 21 a 22 c 23 b
24 c 25 c 26 a 27 c 28 b 29 c 30 b

REVIEW AND CHECK 2

1

1 a 2 c 3 b 4 b 5 a 6 a 7 b 8 c

2

1 a chat   b apologise
2 a moaning   b warn
3 a argue   b gossip
4 a complimented   b boast
5 a shortly   b near
6 a year   b term
7 a long   b short
8 a years'   b Next

3

1 aren't likely to
2 might not
3 may
4 is going to
5 is likely to
6 will
7 won't
8 may
9 are going to
10 could

4

1 a piece of cake
2 in hot water
3 my foot in it
4 close to my heart
5 the rat race
6 give me a hand
7 on my mind
8 my cup of tea
9 keep an eye on
10 run out of time

5

1 catch 2 lost 3 get 4 exactly 5 mean
6 say 7 repeat 8 saying 9 what 10 other

6

1 competitive
2 leader
3 amazing
4 exhausted

5 risk taker
6 freezing
7 fascinating
8 salary
9 boss, fired
10 interview
11 furious
12 hard-working

7A

oOo: successful, delicious, exhausted
Ooo: interview, furious, difficult
Oo: tasty, leader, boiling, freezing
oOoo: competitive, impossible

8

1 has to
2 should
3 mustn't
4 don't have to
5 must / have to
6 mustn't
7 must / have to
8 have to
9 shouldn't
10 don't have to

9

1 remember 2 forgotten 3 left 4 listen
5 hear 6 won 7 funny 8 fun

10A

1 used to live
2 used to work
3 used to study
4 used to have
5 would play
6 would enjoy

B

1 didn't use to have
2 didn't use to work
3 used to enjoy
4 didn't use to wear
5 didn't use to stay
6 would eat

11A

1 that 2 me 3 agree 4 should
5 things 6 don't 7 point 8 about
9 sure 10 suggest 11 What 12 need

B

opinions: I feel that, I think we should think about, The way I see things, Why don't we, How about if we, I suggest we focus on, How about, I think we need to focus on

responses: That's OK by me, I'm not sure that I agree, That's a good point, I'm not sure that's a good idea

TEST

1 b 2 b 3 a 4 c 5 b 6 c 7 b 8 a 9 b
10 c 11 b 12 a 13 c 14 c 15 a 16 b
17 c 18 b 19 a 20 c 21 c 22 b 23 a
24 c 25 a 26 c 27 a 28 b 29 c 30 a

REVIEW AND CHECK 3

1

1 electricity
2 vaccination
3 space travel
4 genetic engineering
5 solar panels
6 computer network
7 nuclear power
8 commercial aeroplanes

2

1 is slightly warmer
2 are far more expensive than
3 the most delicious meal
4 was a lot easier than
5 the simplest
6 much happier
7 a bit shorter than
8 a worse place than

3

1 discuss 2 respond 3 look
4 wondering 5 research 6 investigate
7 inquiries 8 debate

4

1 can't we
2 haven't they
3 won't we
4 do you
5 wasn't it
6 didn't you
7 will you
8 have you

5

1 painful 2 homeless 3 responsible
4 creative 5 hopeless 6 effective
7 thankful 8 messy

6

1 The car's broken down.
2 My phone needs recharging.
3 It's out of order.
4 The printer needs fixing.
5 Try switching it off and on again.
6 It keeps making this strange noise.
7 It doesn't work any more.
8 We have to sort it out.

7

1 tell, of course
2 if there's, sure
3 checking, course
4 see, look

8

1 annoyed 2 relaxed 3 confusing
4 bored 5 embarrassing 6 exhausted
7 worried 8 frightening

9A

1 I'll call 2 don't 3 is 4 will die 5 I'd
6 didn't 7 would 8 don't 9 live
10 get 11 would 12 had

B

1 b 2 c 3 a 4 a 5 c 6 b 7 a 8 c

10

1 up 2 down 3 on 4 on 5 off 6 on
7 off 8 down 9 off 10 down

11

1 b 2 b 3 b 4 c 5 a 6 c 7 b

12

1 c 2 e 3 a 4 g 5 h 6 b 7 f 8 d

3

1 A: I'm sorry to have to **tell** you, but the train has been cancelled.
  B: **That's** annoying.
2 A: I've got **some** good news for you.
  B: **Congratulations!**
3 A: There's something I've got to **tell you.**
  B: Oh. I'm sorry **to** hear that.
4 A: You'll never **guess what.**
  B: **That's fantastic** news!
5 A: **Unfortunately,** I didn't get the job.
  B: That's **a** real shame.

TEST

1 c 2 b 3 a 4 b 5 c 6 c 7 b 8 c 9 b
10 a 11 c 12 a 13 c 14 b 15 b 16 c
17 a 18 c 19 a 20 b 21 c 22 b 23 c
24 a 25 b 26 a 27 c 28 b 29 b 30 c

REVIEW AND CHECK 4

1

1 Our company focuses **on** quality software.
2 ✔
3 It's important that we work **hard** at this.
4 The key is to believe **in** yourself.
5 ✔
6 We'll improve if **we practise** every day.

2

1 known
2 been waiting
3 been reading
4 invited
5 been working
6 been learning
7 seen
8 met

3

1 to 2 to 3 on 4 in 5 for 6 on 7 on
8 about 9 with 10 at / for 11 to
12 to 13 in 14 for 15 in 16 with
17 about 18 for

4

1 Because he's an expert in his subject.
2 Because he has a lot of ability in maths.
3 Because she's gifted at the sport.
4 Because they have a talent for writing scripts.
5 Because he has an aptitude for the game.
6 Because I'm absolutely hopeless at science.

5

1 We can't play
2 She can sing
3 Are you able
4 didn't manage to
5 wasn't able to
6 manage to clean
7 could you speak
8 managed to break

6

1 qualifications 2 licence
3 apprenticeship 4 learning 5 distance
6 online 7 degree 8 Master's

7A

1 view 2 reason 3 For 4 must 5 For
6 another 7 For 8 what 9 said 10 do
11 give 12 said

B

O: 1, 2, 3, 4, 10
E: 5, 6, 7, 11
R: 8, 9, 12

8

2 myself to myself
3 doing me favours
4 your own business
5 over for dinner
6 get on well

9

2 ✔, ✔
3 ✔, **the** best ones
4 ✔, **the** rat
5 **the** party, too **many** people
6 ✔, **a** haircut
7 ✔, **the** Moon
8 too **much** time, ✔
9 ✔, **a** lot of pepper
10 ✔, **Barcelona**

10

2 house 3 calling 4 school
5 apartment 6 news 7 shops 8 flat

11

2 ✔
3 Corporate websites
4 Ratings sites
5 ✔
6 Personal homepages
7 ✔
8 ✔
9 ✔
10 dating sites
11 ✔
12 Blogs

12

1 who I spoke to was very nice
2 which we visited had a wonderful exhibition
3 where she was born is now under water
4 who is in the fashion industry, lives in Paris
5 where I grew up is now a theatre
6 who is my best friend, works with my father
7 which lasted for ten days, is now finished
8 which they went to / where they went served crocodile

13

1 have 2 Be 3 Excuse 4 Make 5 put
6 help

14

1
Pete: Do I need ~~for~~ to bring anything?
Don: No, it's not ~~the~~ necessary.

2
Kat: It's considered ~~be~~ a bit rude.
Kat: It's OK – we can sort it ~~but~~ out.

3
Andre: Is this ~~for~~ a bad time?
Bella: Can you ~~to~~ come back in ten minutes?
Andre: I didn't ~~can~~ realise you were in a meeting.
Bella: Don't ~~to~~ worry about it.

4
Nick: What should we ~~to~~ do?
Tam: No, you'd better ~~be~~ not.

15

2 B: It's **no** problem. I can photocopy mine.
3 B: That's **all right**. It didn't hurt.
4 B: Not **at all**. We usually don't start till 3.15.
5 B: No, **it's** nothing. I didn't even feel it.
6 B: Honestly, **it's** fine. Don't worry about it.

1 b 2 c 3 b 4 a 5 c 6 c 7 c 8 c 9 c
10 a 11 c 12 a 13 b 14 a 15 c 16 b
17 c 18 a 19 a 20 b 21 a 22 b 23 c
24 a 25 c 26 a 27 a 28 c 29 c 30 a

1

1 revolution 2 turning point
3 development 4 spread 5 advance
6 movement 7 invention
8 foundation 9 discovery 10 progress

2

1 hadn't helped, wouldn't have finished
2 would have gone, hadn't rained
3 'd / had studied, wouldn't have failed
4 would have told, 'd / had had
5 hadn't scored, wouldn't have won
6 would you have done, 'd / had missed

3

1 are sold here
2 isn't produced in England
3 is being built
4 was assassinated
5 wasn't written by Samuel Beckett
6 haven't been told anything about the exam

4

1 millennium
2 a decade
3 a fortnight
4 a quarter-century
5 generation
6 the nineties

5

Not possible:
1 well
2 a discussion
3 project
4 homework
5 forward
6 problem
7 money
8 progress

6

1 creative 2 original 3 charismatic
4 exemplary 5 innovative 6 brave
7 inspirational 8 influential

7

2 c i I haven't a clue.
3 a iii I'm fairly sure it's Jane.
4 f iv It's definitely not Sarah.
5 d ii I'm sure it isn't Elizabeth.
6 e vi I have no idea.

8

1 just about 2 Is 3 interesting
4 couldn't

9

1 organic
2 energy-saving, insulated
3 double glazed, on standby
4 pre-prepared, packaging
5 second-hand, recycled

10

2 you didn't know the answer
3 you had been to Germany
4 you could swim
5 you weren't going to university
6 you would be there on Monday
7 you wouldn't be able to help
8 you hadn't spoken to Kevin

11

1 He asked me **when the game started**.
2 He asked me if **I play / played any instruments**.
3 ✔
4 ✔
5 He asked me why **I was crying**.
6 She asked me if **my baby slept all night**.
7 She asked me if **they spoke** English.

12

1 misunderstood, unusual
2 misjudged, overcooked
3 unbelievable, overweight
4 untidy, disobeyed
5 reuse, recycle
6 disapproved, unethical
7 underestimate, renew
8 disappeared, unknown

13

1 David <u>promised</u> (invited) us to his birthday party. Sentence 6
2 The tour guide <u>refused</u> (warned) us about poisonous spiders. Sentence 3
3 The doorman <u>suggested</u> (refused) to let me into the club because I was wearing jeans. Sentence 7
4 I <u>explained</u> (offered) to take her for dinner, to say 'thank you'. Sentence 5
5 The teacher <u>invited</u> (explained) the grammar clearly so everyone understood. Sentence 1
6 My dad <u>warned</u> (promised) to buy me an ice cream if I behaved well. Sentence 2
7 Minty <u>offered</u> (suggested) going to Greece for our holiday. Sentence 4

14

1 that I
2 that
3 me to
4 me
5 to wait
6 to take
7 to give
8 to move
9 to
10 trying

15

1 d 2 a 3 e 4 g 5 b 6 h 7 c 8 f

16

1 the most important thing is to
2 make sure you bring
3 watch out for snakes
4 it's not very common
5 if I were you, I'd start
6 you need to bring
7 have a tendency to bring
8 Whatever you do, don't pack
9 don't forget to bring
10 on the whole
11 be careful to eat
12 you'd better take some

TEST

1 a 2 c 3 b 4 c 5 c 6 b 7 a 8 a 9 c
10 c 11 b 12 b 13 c 14 b 15 c 16 a
17 a 18 c 19 b 20 c 21 c 22 a 23 b
24 c 25 a 26 b 27 b 28 a 29 b 30 b

PART C

Pearson Education Limited
Edinburgh Gate
Harlow
Essex CM20 2JE
England
and Associated Companies throughout the world.

www.pearsonelt.com

First published 2012
Seventh impression 2017

Set in Gill Sans Book 9.75/11.5

Printed in Italy by L.E.G.O.

Illustrated by Sean@kja-artist.com

Damian Williams

speakout

Intermediate
Students' Resource Bank

PAGE	UNIT	PHOTOCOPIABLE	LANGUAGE POINT	TIME
141	1	Who you know	**Vocabulary: family and relationships** • review vocabulary of family and relationships • practise speaking skills by asking and answering questions	25–30
143	1	Similarities	**Grammar: question forms** • practise forming questions • practise speaking skills by asking questions to find similarities	30–40
144	1	Queens and kings	**Grammar: review of verb tenses** • use the present simple, present continuous, past simple and past continuous • practise speaking skills by asking and answering questions	30–40
145	1	Jobs fair	**Functional language: talking about yourself** • practise functional language for talking about yourself in the context of jobs	30–40
146	2	You're the director	**Vocabulary: types of story and the news** • review vocabulary of types of story and the news • practise speaking skills by discussing and presenting ideas for a film	30–40
148	2	Celebrity facts	**Grammar: present perfect/past simple** • practise the present perfect and past simple in a true/false activity	30–40
149	2	In your dreams	**Grammar: narrative tenses** • use the past simple, past continuous and past perfect • practise speaking skills by describing and asking about a dream	30–40
150	2	What happened next?	**Functional language: telling a story** • practise functional language for telling a story and keeping a story going	30–40
152	3	Idiom wars	**Vocabulary plus: idioms** • review idioms in the context of a game	25–30
153	3	The contract of life	**Grammar: the future (plans)** • practise future forms for making plans	20–30
154	3	Inventions	**Grammar: the future (predictions)** • use future forms for making predictions • practise speaking skills by discussing and presenting an invention	30–40
155	3	Sorry, I didn't catch that	**Functional language: dealing with misunderstandings** • practise functional language for dealing with misunderstandings in role-play situations	30–40
156	4	Three jobs	**Vocabulary: personal qualities** • review vocabulary of personal qualities • practise speaking skills by finding out and giving information about jobs	30–40
157	4	Finding the right words	**Vocabulary plus: confusing words** • review vocabulary of confusing words in the context of a correction activity • practise speaking skills by discussing statements	25–35
158	4	Top tips	**Grammar: *must, have to, should*** • use modals of obligation *must, have to* and *should* to give advice	30–40
159	4	Those were the days	**Grammar: *used to, would*** • use *used to* and *would* in the context of talking about your childhood • practise speaking skills by asking about people's childhoods	30–40
160	4	Coalition government	**Functional language: reaching agreement** • practise functional language for reaching agreement in a role-play situation	30–40
161	5	Give us a clue	**Vocabulary: technology** • review vocabulary of technology • practise speaking skills by describing types of technology	25–35
162	5	Word-building race	**Vocabulary plus: word-building: adjectives** • review adjective suffixes in the context of a board game	30–40
163	5	Which phone?	**Grammar: comparatives/superlatives** • use comparatives and superlatives to compare phones • practise speaking skills by discussing and comparing information on phones	30–40
164	5	You're not French, are you?	**Grammar: question tags** • use question tags • practise rising and falling intonation in question tags to check information	25–30
165	5	What's the problem?	**Functional language: polite requests** • practise functional language for polite requests in role-play situations	30–40
166	6	How emotional are you?	**Vocabulary: *-ing/-ed* adjectives** • review *-ing/-ed* adjectives in the context of a questionnaire	30–40
167	6	Guess the verb	**Vocabulary plus: multi-word verbs** • review multi-word verbs • practise speaking skills by describing the meaning of multi-word verbs	25–30

RESOURCE BANK

Index of photocopiables

Worksheet A

1   Read out the sentences for your partner to correct the underlined words.

  I   When I was at junior school, I was a very good <u>employee</u>.

  2   When I meet up with my <u>team-mates</u> after school, we speak English together to get more practice.

  3   I'm a <u>partner</u> of several clubs in my home town.

  4   <u>I'm related to</u> my mother – we look the same and have a similar personality.

  5   I think a good <u>mentor</u> is always ready to listen to his or her employees.

  6   No one has ever asked me to be the <u>great-grandmother</u> of their child.

  7   I've never <u>inherited</u>. I'm still waiting for the right person to come along!

  8   I don't live with my <u>family history</u>, but they all live quite near so I see them often.

  9   I don't know much about my mother's <u>roots</u> of the family.

  10   I don't get to see my <u>ancestors</u> very often. Most of them live in a different city.

2   Are the sentences true or false for you? Discuss with your partner.

Worksheet B

1 Read out the sentences for your partner to correct the underlined words.

   I I like team sports, but success often depends on your <u>classmates</u>.

  2 If I owned a company and an <u>pupil</u> was always late, I would fire them.

  3 My <u>relatives</u> came to my country in the 1800s.

  4 I never knew my <u>godmother</u> – she died a long time before I was born.

  5 I don't know much about my <u>extended family</u> – only back to the 1950s.

  6 To be a good <u>boss</u>, I think you need to know how your pupils learn best.

  7 In class, I like working with a <u>member</u> more than working on my own.

  8 My family's <u>side</u> are in the town which I grew up in.

  9 I <u>take after</u> someone famous – well, my brother was in the local newspaper once!

10 I've never <u>had a fiancé/fiancée</u> anything.

2 Are the sentences true or false for you? Discuss with your partner.

1 Complete the information about yourself. Add three more facts.

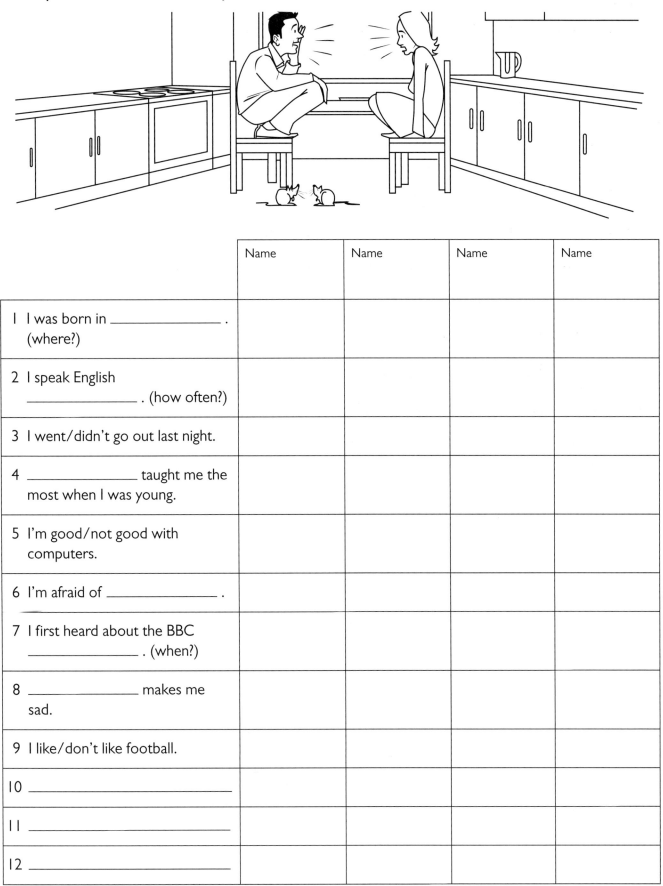

	Name	Name	Name	Name
1 I was born in _____ . (where?)				
2 I speak English _____ . (how often?)				
3 I went/didn't go out last night.				
4 _____ taught me the most when I was young.				
5 I'm good/not good with computers.				
6 I'm afraid of _____ .				
7 I first heard about the BBC _____ . (when?)				
8 _____ makes me sad.				
9 I like/don't like football.				
10 _____				
11 _____				
12 _____				

2 Ask some of your classmates the questions. Tick ✓ if they are the same or cross ✗ if they are different.

Worksheet A

Ask your partner questions to complete the text about Queen Elizabeth II. Then answer your partner's questions about King Juan Carlos I.

Queen Elizabeth II of the United Kingdom

Queen Elizabeth II of the United Kingdom was born in London on the [1] _____ . She has one sister, Princess Margaret. She is married to [2] _____ . They got married on the 20th of November 1947, when they received [3] _____ from around the world. She later had her first child, Prince Charles, while they were [4] _____ in 1948.

While she was [5] _____ in 1952, her father died and she became queen.

In 1977 she celebrated her [6] _____ (twenty-five years), and in 2002 she celebrated her [7] _____ (fifty years). At the moment, she is hoping to become [8] _____ in British history. (This will actually happen on the 10th of September 2015.)

She lives at Buckingham Palace, but it is reported that she prefers [9] _____ .

Currently, she is working hard to [10] _____ .

King Juan Carlos I of Spain

King Juan Carlos I of Spain was born in Rome on the 5th of January 1938. He got married in 1962 to Sofía of Greece and Denmark, and they have three children and eight grandchildren.

In 1969, the dictator Francisco Franco named Juan Carlos as his successor. In 1974 and 1975, while the dictator was suffering from health problems, Juan Carlos was temporary head of state. On the 22nd of November 1975, two days after the death of Franco, Juan Carlos became king.

At the moment he is enjoying popular support from Spanish people, and in 2008 he was voted the most popular leader in all Ibero-American states. At present he is working hard to promote Ibero-American relations.

He speaks Spanish, English, French, Italian and Portuguese. He likes sport and while the Spanish football team were celebrating their 2010 World Cup victory, he told them 'You made our best dreams come true.'

Worksheet B

Ask your partner questions to complete the text about King Juan Carlos I. Then answer your partner's questions about Queen Elizabeth II.

King Juan Carlos I of Spain

King Juan Carlos I of Spain was born in [1] _____ on the 5th of January 1938. He got married in 1962 to [2] _____ , and they have three children and [3] _____ grandchildren.

In 1969, the dictator Francisco Franco named Juan Carlos as [4] _____ . In 1974 and 1975, while the dictator was [5] _____ , Juan Carlos was temporary head of state. On the 22nd of November 1975, two days after the death of Franco, Juan Carlos [6] _____ .

At the moment he is enjoying [7] _____ , and in 2008 he was voted the most popular leader in all Ibero-American states. At present he is [8] _____ Ibero-American relations.

He speaks [9] _____ . He likes sport and while the Spanish football team were celebrating [10] _____ , he told them 'You made our best dreams come true.'

Queen Elizabeth II of the United Kingdom

Queen Elizabeth II of the United Kingdom was born in London on the 21st of April 1926. She has one sister, Princess Margaret. She is married to Prince Philip, the Duke of Edinburgh. They got married on the 20th of November 1947, when they received 2,500 wedding gifts from around the world. She later had her first child, Prince Charles, while they were living near Windsor in 1948.

While she was visiting Kenya in 1952, her father died and she became queen.

In 1977 she celebrated her Silver Jubilee (twenty-five years), and in 2002 she celebrated her Golden Jubilee (fifty years). At the moment, she is hoping to become the longest-reigning queen in British history. (This will actually happen on the 10th of September 2015.)

She lives at Buckingham Palace, but it is reported that she prefers Windsor Castle.

Currently, she is working hard to promote her 600 charities and organisations.

Role card 1

You are an exhibitor at a jobs fair. You are looking to recruit suitable people to train and work for your company. Competition between companies at the jobs fair to recruit new people is high, so think about how you can persuade people to work for you.

First decide on the following information:

Position available: _____

Main duties/tasks of the position: _____

Qualifications needed: _____

Experience required: _____

Personal qualities you are looking for: _____

Typical hours: _____

Working environment: _____

Best things about the position: _____

When you are ready, take your place at the jobs fair and ask and answer questions about the position.

Role card 2

You are looking for a new job and have decided to go to a jobs fair, where different companies are looking to recruit people for positions in their companies. You want to find the best job possible.

First decide on the following information:

Type of job you are looking for: _____

Qualifications you have: _____

Experience you have: _____

Your top three personal qualities: _____

Which **three** of the following are important to you, and why?

working outside   working in an office   working with people   caring for people using computers   physical work   challenging work   being creative   selling things managing people   training people   being competitive   other (say which)

_____

_____

When you are ready, visit the companies and ask questions about the positions available. Choose one you would like to apply for.

1 Choose a type of film and some events.

Types of film

biopic   docudrama   disaster   romantic comedy   period drama   fantasy/science fiction
mystery/crime   action/adventure   psychological thriller

Events

a crash happens   someone attacks the hero   a lot of violence occurs   a fugitive is caught
an earthquake hits the city   X and Y fall in love   the queen dies   X is destroyed
workers go on strike   hostages are taken/released   X gets shot
X causes an economic collapse   Lord X falls ill   X has an affair   other (say which)

2 Complete the storyboard then present your ideas to the class.

1	2	3
Background	Main characters	Problem

4	5	6
Solution	Further problem	Ending – happy or sad?

Worksheet A

Read out your celebrity facts, choosing the correct verb form. Then listen to your partner's facts and say if they are true or false.

1 At the age of ten, Justin Timberlake **has won/won** the 1991 pre-teen Mr America contest. (true)

2 Christina Aguilera **has recorded/recorded** an album in Spanish, but she doesn't speak the language. (true)

3 When he was a child, Jim Carrey **has worn/wore** tap shoes to bed, in case his parents needed cheering up in the middle of the night. (true)

4 Drew Barrymore **has never directed/never directed** a film. (false – she directed her first film *Whip It* in 2009)

5 Samuel L. Jackson **has first appeared/first appeared** in a film when he was two years old. (false – Samuel L. Jackson first appeared in the film *Together for Days* in 1972, when he was twenty-four)

6 Jack Black **has been/was** an actor since 1969. (false – he was born in 1969)

7 The film *Titanic* **has never been/was never** translated into any languages other than English. (false – it has been translated into many languages)

8 Janis Joplin, Jimi Hendrix, Jim Morrison and Kurt Cobain **have all died/all died** when they were twenty-seven. (true)

9 James Bond is a real agent in the British secret service. He **has worked/worked** there for over twenty years. (false – James Bond is a fictional character)

10 Tom Cruise **has studied/studied** to be a priest. (true)

Worksheet B

Listen to your partner's facts and say if they are true or false. Then read out your celebrity facts, choosing the correct verb form.

1 Quentin Tarantino **has directed/directed** but never acted in films. (false – he has appeared in many of his own films)

2 Jennifer Lopez **has started/started** singing and dancing lessons at the age of five. (true)

3 Cuba Gooding Jr's first job **was/has been** as a break-dancer for Lionel Richie at the 1984 Olympics. (true)

4 George Clooney **has had/had** a pet lion when he was a boy. (false – but he did have a pet pig!)

5 Brad Pitt **has never won/never won** an Oscar. (true – but he has been nominated for two)

6 Ex-President Ronald Reagan **has appeared/appeared** in over fifty films from the 1930s to the 1960s. (true)

7 John Wayne **has made/made** more than 200 films before he died in 1979. (true)

8 Steven Spielberg **has appeared/appeared** in the 1984 film *ET*. (false – he directed it)

9 Harrison Ford **has had/had** a species of spider named after him. (true)

10 Jennifer Aniston **has dated/dated** all of the male actors in *Friends* in real life. (false – but she has dated Brad Pitt, who once appeared in *Friends*)

Think of a dream you had recently and make notes in the word webs. Describe your dream to your group. Listen and ask questions to find out more about other students' dreams.

Things you did/ate the day before

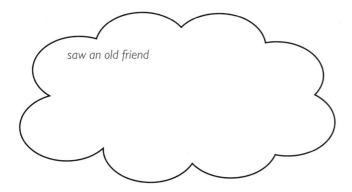

saw an old friend

Background of the dream

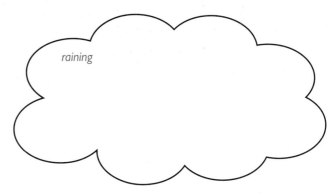

raining

Places in the dream

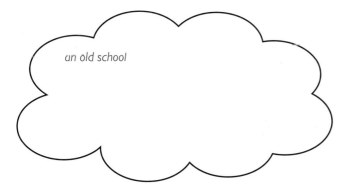

an old school

Clothes you were wearing

a beautiful dress

Main events of the dream

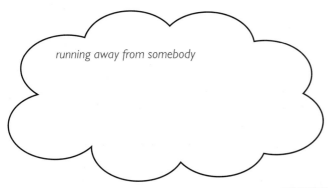

running away from somebody

The end/After the dream

woke up feeling scared

Worksheet A

Two ugly sisters lived in a flat in London.

Suzerella was a university student who worked part-time as a cleaner for the two ugly sisters. The two ugly sisters were very cruel and made her work very hard.

A new nightclub opened, and a very handsome celebrity was going to open it. The ugly sisters and Suzerella really wanted to go and meet him.

The ugly sisters bought their tickets, but wouldn't let Suzerella go. They made her stay at home and clean the floors.

On the opening night, Suzerella was at home, cleaning and feeling very sad. Suddenly, an angel appeared …

Worksheet B

Joe and his mother were very poor. They lived together in a very small house, and didn't have enough food to eat.

One day, they went to a market, so they could sell their TV to buy some food.

While they were there, Joe's mother went to see the other things for sale and asked Joe to stay and try and sell the TV.

A man came up and asked Joe to sell him the TV for some 'magic' beans. Joe thought this was an excellent idea, and sold it to him.

When Joe's mother returned, she was very angry, and couldn't believe Joe had done that. When they got home, she threw the beans into the garden.

The next morning, when Joe woke up, a huge, tree had grown in the garden. Joe decided to climb it …

Student A

Put these idioms somewhere in the grid, one word per square:

We're in hot water.   It's not my cup of tea.   We're working against the clock.
He's a bit of a dark horse.   Can you keep an eye on her?

	1	2	3	4	5	6	7	8
A								
B								
C								
D								
E								
F								
G								
H								

Miss!

Hit '...'!

You've hit the idiom '...'!

Student B

Put these idioms somewhere in the grid, one word per square:

I really put my foot in it.   It's a piece of cake.   We're running out of time.
I've had enough of the rat race.   Could you give me a hand?

	1	2	3	4	5	6	7	8
A								
B								
C								
D								
E								
F								
G								
H								

Miss!

Hit '...'!

You've hit the idiom '...'!

The Contract of Life

I, _____ , hereby promise that:

This weekend I'm ____-ing _____ .

Before the end of the month I'm going to _____ .

This year I'll definitely _____ .

Next week I might _____ .

In the next ten years I'm going to _____ .

This evening I might _____ .

Next year I'll definitely _____ .

Tomorrow I'm ____-ing _____ .

Before I'm sixty-five _____ .

(your own promise) _____ .

(your own promise) _____ .

Signed _____

Witness 1

Name _____   Signed _____

Witness 2

Name _____   Signed _____

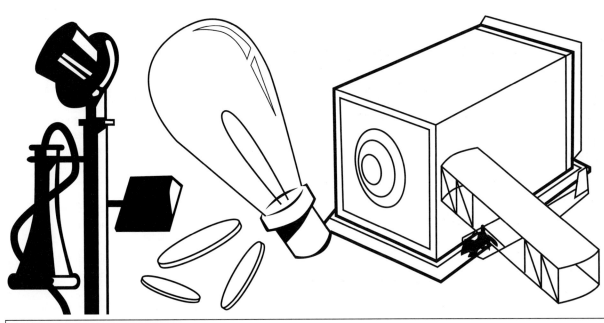

Name of invention _____

What your invention looks like:

What will your invention do? _____

How is it going to transform the way we live? _____

Is it likely to be popular for everybody, or will it be a luxury product? _____

Which current inventions could it be more popular than? _____

Other details _____

Role card 1A

You are a market researcher. You need to ask people in the street to answers these questions. If they do the questionnaire, they can win a free mobile phone. Be polite!

Market research questionnaire

1 How old are you?

   a) under 20   c) 36–49

   b) 21–35   d) over 50

2 Which profession do you work in?

   a) food and drink   c) manufacturing

   b) education   d) administration

3 How many people do you live with?

   a) alone

   b) my immediate family

   c) my extended family

4 What do you use the internet for?

   a) email   c) social networking

   b) news   d) shopping

5 How much do you earn?

   a) under 20,000 a year

   b) 20,000–35,000 a year

   c) over 35,000 a year

Role card 2A

Your name is Jane/John. You called your friend Louisa/Louis earlier, but they weren't in, so you left a message with their flatmate. You were calling to see if your friend had the receipt for some pink shoes they bought you for your birthday. The shoes don't fit. You can go over to your friend's place to pick up the receipt later, if it's convenient. You finish work at 7p.m. and would like to go over then.

Additional information:

- It's really important that you get the receipt tonight. The only chance you have to take the shoes back is tomorrow morning before work.

- The shoes actually fit perfectly, but you just don't like them. Don't let your friend know this, though.

Role card 1B

You are in a hurry as you're late for work. A market researcher stops you and asks you to do a questionnaire. You don't really want to, but if you do, you might win a mobile phone, and your current one is very old. Answer the questions, but try to be as quick as possible.

This is your profile:

- You are twenty years old, but it's your birthday tomorrow.
- You are a business management consultant (you give advice to managers of small businesses).
- You live with your husband/wife, and their son from a previous marriage.
- You only ever use the internet for business research.
- Your salary varies. You get paid for each project you work on – about 10,000 per project. You do three to four projects a year.

Role card 2B

Your name is Louisa/Louis. You have just got home and found the following phone message, taken down by your flatmate. Call your friend Jane/John to check the details.

Your friend Joan?/Shaun? called to ask if you have the recipe for pigs' feet, which you made for their birthday. If you do, can you take it over to their place at 7a.m. before they go to work?

See you later.

Additional information:

- You're going out with friends in a few minutes, and won't be back until very late.
- You love giving your friends gifts, and if they don't like them, you get very upset. You are usually really good at buying presents, though.

Role card 1A

You are a Human Resources Manager for a company that produces new technology for the computer industry. Read about these three jobs that are available at your company, then answer your partner's questions.

Trainer

The successful candidate will be responsible for training new staff in company practices, giving workshops and writing a training programme. He/She will be decisive, a good communicator and a good leader.

Inventor

We are looking for an inventor, who will work as part of a team to create new technology for the computer industry, and help develop existing technology. The ideal person must be able to think outside the box, highly motivated and hard-working.

Sales representative

We need someone to work in our sales team, finding new customers and selling new technology to our existing customers. He/She must be competitive, a real risk-taker and ambitious

Role card 2A

You are interested in working for six months on a cruise ship. You know that these three jobs are available, and you want to find out more information. Ask your partner – a recruitment agent at the cruise company – questions to get the missing information. Then decide which job you will apply for.

Entertainments manager

Main duties:

Personal qualities needed:

Deckhand/Caretaker

Main duties:

Personal qualities needed:

Travel agent

Main duties:

Personal qualities needed:

Role card 1B

You are interested in working for a company which produces new technology for the computer industry. You know that these three jobs are available, and you want to find out more information. Ask your partner – the Human Resources Manager – questions to get the missing information. Then decide which job you will apply for.

Trainer

Main duties:

Personal qualities needed:

Inventor

Main duties:

Personal qualities needed:

Sales representative

Main duties:

Personal qualities needed:

Role card 2B

You are a recruitment agent for a cruise company. Read about these three jobs that are available on a six-month cruise of the Pacific islands, then answer your partner's questions.

Entertainments manager

We are looking for an entertainments manager for our wonderful entertainment programme. You will find new acts and plan interesting activities for the guests for the six-month cruise. You will be a good leader, a risk-taker and able to think outside the box.

Deckhand/Caretaker

The successful candidate will be responsible for the general maintenance of the ship, with duties to include cleaning and repairs. He/She will be hard-working and motivated.

Travel agent

This job will involve selling the cruise package before departure and finding new customers. After the cruise departs, this person will be available on board to help guests with their questions. He/She must be a good communicator, competitive and decisive.

Worksheet A

1 Read out your sentences.

1 I like being busy. When I have a lot of <u>job</u> to do, it stops me getting bored. ✗
(work)

2 I'm quite forgetful. I always have to get other people to <u>remember</u> me to do things. ✗
(remind)

3 I sometimes find it difficult to <u>listen</u> what people say to me in English. ✗
(hear)

4 I never <u>forget</u> people's birthdays. ✓

5 For me it's more important to have an enjoyable job than to <u>win</u> a lot of money. ✗
(earn)

6 We had a <u>fun</u> day out last Saturday – we went to a music festival. ✓

2 Listen to your partner's sentences and say if they are right or wrong.

3 Discuss which sentences are true for you.

Worksheet B

1 Listen to your partner's sentences and say if they are right or wrong.

2 Read out your sentences.

    1   I've never <u>earnt</u> any money in the lottery. ✗

         (won)

    2   I'd like to try lots of different <u>jobs</u> in my lifetime. ✓

    3   I always <u>remember</u> to charge my mobile phone battery. ✓

    4   I like <u>hearing</u> classical music. ✗

         (listening to)

    5   I <u>forgot</u> my book at home today, by mistake. ✗

         (left)

    6   My teacher is <u>fun</u> – he/she always tells good jokes. ✗

         (funny)

3 Discuss which sentences are true for you.

Grammar: *must, have to, should*

How to ______

1 You must ______

2 You don't have to ______

3 You shouldn't ______

4 You mustn't ______

5 You should ______

6 You have to ______

How to ______

1 You must ______

2 You don't have to ______

3 You shouldn't ______

4 You mustn't ______

5 You should ______

6 You have to ______

How to ______

1 You must ever el crush de mario 7u7

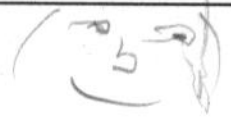

2 You don't have to ______

3 You shouldn't ______

4 You mustn't ______

5 You should ______

6 You have to ______

How to ______

1 You must ______

2 You don't have to ______

3 You shouldn't ______

4 You mustn't ______

5 You should ______

6 You have to ______

Write sentences about when you were a child, using *used to* or *would*.
Then ask questions to find people with the same information.

		Name
Pets	∄ I used to have a dog and 2 a rabbits ~~dog~~	Diana ♡
1	_____ .	_____
Home	I used to live in Chadacayo d parends my bedroom used to be light blue Diana	
2	_____ .	_____
3	_____ .	_____
Family	I used to live with my grandparends Andrea I used to have one cousin now i have two Andrea	
4	_____ .	_____
5	_____ .	_____
What you were(n't) afraid of	I used to be afraid of clouns ~~I was afra clou~~ I used to be afraid of the insects Carla	
6	_____ .	_____
7	_____ .	_____
Sports and games	I used to swim a lot Carla I used to rollerblading Diana	
8	_____ .	_____
9	_____ .	_____
Ambitions and dreams	I ~~used~~ want to be a astronaut I ~~used~~ want to be a famous fothography	
10	_____ .	_____
11	_____ .	_____
Food	I used to eat a lots of candies Diana	
12	_____ .	_____

Worksheet A

The Education party

You are the leader of the Education party. You have just won equal votes in the recent general election in Politicaria, and must now form a coalition government with the Freedom party. You both need to agree on the country's new laws, but first, decide what your priorities are.

You want the following:

- More money spent on state education, and less on hospitals.

  Reasons:

- Higher taxes for the rich.

  Reasons:

- Strong law and order, with more money spent on the police.

  Reasons:

- Big investment in the environment and renewable energy.

  Reasons:

Worksheet B

The Freedom party

You are the leader of the Freedom party. You have just won equal votes in the recent general election in Politicaria, and must now form a coalition government with the Education party. You both need to agree on the country's new laws, but first, decide what your priorities are.

You want the following:

- More money spent on hospitals, and less on state education.

  Reasons:

- Lower taxes for everyone.

  Reasons:

- More freedom for people in general, restricting the powers of the police.

  Reasons:

- Big investment in nuclear power.

  Reasons:

Crossword A

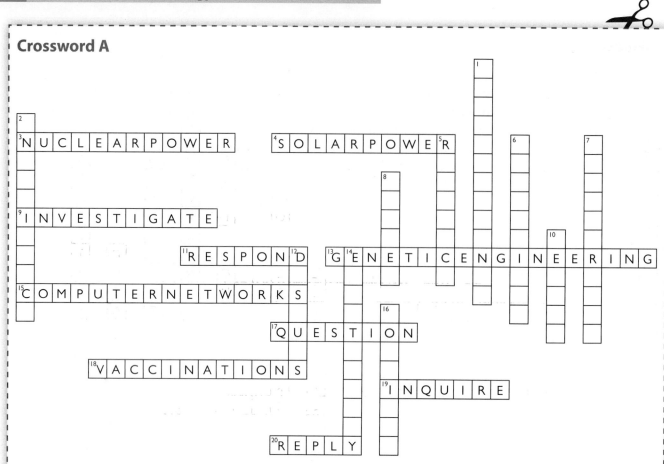

Crossword B

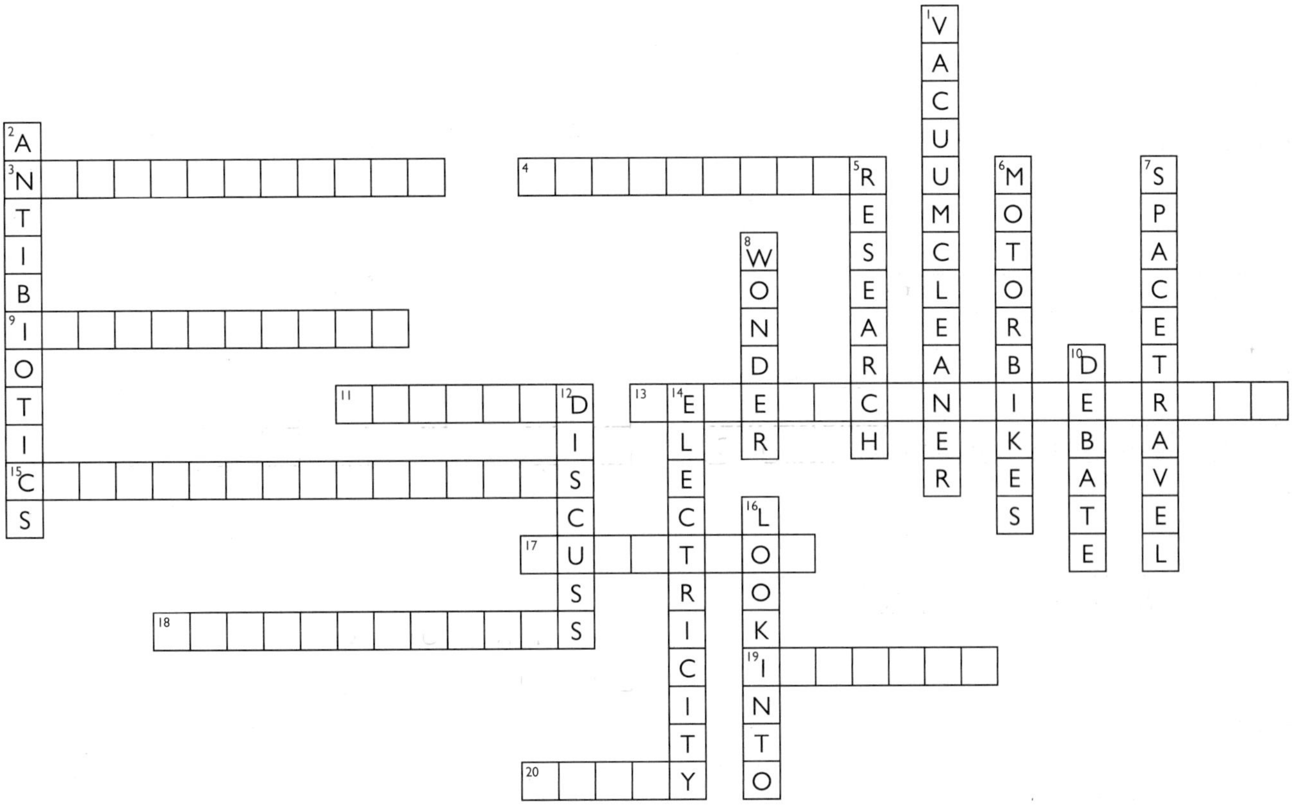
VACUUMCLEANER
ANTIBIOTICS
RESEARCH
MOTORBIKES
SPACETRAVEL
WONDER
DEBATE
DISCUSS
ELECTRICITY
LOOKINTO

Vocabulary plus: word building: adjectives

I love cats: they're so cute and (love).

-less

I like films which are (drama).

There aren't many (home) people in my country.

The most (effect) plans are often the simplest.

Free square!

I hate horror films. They're too (scare).

I'm a very (talk) person – I talk too much sometimes!

-ful

English grammar is always (logic).

-ic/-ical

I think I'm a (response) person.

Free square!

I can't cook. When I do, my food is never (eat)!

Going to the dentist can be (pain).

There are some very (poet) traditional stories from my country.

There have been a lot of (explode) scandals in my country recently.

I like work that is (create).

-able/-ible

I have a friend who is a (care) driver. He/she's always nearly having accidents.

I'm (hope) that my English will improve in the next year.

I'm quite a (mess) person!

Art classes at school were (use). I never learnt anything!

Happiness is more (value) than money.

FINISH

-y

Learning English is (ease).

I'm (hope) at music. I can't sing or play any instruments.

My favourite kind of holiday is one which is (peace) – I like to relax.

START

It doesn't matter what job you do, as long as you are (success).

-ive

I love (rain) days.

Free square!

I'd love to travel and do (biology) research – just like Darwin!

Role card 1

You are looking for a new mobile phone. You want a phone with a lot of different functions, but you also want one that's very small, and that you can carry around easily. You don't want to spend too much money, but you don't mind paying a bit more for extra functions.

Compare the information below with your partner's phones. Then choose which phone you are going to buy.

Econofon 3000

Price: *$10.00*

Size: *15cm x 7cm*

Easy/difficult to use: *very easy*

Functions: *calls and text messages only*

Battery life: *12 hours*

Internet speed: *no internet*

Supertech 7120i

Price: *$699.99*

Size: *10cm x 7cm*

Easy/difficult to use: *very difficult*

Functions: *calls, text messages, internet, email, camera, video camera, organiser, games and many more*

Battery life: *8 hours*

Internet speed: *fast*

Surfista XS

Price: *$150.00*

Size: *10cm x 6cm*

Easy/difficult to use: *quite difficult*

Functions: *calls, text messages, internet, email, camera, video*

Battery life: *10 hours*

Internet speed: *very fast*

Role card 2

You are looking for a new mobile phone. You don't have much money, so you can't buy a very expensive phone. You travel a lot, so you want a phone that can connect to the internet almost anywhere. You also like playing games on your phone on long bus journeys.

Compare the information below with your partner's phones. Then choose which phone you are going to buy.

Gamesmart 999

Price: *$299.99*

Size: *12cm x 15cm*

Easy/difficult to use: *easy*

Functions: *calls, text messages, internet, lots of games*

Battery life: *5 hours*

Internet speed: *medium*

Micro 272X

Price: *$350.00*

Size: *5cm x 3cm*

Easy/difficult to use: *medium*

Functions: *calls, text messages, camera, video*

Battery life: *9 hours*

Internet speed: *no internet*

Traveller 900

Price: *$99.99*

Size: *8cm x 6cm*

Easy/difficult to use: *easy*

Functions: *calls, text messages, camera, video, simple games; internet available on the 901 model, which costs 250.00*

Battery life: *24 hours*

Internet speed: *slow, where available*

Complete the sentences with the names of your classmates.
Use question tags to check the information.

	✓ or ✗?
1 _____ came to class by car today.	
2 _____ likes studying English.	
3 _____ doesn't like eating fish.	
4 _____ went out with friends last night.	
5 _____ has got a boy/girlfriend.	
6 _____ is a student.	
I'm fairly sure …	
7 _____ .	
8 _____ .	
9 _____ .	
I'm not sure …	
10 _____ .	
11 _____ .	
12 _____ .	

Worksheet A

Role card 1A

You have just bought a new computer, which was very expensive. When you got home, you set it up, following the instructions. You switched it on, but nothing happened. You have tried everything, and connected all the cables correctly, but nothing has worked. Call the support line and ask for help. You either want a new computer or a full refund.

Role card 2A

You work for a mobile phone company. A customer calls to complain that the payment for their bill has left their bank four days early. It is because of a problem with your computer system. However, don't tell them this, and tell them it's not your company's policy to give refunds. Suggest another solution.

Role card 3A

You recently bought a new MP3 player, and the shop assistant told you it would work with any computer. However, when you got home and tried to connect it, a message came up saying 'Player not compatible with this software'. Your computer uses Supersystem1 software. Take it back to the shop to complain, and ask for a refund.

Worksheet B

Role card 1B

You are a computer engineer and work for the support line of a computer company. You have nearly finished for the day, and are keen to get home quickly because it's your daughter's birthday today. A customer calls you to complain about a new computer that she can't get to work. Ask her questions to find out what's wrong and make sure she checks all the cables are connected. After trying everything, it still won't work. However, your company doesn't give refunds or replacement computers, so try to find another solution.

Role card 2B

You are having a bad day. First your alarm clock didn't go off this morning, and so you were late. Then you just missed the bus and had to walk two kilometres to work. You were late for work and your boss was angry. You have just checked your bank statement and noticed that the payment for your mobile phone bill has come out of your account four days early, leaving you with no money for the weekend until you get paid on Monday. Call the mobile phone company to complain, and ask them to refund you.

Role card 3B

You work in an electronics shop. A customer recently bought an MP3 player, which you know can be used with any computer. However, it is only compatible with Supersystem2 software. The customer comes to your shop to complain that it wouldn't work with their computer. Find out as much as you can and try to solve the problem. Your company doesn't give refunds, though.

Worksheet A

1 Underline the correct adjective, and write one more question.

1 It's Thursday. You have to finish a project by the end of the week. How do you feel?

   a) _Relaxed/Relaxing_. You'll get it done.

   b) A bit **stressing/stressed**, but you'll get it finished somehow.

   c) Very, very **worried/worrying**. You don't have enough time left.

2 You've just seen a new horror film at the cinema.

   a) It was **boring/bored**. Not scary at all.

   b) You feel **embarrassing/embarrassed**. You think your friends saw you were scared.

   c) It was so **frightening/frightened** that you won't be able to sleep tonight!

3 Someone jumps the queue in front of you at the supermarket.

   a) You're **surprised/surprising** that someone could do that, but it's OK.

   b) It's a bit **annoying/annoyed**, but you don't say anything.

   c) You're **disgusting/disgusted** at their behaviour, and tell them angrily to wait.

4 You find out that your English teacher is giving you a test this week. How do you feel?

   a) _Pleased/Pleasing_. It will be good to see your progress.

   b) A bit **confusing/confused**. You're not sure what to study.

   c) **Terrified/Terrifying**. You hate tests!

5 _____

   _____

   _____

   _____

Student B's answer:

_____

_____

2 Look at your partner's answers and read the analysis. Do you agree?

Mostly a) answers
You're a very calm person who rarely gets excited. You're good in a crisis, but you should open up at times – don't let life get boring!

Mostly b) answers
You manage your emotions well, and you don't let them get out of control. Perhaps you should become a therapist!

Mostly c) answers
You're a very passionate person, but need to learn to control your emotions. Slow down sometimes!

Worksheet B

1 Underline the correct adjective, and write one more question.

1 It's Friday afternoon. How do you feel?

  a) **_Pleased_/Pleasing**, because it's the end of the week.

  b) This time of the week is **excited/_exciting_**. Here comes the weekend!

  c) I feel absolutely **exhausting/_exhausted_**. It's been a very emotional week (again)!

2 Your friend calls you to tell you his/her pet has just died.

  a) You're **confusing/_confused_** about why he/she is so upset. It's only a pet.

  b) The situation is a little **_worrying_/worried**. You know your friend is going to be upset.

  c) You're **_devastated_/devastating**. Why did it have to die?

3 It's your birthday, but nobody remembered.

  a) It's fine. In fact, you're quite **_pleased_/pleasing** because you don't like lots of attention.

  b) It's not a problem; it's just a bit **annoyed/_annoying_** that nobody remembered.

  c) You are **disgusting/_disgusted_** with them. They call themselves 'friends'?

4 You arrive at a party and don't know anyone.

  a) You know it's going to be **bored/_boring_**. You have nobody to talk to, so you leave.

  b) You feel a little uncomfortable, but it's **_interesting_/ interested** to meet new people.

  c) You feel really **_embarrassed_/embarrassing** about being alone and panic!

5 _____

  _____

  _____

  _____

Student A's answer:

_____

2 Look at your partner's answers and read the analysis. Do you agree?

Mostly a) answers
You're a very calm person who rarely gets excited. You're good in a crisis, but you should open up at times – don't let life get boring!

Mostly b) answers
You manage your emotions well, and you don't let them get out of control. Perhaps you should become a therapist!

Mostly c) answers
You're a very passionate person, but need to learn to control your emotions. Slow down sometimes!

Worksheet A

Describe each multi-word verb to your partner but do <u>not</u> use the words in italics. Your partner will try and guess the verb.

chat somebody up *talk speak man woman like*	**scroll up** *website computer mouse move top*	**dress up** *clothes formal wear smart down*
get on *like friend relationship good well*	**click on** *mouse computer icon link move*	**try on** *clothes shop test fit size*

Worksheet B

Describe each multi-word verb to your partner but do <u>not</u> use the words in italics. Your partner will try and guess the verb.

settle down *old family calm home live*	**shut down** *computer finish off power close*	**take off** *clothes remove finish bed on*
go off somebody *stop like relationship finish friend*	**log off** *website computer close leave exit*	**dress down** *clothes informal up wear jeans*

Worksheet A

1 Ask your partner questions using the prompts below.

	Partner 1	Partner 2
1 / work / hard / school? *(Do you ... at)*		
2 How often / practise / swimming ? *(do you)*		
3 / know anyone / expert / in art ? *(Do you)*		
4 / aptitude / computers? *(Do you have an for ... who is and)*		
5 / believe / ability / succeed? *(you had and to for)*		
6 Who / most / talented musician / you know? *(Do you spend with ... do you thing is the)*		
7 / know anyone / ability / in sports ? *(that ... Do you that has an)*		
8 / anything / you / hopeless / ? *(that are at)*		

2 Now change partners and ask your questions again. Do they have anything in common?

Worksheet B

1   Ask your partner questions using the prompts below.

	Partner 1	Partner 2
1 What things / practise / regularly?		
2 / know anyone / natural talent / languages?		
3 For which jobs / need to be / skillful communicator?		
4 / know anyone / gifted / art?		
5 / find it easy / focus / problems?		
6 / you / high achiever / school?		
7 / ever have / opportunity / _____ ?		
8 / anything / you / useless / ?		

2   Now change partners and ask your questions again. Do they have anything in common?

	My answer	Name
1 Who do you most depend __on__ in your life?		
2 How many hours a day do you put __in__ to your work/studies?		
3 Who do you have a lot in common __with__ ?		
4 Do you believe __in__ ghosts?		
5 What do you have a talent __for__ ?		
6 Who was the last person you argued __with__ ?		
7 What was the last TV show you laughed __at__ ?		
8 Who in your family do you usually agree __with__ ?		
9 What sport is your country world-class __at__ ?		
10 Do your parents have access __to__ the internet at home?		
11 What kind of art/photography do you like looking __at__ ?		
12 Does your work/Do your studies give you a lot to think __about__ at the moment?		
13 On a date, do you think the man, woman, or both should pay __for__ the meal?		
14 What organisations/clubs do you belong __to__ ?		
15 Who did you rely __on__ most when you were younger?		
16 What one thing in your life do you worry __about__ most?		
17 Are you good at picking up __on__ other people's problems?		
18 If you receive bad service in a shop/restaurant, do you usually complain __about__ it?		

Worksheet A

Film star 1A

1 She was born on 30th August 1972 in San Diego, USA.

2 She / previously / work / model.

3 She / act / major roles / since / first appeared in *The Mask* in 1994.

4 She / win / many awards / but / never win / an Oscar.

5 She / previously / date / Justin Timberlake and Matt Dillon.

6 She / recently / appear / *There's Something About Mary, Charlie's Angels* and *Shrek* in comedy roles.

Answer:
Cameron Michelle Diaz

Student B's score: _____

Film star 2A

1 He was born on 19th March 1955 in Idar-Oberstein, Germany.

2 As well / acting, he / also work / nuclear power plant.

3 He / go bald / since / 1980s.

4 He / previously / be married / Demi Moore.

5 He / win / many awards / but / never win / an Oscar.

6 He / appear / many action films / *Armageddon* and *The Sixth Sense,* and sitcoms such as *Moonlighting* and *Friends*.

Answer:
Walter Bruce Willis

Student B's score: _____

Film star 3A

1 She was born on 5th October 1975 in Reading, England.

2 She / act / major roles / since / first appeared in *Sense and Sensibility* in 1995.

3 She married Sam Mendes / 2003 / but they / recently / split up.

4 She / recently / win / an Oscar / *The Reader.*

5 She / act / one of / best-selling films of all time / Leonardo DiCaprio.

6 She / appear / other films / *Iris, Enigma* and *Flushed Away*.

Answer:
Kate Elizabeth Winslet

Student B's score: _____

Worksheet B

Film star 1B

1 He was born on 17th August 1943 in New York, USA.

2 He / be / member of a real street gang.

3 He / be married / Grace Hightower / since 1997.

4 Since 1989 / he / invest / TriBeCa district of New York.

5 He / win / two Oscars / *The Godfather II* and *Raging Bull*.

6 He / mainly / act / serious roles / but recently / act / comedy roles / *Meet the Fockers* and *Stardust*.

Answer:
Robert De Niro, Jr.

Student A's score: _____

Film star 2B

1 She was born on 26th March 1985 in Teddington, England.

2 She / act / major roles / since / first appeared in *Bend it Like Beckham* in 2002.

3 She / always / want / act / since she was three.

4 She / recently / do / charity work / Amnesty International.

5 Although she / be nominated / she / never win / an Oscar.

6 She / act / major series of films about pirates with Johnny Depp and Orlando Bloom.

Answer:
Keira Christina Knightley

Student A's score: _____

Film star 3B

1 He was born on 23rd July 1989 in London, England.

2 He / act / 'with magic' / since 2001.

3 He / act / in films, on TV and at the theatre.

4 He / win / many awards / but / never win / an Oscar.

5 He / appear / Sunday Times Rich List as one of the richest young people in England.

6 He / recently / act / in the theatre.

Answer:
Daniel Jacob Radcliffe

Student A's score: _____

Role card 1

You are one of the directors of *Y-Starz*, a clothing company aimed at the teenage market. Last year you made record profits, and now you have to decide how you are going to spend the money this year.

You believe the best option is to spend at least 75% of the money on paying rewards to shareholders, for the following reasons:

- You didn't pay them last year, and they are expecting to receive some money this year.

- The economy is going to get worse this year, and if you don't pay them, they might sell their shares.

- _____

- _____

Role card 2

You are one of the directors of *Y-Starz*, a clothing company aimed at the teenage market. Last year you made record profits, and now you have to decide how you are going to spend the money this year.

You believe the best option is to spend at least 75% of the money on improving the environmental aspects of the company, such as eco-friendly machinery, reducing pollution, etc. for the following reasons:

- Your competitors have recently invested a lot of money in this, and if you don't, you might get a bad reputation with your customers.

- The government has announced plans to give tax cuts to companies investing in the environment, and you would receive this money next year if you invest now.

- _____

- _____

Role card 3

You are one of the directors of *Y-Starz*, a clothing company aimed at the teenage market. Last year you made record profits, and now you have to decide how you are going to spend the money this year.

You believe the best option is to 'go global', by spending at least 75% of the money on setting up factories and shops in places such as China and Brazil, for the following reasons:

- These markets are growing, and it would mean growing the business over the next few years.

- The economy in the country where you are based is predicted to get worse this year.

- _____

- _____

Role card 4

You are one of the directors of *Y-Starz*, a clothing company aimed at the teenage market. Last year you made record profits, and now you have to decide how you are going to spend the money this year.

You believe the best option is to spend at least 75% of the money on new technology, for the following reasons:

- There have been a number of new innovations in machinery for producing clothes, which can cut costs.

- Your competitors are also doing this at the moment.

- _____

- _____

Worksheet A

1   **Read out the questions and replace the underlined phrase with the one your partner gives you.**

   1   Are you good friends with your neighbours, or do you prefer to <u>be alone</u>?

   2   Are you a <u>very curious</u> person?

   3   Do you find it easy to <u>start a good relationship with</u> new people you meet?

   4   Do you have any neighbours who <u>interrupt your privacy</u>?

   5   Have you <u>helped</u> anyone recently?

   6   What kind of behaviour <u>annoys you</u>?

2   **Now listen to your partner's questions and give them the correct phrase from the box.**

get on well with	mind their own business	a nuisance	invite your neighbours over
ask a favour of	get to know		

3   **Discuss your answers to the questions.**

Worksheet B

1 **Listen to your partner's questions and give them the correct phrase from the box.**

| keep yourself to yourself | disturb you | gets on your nerves | make friends with |
| done favours for | nosy | | |

2 **Now read out the questions and replace the underlined phrase with the one your partner gives you.**

1 Do you <u>have a good relationship with</u> everyone in your family?

2 Do you ever <u>ask your neighbours if they want to come to your house</u> for a coffee?

3 When you have a problem, do you like people to help or do you prefer them to <u>not get involved</u>?

4 In your work/studies, is there anything which is <u>annoying</u>?

5 How do you <u>find out about</u> people you've just met?

6 Do you find it easy to <u>ask for help from</u> other people?

3 **Discuss your answers to the questions.**

Worksheet A

1 **Read out the sentences. Your partner will try to correct them.**

   1 There aren't much primary schools in my area.
     (~~much~~ – many)

   2 I have a good local supermarket close to where I live. It's a best in the area.
     (a – the)

   3 In my city there are lot of housing estates.
     (~~lot of~~ – a lot of)

   4 There are none swimming pools in my area.
     (~~none~~ – no)

   5 How many graffiti is there in your area? A little bit or a lot of?
     (~~many~~ – much, ~~a lot of~~ – a lot)

   6 High Street in my town gets very busy at the weekend. Plenty people come there to do their shopping.
     (~~High Street~~ – The High Street, ~~Plenty~~ – plenty of)

   7 Every the buildings in my city are modern.
     (~~Every~~ – All)

   8 There aren't much car parks in my area, and parking is a problem.
     (~~much~~ – many)

2 **Now listen to your partner's sentences and try to correct them.**

3 **Discuss which sentences are true for you.**

Worksheet B

1   Listen to your partner's sentences and try to correct them.

2   Now read out the sentences. Your partner will try to correct them.

   1   There is the big park in the centre of my city.
     (~~the~~ – a)

   2   My city gets plenty tourists in the summer, but in the winter there are no.
     (~~plenty~~ – plenty of, ~~no~~ – none)

   3   How much shopping centres are there in your area?
     (~~much~~ – many)

   4   There are lots of one-way streets in my area, and we get so many traffic during rush hour.
     (~~many~~ – much)

   5   I like buying food at an outdoor market. A one where I live is small, but there are several types of food available.
     (~~A~~ – The)

   6   I have a nicest neighbour in the world. She's an teacher!
     (~~a~~ – the, ~~an~~ – a)

   7   The New York is much more famous than my city.
     (~~The New York~~ – New York)

   8   There aren't much things for young people to do in my area in the evening.
     (~~much~~ – many)

3   Discuss which sentences are true for you.

Worksheet A

1 **Read out the sentence halves for your partner to complete.**

 1 YouTube <u>is a website where you can</u> …

 2 <u>I visit my favourite website, which is</u> flash.com, …

 3 <u>My mother, who is a</u> web designer, …

 4 Findit.com <u>is the website which I always use for</u> …

 5 <u>The internet company which I most respect is</u> …

 6 <u>Today's children, who spend too long on the internet,</u> …

2 **Now listen to your partner's sentence halves and complete them with your endings.**

 A … help you with technical problems related to your computer.

 B … information about a particular company.

 C … every day.

 D … humour online.

 E … has a lot of animation.

 F … share opinions on your favourite websites.

3 **Using the underlined phrases, make sentences that are true for you.**

Worksheet B

1   Listen to your partner's sentence halves and complete them with your endings.

A … at least three times a day.

B … loves her job.

C … share videos.

D … searches.

E … will have problems with communication later in life.

F … savetheplanet.com.

2   Now read out the sentence halves for your partner to complete.

I   <u>My personal homepage, which I use for</u> homework projects, …

2   Cyberforum.com <u>is a new website where you can</u> …

3   <u>A</u> support technician <u>is a person who can</u> …

4   SN.com, <u>which is a social networking website, is the first website I visit</u> …

5   LOL, <u>which means</u> 'laughing out loud', <u>is the best way to express</u> …

6   <u>A</u> corporate <u>website is a place where you can go to find out</u> …

3   Using the underlined phrases, make sentences that are true for you.

Worksheet A

Situation 1A
You're having a party at your house. Student B starts smoking, and you'd like them to go outside.

Situation 2A
You are sitting on the train, reading the newspaper, when Student B enters.

Situation 3A
You invite Student B over to your house, and they arrive an hour late.

Situation 4A
You buy something in a shop and the shop assistant (Student B) gives you too much change.

Situation 5A
You call Student B for a chat, but they sound really busy.

Situation 6A
You are at Student B's house for a dinner party. They offer you a dish which has taken them ages to prepare, but you can't eat it as you don't like it.

Situation 7A
You are in class and Student B wants to open the window. You are cold and want to keep it closed.

Situation 8A
You arrive at a party at Student B's house and everyone is wearing smart clothes. You are wearing jeans and a T-shirt.

Situation 9A
You are sitting in your car, about to drive away from a car park, when Student B's car hits yours. There isn't much damage.

Situation 10A
You borrow a DVD from Student B, but accidentally break it.

Situation 11A
You are waiting to be served in a shop, when Student B goes in front of you.

Situation 12A
You are in a meeting with Student B and put your feet up on the desk.

Worksheet B

Situation 1B
You're at a party at Student A's house. You've just finished dinner, relax and smoke a cigarette.

Situation 2B
You get on the train and want to sit down, but Student A is taking up two seats.

Situation 3B
Student A invites you over to their house and you arrive an hour late.

Situation 4B
You are working in a shop and the customer (Student A) tells you you've given them too much change.

Situation 5B
Student A calls you for a chat, but you are very busy and can't talk right now.

Situation 6B
You are having a dinner party. You have prepared a dish which took you ages, but Student A doesn't want to eat it.

Situation 7B
You are in class and are really hot. You want to open the window.

Situation 8B
You are having a formal party at your house, and everyone is wearing smart clothes. Student A arrives, wearing jeans and a T-shirt.

Situation 9B
You accidentally hit Student A's car while trying to park. There isn't much damage.

Situation 10B
Student A borrows a DVD from you, but when they return it, it's broken.

Situation 11B
You are next in line in a shop and start talking to the shop assistant.

Situation 12B
You are in a meeting with Student A, when they put their feet up on the desk. You think this is very rude and don't want them to do it.

THE HISTORY OF MY COUNTRY

Vocabulary: history and periods of time

1 Work in pairs. Invent the name of a country and think of the main events in its history. Use the ideas in the box to help you, and add your own ideas.

progress in ________	the discovery of ________	the foundation of ________, which caused ________	
was invaded by ________	was colonised by ________	the invention of ________, by ________	
the ________ movement	advances in ________	the spread of ________	a period of development
a great turning point	the ________ revolution	independence	under the leadership of ________
________, the founder of ________			

The history of ________ (name of country)

The 1700s: The age of ________
The 1800s: The ________ era
The early 1900s: A period of ________
The 1950s to the 1990s: The modern era
The new millennium: The ________

2 Present your history to the class.

Worksheet A

Read out the sentences using the correct tense and form of the verb in brackets (active or passive). Your partner will guess if they are true or false.

1 Acupuncture _____ (first use) in 2700 bc by Chinese Emperor Shen Nung. (true)

2 Christmas _____ (become) a national holiday in the USA in 1918. (false, all states recognised it as a holiday by 1890)

3 In the Middle Ages, it _____ (believe) the heart was the centre of intelligence. (true)

4 In 1892, Italy _____ (raise) the minimum age of marriage for girls to 16. (false, it was 12)

5 Roman coins _____ (discover) in the USA. (true)

6 One percent of the world's surface _____ (permanently cover) by ice. (false, it's ten percent)

7 More than half of the world's oxygen _____ (produce) by the Amazon rainforest. (false, it's twenty percent)

8 According to a US journal, by 2040 the Arctic Ocean _____ (have) no ice. (true)

Worksheet B

Read out the sentences using the correct tense and form of the verb in brackets (active or passive). Your partner will guess if they are true or false.

1 The first coins _____ (use) by the Romans. (false, it is thought the first coins were used by the Lydians, around 600 bc)

2 National beauty contests _____ (cancel) in Canada in 1992. (true)

3 John F Kennedy _____ (visit) China in 1972, the first US President to do so. (false, it was Richard Nixon)

4 The 'Black Death' _____ (reduce) the population of Europe by half from 1347 to 1351. (false, it was by one third)

5 The first modern Olympics _____ (hold) in Athens in 1896. (true)

6 All gondolas in Venice _____ (paint) red. (false, they are painted black)

7 Mount Everest _____ (grow) by five millimetres every year. (true)

8 According to National Geographic, in twenty years the Amazon rainforest _____ (reduce) by forty percent. (true)

The _____ School Quiz

Team name: _____

1 How many teachers are there in your school?	
2 How many students are there in your school?	
3 When did your school first open?	
4 When is your teacher's birthday?	
5 How many levels of general English does your school offer?	
6 Does your school offer any specialist English courses? If so, which ones?	
7 Does your school have any other branches? If so, where?	
8 Is your school open all year round?	
9 Has your teacher worked in any other countries? If so, which ones?	
10 How many classrooms does your school have?	
11 Does your school have computers for students to use? If so, how many?	
12 How many secretaries are there?	
13 Does your school have a course for complete beginners?	
14 Is there a minimum age to study at your school? If so, what is it?	
15 Is there a maximum age to study at your school? If so, what is it?	
16 What is the school director's name?	
17 Can you name five teachers who work at your school?	
18 What exams can you study for at your school?	
19 How many TVs are there in your school?	
20 What time does your school open in the morning?	

10 'GREEN TEST' YOUR SCHOOL

Vocabulary: the environment

		Yes	No
1	Is there somewhere to recycle paper?		
2	Is there somewhere to recycle glass?		
3	Is there somewhere to recycle plastic?		
4	Is there somewhere to recycle aluminium cans?		
5	Is there somewhere to recycle food waste?		
6	Does the school sell secondhand books?		
7	Are there enough litter bins?		
8	Does your teacher switch off the lights when he/she leaves the classroom?		
9	Is the food in the canteen organic?		
10	Does your teacher avoid driving a car to school?		
11	Are the windows double-glazed? *Or*, If your school is in a hot climate, do the classrooms have fans (instead of air-conditioning)?		
12	Does the school do anything to promote environmental awareness?		
13	Do all the classrooms have energy-saving light bulbs?		
14	______________________________?		
15	______________________________?		

Recommendations

I'd make my school more eco-friendly by …

- ______________________________
- ______________________________
- ______________________________
- ______________________________
- ______________________________

Worksheet A

1 **Read out the sentences and replace the phrase in brackets with the word your partner gives you.**

	Me ✓ or ✗	Partner ✓ or ✗
1 I always (process so that it can be used again) food packaging.		
2 I'm quite an (messy) person. I don't clean up as often as I should.		
3 If I had a (physical problem), I think I would cope with it.		
4 I'm terrible at cooking. I always (leave in the oven for too long) things.		
5 I find speaking English difficult as I often (say the sounds of words incorrectly) words.		
6 My hometown is (not familiar) to most of the world.		
7 I was quite a naughty child and would often (not follow the instructions) my parents.		
8 I should be more confident. Sometimes I (think they are less than they really are) my own abilities.		

2 **Now listen to your partner's sentences and give them the correct word and prefix from the boxes.**

| re-   dis-   mis-   under-   over-   un- |

| weight   judge   understand   believable   estimate   agree   new   appear |

3 **Do you agree with the sentences? Does your partner agree? Mark the boxes with a ✓ or a ✗.**

Worksheet B

1 Listen to your partner's sentences and give them the correct word and prefix from the boxes.

| re- | dis- | mis- | under- | over- | un- |

| cook | cycle | estimate | tidy | obey | pronounce | ability | known |

2 Now read out the sentences and replace the phrase in brackets with the word your partner gives you.

	Me ✓ or ✗	Partner ✓ or ✗
1 I think being (not heavy enough) is unattractive.		
2 Some of my government's policies at the moment are (impossible to take seriously).		
3 If I (don't understand properly) someone in English, I sometimes just pretend I've understood.		
4 If I (have a different opinion) with someone, I always tell them.		
5 I think experts (calculate as too high) the negative effects of eating fast food.		
6 Many types of animals will (not exist) in the future if we don't look after them.		
7 In my country you have to (make valid again) your passport every five years.		
8 I hate it when people (have the wrong idea about) me.		

3 Do you agree with the sentences? Does your partner agree? Mark the boxes with a ✓ or a ✗.

Horse: _____   **Total:** $1000

1 'I'm having lunch with my mum tomorrow.'
   (two days later) She said she was having lunch with her mum tomorrow.
   _____ $ _____

2 'We won't know the full effects for a long time.'
   They said they wouldn't know the full effects for a long time.
   _____ $ _____

3 'I've never been to Egypt.'
   He said that he never goes to Egypt.
   _____ $ _____

4 'I go running every day.'
   She said she went running every day.
   _____ $ _____

5 (Father to Son) 'I've told you twice already.'
   (Son) Dad said he'd told you twice already.
   _____ $ _____

6 'What do you want for your birthday?'
   She asked me what did I want for my birthday.
   _____ $ _____

7 'Have you ever seen anything so ridiculous?'
   He asked me had I ever seen anything so ridiculous.
   _____ $ _____

8 'Next year I'm going to study abroad.'
   (the same year) She told us that she was going to study abroad next year.
   _____ $ _____

9 'I sent it last week.'
   (a week later) She said she had sent it last week.
   _____ $ _____

10 'Will you marry me?'
   She asked me if I will marry her.
   _____ $ _____

11 'I haven't eaten broccoli for years.'
   He said he didn't eat broccoli for years.
   _____ $ _____

12 'How was your holiday?'
   He asked me how my holiday had been.
   _____ $ _____

1 Would you like me to help you with your homework?

Hint: offer

2 If I were you, I'd leave early.

Hint: recommend

3 If you want, you can stay with me while you're in town.

Hint: invite

4 Black shoes or blue shoes? I know, I'll wear the black ones.

Hint: decide

5 You want a lift home? Of course it's no problem!

Hint: agree

6 I'll definitely do my homework for tomorrow.

Hint: promise

7 Why don't you hire a car?

Hint: suggest

8 No! I won't eat my broccoli!

Hint: refuse

9 If you stay in a hostel it will be cheaper.

Hint: explain

10 If you're going out at night, you should be careful.

Hint: warn

11 I'll help you with your bags, if you like.

Hint: offer

12 What about going to the cinema tonight?

Hint: suggest

13 I'll always love you.

Hint: promise

14 Would you like to come with me?

Hint: invite

15 I think I'll have fish for lunch.

Hint: decide

16 I wouldn't take a taxi, if I were you.

Hint: warn

17 It's my first visit here.

Hint: explain

18 You should visit the fantastic local restaurants.

Hint: recommend

1 Complete the sentences to make advice for visitors to a country, city or region you know well. Use the ideas in the box to help you.

crime	taxis	health	food and drink	public transport	time
climate	complaining	making jokes	shopping	going out alone	animals

If you visit _____ for the first time ...

1 Make sure you _____

2 You need to _____

3 Be careful _____

4 Don't _____

5 Watch out for _____

6 You'd better _____

7 Whatever you do, _____

  or else you could _____

8 The most important thing is to _____

9 If I were you, I'd _____

10 Don't forget to _____

11 _____

12 _____

2 Share your ideas with your group.

Tests index

LISTENING

1 ▶ **44 Listen and circle the correct answer: a), b) or c).**

1 Jo thinks she could be ____ Native American.
   a) 5%   b) 15%   c) 50%

2 The woman felt the bed moving so she got up and ____.
   a) got under the table   b) went outside   c) got dressed

3 The girl's going to save ____ to go to the Moon.
   a) $1m   b) for a long time   c) for 25 years

4 Jack ____ Nick's idea for a new business.
   a) likes   b) agrees with   c) doesn't agree with

5 The shop doesn't have a ____.
   a) price list   b) computer   c) dishwasher

6 The woman says she couldn't live without a ____.
   a) fridge   b) cooker   c) tin opener

[ ] **10**

PRONUNCIATION

2 ▶ **45 Listen and cross out the word with a different vowel sound in bold.**

1 family ~~drama~~ married ambitious

2 inquiry risk science fiction

3 romantic forgot comedy job

4 genetic remember engineering period

5 hear earn leader freeze

6 fun discussion furious wonderful

[ ] **5**

VOCABULARY AND GRAMMAR

3 Match the compound nouns.

1 great-   _d_   a) power
2 romantic   ____   b) taker
3 washing   ____   c) family
4 risk   ____   d) ~~grandparents~~
5 psychological   ____   e) networks
6 solar   ____   f) comedy
7 genetic   ____   g) drama
8 extended   ____   h) fiction
9 period   ____   i) machine
10 computer   ____   k) thriller
11 science   ____   l) engineering

[ ] **5**

4 Underline the correct preposition.

1 I'm meeting them _at_ / in lunchtime.

2 He complimented her on / of her new hairstyle.

3 I dialled the wrong number for / by mistake.

4 We can't possibly predict what changes will take place in / on ten years' time.

5 You haven't said a word for an hour. What's at / on your mind?

6 He couldn't stop for a chat because he was from / in a hurry.

7 I warned him about / from the traffic jams.

8 She had to apologise on / for forgetting the time of the meeting.

9 He couldn't finish the exam because he ran up / out of time.

10 I think the situation will get slightly worse of / in the short term.

11 She forgot to switch up / off the lights when she left the house.

[ ] **5**

5 Complete the sentences. Use the correct form of the word in capitals.

1 He's been ____unemployed____ for six months. He can't find a job. EMPLOY

2 They're trying to find a _____ solution to the conflict. PEACE

3 I can't use my mobile. The battery needs _____. CHARGE

4 They had to close the business because it had become _____. PROFIT

5 There are fewer _____ people sleeping on the streets now there are more shelters for them. HOME

6 Commuting to work in big cities is more _____ than it used to be. EXHAUST

[ ] **5**

6 Correct <u>two</u> mistakes in each sentence.

1 My students don't hear me and that's why they do mistakes.

<u>My students don't **listen to** me and that's why they</u>
<u>**make** mistakes.</u>

2 My ancestors are coming for lunch today. My uncle says very funny stories.

_____

3 He got fired from his boss so he's looking for a new work.

_____.

4 I said him I'd be late because I forgot my purse at home.

_____.

5 You didn't remember me about Alan's birthday and now I'm in boiling water!

_____.

6 She made medical research after university, but she didn't win much money.

_____.

☐ **5**

7 Write questions for the answers in *italics*.

1 He was *talking on his mobile* when I saw him.
What <u>was he doing when you saw him</u>_____?

2 I used to play *tennis and hockey* before I broke my leg.
Which _____?

3 They were looking for *you* just now.
Who _____?

4 *The Arsenal football team* is likely to win the championship.
Which _____?

5 He realised *later* that he'd given her the wrong address.
When _____?

6 *Maria* sent me a beautiful card for my birthday.
Who _____?

☐ **5**

8 Complete the second sentence so that it means the same as the first. Use the word in brackets.

1 You can't smoke in the office. (must)
You <u>mustn't smoke in the office</u>_____.

2 His flat's not as messy as it used to be. (less)
His flat _____.

3 The plane will probably be late. (likely)
The plane _____.

4 This one's a bit more expensive. (slightly)
This one _____.

5 I told him not to forget to buy the bread. (remind)
I _____.

6 We used to have a family lunch every Sunday. (would)
We _____.

☐ **5**

9 Circle the correct answer: a), b), c) or d).

1 You ____ eat so much junk food.
a) might   b) shouldn't   c) must   d) have to

2 We ____ to stay with friends when we get to Sydney.
a) will   b) would   c) likely   d) 're going

3 I've never been to China, but I ____ to Japan last year.
a) went   b) 've been   c) used to go   d) gone

4 He ____ her name now.
a) isn't remembering   b) don't remember
c) doesn't remember   d) remember

5 When she got to the airport, she realised she ____ her passport at home.
a) left   b) forgot
c) 'd forgotten   d) 'd left

6 We met them ____ we were living in Tanzania.
a) during   b) until   c) while
d) as soon as

7 My ancestors ____ from Ireland.
a) came   b) comes
c) lived   d) are coming

8 Have you seen his latest play ____?
a) just   b) yet   c) ever   d) last night

9 When we were children, we ____ in the garden all day.
a) 'd played   b) 'd play
c) were playing   d) 've played

10 You ____ to go now. You can go later.
a) don't have   b) must   c) mustn't   d) ought

11 The house was ____ more beautiful than he remembered.
a) very   b) little bit   c) far   d) not as

☐ **5**

10 Complete the article with <u>one</u> word in each gap.

New words from old

The English [1] _language_ is constantly growing in response to changes in the world around us, and new [2] _____ are added every day. The word 'framily' for example, first came into use in 2006 and is made [3] _____ two words: 'family' and 'friends'. It refers to close friends who [4] _____ become like a family, providing company and support to each other.

The concept has probably developed as a result [5] _____ changes in our society, where people don't live as near to [6] _____ families as they [7] _____ to. The word 'framily' has been used in the USA [8] _____ quite a while, especially by younger people living [9] _____ cities, as reflected in popular TV shows like *Friends*. If you like being with both 'framily' and family, you might want [10] _____ try 'togethering', which means to go on holiday with both your extended [11] _____ and friends!

☐ **5**

READING

11 Match gaps 1–6 in the text with sentences a)–f) opposite.

LIVING TOMORROW

If you want to find out what houses might look like in the future, you should visit the *Living Tomorrow* exhibition. It's a permanent exhibition near Brussels in Belgium, where you can see for yourself how tomorrow's technologies will integrate into our daily lives.

¹ _c_ . Everything works via remote control, from warming up food, to authorising access to the supermarket delivery man. The living room has touch screens which control the light, music and windows. You might want to read, relax or just chat to friends there. ² ___ . You'll find out why when you go upstairs.

The kitchen can be whatever you want it to be. Appliances like the oven, fridge and dishwasher slide in or out of view as needed. They even change colour automatically when you adjust the lighting. ³ ___ . The only thing that doesn't move here is the flat screen on the wall. Among other things, you can use this screen to do your shopping easily and safely online.

Upstairs is the 'home theatre', with specialised acoustics and large screens. The latest 3D technology makes watching TV a whole new experience! ⁴ ___ .

The bathroom, which has water-free toilets and voice-controlled taps, is also equipped with an 'intelligent mirror'. This acts as both a mirror and an electrically controlled screen. ⁵ ___ . The mirror will even check your blood pressure and temperature, and remind you to take your medicine if necessary!

Finally, there's the 'home office'. ⁶ ___ . This means that the office will become much more central to our lives. In fact, in 'the house of the future', it will hardly be necessary to leave home at all!

a) You can watch the news on it, check the weather forecast or listen to music while you clean your teeth.

b) Next to this, in the 'sleeping space', you can try out a bed that adapts to your size and shape.

c) ~~The 'House of the Future' consists of a living room, bathroom, kitchen, home theatre, sleeping space and office.~~

d) Thanks to tomorrow's interactive multimedia technology, more and more people will be working from home.

e) The oven and microwave are designed to recognise different kinds of food and decide automatically how to cook them.

f) However, you won't see a TV there.

| | 10 |

12 Read the text in Exercise 11 again and circle the correct answer: a), b) or c).

1 The Living Tomorrow exhibition ___ .
   a) shows what daily life will be like in the future
   b) is only going to be on for a short time
   c) shows you what houses will be like in the future ⟵ (circled)

2 In the 'House of the Future', you ___ .
   a) won't have to switch the lights on
   b) can watch TV in the living room
   c) will have to open the door when your shopping is delivered

3 In the kitchen, ___ .
   a) the fridge and dishwasher are white
   b) you can move the domestic appliances around
   c) the oven decides what food you'll eat

4 There's a 'home theatre' upstairs ___ .
   a) where you can watch 3D TV
   b) which has an 'intelligent mirror'
   c) where you can sleep

5 In the bathroom, ___ .
   a) the taps turn on automatically
   b) music starts playing when you clean your teeth
   c) you can check what the weather is like outside

6 In the future, ___ .
   a) people won't be able to go outside very much
   b) the 'home office' will be more essential than it is now
   c) people won't need to work

| | 5 |

SPEAKING

13 **Cross out the response that is <u>not</u> possible.**

1 So should I dress smartly for the interview?
~~a) I see.~~   b) Of course.   c) That's right.

2 Anyway, in the end, we had to sleep in the airport!
   a) I don't believe it.   b) You must be joking.
   c) What did you do?

3 A: I'm sorry, sir, but we have no more rooms available.
   B: ___ you didn't get my booking?
   a) Do you mean to say   b) Didn't you say
   c) So you're saying

4 Would you mind calling a taxi for me?
   a) Sure.   b) Yes, please.   c) Of course not.

5 ___ the name of our new product.
   a) Let's sum up   b) Let's focus on
   c) I think we need to come back to

6 Do you know if the train's on time?
   a) I'm not sure.   b) Yes, I can.   c) I think so.

| 5 |

14 **Match gaps 1–11 in the conversation with a)–k) below.**

A: First of ¹ <u>a</u> , we need to decide when to have the conference.

B: I think June's the best time – before the summer holidays start.

A: Yes, ² ___ a good point. May's too early.

B: Exactly. But ³ ___ me, the most important thing is *where* to have it. The way I see it, we should book somewhere as soon as possible.

A: Yes, I ⁴ ___ . We'll need a hotel with conference facilities for fifty people.

B: How ⁵ ___ I call James? He works at the Plaza. He'll be able to advise us.

A: OK, go ahead. That's OK ⁶ ___ me.

B: So moving ⁷ ___ the next point. Who are we going to invite as speakers?

A: You've ⁸ ___ now. I thought *we* were going to do all the presentations?

B: Did ⁹ ___ that? Well, I think we need someone who specialises in marketing.

A: I'm ¹⁰ ___ I agree, actually. I have plenty of marketing experience.

B: OK. Why don't ¹¹ ___ back to that later? Let's recap: what have we decided so far?

a) ~~all~~   g) for
b) I say   h) we come
c) about if   i) on to
d) that's   j) by
e) lost me   k) agree
f) not sure

| 10 |

WRITING

15 **Underline the correct alternative.**

1 <u>In general</u> / *the whole*, the good points outweigh the bad points.

2 I like eating pre-prepared food. *However / Although,* it isn't very healthy.

3 He never gets up *while / until* his alarm clock goes off.

4 *As soon as / By the time* I got home, it had stopped raining.

5 We talked on the phone *for / during* hours last night.

6 *Although / As well as that* he knows he should find a better job, he isn't ambitious enough.

| 5 |

16 **Write an essay about the advantages and disadvantages of mobile phones. Use the prompts below to help you. Write 120–150 words.**

It's easy to see the advantages of mobile phones in our everyday lives. _____
_____
_____
_____
_____

One of the main advantages _____
_____
_____
_____
_____

The problem is that, on the other hand, _____
_____
_____
_____
_____

In my opinion, _____
_____
_____
_____
_____
_____

| 10 |

Total: | 100 |

LISTENING

1 ▶ 38 **Listen to a teacher talking about a school trip and complete the notes.**

Visit to the Science Museum

Date: ¹ _27th May_
Coach leaves at: ² ____ a.m.

Museum opens: ³ ____ a.m. to 6p.m.
1st guided tour at: ⁴ _____
Name of exhibition: Antenna
⁵ _____ break at: 11a.m.
Number of themed galleries: 20
Recommended: ⁶ _____ the Modern World
and The Secret Life of the ⁷ _____
Lunch: in picnic area at ⁸ _____ p.m.
IMAX film at: 1.15p.m.
Name of film: ⁹ _____ Station
2nd guided tour at: 2.45p.m.
Name of exhibition: Fast ¹⁰ _____
Free time: ¹¹ ____ to 5.30p.m.
Home by: 8.00p.m.

`[ 5 ]`

2 Listen again. Are the sentences true (T) or false (F)?

1 The teacher advises his students to be in the car park by 7.30a.m. _F_

2 They've all been to the museum before. ____

3 The Wellcome Wing had been closed until last week. ____

4 The teacher recommends two exhibitions about gadgets in the home. ____

5 They'll watch a film about what it's like to live and work in space. ____

6 The afternoon guided tour is about the development of Formula One cars. ____

`[ 5 ]`

PRONUNCIATION

3 ▶ 39 **Listen and write the number of words in each sentence. Contracted forms count as one word.**

1 _7_   4 ____
2 ____   5 ____
3 ____   6 ____

`[ 5 ]`

VOCABULARY AND GRAMMAR

4 Match 1–11 with a)–l).

1	organic	_d_	a)	learning
2	traffic	____	b)	out
3	search	____	c)	taker
4	print	____	d)	~~food~~
5	high	____	e)	pass
6	period	____	f)	engine
7	distance	____	g)	lights
8	risk	____	h)	on
9	driving	____	i)	achiever
10	try	____	k)	drama
11	boarding	____	l)	licence

`[ 5 ]`

5 Complete the sentences with the prepositions in the box. Use some words more than once.

with   at   in   to   on   by   down   up

1 I haven't made friends ___with___ many people at work.

2 We try to save energy by not leaving electrical appliances _____ standby.

3 The letter didn't arrive because it was delivered to the wrong house _____ mistake.

4 Do you believe _____ magic?

5 You'll get better _____ playing the piano if you practise every day.

6 Unfortunately, speaking a foreign language doesn't come naturally _____ me.

7 If you got up earlier, you might arrive _____ time.

8 You shouldn't forget to shut _____ your computer at night.

9 Did you know that Ben's split up _____ Jo?

10 When I get home from work, I like to relax and put my feet _____.

11 He succeeded _____ passing the exam after a lot of hard work.

`[ 5 ]`

6 Complete the sentences. Use the correct form of the word in capitals.

1 She's been ___unemployed___ for six months. She can't find a job. EMPLOY

2 The job market for university graduates is much more _____ these days. COMPETE

3 My son wants to specialise in _____ engineering. GENE

4 I heard a _____ talk about the meaning of dreams. FASCINATE

5 They were sent home from school for _____ the teacher. OBEY

6 I didn't get an interview because I didn't have the right _____. QUALIFY

`[ 5 ]`

7 Correct <u>one</u> mistake in each question.

1 What for did you do that?
   What did you do that for?

2 Who did gave you those lovely flowers?
   _____

3 If you saw him, what would you said?
   _____

4 Where were made these shoes?
   _____

5 Who's the man that he stole your bag?
   _____

6 Have you speak to her last night?
   _____

   [ ] **5**

8 Circle the correct answer: a), b), c) or d).

1 We don't ____ eat out on Tuesdays.
   a) easily   b) early   c) usually   d) never

2 I couldn't leave at six because I ____ finished the report.
   a) had   b) hadn't
   c) wasn't   d) wouldn't

3 We talked for hours about ____ we used to live.
   a) where   b) which   c) that   d) what

4 She ____ to get promoted before me.
   a) should   b) might not
   c) won't   d) isn't likely

5 Your order ____ sent by first class post and will arrive tomorrow.
   a) is being   b) has being   c) will   d) is

6 He asked me what time ____ arrive.
   a) we'll   b) we'd   c) would we   d) we have

7 If I'd seen you, I ____ hello.
   a) 'd say   b) 'll say
   c) would've said   d) had said

8 We ____ them since we were children.
   a) know   b) knew
   c) 've been knowing   d) 've known

9 While we ____ to check in, they announced that our plane was delayed.
   a) waited   b) are waiting
   c) were waiting d) had waited

10 He's been working there since ____.
   a) five months   b) March
   c) two years   d) a long time.

11 ____ we arrived, the concert had started.
   a) While   b) Until
   c) As soon as d) By the time

   [ ] **10**

9 Complete the second sentence so that it means the same as the first.

1 We last saw each other six months ago.
   We *haven't seen each other* for six months.

2 There aren't many nice places to eat here.
   There are only _____.

3 If sales don't improve, I'll lose my job.
   Unless _____.

4 They're building a new factory near the river.
   A new factory _____.

5 He told them they shouldn't smoke so much.
   He warned_____.

6 I wasn't able to get in touch with her.
   I didn't _____.

   [ ] **5**

10 Complete the text about popular words with <u>one</u> word in each gap.

Do you tweet on Twitter?

It [1] *will* probably come as no surprise that not only was Twitter the fastest growing website [2]_____ 2009, but 'twitter' was also the most widely used word in the media. 'Obama' was in [3]_____ place and 'H1N1', the name of the swine flu virus that spread all over [4]_____ world, was in third. More surprisingly, the success of Stephenie Meyer's *Twilight* series of [5]_____ and films pushed the word 'vampire' into fifth place.

The popularity of the [6]_____ 'twitter' summed up the rise of social networking on the internet. It was also a 'fun' word, [7]_____ led to the creation of a whole new set of vocabulary. For example, 'tweet', 'tweetaholic' and even 'tweet up', which means to arrange to [8]_____ up with your friends.

If further proof of social networking as [9]_____ huge cultural force was needed, the New Oxford American Dictionary chose 'unfriend' as its 2009 Word of the [10]_____. To 'unfriend' means to remove someone as a friend on a social networking [11]_____ like Facebook. Have you unfriended anyone recently?

   [ ] **5**

READING

11 Match gaps 1–6 in the text with sentences a)–g) opposite. There is <u>one</u> extra sentence you do not need.

Teenage boy climbs Everest

In May 2010, American teenager Jordan Romero made history by becoming the youngest person to climb the highest peak in the world, Mount Everest (8,848m). ¹ _e_ . The first thing he did when he reached the summit was to make a phone call, saying, 'Mom, I'm calling you from the top of the world!'

Jordan made the climb with his father Paul, his stepmother Karen Lundgren and three Sherpa guides, all experienced mountaineers. However, despite Jordan's age, he was by no means an inexperienced climber. In fact, this was his sixth major achievement in his dream to climb the Seven Summits, the highest peaks on all seven continents.

² ___ . Between 2007 and 2009, he climbed five others in North and South America, Australia and Europe. Having climbed the Asian one, this left only the Vinson Massif (4,892m) in Antarctica to achieve his dream of being the youngest person to climb all seven.

³ ___ . There was a painting on a corridor wall in his California school which showed the highest point on every continent, and it fascinated him. He did some research and then one day he said to his father, 'Dad, I want to climb the Seven Summits.' His father immediately started training him and the following year they climbed Kilimanjaro.

Despite Jordan's achievements, the Everest climb also attracted criticism from people who said he was too young to take such risks. It is true that climbing at such high altitudes can be dangerous. ⁴ ___ Furthermore, a previous record holder for the youngest person to climb Mount Everest, 16-year-old Temba Tsheri from Nepal, lost five fingers from frostbite during his climb due to the extreme cold.

But Jordan's father rejected the criticisms, saying, 'We were so prepared, everything went absolutely perfectly. ⁵ ___ '. He said they'd spent several weeks getting used to the high altitude. He thought Jordan had trained hard and had been ready for the challenge.

Jordan himself said, 'I'm the one who started this project. ⁶ ___ . I know it's a big goal and luckily for me, my family is supporting me every step of the way. In fact my family is my team.'

He hopes his adventure will inspire young people around the world to set themselves challenges – to get fit and aim high.

a) The cold and the lack of oxygen has killed many climbers in the past.

b) It's my dream we are following.

c) Their knowledge and experience of the mountain will help keep us all safe.

d) He conquered the first one, Mount Kilimanjaro (5,895m), in Africa when he was ten.

e) ~~Jordan was 13 years old.~~

f) Age has nothing to do with anything.

g) Jordan says he was first inspired to climb at the age of nine.

> | 10 |

12 Read the text again and choose the correct answer: a), b) or c).

1 When Jordan got to the top of Everest, he called his ___ .
  a) father
  b) friends
  c) mother ⟵ (circled)

2 He'd already climbed ___ of the highest mountains in the world.
  a) five
  b) six
  c) seven

3 Jordan climbed Kilimanjaro when he was ___ .
  a) seven
  b) nine
  c) ten

4 Some people thought Jordan shouldn't climb Everest because ___ .
  a) he would get frostbite
  b) the mountain was too high
  c) he wasn't old enough

5 Before the climb, ___ .
  a) Jordan trained very hard
  b) he spent several months on Everest
  c) his father was very worried

6 Jordan would like ___ .
  a) everybody to climb mountains
  b) to inspire other teenagers
  c) to find more challenges

> | 5 |

SPEAKING

13 Cross out the option or response that is <u>not</u> possible.

1 So should I dress smartly tonight?
   ~~a) I see.~~   b) Of course.   c) That's right.

2 I'm afraid the party's been cancelled.
   a) Really?   b) Well done.   c) That's a shame.

3 A: Do you recommend taking a sweater?
   B: Yes, ____ quite cold in the evenings.
   a) it's generally   b) on the whole, it's
   c) it tends to

4 A: That was a fantastic meal, wasn't it?
   B: Yes, but I ____ the food was overpriced.
   a) for one thing   b) do think   c) must say

5 Did you know that if you listen to Bach, it helps you to learn better?
   a) Oh, really?   b) I have no idea.
   c) Does it? That's interesting.

6 What should we get Harry and Sara for their wedding anniversary?
   a) Don't forget to buy them a plant.
   b) I don't know.
   c) If I were you, I'd just send them a card.

☐ **5**

14 Match gaps 1–11 in the conversation with a)–k) below.

A: ¹Have _a_ my car keys, Anna?

B: I'm ²____ sure I left them on the table.

A: No, I've looked there. Did you put them in your handbag?

B: Maybe. I ³____. Where *is* my handbag anyway?

A: I haven't got ⁴____. You know, I think we should buy a red carpet!

B: ⁵____? Why red?

A: I read an article about it. Apparently red helps you remember details better.

B: You've ⁶____.

A: Well, ⁷____ thing, we're getting very forgetful these days.

B: Yes, but ⁸____ I see it, that's because we spend too much time using computers.

A: Exactly! I think I'll try using a red screen on mine.

B: OK, but whatever ⁹____, don't buy a red carpet!

A: Don't worry. Hey, you'll ¹⁰____ what!

B: You found the keys?

A: Yes, in my pocket …

B: ¹¹____ joking!

a) ~~you seen~~   g) Really
b) the way   h) a clue
c) you do   i) lost me
d) fairly   j) can't remember
e) never guess   k) for one
f) You're

☐ **10**

WRITING

15 Underline the correct alternatives.

The best meal of my life!

What's the ¹*more* / <u>*most*</u> delicious food you've ever eaten? Mine was chicken soup. ²*In general* / *In all likelihood* it wasn't just the soup itself, but where and ³*what* / *when* it was eaten. It happened when I was working in Morocco ⁴*while* / *during* Ramadan, when Muslims don't eat ⁵*or* / *but* drink anything from sunrise to sunset, and never complain.

⁶*Although* / *However* I'm not a Muslim, I admired the willpower of my friends so much ⁷*than* / *that* one day I decided to share the experience with them. It was one of the most memorable days of my life, full of unexpected feelings and emotions.

⁸*Finally* / *By the time* the sun was setting, I'd joined the crowds of people in the square, ⁹*which* / *where* the cafés had prepared bowls of steaming chicken soup ¹⁰*as well as* / *also* deliciously sweet desserts. Everyone had a bowl of soup in front of them and held their spoons ready to eat. ¹¹*After that* / *As soon as* the sun went down, we lifted our spoons. Food had never tasted so good.

☐ **5**

16 Choose <u>one</u> of the topics below and write an essay / a story on a separate piece of paper. Use the paragraph notes to help you. Write 130–150 words.

Topic A

If you could choose to be a famous person from history, who would you choose?

Para 1: say who the person is and what they are famous for

Para 2: give two or three reasons why you would like to be them

Para 3: say what things you would do differently from them, and why

Topic B

Write a story beginning with these words:

It was the most important day of my life.

Para 1: say why the day was important

Para 2: describe what happened on this day

Para 3: say what the conclusion was – positive or negative

☐ **10**

Total:	100

LISTENING

1 ▶ **44 Listen and circle the correct answer a), b) or c).**

1 Jo thinks she could be ____ Native American.
   a) 5%   b) 15%   c) 50%

2 The floor stopped moving after the woman ____.
   a) got dressed   b) went outside   c) got under the table

3 The girl's going to save ____ to go to the Moon.
   a) $1m   b) for 50 years   c) for a long time

4 Jack thinks Nick's idea for a new business is ____.
   a) great   b) original   c) mad

5 The shop doesn't have a ____.
   a) computer   b) price list   c) dishwasher

6 The woman thinks the most important invention for the kitchen is a ____.
   a) tin opener   b) cooker   c) fridge

	10

PRONUNCIATION

2 ▶ **45 Listen and cross out the word with a different vowel sound in bold.**

1 family ~~drama~~ married ambitious

2 inquiry risk science fiction

3 romantic forgot comedy job

4 genetic remember engineering period

5 hear earn leader freeze

6 fun discussion furious wonderful

	5

VOCABULARY AND GRAMMAR

3 **Match the compound nouns.**

1 great-   ____   a) power
2 risk   ____   b) ~~grandparents~~
3 computer   ____   c) thriller
4 science   ____   d) engineering
5 psychological ____   e) networks
6 extended   ____   f) fiction
7 period   ____   g) cleaner
8 romantic   ____   h) taker
9 vacuum   ____   i) family
10 nuclear   ____   j) comedy
11 genetic   ____   k) drama

	5

4 **Underline the correct preposition.**

1 I'm meeting them *at* / *in* lunchtime.

2 She's always gossiping *about* / *from* other people.

3 He apologised *on* / *for* forgetting to call me.

4 I couldn't finish the test because I ran out *of* / *of the* time.

5 The situation will improve *at* / *in* the long term.

6 Don't forget to switch *on* / *up* the computer before you start.

7 He complimented the students *on* / *of* their excellent exam results.

8 Some authors write their novels *in* / *by* hand.

9 You can't predict what changes will take place a long time *of* / *from* now.

10 She's hardly opened her mouth tonight. What's *at* / *on* her mind?

11 He couldn't stay because he was *from* / *in* a hurry to get to work.

	5

5 **Complete the sentences. Use the correct form of the word in capitals.**

1 He's been ____unemployed____ for 6 months. He can't find a job. EMPLOY

2 Fewer _____ people are living on the streets because there are special places for them to sleep. HOME

3 Commuting to work every day is making me feel completely _____. EXHAUST

4 I hope they find a _____ solution to the conflict. PEACE

5 My mobile's not working. It must need _____. CHARGE

6 This new detergent is much more _____ than the old one. EFFECT

	5

6 Correct <u>two</u> mistakes in each sentence.

1 My students don't hear me and that's why they do mistakes.

   *My students don't **listen to** me and that's why they*
   ***make** mistakes.*

2 You forgot to remember me about mum's birthday, so I'm on hot water now!

   _____.

3 She made her best with the project, but it looked a bit short when she printed it on.

   _____.

4 I don't like many of my ancestors much, but my Uncle Tom is great funny to be with.

   _____.

5 He used to win a good salary, but then he lost his work. Now he's unemployed.

   _____.

6 I said her I'd be late because I had to make some shopping.

   _____.

   [5]

7 Write questions for the answers in *italics*.

1 He was *talking on his mobile* when I saw him.

   What *was he doing when you saw him* _____?

2 She realised *later* that she'd given him the wrong phone number.

   When _____?

3 *David* sent me these beautiful flowers.

   Who _____?

4 He used to play *rugby and tennis* before he had the accident.

   Which _____?

5 I was looking for *my friends*.

   Who _____?

6 *The Barcelona football team* is likely to win the championship.

   Which _____?

   [5]

8 Complete the second sentence so that it means the same as the first. Use the word in brackets.

1 You can't smoke in the office. (must)

   You *mustn't smoke in the office* _____.

2 I told him to remember to buy cheese. (remind)

   I _____.

3 We used to meet for lunch every Sunday. (would)

   We _____.

4 His room's not as messy as mine. (less)

   His room _____.

5 They'll probably be late again. (likely)

   They _____.

6 The red ones are a bit cheaper. (slightly)

   The red ones _____.

   [5]

9 Circle the correct answer: a), b), c) or d).

1 Have you seen his latest play ____?

   a) just   b) yet   c) ever   d) last night

2 My parents ____ from Ireland.

   a) lived   b) are coming   c) come   d) comes

3 When we were children, we ____ outside all the time.

   a) 'd play   b) 'd played
   c) were playing   d) 've played

4 You ____ eat so much junk food.

   a) might   b) shouldn't   c) must   d) have to

5 The house was ____ smaller than he remembered.

   a) very   b) little bit   c) far   d) not as

6 We ____ to stay in a hotel when we get to Toronto.

   a) will   b) would   c) likely   d) 're going

7 I've never been to India, but I ____ to China last year.

   a) went   b) 've been
   c) used to go   d) gone

8 They ____ her address any more.

   a) aren't remembering   b) don't remember
   c) doesn't remember   d) remember

9 You ____ to go now. You can go later.

   a) don't have   b) must   c) mustn't   d) ought

10 When he got to the airport, he realised he ____ his plane ticket.

   a) left   b) forgot
   c) 'd forgotten   d) 'd left

11 He met them ____ he was living in Warsaw.

   a) during   b) until
   c) while   d) as soon as

   [5]

10 Complete the article with <u>one</u> word in each gap.

New words from old

The English [1] *language* is constantly growing in response to changes in the world around us, and [2]_____ words are created every day. The word 'framily', for example, first came into use in 2006 and is made from [3]_____ words: 'family' and 'friends'. It refers to close friends [4]_____ have become like a family, providing company and support. The concept has probably developed [5]_____ a result of changes in our society, where people [6]_____ live as near to their families as they used [7]_____. The word 'family' has been used in the USA for quite a while, especially by younger [8]_____ living in cities; this is reflected [9]_____ popular TV shows like *Friends*. If you like being with both 'framily' and family, you might want to try 'togethering', which [10]_____ to go on holiday with both your extended family and [11]_____!

   [5]

READING

11 Match gaps 1–6 in the text with sentences a)–f) opposite.

LIVING TOMORROW

If you want to find out what houses might look like in the future, you should visit the *Living Tomorrow* exhibition. It's a permanent exhibition near Brussels in Belgium, where you can see for yourself how tomorrow's technologies will integrate with our daily lives.

¹ _b_. Everything works via remote control, from warming up food, to authorising access to the supermarket delivery man. The living room has touch screens which control the light, music and windows. You might want to read, relax or just chat to friends there. However, you won't see a TV. ² ___.

The kitchen can be whatever you want it to be. Appliances like the oven, fridge and dishwasher slide in or out of view as needed. ³ ___. The oven and microwave are designed to recognise different kinds of food and decide automatically how to cook them. The only thing that doesn't move here is the flat screen on the wall – which, among other things, allows you to do your shopping easily and safely online.

Upstairs is the 'home theatre', with specialised acoustics and large screens. ⁴ ___. Next to this, in the 'sleeping space', you can try out a bed that adapts to your size and shape.

The bathroom, which has water-free toilets and voice-controlled taps, is also equipped with an 'intelligent mirror'. ⁵ ___. You can watch the news on it, check the weather forecast or listen to music while you clean your teeth. The mirror will even check your blood pressure and temperature, and remind you to take your medicine if necessary!

Finally, there's the 'home office'. Thanks to tomorrow's interactive multimedia technology, more and more people will be working from home. ⁶ ___. In fact, in 'the house of the future', it will hardly be necessary to leave home at all!

a) This means that the office will become much more central to our lives.

b) ~~The 'House of the Future' consists of a living room, bathroom, kitchen, home theatre, sleeping space and office.~~

c) This acts as both a mirror and an electrically controlled screen.

d) The latest 3D technology makes 'watching TV' a whole new experience.

e) You'll find out why when you go upstairs.

f) They even change colour automatically when you adjust the lighting.

| | 10 |

12 Read the text in Exercise 11 again and circle the correct answer: a), b) or c).

1 The Living Tomorrow exhibition ___.
   a) shows what houses will be like in the future
   b) shows what daily life will be like in the future
   c) is only showing for a short time

2 In the 'House of the Future', you ___.
   a) will have your shopping delivered automatically
   b) won't have to know how to cook much
   c) can watch TV in the living room

3 In the kitchen, ___.
   a) you can move the domestic appliances around
   b) the oven decides what food you'll eat
   c) the fridge and dishwasher are white

4 There's a 'home theatre' upstairs ___.
   a) which has an 'intelligent mirror'
   b) where you can sleep
   c) where you can watch films

5 In the bathroom, ___.
   a) music starts playing when you clean your teeth
   b) you can check if it's raining outside
   c) the taps turn on automatically

6 In the future, ___.
   a) the 'home office' will be more essential than it is now
   b) people won't have to work
   c) people won't be able to go outside very much

| | 5 |

SPEAKING

13 Delete the response that is <u>not</u> possible.

1 So should I dress smartly for the interview?
a) ~~I see.~~   b) Of course.   c) That's right.

2 _____ the name of our new company.
a) Let's focus on   b) I think we need to come back to
c) Let's sum up

3 Do you know if the train's left yet?
a) Yes, I can.   b) I think so.   c) I'm not sure.

4 Anyway, in the end, we had to sleep on the floor!
a) You must be joking.   b) What did you do?
c) I don't believe it.

5 A: Sorry, sir, but we have no tables available.
B: _____ you didn't get my booking?
a) Didn't you say   b) So you're saying
c) Do you mean to say

6 Would you mind calling him for me?
a) Of course not.   b) Yes, please.   c) Sure.

[5]

14 Match gaps 1–11 in the conversation with a)–k)
below.

A: First of ¹ _a_ , we need to decide when to have the
conference.

B: I think June's the best time – before the summer holidays
start.

A: Yes, that's a good ² ___. May's too early.

B: ³ ___. But for me, the most important thing is *where* to
have it. The ⁴ ___ see it, we should book somewhere at
once.

A: Yes, ⁵ ___. We'll need a hotel with conference facilities
for fifty people.

B: How about if I call James? He works at the Plaza. He'll be
able to advise us.

A: OK, go ⁶ ___. That's OK by me.

B: So ⁷ ___ to the next point. Who are we going to invite as
speakers?

A: You've lost me now. I thought *we* were going to do all the
presentations?

B: ⁸ ___ say that? Well, I think we need someone who
specialises in marketing.

A: I'm not ⁹ ___ agree, actually. I have plenty of marketing
experience.

B: OK. Why ¹⁰ ___ come back to that later? ¹¹ ___ recap:
what have we decided so far?

a) ~~all~~   g) way I
b) ahead   h) point
c) Exactly   i) Did I
d) I agree   j) sure I
e) Let's   k) moving on
f) don't we

[10]

WRITING

15 Underline the correct alternative.

1 In *general* / *the whole*, the good points outweigh the bad
points.

2 We talked on the phone *for* / *during* hours last night.

3 *Although* / *As well as that* he isn't ambitious, he knows he
should find a better job.

4 I like eating organic food. *However* / *Although,* it's much
more expensive.

5 They never listen to music *while* / *during* they're studying.

6 *As soon as* / *By the time* he got home, it was nearly
midnight.

[5]

16 Write an essay about the advantages and
disadvantages of mobile phones. Use the prompts below
to help you. Write 120–150 words.

It's easy to see the advantages of mobile phones in our
everyday lives. _____
_____
_____
_____
_____
_____

One of the main advantages _____
_____
_____
_____
_____
_____

The problem is that, on the other hand, _____
_____
_____
_____
_____
_____

In my opinion, _____
_____
_____
_____
_____
_____

[10]

| Total: | 100 |

LISTENING

1 ▶ 38 Listen to a teacher talking about a school trip and complete the notes.

> **Visit to the Science Museum**
>
> Date: ¹ _27th May_
> Coach leaves at: ² ____ a.m.
> Museum opens: 10a.m. to ³ ____ p.m.
> 1st guided tour at: ⁴ _____
> Name of exhibition: Antenna
> Coffee break at: ⁵ _____ a.m.
> Number of themed galleries: ⁶ _____
> Recommended: Making the ⁷ _____ World
> and The Secret Life of the Home
> Lunch: in ⁸ _____ area at 12.30p.m.
> IMAX film at: 1.15p.m.
> Name of film: Space ⁹ _____
> 2nd guided tour at: 2.45p.m.
> Name of exhibition: ¹⁰ _____ Forward
> Free time: 3.45 to ¹¹ _____ p.m.
> Home by: 8.00p.m.

[ ] 5

2 Listen again. Are the sentences true (T) or false (F)?

1 The teacher advised his students to be in the car park by 7.30a.m. _F_

2 The Wellcome Wing has exhibitions about modern art and science. ____

3 The teacher recommended two permanent exhibitions about contemporary science. ____

4 The students will watch a film about daily life on the International Space Station. ____

5 *Fast Forward* is an exhibition about how Formula One technology is being adapted for use in daily life. ____

6 The visit will end with a guided tour of some interesting new galleries. ____

[ ] 5

PRONUNCIATION

3 ▶ 39 Listen and write the number of words in each sentence. Contracted forms count as one word.

1 _7_   4 ____
2 ____   5 ____
3 ____   6 ____

[ ] 5

VOCABULARY AND GRAMMAR

4 Match 1–11 with a)–l).

1 organic	_d_	a)	money
2 natural	____	b)	off
3 hand	____	c)	course
4 dating	____	d)	~~food~~
5 genetic	____	e)	research
6 romantic	____	f)	luggage
7 log	____	g)	talent
8 raise	____	h)	estate
9 online	____	i)	site
10 council	____	k)	comedy
11 do	____	l)	engineering

[ ] 5

5 Complete the sentences with the prepositions in the box. Use some words more than once.

> with   in   to   on   down   up   for   at

1 I haven't made friends ___with___ many people at work.

2 Please come in and make yourself _____ home.

3 Ben's always had an aptitude _____ cooking.

4 I don't think it'll work. She has so little in common _____ him.

5 Since they got back from Singapore, they haven't been able to settle _____ again.

6 His teacher thinks Tim's not paying enough attention _____ his homework.

7 If they'd left earlier, they would've been able to check _____ for their flight on time.

8 I was embarrassed because I was wearing my jeans, but everybody else had dressed _____ for the party.

9 I wouldn't rely _____ him if I were you.

10 I know you didn't do it _____ purpose.

11 Unfortunately, dancing doesn't come naturally _____ him.

[ ] 5

6 Complete the sentences. Use the correct form of the word in capitals.

1 She's been ___unemployed___ for six months. She can't find a job. EMPLOY

2 They _____ the teacher so they had to do extra homework. OBEY

3 The problem is that she's too good. She's _____ for the job. QUALIFY

4 I think he's got a very _____ job in the government. INFLUENCE

5 Please accept my apologies. I _____ what you said. UNDERSTAND

6 If you'd arrived on time, he wouldn't have been so _____. ANNOY

[ ] 5

7 Correct one mistake in each question.

1 What for did you do that?
  What did you do that for?

2 Who's the woman that she was so rude to you?
  _____

3 Have you see them last weekend?
  _____

4 Who did sent you that lovely card?
  _____

5 If he'd spoke to you, what would you have done?
  _____

6 How is made this table?
  _____

  ☐ 5

8 Circle the correct answer: a), b), c) or d).

1 We don't ____ eat out on Tuesdays.
  a) easily   b) early   c) usually   d) never

2 She ____ them since she was at primary school.
  a) knows   b) knew
  c) 's been knowing   d) 's known

3 While they ____ at the gate, they found out the flight would be five hours late.
  a) waited   b) are waiting
  c) were waiting   d) had waited

4 I've been working here for ____.
  a) five months   b) March
  c) two years ago   d) last year

5 ____ we arrived, the concert started.
  a) While   b) Until
  c) As soon as   d) By the time

6 He couldn't leave work early because he ____ asked his boss.
  a) had   b) hadn't
  c) wasn't   d) wouldn't

7 We talked for hours about ____ we used to play together in a band.
  a) when   b) which   c) that   d) who

8 I ____ to get promoted before him.
  a) should   b) might not
  c) won't   d) 'm not likely

9 Your order ____ sent by first class post and will arrive tomorrow.
  a) 's been   b) has being   c) will   d) is

10 She asked them what time ____ leave.
  a) they'll   b) they'd
  c) would they   d) they have

11 If I'd met you, we ____ had lunch.
  a) would   b) won't have   c) could've   d) might

  ☐ 10

9 Complete the second sentence so that it means the same as the first.

1 We last saw each other six months ago.
  We _haven't seen each other_ for six months.

2 They're delivering the furniture tomorrow.
  The furniture _____.

3 She told us it would be a good idea to take a taxi.
  She advised _____.

4 The quality isn't as good as it used to be.
  The quality is _____.

5 There wasn't much food left after the party.
  There was only _____.

6 If it doesn't stop raining, we won't be able to go for a walk.
  Unless _____.

  ☐ 5

10 Complete the text with one word in each gap.

Do you tweet on Twitter?

It ¹ _will_ probably come as no surprise that not only was Twitter ² _____ fastest growing website in 2009, but 'twitter' was also the ³ _____ widely used word in the media. 'Obama' was in second place and 'H1N1', the name of the swine flu virus that spread all over the world, was in ⁴ _____. More surprisingly, the success of Stephenie Meyer's _Twilight_ series of books and ⁵ _____ pushed the word 'vampire' into fifth place.

The popularity of the word 'twitter' summed up the rise of ⁶ _____ networking on the internet. It was also a 'fun' word, which led to the creation of a whole new set of vocabulary. For example, 'tweet', 'tweetaholic' and even 'tweet up', ⁷ _____ means to arrange to meet ⁸ _____ with your friends.

If further proof of social networking as a huge cultural force was needed, ⁹ _____ New Oxford American Dictionary chose 'unfriend' as its 2009 Word of the Year. To 'unfriend' means to remove someone as a ¹⁰ _____ on a social networking site like Facebook. ¹¹ _____ you unfriended anyone recently?

  ☐ 5

READING

11 Match gaps 1–6 in the text with sentences a)–g) opposite. There is <u>one</u> extra sentence you do not need.

Teenage boy climbs Everest

In May 2010, American teenager Jordan Romero made history by becoming the youngest person to climb the highest peak in the world, Mount Everest (8,848m). ¹ _a_ . The first thing he did when he reached the summit was to make a phone call, saying, 'Mom, I'm calling you from the top of the world!'

Jordan made the climb with his father Paul, his stepmother Karen Lundgren and three Sherpa guides, all experienced mountaineers. However, despite Jordan's age, he was by no means an inexperienced climber. In fact, this was his sixth major achievement in his dream to climb the Seven Summits, the highest peaks on all seven continents.

² ____ . Between 2007 and 2009, he climbed five others in North and South America, Australia and Europe. Having climbed the Asian one, this left only the Vinson Massif (4,892m) in Antarctica to achieve his dream of being the youngest person to climb all seven.

³ ____ . There was a painting on a corridor wall in his California school which showed the highest point on every continent, and it fascinated him. He did some research and then one day, he said to his father, 'Dad, I want to climb the Seven Summits.' His father immediately started training him and the following year they climbed Kilimanjaro.

Despite Jordan's achievements, the Everest climb also attracted criticism from people who said he was too young to take such risks. It is true that climbing at such high altitudes can be dangerous. ⁴ ____ . Furthermore, a previous record holder for the youngest person to climb Mount Everest, 16 year old Temba Tsheri from Nepal, lost five fingers from frostbite during his climb due to the extreme cold.

But Jordan's father rejected the criticisms, saying, 'We were so prepared, everything went absolutely perfectly. ⁵ ____ .' He said they'd spent several weeks getting used to the high altitude. He thought Jordan had trained hard and had been ready for the challenge.

Jordan himself said, 'I'm the one who started this project. ⁶ ____ . I know it's a big goal and lucky for me, my family is supporting me every step of the way. In fact my family is my team.'

He hopes his adventure will inspire young people around the world to set themselves challenges – to get fit and aim high.

a) ~~Jordan was 13 years old.~~

b) Age has nothing to do with anything.

c) Jordan says he was first inspired to climb at the age of nine.

d) The cold and the lack of oxygen has killed many climbers in the past.

e) It's my dream we are following.

f) Their knowledge and experience of the mountain will help keep us all safe.

g) He conquered the first one, Mount Kilimanjaro (5,895m), in Africa when he was ten.

| 10 |

12 Read the text again and choose the correct answer: a), b) or c).

1 When Jordan got to the top of Everest, he called his ____.
   a) father
   b) friends
   c) mother

2 He hasn't climbed the highest mountain in ____ yet.
   a) Africa
   b) Asia
   c) Antarctica

3 Jordan first got interested in climbing when he was ____.
   a) at school
   b) seven
   c) a teenager

4 The main criticism of Jordan's Everest climb was ____.
   a) the cold
   b) his age
   c) the lack of oxygen

5 Before the climb, ____.
   a) Jordan did a lot of training
   b) Jordan's father was very worried
   c) Jordan had frostbite

6 Jordan wanted to climb Everest because ____.
   a) it was what he dreamt of
   b) his family wanted him to do it
   c) he wanted to encourage young people to keep fit

| 5 |

SPEAKING

13 Cross out the option or response that is <u>not</u> possible.

1 So should I dress smartly tonight?

~~a) I see.~~   b) Of course.
c) That's right.

2 Did you know that if you miss breakfast, you can't concentrate so well?

a) Oh, really?   b) I have no idea.
c) Can't you?

3 What should I get them as a wedding present?

a) Don't forget to send them a card.
b) I don't know.
c) If I were you, I'd give them some money.

4 I'm afraid our flight has been cancelled.

a) You can't be serious.   b) Well done.
c) That's terrible!

5 A: Would you suggest taking a swimsuit?

B: Yes, ___ quite hot in June.

a) it's generally   b) on the whole, it's
c) it tends to

6 A: That was a fantastic play, wasn't it?

B: Yes, but I ___ the seats were overpriced.

a) for one thing   b) do think   c) must say

[5]

14 Match gaps 1–11 in the conversation with a)–k) below.

A: ¹ Have _a_ my car keys, Anna?

B: I'm fairly ²___ I left them on the table.

A: No, I've looked there. Did you put them in your handbag?

B: It's ³___. I can't remember. Where *is* my handbag anyway?

A: I ⁴___ a clue. You know, I think we should buy a red carpet!

B: Really? Why red?

A: I read an article about it. Apparently red helps you remember details better.

B: What exactly ⁵___ mean?

A: Well, for one ⁶___, we're getting very forgetful these days.

B: Yes, but the way I ⁷___, that's because we spend too much time using computers.

A: ⁸___! I think I'll try using a red screen on mine.

B: OK, but ⁹___ you do, don't buy a red carpet!

A: OK, don't worry. Hey! ¹⁰___ guess what!

B: You found the keys?

A: Yes, they were in my pocket …

B: You're ¹¹___!

a) ~~you seen~~   g) Exactly
b) whatever   h) joking
c) possible   i) haven't got
d) thing   j) do you
e) You'll never   k) see it
f) sure

[10]

WRITING

15 Underline the correct alternatives.

The best meal of my life!

What's the ¹*more* / <u>*most*</u> delicious food you've ever eaten? Mine was chicken soup. ²*In all probability* / *On the whole*, it wasn't just the soup itself, but where and when it was eaten. It happened ³*during* / *while* I was working in Morocco during Ramadan, ⁴*which* / *when* Muslims don't eat or drink anything from sunrise ⁵*until* / *by* sunset, and never complain.

I'm not a Muslim, ⁶*however* / *also* I admired the willpower of my friends ⁷*so* / *such* a lot that one day I decided to share the experience with them. It was one of the most memorable days of my life, full of unexpected feelings ⁸*or* / *and* emotions.

⁹*Finally* / *As* the sun was going down, I joined the crowds of people in the square, ¹⁰*which* / *where* cafés had prepared bowls of steaming chicken soup and sticky, sweet desserts. Everyone had a bowl of soup and held their spoons, ready to eat. ¹¹*As soon as* / *As well as* the sun set, we lifted our spoons. Food had never tasted so good.

[5]

16 Choose <u>one</u> of the topics below and write an essay / a story on a separate piece of paper. Use the paragraph notes to help you. Write 130–150 words.

Topic A

If you could choose to be a famous person from history, who would you choose?

Para 1: say who the person is and what they are famous for

Para 2: give two or three reasons why you would like to be them

Para 3: say what things you would do differently from them, and why

Topic B

Write a story beginning with these words:

It was the most important day of my life.

Para 1: say why the day was important

Para 2: describe what happened on this day

Para 3: say what the conclusion was – positive or negative

[10]

Total: [100]

ENGLISH PHONEMES

CONSONANTS

p /pen/ pen	**b** /bʊk/ book	**t** /tiː/ tea	**d** /deɪ/ day
tʃ /tʃeə/ chair	**dʒ** /'dʒɜːmən/ German	**k** /kæt/ cat	**g** /gʊd/ good
f /fɔː/ four	**v** /'verɪ/ very	**θ** /θɪŋk/ think	**ð** /ðæt/ that
s /sɪks/ six	**z** /zuː/ zoo	**ʃ** /ʃiː/ she	**ʒ** /'telɪvɪʒən/ television
m /mæn/ man	**n** /naɪs/ nice	**ŋ** /θɪŋ/ thing	**h** /'hæpi/ happy
l /lʊk/ look	**r** /red/ red	**w** /wɒnt/ want	**j** /jes/ yes

VOWELS

iː /siː/ see	**ɪ** /hɪz/ his	**ʊ** /lʊk/ look	**uː** /juː/ you
e /ten/ ten	**ə** /əbaʊt/ about	**ɜː** /hɜː/ her	**ɔː** /mɔːnɪŋ/ morning
æ /bæd/ bad	**ʌ** /bʌt/ but	**ɑː** /kɑː/ car	**ɒ** /hɒt/ hot

DIPHTHONGS

ɪə /hɪə/ hear	**eɪ** /neɪm/ name

ʊə /'tʊərɪst/ tourist	**ɔɪ** /bɔɪ/ boy	**əʊ** /nəʊ/ no
eə /weə/ where	**aɪ** /maɪ/ my	**aʊ** /haʊ/ how